CHARLEMAGNE

D1250127

Charlemagne is often claimed as the greatest ruler in Europe before Napoleon. In this magisterial new study, Rosamond McKitterick re-examines Charlemagne the ruler and his reputation. She analyses the narrative representations of Charlemagne produced after his death, and thereafter focuses on the evidence from Charlemagne's lifetime concerning the creation of the Carolingian dynasty and the growth of the kingdom, the court and the royal household, communications and identities in the Frankish realm in the context of government, and Charlemagne's religious and cultural strategies. She offers a completely fresh and critical examination of the contemporary sources and in so doing transforms our understanding of the development of the Carolingian empire, the formation of Carolingian political identity, and the astonishing changes effected throughout Charlemagne's forty-six-year period of rule. This is a major contribution to Carolingian history which will be essential reading for anyone interested in the medieval past.

ROSAMOND MCKITTERICK is Professor of Medieval History at the University of Cambridge and a Fellow of Sidney Sussex College. Her previous publications include *Atlas of the Medieval World* (2003), *History and Memory in the Carolingian World* (2004) and *Perceptions of the Past in the Early Middle Ages* (2006).

CHARLEMAGNE

The Formation of a European Identity

ROSAMOND McKITTERICK

*Professor of Medieval History at the University of Cambridge
and Fellow of Sidney Sussex College*

CAMBRIDGE
UNIVERSITY PRESS

CAMBRIDGE UNIVERSITY PRESS
Cambridge, New York, Melbourne, Madrid, Cape Town, Singapore, São Paulo, Delhi

Cambridge University Press
The Edinburgh Building, Cambridge CB2 8RU, UK

Published in the United States of America by Cambridge University Press, New York

www.cambridge.org
Information on this title: www.cambridge.org/9780521716451

Originally published in German as *Karl der Große* by Wissenschaftliche Buchgesellschaft,
Darmstadt, 2008

© Wissenschaftliche Buchgesellschaft, Darmstadt, 2008

First published in English as *Charlemagne: The Formation of a European Identity* by
Cambridge University Press, 2008

English edition © Cambridge University Press 2008

First published 2008
Third printing 2009

Printed in the United Kingdom at the University Press, Cambridge

A catalogue record for this publication is available from the British Library

Library of Congress Cataloguing in Publication data
McKitterick, Rosamond.
Charlemagne: the formation of a European identity / Rosamond McKitterick.
p.   cm.
Includes bibliographical references and index.
ISBN 978-0-521-88672-7
1. Charlemagne, Emperor, 742–814.   2. France – Kings and rulers – Biography.   3. Holy Roman
Empire – Kings and rulers – Biography.   4. Carolingians – History.   5. France – History –
To 987.   6. Holy Roman Empire – History – To 1517.   I. Title.
DC73.M38 2008
944'.0142092–dc22[B]   2008000621

ISBN 978-0-521-88672-7 hardback
ISBN 978-0-521-71645-1 paperback

To the medievalists in the Attic, NIAS 2005–6

Contents

Maps

Tables

Preface

In this book I have investigated both what we can know about
Charlemagne and what we think we know. I have taken a fresh look at
the beginnings of the Carolingian empire, and have tried to free
Charlemagne's reign from the clutter of arguments, assumptions and
hypotheses that have somehow become facts. In charting the formation of
a European identity during Charlemagne's reign, I have explored the interaction between the practical consequences of the expansion of the Frankish
empire into totally new territory and Frankish perceptions and uses of the
past. The degree to which Charlemagne and the Franks at the end of the
eighth century and the beginning of the ninth communicated with the past
in order to form or to inform their own contemporary concerns, to heighten
their sense of identity and cultural affiliations and to shape their political
purpose form the conceptual framework of this book. I have endeavoured
to avoid ascribing without question a phenomenon loosely described as
'Carolingian' to his period of rule rather than to those of his successors.
Instead, I have attempted to capture the dynamism of the reign and to
document the astonishing changes effected throughout the period from
768 to 814. In all this I offer a critical reassessment of the sources first
produced between 747/8 and 814, not because they may or may not be
more truthful than accounts produced after Charlemagne's death, from
Einhard's *Vita Karoli* onwards, but because they have at least the merit of
being contemporary. They therefore reflect something of perceptions and
conditions during his reign. I have been very conscious of parallel work in
progress on the Carolingian period, with books in preparation from
Mayke de Jong on the reign of Louis the Pious, Stuart Airlie on the
Carolingian aristocracy, Jinty Nelson on Charlemagne, and David Ganz
on Einhard. Consequently, I have endeavoured to avoid trespass or
overlap. The book is divided into five sections, addressing narrative
representations of Charlemagne, the creation of the Carolingian dynasty
and the growth of the kingdom, the court and the royal household,

communications and identities in the Frankish realm in the context of government, and Charlemagne's religious and cultural strategies.

I have benefited greatly from past scholarship on Charlemagne, most particularly the spate of books and collections of papers over the past decade devoted to different aspects of the man and his times. A simple list of these historical analyses would occupy a substantial book on its own, but I have tried both to be up to date and comprehensive in my treatment of all the topics tackled in this book and to pay due respect both to more recent scholarship and to the path-breaking work of the nineteenth and early twentieth centuries. That I have disagreed with much of it, whether on points of detail or major traditions of interpretation, does not diminish my admiration and gratitude for all the work of my predecessors. Many, both among the departed and those I am fortunate enough to have as my colleagues, have been of enormous assistance in the endeavour to make sense of rebarbative, dispersed, lacunose, opaque, ambiguous but always fascinating primary sources. For practical reasons the references in the notes and the Bibliography have had to be selective, but those cited will provide the means for any reader to explore further. It is a testimony to the richness of Charlemagne's reign that study of it shows no signs of being exhausted. New texts are continually being added to the spectrum of material that needs to be taken into account, quite apart from the questioning of what has for too long been accepted without question.

An enterprise such as this can be completed only with a great deal of support. I am indebted first of all to the Wissenschaftliche Buchgesellschaft, to Peter Herde, the editor of the series Gestalten des Mittelalters, and to the desk editor in Darmstadt, Harald Baulig, for inviting me to write this book, and for their encouragement and extreme patience during its long gestation. I am also very grateful to Cambridge University Press for suggesting that they might publish the English version, and especially to Bill Davies, Simon Whitmore and Michael Watson at the Press for all the interest they have shown in the project. Without the award of a Visiting Fellowship for ten productive and happy months during the academic year 2005–6, in the ideal and idyllic working conditions at the Netherlands Institute of Advanced Study in Wassenaar, the Netherlands, this book would certainly have taken very much longer. I am very grateful to the Directorate, staff and Fellows of NIAS 2005–6 for all their support and to the library and computing staff for procuring so much of what I needed. Most particularly I wish to thank the other medievalists among the Fellows there, both the research group on Carolingian political identity, namely Mayke de Jong, David Ganz, Els Rose and Helmut Reimitz, and

Anu Mand, Joseph Harris, Arjo Vanderjagt and Jan Ziolkowski for inspiring discussions and help on many points. In addition, Mayke de Jong and Helmut Reimitz kindly read all my draft chapters and I have benefited immeasurably from their critical commentary and suggestions. Some of the preparatory work for this book was completed in 2002 while I was resident for three months at the British School at Rome as Hugh Balsdon Fellow. It is a pleasure here, therefore, to record my debt to the Director, staff and fellow scholars and artists of the School who contributed so much to the development of this book's arguments and perspective. In the Netherlands and Rome, I was fortunate to be able to explore the riches of Leiden Universiteitsbibliotheek and the Biblioteca Apostolica Vaticana respectively, and I am especially grateful to André Bouwman in Special Collections and Paul Hoftijzer in the Scaliger Instituut in Leiden Universiteitsbibliotheek and to Christine Grafinger in the Vatican library for all their help and hospitality. Visits to the Bibliothèque Nationale de France in Paris, the Deutsche Staatsbibliothek in Berlin, the Österreichische Nationalbibliothek in Vienna, the Bibliothèque royale in Brussels, the Bayerische Staatsbibliothek in Munich and the Stiftsarchiv and Stiftsbibliothek in St Gallen were similarly fruitful. At home in Cambridge the University Library and its staff were, as always, unfailingly helpful and the resources they made available were quite remarkable. In an earlier stage of work on the book, the Principal and Fellows of Newnham College, Cambridge, offered invaluable support. In the final stages of the book I have enjoyed the congenial company and excellent working conditions provided by the Master and Fellows of Sidney Sussex College.

Many friends, colleagues and students have assisted me in this enterprise, by generously sending me offprints or books, answering queries, listening (sometimes unwittingly) to sections of the book when I sought reactions to particular interpretations, and contributing a range of questions and reflections on major sources which were immensely stimulating. Among these I particularly want to mention David Bates, Matthias Becher, Philippe Bernard, Jesse Billett, François Bougard, Geneviève Bührer-Thierry, Caroline Burt, Guglielmo Cavallo, Benedict Coffin, John Contreni, Richard Corradini, Marios Costambeys, Georges Declercq, Philippe Depreux, Jean-Pierre Devroey, Alain Dierkens, Max Diesenberger, Bruce Eastwood, Peter Erhart, Arnold Esch, Nicholas Everett, Tom Faulkner, Michele Ferrari, Sarah Foot, Stefano Gasparri, Hans Werner Goetz, Carl Hammer, Wolfgang Haubrichs, Yitzhak Hen, Julian Hendrix, Paul Hilliard, Dominique Iogna-Prat, Tom Kitchen, Cristina La Rocca, Sally Lamb, Regine Le Jan, Uwe Lobbedey, Natalia Lozovsky, Federico Marazzi,

Andrew Merrills, John Morrill, Larry Nees, Tom Noble, Eric Palazzo, Michael Reeve, Flavia de Rubeis, Jean-Marie Sansterre, Peter Sarris, Anton Scharer, Rudolf Schieffer, Elina Screen, Josef Semmler, Julia Smith, Francesco Stella, Wesley Stevens, Joanna Story, Benoît-Michel Tock, Chris Wickham, Annette Wiesheu, Herwig Wolfram and Ian Wood. I am especially grateful to those who joined the Carolingian 'workshops' in NIAS: Stuart Airlie, Carmela Vircillo Franklin, Matthew Innes, David Mitchell, Jinty Nelson, Walter Pohl, Christina Pössel, Janneke Raaijmakers, Irene van Renswoude, Carine van Rhijn, Mariken Teeuwen and Charles West. But as always my final thanks are to my husband David. The book could not have been written without his critical engagement with it, and his constant encouragement in every respect.

Abbreviations

Apart from the following, all works are cited in full at the first reference to them and susbsequently in short-title form in each chapter. Full details may also be found in the Bibliography.

799 Kunst und Kultur	C. Stiegemann and M. Wemhoff (eds.), *799 Kunst und Kultur der Karolingerzeit: Karl der Große und Papst Leo III. in Paderborn*, 3 vols. (Mainz, 1999)
Annales fuldenses	*Annales fuldenses sive Annales regni francorum orientalis*, ed. F. Kurze, *MGH SRG* 7 (Hanover, 1891)
Annales mettenses priores	*Annales mettenses priores*, ed. B. von Simson, *MGH SRG* 10 (Hanover, 1905)
ARF	*Annales regni francorum unde ab. a. 741 usque ad a. 829, qui dicuntur Annales laurissenses maiores et Einhardi*, ed. F. Kurze, *MGH SRG* 6 (Hanover, 1895)
BAV	Rome, Biblioteca apostolica Vaticana
BnF	Bibliothèque nationale de France
Codex epistolaris carolinus, ed. Gundlach	*Codex epistolaris carolinus*, ed. W. Gundlach, *MGH Epp.* III, *Epistolae merowingici et karolini aevi*, I (Hanover, 1892)
CCSL	*Corpus Christianorum, Series Latina* (Turnhout, 1952–)
ChLA	*Chartae latinae antiquiores, Facsimile edition of the Latin charters prior to the ninth century*, I–, ed.

	A. Bruckner *et al.* (Olten and Lausanne, 1954–98)
ChLA2	*Chartae latinae antiquiores, Facsimile edition of the Latin charters,* 2nd series: *ninth century,* 1–, ed. G. Cavallo, G. Nicolaj *et al.* (Olten and Lausanne, 1997–)
CLA	E. A. Lowe, *Codices latini antiquiores: a palaeographical guide to Latin manuscripts prior to the ninth century,* 11 vols. plus Supplement (Oxford, 1935–71)
Clm	Codices latini monacenses
Davis, *Lives*	R. Davis (trans.), *The lives of the eighth-century popes* (*Liber pontificalis*) (Liverpool, 1992)
Depreux, *Prosopographie*	P. Depreux, *Prosopographie de l'entourage de Louis le Pieux (781–840),* Instrumenta 1 (Sigmaringen, 1997)
Deutsches Archiv	*Deutsches Archiv für Erforschung des Mittelalters*
DKar. I	E. Mühlbacher (ed.), *Die Urkunden der Karolinger,* I: *Urkundens Pippins, Karlmanns und Karl der Großen, MGH Diplomata karolinorum* (Hanover, 1906)
Einhard, *Vita Karoli*	Einhard, *Vita Karoli,* ed. L. Halphen, *Eginhard: vie de Charlemagne,* 2nd edn (Paris, 1947)
KdG	W. Braunfels (ed.), *Karl der Große: Lebenswerk und Nachleben,* 4 vols. I: H. Beumann (ed.), *Persönlichkeit und Geschichte*; II: B. Bischoff (ed.), *Das geistige Leben*; III: W. Braunfels and H. Schnitzler (eds.), *Karolingische Kunst*; IV: W. Braunfels and P. E. Schramm (eds.), *Das Nachleben* (Dusseldorf, 1965)
LP, ed. Duchesne	*Liber pontificalis,* ed. L. Duchesne, *Le liber pontificalis: texte, introduction et commentaire,* 2 vols. (Paris, 1886–92)

McKitterick, *History and memory*	R. McKitterick, *History and memory in the Carolingian world* (Cambridge, 2004)
McKitterick, *Perceptions of the past*	R. McKitterick, *Perceptions of the past in the early middle ages* (Notre Dame, 2006)
MGH	*Monumenta Germaniae Historica*
Cap.	*Capitularia, Legum Sectio* II, *Capitularia regum francorum*, I ed. A. Boretius (Hanover, 1883)
Conc.	*Concilia, Legum Sectio* III, *Concilia*: II, ed. A. Werminghoff (Hanover, 1906–8); III, ed. W. Hartmann (Hanover, 1984)
Epp.	*Epistolae* III–VII (= *Epistolae merowingici et karolini aevi* (Hanover, 1892–1939)
Epp. Sel.	*Epistolae Selectae in usum scholarum*, 5 vols. (Hanover, 1887–91)
Fontes	*Fontes iuris germanici antiqui in usum scholarum ex monumentis germaniae historicis separatim editi*, 13 vols. (Hanover, 1909–86)
Formulae	*Formulae merowingici et karolini aevi* (Hanover, 1882–6)
Leges nat. germ.	*Leges nationum germanicarum*, ed. K Zeumer (*Lex Visigothorum*); L. R. de Salis (*Leges Burgundionum*); F. Beyerle and R. Buchner (*Lex Ribuaria*); K. A. Eckhardt (*Pactus Legis Salicae* and *Lex Salica*); E. von Schwind (*Lex Baiuariorum*), 6 vols. in II parts (Hanover, 1892–1969)
Poet.	*Poet. latini aevi carolini*, ed. E. Dummler, L. Traube, P. von Winterfeld and K. Strecker, 4 vols (Hanover, 1881–99)
SRG	*Scriptores rerum germanicarum in usum scholarum separatim editi*, 63 vols. (Hanover, 1871–1987)
SRL	*Scriptores regum langobardicarum et italicarum saec. VI–IX*, ed. G. Waitz (Hanover, 1898)

SRM	*Scriptores rerum merovingicarum*, ed. B. Krusche and W. Levison, 7 vols. (Hanover, 1885–1920)
SS	*Scriptores* in folio, 30 vols. (Hanover, 1824–1924)
MIÖG	*Mitteilungen des Instituts für Österreichische Geschichtsforschung*
Mordek, *Bibliotheca*	H. Mordek, *Bibliotheca capitularium regum francorum manuscripta: Überlieferung und Traditionszusammenhang der fränkischen Herrschererlasse*, MGH Hilfsmittel 15 (Munich, 1995)
NCMH II	R. McKitterick (ed.), *The new Cambridge medieval history*, II: *c. 700–c. 900* (Cambridge, 1995)
ÖNB	Vienna, Österreichische Nationalbibliothek
PL	*Patrologia Latina*, J.-P. Migne (ed.), *Patrologiae cursus completus, series Latina*, 221 vols. (Paris, 1841–64)
RVARF	*Annales regni francorum unde ab. a 741 usque ad a. 829, qui dicuntur Annales laurissenses maiores et Einhardi*, ed. F. Kurze, *MGH SRG* 6 (Hanover, 1895)
Settimane	Settimane di Studio del Centro italiano di studi sull' alto medioevo (Spoleto, 1954–)

CHAPTER I

Representations of Charlemagne

INTRODUCTION

Charlemagne, king of the Franks from 768 to 814, is one of the few major rulers in European history for whom there is an agreed stereotype. According to this he was a great warrior, and with his conquests he expanded his realm from a region smaller than France to include most of what we now know as western Europe. He promoted Christianity, education and learning. He was crowned emperor by the pope on Christmas Day 800, and provided thereby both the essential ideological potential for subsequent imperial ambitions among the medieval and early modern rulers of western Europe and a link between the 'germanic' and Roman political worlds. He was already hailed as the 'father of Europe' by a poet of his own day.[1] Modern scholars in search of Europe's linguistic core have proposed a 'Charlemagne *Sprachbund*', for the area where French, German, Italian and Dutch are spoken.[2] With the modern *International Karlspreis / Prix International de Charlemagne* for services to European peace and unity, first awarded in 1950, this Frankish ruler has also attained status as a symbol of European unity and integration. The prize itself was even awarded to the Euro in 2002.

Throughout the history of France and Germany and even in the new kingdom of the Belgians in the nineteenth century, this stereotype of Christian emperor, mighty conqueror and patron of learning also served as a focus of national identity. A liturgical feast in honour of St Charlemagne

---

[1] *Karolus magnus et Leo papa*, ed. E. Dümmler, *MGH Poet.* I (Berlin, 1881), pp. 366–79; and W. Hentze, *De Karolo rege et Leone papa: der Bericht über die Zusammenkunft Karls des Großen mit Papst Leo III in Paderborn 799 in einem Epos für Karl den Kaiser* (Paderborn, 1999).

[2] J. van de Auwera, *Adverbial constructions in the languages of Europe* (Berlin, 1998), pp. 823–5. This *Sprachbund* is also known as SAE or Standard Average European. See also R. Thieroff, 'The German tense-aspect-mood system from a typological perspective', in S. Watts, J. West and H.-J. Solms (eds.), *Zur Verbmorphologie germanischer Sprachen*, Linguistische Arbeiten 146 (Tübingen, 2001), pp. 211–30 at p. 228, and B. Heine and T. Kuteva (eds.), *The changing languages of Europe* (Oxford, 2006), p. 8.

was actually instituted in 1165 when Pope Alexander III canonized him and a cult of Charlemagne spread across western Europe.[3] It was at a later stage that Charlemagne's bones were translated into the gaudy gold reliquary commissioned for the purpose by the Emperor Frederick II.[4] In literature, too, Charlemagne enjoyed every variant of valiant Christian warrior in any number of medieval Latin and vernacular epics, such as the Old French *Chanson de Roland,* the Irish *Gabáltais searluis móir* and the German *Kaiserchronik.*[5] The Carolingian emperors, most particularly Charlemagne but increasingly because he was seen as a sort of composite super-emperor, moreover, provided political ideologues with a powerful model. This was not just a matter of claiming Frankish descent, though that happened too. Robert Peril's genealogies of the emperors of Austria published in 1535 in French, Spanish, Latin and Dutch versions, for example, did precisely that.[6]

It was not only a Carolingian imperial ideal and its resonance with the Roman empire that proved so powerful throughout the middle ages and into the early modern period, as Dürer's famous imaginary imperial portrait of 1512/13 (still in Nürnberg),[7] and Cointin's *Charlemagne et le rétablissement de l'empire romain,* published in 1666, indicate.[8] The imagination of political leaders was also fired by what they understood of his achievements. No less a leader than Napoleon thought of himself as a second Charlemagne in his relations with the pope and the church.[9] In the procession which formed part of a spectacle organized in Aachen in June 1811, a colossal effigy of Charlemagne bore the legend 'Nur Napoleon ist grösser als ich' (Only

[3] R. Folz, *Etudes sur la culte liturgique de Charlemagne dans les églises de l'empire* (Paris, 1951).

[4] H. Müllejans, *Karl der Große und sein Schrein in Aachen: eine Festschrift* (Aachen, 1988).

[5] See R. Folz, *Le souvenir et la légende de Charlemagne dans l'empire germanique médiéval* (Paris, 1950); *Gabáltais searluis móir (The conquests of Charlemagne),* ed. D. Hyde, Irish Texts Society (London, 1917); and K.-E. Geith, *Carolus Magnus: Studien zur Darstellung Karls des Großen in deutschen Literatur des 12. und 13. Jahrhunderts* (Munich, 1977). See also B. Bastert (ed.), *Karl der Große in den europäischen Literaturen des Mittelalters: Konstruktion eines Mythos* (Tübingen, 2004).

[6] R. Peril, *La généalogie et descente de la très illustre maison Dautriche* (Antwerp, 1535). See J. Voss, *Das Mittelalter im historischen Denken Frankreichs: Untersuchungen zur Geschichte des Mittelalterbegriffes und der Mittelalterbewertung von der zweiten Hälfte des 16. bis zur Mitte des 19. Jahrhunderts* (Munich, 1972); R. McKitterick, 'The study of Frankish history in France and Germany in the sixteenth and seventeenth centuries', *Francia* 8 (1980), pp. 556–72; and R. Morrissey, 'Charlemagne', in the section 'De l'archive à l'emblème', in P. Nora (ed.), *Les lieux de mémoire,* III: *Les Frances* (Paris, 1992, repr. 1997), pp. 4389–425.

[7] P. Schoenen, 'Das Karlsbild der Neuzeit', *KdG,* IV, pp. 274–305.

[8] A useful introduction is R. Folz, *The concept of empire in western Europe from the fifth to the fourteenth century* (London, 1969) from the 1953 French edition.

[9] R. Morrissey, *Charlemagne and France: a thousand years of mythology,* trans. C. Tihanyi (Chicago, 2003) (from the French edition of 1997).

Napoleon is greater than I).[10] Contemporaries were not slow to find super-ficial comparisons: the famous equestrian portrait of Napoleon crossing the Alps by Jacques-Louis David in the Belvedere in Vienna, for example, explicitly reminds the viewer in inscriptions on the rocks under the horse's feet that Napoleon was literally following in the footsteps of both *Annibal* and *Carolus Magnus*. Both Charlemagne and Napoleon were described by the author in his preface to a study of Charlemagne published in Brussels in 1848 as 'veritable demi-gods who, like Alexander the Great and other ancient conquering heroes, changed the course of history'.[11] It was Napoleon who appropriated, for his triumphal procession in Paris in 1798, the magnificent sarcophagus in which Charlemagne is thought to have been buried. This tomb, returned to Aachen in 1815, was one of the highlights of the remarkable exhibition mounted in Paderborn in 1999 to celebrate the meeting between Charlemagne and Pope Leo in 799. It is 2.15 m long, 62 cm high and 65.5 cm broad, made of Carrara marble in the third century A D, and carved with a bas-relief sculpture depicting the Rape of Proserpina and her descent into the Underworld.[12]

Statues and paintings of Charlemagne abound in many of the cities of Europe, whether major capitals such as Paris or towns that have often long since lost their political pre-eminence. Thus Charlemagne graces the market place in Aachen itself (the venue for no fewer than thirty-eight coronations of German kings between 813 and 1531),[13] and the cathedrals of Bremen, Frankfurt and Halberstadt. He surveys the cities of Zürich, Dinant and Liège, and he sits astride his horse in front of Notre Dame in Paris.[14] In the frescoes by Melchior Steidl in the Kaisersaal of the Neue Residenz in Bamberg, completed in 1707–9, Charlemagne assumes a place alongside other Roman and German emperors, such as Julius Caesar and Constantine, and Henry II, Rudolf II, Joseph I and Leopold I. Just as Julius Caesar has the famous quotation attributed to him – *veni vidi vici* – in the

[10] S. Tanz, 'Aspekte der Karlsrezeption im Frankreich des 19. Jahrhunderts', *Das Mittelalter* 4/2 (1999), pp. 55–64 at p. 58.

[11] Anon., *Charlemagne* (Brussels, 1848). See also T. Verschaffel, *Beeld en geschiedenis: het Belgische en Vlaamse verleden in de romantische boekillustraties* (Turnhout, 1987), p. 59 (Charlemagne crossing the Alps).

[12] *799 Kunst und Kultur*, II, X.41, pp. 758–63: 'mit an Sicherheit grenzender Wahrscheinlichkeit im Jahr 814 als Grablege für Karl den Großen verwendet'. Such iconography was a common feature of late antique sarcophagi; a very similar sarcophagus, in date and decoration, albeit somewhat smaller, for example, is to be found in the Kunsthistorisches Museum in Vienna, Griechische-Römische Antiquitäten-Abteilung, Inv. Nr. I 1126.

[13] *Krönungen Könige in Aachen: Geschichte und Mythos*, Austellungs Katalog (Mainz, 2000).

[14] D. Kötzsche, 'Darstellungen Karls des Großen in der lokalen Verehrung des Mittelalters', *KdG* IV, pp. 155–214; E. G. Grimme, 'Karl der Große in seiner Stadt', *KdG* IV, pp. 228–73.

inscription under the painting, so under Charlemagne the text displayed is that of the imperial *laudes* of the medieval coronation liturgy: *Christus regnat. Christus vincit. Christus triumphat.*[15] In the memorial of the heroes of the French nation in the Panthéon in Paris, the huge frescoes by Puvis de Chavannes include the coronation of Charlemagne as emperor alongside other medieval events perceived as formative in French history, namely, the baptism of Clovis and his victory at Tolbiac, and the careers of Sainte Geneviève and Jeanne d'Arc.

At a more local level, Alfred Rethel's Charlemagne frescoes in the Aachen Rathaus, regarded as one of the most important examples of nineteenth-century German monumental art, were originally planned by him in 1840 as a result of his reading of the eighth- and ninth-century sources, to depict Charlemagne above all as a Christian emperor.[16] Thus his chosen scenes, of which he completed only five, were the destruction of the Saxon Irminsul, the battle at Cordoba against the Saracens, the baptism of Widukind, the Synod of Frankfurt, the imperial coronation in Rome, the coronation of Louis the Pious by Charlemagne in 813, and the visit paid by Otto III to the grave of Charlemagne in 1000. Rethel later added Charlemagne's capture of Pavia in 774 and the building of the chapel at Aachen.

In Rome, on the other hand, the emphasis was on the papal coronation of Charlemagne and the special relationship between pope and emperor. The latter was proclaimed in the association between Pope Hadrian VI and the Emperor Charles V, and their preservation of the wonderful late eighth-century epitaph for Pope Hadrian I commissioned by Charlemagne in Francia after the pope's death in 795. It was saved from the destruction of Old St Peter's in Rome and is now to be found above the left portico of the new basilica.[17] Raphael's painting of the coronation of Charlemagne by Pope Leo III, moreover, adorns the walls of the Stanza dell'Incendeio di Borgo (1514–17) in the Stanze di Rafaello in the Vatican.

The imaginations of rulers, artists, sculptors and poets alike have been fired by Charlemagne. Yet he is not simply the Charlemagne of legend, for

[15] L. E. Saurma-Jeltsch (ed.), *Karl der Große als vielberufener Vorfahr: sein Bild in der Kunst der Fürsten, Kirchen und Städte*, Schriften des historischen Museums: im Auftrag des Dezernats für Kultur und Freizeit 19 (Sigmaringen, 1994). See also the essays in the section on 'Rezeption und Wirkungen' in F.-R. Erkens (ed.), *Karl der Große und das Erbe der Kulturen* (Berlin, 2001).
[16] H. von Erinem, 'Die Tragödie der Karlsfresken Alfred Rethels', *KdG* IV, pp. 306–25.
[17] It was remounted there on the orders of Pope Gregory XIII in 1574. J. Story, *Charlemagne and Rome: the epitaph of Pope Hadrian I* (Oxford, forthcoming); and see J. Story, J. Bunbury, A. C. Felici, G. Fronterotta, M. Piacentini, C. Nicolais, D. Scacciatelli, S. Sciuti and M. Vendittelli, 'Charlemagne's black marble: the origins of the Epitaph of Pope Hadrian I', *Papers of the British School at Rome* (2005), pp. 157–90.

historians have played a crucial role in establishing the contours of this stereotype. Thus scholars too have highlighted his exploits, painstakingly reconstructed the possible limits of his power, elucidated the ideological significance of his reign, and used him to serve particular political purposes. With 1,200 years of storytelling and myth-making as well as of serious and productive scholarship about Charlemagne, not least that of the decades since the Council of Europe's Charlemagne exhibition in 1965,[18] the Paderborn exhibition in 1999,[19] the spate of popularizing biographies[20] and scholarly essay collections issued to mark the 1,200th anniversary of the imperial coronation,[21] it may seem superfluous to present yet another study of his reign. But it is precisely because the stereotype of him is so dominant and his role in relation to a sense of European identity is so pervasive that a fresh look can be justified.

Charlemagne, in short, has been the object of commentary and study for the past 1,200 years, some of it very nationalistic and celebratory in tone.[22] On the one hand there are contemporary or near contemporary representations of the ruler and, on the other, as we have seen, Charlemagne has come to symbolize the common roots of European political and legal culture, with an impact on ideology and imagination that can be traced across the 1,200 years since he died. Yet both aspects demonstrate that among the formative elements of political identity, as well as the means of articulating it, are a people's knowledge and use of the past. This has been amply demonstrated in contexts as widely separated as the writing of deuteronomic history and exile in ancient Israel,[23] the mixing of cultures

---

[18] Council of Europe exhibition catalogue: W. Braunfels (ed.), *Karl der Große / Charlemagne* (Aachen, 1965).

[19] C. Stiegemann and M. Wemhoff (eds.), *799 Kunst und Kultur der Karolingerzeit: Karl der Große und Papst Leo in Paderborn*, 3 vols. (Mainz, 1999).

[20] The best of these is M. Becher, *Karl der Große* (Munich, 1999), English trans. D. Bachrach (New Haven, 2003). See also, for example, R. Collins, *Charlemagne* (London, 1998); A. Barbero, *Charlemagne: father of a continent* (New Haven, 2004), trans. from the Italian edn of 2000 by A. Cameron, D. Hägermann, *Karl der Große: Herrscher des Abendlandes. Biographie* (Berlin, 2000); J. Favier, *Charlemagne* (Paris, 2000).

[21] F.-R. Erkens (ed.), *Karl der Große und das Erbe der Kulturen* (Berlin, 2001); P. Godman, J. Jarnut and P. Johanek (eds.), *Am Vorabend der Kaiserkrönung: "Das Epos Karolus Magnus et Leo Papa" und der Papstbesuch in Paderborn 799* (Berlin, 2002); R. Schieffer (ed.), *Schriftkultur und Reichsverwaltung unter den Karolingern* (Opladen, 1996); J. Story (ed.), *Charlemagne: empire and society* (Manchester, 2005).

[22] See, for example, *Karl der Große oder Charlemagne? Acht Antworten deutscher Geschichtsforscher* (Berlin, 1935); and the review by P. E. Schramm, 'Karl der Große oder Charlemagne? Stellungnahme Deutscher Historiker in der Zeit des Nationalsozialismus', in P. E. Schramm, *Kaiser, Könige und Päpste: Gesammelte Aufsätze zur Geschichte des Mittelalters*, I (Stuttgart, 1968), pp. 342–4.

[23] E. T. Mullen, *Narrative history and ethnic boundaries: the deuteronomistic historian and the creation of Israelite national identity* (Atlanta, Georgia, 1993).

in Hellenic Palestine,[24] the processes of ethnogenesis in Latin America,[25] the dynamic reworkings of the court's historical knowledge in the seventeenth- and eighteenth-century Qing empire in China,[26] the Irish-origin legends which furnished kingship in medieval Scotland with a legitimating antiquity,[27] the imperial expansion of early modern Britain,[28] competing discourses on national history and the efforts to disseminate them through the medium of the schools in nineteenth- and twentieth-century Spain,[29] and the politics of identity in modern Germany since reunification.[30] The degrees to which a people communicates with the past in order to form or to inform its own contemporary concerns, to heighten its sense of identity and cultural affiliations, and to shape its political purpose, are therefore among the underlying themes of this book.[31]

I aim to chart the formation of Frankish political identity during the reign of Charlemagne. I shall explore the interaction between the practical consequences of the expansion of the Frankish empire into totally new territory and Frankish perceptions and uses of the past.[32] I shall take a fresh look at the development of the Carolingian empire from its beginnings and attempt to free the reign of Charlemagne from the clutter of accumulated arguments and of hypotheses that have somehow become facts. Many

[24] D. Mendels, *Identity, religion and historiography: studies in Hellenistic history*, Journal for the Study of the Pseudepigrapha, Supplement series 24 (Sheffield, 1998), pp. 13–34.
[25] J. D. Hill (ed.), *History, power and identity: ethnogenesis in the Americas, 1492–1992* (Iowa City, 1996).
[26] P. Kyle Crossley, *A translucent mirror: history and identity in Qing imperial ideology* (Berkeley, 1999) (the entire Qing period is 1636–1912).
[27] D. Broun, *The Irish identity of the kingdom of the Scots in the twelfth and thirteenth centuries*, Studies in Celtic History (Woodbridge, 1999), which focusses in particular on John of Fordun's Chronicle. See also Bruce Webster, *Medieval Scotland: the making of an identity* (London, 1997).
[28] K. Wilson (ed.), *A new imperial history: culture, identity and modernity in Britain and the empire, 1660–1840* (Cambridge, 2004).
[29] C. P. Boyd, *Historia patria: politics, history, and national identity in Spain, 1875–1975* (Princeton, 1997).
[30] See K. Jarausch, 'Normalization or renationalization? On reinterpreting the German past', in R. Alter and P. Monteath (eds.), *Rewriting the German past: history and identity in the new Germany* (Atlantic Highlands, NJ, 1997). See also M. Fulbrook and M. Swales (eds.), *Representing the German nation: history and identity in twentieth-century Germany* (Manchester, 2000).
[31] In addition to my own *History and memory in the Carolingian world*, (Cambridge, 2004), see more generally J. G. A. Pocock, *Barbarism and religion*, 3 vols. (Cambridge, 1999–2003), esp. 'Prelude: the varieties of early modern historiography', II, pp. 7–25; B. Lewis, *History remembered, recovered, invented* (Princeton, 1975); A. D. Smith, *The ethnic origins of nations* (Oxford, 1986); P. Geary, *The myth of nations: the medieval origins of Europe* (Princeton, 2002); and E. Hobsbawm and T. Ranger, *The invention of tradition* (Cambridge, 1983).
[32] For discussions of this see also my *History and memory* and *Perceptions of the past*; and more generally Y. Hen and M. Innes (eds.), *The uses of the past in the early middle ages* (Cambridge, 2000); and A. Scharer and G. Scheibelreiter (eds.), *Historiographie im frühen Mittelalter*, Veröffentlichungen des Instituts für Österreichischen Geschichtsforschung 32 (Vienna and Munich, 1994).

of our inherited certainties about it may thereby be undermined.[33] Charlemagne himself, as we shall see, becomes far less solid and more elusive. The reign of Charlemagne needs to be stripped right down to what we can know or might be able to reconstruct from contemporary sources. I shall, therefore, examine the primary evidence anew. I shall discard the prevalent and somewhat static picture of a forty-six-year reign still understood to too great an extent in terms both of the situation prevailing at the end of Charlemagne's reign and of far too narrow a preoccupation with the coronation of 800. Instead, I shall attempt to capture the dynamism of the reign and to chart the pace of change, for so much was developed on the hoof in order to cope with the opportunities and problems created by both the peculiar position of the Carolingian family within the Frankish kingdom and such rapid, and often unplanned, expansion of the realm.

NINTH-CENTURY NARRATIVE IMAGES OF CHARLEMAGNE: EINHARD, THE ASTRONOMER AND THE POETA SAXO

Ninth-century accounts of Charlemagne played a major role in shaping the subsequent knowledge and simplified understanding alluded to above. Of the many such narratives constructed after Charlemagne's death, I take three representative examples, one from soon after his death in 814, one from the middle of the ninth century, and one from the end of the ninth century.

Einhard's Vita Karoli

Perhaps the most seductive and influential of the representations of Charlemagne has proven to be that created by his courtier Einhard within a few years of Charlemagne's death. Its eloquence and Ciceronian Latin were a major factor in securing both its success and the fame of its subject; the *Vita Karoli* has had a remarkably wide and prolonged history of dissemination in manuscript and printed versions from the time of its initial production.[34]

---

[33] I. N. Wood, 'In praise of uncertainty', in W. Pohl and M. Diesenberger (eds.), *Integration und Herrschaft: ethnische Identitäten und soziale Organisation im Frühmittelalter* (Vienna, 2002), pp. 303–14.

[34] M. Tischler, *Einharts Vita Karoli: Studien zur Entstehung, Überlieferung und Rezeption, MGH Schriften* 48 (Hanover, 2002).

The *Vita Karoli* was written, or so Einhard tells us, in order to celebrate the king's life, his way of life (*vita et conversatio*), his many accomplishments (*res gestas*), his deeds and his habits (*actus et mores*).[35] Einhard was moved to write the life 'of the most splendid and greatest of all men' out of gratitude to the king he regarded as his *nutritor*. Einhard thought it better to risk criticism for his inadequacies than to neglect the memory of one so great. He stressed the fact that he knew the king personally and thus gave his account greater authority. He added to this effect by explaining that by contrast he knew too little about the king's early life to write about it. That Einhard was closely involved in royal business, at least in the latter part of Charlemagne's reign, is suggested by the claim that it was he who took the *Divisio regnorum* of 806 to Pope Leo III in Rome so that the pope might subscribe it.[36]

The life starts with a short sketch of how the Carolingian family members had once served as mayors of the palace to the Merovingian kings and how Charles succeeded to the kingship secured by his father Pippin from the Merovingians. Einhard then outlines the structure of his book, stating that he would write about Charlemagne's deeds within and without the kingdom, his habits and interests, his administration of the kingdom and his death. There is a long section in which the various wars and conquests of Charlemagne against the Aquitainians, Lombards, Saxons, Saracens, Bretons, Bavarians, Slavs, Avars and Danes are set out in the chronological order of their completion. This is rounded out with an expansive ethno-geographical account of the huge area now ruled by Charlemagne, as if to echo the formulation of the poet of the 'Paderborn epic' in *c.* 799 of Charlemagne as the 'Father of Europe'.[37] The impressiveness of these conquests is then further enhanced by Einhard's stress on the recognition Charlemagne received from other rulers in the far west, the south and the east – from Ireland, the Asturias in Spain, the Persians and Byzantium. Some of the building work Charlemagne undertook to 'improve and beautify the kingdom' is described, such as the chapel at Aachen, the bridge at Mainz and the two great palaces at Ingelheim and Nijmegen, the construction of a fleet and of the defences against Danes and

---

[35] Einhard, *Vita Karoli*, O. Holder-Egger, *MGH SRG* 25 (Hanover, 1911); ed. L. Halphen; and *Eginhard: vie de Charlemagne* (Paris, 1947), trans. P. Dutton, *Charlemagne's courtier: the complete Einhard* (Peterborough, ON, 1998). A new Penguin translation by David Ganz is in preparation.

[36] 'Atque haec omnia litteris mandata sunt et leoni papae, ut his sua manu subscriberet, per Einhardum missa.' Kurze notes that Einhard would appear to be the author of the annals from 795 to 820: *ARF*, ed. Kurze, p. vii.

[37] D. Ganz, 'Einhard's Charlemagne: the characterization of greatness', in Story (ed.), *Charlemagne*, pp. 38–51, makes this point.

Saracens. Thus to the image of the mighty and successful conqueror is added that of the protector of his people.

From this military portrait, Einhard turned to more personal matters. High praise is offered of Charlemagne's character, his family life, his religious devotion and friendship with Pope Hadrian, and his interest in learning and the scholars who served as his teachers. Einhard reports the king's knowledge of Latin and Greek as well as his native Frankish, and that his favourite reading was Augustine's *City of God*. In a disarming sketch provided of Charlemagne's appearance, we are told of the king's great height, incipient pot belly, small head and high-pitched voice, of the lameness in one foot he developed in old age, his love of swimming in the hot springs at Aachen, his preference for simple Frankish clothes, and his personal habits. These included his wakefulness at night and his fondness for red meat. Even within the household he gave his attention to ruling and the administration of justice.

Einhard then referred briefly to the king's attempt to remedy the defects of the laws of the realm, his move to have ancient poems of his kingdom written down, and his fostering of a grammar of his own language with new names for the months and the winds. The paragraphs on the king's personal piety and interest in education is augmented further by sections on almsgiving, his devotion to St Peter and his visits to Rome. According to the concluding portions of the *Vita*, Charlemagne made his sole surviving son Louis (the Pious) his heir, and crowned him emperor at Aachen. Finally, Charlemagne's last illness, death and burial are described. This is followed by an account of the portents of his death and full details of his will, including a list of the magnates who witnessed it. The *Vita* ends with an assurance of the faithfulness with which his son Louis discharged the provisions of the will.[38]

From this short summary it should be clear that Einhard certainly provided an effective and comprehensive biography of the ruler in terms of topics covered, even if the treatment of each topic is brief and omissions and silences have been detected in relation to other information we possess. We should remind ourselves, however, that what we now perceive as omissions and silences would not necessarily have appeared so at the time, for the life's immediate and contemporary audiences would have been able to supplement Einhard's interpretative celebration of the ruler from their own memory and documentation, whether relating to details of

[38] See M. Innes, 'Charlemagne's will: piety, politics and the imperial succession', *English Historical Review* 112 (1997), pp. 833–55.

the wars, what it was like to cross the Alps, life at court, or the huge amount of administrative communications and legislation associated with the ruler. Einhard himself clearly exploited the other written information and narrative sources which will be discussed later in this chapter, but it is also very likely that he simply drew on his memory of what he had seen or what he had been told. It is odd to criticize Einhard for failing to omit detail we find in contemporary sources of information on which he undoubtedly drew, for these were also available in principle to his readers. What he did was to provide a digested, carefully crafted, interpretative essay from an historical perspective. To some extent, therefore, Einhard's account could have served as a mnemonic in that it addressed its immediate audience on a subject they knew.

Einhard, nevertheless, began a process of distortion simply by writing from hindsight, after the king's death. His strongest memories are inevitably of the king in his latter years, and much is presented as having been brought to a conclusion. His literary skill has rounded the life out, imposed order upon it, and offered a considered assessment. Einhard thus followed, to a greater or lesser extent, the ideal form of history implied at various points by Cicero in his *Orator* and *De oratore*: chronological arrangement, geographical precision, a clear narrative of doings and sayings, an exposition of causes and consequences, biographical details about the character's life and a notion of what the author himself approved.[39]

The scholarly reaction to Einhard's account has ranged from uncritical acceptance to outright rejection of its historical validity.[40] As a response to Charlemagne's personality and achievement, and as a reflection of perceptions of Charlemagne and knowledge available about him at the time Einhard wrote, however, it is immensely valuable. This is not the place to engage fully with the great diversity of discussion about Einhard's *Vita Karoli* or Einhard himself, and he has become in any case the focus of renewed attention from a number of different perspectives.[41] A few comments on the date, on the character of the work as 'secular biography', and on its sources and models of inspiration are nevertheless necessary.

---

[39] See, for example, Cicero, *Orator*, XIX.66 and XXXIV.120, ed. H. M. Hubbell, in *Cicero, Brutus, Orator*, ed. and trans. G. L. Henderson and H. M. Hubbell (Cambridge, Mass., 1962), pp. 354 and 394. On the Carolingian witnesses to Cicero's texts on rhetoric see L. R. Reynolds, *Texts and transmission: a survey of the Latin classics* (Oxford, 1983), pp. 102–9.

[40] Halphen, for example, rejected it. See Halphen (ed.) *Eginhard*, especially pp. ix–x and xiii.

[41] Tischler, *Einharts Vita Karoli*; Dutton, *Charlemagne's courtier*, J. M. H. Smith, 'Einhard: the sinner and the saints', *Transactions of the Royal Historical Society*, 6th series 13 (2003), pp. 55–77; H. Schefers (ed.), *Einhard: Studien zu Leben und Werk* (Darmstadt, 1997); D. Ganz, *Einhard*, forthcoming.

First, the date: this matters, for it affects the context in which the text is to be understood and the purpose for which it was written.[42] Unfortunately the precise date of composition cannot be established, and it has become a matter of what scholars think most likely in relation to their understanding of the emphases of the text itself. It used to be supposed simply that Einhard had completed his *Vita Karoli* between 817 and 829/30, with the earlier date proposed in relation to a revolt of the Abodrites and the collapse of a portico in the palace at Aachen, and the later in relation to an allusion to it by Lupus of Ferrières in a letter to Einhard usually dated 829/30.[43]

Such a span is unsatisfactory, for it fails to take into account either the remarkable strength of the text itself, or the degree to which it might have functioned effectively as a funeral oration and celebration of the king soon after his death. The *Vita Karoli* had a political purpose. That purpose was to celebrate Charlemagne and, in its final paragraphs, to underscore Louis the Pious's legitimacy, imperial rule and the regularity of the succession. It is significant that the narrative stops with Charlemagne's death and the secure succession of his son, with no inkling at all of what might have happened next. Einhard was closely associated with both Charlemagne and Louis the Pious as well as with the leading lay and ecclesiastical magnates of the realm. This portrait of Charlemagne, so crucial for contemporary understanding of the new political configuration of the Frankish realm that had been totally transformed within a space of just under half a century, was an important political statement and description of the Frankish realm at a precise moment. Subsequent reception certainly indicates that the text was recognized as such. There are allusions to Einhard's work within a few years of its completion (the earliest may be 821), though the lack of surviving copies from less than about fifty years after its composition unfortunately makes it impossible to chart its initial impact with certainty. Books containing the *Vita Karoli* can be linked with the royal court and royal monasteries. The manuscripts are so dispersed, however, and reflect different interventions in the process of dissemination, including Walafrid Strabo's preface and insertion of chapters, as to

---

[42] The arguments for an early date of M. Innes and R. McKitterick, 'The writing of history', in McKitterick, *Carolingian culture*, pp. 203–8, have not found universal favour. See the summary of the most recent debate in McKitterick, *History and memory*, pp. 29–30.

[43] On the Abodrites see R. Ernst, 'Karolingische Nordostpolitik zur Zeit Ludwigs des Frommen', in C. Goehrke, E. Oberländer, D. Wojtecki (eds.), *Östliches Europa: Spiegel der Geschichte. Festschrift für Manfred Hellmann zum 65. Geburtstag*, Quellen und Studien zur Geschichte des östlichen Europa 9 (Wiesbaden, 1977), pp. 81–107; and Lupus of Ferrières, *Ep.* 1, ed. L. Levillain, *Loup de Ferrières: correspondance* (Paris, 1964), p. 6.

indicate rapid and extensive manuscript transmission soon after the text's composition.[44]

An early date provides the most appropriate context for this celebratory text about a ruler who has recently died. On closer scrutiny, even the confidence in 817 as the earliest possible date the *Vita Karoli* could have been written proves to be ill-founded. Ganshof's robust common sense long ago undermined the value of the reference to the portico. He proposed that Einhard's knowledge of building should be given greater credit, and that his reference to the collapse of the heavy gallery between the palace and the chapel, probably of stone, was not the same as that mentioned in the *Annales regni francorum* for 817; the latter was a lighter, probably wooden, structure that replaced it. Whether this conjecture about the building material being referred to is sustainable or not, the archaeological indications are that Aachen remained a building site well into Louis the Pious's reign. Occasional collapses of parts of new buildings, especially in a region of thermal springs, seem likely. The portico certainly cannot provide a secure basis for dating the *Vita Karoli*.[45]

The reference to the Abodrites is also inconclusive. Between the murder of Thrasco, *dux* of the Abodrites in 809, and the allusion in the annals for 817, there is no reference to the Abodrites at all in any extant text. Thrasco had been Charlemagne's ally, elevated to a position of leadership among what seems to have been a conglomerate group of Abodrites in the Baltic sea region.[46] The fluctuations of alliances and hostilities among the Abodrites, Danes and Wiltzites in that region, and the difficulties posed for the Franks in ensuring some kind of influence on the political leadership among the Abodrites after Thrasco's death, open up several years of

---

[44] The chapters inserted by Walafrid Strabo were not part of Einhard's original intentions; see Ganz, 'Einhard's Charlemagne', pp. 38–9.

[45] F. L. Ganshof, 'Eginhard, biographe de Charlemagne', *Bibliothèque d'Humanisme et Renaissance* 13 (1951), pp. 217–30, trans. J. Sondheimer, 'Einhard, biographer of Charlemagne', in F. L. Ganshof, *The Carolingians and the Frankish monarchy* (London, 1971), pp. 1–16, esp. note 42.

[46] In addition to the references cited in note 43 above, see W. F. Fritze, 'Die Geographicus Bavarus und die Stammesverfassung der Abodriten', *Zeitschrift für slavische Philologie* 21 (1952), pp. 326–42, and see below, pp. 129–30. Fritze reports a suggestion of the Polish scholar E. Kucharski, made in 1929, that the list of Slav peoples and *civitates* in Munich, Bayerische Staatsbibliothek, Clm 560, fols. 149v–150r (the so-called *Geographicus bavarus*), was an official report compiled in preparation for the Avar war from 797 and the limits set on merchant travel to Avars and Slavs in the Thionville capitulary of 806 (see below, p. 255). The manuscript itself is dated by B. Bischoff, *Katalog der festländischen Handschriften des neunten Jahrhunderts (mit Ausnahme der wisigotischen)*, Teil II: Laon–Paderborn (Stuttgart, 2004), pp. 221–2, No. 2928, to the last quarter of the ninth century. Fritze prefers a date for the original text between 844 and 862 and links it with Louis the German. For a facsimile of the *Geographicus Bavarus* text see M. Hellmann, 'Karl und die slawische Welt zwischen Ostsee und Böhmerwald', *KdG* 1, pp. 708–18 at 712–13.

instability among the Abodrites between 809 and 817. The allusion Einhard makes to the Abodrites formerly being allies of the Franks is as likely to be a reference to the situation after 809, when they had become tributaries of the Danes, as to 817. Thus 817 ceases to be a secure *terminus a quo*; instead, Einhard's *Vita Karoli* was written after January 814.

The agenda for ruling implicit in the *Vita Karoli* can be read as a manifesto in support of the settlement of 813–14 at a time early in Louis's reign when it would have had the greatest political impact. As Matthew Innes and I argued in 1994, the *Vita Karoli* needs to be placed in the context of the preparation of the *Ordinatio imperii* of 817 and the association between Louis the Pious and the papacy in 815–16. The will and its signatories included by Einhard enhanced the function of the final paragraphs of his text. These stress the legitimacy and regularity of Louis's succession, both in the account of Charlemagne's admonition to Louis and the crowning of his son, and in the comment on Louis's responsibility for seeing that his father's wishes, as expressed in the will, were followed after his death. Einhard tells us far more about Charlemagne's coronation of Louis in 813 than he does about Charlemagne's coronation at the hands of Pope Leo III in 800. Einhard's text also contains a clear statement about the inheritance of Bernard of Italy, a grandson of Charlemagne whom Louis subsequently disinherited in the *Ordinatio imperii* of 817. An instant objection might be to ask why the text continued to circulate, if so placed in terms of its political purpose and sympathies in relation to Bernard of Italy. This can be countered by pointing out that there continued to be doubts among the Franks about Bernard's responsibility for his own downfall and Louis's complicity in Bernard's blinding and subsequent death.[47] A text that seems to make such a strong case for Louis's succession would continue to have a positive function, for it made clear that Louis was in every respect Charlemagne's rightful heir and that his sons' right to rule in their respective kingdoms was also confirmed.[48]

The most plausible of the cases for alternative dates that have been made is that connecting the composition of the Life with the birth of Charlemagne's namesake Charles (subsequently the Bald, and king of the west Franks from 840 to 877) as a fourth son to Louis the Pious in 823.[49] Yet these arguments could provide an equally persuasive case for a special copy

---

[47] See McKitterick, *History and memory*, pp. 265–9.
[48] M. Innes and R. McKitterick, 'The writing of history', in R. McKitterick (ed.), *Carolingian culture: emulation and innovation* (Cambridge, 1994), pp. 193–220.
[49] K. H. Krüger, 'Neue Beobactungen zur Datierung von Einhards Karlsvita', *Frühmittelalterliche Studien* 32 (1998), pp. 124–45.

of an existing text being made and presented to Charlemagne's namesake. Arguments for later dates than this that have been offered, notably for 828–30, are less persuasive and too much dominated by the mistaken notion that the text is to be seen as a critique of Louis rather than as a celebration of Charlemagne.[50] In short, I maintain that the *Vita Karoli* was produced early in Louis's reign, most likely before 817 but certainly no later than 823, and that the very particular representation of Charlemagne it offered was valued and drawn on from then on.

Modern characterization of the work as secular biography might be regarded as puzzling in the light of its references to Charlemagne's piety and personal devotion as a Christian ruler. The 'secular' in this instance, however, appears to be an attempt on the part of past historians to signal the principally classical, rather than Christian, precedents for this kind of work. Einhard, indeed, has been credited with inventing, for the early middle ages at least, a new form of Life. This has been seen as a deliberate reaction against the genre of saint's Life merely because it is a biography of a lay contemporary ruler.[51] It is unnecessary to go so far, for the character of the text is surely more determined by its subject, in this case a secular ruler, than by the sub-genre to which it might be assigned.

Einhard's purpose was manifestly not to make Charlemagne into a saint, unlike some Merovingian hagiographers before him who had set themselves with great determination to turn unpromising subjects into saints.[52] For one thing, he may not in any case have seen hagiography and secular biography as such distinct genres. In his own monastery at Fulda, where he was educated, he is most likely first to have encountered the classical and Christian texts which formed his intellect and shaped his style of writing. There, Einhard would have been familiar at the very least with the *Vita Bonifatii*, an account of Boniface's career by an author who had access to letters written by Boniface as well as the personal recollections of his subject by people who had known him. Secondly, the notions of sainthood or hagiography may not have crossed his mind. Early medieval rulers had played a prominent role in early medieval historical narratives before, if we think only of the portrait of Clovis in Gregory of Tours's *Historiae*,[53]

---

[50] See, for example, Tischler, *Einharts Vita Karoli*, pp. 163–4, and the strong counterarguments by M. de Jong, *The penitential state* (Cambridge, forthcoming).

[51] Ganz, 'Einhard's Charlemagne', p. 40.

[52] P. Fouracre, 'Merovingian history and Merovingian hagiography', *Past and Present* 127 (1990), pp. 3–38.

[53] See J. M. Wallace-Hadrill, 'Gregory's kings' in J. M. Wallace-Hadrill, *The long-haired kings and other studies in Frankish history* (London, 1962), pp. 185–206; and M. Heinzelmann, *Gregor von Tours*

the structure of Paul the Deacon's *Historia langobardorum*, in which the central figures of the kings Alboin, Authari, Agilulf, Grimoald and Liutprand link each successive book of the history,[54] and the focus on Charles Martel and Pippin provided in the early stages of the Continuation of the Chronicle of Fredegar, let alone the deeds of Charlemagne related in the Royal Frankish annals in both the original and the Revised Version.[55] All these provide vivid thumbnail sketches and a variety of approaches to relating the deeds of the kings and rulers concerned. Certainly their structure was not the same as a biography, but they did at least provide examples of how to discuss the *gesta* of kings. Thirdly, it is mistaken to suppose that writers in the early middle ages might have been unfamiliar with the idea of a secular biography, for the Life of a saint was not the only contemporary model to hand. Ancient models of praise of rulers and 'illustrious men' and biographies from antiquity were available as well. Some at least of these older texts were in effect also part of Einhard's contemporary intellectual equipment and those of his peers. What is obvious, however, is that Einhard's rhetorical eloquence, as well as his borrowing of phrases and vocabulary, reinforced his text's character as biography according to classical models, created associations with Roman texts of a similar kind, and thereby extended the imaginative horizons and frame of reference for contemporary memories of Charlemagne.

Since Einhard's use of Suetonius' Lives of the Twelve Caesars, and especially the life of Augustus, was first spotted by Isaac Casaubon (1559–1614), one of Einhard's classical models has been acknowledged to be Suetonius' *De vita caesarum*, even though the appropriateness of such a set of pagan emperors, who claimed divinity, as patterns for a Christian king, is questionable.[56] Einhard's use of Suetonius was mainly confined to the verbal echoes from the lives of Augustus, Nero and Caligula in the sections about appearance and personal habits, and to an adaptation of the structure of each imperial biography and method of proceeding partly by topic rather than in a strictly chronological order. The parallels in subject matter between Augustus (according to Suetonius) and Charlemagne (according to Einhard) are undoubted, not least the interest in learning

(538–594): *Zehn Bücher Geschichte Historiographie und Gesellschaftskonzept im 6. Jahrhundert* (Darmstadt, 1994), pp. 57–68, trans. C. Carroll, *Gregory of Tours: history and society in the sixth century* (Cambridge, 2001), pp. 60–75.
[54] McKitterick, *History and memory*, pp. 71–4.   [55] See further below, pp. 107–11.
[56] For a positive assessment see L. Hageneier, *Jenseits der Topik: die karolingische Herrscherbiographie*, Historische Studien 483 ((Husum, 2004), pp. 32–128.

and the honoured presence in his own household of scholars.[57] Other
parallels are the treatment of the personal appearance and domestic habits
of both (even to liking a nap after lunch), clothes, family, personal devotion
to learning, linguistic abilities and religious faith, the omens and portents
before death, the last illness and death, and the will. We also know there
was a copy of Suetonius at Tours (Paris BnF lat. 6115) dated to *c.* 820,
though no one has ever suggested that this was a manuscript Einhard knew.

Yet subsequent historians have become somewhat fixated on Suetonius
as the *exempla* for the *Vita Karoli* and have seen it as Einhard's only classical
model rather than considering Einhard's emulation of other texts. The
rhetorical tradition to which Einhard's text belongs includes the praise of
famous men, panegyric and *laudationes*, for which the ideal scheme was
proposed by the Greek rhetor Menander – including a Prooimion and such
topics as fatherland, family, birth and upbringing, deeds (starting with
war), bravery, justice and temperance, the king and his enemies, his battles,
appearance, other successes, wisdom, philanthropy and justice, deeds in
peace (including government) and concern for the succession. These
prescriptions were adapted among the Roman orators and rhetoricians,
not least Quintilian in a section of his *Institutio oratoria* on the praise of
men and, more generally, by Cicero in his *De oratore*.[58] The influence of
Cicero on Einhard's Latin style is the one thing about Einhard on which all
scholars are agreed.[59] Cicero's *De oratore*, moreover, was at Fulda when
Einhard was there.[60] In his discussion of the panegyric, Cicero mentioned
topics such as family, good looks, bodily strength, resources, riches and
other gifts of fortune, as well as mercy, justice, kindness, fidelity, and
courage in common dangers that could be addressed. Cicero referred to
the deeds (*facta*) and the achievements (*res gesta*) that could also be praised
by the panegyricist. These are the words Einhard invokes in his preface to
the *Vita Karoli*.[61] It was not only theory that guided Einhard. He also had
other practical examples of the praise of illustrious men to hand. Einhard in
806 and others in the royal entourage on other occasions, for example,

---

[57] Compare Einhard, *Vita Karoli*, ed. Halphen, c. 18, p. 54, and Suetonius, *Augustus*, c. 89, ed. J. C. Rolfe,
     Suetonius (Cambridge, Mass., 1970), pp. 256–8.
[58] C. E. V. Nixon and B. Saylor Rodgers, *In praise of later Roman emperors: the Panegyrici Latini.
     Introduction, translation and historical commentary with the Latin text of R. A. B. Mynors* (Berkeley,
     1994), pp. 12–13.
[59] For a useful summary see M. S. Kempshall, 'Some Ciceronian aspects of Einhard's Life of
     Charlemagne', *Viator* 26 (1995), pp. 11–38.
[60] Lupus, *Ep.* 1, ed. Levillain, p. 8.
[61] Cicero, *De oratore*, II, 84–5, ed. E. W. Sutton and H. Rackham (Cambridge, Mass., and London,
     1976), pp. 458–63.

could have seen the visual narratives of an emperor's exploits on such monuments as the Arch of Titus and Trajan's column in Rome.

As far as knowledge of texts is concerned, Einhard's use of a rare word *dicaculus* (talkative) from the Life of the Emperor Hadrian in the *Scriptores Historiae Augustae* has been noted by David Ganz.[62] Given the existence of a Fulda copy of the *Scriptores Historiae Augustae* copied in the second quarter of the ninth century from a north Italian manuscript of the first half of the ninth century, it is possible that Einhard at some stage had direct access to this late antique set of imperial biographies as well.

There is one other crucial text to be mentioned. Although ignored hitherto in relation to Einhard's *Vita Karoli*, it has as many, if not stronger, parallels with the *Vita Karoli* as Suetonius and was an important precursor of Suetonius. It provided the essential structure, standard in ancient biographies, for the biography of a secular leader. This is the *Agricola* by Tacitus, son-in-law of his subject, completed in AD 97–8, and thus about two decades before Suetonius' *De vita caesarum*.[63]

Agricola himself held office during the careers of seven of the caesars discussed by Suetonius – Nero, Galba, Otho, Vitellius, Vespasian, Titus and Domitian. Completed within four years of Agricola's death, the text is a brilliant piece of rhetoric and historical narrative. It has an element of panegyric and a sensitivity to the recent political past it portrays. The narrative style draws on Sallust and Livy.[64] Tacitus was conscious of joining a tradition of writing about the works and ways, deeds and habits, of famous men – *clarorum virorum facta moresque* – and therefore set out to write a *vita*, a Life, of his father-in-law Gnaeus Julius Agricola out of filial piety.[65] Agricola still inspires admiration as a military genius and able administrator, particularly skilled at strategic geography and with an unexpected sympathy, as articulated by Tacitus, with those he was beating into submission, which made him dangerously successful. Agricola was a provincial, born in Forum Julii (Fréjus) in *Gallia Narbonensis*, and had a remarkable career, serving in Britain on three separate occasions as well as in *Asia* and *Aquitania*. He also acted as *quaestor* in AD 64, tribune of the

[62] Ganz, 'Einhard's Charlemagne', in Story (ed.), *Charlemagne*, p. 49.
[63] I am grateful to Alexander Murray, member of Harrow School's Sixth Form History and Classics set in 1989–90, for planting this idea, sprung from his own reading of both texts, in discussion after a talk on Charlemagne I gave to the group at Harrow School in 1990.
[64] Tacitus, *Agricola, Germania and Dialogus*, ed. and trans. R. M. Ogilvie, E. H. Warmington and M. Winterbottom (revised from M. Hutton and W. Peterson's translations) (London and Cambridge, Mass., 1970), p. 19.
[65] Tacitus, *Agricola* c. 1 and 3, in Tacitus, *Agricola, Germania and Dialogus*, ed. and trans. Ogilvie, Warmington and Winterbottom, p. 30.

plebs in AD 66, *praetor* in AD 68, was elected a patrician in AD 74 and served as consul in AD 77. Agricola was in Britain at the time of the revolt of Boudicca in AD 60. At a later stage he was appointed by the Emperor Vespasian to command the Twentieth Legion stationed at Wroxeter in AD 70 and he returned as governor of Britain in AD 78.

After the introduction explaining his motives for writing the biography, Tacitus gives a brief account of Agricola's family, grandfathers and father (c. 4)[66] and how his apprenticeship to war was in Britain (c. 5). More personal detail is given in an account of his virtues and of his (happy) marriage (c. 6), while in c. 7 there is the reporting of the murder of his mother, his loss of estates, and the problems of serving under different emperors. Tacitus then takes Agricola back to Britain in AD 78. The central section telling of his governorship and extensive military campaigns against the British tribes (cc. 18–39) is marked off by the introduction on the ethnography and history of Britain (cc. 10–12, 13–17). This includes the description of the length of the days and nights in Britain and an imaginative reconstruction of how the Britons would have felt about being ruled by Rome.[67] Tacitus emphasizes Agricola's evenhandedness and attention to justice to civilians. He offers praise of his wise ruling and details of his military leadership in terms of straightforward organization (choice of camps, estuaries and forests) and how many states 'were induced to give hostages and abandon their hostility'.[68] There is also an account of the method by which he started the process of the Romanization of the Britons, reminiscent of the process by which Charlemagne and the Franks 'frankicized' the Saxons: Agricola 'began to train the sons of the chieftains in liberal education and to give a preference to the native talents of the Briton against the trained abilities of the Gaul. As a result, the nation which used to reject the Latin language began to aspire to rhetoric' . . . (they wore togas, learnt about baths, the dinner table, etc.) . . . 'the simple natives gave the name of culture to this fact of their slavery'.[69]

Final sections recount Agricola's last illness and death. There is an account of the will which named the Emperor Domitian as co-heir. At

---

[66] Ibid., c. 4 pp. 31–33.   [67] Ibid., cc. 12 and 15, pp. 48 and 52–6.
[68] Ibid., c. 20, p. 64: 'quibus rebus multae civitates, quae in illum diem ex aequo egerant, datis obsidibus iram posuere et praesidiis castellisque circumdatae' (and how he carefully and skilfully surrounded them with Roman garrisons and forts).
[69] Ibid., c. 21, p. 66: 'iam vero principum filios liberalibus artibus erudire, et ingenia Britannorum studiis Gallorum anteferre, ut qui modo linguam Romanam abnuebant, eloquentiam concupiscerent. Inde etiam habitus nostri et frequens toga; paulatimque discessum ad delenimenta vitiorum, porticus et balinea et conviviorum elegantiam. Idque apud imperitos humanitas vocabatur, cum pars servitutis est.'

this stage Tacitus gave a description of Agricola's personal appearance, and the text ends with a lament for the loss of Agricola and tells how his deeds, whose story is told by Tacitus, will outlive death.[70]

In structure the *Vita Karoli* resembles *Agricola* and on a number of points of detail the text also begs comparison with Einhard's account. *Agricola* starts with Tacitus' explanation of his wish to hand down to posterity the works and ways of famous men which, out of filial piety, he dedicates to the glory of his father-in-law.[71] One is here reminded of Einhard's statement at the outset of his preface to his *vita* of Charles, who had been his lord and *nutritor*, and how he had decided to describe 'the life and character and many of the accomplishments of . . . Charles, that most outstanding and deservedly famous king'. The persistent way the British campaign is conducted by Agricola year after year can also be compared with Charlemagne's long-drawn-out series of campaigns against the Saxons, the subjection of different groups or tribes, strategic tactics, taking of hostages, large-scale displacement and deportation of the people and conversion as well as the establishment of new Frankish garrisons. Agricola spent the winter of AD 79 in supervising the Romanization of the province, encouraging in particular the development of urban centres and the spread of Latin education. Season after season of campaigns in the north and northwest of Britain, including the strategic capture of Anglesey and southern Scotland, culminated in the dramatic victory of Mons Graupius.[72] Archaeological evidence confirms Tacitus' claims about the extent to which garrisons and forts were built to consolidate the conquest and establish a military presence. Further, Tacitus' digression on the ethnography of Britain, the bringing under Roman rule of which is the mark of Agricola's success, bears direct comparison with the two ethno-geographical digressions of Einhard on the peoples of the Baltic, and the summary of the territorial extent of Charlemagne's conquests and the peoples brought under Frankish rule.[73]

Tacitus' *Agricola* could have influenced Einhard directly, for the earliest extant manuscript of it, and conceivably therefore also the exemplar from which it was copied, are associated with Fulda. This codex was formerly Codex Aesinas lat. 8 in a private library in Jesi. Written at Fulda, it is dated palaeographically to s.IX 2/4 and s.XV. It contains Dictys Cretensis, *Bellum Troianum* as well as the *Germania* and *Agricola* of Tacitus, but the *Agricola*

---

[70] Ibid., cc. 45 and 46, pp. 110–14.   [71] Ibid., cc. 1 and 3, pp. 26–7, 30–1.   [72] Ibid., c. 21, p. 66.
[73] Ibid., cc. 10–12, pp. 42–50; and Einhard, *Vita Karoli*, c. 15, ed. Halphen, pp. 44–6.

(fols. 56–63) is now the only Carolingian portion of the book. It also has contemporary corrections in a different hand. The rest of the book comprises copies of the *Germania* and Dictys Cretensis made by the Italian humanist Guanieri, supposedly from another ninth-century exemplar. Guanieri appears to have attempted to make his copy look as much like his ninth-century exemplar in layout and headings as he could.[74] A wider knowledge of this text in Frankish intellectual circles is suggested not only by this text and its exemplar but also by the third copy, which appears to have been the source of the corrections. The Jesi codex was discovered by Cesare Annibaldi in 1904, attracted the attention of Adolf Hitler (who vainly asked Mussolini for it) in 1936, was published in facsimile in 1943,[75] and was lost sight of for decades subsequently, but is now in Rome, Biblioteca Nazionale Cod. Vitt. Em. 1631.[76]

Einhard, therefore, was able to draw on a wide range of sources for ideas about how to present Charlemagne. In this sense he could be said to have created Charlemagne,[77] or at least an extraordinarily influential representation of Charlemagne that might also have been read as a model for rulership. That later readers nevertheless wanted more detail on specific points and supplementary topics and used the royal portrait in different ways is suggested by the manuscript contexts in which the life is so often found, that is, in books which are effectively dossiers on Charlemagne or on Carolingian kings and Frankish history more generally. Thus Einhard's *Vita Karoli* is sometimes accompanied by the Royal Frankish annals, or Notker Balbulus's entertaining but instructive collection of anecdotes, written for the Emperor Charles the Fat,[78] or is set beside the Lives of Louis the Pious by Thegan[79] and the Astronomer.[80]

---

[74] Reynolds, *Texts and transmission*, p. 410. Heiric made some excerpts, see M. Ihm, 'Beitrage zur Textgeschichte des Sueton', *Hermes* 36 (1901), pp. 343–63.

[75] R. Till, *Handschriftliche Untersuchungen zu Tacitus Agricola und Germania* (Berlin and Dahlem, 1943).

[76] See the useful summary by R. Pearse, <www.tertullian.org/rpearse/tacitus>.

[77] Ganz, 'Einhard's Charlemagne'.

[78] For orientation in the massive amount of literature on Notker see H. Löwe, 'Das Karlsbuch Notkers von St Gallen und sein zeitgeschichtliche Hintergrund', *Schweizerische Zeitschrift für Geschichte* 20 (1970), pp. 269–302; D. Ganz, 'Humor as history in Notker's *Gesta Karoli magni*', in E. B. King (ed.), *Monks, friars and nuns in medieval society* (Sewanee, 1989), pp. 171–83; and S. MacLean, *Kingship and politics in the late ninth century: Charles the Fat and the end of the Carolingian empire*, Cambridge Studies in Medieval Life and Thought (Cambridge, 2003), pp. 199–229.

[79] On Thegan see Ernst Tremp, *Studien zu den Gesta Hludowici imperatoris des Trierer Chorbischofs Thegan*, MGH Schriften 32 (Hanover, 1988).

[80] On other examples of 'Karlskompendien' see Tischler, *Einharts Vita Karoli*, esp. pp. 592–606. On the manuscript transmission of the Astronomer see E. Tremp, *Die Überlieferung der Vita Hludowici imperatoris des Astronomus*, MGH Studien und Texte 1 (Hanover, 1991).

Charlemagne in the Astronomer's Gesta Hludowici imperatoris

The Astronomer's Life of Louis the Pious offers a perception of Charlemagne from the early 840s,[81] though his chosen subject was the deeds and life of the orthodox emperor Louis. Consequently, chapters 2–20 refer to Charlemagne only incidentally. The Astronomer's overall purpose is indicated by his reference to remembering the 'good and bad deeds of the ancients, especially princes', for this had a two-fold advantage, to benefit or edify, and to warn.[82] He noted that older records were zealous to instruct posterity how each prince travelled a moral journey. His task was to be neither careless to the present nor begrudging to the future. In the first chapter of his work, Charlemagne's career is presented in a summary fashion as a prelude to that of his son, so much so that the coronation of 800 is mentioned in passing: while Charles was going to Rome and receiving the imperial insignia, Louis stayed in Toulouse and then marched into Spain.[83] Charlemagne assumed sole rule in 771, and the Astronomer emphasized the peace and concord of the church and the need to bind peaceful people together into fraternal union, strike down rebels, bring hope to those oppressed by pagans and even lead pagans to truth. The Astronomer was clear that God assisted Charlemagne, for it was with God's help that Charlemagne settled the affairs of Francia. Hannibal was invoked as a comparison when Charlemagne crossed the Pyrenees, and the defeat at Roncesvalles was mentioned only obliquely.

A further instance of the Astronomer's insistence on Louis as the designated heir from the beginning is the account of the birth of Louis. Here the Astronomer claims that Charlemagne handed over the kingdom which he had assigned to him at birth and he describes the arrangements made for the administration of the kingdom. Charlemagne is portrayed in consequence as a wise king, treating the kingdom like a body, and making sensible, practical administrative arrangements for good government. Further, in chapter 4, the Astronomer noted that Charles took Louis to Rome to receive the royal insignia from the pope and later on summoned him successively to Paderborn, Worms, Ingelheim, Regensburg and Salz. In 791 Louis spent Christmas in Ravenna and on campaign in Benevento with his brother Pippin, and he is mentioned as coming to Tours in 800, to

---

[81] Dated winter 840/1 or 842–3. See E. Tremp, *Thegan: die Taten Kaiser Ludwigs. Astronomus: das Leben Kaiser Ludwigs, MGH SRM* 64 (Hanover, 1995), pp. 66–9 for the earlier date; and H. Doherty, 'The maintenance of royal power and prestige in the Carolingian *regnum* of Aquitaine under Louis the Pious', unpublished MPhil dissertation, University of Cambridge (1998), for the later.

[82] Prologus, ed. Tremp, *Astronomus*, p. 280.   [83] Ibid., c. 10, pp. 298–300.

the general assembly at Aachen in 802, and to Saxony in 804. This seems designed to demonstrate how Charlemagne was schooling his son for the succession, and certainly for his role as king in Aquitaine. The Astronomer spelt this out in col. 6: the royal father was especially concerned that the royal son should not lack an honourable upbringing, and that foreign customs would not dishonour him. It was Charlemagne, moreover, who forbade Louis to relinquish rule and become a monk. This section of the work culminates in Louis's summons to Aachen in 813 to be crowned by his father and be given advice on how to be king. It is followed by a very striking insistence on the 'almost unshakeable sorrow Charlemagne's death caused in the kingdom of the Franks'. *Ecclesiasticus* 30.4 is invoked: 'The just man is dead and yet he is not dead for he has left behind a son like himself as an heir.'

The principal characteristics of Charlemagne as he was represented by the Astronomer are as follows: he was a wise king and governor; he was a wise father, schooling his son Louis in kingship so that from 813 complete authority within his own household is ceded to Louis; he was the conqueror of the Saxons, an achievement with which Louis is associated.[84] The succession is presented as the climax of all these preparations in 813 as the Old King contemplated his decline. The Astronomer's parting shot for this section is to stress that Louis the son is like his father Charlemagne.

The Poeta Saxo

It is the Poeta Saxo who provides us with a remarkable demonstration of how much the earlier narrative and descriptive accounts of Charlemagne's reign had been absorbed and digested by the end of the ninth century in Saxony. He presented Charlemagne in an extraordinary and distinctive way as an apostle bringing the Christian faith to the gentiles: just as the Ethiopians had Matthew, and Thomas went to India, so the Saxons had Charlemagne.[85] His other major theme was that the Franks and the Saxons formed one *gens*, an outcome also stressed by Einhard in his statement that the Saxon wars concluded with terms laid down by the king and accepted by the Saxons, namely, that they would reject the worship of demons, take up the Christian faith, and unite with Franks in order to form a single people.[86]

---

[84] Ibid., c. 11, pp. 310–12.
[85] Poeta Saxo, *Annales de gestis Caroli: magni imperatoris*, ed. P. von Winterfeld, *MGH Poet.* IV (Berlin, 1899), pp. 1–71.
[86] Einhard, *Vita Karoli*, ed. Halphen, c. 7, p. 22.

Frustratingly little is known about the Poeta Saxo. He was a Corvey monk, writing between 888 and 891 in the reign of Arnulf, who is mentioned in the text as still the reigning monarch. The poem might even have been presented to King Arnulf, but there is no clear evidence that it was known outside Corvey itself. The manuscript in Wolfenbüttel, Herzog August Bibliothek, Helmstedt. 553, is apparently eleventh-century.[87] Only subsequent use by the tenth-century Saxon historian Widukind assured the Poeta Saxo's representation of Charlemagne a far longer life. Corvey itself was a productive place in the ninth century. Adalhard of Corbie was its first abbot, and a number of important saints' Lives were written there, not least Rimbert's Life of St Anskar. Efforts to identify the Poeta Saxo with Agius of Corvey, author of the *Vita Hathumodi*, were dismissed by Strecker and attempts to resuscitate the attribution have not found favour.[88]

The Poeta Saxo wrote versified history in hexameters, the metre for epic poetry. One precedent for this was Alcuin's York Poem, in large part a versification of Bede's *Historia ecclesiastica*. Similarly, the Poeta Saxo's work rendered the *Annales regni francorum* into verse, with an emphasis on the Christianization of the Saxons. Even under 782, the year of Widukind's rebellion and the terrible slaughter of 4,500 Saxons at Verdun, the Poeta Saxo simply comments that after meting out this punishment the 'greatest of kings' returned to Thionville. Other killing and destruction by fire and sword are presented as incidental means for the procuring of a people for the new faith. An account of the establishment of a new people is also of course the principal theme of Virgil's *Aeneid*, and this may have been a further inspiration for the Poeta Saxo.[89] The first four books of this fascinating poem are usually disregarded, except for the singling out of his reference to the tripartite division of the Saxon people and his account of the peace of Salz.[90]

The work is divided into five books. Books I to IV divide up Charlemagne's reign into decades, and the poem is presented in a year-by-year sequence just like the Royal Frankish annals.[91] Book I begins in

[87] Poeta Saxo, ed. Winterfeld, *MGH Poet.* IV, pp. 2–3.
[88] K. Strecker, 'Studien zu karolingischen Dichtern', *Neues Archiv* 43 (1922), pp. 477–511 at pp. 490–92; H. Löwe, 'Lateinisch-christliche Kultur im karolingischen Sachsen', in *Angli e Sassoni al di qua e al di là del mare*, Settimane 32 (Spoleto, 1986), pp. 491–531; B. Bischoff, 'Das Thema des Poeta Saxo', *Mittelalterliche Studien* 3 (Stuttgart, 1981), pp. 253–59; and J. Bohne, *Der Poeta Saxo in der historiographischen Tradition der 8.–10. Jahrhundert* (Frankfurt, 1965).
[89] I am grateful to the participants in the discussion at the NIAS workshop on 21 February 2006 on the Astronomer's Life of Louis the Pious for their helpful suggestions.
[90] M. Becher, 'Die Sachsen im 7. und 8. Jahrhundert: Verfassung und Ethnogenese', in *799 Kunst und Kultur*, I, pp. 188–94.
[91] See below, pp. 31–6.

771; it takes Charlemagne's career to the return from Spain and the Saxons' feigning to believe in Christ. Book II starts with the visit to Rome in 781 and the baptism of Pippin. It is in keeping with the poet's theme of baptism and faith that no reference here is made to the anointing of either Pippin or Louis as (sub-)kings of Italy and Aquitaine respectively. It treats the downfall of Tassilo very summarily, and omits the material in the revised *Annales regni francorum* on Theuderic, on the death of Bertrada, and concerning Byzantium, though it does include the revolt of Hardrad of 785. On Tassilo, the Poeta Saxo offers the terse judgment that such a penalty comes deservedly to anyone who has followed a woman's advice.

The third book includes verses for 799 which bewail the evils of humans, before telling the story of Leo and the happy days the pope spent with Charlemagne at Paderborn. Charlemagne reaches Rome and Book IV starts with the imperial coronation. A large amount of space is devoted to the year 803 and the final conclusion of peace between Charlemagne and the Saxons. The terms of the peace are provided in detail and great weight is placed upon the hope that they should now be one people. Under 806 the king is at Aachen. The poet gave a full account of the rationale for the *Divisio regnorum*. The king wanted to maintain peace, prevent dissension and avoid schism. He devised a division of the kingdom, giving portions to each one as he wished, for he hoped to prevent his sons quarrelling. The Poeta Saxo emphasized that Charles the Younger was intended to be the successor to the kingdom of the Franks. It is from this year, moreover, that Charlemagne is said to have based himself at Aachen and his military exploits ceased. In 810 and 811 Charlemagne's grief at the death of his sons Pippin of Italy and Charles the Younger gets more sympathetic treatment than in any other source. The rightful inheritance of Bernard, son of Pippin, in 811 is also stressed. The emphasis Einhard and the Astronomer placed on the succession of Louis is reiterated here, for Charlemagne increased his kingdom and surrendered it to his prudent and peace-loving son Louis. Book V is a lament on the death of Charlemagne who 'caused my nation (the Saxons) to know the light of faith and to cast off the darkness of perfidy. Almost all the peoples of Europe, says the author, remember his great effort even to this day.'[92]

These three ninth-century texts have in common their primarily literary purpose and a particular style of interpretation of political events as a consequence of their being from hindsight. All are, moreover, dependent to a greater or lesser extent on information provided either in the *Annales*

---

[92] Poeta Saxo, ed. Winterfeld, *MGH Poet.* IV, p. 70.

regni francorum for the years 741–814 or in the Revised Version of the annals for the years 741–801, both texts which, as we shall see below, are more directly contemporary with the events on which they report and which have a different kind of historical validity.[93] That being the case, the Poeta Saxo quite clearly used the *Annales regni francorum* primarily in the Revised Version and possibly also in the original version for Books I, II and III, as well as summarizing Einhard's *Vita Karoli* in Book V of his poem. After his account of the imperial coronation of Charlemagne in Book IV, however, he diverged ever further from the Revised Version of the *Annales regni francorum* which have been his base text hitherto, to such an extent that I suspect he had access only to a text of the annals running to 801, that is the section actually revised. There is a great deal of material in the fourth book, covering the last years of Charlemagne's life, which is not to be found elsewhere. He also appears to have drawn on the Lorsch annals; or at least he chooses to discuss the law giving of the king, an account of which is also to be found in the Lorsch annals entry for 802.[94] Yet the Poeta Saxo's own purpose was distinct, and he used his sources to enable him to stress the conversion of the Saxons rather than their conquest, and to paint an idealized and apostolic portrait of the mighty emperor.

For the section before 814, by contrast, it is striking what little use the Astronomer made of the *Annales regni francorum* as opposed to his extensive use of the section of the *Annales regni francorum* for 814–29 when writing about Louis's reign once he had succeeded his father as emperor. Presumably this is partly because that text provided so little on the early career of Louis, or was all that was available to him apart from the comments he reports having received from 'Ademar'. But the Astronomer's representation can also be read as a conscious decision about the use of, and reactions to, the narrative supplied by the *Annales regni francorum*.

Further, each author was perfectly capable of adding local and individual memories or a personal selection of documentary material to his narrative. Thus Einhard, although apparently drawing much of his information from the Revised Version of the *Annales regni francorum*, and once even credited with being the Reviser himself, adds comments about particular events.[95] The most famous of these are his portrait of the last and ludicrous Merovingian king, reduced to travelling around in an ox cart, and his

---

[93] See below, pp. 27–36.

[94] McKitterick, *History and memory*, pp. 104–10. See also R. Collins, 'Charlemagne's imperial coronation and the annals of Lorsch', in Story, *Charlemagne*, pp. 52–70.

[95] See L. Halphen, *Etudes critiques sur l'histoire de Charlemagne* (Paris, 1921), pp. 78–81; and M. Manitius, 'Zu den Annales Laurissenses und Einhart', *MIÖG* 13 (1892), pp. 225–38.

claim that Charlemagne protested that he would never have entered
St Peter's church in Rome on Christmas Day 800 had he known of the
pope's intentions.[96] There are many smaller additions and omissions.
Foreign embassies from the Persian ruler, the Greeks, Alfonso, king of
Galicia and the Asturias, and monks from Jerusalem are certainly men-
tioned in the *Annales regni francorum* from 798. But so are many more that
Einhard does not mention. Equally Einhard refers to the Irish kings who
are not mentioned in the annals.

The Poeta Saxo, for his part, added occasional comments on protagonists in his story, his own knowledge about his people, and the long
account of the terms agreed between Charlemagne and the Franks at the
conclusion of the three decades of war and attrition. How strong local
memories might be is also suggested by the Astronomer's comment, a full
seventy years after the event, that he had no need to provide details of the
names of those killed at Roncesvalles in the Pyrenees because they were
widely known.[97]

The use of narrative accounts from the reign of Charlemagne itself raises
the question of influence and how this should be understood. By 'influence' I do not mean the old game of spotting textual borrowing and
omission or inclusion of particular details. That of course is something
that has to be done, as I have indicated above, and is certainly interesting in
itself. It is essential, however, to move to the next stage and to think in
terms not so much of how particular texts influenced subsequent authors
but more of what these authors did to these texts and how they used them.
Further, does Einhard, the Astronomer, or the Poeta Saxo need to have a
single specific *textual* source for the information he includes? Could each
not also have benefited from the same sources – personal memory, written
records and other narratives, oral communication of other people's memories and information, gossip and so on – as the Reviser?

Why should this be important? Did these authors have a choice, or does
this merely reflect different distribution patterns of the text on which they
drew? If, on the other hand, both the original and revised texts of the
Annales regni francorum were available, as seems to have been the case for all
these authors, the version of one being preferred over the other assumes
greater significance. Yet what matters more than the sources from which
each new text was constructed is the image of Charles thereby created. In
other words, my underlying theme is use and transformation as processes

---

[96] See *Vita Karoli*, ed. Halphen, c. 28, pp. 80–1.
[97] Astronomer, *Vita Hludowici*, c. 2, ed. Tremp, *Astronomus*, p. 288, and compare below, p. 134.

in the creation of an image of Charlemagne and his achievements. Even so, neither should we underestimate the independence of each author. Given that the *Annales regni francorum* were used by the author of the Revised Version of the *Annales regni francorum* to create his own text, some discussion of the consequent transformation of the overall image of Charlemagne effected by the Reviser is necessary before we address the topic of the *Annales regni francorum* themselves.

THE REVISED VERSION OF THE *ANNALES REGNI FRANCORUM*

The Revised or E Version of the *Annales regni francorum* comprised a reworked version of the *Annales regni francorum* for the years 741 to 801 plus what I shall denote as the 'common continuation' of both the *Annales regni francorum* and the Revised Version, namely the section covering the years 802–29.[98] Scholars remain undecided about whether it was completed shortly after 801 (my own view), between 814 and 817, or as late as *c.* 829.[99] The manuscript distribution suggests different spheres of influence, with *Annales regni francorum* apparently concentrated in Rhineland and westwards, but the Revised Version being mostly extant in manuscripts of the second half of the ninth century and later present in the Rhineland and eastwards. Its earliest complete manuscript, now in Vienna ÖNB 510, dates from the s.X/XI, but an earlier fragment of the text, as found in E manuscripts but with some variants and dated s.IX 1/3, survives in Cologne (Sankt Maria in Kapitol AII/18; this fragment is also associated with the court.[100] It is far from impossible to imagine two different versions of the same events in circulation, for the Lorsch annals offer another alternative, as do, for that matter, all the so-called minor annals. The spectrum of political opinion represented in the circulation of modern newspapers is a possible parallel. The crux appears to be that it might be possible to chart a change in court preference in the time of Charles the Bald and Louis the German.

The Revised Version alters the emphasis of the narrative and offers us a different perspective – sometimes subtly different and sometimes less so. In

---

[98] See the clear account of the discussion of this text in S. Kaschke, *Die karolingische Reichsteilungen bis 831: Herrschaftspraxis und Normvorstellungen in zeitgenössischer Sicht* (Hamburg, 2006), pp. 283–90; and see also McKitterick, *History and memory*, pp. 116–18. See also below, pp. 49–54.

[99] T. Reuter, in an unpublished Cambridge paper delivered in 1998, thought there were some stylistic deviations in the E family sufficient to distinguish it from B, C, D to 'about 812'.

[100] R. Collins, 'The "Reviser" revisited; another look at the alternative version of the *Annales regni francorum*', in A. C. Murray (ed.), *After Rome's fall: narrators and sources of early medieval history. Essays presented to Walter Goffart* (Toronto, 1998), pp. 191–213 at p. 213.

comparison with the *Annales regni francorum* for 741–801 the Reviser chose to mention episodes excluded from the original version, such as the account of the claims of Grifo to share rule with his brothers Pippin III and Carloman, the rebellion of Hardrad in 785 and the rebellion of Pippin the Hunchback in 792, and the Frankish military campaigns in Benevento. There are a number of minor differences that can be noted, such as the form of some place and personal names. Thus the Reviser wrote *Franci orientales* rather than *Franci austrasiorum*. There are literary debts to and vocabulary from classical authors in the Revised Version (and from 808 in the *Annales regni francorum*) to Livy, Tacitus, Quintus Curtius Rufus, Justinus, Velleius Paterculus, Caesar and Florus. The reviser very occasionally used rare words such as *foedifragus* (775, 798) and *obnubilo* (778), both from Aulus Gellius' *Noctes Atticae*, and he tended to prefer a more correct, or more classical, form of a place name. A variant choice of vocabulary is generally more classical.[101] For 'assembly' the Reviser used *conventus generalis* rather than the *Annales regni francorum*'s *placitum* and *synodus*. There is apparently a more exact version of place and personal names, especially in the rendering of Slavic names; names are supplied where lacking and additional people are mentioned by name.

Three further instances of the treatment of particular incidents – the conquest of the Lombard kingdom in 773–4, the events leading up to the execution of 4,500 Saxons at Verdun in 782, and the references to Rome in 796 – serve to demonstrate how the Reviser built his own account.

According to the *Annales regni francorum*, the legate Peter sent by Pope Hadrian arrived in 773 to urge the king and the Franks to help him against Desiderius, king of the Lombards. Charlemagne took counsel with the Franks and agreed to do what was requested; he then went and gathered the army at Geneva and divided it, with his uncle Bernard leading one wing across the Great St Bernard pass while Charles went via Mont Cenis. The king pitched his camp with the Franks below the pass, where Desiderius set out to meet him, but then retreated without an engagement. Charles with the Franks and all his *fideles* entered Italy and besieged Pavia.

The Reviser changed the emphasis by starting with Hadrian finding the oppression of the Lombards intolerable and deciding to seek Charlemagne's aid. The papal legate Peter comes to the king but Charlemagne alone investigates what is happening between Romans and Lombards, and decides to wage war. He comes with his army of Franks to Geneva and only at that stage takes counsel about the conduct of the war. Thus the

---

[101] See the useful list in ibid., pp. 203–4.

Reviser made more of the papal position by means of some imaginative glossing, which, incidentally, may indicate he had access to the copies of letters from Pope Hadrian in the *Codex Carolinus*. He stressed that the Lombard campaign is Charlemagne's decision, the Franks just do what they are told, and the Lombard king Desiderius' resistance is even weaker than before.

Under 782, the *Annales regni francorum* recorded that Charles set out on a military campaign, crossed the Rhine at Cologne, and held a *synodus* at Lippspringe. All the Saxons save the rebel Widukind came to Charlemagne there, and there were also legates from Halfdan of the Danes and from the Avars. The Saxons under Widukind rebelled, but Charlemagne, unaware of this, sent an army of Franks *and* Saxons against some Slavs. *En route* the leaders of this army, Adalgis, Geilo and Warin, heard about the Saxon rebellion, so without telling Charles they diverted, went to meet the Saxons in the Süntel mountains and were killed. The implication is that this was a punishment for going behind the king's back or not consulting him. Charlemagne heard about this and sent another army of Franks. The Saxons then assembled docilely, subjected themselves to the power of the lord king, and handed over to Charlemagne the rebels, except for Widukind, who had fled to the Northmen. The account continues in this neutral way: 4,500 Saxons were to be put to death, the sentence was carried out and when all this had been done the king returned to Francia.

The Reviser's version of this story starts with some scene-painting and auspicious weather (good weather for good kings is a recurrent motif): summer arrives and this means fodder for an army, so Charlemagne decided to hold an assembly in Saxony just as he had been accustomed to do every year in Francia. The king received news of a rebellion of Sorbs in Thuringia and sent Adalgis the *camerarius*, Geilo the *comes stabuli* and Warin the *comes palatii* to take the eastern Franks and Saxons (in an army) to repress the Slavs. Adalgis, Geilo and Warin accordingly crossed the Saale, heard about the Saxon rebellion and decided to go and deal with it themselves, but without informing the king. They were joined in Saxony, however, by Theodoric, a relative of the king, and Theodoric's troops gathered together when he had heard about the Saxon rebellion. The relationship claimed by use of the words *propinquus regis* for Theodoric was actually that of a grandson of a sister of both Plectrud, wife of Pippin II and the elder Bertrada, grandmother of Charlemagne's mother Bertrada.[102] Theodoric met the other Frankish army and advised them to reconnoitre.

---

[102] E. Hlawitschka, 'Die Vorfahren Karls des Großen', *KdG* I, pp. 51–82 at pp. 76–8.

He set up camp at the foot of the Süntel mountains whereas the other army crossed the river. At this stage the palatine counts decided that they wanted to do this on their own, for they feared that otherwise Theodoric would get all the credit. They thereupon attacked the Saxons without Theodoric and disaster (of course) ensued. Adalgis and Geilo were killed together with four other counts, twenty *fideles* and men who chose to die at their sides rather than survive them: *Praeter ceteros qui hos secuti potius cum eis perire quam post eos vivere maluerunt.* The king then received news of what had happened and decided to gather an army, and when he had arrived he questioned the *primores* of the Saxons whom he had summoned to him about who was responsible for the rebellion. They said 'Widukind', but they could not give him up because he had fled to the Northmen. No fewer than 4,500 of the others who had fallen in with him and committed this 'gross outrage', however, were handed over and at the king's command all were beheaded in a single day.

Not only is there a stronger moral tone and elegiac element for the fallen (led astray by their disobedient leaders); there is also again more emphasis on the personal role of the king himself.

A further example is the entry for 796. The Revised Version reads as follows:

At Rome [Leo] assumed the pontificate on the death of Pope Hadrian. He soon sent his legates to the king with the keys of the *confessio* of St Peter, the standard of the city of Rome and other gifts and asked him to despatch one of his *optimates* (leading men) to Rome to secure the Roman people's fidelity and subjection to him by oaths. Angilbert, abbot of the monastery of St Riquier was sent for this purpose.

The original version, however, makes no mention of securing the fidelity of the Roman people, their oaths, or that Angilbert was sent to receive the oaths. What Angilbert went to Rome for, according to this annalist, was to take the pope some of the Avar treasure as a gift.

As one proceeds through the whole Revised Version of the *Annales regni francorum*, it conveys an impression of Charlemagne the king, the role of the Franks and the regime he created, very different from that created by the text on which it is based. The focus is far more on the king himself and less on the triumphal role of the Franks as essential to the king's success. The hindsight inevitable because of the later date of creation apparently enabled the author/compiler to talk about the entire realm ruled by Charles in a much more integrated manner. Charles emerges as far more obviously the principal actor in the version made by the Reviser. The Reviser was a wholehearted admirer of Charlemagne, even of his ruthlessness when dealing with rebellions. As I have stressed elsewhere, the Reviser further enhances the legitimacy of Carolingian and Frankish rule over many peoples.[103]

All these later representations of Charlemagne appear to have been adjusted according to contemporaries' needs, and they relied for some of their effect on their audience's recognition of parallels and implied allusions to their own memory of events. They offer precious insights into the processes of the reception of news and the augmentation of the construction of the Frankish past to be found in the *Annales regni francorum*, and it is to this fundamental text that I now turn.

THE *ANNALES REGNI FRANCORUM*

The text known as the *Annales regni francorum* is the most substantial, as well as the most influential, of the contemporary narratives for the history of the Frankish kingdoms under the early Carolingian rulers. The annals form a powerful triumphalist narrative about the Franks and their rulers, and the text's influence can be traced, as we have seen, throughout the ninth century.[104] The *Annales regni francorum* run from 741 to 829, that is, dated by the year of the Incarnation and starting with the death of Charlemagne's grandfather Charles Martel. The structure of year-by-year entries is most probably modelled on that of the *Chronicon* of Eusebius-Jerome, which was widely known and copied in the early Carolingian period. The fine copy of the first quarter of the ninth century, Leiden Universiteitsbibliotheek Scaliger 14, has even been connected with the court.[105]

The annals are the closest thing to 'official history' we have from the early Carolingian period, and were first recognized as closely associated with the royal court by von Ranke, though I do not think it is possible to be as positive as Wattenbach and Levison that the annals must have been written *at* the court.[106] The court connection has been accepted by subsequent scholars because the annals in both the original and the Revised Version do indeed seem to be by someone writing about the deeds of the

---

[103] McKitterick, *History and memory*, p. 118.   [104] Ibid., pp. 84–119.
[105] Bischoff, *Katalog* II, No. 2179, p. 48; see also McKitterick, *Perceptions*, pp. 14–22, and below, p. 358.
[106] W. Wattenbach, W. Levison and H. Löwe, *Deutschlands Geschichtsquellen im Mittelalter: Vorzeit und Karolinger II. Heft Die Karolinger vom Anfang des 8. Jahrhunderts bis zum Tode Karls des Großen* (Weimar, 1953), pp. 245–54 at p. 248: 'Am Hofe müssen die Annalen geschrieben sein.'

Frankish kings who was, for the most part, very well informed about the central affairs of the Frankish kingdoms. He wrote, moreover, from a court, rather than from a monastic, perspective. There are also indications in the surviving manuscripts that the court was implicated in the distribution of the text.[107] Thus I do not propose to challenge the nineteenth-century label, provided it is understood that this is descriptive of the content and form of the text, though the question of the court connections of the authors is closely linked to the way in which the annals have survived.

Although organized as entries for a succession of years, it is generally agreed that these annals present a composite text: they were written in batches by a few anonymous individuals; they were not compiled on a year-by-year basis. Arguments have centred, therefore, on how these batches of year entries were grouped, when they were compiled, and how the manuscript tradition may help to determine either of these things. The grouping of years as well as the dates of compilation may illuminate what the intended impact and political purpose of each batch might have been at the time of composition. The effect on the preceding sections of adding a section, quite apart from the role played by the later permutations and combinations of the text we find in the extant manuscripts, also needs to be considered.[108] These matters affect the attitude we should have towards the information they contain.

In the remainder of this chapter, my principal concern is with the production and content of the sections of the *Annales regni francorum* covering Charlemagne's reign, that is, to 814. It is also necessary, however, to address two general issues. Firstly, there is the question of the structure of the narrative in terms of possible changes of author. Secondly, and as a consequence of the apparent method for the production of the annals, the section covering Charlemagne's last fifteen years or so differs markedly in emphasis from the account up to *c.* 798 and merits separate discussion. Because the Reviser stopped in 801, there is only one *Annales regni francorum* account of the last fourteen years of Charlemagne's reign rather than two. This in itself is a further reason to look at this section rather more

---

[107] McKitterick, *History and memory*, pp. 21–2.
[108] H. Reimitz, 'Der Weg zum Königtum in historiographischen Kompendien der Karolingerzeit', in M. Becher and J. Jarnut (eds.), *Der Dynastiewechsel von 751: Vorgeschichte, Legitimationsstrategien und Erinnerung* (Münster, 2004), pp. 283–326; and H. Reimitz, 'Ein fränkisches Geschichtsbuch aus Saint-Amand. Der Codex Vindobonensis palat. 473', in C. Egger and H. Weigl (eds.), *Text–Schrift–Codex: Quellenkundliche Arbeiten aus dem Institut für Österreichische Geschichtsforschung*, MIÖG Ergänzungsband 35 (Vienna and Munich, 2000), pp. 34–90.

closely. It may be helpful, therefore, to summarize current scholarship on the survival and production of the annals.[109]

The *Annales regni francorum* survive in four different recensions of the presumed 'original' version, plus the Revised or 'E' Version already discussed. The four different recensions of the 'original' *Annales regni francorum* were labelled A, B, C and D by the *MGH* editor Kurze, according to both variants between the recensions and the degree of completeness of the text in the extant manuscripts. Each of the versions B to E, moreover, has ninth-century manuscript witnesses and the distribution of extant copies indicates that the *Annales regni francorum* was disseminated right across the Frankish realm from Brittany to Bavaria.[110] Obvious questions are, first of all, how much of the *Annales regni francorum* might have been written in the early years of the reign of Louis the Pious, say, *c.* 817, *c.* 823, or soon after 829. A further question concerns the distribution of the text in terms of year entries in the extant versions and their surviving manuscripts, for the latter are divided more or less according to the number of years included in the different manuscript recensions. They may be a reflection of the stages in which composition was completed. While conceding that the text was designed to be continuous, scholars such as Monod, Halphen, Bloch, Manitius, Kurze and Collins have proposed different authors for sections which effectively split the text into portions as follows: 741–88, 789–94, 795–801, 802–5 and 806/7–29.[111] Sometimes the sections 789–93 and 801–6 have been described as 'bridging' sections, though the obvious danger with such a description is the relegation of the contents to the background.[112]

---

[109] Mayke de Jong's formulation, i.e. 'court-related annals', seems to me to be the most helpful: see her *The penitential state* (Cambridge, forthcoming).

[110] McKitterick, *History and memory*, pp. 19–22.

[111] Halphen, *Etudes*; G. Monod, *Etudes critiques sur les sources de l'histoire carolingienne*, Bibliothèque de l'Ecole des hautes études 119 (Paris, 1898); H. Bloch, review of Monod, 'Etudes critiques', *Göttingische gelehrte Anzeigen* 163 (1901), pp. 872–97; F. Kurze, 'Über die karolingischen Reichsannalen von 741–829 und ihre Überarbeitung', *Neues Archiv* 19 (1894), pp. 295–339; 20 (1895), pp. 9–49; and 21 (1896), pp. 9–82; F. Kurze, 'Zur Überlieferung der karolingischen Reichsannalen und ihrer Überarbeitung', *Neues Archiv* 28 (1903), pp. 619–69; Wattenbach, Levison and Löwe, *Deutschlands Geschichtsquellen*, II, pp. 245–65; H. Hoffmann, *Untersuchungen zur karolingischen Annalistik*, Bonner historische Forschungen 10 (Bonn, 1958); M. Becher, *Eid und Herrschaft: Untersuchungen zum Herrscherethos Karls des Großen* Vorträge und Forschungen Sonderband 39 (Sigmaringen, 1993).

[112] Collins, 'The "Reviser" revisited'. Kurze suggested that the author of the section to 788 himself added the entries to 795. Thus his suggestion was: 741–88 + 789–95 (these latter portions by the same author as the beginning section) 796–813; 814–29. On the basis of style, syntax and vocabulary, H. Wibel, *Beiträge zur Kritik der Annales regni francorum und der Annales q. d. Einhardi* (Strasbourg, 1902), and Bloch, review of Monod, proposed the following divisions: 741–94, 795–807, 808–29; but Halphen, *Etudes critiques*, suggested that if their criteria were rigorously applied one also got changes of author at 789, 792, 796, 797, 801, 807, 814, 816, 820, etc!

We also need to ask why the Reviser stopped revising his text at 801. It may be the case that the section of the *Annales regni francorum* running to 801 had been widely circulated, and that the Revised Version was intended as a specific substitute for it. Further support for the notion of an earlier section of the *Annales regni francorum* (that ran to somewhere in the 790s or even up to 801) being disseminated and a portion subsequently added might be derived from the Lorsch annals, composed in 803. My impression is that the narrative in the Lorsch annals diverges most substantially, in terms of additional topics and information from the *Annales regni francorum*, in the entries for 795 onwards, not least of course in its famous account of the inscription for Pope Hadrian, the reasons for Charlemagne's coronation in the entry for 801, and the compilation and dissemination of the law in that for 802.[113]

The various recensions are as follows. The A version survives in the edition made by Canisius, published in 1603 and based on a now lost Lorsch manuscript. It apparently ran to 788. Hence the proposal that this was the point at which the annals were first compiled or written (though Canisius added some more text from 788 up to 793 from the so-called Lorsch annals in his edition). The current *MGH* entry for 788, however, has an extra paragraph (taken from the B, C and D versions but not in Canisius) which begins:

Post haec omnia domnus rex Carolus per semetipsum ad Raganesburg pervenit et ibi fines vel marcas Baioariorum disposuit, quomodo salvas Domino protegente contra iamdictos Avaros esse potuissent. Inde vero reversus celebravit natalem Domini in Aquis palatio, pascha similiter. Et inmutavit se numerus annorum in DCCLXXVIIII.

After all this the lord king Charles went in person to Regensburg and there ordered the Bavarians' territories and frontier regions so that these could be safe, with the Lord's protection, against the aforesaid Avars. But returning from there he celebrated the Lord's birthday at the palace of Aachen, and Easter likewise. And the count of the years changed to 789.

This is the kind of summing-up paragraph which could have been added by an author of a subsequent section. It does not preclude the notion that the 'original text' ended before it with the account of a great defeat against the Avars.[114] On the other hand, one of the constant features of the *Annales regni francorum* from 759 up to this point has been the rounding out of

---

[113] McKitterick, *Perceptions*, pp. 75–8; and Kaschke, *Die karolingische Reichsteilungen*, pp. 134–45 and 283–90.

[114] Incidentally the Revised Version uses different words: 'Rex autem in Baioariam profectus eandem *provinciam* cum suis *terminis ordinavit* atque disposuit; atque inde regressus in Aquisgrani palatio

each entry by a reference to where the king spent Christmas and then Easter, and the announcement of the change of year, in precisely the formulaic manner of the completion provided by the other recensions. A more likely possibility, therefore, is that the account of the drowning of Avars in the Danube which ends the Canisius text came at the bottom of the page or the end of the quire in Canisius' manuscript or its exemplar, and the next page or next quire with the final paragraph of the 788 entry simply got detached. This would lend the year 788 no particular significance in relation to the distinctness of portions.

The B version is represented in the Carolingian manuscripts Vat. reg. lat. 617 (where it runs from 777 to 813) and Vat. reg. lat. 213 (where it runs from 791 to 806). It begins in mid-sentence in the former and ends before the final paragraph about the war waged by the Emperor Michael of Byzantium against the Bulgars, presumably from a copy which also ran from 741 to 813. There is an eleventh-century copy running from 741 to 813 and a sixteenth-century edition from a lost manuscript which ran to 807.[115] It is this B version which Regino used for his *Chronicon* for the years 741–813 in the tenth century. Again, therefore, possible explanations for the lack of Christmas notes aside, this B version may stem from a once complete version and 813 may be of no particular significance.

The C version contains the complete text to 829, includes some substantial paragraphs not found in other versions, and is divided into two classes of manuscript according to the company they keep. The first of these, represented by its earliest manuscript Paris, BnF lat. 10911, c. 830, has the text accompanied by the *Liber historiae francorum* and part of the Continuations of Fredegar, and thus offers a codex with a history of the Franks from their Trojan origins to the Carolingian kings. The second group is represented by its earliest manuscript, St Omer, Bibliothèque Municipale MS 697 + 706 of the tenth century. It continues the *Annales regni francorum* with the addition of the *Annales Bertiniani* to 882, though, in the case of the St Omer codex, Eutropius, the *Chronicle* of Count Marcellinus, the *Notitia provinciarum*, Gregory of Tours's *Historiae* and some of Fredegar are included. All these act as a Roman and Merovingian prolegomenon to the *Annales regni francorum*'s rendering of the history of the Carolingian rulers.[116]

---

suo, *ubi hiemaverat* et Diem Domini natalicium sanctumque pascha *more solemni* celebravit,' *RVARF* 788, ed. Kurze, p. 85. It omits the reference to the Avars. Translation of *ARF* 788 in King, *Charlemagne*, p. 87.

[115] *ARF*, ed. Kurze, p. x. This is also known as the *Annales Tiliani*.
[116] McKitterick, *History and memory*, pp. 50–1.

The D version survives in a fragment in Leiden of s.IX 2/4 from the court or Rhineland area, and in full form running from 741 to 829 in Vienna ÖNB 473, which Helmut Reimitz and I have associated with Charles the Bald and Reimitz has dated *c.* 869.[117] Various derivatives of the D version do not include the full text. Like the C text, the D version offers a number of interesting variants and additions to versions A, B and C, though it can be quite a tussle to extricate many of these from Kurze's *apparatus criticus.* I have also explained elsewhere that Kurze's attempt to produce a single edition of this complicated text is probably misguided and anachronistic, and that the codicological context of each manuscript witness of the annals needs to be taken into account, for each Frankish history book or manuscript compilation offers the text to us in a different historiographical context, such as those of the two groups of C-text manuscripts. The codicological context alters the emphasis and message of the text itself.[118]

It should also be stressed that the *Annales regni francorum* are part of a veritable explosion of history-writing in the Carolingian period, with all kinds of new genres developed and older forms reconfigured and adapted to record contemporary history. In addition to the so-called 'major' annals such as the *Annales regni francorum*, and the continuations of these in the west and east Frankish kingdoms known as the Annals of St Bertin and the Annals of Fulda respectively, there is the large and motley collection of so-called 'minor' annals regarded as emanating from a number of different centres throughout the Frankish realm and most of them terminating their narratives between 790 and 806/7. Roger Collins in stressing this point has also suggested that this spate of annal-making was all in some way officially encouraged, but that these local efforts gave way to the 'centrally produced record in the form of the *Annales regni francorum* by about 807/808 at the latest'. The implications of this suggestion merit fuller consideration than is possible in this chapter.[119]

The local histories include the prior Metz Annals (that is the *Annales mettenses priores*), the *Annales Alemannici, Guelferbytani, Tiliani, Petaviani* and so on. These labels 'major' and 'minor' are in effect modern value-judgments as distinct from usable categorizations.[120] Many of the so-called

---

[117] Ibid, pp. 120–32. See also Reimitz, 'Ein fränkisches Geschichtsbuch'.

[118] McKitterick, *History and memory*, pp. 50–1.

[119] Collins, 'Charlemagne's imperial coronation', pp. 58–9.

[120] For constructive suggestions about the potential value of thirty-eight of these 'minor' annals see J. Davis, 'Conceptions of kingship under Charlemagne', unpublished M Litt thesis, University of Cambridge (1999).

'minor' annals survive essentially in single manuscripts from the ninth century which can rarely be precisely located. Some can, and reflect local perceptions of the past, but that is another story.[121]

Past discussion has rather sterilely focussed on whether the 'major' annals, and specifically the *Annales regni francorum*, drew on information in the 'minor' annals or the 'minor' annals adapted the *Annales regni francorum*. I have in the past followed Halphen in regarding the *Annales regni francorum* as an original composition on which other annal texts drew, or could have drawn, and I am still of that opinion. The role of the *Annales regni francorum* in supplying information seems clear and has acted as one means of associating groups of annal texts, that is, several appear to use the same stem text of annal entries.[122] Some scholars have also tried to group sets of annals in different manuscripts according to their stylistic features, though this has been notably inconclusive.[123] A grouping of annal texts might be more usefully proposed on the basis of networks of information, geography, and networks of centres. Thus the use made by these 'minor' annal compilers of the *Annales regni francorum* is supplemented by information drawn from alternative sources with the intention and effect of providing a different perspective on events. These could include administrative documents, letters, and knowledge and gossip acquired by word of mouth at political or legal assemblies, in relation to the movement or armies, or disseminated by messengers, missionaries, pilgrims, merchants, ambassadors and other travellers.[124]

In this connection it should be recalled that the compilation of the *Codex epistolaris carolinus* in 791 coincides with the chronological range of possibility for the first stage of the *Annales regni francorum*. Compiled on Charlemagne's orders in order to preserve the papal correspondence to the king himself as well as to his father and grandfather, and reflecting, in answers to letters sent by the king, the letter-writing activity of Charlemagne's royal notaries, the collection is largely preoccupied with the pope's efforts to persuade the Franks to offer the popes military support against the

---

[121] See, for example, McKitterick, *Perceptions*, pp. 63–89, some of the arguments of which I repeat here.

[122] See K. Brunner, *Oppositionelle Gruppen im Karolingerreich*, Veröffentlichungen des Instituts für Österreichische Geschichtsforschung 25 (Vienna, 1979), pp. 47–52; W. Lendi, *Untersuchungen zur frühalemannischen Annalistik: die Murbacher Annalen, mit Edition*, Scrinium Friburgense 1 (Freiburg in der Schweiz, 1971); and Kaschke, *Die karolingische Reichsteilungen*, pp. 131–72.

[123] Davis, 'Conceptions of kingship', p. 176.

[124] Ibid., p. 177. See also M. Innes, *State and society in the early middle ages: the middle Rhine valley 400–1000* (Cambridge, 2000), pp. 118–24 and 143–53; and C. Pössel, 'Symbolic communication and the negotiation of power at Carolingian regnal assemblies, 814–840', unpublished PhD thesis, University of Cambridge (2003).

Lombards, and the working relationship between the Frankish king and the popes consequent upon Charlemagne's conquest of the kingdom of the Lombards. The *Codex epistolaris carolinus* witnesses to the efficiency of the palace archive, with letters dating back forty years. Yet this collection of papal letters is also part of the same historical endeavour of those close to court circles and even the king himself to preserve historical records. It is a distinctive historical collection of correspondence concerned with the recent political past.[125]

Despite all the discussion of the *Annales regni francorum* to date, two further issues remain to be considered. Firstly, are there any indications in the text itself of sufficiently distinct changes of style to posit a change or changes of authorship? Neil Wright, for example, has identified a certain peculiarity of style, including a propensity to finish sentences with a compound perfect form of passive verbs, that seems to pinpoint a change of author between 819 and 820. Are there other differences in the earlier sections of the text to indicate similar changes? Roger Collins has offered the observation that up to and including the year 788 the writer makes frequent use of the word *tunc* and all references to the ruler are relatively elaborate, employing such formulae as *Domnus Carolus gloriosus rex* and *Domnus Carolus benignissimus rex*, after which the simpler *rex* becomes standard. Collins notes the use of the formula *Domino adiuvante* or *Domino auxiliante* up to 789.[126] Manitius identified a change of author *c.* 795 and legal and Romance words and phrases from charters. This view was corroborated by Adams, whose meticulous study of the vocabulary in the annals identified many instances of words foreshadowing Romance forms in the section up to 795. He suggested that the subsequent avoidance by the Reviser of particular words and the substitution of classicizing vocabulary could constitute evidence of the original Romance words' currency in ordinary speech at the end of the eighth and beginning of the ninth century. Adams further proposed that the author of the first section of the original annals was someone of Germanic or Frankish origin, or at least

---

[125] *Codex epistolaris carolinus*, ed. Gundlach, pp. 469–657. See F. Hartmann, *Hadrian I (772–795)*, Päpste und Papsttum 34 (Stuttgart, 2006), pp. 29–36, who announces the study by A. T. Hack, *Codex carolinus: Studien zur päpstlichen Epistolographie im 8. Jahrhundert*, Päpste und Papsttum (Stuttgart, forthcoming) which I have not seen. I have also benefited from B. Coffin, 'The production of the *Codex carolinus* in its historical context', unpublished short essay produced for the MPhil in Medieval History, University of Cambridge (2003), and am grateful to him for allowing me to cite it. Facsimile edn, F. Unterkircher (ed.), *Codex epistolaris carolinus*, Codices Selecti 3 (Graz, 1962).

[126] Collins, 'The "Reviser" revisited', p. 193.

familiar with Christian communities in Germany, but also in contact with the Romance forms of ordinary speech in Frankish Gaul.[127]

Even taking such stylistic quirks into account, it might be most helpful to think in terms of the structure and emphases of the text as a whole, with successive authors capable of picking up the narrative baton and running their sections of the Frankish history relay race essentially down the same track.

Secondly, what is striking about the account of the years 799–814? I have commented elsewhere that I think that there are many efforts in the post-800 entries to keep alive themes addressed in the earlier sections, notably the interaction on the part of the Franks with a host of non-Franks. This needs, however, to be explored in further detail, as does the sympathy between the earlier and later sections of the text, if one thinks of the pre- and post-799 portions. The account of these years may have been produced in the reign of Louis the Pious. If so, then it needs to be placed alongside other texts emanating from the earlier part of Louis's reign.

I turn therefore to the possible changes of author and how significant they might be. I shall then consider the account of the years 799–814 more closely.

The *Annales regni francorum* and its authors

Two striking features of the *Annales regni francorum* are its apparently habitual recording of where the king spent Christmas and Easter and the formula *Et inmutavit se numerus annorum in* before the next date is supplied. Where this is not the case needs to be noted. Further, the beginning of the year could be reckoned from or after Christmas, or from after Easter (despite its being a moveable feast), so whether an annal entry includes the record of where the king spent Christmas of that year and the Easter of the following year needs also to be registered.[128]

Christmas and Easter, therefore, are recorded in the *Annales regni francorum* for most of the years 759–807, but with the following variants: from 768 to 771 only Charlemagne's location at Christmas and Easter is

---

[127] M. Manitius, 'Zu den Annales Laurissenses maiores', *MIÖG* 10 (1889), pp. 410–27; M. Manitius, 'Zu den Annales laurissenses und Einharti (zur Sprache und Entstehung)', *MIÖG* 13 (1892), pp. 232–8; and M. Manitius, *Geschichte der lateinischen Literatur des Mittelalters*, 1: *Von Justinian bis zur Mitte des 10. Jahrhunderts* (Munich, 1911), pp. 646–7. See also J. N. Adams, 'The vocabulary of the *Annales regni francorum*', *Glotta* 55 (1977), pp. 257–82.

[128] Christmas in the year date of the annals + Easter of the following year except for 775, 780, 790, 799–802 (when only Christmas is recorded and Easter is put into the correct calendar year).

noted, not Carloman's; in 792 Christmas and Easter at Regensburg is repeated, and in 793 Christmas only is recorded. The next year entry, however, starts with Easter at Frankfurt on 23 March 794 and then also includes Christmas in 794 and Easter on 12 April 795. Between 794 and 798 Christmas and Easter of the following year are recorded, while between 799 and 802 Christmas is noted as the end of the year with Easter noted in the next year. A further peculiarity is that the annal entry for the year 800 ends with Christmas in Rome, but the following entry, for 801, starts with Christmas in Rome. For the four years from 803 to 806, only Christmas is recorded, and for 807 Easter and Christmas of the same year are recorded, that is, with Christmas coming at the close of the year. After 807 some other differences occur, in that for the years 808, 811, 813, 816, 818–22, 824–5 and 828, winter is noted but not the liturgical feasts. In 829, however, Easter and Christmas are in the same calendar year.

The formula for the change of the year between 758 and 808 remains *Et inmutavit se numerus annorum in . . .* and is omitted thereafter.

In addition to the register of Christmases and Easters and the end-of-the-year formula, different emphases in subject matter are apparent, such as the record of military campaigns. These occur in the following years: 742–4, 747, 748, 753, 755, 756, 758, 760–4, 767–8, 768–89, 791, 794–802, 804, 806–11. The record of the convening of an assembly also includes a significant change in the word used for 'assembly', if it is explicitly mentioned at all. For the years 758, 761, 763–6 it is *placitum*; for 767, 770, 771, 772, 776, 777, 778, 787, 785–8 and 794 it is *synodus*, and in 795 and 811 it is *placitum* again.[129] But in 806 the word is *conventus*[130] and for the years 813–815, 817, 818, 819 (×2), 820, 821 (×3), 826, 827 (×2), 828 and 829 the term used is *conventus generalis*.

The reports of legates and embassies from foreign rulers to the king before 797 are mostly concerned with initiating or following up campaigns, except in 757 and 777. In these years diplomatic visits with presents brought by the legates are mentioned. There are many such gift-bearing embassies from 798 onwards. Similarly, the receipt of foreign news and of events in Italy, the Balearic islands, Rome, Constantinople, Ireland and elsewhere occurs from 798.[131]

Observations about astronomical or meteorological phenomena are introduced from 798 onwards. In the entry for 807 there is a full account

---

[129] 811 . . . *et placito generali secundum consuetudinem Aquis habito*: ARF, ed. Kurze, p. 134.
[130] This or *conventus generalis* is used for assembly in the RVARF, 741–801; see below, pp. 222–31.
[131] See below, pp. 49–54.

of the eclipses of the moon and other eclipses are noted thereafter. Explicit attention is paid to the production of written records or the palace archive in the entries for 794, 803, 806 and 813, and the reports about the king going hunting are included in the accounts for 802, 804, 805, 809 and 813.[132]

A change of author or authors may be indicated by the appearance from 797, that is in the entries for the years 797, 799, 802, 806, 807, 812, 817, 818, 820 and 826–9, of words suggesting a sympathetic identification of the writer with the Franks. This is signalled by the use of such words as *nos*, *nostros* and *nobis* referring to military victories achieved by 'our men'.

The overlapping of different interests and categories evident in this survey is clear. There are many signs that the continuators of the first section made every effort to preserve the original formulaic phrases and conventions of subject matter. Some of the changes in emphasis may well be attributable to actual changes in the character and emphases of the reign. After 800 there were fewer campaigns. Perhaps, too, there was indeed a greater number of embassies as Charlemagne's power became more widely known and as the expansion of his territories meant that the Frankish empire impinged on many more new groups of peoples.[133]

All the same, there are some interesting recurrences and differences. As we have seen, there is the change of styling in the year running from Easter to Easter to one from Christmas to Christmas. This may indicate a change in Carolingian understanding of the course of the year, perhaps accompanying the interest in computing and consequent compilations of Encyclopaedias of time between 792 and 809.[134] The introduction of astronomical observations and weather reports may also be due to a change of author, as may the inclusion of news from elsewhere and the details about the foreign diplomatic visits and the presents they brought.

There is also a certain coincidence of changes in terms of categories of subject matter from 798 onwards which might suggest a new author taking over. In 798, as recorded above, there is the beginning of references to astronomical and meteorological phenomena. There may be a case for another change for the section 807–17, because of the wealth of detail about eclipses. Other indications of a possible takeover of the narrative at

---

[132] See below, p. 45.   [133] See below, pp. 135–6 and 288–91.

[134] B. Krusch, 'Das älteste fränkische Lehrbuch der dionysianischen Zeitrechnung', *Mélanges offerts à Emile Chatelain* (Paris, 1910), pp. 232–42; A. Borst, 'Alkuin und die Enzyklopädie von 809', in P. L. Butzer and D. Lohrmann (eds.), *Science in western and eastern civilization in Carolingian times* (Basle, Boston and Berlin, 1993), pp. 53–78; and A. Borst, *Die Karolingische Kalenderreform*, MGH Schriften 46 (Hanover 1998); and see also below, p. 323.

particular points are the repetitions of information, though these might be attributed to a failure of concentration. In 791 and in 792, for example, Christmas and Easter at Regensburg are repeated, so that the entry for 792 has four feasts celebrated, rather than two. In 798 the visit of Froia, the ambassador for King Alfonso of Galicia, is recorded twice, once at the beginning and a second time at the end of that year's entry. Incidentally, the Revised Version tidied this into one visit and described the presents Froia brought in some detail. Such repetition happens again in the entries for 816 and 817 with reference in each to the same visit of the legates from Abd al-Rahman, the ruler of Al-Andalus.

From 797, as indicated in the survey above, there is occasionally the more personal association of the author with Frankish success. Thus under 797 Barcelona is noted as a city which had long since seceded 'from us', and the Balearic islands surrendered themselves in 799 'to us after requesting and receiving aid from our men and with God's help were protected by our men from the pirates' attack' (*postulato atque accepto a nostris auxilio nobis se dediderunt et cum Dei auxilio a nostris a praedonum incursione defensi sunt.*) Under 802 the annalist notes that a garrison of 'our men' was installed at Ortona in Italy, and in 806, again in Italy, one of our men (*unus tamen nostrorum*), Hadumar, count of Genoa, was killed by Saracens. A third Italian military context is the reference in 812, when Wala, son of the king's paternal uncle Bernard, was sent by Charlemagne to remain in Italy with Bernard, the king's grandson, until such time as the circumstances had removed the danger from 'our people' (*quoadusque rerum eventus securitatem nostris adferret*).[135] A variant from the military context is observed in 807 when the eclipse of the moon was observed 'by us'.[136]

The sudden burst of dramatic detail and emotional comments in 787 and 796 is also notable. In 787 there is an account of Charlemagne's campaign in Benevento, and the portrayal of Duke Arichis as too terrified of Charlemagne to meet him himself, so he sent *missi* to meet the king. There is also considerable detail about the *missi* from Duke Tassilo of Bavaria in Rome with an attempt to characterize the reason for the pope's response in his recognition of the 'inconstancy and hypocrisy of the *missi*'. The most striking passage in this entry is the account of how Charlemagne joined his wife Fastrada in Worms, where they 'rejoiced and were happy in

---

[135] *ARF*, ed. Kurze, pp. 100, 108, 117, 122, 137. See also for further references to 'our men' *et sim.* in military contexts (against Danes, Bulgars, Saracens *et al.*), *s. a.*, 817, 818, 820, 826, 827, 828 and 829; ibid., pp. 147, 149, 153, 170, 173, 175 and 177.

[136] Ibid., p. 123.

one another's company and together praised God's mercy' (*et ibi ad invicem gaudentes et laetificantes ac dei misericordiam conlaudantes*).[137] In 796 Angilbert is described as Charlemagne's most beloved abbot (*misit per Angilbertum dilectum abbatem suum*), the king joyfully witnessed (*laetus aspexit*) the return of his son Pippin, and the king himself is described as this most prudent and generous man, God's steward (*vir prudentissimus atque largissimus et dei dispensator*).[138]

A further dimension to the issue of authors and possible changes in authorship linked with these emotional outbursts, and the phrases in which the author identifies himself with the Frankish armies, is offered by the letter of Charlemagne to his wife Fastrada dated 8 September 791. In this he told her about the three-day fast and litanies on the Avar campaign which are also recorded in the *Annales regni francorum*,[139] and asked her to see to the performance of further litanies, presumably at Regensburg.[140] The army's special fasts and prayers certainly would have been common knowledge, but let us pause for a moment to consider how this letter has survived.

The St Denis letter collection

Charlemagne's letter to Queen Fastrada is part of the letter collection in Paris, BnF lat. 2777, fols 43–61 at fol 61r–v. This codex was compiled at St Denis during the abbacy of Fardulf, abbot of St Denis and former *capellanus*.[141] According to the Revised Version, Fardulf had been granted the abbacy in 792 for his loyalty after he had exposed the revolt of Pippin

[137] Ibid., p. 76; and see J. L. Nelson, 'The siting of the council at Frankfort: some reflections on family and politics', in R. Berndt (ed.), *Das Frankfurter Konzil von 794: Kristallisationspunkt karolingischer Kultur*, Quellen und Abhandlungen zur mittelrheinischen Kirchengeschichte 80, 2 vols. (Mainz, 1997), I, pp. 148–65; and below, p. 47.

[138] *ARF* 796, ed. Kurze, p. 98.

[139] Compare also *MGH Conc.* II.i, No. 18, pp. 108–9. For a general context see M. McCormick, 'A new ninth-century witness to the Carolingian mass against the pagans', *Revue Bénédictine* 97 (1987), pp. 68–86; and D. Bachrach, *Religion and the conduct of war, c. 300–c. 1215* (Woodbridge, 2003), pp. 32–63.

[140] *MGH Epp.* IV, pp. 528–29; and see also Bachrach, *Religion*, pp. 34 and 39.

[141] W. Levison, 'Das Formulbuch von Saint-Denis', *Neues Archiv* 41 (1919), pp. 283–304. Differing explanations for the inclusion of the Cathwulf letter and incidental references to the Fastrada letter are offered by M. Garrison, 'Letters to a king and biblical exempla: the examples of Cathwulf and Clemens *peregrinus*', in M. de Jong (ed.), *The power of the word: the influence of the Bible on early medieval politics*, special issue of *Early Medieval Europe* 7 (1998), pp. 305–28; and J. Story, 'Cathwulf, kingship and the royal abbey of Saint Denis', *Speculum* 74 (1999), pp. 1–21. On the manuscript see also D. Nebbiai Dalla Guarda, *La bibliothèque de l'abbaye de Saint-Denis en France du IXe au XVIIIe siècle* (Paris, 1985), pp. 301–2.

the Hunchback.[142] Fardulf held the abbacy until his death in 806. Mary Garrison has suggested that Charlemagne's letter to Fastrada or a copy of it may have been brought back from Regensburg by Fardulf in 792, for it would have been he who would have been at least partly responsible for putting into effect the liturgical requirements for litanies in relation to Charlemagne's victories over the Avars.[143] The letter collection also includes the letter of Cathwulf to Charlemagne, praising the king who had been exalted by God in honour with glory to the kingdom of Europe (*Quod ipse te exaltavit in honorem glori regni Europae*). Cathwulf's letter went on to offer eight reasons for the crown of glory and to describe the eight columns of good government. The reasons include references to the amicable division of the kingdom between Carloman and Charles in 768, the death of Carloman and Charlemagne's assumption of the whole kingdom in 771, the flight of the Lombard army in 773, the capture of Pavia, Desiderius and his treasures, and the conquest of the Lombard kingdom in 774. These incidents constitute a brief history of Charlemagne's career and follow closely the account in the Royal Frankish annals.

The other letters, apparently gathered together by the recipients, comprise letters from Pope Stephen II and Hadrian to Abbots Fulrad (751–84) and Maginarius (784–92). Both Fulrad and Maginarius had served at court; both had been *capellani* and notaries, and both had served as the king's *missi* to Rome.[144] There is also some seventh- and earlier eighth-century material relating to Tours which is presumed to have come via Hitherius, abbot of Tours until 796, because of his association with Maginarius. It is also this collection which includes the earliest text of the notorious Donation of Constantine, as well as a letter from Pope Zacharias to all the Frankish clergy, a letter, possibly from Fardulf of St Denis, to Pippin of Italy, one from Theodulf of Orleans to Pippin of Italy, and from Theodulf to his friend Fardulf on the latter's fidelity.[145]

The close association between information provided in these letters and reflected in the *Annales regni francorum* on the one hand, but also the connection between the Carolingian rulers and St Denis is significant. It was, after all, where Pippin III had been educated and where he and his

[142] For Fardulf's career as chaplain see J. Fleckenstein, *Die Hofkapelle der deutschen Könige*, *1: Grundlegung: die karolingische Hofkapelle*, *MGH* Schriften 16, 1 (Stuttgart, 1959), pp. 105–6, 108.

[143] *RVARF* 792, ed. Kurze, pp. 91–3; Garrison, 'Letters to a king', and M. McCormick, 'The liturgy of war in the early middle ages: crisis, litanies and the Carolingian monarchy', *Viator* 15 (1984), pp. 1–23.

[144] See A. Stoclet, *Autour de Fulrad de Saint-Denis 710–784* (Geneva, 1993), pp. 463–7.

[145] Garrison, 'Letters to a king', pp. 318–21. See H. Fuhrmann (ed.), *Constitutum Constantini*, *MGH Fontes* 10 (Hanover, 1968), and J. Fried, *Donation of Constantine and Constitutum Constantini* (Berlin, 2007).

family were anointed as the new dynasty for Francia by Pope Stephen II in 754.[146] Pippin died there and chose to be buried there, and the fact of his death is recorded, in an interesting phrase in the *Annales regni francorum*, as a completion of his career in association with St Denis: *ad sanctum Dionisium usque pervenit ibique diem obiens finivit*.[147] It was also on the bones of St Denis that Tassilo was made to swear his oath in 757, similarly recorded in the *Annales regni francorum*.[148] Gifts to the abbey are a striking feature of the early charters of Charlemagne.[149] St Denis was a royal abbey and retained a close relationship with the Carolingian royal family throughout the later eighth and the ninth centuries.[150] Not only was there the close association between the palace archives and the *capella, capellani* and notaries in the writing office, long ago emphasized by Fleckenstein, but such archives would, of course, also furnish access to essential information relating to the rulers of the kind incorporated into the *Annales regni francorum*'s narrative.[151] We should recall that it was in 791 that the *Codex carolinus*, containing the letters between the popes and the Carolingian rulers, was compiled, and this would have been a valuable source of information.[152] Recent excavations have even indicated that a Carolingian royal palace formed part of the St Denis monastic complex, built some time after the dedication of the splendid new basilica in 775 at which the king had also been present.[153] From the fragments of carved stone work and painted plaster that survive of this building, as well as a description made in 798–9 and preserved in a manuscript from Reichenau, it is clear that this was once an impressive basilica and may be an indication of the quality of the palace building as well.[154]

The letter collection in Paris BnF lat. 2777 could be regarded simply as a formulary, but it also has a claim to be regarded as a dossier of material useful for the compiling of history. In other words, it may be to St Denis

---

[146] See below, pp. 292–3 (events of 754), and 75 (charters).

[147] *ARF* 768, ed. Kurze, p. 26 (he reached St Denis and there he ended his days).

[148] *ARF* 757, ed. Kurze, p. 16.   [149] This point is stressed also by Story, 'Cathwulf', p. 20.

[150] See G. Brown, 'Politics and patronage at the abbey of St Denis (814–898): the rise of a royal patron saint', unpublished DPhil dissertation, University of Oxford (1989).

[151] See Fleckenstein, *Die Hofkapelle*, I, pp. 80–1; and compare D. Bullough, '*Aula renovata*: the Carolingian court before the Aachen palace', in Bullough, *Carolingian renewal: sources and heritage* (Manchester, 1991), pp. 123–60 at p. 133. See also Garrison, 'Letters to a king', pp. 317.

[152] *Codex epistolaris carolinus*, ed. Gundlach, see p. 476.

[153] M. Wyss, 'Saint-Denis', in *799 Kunst und Kultur*, III, pp. 138–41; and on the remains of 'Fulrad's basilica' see S. M. Crosby, *The royal abbey of Saint-Denis from its beginning to the death of Suger, 475–1151*, ed. P. Blum (New Haven, 1987); and J. van der Meulen and A. Speer, *Die fränkische Königsabtei Saint-Denis: Ostanlage und Kultgeschichte* (Darmstadt, 1988).

[154] A. Zettler, 'Eine Beschreibung von Saint-Denis aus dem Jahre 799', in Zettler, *Die Franken* (Mannheim/Mainz 1996), I, pp. 435–7. For Charlemagne's palaces generally see below, pp. 157–71.

and the former *capellani*, then abbots, that we need to look as potential compilers of the earlier sections of the *Annales regni francorum*.[155] The St Denis abbots' responsibility for the *Annales regni francorum* may be one reason why Fulrad is accorded a prominent role in the supposed visit to Pope Zacharias in 749 to ask him about who should be the rightful king of the Franks.[156] After 768 he was Carloman's *capellanus*, and he is specifically recorded as becoming Charlemagne's man in 771.[157] The St Denis abbots as royal chaplains certainly had the knowledge of central affairs at court, and the experience of different regions of the empire provided by their acting as *missi*. There are also the indications provided by correlations between the charters and the narrative evidence. In 775, for example, the *Annales regni francorum* recorded the king spending Christmas at Selestat, and an original charter survives of the settlement of a dispute in the presence of the king there.[158] It may not be going too far, therefore, to envisage the author checking the register of royal charters in order to compile his narrative. There are parallels of administrative documents being used to construct a narrative in the *Liber pontificalis*, when the papal letter register provides some information for the biographer of Leo and Hadrian, and in the case of the Life of Boniface by Willibald it seems clear that Willibald made use of a collection of Boniface's letters in order to compose his Life.[159]

The dates for the terms of office of Maginarius and Fardulf as abbot coincide with some at least of the indicators of detectable changes in the course of the text. The Lombard Fardulf's sympathy with Italy might account for the close identification with Frankish enterprise in Italy noted after 798. He also may have had a special link with Fastrada as a consequence of the exposing of the conspiracy of Pippin the Hunchback, for it was Fastrada's cruelty that is sometimes blamed as one cause of the rebellion.[160] These may well be reflected in the far greater prominence of Fastrada and sympathy towards her in the *Annales regni francorum*'s narrative, especially when compared with the Revised Version of the year

---

[155] Stoclet, *Autour de Fulrad*; and M. Tangl, 'Das Testament Fulrads von Saint-Denis', *Neues Archiv* 32 (1907), pp. 167–217, repr. in Tangl, *Das Mittelalter in Quellenkunde und Diplomatik: Ausgewählte Schriften*, I (Berlin, 1966), pp. 540–81.

[156] First suggested in R. McKitterick, 'The illusion of royal power in the Carolingian annals', *English Historical Review* 115 (2000), pp. 1–20, but see the expanded argument in McKitterick, *History and memory*, pp. 84–119.

[157] *ARF* 771, ed. Kurze, p. 32.   [158] *DKar.* I, No. 110, and see below, pp. 190–2.

[159] H. Geertman, *More veterum: il Liber pontificalis e gli edifici ecclesiastici di Roma nella tarda antichità e nell'alto medioevo*, Archaeologia Traiectini 10 (Groningen, 1975); and Hartmann, *Hadrian I*, pp. 19–28.

[160] Einhard, *Vita Karoli*, c. 20, ed. Halphen, p. 65; and see Nelson, 'The siting of the council at Frankfort', p. 163; and Story, 'Cathwulf', p. 18.

entries in which Fastrada is mentioned.[161] 'In 783, after the death of Hildegard, Charlemagne married the lady Fastrada. Four years later the same most gentle king joined his wife, the lady queen Fastrada in the city of Worms, where they rejoiced and were happy in one another's company and together praised God's mercy.' Such effusion is somewhat unusual, though I have already noted the other little patch of it in 796. The Revised Version omits it and simply says instead that the king joined his wife Fastrada, his sons and daughters and all the court dignitaries at Worms. Then in 794 the *Annales regni francorum* notes Fastrada's death and burial in St Alban's, Mainz.

Fardulf himself was succeeded as abbot by two more royal *capellani*, Waldo (abbot 806–19, who also became abbot of St Gallen and Reichenau), and Hilduin (abbot 819–40).[162] Such an association, of course, would also chime in with the efforts of former scholars to assign responsibility for a later portion of the annals to Hilduin, abbot of St Denis from 814 and *capellanus* in succession to Hildebold of Cologne from 819 to 830.[163] Hilduin was with Louis the Pious for the expedition into Brittany in 818, and organization of the translation of the relics of St Sebastian to Saint-Médard of Soissons is also recorded in the *Annales regni francorum*.[164] He is noted by Einhard as someone who delivered news to the emperor, and it used to be Hilduin's involvement in the revolt of 830 which was produced as a reason for the original *Annales regni francorum* stopping in 829.[165] A link between St Denis and the *Annales regni francorum*, given the abbots' range of connections across the empire, might also help to explain the rapid dissemination of the annals. Further, a St Denis connection could provide a context for the production in a script of the Paris region of one of the earliest extant manuscripts of the *Annales regni francorum*, namely BnF lat. 10911.

As an indication of the unresolved uncertainties of the text, one could add all the indications about a connection between the abbots of St Denis, royal chaplains and the queen, to the arguments about the groups of year entries, some of which, as we have seen, propose breaks at 794 and 801.

---

[161] See Nelson's comments on the 'affective language of the 787 entry' in particular, 'The siting of the council at Frankfort', pp. 158–9.

[162] Fleckenstein, *Die Hofkapelle*, I, pp 107–8.

[163] On Hilduin, see Depreux, *Prosopographie*, pp. 250–6; Brown, 'Politics and patronage', and Fleckenstein, *Die Hofkapelle*, I, pp. 51–3. Wattenbach, Levison and Lowe, *Deutschlands Geschichtsquellen*, II, p. 251, thought of a connection with a chaplain, and Angilram of Metz was a candidate (769–91); so were his successors Hildebold and Hilduin.

[164] *ARF* 818 and 826, ed. Kurze, pp. 148 and 171.

[165] See Kaschke, *Die karolingische Reichsteilungen*, pp. 290–6.

Then there are such coincidences of information in the annals with other texts by Charlemagne as the letter of Charlemagne to his wife Fastrada in 791, mentioned earlier.[166] Fastrada died in 794, and Liutgard, the next and last of Charlemagne's queens, died on 4 June 800, so before Charlemagne went to Rome. A scenario that has not to my knowledge been considered, except in relation to the authorship by Gisela at Chelles of the *Annales mettenses priores*,[167] is that of the queen being responsible for the production of the royal annals or overseeing their production. If one were to go so far as to envisage queenly authorship as distinct from general oversight, that would imply that when Fastrada died, Liutgard took over but may only have settled to it shortly before she died. When she died there was no queen, so at that point or thereabouts a *cancellarius* decided to tidy up the queen's Latin and continue the story from 799, but with a new set of emphases. However fanciful this scenario may seem, it is salutary to remember that there is as little to prove that it is false as there is in favour of all the other explanations proposed. The responsibility of women to carry the memory of their family's history has been documented elsewhere in the middle ages.[168] It may also, therefore, have been part of the Carolingian queen's role, with some overall responsibility for production falling to the queen while the actual writing or editing was allocated to past or current members of the royal writing office.

Let me summarize the discussion so far. The initial production and subsequent dissemination of the *Annales regni francorum* are problems that look increasingly intractable the more one looks at them. Some indications seem mutually contradictory. What can be said can be briefly summarized as follows. The first section of it was put together after 788 and by 795. Possible changes of author in the *Annales regni francorum* are not matched sufficiently clearly by changes in vocabulary, content and a range of other differences to make the customary demarcations definitive, though there may be a case for positing a change of author for the section 798–806. The section covering 799/801–14 was produced early in Louis the Pious's reign, say by 817. This might then support the implications of the existence of the Revised Version discussed above, viz. that the *Annales regni francorum* to c. 795 or even to 801 had an independent and early circulation in the late

[166] *MGH Epp.* IV, pp. 528–9.
[167] I. Haselbach, *Aufstieg und Herrschaft der Karolinger in der Darstellung der sogenannten Annales mettenses priores*, Historische Studien 12 (Lübeck, 1970).
[168] E. van Houts, 'Women and the writing of history: the case of Abbess Matilda of Essen and Aethelweard', *Early Medieval Europe* 1 (1992), pp. 53–68; and van Houts, *Memory and gender in medieval Europe 900–1200* (Basingstoke, 1999).

eighth and early ninth centuries. The many minor annals support this. This has the effect of making the imperial coronation in 800 appear more like a turning point as far as the narrative is concerned. The possibility of the production of the *Annales regni francorum* under the auspices of, or by former royal chaplains in, St Denis is of course speculation, as is the possible association with the Carolingian queens. Nevertheless, the links with possible sources of information I have explored in relation to the St Denis letter collection need to be taken seriously.

I should stress that I am not returning to Monod's notion of a year-by-year chaplain's duty at the palace to set out the annal record.[169] Even if my conjecture about the role of the St Denis abbots / royal chaplains were correct, it would still not be of great assistance in establishing the date of the redaction of particular sections. This can only be hazarded on the basis of use elsewhere, such as the Northumbrian, Rhineland and southern Alamannic knowledge of the earlier portion of the annals to *c.* 790 or the Poeta Saxo's use of a text that seems to have stopped in *c.* 801.[170] As I indicated earlier, I do not think in any case that the question of authorship and responsibility for sections is the most important aspect of the production of the annals in the light of the authors' evident wish for anonymity. Such anonymity was a reflection of humility that was so widespread, at least in monastic circles, in the early middle ages. It would have added the semblance of objective authority to their account. One might consider, too, the mnemonic function of a year-by-year narrative structure.[171]

On the contrary, an analysis of the annals by categories of topic exposes an important shift in emphasis in the last thirteen to fifteen years of the reign of Charlemagne. It is on the narrative of Charlemagne's final years, therefore, that I shall now focus.

CHARLEMAGNE'S LATER YEARS

The Vienna, ÖNB cod. 473 copy of the *Annales regni francorum* makes a clear distinction between the section on Charlemagne's reign

---

[169] Monod, *Etudes critiques*, p. 153.

[170] On the Northumbrian links see J. Story, *Carolingian connections: Anglo-Saxon England and Carolingian Francia, c. 750–870* (Aldershot, 2003), pp. 93–134.

[171] See P. Klopsch, 'Anonymität and Selbstnennung mittellateinischer Autoren', *Mittellateinisches Jahrbuch* 4 (1967), pp. 9–25; and P. G. Schmidt, 'Perchè tanti anonymi nel medioevo? Il problema della personalità dell'autore nella filologia mediolatina', *Filologia mediolatina* 6–7 (1999–2000), pp. 1–8. I owe these suggestions and references to Jan Ziolkowski in discussion at the NIAS workshop on 'Carolingian political identity: historiography and hagiography', NIAS, 25 November 2005.

and that of Louis. It completes the account of Charlemagne's death after the first few lines of the entry for 814 as follows (fol. 143v): 'FINIUNT GESTA DOMNI KAROLI MAGNI ET PRAECELLENTISSIMI FRANCORUM IMPERATORUM.' The portion of Einhard's *Vita Karoli* concerning Charlemagne's marriage to Hildegard follows (fols 144r–151v) as if, as I have suggested elsewhere, to reinforce the legitimacy of Louis's succession as the son of Charlemagne and Hildegard. The text of the annals then resumes with the heading (fol. 152r): 'INCIPIT GESTA HLUDOVICI IMPERATORIS FILII MAGNI IMPERATORIS.' In the Paris manuscript, BnF lat. 10911, the annals are also divided by reign, with Charles Martel, Pippin and Charlemagne occupying text that is numbered in chapters I–LXXII parallelling the year entries 741–813; the entries for 814–29 for Louis the Pious follow without such a chapter sequence; they simply have the year numbers.

The presentation of the text of the *Annales regni francorum* in the manuscripts of the later ninth century undoubtedly requires further consideration. It is not the later manuscripts' possible directives to the reader about the principal purport of the text up to 814 that are my concern here, but the account actually offered of the later years of Charlemagne in the *Annales regni francorum* in the light of the manuscripts' apparent invitation to see the entire reign as a preface to the *Gesta* of Louis. This is particularly necessary, with reference to the composite structure and authorship of the *Annales regni francorum* and the added complications of the manuscript transmission, because the narrative for Charlemagne's last fifteen years or so differs so markedly in emphasis from the account up to *c.* 798. If one looks at the entries between 788 and 798, what is most striking is how many long-running episodes are brought to a conclusion.

The annexation of Bavaria and downfall of Tassilo in 788 completed a story begun in the *Annales regni francorum* in 757. Saxony is conquered and the affairs of Saxony are all described as being settled in 797. The Avars are destroyed, their treasure brought to Francia in triumph and then distributed by Charlemagne, and peace is concluded in 797 (though there is a further rebellion quelled in 799). The Nordliudi and Wilzi are dealt with for the time being. An embassy is received from Empress Irene offering peace in 798, and the legates from the ruler of Al-Andalus and from Alphonso in Galicia seem at least to mark the completion of a stage in the relations with the various polities in Spain. In the religious sphere, Adoptionism is finally settled in 792 and 794, and the relationship with the papacy seems to reach one climax on Hadrian's death in 795 with the sending to Charlemagne of the keys to the *confessio* of St Peter and the standard of the city of Rome.

In 799, however, as well as the subjection of Brittany, described as something which had never occurred before (*quod nunquam antea a francis subjugata est*), a new phase in relations with the pope is launched, with the excitement of the attack on Pope Leo and the king receiving the pope at Paderborn, in Saxony. This is a dramatic symbol of the new status of Saxony as a fully integrated part of the Frankish empire with Paderborn as its principal palace. The papal visit, of course culminates in Charlemagne's visit to Rome, the trial of the pope in Rome and the coronation of Charlemagne as emperor. In the most obvious change in the entire text, Charlemagne is thereafter described as *imperator*. But the relationship with Leo is consolidated by the papal visit to Charlemagne for Christmas in 804. The emperor's religious status is enhanced by the arrival of a monk from Jerusalem in 799 with the blessing of the patriarch and with sacred relics, subsequently augmented (in the following year) by the keys of the holy sepulchre and of Calvary, and the keys and standard of the city of Jerusalem itself.[172] As I noted earlier, the long series of descriptions of the visits of legates on diplomatic visits, as distinct from concluding peace after long and bitter campaigns, begins in 799 as well, with legates received from and sent to the Arabic rulers in Spain, the ruler of Persia (with the famous elephant and the wonderful clock), the Huns (Avars), the Danish kings, Venice, Dalmatia, Jerusalem, Northumbria and, most spectacularly, the Greeks. It is the legates from the last named who bring Charlemagne the Byzantine recognition in the form of acclamation and calling him emperor and *basileus*.

The narrative of these last fifteen years of Charlemagne's reign, moreover, is constructed as a succession of reports of legates coming to the palace, and reports of various events in Bavaria, Bohemia, Pannonia, Denmark, Frisia and Schleswig, the northern Slav regions, Spain, Sardinia, Corsica, the Balearic islands, Benevento, Ireland, Moesia, Byzantium and Bulgaria, as well as of raids by northern and Moorish pirates.

Essentially, therefore, the emphasis has shifted away from Charlemagne himself and is placed more on a style of explicitly imperial rulership with the palace as the centre of affairs, the acknowledgment of his power and renown in the form of constant streams of embassies bearing gifts, and a succession of events on the outer rim of the empire to contrast with the

---

[172] See below, p. 371.

relative peace and stability of the Frankish realm itself, where embassies are received and news from the surrounding world is regularly reported.[173]

Such an emphasis on the importance of internal stability and outside recognition as a sign of power and status is also developed in a remarkable passage in the *Annales mettenses priores* which was surely inspired by observation of Charlemagne's practice. It was written in 805 or 806 with a clear agenda to promote his royal and imperial power.[174] There it is first adumbrated with reference to Pippin II, Charlemagne's great-grandfather. He is described with regal vocabulary, albeit still a mayor, and his special status is portrayed in the text as follows:

... with divine help as his companion governed the kingdom of the Franks internally with justice and peace and externally with most prudent policies and unconquerable protection of arms, with the Lord helping. Delegations of the nations living round about, that is, the Greeks, Romans, Lombards, Huns, Slavs and Saracens, poured in to him. And the fame of his victory and triumphs so went out among all peoples that, deservedly on account of his virtue and prudence, all the nations round about sought his friendship with great gifts and rewards ... And he with no less speed, sending his own legates though the various regions at the right moment for the well-being of his realm, obtained peace and friendship from the surrounding peoples with the greatest goodwill.[175]

Of further significance is the meagre attention devoted to the children of Charlemagne before 813. The anointing of Pippin and Louis is noted in 781, as is Gisela's baptism in Milan. Thereafter there is a series of brief references to Charles the Younger's career as a military commander. He was sent to Westphalia in 784 (when still only eleven or twelve years old) and subsequently led an expedition in Saxony (794), against the Slavs (798, 805, 806) and against the Danes (808). In 804 it was Charles who was sent to greet Pope Leo III at St Maurice d'Agaune and escort him to Rheims. Charles's presence at Thionville in 806 is indicated when the *Divisio regnorum* was drawn up, but the annal entry is notably deficient in detail about this. It says merely that the assembly was concerned with the establishment and preservation of peace between Charlemagne's sons, and with the division of the realm into three parts, so that each son would know which part he must defend and rule should he outlive his father. It then adds that each of the sons was then dismissed, Pippin and

[173] See below, pp. 127–35.
[174] See Hoffman, *Untersuchungen zur karolingischen Annalistik*, pp. 10 and 58; Haselbach, *Aufstieg und Herrschaft der Karolinger*, p. 12. See also below, pp. 60–5.
[175] English trans. P. Fouracre and R. A. Gerberding, *Late Merovingian France: history and hagiography 640–720* (Manchester, 1996), p. 361, and see their discussion of the text, pp. 330–49.

Louis to their allotted kingdoms and Charles to fight the Slavs.[176] Under 811 there is a bald notice of Charles the Younger's death, which reads like an extract from a necrology; it has no comments about how Charles died, whether the emperor grieved at the death of his eldest son, or even where he was buried. That Charles had spent his life with his father rather than being allotted a little kingdom like Louis, and that he had been given by far the most important parts of the realm in the *Divisio* of 806, is simply not mentioned.

An even more crucial indication of Charles's status, that he had been anointed by Pope Leo as king immediately after his father had been crowned emperor in St Peter's church on Christmas Day 800, is not mentioned in the *Annales regni francorum* entry for 801 at all.[177] Peter Classen has also drawn attention to the sympathetic treatment received by Charles the Younger in the *Annales mettenses priores*. This narrative history records Charles as holding the *ducatus cenomannicus* as early as 789. The *Annales sancti Amandi* mentions that Charles took over the *regnum ultra segona* (kingdom beyond the Seine).[178] Paul the Deacon's *Gesta episcoporum mettensium*, written c. 784, also reflects a much more positive future for Charles as the heir to Charlemagne.[179]

There is a similar downplaying in the *Annales regni francorum* of the role of Pippin. His campaigns in Pannonia in 796, against the Beneventans in 801, dealing with the Greeks in 806, 807 and 809 and with Venice in 810 are all noted, but his death on 8 July 810, too, is recorded simply as one among many matters reported to Charlemagne in his camp on the River Aller, whither the emperor had gone to deal with the Danes. We might also note the laconic reporting of the death of Charlemagne's daughter Rotrud in the same year as her brother Pippin. The annals define the position of Bernard,

---

[176] *ARF* 806, ed. Kurze, p. 121: 'De pace constituenda et conservanda inter filios suos et divisione regni facienda in tres partes, ut sciret unusquisque illorum, quam partem tueri et regere debuisset, si superstes illi eveniret.'

[177] *LP*, Life 98, c. 24, ed. Duchesne, II, p. 7. Compare Alcuin's reference in his congratulatory letter to Charles, specifying that Charles was crowned: *MGH Epp.* IV, No. 217, p. 360: 'regium nomen cum corona regiae dignitatis.'

[178] P. Classen, 'Karl der Große und die Thronfolge im Frankenreich', in *Festschrift für Hermann Heinrich Heimpel*, Veröffentlichungen des Max-Planks-Instituts für Geschichte 36/3 (Göttingen, 1973), pp. 109–34. On the *Annales mettenses priores* see Haselbach, *Aufstieg und Herrschaft*; Y. Hen, 'The Annals of Metz and the Merovingian past', in Y. Hen and M. Innes (eds.), *The uses of the past in the early middle ages* (Cambridge, 2000), pp. 175–90; and Kaschke, *Die karolingische Reichsteilungen*, pp. 203–48.

[179] W. Goffart, 'Paul the Deacon's *Gesta episcoporum Mettensium* and the early design of Charlemagne's succession', *Traditio* 42 (1986), at pp. 89–91; and D. Kempf, 'Paul the Deacon's *Liber de episcopis mettensibus* and the role of Metz in the Carolingian realm', *Journal of Medieval History* 30 (2004), pp. 279–99.

Pippin of Italy's son, with great care, for the entry for 813 makes it clear that Charlemagne granted the rule of Italy to Bernard. The entry for 814 also insisted on Louis, after Charlemagne's death, summoning his nephew Bernard and sending him back to his kingdom with gifts. This acknowledgment seems to prepare the way for the presentation of Bernard's rebellion in 817 as a shocking and unprovoked rebellion against his uncle.

In the section after 799, Louis the Pious gradually emerges from the shadows. After Christmas spent with his father and brothers in 805 and the settling of the *Divisio regnorum* in 806, Louis appears again in a campaign in Spain in 809, and then, after the death of his brothers, it is he who is recognized as sole heir in 813, summoned to the palace and crowned by his father. The entry for 814 also made a point of telling his audience that Louis succeeded his father with the fullest agreement and approval of all the Franks (*summoque omnium francorum consensu ac favore patri successit*).

It is a cleverly orchestrated narrative. Not only is Louis introduced as the new principal protagonist and a fitting heir to his father, even to the enjoyment of hunting in the Vosges and Ardennes, but many of the themes of his reign are initiated and then developed further in the entries from 814 onwards, such as the focus on Aachen, the relations with the papacy, the issue of the kingdom of Italy and Bernard, the problem of Brittany, the complicated series of negotiations with the Danes, the uneasy peace with the Arab rulers of Spain, the integration of Saxony and Bavaria, the continuation of volatile agreements with the Slavs and the remarkable range of diplomatic relations with the Franks' neighbours to north, south, west and east. All these are striking features of Louis's reign as it is represented in the *Annales regni francorum* up to 829.

CONCLUSION

Although the imperial coronation of Charlemagne, as we shall see, made little actual difference to his power or territorial possessions, it needs to be acknowledged here that the *Annales regni francorum* in the section between 799 and 814 constitutes an important contribution to imperial ideology. It serves to highlight, or even introduce, many themes subsequently included and developed in the annals' account of Louis's reign itself. In addition to being the culmination of the overall triumphalist narrative of Frankish expansion and Carolingian success, especially of Pippin III and Charlemagne, it offers a very impressive backing for imperial ideology and Louis the Pious's reign. The account of the years from 799 to 814, the last fifteen years of Charlemagne's reign, also plays a significant role in the

Annales regni francorum as a whole and can be interpreted as a clearly articulated and controlled overture to the reign of Louis within the narrative. This account of Charlemagne's last years may have been produced in the reign of Louis the Pious, probably as early as 817 but certainly no later than the earliest surviving manuscripts of the text, that is, soon after 829. Yet those very manuscripts' perception of the text's structure and central message, in presenting the *Annales regni francorum*'s account of Pippin and Charlemagne as effectively an overture to the reign of Louis the Pious, is reflected in the content of the central portion, in every sense, covering the years 799–814.

All the overlapping and sometimes contradictory positions adopted with regard to the chronology of composition of the *Annales regni francorum* make it impossible to pinpoint the stages of composition of the entries for these years. It would make most sense to posit the representation of Louis as the rightful heir and successor to so many of his father's policies as the product of the years immediately following on his succession. The harking back to themes of the earlier annals is particularly strong in the years between 815 and 818. The repetition about the legates from Al-Andalus and the fall of Bernard of Italy recorded in 817, moreover, might indeed be an appropriate moment for the composition of the text. This would of course fit in with the argument mounted earlier with reference to the composition of the *Vita Karoli* by Einhard. Indeed, that argument might even be felt to be more appropriate, and more persuasive, when applied to the section 799–814 in the *Annales regni francorum* than to the *Vita Karoli* itself. If Neil Wright is correct in his detection of grammatical quirks, then it could have been between 818 and 819 that one person's portion of the text ended and another's began. But someone taking over the composition of a text at a certain point in that *text* need not be taking over in that *year*. Similarly, when Hincmar of Reims wrote his famous remark in the so-called *Annales Bertiniani* (which comprise the Continuation to the *Annales regni francorum*) about the point at which Prudentius of Troyes had ceased his narrative, we cannot assume that Hincmar then started to write in 862.

The authors and scribes of the *Annales regni francorum*, nevertheless, manage to present the narrative from 741 as a continuous sequence and developing story of Carolingian and Frankish success. It is the earlier portion of the text, with all its problems of interpretation, which provides one of the principal sources of information for the analysis of the establishment of the Carolingian family as rulers of the kingdom of the Franks. The foregoing analysis serves to demonstrate both the problematic nature of the information the annals provide and how ninth-century texts started the process of the transformation and interpretation of the story told in the *Annales regni francorum*. Of course there are many other shorter narratives and a great variety of other kinds of documentary and material evidence emanating from the reign. In them Charlemagne's own voice, and that of his immediate contemporaries, may be heard. These will be discussed in subsequent chapters. They may enable us to get closer to Charlemagne and his achievements, not least in his early career with which the next chapter begins.

CHAPTER 2

Pippinids, Arnulfings and Agilolfings: the creation of a dynasty

INTRODUCTION: PERCEPTIONS OF THE EIGHTH CENTURY AND THE RISE OF THE CAROLINGIANS

Charlemagne's forebears, the Pippinids, rather than the Merovingian kings, dominate court-associated history, family histories and local annals alike in the later seventh and the eighth centuries. Charlemagne's great-grandfather and grandfather, Pippin II and Charles Martel, served as mayors of the Merovingian royal palace and were descended from the union between Ansegisel, son of Arnulf, bishop of Metz, and Begga, daughter of Pippin I (hence Pippinids)[1] (see Table 1). Thus the court-associated narrative of the *Annales regni francorum*, discussed in the preceding chapter, begins in 741 with the death of Charles Martel, Charlemagne's grandfather. Einhard, as we have seen, opened his *Vita Karoli* with the taking of the kingship by Pippin III, son of Charles Martel, and the notorious portrait of the last Merovingian king who merely sat on his throne and played at being a ruler. In this way, Einhard heightened the contrast between the strong Pippinids and the feeble dynasty of Merovingian kings that Pippin III replaced.[2] Even the narrative of the

---

[1] E. Hlawitschka, 'Die Vorfahren Karls des Großen', *KdG* I, pp. 51–82, and see Table 1. In the early ninth century this family is described as that of Pippin, hence the word 'Pippinid', though the term 'Carolingian' or 'Karoling', from Charles (Karl) Martel, is regarded by many as the name of the family consequent upon the union of descendants of Arnulf and Pippin. In describing the Neustrian pact with Radbod of the Frisians against the Pippinids, the *Annales mettenses priores* uses the phrase *contra Pippinios*: *Annales mettenses priores*, p. 20. This seems to be the earliest use of a collective name for the family. Some historians have preferred the term 'Arnulfing', stressing the descent from Bishop Arnulf. Apart from Ansegisel and Bishop Chlodulf of Metz, however, Arnulf had no other descendants, whereas the Pippinid family formed many links across the Frankish kingdoms. Carolingian/Karlinger seems to be attested only from the tenth century.

[2] Einhard, *Vita Karoli*, c. 1, ed. Halphen, pp. 8–10, and see above, pp. 25–6. On the beginning of the *Annales regni francorum* see M. Becher, 'Eine verschleierte Krise: die Nachfolge Karl Martells 741 und die Anfänge der karolingischen Hofgeschichtsschreibung', in J. Laudage (ed.), *Von Fakten und Fiktionen: Mittelalterliche Geschichtsdarstellungen und ihre kritische Aufarbeitung* (Cologne, Weimar and Vienna, 2002), pp. 95–134.

Table 1 *The family of Charlemagne*

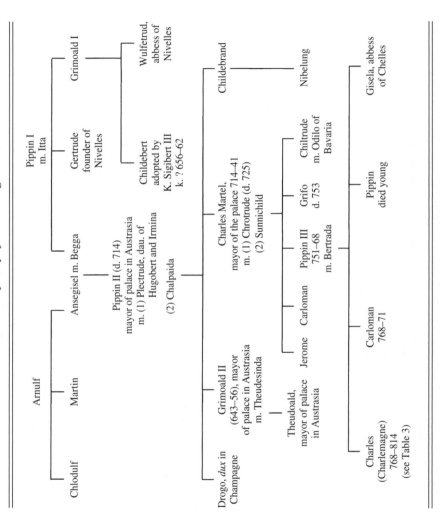

Liber historiae francorum, completed *c.* 727 and usually classified as a non-Carolingian source, concedes much of its space in the later chapters of the work to the Pippinid mayors, and concludes with the initial triumph of Charles Martel over Ragamfred, the Neustrian mayor of the palace, and King Chilperic.[3] Carolingian scribes, moreover, such as the person responsible for the Frankish history book now in Paris, BnF lat. 10911, contrived by clever juxtapositioning to present the *Liber historiae francorum* from the Carolingian perspective.[4] This codex also incorporated sections of the Continuations of Fredegar's Chronicle, that is, the partial (in both senses) record of the triumphant careers of Pippin II, and of Charles Martel and his sons written under the auspices of Charles Martel's half-brother Childebrand and Childebrand's son Nibelung.[5] These Continuations take up the story of the faction-ridden politics of Francia in the seventh century at the point of the Neustrian King Clovis II's marriage to Balthild, and gallop in two chapters through forty years of Neustrian history before moving to recount the fortunes of Austrasia. It is at this point that Duke Martin and Pippin (II) son of the noble Ansegisel are introduced and the successes of the latter become increasingly prominent, with his death recorded as coming at the end of twenty-seven years of rule of the Franks: *rexitque populum Francorum ann. 27.*[6]

Further assessments of the political success of Charlemagne's family are indicated with the choice by annal compilers of alternative beginnings for the Pippinids' political prominence, even if the account of the Pippinids after 741 is usually heavily dependent on the information summarized in the *Annales regni francorum*. Thus the *Annales fuldenses* start with the death of Pippin II, Charles Martel's father, in 714, but texts of the 'Murbach group' of local annals, such as the *Annales alemannici*, and *Annales nazariani*, record as their first entry the death of Drogo (708/9), Pippin II's legitimate son by Plectrude.[7] The so-called minor annals group, comprising the *Annales petaviani*, *Annales sancti Amandi* and *Annales laubacenses*, start with brief entries for 687 and 708 in the case of the first two, and 707

[3] R. Gerberding. *The rise of the Carolingians and the* Liber historiae francorum (Oxford, 1987).
[4] McKitterick, *History and Memory*, pp. 13–19.
[5] See R. Collins, *Fredegar*, Authors of the Middle Ages 4, No. 13 (Aldershot, 1996); and R. Collins, 'Deception and misrepresentation in early eighth-century Frankish historiography: two case studies', in J. Jarnut, U. Nonn and M. Richter (eds.), *Karl Martell in seiner Zeit*, Beihefte der Francia 37 (Sigmaringen, 1994), pp. 227–48.
[6] *Chronicarum quae dicuntur Fredegarii Continuationes*, ed. H. Haupt and H. Wolfram, *Quellen zur Geschichte des 7. und 8. Jahrhunderts* (Darmstadt, 1982), pp. 274–80, cc. 3–8, especially c. 8, p. 280.
[7] W. Lendi, *Untersuchungen zur frühalemannischen Annalistik: die Murbacher Annalen, mit Edition*, Scrinium Friburgense 1 (Freiburg in der Schweiz, 1971), pp. 146–7.

and the death of Duke Hildulf in the case of the third. The fourth member
of this group, the *Annales tiliani*, starts like those of the 'Murbach group'
with Drogo's death in 708.[8]

Eighth- and ninth-century perceptions of Charlemagne's background,
therefore, give different weight to the contribution and importance of
particular members of the family and mark different events as turning
points. Pippin II's sons by his first wife Plectrude are superseded by the son
of the woman claimed as his second wife, Chalpaida.[9] That Plectrude's
own family remained in the political arena and the Pippinid social orbit,
however, is suggested by the subsequent marriage between Plectrude's
great-niece Bertrada to Charles Martel's son Pippin III and support given
Charles Martel and his heirs by kinsmen of his half-brothers and stepmother, such as Hugh, archbishop of Rouen, and Count Theoderic.[10]
Given that the various narratives highlight the careers and claims to leadership of some members of the family at the expense of others, the various
opinions about who established the family's fortunes may be attributed to
different branches of the family, if not factions.[11]

Still another assessment is implied by the *Annales mettenses priores*, which
starts with the career of Pippin II. It claims, for example, that Pippin I had
no sons, so that it was the son of his daughter Begga to whom he
bequeathed his name and his leadership (*nepoti suo Pippino superstiti
nomen cum principatu dereliquit*). Further, in the next generation, it sets
the line of Pippin II's sons Drogo and Grimoald aside by stating that
Grimoald's son Theudoald had died after a revolt among the Neustrian

---

[8] N. Schröer, *Die Annales S. Amandi und ihre Verwandten. Untersuchungen zu einer Gruppe karolin-
gischer Annalen des 8. und frühen 9. Jahrhunderts*, Göppinger Akademischer Beiträge 85 (Göppingen,
1975); and S. Kaschke, *Die karolingischen Reichsteilungen bis 831: Herrschaftspraxis und
Normvorstellungen in zeitgenössischer Sicht* (Hamburg, 2006), pp. 145–68; *Annales sancti Amandi,
Annales Petaviani, Annales Tiliani*, ed. G. Pertz, *MGH SS* 1 (Hanover, 1826), pp. 3–13; and
M. Becher, 'Drogo und die Königserhebung Pippins', *Frühmittelalterliche Studien* 23 (1989), pp. 131–51.

[9] I. Wood, 'Genealogy defined by women: the case of the Pippinids', in L. Brubaker and
J. M. H. Smith (eds.), *Gender in the early medieval world, east and west, 300–900* (Cambridge,
2004), pp. 234–56.

[10] On Hugh, see *Gesta abbatum Fontanellensium* c. 8, *MGH SS* 2, p. 280; and *Gesta fontanellensis
coenobii*, ed P. Pradié, *Chronique des abbés de Fontenelle (Saint-Wandrille)* (Paris, 1999), pp. 58–66;
and on Count Theoderic see above, pp. 29, 30.

[11] Compare also the letter of Boniface to Pope Zacharias in 741 referring to the killing of an uncle of the
Frankish *dux* by a member of Plectrude's family: Boniface, *Epistolae*, No. 50, ed. M. Tangl, *Die Briefe
des Heiligen Bonifatius und Lullus, MGH Epp. Sel.* 1 (Berlin, 1916), p. 82; and see M. Tangl, 'Studien
zur Neuausgabe der Briefe des Hl. Bonifatius und Lullus, Teil 1', *Neues Archiv* 40 (1916), pp. 639–790
at pp. 767–71. For essential background see M. Werner, *Adelsfamilien im Umkreis der frühen
Karolinger: die Verwandschaft Irminas von Oeren und Adelas von Pfalzel*, Vorträge und
Forschungen Sonderband 28 (Sigmaringen, 1982).

nobility.[12] The *Annales mettenses priores* is ostensibly a family history, and is certainly distinctive for the amount of independent information it provides about both Charlemagne's great-great-grandfather and late Merovingian politics, the inclusion of what amounts to a biography of Pippin II, and a eulogistic affirmation of the legitimacy of Charles Martel. The first phase of the narrative, composed *c.* 805, runs from 687 to 805. A second stage, largely taken over from the *Annales regni francorum*, was added for 806–29, and a dramatic and totally independent entry about the Empress Judith was added for the year 830.[13]

The composition of the *Annales mettenses priores* has been attributed most persuasively to someone in the convent of Chelles, presided over by Charlemagne's learned sister Gisela.[14] This would certainly accord with the knowledge and interests expressed in the text in relation to the resources and capabilities of Chelles. It is known to have been an active centre of book production, quite apart from housing Charlemagne's sister, two of his daughters, and other high-ranking women.[15] Yet Chelles was not the exclusive possessor of royal or court connections or of a scriptorium. Nor were members of its community the only ones with sufficient political knowledge and levels of intellectual activity, let alone an interest in the chief protagonists of the narrative, such as the Pippinid leaders, or less prominent figures, such as the queens Bertrada and Hildegard or Charlemagne's son Charles the Younger. Although the vocabulary used is indeed 'thick with royal innuendo', it has this in common with the other narrative accounts of the Pippinid mayors of the palace of the late eighth and early ninth centuries already mentioned.[16] There are, in short, other

---

[12] *Annales mettenses priores*, pp. 2–3; Collins, 'Deception and misrepresentation, pp. 229–35; and Y. Hen, 'The annals of Metz and the Merovingian past', in Y. Hen and M. Innes (eds.), *The uses of the past in the early middle ages* (Cambridge, 2000), pp. 175–90.

[13] For a useful summary of scholarship on the *Annales mettenses priores* see P. Fouracre and R. Geberding, *Later Merovingian France: history and hagiography, 640–720* (Manchester, 1996).

[14] H. Hoffmann, *Untersuchung zur Karolingischen Annalistik*, Bonner Forschungen 10 (Bonn, 1958), pp. 55–61, supported by I. Haselbach, *Aufstieg und Herrschaft der Karolinger in der Darstellung der sogenannten Annales mettenses priores*, Historische Studien 12 (Lübeck, 1970) and J. L. Nelson, 'Gender and genre in women historians of the early middle ages', in Nelson, *The Frankish World, 750–900* (London, 1996), pp. 183–97, and 'Perceptions du pouvoir chez les historiennes du haut moyen âge', in M. Rouche (ed.), *Les femmes au moyen âge* (Paris, 1990), pp. 77–85.

[15] B. Bischoff, 'Die Kölner Nonnenhandschriften und das Skriptorium von Chelles', in Bischoff, *Mittelalterliche Studien*, 1 (Stuttgart, 1966), pp. 16–34; and R. McKitterick, 'Nuns' scriptoria in England and Francia in the eighth century', *Francia* 19/1 (1992), pp. 1–35, repr. in McKitterick, *Books, scribes and learning in the Frankish kingdoms, 6th–9th centuries* (Aldershot, 1994), Chapter VII; and McKitterick, 'The Rorigo Bible in its ninth-century context', in L. Gatto and P. Supino Martini (eds.), *Studi sulle società e le culture del medioevo per Girolamo Arnaldi* (Rome, 2002), pp. 409–22.

[16] See Fouracre and Gerberding, *Later Merovingian France*, pp. 340–1.

centres, not least St Denis or even Metz,[17] for which a case for the production of the *Annales mettenses priores* could plausibly be made in what Thomas Faulkner has described as 'a context of widespread interest in, support for, identification with, or commemoration of' the Pippinids'.[18] Thus the *Annales mettenses priores* could have been produced in any one among a number of leading centres closely associated with the royal court. Nevertheless, Chelles remains the strongest possibility. The *Annales mettenses priores*, while not so court-centred as the *Annales regni francorum*, can be read as a further witness to the creative response to the latter, its principal source, with a readiness to adapt, modify and augment that text to reflect an alternative point of view.[19]

Even so, the *Annales mettenses priores* only superficially resembles the other court- or family-associated histories from the later eighth and early ninth centuries already mentioned, not least the Continuations of the Chronicle of Fredegar and the *Annales regni francorum*. Despite the organization into year-by-year entries, there is a clear thematic structure underlying the text, and strong arguments have been mounted for its ideological importance. It has, for example, been associated with the thinking behind the *Divisio regnorum* of 806 and is thought to have been intended for an aristocratic audience needing to be persuaded of the legitimacy of Carolingian power in the early ninth century.[20] Certainly, the principal focus of the *Annales mettenses priores* is the glorious success of the male leaders of the Pippinid family. Yet it offers very distinctive comments on the legality and fitting nature of Pippinid rule of the Frankish kingdoms, both in the time of the Merovingian kings and after Pippin's usurpation of the throne, on rulership in general, on the specific line of succession from Pippin II, Charles Martel and Pippin III to Charlemagne, and on the much wider network of support from the female and other male members of the family. As a version of the Frankish past which claims the front of the

---

[17] On St Denis see above, pp. 43–9. On Metz see O.-G. Oexle, 'Die Karolinger und die Stadt des heiligen Arnulf', *Frühmittelalterliche Studien* 1 (1967), pp. 249–364; and D. Kampf, 'Paul the Deacon's *Liber de episcopis Mettensibus* and the role of Metz in the Carolingian realm', *Journal of Medieval History* 30 (2004), pp. 279–99, arguing against W. Goffart, 'Paul the Deacon's *Gesta episcoporum mettensium* and the early design of Charlemagne's succession', *Traditio* 42 (1986), pp. 59–94.

[18] I am grateful to T. W. G. Faulkner for permission to cite his unpublished essay which discusses this wider context, 'The representation of the past in the *Annales mettenses priores*', submitted as part of the requirements for the MPhil in Medieval History in the University of Cambridge (2005).

[19] See above, pp. 7–27, with reference to other ninth-century representations of Charlemagne which also drew on the *Annales regni francorum*.

[20] See Hen, 'The annals of Metz'; and Kaschke, *Die karolingischen Reichsteilungen*, pp. 203–48; see also below, pp. 96–8.

political stage for an entire family it merits fuller attention, but it also has important implications for any assessment of the strength of Charlemagne's position in the later eighth and early ninth centuries. I shall focus in what follows, therefore, less on the unfolding of early eighth-century events, for this is adequately covered elsewhere, than on the themes which emerge.[21]

THE PIPPINIDS AND THEIR RISE TO POLITICAL PROMINENCE

The first section of the *Annales mettenses priores* begins with an exultant sketch of Pippin II, son of Ansegisel, and his military successes, including a heroic account of the battle of Tertry in 687. The author makes very specific claims about the extent of the authority of the Pippinid mayors of the palace, to the extent of representing the Merovingian kings as ruling under the Pippin mayors rather than *vice versa*. After the defeat of the Merovingian king of Neustria at Tertry, for instance, Pippin II, up to then the mayor of the palace in Austrasia, is described as taking over the sole leadership of the Franks and reserving the name of king for Theuderic 'with unimaginable faithfulness ... lest he should seem to exercise tyranny or cruelty. But he retained the right to judge cases in the *placitum* or judicial court, the governance of the whole kingdom, the royal treasure and the command of all the army.'[22] In a similar definition of the relative degrees of power Charles Martel graciously conceded the royal throne to Chilperic II under Charles's own authority after his success in 716.[23]

The *Annales mettenses priores* also reflects the author's understanding of rulership. The account of the preparation of Pippin II as a leader of the family enterprise refers as a matter of course to the crucial contribution of the women of the family. Begga, Pippin's mother, is described as teaching him the responsibilities of rule and supporting him in the administration of the kingdom after the murder of her husband Ansegisel. Pippin II may

[21] See I. Wood, *The Merovingian kingdoms* (London, 1994); P. Fouracre, *The age of Charles Martel* (Harlow, 2000); P. Fouracre, 'Observations on the outgrowth of Pippinid influence in the "Regnum Francorum" after the Battle of Tertry (687–715)', *Medieval Prosopography* 5 (1984), pp. 1–31; the various essays in J. Jarnut, U. Nonn and M. Richter (eds.), *Karl Martel in seiner Zeit*, Francia Beihefte 37 (Sigmaringen, 1994); and T. Kölzer, 'Die letzen Merowinger: rois fainéants', in M. Becher and J. Jarnut (eds.), *Die Dynastiewechsel von 751: Vorgeschichte, Legitimationsstrategien und Erinnerung* (Münster, 2004), pp. 33–60.

[22] *Annales mettenses priores*, p. 12. I have used the translation of Fouracre and Geberding, *Later Merovingian France*, p. 359, but note the difficulty of translating what is meant by *propriae facultatis iure disponenda*. They translate this phrase as 'he retained the ordering of private property in law' and add that this perhaps means the *placita*, the formal law cases heard in the royal court.

[23] Ibid., p. 370.

even have been still a minor, with mayoral authority in the hands of his mother, who acted as a kind of regent at this stage. Arnulf, Pippin's grandfather, though described here merely as a 'close relative', appears to have 'strengthened him with sacred admonitions and divine and human learning', while his maternal aunt Gertrude, abbess of Nivelles, took care of her nephew's spiritual and religious instruction and 'watered the young man's spirit with her fruitful stream of heavenly teaching'. The theme of education for princes is maintained later in the narrative in the account of Pippin's grandson Hugh, who was taught by his maternal grandmother Ansfled.[24]

By 687 Pippin II was ready to rule and assumed leadership of the eastern Franks, or *Osterliudos* (eastern people). More training for a princeling is implied in the vivid descriptions of battles. Most crucial among these are the account of how as a youth Pippin II had sought out his father's murderer, the 'tyrant' Godoin, and killed him, like David destroying Goliath. Once he had assumed the leadership of the eastern Franks, however, he conducted a righteous war against King Theuderic which culminated, as already stated above, in Pippin's triumph at the Battle of Tertry in 687. The importance of war leadership is reiterated in the passages concerning Charles Martel's wars, with a zest reminiscent of the combat scenes in the epic poem *Waltharius*.[25]

The careers of Pippin II and Charles Martel are clearly used by the author of the *Annales mettenses priores* to provide a series of precedents for the actions and status of the Carolingian ruler in the author's own day. The themes are continuity and a long tradition. Thus Pippin II receives delegations from Greeks, Romans, Lombards, Slavs and Saracens, and inflicts defeat on the Frisians. Pippin II and his son Charles Martel set out to restore Frankish control over the Saxons, Frisians, Alemans, Bavarians, Aquitainians, Gascons and Bretons; all of them had once been subject to the Franks but had become independent because of the idleness of the Merovingian kings. The text insists on the extension of Pippinid control over Neustria and further claims that Pippin II exerted his authority over

---

[24] *Annales mettenses priores* 693, p. 16. See also Werner, *Adelsfamilien im Umkreis der frühen Karolinger*, and Kölzer, 'Die letzen Merowinger'.

[25] *Waltharius*, ed. K. Strecker, *MGH Poet.* VI, pp. 1–85; and see J. M. Ziolkowski, 'Fighting words: wordplay and swordplay in the Waltharius', in K. E. Olsen, A. Harbus and T. Hofstra (eds.), *Germanic texts and Latin models: medieval reconstructions* (Leuven, Paris and Stirling, VA, 2001), pp. 29–51; and J. M. Ziolkowski, 'Blood, sweat and tears in the 'Waltharius', in G. R. Wieland, C. Ruff and R. G. Arthur (eds.), *Insignis sophiae arcator: medieval Latin studies in honour of Michael Herren on his 65th birthday*, Publications of the Journal of Medieval Latin 6 (Turnhout, 2006), pp. 149–64.

Saxons, Bavarians and Suabians. The mayors' leadership of the army, support of the church, and protection of widows and orphans, and their ability to summon assemblies and to convene synods, were clearly really royal functions. The war against King Theuderic, moreover, was justified in terms of restoring political exiles to their homes and returning their patrimonies. It was the mayors, therefore, who set the social order to rights. In so doing, they won the support and acquiescence of the Frankish nobles for their leadership. Indeed, this emphasis on the consensus and support of the Franks is also a prominent feature of the *Annales regni francorum*'s account of the reigns of Pippin and Charlemagne.

Some scholars might wish to discount this characterization of Charlemagne's forebears as Merovingian kings in all but name as fanciful back projection, or, at best, a construction designed not only to reinforce the legitimacy of the Pippinids' position but also to inspire the present occupants of the Frankish throne. There is no doubt, however, that when King Theuderic IV died in 737, Charles Martel made no move to place another member of the Merovingian family on the throne.[26] The terms in which other sources refer to the mayors, moreover, such as letters addressed to the Pippinid mayors of the palace, incidental references in external sources to events within the Frankish realm, the Pippinids' own charters as mayors, and the numismatic evidence, appear to attest to the respect they had won while they held office as mayors, the external perception of the power they exercised, and the extent to which they maintained the traditions of late Merovingian government.

Several letters in Boniface of Mainz's letter collection, for example, give a clear indication that it was from the Pippinid mayors that the English missionary sought and found political support for his enterprise. His letter of 742–6 to Bishop Daniel of Winchester, stating that it would have been impossible to have done his work without the support of Charles Martel and the fear he inspired, is supported by the surviving letter of 723 in which Charles Martel, *Carlus maior domus*, takes Boniface under his protection.[27] Elsewhere Boniface refers to Charles as *patricius*, to Carloman as *dux francorum*, and to Carloman and Pippin as *principes*.[28] In a letter dated 747 Boniface refers to Pippin as the most excellent Pippin, *maior domus* of

[26] See P. Fouracre, *The age of Charles Martel* (Harlow, 2000), pp. 157–8.

[27] Boniface, *Epistulae*, ed. M. Tangl, *Die Briefe des heiligen Bonifatius und Lullus, MGH Epp. Sel.* 1 (Hanover, 1916), Epp. 22 and 63, pp. 36–8 and 130; and compare H. Wolfram, *Intitulatio,* 1: *Lateinische Königs- und Fürstentitel bis zum Ende des 8. Jahrhunderts, MIÖG* Ergänzungsband 21 (Graz, Vienna and Cologne, 1967), pp. 141–54.

[28] Boniface, *Epistulae*, ed. Tangl, Epp. 24, 28, 50, 78, 86, pp. 42, 50, 82, 165, 193.

the Frankish people.[29] Pope Gregory III in a letter to Boniface in 739 calls Charles Martel *princeps francorum*.[30] Boniface also addresses Grifo, son of Charles Martel, at a stage soon after Charles Martel's death, when the succession and Grifo's position appear not to have been entirely clear, and requests the maintenance of mayoral support for his work in Thuringia.[31] The *Concilium germanicum* of 742/3, presided over by Boniface and Carloman, Pippin III's brother, is the most famous statement of the mayors' leadership in church matters, for it was convened by Carloman, *dux et princeps francorum*, and dated not by a regnal year (for at that stage there was still no king) but by the year of the Incarnation.[32] The succeeding synod at Soissons in 744, held under Pippin's auspices, also describes Pippin III as *dux et princeps francorum*. Pippin III's letter (written 748–51) accompanying a gift to the monastery of Flavigny gives himself the style *vir inluster Pippinus, maior domus*.

Similarly the three papal letters to the mayors preserved in the *Codex epistolaris carolinus* style Charles Martel as *subregulus* and Pippin as *maior domus*, with the latter being besought by the pope for help against the Lombards in 753–6.[33] It has to be acknowledged that the letters in this collection may not be as clean of Carolingian interference as might be supposed. According to the preface to the *Codex epistolaris carolinus*, the letters were gathered from the time of 'the principate of Charlemagne's grandfather Charles Martel to Charlemagne's own day', and were preserved and carefully selected on Charlemagne's orders in 791 for the benefit of his successors.[34] This does not seem to have been a simple process of recopying, for some of the original letters, no doubt written on papyrus, were said to be in very poor condition and there was an effort both to *renew* (*renovare*) and *rewrite* (*rescribere*) the texts from memory onto parchment.[35]

---

[29] Ibid., *Ep.* 77, p. 160.   [30] Ibid., *Ep.* 45, p. 72.

[31] Ibid., *Ep.* 48, p. 77. On Grifo see G. Wolf, 'Grifos Erbe, die Einsetzung König Childerichs III. und der Kampf um die Macht: zugleich Bemerkungen zur karolingischen, Hofhistoriographie'', *Archiv für Diplomatik* 38 (1992), pp. 1–16; S. Airlie, 'Towards a Carolingian aristocracy', in Becher and Jarnut, *Der Dynastiewechsel von 751*, pp. 109–28; and Becher, 'Ein verschleierte Krise'.

[32] Boniface, *Epistulae*, ed. Tangl, Ep. 56, p. 98.

[33] *Codex epistolaris carolinus*, ed. Gundlach, pp. 476–7.

[34] Ibid., p. 476, 'ut nullum penitus testimonium sanctae ecclesiae profuturum suis deesse successoribus videatur'. See F. Hartmann, *Hadrian I (772–795)*, Päpste und Papsttum 34 (Stuttgart, 2006), pp. 29–36. Hartmann announces the forthcoming publication by T. Hack, *Codex carolinus: Studien zur päpstlichen Epistolographie im 8. Jahrhundert*, Päpste und Papsttum (Stuttgart, 2007). I have benefited from B. Coffin, short essay on 'The production of the *Codex carolinus* in its historical context, produced for the MPhil in Medieval History, University of Cambridge (2003), and am grateful to him for allowing me to read it. See also above, pp. 45–7, for the context of history-writing.

[35] *Codex epistolaris carolinus*, ed. Gundlach, p. 476: 'Denuo memorabilibus membranis summo cum certamine renovare ac rescribere decrevit'.

Further influence may have been exerted over the character of the collection by omission of entire letters. In the absence of surviving papal registers from the eighth-century popes, it is not possible to know whether or not any letters were addressed by the pope to the Merovingian kings, or whether these were also simply excluded from the Carolingian collection. The only surviving manuscript of these papal letters to the Pippinid mayors and to the kings Pippin and Charlemagne was copied for Archbishop Willibert of Cologne (870–89) in the later ninth century. It is possible, therefore, that a further selection was made by Willibert's copyists. Certainly the letters from Byzantium referred to in the preface are not to be found in this compilation.[36] On the other hand, the Lives of the popes between 670 and 750 in the *Liber pontificalis* mention very few instances in which letters could have been part of the exchange of news or brought by legates. The Life of Gregory II mentions a letter to the pope from Eudo of Aquitaine telling him of the defeat of the Saracens and referring to presents sent by the pope to Eudo the previous year; and the Life of Stephen II claims that Gregory II, Gregory III and Zacharias had all sent messages to Charles Martel asking him to intervene to help the pope against the Lombards.[37]

Some laudatory references to the leaders of the Franks, such as the description of Charles Martel as 'the shrewd man who then ruled the kingdom of the Franks' (*partibus Franciae Carolo sagacissimo viro, qui tunc regnum regebat Francorum*) are in fact to be found only in the ninth-century Frankish version of the *Liber pontificalis*.[38] But others are in the so-called Lombard recension as well, presumably because of Charles Martel's cordial relations with King Liutprand, and these give the Pippinid mayors the title of king. Thus there is a description of Carloman, son of Charles (Martel), king of the Franks, in the Life of Zacharias, and Charles Martel is again described as king in the Life of Stephen II.[39] Bede's *Historia ecclesiastica*, completed *c.* 731, provides some further indication of the power of Pippin II, for it is he whose conquest of the southern Frisians made it possible for Christianity to be introduced into the region, who gave permission to Willibrord to preach, granted him Utrecht to serve as his

[36] Vienna ÖNB 449, facsimile edn F. Unterkircher, *Codex epistolaris carolinus*, Codices Selecti 3 (Graz, 1962).

[37] Compare *LP*, Life 91 (Gregory II), c. 11, ed. Duchesne, I, p. 399, trans. Davis, *Lives*, p. 8; and *LP*, Life 94 (Stephen II), c. 15, ed. Duchesne, I, p. 444, trans. Davis, *Lives*, p. 58.

[38] *LP*, Life 92 (Gregory III), c. 14, ed. Duchesne, I, p. 420, trans. Davis, *Lives*, p. 27.

[39] *LP*, Life 93 (Zacharias), c. 21, ed. Duchesne, I, p. 433, trans. Davis, *Lives*, p. 46; and *LP*, Life 94, c. 15, ed. Duchesne, I, p. 444, trans. Davis, *Lives*, p. 58.

episcopal seat, and sent Clemens-Willibrord off to Rome to be consecrated by Pope Sergius.[40]

The twenty-three genuine Arnulfing/Pippinid charters extant, dating from between *c.* 650 and 751, with a further forty-eight *deperdita*, as Ingrid Heidrich has long since established, witness not only to the steady build-up of wealth and connections on the part of the mayors and other members of the family, especially in Alemannia and Frisia, but also to the vagaries in their own political fortunes. The charters reflect the mayors clinging to their own position and attempting to deal with the problems of succession, notably between 709 and 715. They constitute an unprecedented and unparalleled quantity of charters from a single private family, with thirty-seven from Pippin II and Charles Martel between 691 and 741 alone. Those for Charles Martel even exceed the number of surviving Merovingian royal charters from the same period.[41] The establishing of a relationship with the royal monastery of St Denis by Charles Martel, culminating in the gift to St Denis of the royal villa of Clichy shortly before his death, is particularly notable.[42]

The production of coinage in the eighth century reflects the real power of the mayors, as well as their close involvement in the regulation of the economy, in both Neustria and Austrasia. This is especially significant in the light of the lack of central control over the minting of coinage throughout the Merovingian period before the 670s.[43] After that decade, gold coinage appears to have been abandoned in favour of silver. A strong case has been made for the monetary revolution which brought about the change to the independent silver denier being effected by Ebroin, mayor of the palace in Neustria, with the chief mints probably at Rouen, Amiens, Paris and Tours.[44] The use of the silver denier was subsequently adopted in Austrasia, Burgundy and Provence, largely in the train of the extension of Pippin II's authority after 687. In Austrasia, in so far as this can be

---

[40]   Bede, *Historia ecclesiastica gentis anglorum*, ed. B. Colgrave and R. A. B. Mynors, *Bede's Ecclesiastical history of the English people* (Oxford, 1969), Book 5, cc. 10 and 11, pp. 484 and 485. The *Liber pontificalis* account of Pope Sergius (687–701), *LP*, Life 86, c. 16, ed. Duchesne, p. 376, only records the consecration of Willibrord for the Frisians.

[41]   I. Heidrich (ed.), *Die Urkunden der Arnulfinger* (Bad Münstereifel, 2001); and see also the website created with great personal generosity by Carl and Ingrid Heidrich in order to make these charters accessible on line, <www.igh.histsem.uni-bonn.de>; and I. Heidrich, 'Titulatur und Urkunden der arnulfingischen Hausmeier', *Archiv für Diplomatik* 11/12 (1965/6), pp. 71–279. See also I. Heidrich, 'Die Urkunden Pippins d.M und Karl Martells: Beobachtungen zu ihrer zeitlichen und räumlichen Steuerung', in Jarnut, Nonn and Richter, *Karl Martell in seiner Zeit*, pp. 23–34.

[42]   See Heidrich, *Die Urkunden der Arnulfinger*, No. 14, pp. 90–1.

[43]   P. Grierson and M. A. S. Blackburn, *Medieval European coinage with a catalogue of the coins in the Fitzwilliam Museum, Cambridge*, 1: *The early middle ages (5th–10th centuries)* (Cambridge, 1986), p. 102.

[44]   Ibid., pp. 94–5 and 138.

determined from the very few hoards and single finds, the main mints were at Reims and Metz. The introduction of a lower denomination of money is linked to the proliferation of local markets, notably that associated with St Denis, to which freedom of tolls was granted.[45] Royal names are almost never to be found on this silver coinage, though, apart from two early silver coins bearing the name of Ebroin, they are not replaced by those of the mayors of the palace.[46] Even so it would appear that the mayors in the early eighth century re-established central control of minting on the Roman model and successfully imposed uniformity in weight and design, though it was only from 754–5 that there is legislation surviving from Pippin III's reign on the subject. This provided for a heavier silver coin than the earlier Merovingian coin in stating that not more than twenty-two solidi, that is, 264 deniers (allowing for seigneurage of twenty-four deniers), should be struck to the pound by weight. Although not stipulated in the legislation, a royal legend was introduced onto the coinage under Pippin.[47]

The evidence is undoubtedly meagre, but it all supports an understanding of the power of the mayors as equivalent to that enjoyed by kings. Even if they were not actually kings themselves, they ruled as if they were Merovingian kings. It is clear from the Merovingian royal charters and from the dating clauses of local 'private' charters, however, that there is no sense in which contemporaries failed to distinguish the difference between the positions of king and *maior domus*, even if the actual power and authority of the *maiores* were recognized.[48] Nevertheless, what needs to be emphasized above all is that the models for the Pippinid mayors themselves had been the seventh-century Merovingian kings they served, even though the pro-Pippinid and Carolingian narratives subsequently exaggerated Merovingian decline to justify the Pippin takeover. In this respect continuity in the style of rulership was indeed maintained by the Carolingian mayors, not so much on Pippin III's usurpation in 751 but from the later seventh century, when Pippin II is first described as ruling the kingdom. The mayors ruled from the royal palace and were in charge of the household, all aspects of royal administration, justice, the treasure and

---

[45] T. Kölzer, *Die Urkunden der Merovinger, MGH Diplomata* regum francorum e stirpe Merovingica (Hanover, 2001), Nos. 123 and 156; and *DKar.* 1, No. 6 K; and see I. Wood, 'Usurpers and Merovingian kingship', in Becher and Jarnut, *Die Dynastiewechsel von 751*, pp. 15–32.

[46] Grierson and Blackburn, *Medieval European coinage*, pp. 94 and 145–6.

[47] Ibid., pp. 203–4, Catalogue No. I.719, and compare No. 720, p. 520 and Plate 33.

[48] See the examples from Weissenburg, St Wandrille and the upper Rhine region provided by Heidrich, 'Die Urkunden Pippins d.M und Karl Martells', p. 28. On the Weissenburg charters see also H. Hummer, *Politics and power in early medieval Europe: Alsace and the Frankish realm, 600–1000* (Cambridge, 2005), pp. 26–55.

the army. They ruled the kingdoms together with the bishops and secular magnates just as the Merovingian kings had done.[49] From the late seventh century onwards, the political importance and role of the Merovingian kings themselves were very much diminished.

Underlying the portrayal of the Pippinid mayors within the political framework of Merovingian rule, however, is an implicit sense of continuity and historical consciousness in terms of political control and the identity of the kingdom. This is made explicit in a number of curious texts given the collective title of *Catalogi regum francorum*, the earliest versions of which date from early in Charlemagne's reign and, significantly, in manuscripts containing either the Roman law Breviary of Alaric or the *Lex Salica*, or both. In Bern Burgerbibliothek MS 263, for example, a manuscript from the upper Rhine region, Theuderic IV's rule and an interregnum of seven years thereafter are noted. Chilperic III's reign of nine years is recorded and a total totted up of kings between Theuderic and Chilperic III as seventy-nine years. Then *Pippinus rex* is recorded as having reigned for eighteen years. The same sequence, including the interregum after Theodoric, is preserved in St Gallen, Stiftsbibliothek MS 731, in which the layout and introductory word *Regn(avit)* for the Merovingian kings and the Pippinid successors are exactly the same. In Bern, Burgerbibliothek MS 83, a late ninth-century adaptation of this list, there is a still more interesting presentation of the sequence of rule, for here the kings and the Pippinid mayors, all under the heading *NOM(ina) REG(um) FRANCOR(um)* are interleaved as rulers and it is simply noted they are *maior domus*, with the distinction between them and the kings lying in the lack of regnal years given for the mayors before Pippin III.[50] The mocking description of the

---

49 See Fredegar, ed. J. M. Wallace-Hadrill, *The fourth book of the Chronicle of Fredegar with its continuations* (London, 1960), p. 85. On Merovingian government see I. N. Wood, *The Merovingian kingdoms, 482–751* (London, 1994). On the essential co-operation between the secular and ecclesiastical leaders with the king see the important remarks by M. de Jong, '*Ecclesia* and the early medieval polity', in S. Airlie, W. Pohl and H. Reimitz (eds.), *Staat im frühen Mittelalter*, Österreichische Akademie der Wissenschaften, phil.-hist. Klasse Denkschriften 334 (Forschungen zur Geschichte des Mittelalters 11) (Vienna, 2006), pp. 113–33, esp. pp. 124–9.

50 *Regum francorum genealogiae*, ed. G. Pertz, *MGH SS* 2, pp. 304–14. See E. Ewig, 'Die fränkischen Königskataloge und der Aufstieg der Karolinger', *Deutsches Archiv* 51 (1995), pp. 1–28; H. Reimitz, 'Anleitung zur Interpretation: Schrift und Genealogie in der Karolingerzeit', in W. Pohl and P. Herold (ed.), *Vom Nutzen des Schreibens: Soziales Gedächtnis, Herrschaft und Besitz*, Österreichische Akademie der Wissenschaften, phil.-hist. Klasse, Denkschriften 306 (Forschungen zur Geschichte des Mittelalters 5) (Vienna, 2002), pp. 167–81; and Reimitz, 'Die Konkurrenz der Ursprünge in der fränkischen Historiographie', in W. Pohl (ed.), *Die Suche nach den Ursprüngen: von der Bedeutung des frühen Mittelalters*, Österreichische Akademie der Wissenschaften, phil.-hist. Klasse, Denkschriften 322 (Forschungen zur Geschichte des Mittelalters 8) (Vienna, 2004), pp. 191–209. On the importance of Novalesa as a focus of Pippinid support, see below, p. 82.

last Merovingian king aside, Einhard's characterization of the structures and balance of power under the late seventh- and early eighth-century Merovingian kings, therefore, appears to be accurate. He expressed a contemporary perception in the early ninth century, grounded in reality, of a far more gradual transition between Merovingian and Carolingian rule, and the steady assumption of royal power by the mayors that eventually enabled them to replace the dynasty. There is a further theme, however, to be extracted from the eighth-century narratives. Not everyone supported the Pippinids, and there was, as we shall see below, a constant element of local disaffection and division within the realm which occasionally erupted.[51]

PREPARATION FOR KINGSHIP: PIPPIN III AND CHARLEMAGNE

Pippin III's decision between 749 and 751 to depose the Merovingian ruler Childeric III, whom Pippin himself and his brother Carloman had set upon the throne in 743, was supported by a sufficient number of Frankish magnates to secure his position. The event is presented by later commentators as an obvious step to take in relation to the ineffectiveness of the Merovingian ruler. Although Pippin's elevation to the kingship is accepted as having been effected by 751 (though some sources date it a year later), many of its details, not least whether the king was anointed or simply consecrated,[52] and whether the pope's opinion about the elevation of Pippin to the kingship was sought or offered, are disputed.[53] The Continuator of Fredegar's Chronicle, for example, reports *consecratio*, not anointing, of Pippin in 751, whereas the *Annales regni francorum* records episcopal anointing of Pippin in 751 and the papal anointing of Charles and Carloman in 754.[54] What is at issue is the legitimacy of

---

[51] See above, note 21, and P. J. Geary, *Aristocracy in Provence: The Rhône basin at the dawn of the Carolingian age*, Monographien zur Geschichte des Mittelalters 31 (Stuttgart, 1985), esp. pp. 148–51, on an anti-Pippinid group in Provence represented by Maurontus, who was eliminated by Abbo in the 730s.

[52] J. Semmler, 'Zeitgeschichtsschreibung und Hofhistoriographie unter den frühen Karolingern', in Laudage, *Von Fakten und Fiktionen*, pp. 135–64; and J. Semmler, *Der Dynastiewechsel von 751 und die fränkische Königssalbung*, Studia humaniora 6 (Düsseldorf, 2003). Compare W. Affeldt, 'Untersuchungen zur Königserhebung Pippins', *Frühmittelalterliche Studien* 14 (1980), pp. 95–187.

[53] See R. McKitterick, 'The illusion of royal power in the Royal Frankish annals', *English Historical Review* 115 (2000), pp. 1–20; McKitterick, *History and memory*, pp. 133–55; and Becher and Jarnut, *Der Dynastiewechsel von 751*.

[54] See the discussion by P. Buc, 'Nach 754: warum weniger die Handelnden selbst als eher die Chronisten das politische Ritual erzeugten – und warum es niemanden auf die wahre Geschichte ankam', in B. Jussen (ed.), *Die Macht des Königs: Herrschaft in Europa vom Frühmittelalter bis in die Neuzeit* (Munich, 2005), pp. 27–37, albeit he unaccountably omits the *Clausula de unctione Pippini* from his discussion. On the *Clausula*, see A. I. Stoclet, 'La "Clausula de unctione Pippini Regis":

Pippin's position and steps taken on his part or on that of his lay and ecclesiastical supporters to enhance it.[55] One major event in this respect was the visit of Pope Stephen II to the Frankish kingdom in 753–4, which appears to have been a papal initiative in order to seek Frankish assistance against the Lombards. At St Denis in January 754, according to the *Clausula de unctione Pippini*, allegedly written in 767, the pope anointed Pippin and his wife Bertrada as well as his two sons Charles (Charlemagne) and Carloman. Pope Stephen also confirmed that Pippin and his family were henceforth the only rightful rulers of the Frankish kingdom.[56] This ritual was designed to establish the authority and legitimacy of the new royal family on the throne and to create a dynasty.

The Life of Stephen II (Life 94) in the *Liber pontificalis*, the text written closest in time to the events, adds details about the protocol of the reception of the pope in the Frankish realm. Not only did this include the pope being escorted from St Maurice d'Agaune near the Alpine pass to the king at the royal palace of Ponthion near Paris, by Abbot Fulrad of St Denis and Duke Rothard, but Pippin sent his son Charles with some of his great men 'nearly one hundred miles' (*ad centum milia*) to meet the pope.[57] Even if the events were not actually as described, this is the representation of them current by the time Charlemagne himself succeeded to the kingship. That anointing of the princes was part of the ritual, moreover, is reiterated in a later letter from Pope Stephen III to Charlemagne and Carloman and may even explain the inclusion of this detail in the *Annales regni francorum*.[58]

These reports of the papal visit in 754, therefore, both effect the transformation of the Pippinids into a royal family and introduce Charlemagne and Carloman into the historical record. Next to nothing otherwise is known about Charlemagne's childhood. His birth date is not certain, though most now agree it was 747 or 748.[59] It was thus not until

---

mises au point et nouvelles hypothèses', *Francia* 8 (1980), pp. 1–42; and, arguing for the document's authenticity against Stoclet's hypothesis, O. Schneider, 'Die Königserhebung Pippins 751 in der Erinnerung der karolingischen Quellen: Die Glaubwürdigkeit der Reichsannalen und die Verformung der Vergangenheit', in Becher and Jarnut, *Der Dynastiewechsel von 751*, pp. 243–75 at pp. 268–75. See also below, pp. 292–3.

[55] See P. Fouracre, 'Conflict, power and legitimation in Francia in the late seventh and eighth centuries', in I. Alfonso, H. Kennedy and J. Escalona (eds.), *Building legitimacy: political discourses and forms of legitimacy in medieval societies*, The Medieval Mediterranean 53 (Leiden, 2004), pp. 3–26.

[56] On Bertrada, see J. L. Nelson, 'Bertrada', in Becher and Jarnut, *Der Dynastiewechsel von 751*, pp. 93–108.

[57] *LP*, Life 94, c. 25, ed. Duchesne, I, p. 447.

[58] *Codex epistolaris carolinus*, ed. Gundlach, Ep. 45, p. 561.

[59] K. F. Werner; 'Das Geburtsdatum Karls des Großen', *Francia* 1 (1973), pp. 115–57; M. Becher, 'Neue Überlegungen zum Geburtsdatum Karls des Großen', *Francia* 19 (1992), pp. 37–60.

Charlemagne was three or four years old that his father Pippin III usurped the Merovingian throne. He would only have been six or seven years old at the time of the papal visit and the remarkable responsibility apparently given to this newly minted prince of representing his father in honouring the pope. The recent change of status of the family means that neither Charlemagne nor his brother Carloman was necessarily groomed for kingship in their earliest years, though the Pippinid males, as we have seen, had long been accustomed to ruling. Even after 751, furthermore, there would have been no surety that either boy would succeed to the kingship.

From 754, however, we may suppose that the hope on Pippin's part was that thereafter there would be rather more confidence in the future role of the young prince Charlemagne, together with that of his brother. Attention would also have been focussed on the ideological bolstering of the new dynasty's position, and on the difference being a king rather than a mayor might have made. The process by which Charlemagne and his brother may have been trained to rule is unknown. Although Pippin himself had been taught at the monastery of St Denis, it is unknown where his sons were educated. It is conceivable that they were trained at court and that their mother Bertrada as well as the chaplains may have had something to do with their intellectual and spiritual development, and thus the instilling in them, and in Charlemagne in particular, of respect for learning and its potential. Ardo's Life of Benedict of Aniane, for example, refers to the group of scholars gathered at Bertrada's court, and Gisela, Charlemagne's sister, also acquired an education sufficient to be the recipient and commissioner of treatises by Alcuin in later years.[60]

Between 754 and Carloman and Charlemagne's succession in 768, there is only occasionally a passing reference to Charlemagne in the *Annales regni francorum*, and none to Carloman. While still in their minority they are likely to have been members of the royal household, so that references to Pippin and Bertrada in a place together may be supposed to include their boys. Thus when Tassilo of Bavaria came to swear loyalty to Pippin and his sons at the assembly at Compiègne in 757, it is likely that Charlemagne and his brother were there and that customary attendance at the annual assemblies was something Pippin required as part of the boys'

---

[60] On Gisela of Chelles see Alcuin, *Epistulae*, ed. Dümmler, Epp. 84, 154, 195, 216, *MGH Epp.* IV (Berlin, 1895), pp. 127, 29, 322–33, 359–60; and R. McKitterick, 'Les femmes, les arts et la culture en occident dans le haut moyen âge' in S. Lebecq, A. Dierkens, R. Le Jan and J.-M. Sansterre (eds.), *Femmes et pouvoirs des femmes à Byzance et en occident (VIe–XIe)* (Villeneuve d'Ascq, 1998), pp. 149–61. And see above on Chelles and the *Annales mettenses priores*, pp. 60–5, and below, pp. 362–3.

apprenticeship for rulership. If that is the case, then Pippin's major assemblies and pieces of legislation, such as the assemblies at Ver in 755, Compiègne in 757 and Attigny in 762, and thus of their father's activities in matters concerning administration of justice, control of coinage and reform of the church, would have been something of which they had some direct experience in addition to the knowledge of them through written records on which they were later able to draw. As difficult to document precisely is either Carloman's or Charlemagne's acquaintance with the leading members of their father's entourage and circle of supporters and their familiarity with the running of the royal household; both would have been crucial in securing their own positions when each became king.[61]

Charlemagne first appears in the charter record in a grant of royal protection and immunity to the monastery of St Calais in 760, coinciding with his year of majority under Frankish law.[62] In the military expedition of the following spring, Charlemagne accompanied his father Pippin for the first time and thereafter he was probably included in Pippin's military campaigns to subdue Aquitaine, though he is not specifically mentioned as doing so.[63] Later, Charlemagne's campaign in Saxony in 772 is claimed as his first.[64] It was in these years before 768, therefore, that he probably received his education and learnt to value learning and the Christian faith as well as martial prowess. That Carloman received similar treatment is indicated by a charter of 13 August 762 at Trisgodros, when Carloman, presumably because he too had now reached his majority, joined his brother and mother as witnesses when Prüm was taken under royal protection and was granted freedom of election to the abbacy and its earlier gifts were confirmed.[65] When Pippin died at St Denis, it was Carloman who confirmed and added to Pippin's gifts in charters of his own in 769.[66]

Pippin III's untimely death marked the conclusion of his season of campaigning in Aquitaine and the successful subjugation of that region. He fell ill at Saintes, where he had been joined by his wife and household, and travelled north via Tours, where he prayed at the shrine of St Martin, before reaching St Denis, where he died on 24 September aged forty-four.

---

[61] See the survey of Pippin III's probable supporters provided by Semmler, in Becher and Jarnut, *Der Dynastiewechsel von 751*, pp. 58–86.
[62] *DKar.* 1, No. 14. Unfortunately this survives only in a seventeenth-century copy.
[63] *ARF* 761, ed. Kurze, p. 18. The Revised Version adds the extra note that Charles was Pippin's firstborn son and given supreme rule over the whole empire after his father's death, ibid., p. 21.
[64] *ARF* 772, *prima vice*, ed. Kurze, p. 32. [65] *DKar.* 1, No. 16. [66] *DKar.* 1, Nos. 43, 44, 46, 53.

It was there that he was buried, at his own request, close to the saint himself and in the community presided over by Abbot Fulrad, his chaplain and one of his staunchest political allies.[67] The bald account in the annals can be supplemented by a clutch of Pippin's charters for St Denis, confirming the freedom of election to the abbacy and the monastery's immunity as well as granting Abbot Fulrad lands in Alsace and Ortenau and further land to the monastery in recognition that St Denis was to be his burial place.[68] The choice of St Denis as his last resting place not only built on the relationship Pippin himself and his father Charles Martel had established with the monastery, but was also another manifestation of the continuities constructed by the Pippinids with their Merovingian predecessors. In his charters recording gifts to St Denis, Pippin had already shown his consciousness of confirming and continuing the royal munificence towards the saint and the monastery on the part of his predecessors.[69] Now in death he joined some of them, for St Denis was also the burial place of at least the sixth-century queen Arnegundis and the seventh-century Merovingian kings Dagobert I (and his wife Nantechild) and Clovis II, quite apart from that of Charles Martel.[70] Saint Denis, the Merovingian royal saint, was appropriated by the Pippinids. A tradition of prayers requested from the monks for the family and the kingdom was established by Pippin III soon after he became king.[71] It was on the feast day of St Denis, moreover, that is, 9 October 768, that Charlemagne and Carloman were crowned kings in succession to their father.[72]

CHARLEMAGNE AND CARLOMAN 768–771: JOINT RULE

Charlemagne was twenty or twenty-one years old when he succeeded so abruptly to the kingship in 768 and shared his father's inheritance with his

---

[67] See A. Dierkens, 'La mort, les funérailles et la tombe du roi Pépin le Bref (768)', *Médiévales* 31 (1996), pp. 37–52; for the wider context see J. L. Nelson, 'Carolingian royal funerals', in F. Theuws and J. L. Nelson (eds.), *Rituals of power from late antiquity to the early middle ages*, The Transformation of the Roman World 8 (Leiden, 2000), pp. 131–84. On Fulrad and Pippin see J. Semmler, 'Verdient um das karolingische Königtum und den werdenden Kirchenstaat: Fulrad von St Denis', in O. Münsch and T. Zotz (eds.), *Scientia veritatis: Festschrift für Hubert Mordek zum 65. Geburtstag* (Stuttgart, 2004), pp. 91–115.

[68] *DKar.* I, No. 28.

[69] *DKar.* I, Nos 16, 7, 8, 22, 23, 25, 26, 27. On the St Denis archive see below, pp. 198–9.

[70] K. H. Krüger, *Königsgrabkirchen: der Franken, Angelsachsen und Langobarden bis zur Mitte des 8. Jahrhunderts. Ein historischer Katalog*, Münstersche Mittelalter-Schriften 4 (Munich, 1971), pp. 31, 35 and 171–89; and Nelson, 'Carolingian royal funerals', pp. 140–2.

[71] Ibid, at pp. 184–6; and see DKar I, Nos. 6, 8, 22, 25, 26, and compare Nos. 53, 55 and 92.

[72] For comment see U. Nonn, 'Zur Königserhebung Karls und Karlmanns', *Rheinische Vierteljahrsblätter* 39 (1975), pp. 386–7.

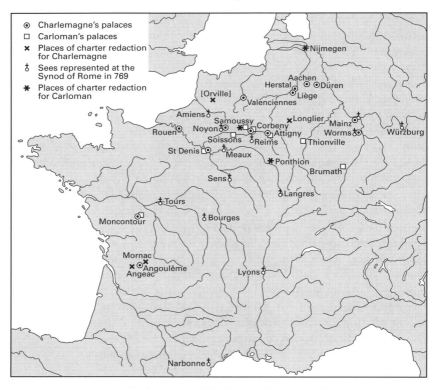

⊙	Charlemagne's palaces
☐	Carloman's palaces
✗	Places of charter redaction for Charlemagne
♂	Sees represented at the Synod of Rome in 769
✳	Places of charter redaction for Carloman

Map 1 Charlemagne and Carloman: joint rule, 768–771

brother Carloman, who was probably, but not certainly, his junior by a
year or two[73] (Map 1). That inheritance, as spelt out by the *Annales regni
francorum*, comprised, above all, training for kingship by example.[74] This
can be surmised because so many of Pippin's policies and methods in the

---

[73] For reflections on the rights of inheritance of the two brothers in relation to the kingship see
G. Wolf, 'Die Königssöhne Karl und Karlmann und ihr Thronfolgerecht nach Pippins
Königserhebung 750/51', *Zeitschrift der Savigny Stiftung für Rechtsgeschichte: Germanistische
Abteilung* 108 (1991), pp. 282–96. J. Semmler describes Carloman as the elder of the two brothers:
see J. Semmler, 'Der Neubau Karls des Großen: die fränkische Reichskirche', in J. Laudage (ed.), *Isti
moderni: Erneuerungskonzepte und Erneuerungskonflikte in Mittelalter und Renaissance* (forthcoming). I am grateful to Josef Semmler for sending me his paper in advance of publication.
[74] See P. Classen, 'Karl der Große und die Thronfolge im Frankenreich', in *Festschrift für Hermann
Heimpel*, Veröffentlichungen des Max-Planck-Instituts für Geschichte 36/3 (Göttingen, 1972),
pp. 109–34, repr. in J. Fleckenstein (ed.), *Peter Classen, Ausgewählte Aufsätze*, Vorträge und
Forschungen 28 (Sigmaringen, 1983), pp. 205–29. See also McKitterick, *History and memory*,
pp. 152–3.

spheres of relations with the papacy and Byzantium, towards the Lombard kingdom, church reform, control of coinage, family strategies and military expansion, as we shall see, were continued and further developed by Charlemagne. Carloman's reign was too short to reflect much of this.[75] Both sons also inherited the network of Pippinid and Agilolfing family ties, the special links with such major monasteries as St Denis, St Wandrille, Prüm and Echternach, and a wide spectrum of aristocratic support. Although it was left to his sons to conclude the arrangements for the administration of Aquitaine, the kingdom Pippin III left them comprised, in theory at least, an extended Frankish realm, stretching south to the Pyrenees, east into Alemannia and north to southern Frisia.

The revised version of the *Annales regni francorum* implies that Pippin had not made, or had not had the time to make, any formal arrangements for the succession, for the author claims that there was a formal division decided at an assembly after Pippin's death, with Charlemagne receiving Austrasia and Carloman Burgundy, Provence, Aquitaine, and Alemannia. No reference is made to Neustria. Only the Continuation to the Chronicle of Fredegar, echoed by the *Annales mettenses priores*, attributes the division to Pippin III before he died.[76]

Short as the period was before Carloman died in 771, it is difficult to determine whether or not the kingdom was divided between them in terms of a partition of territory, let alone its true extent. It looks much more like joint rule, albeit with separate spheres of responsibility, within a very limited area. Since the late sixth century, partition of the Frankish kingdom between kings' sons, according to the Frankish custom of partible inheritance, had been in terms of the kingdoms of Neustria, Austrasia and Burgundy, and this seems to have been the principle on which Pippin III and his brother Carloman had divided their areas of political control as well. Certainly Charlemagne and his brother Carloman were separately consecrated as king, but in the same ecclesiastical province of Reims, with Charlemagne at Noyon and Carloman at Soissons. Certainly, too, they used a different set of palaces in both Neustria and Austrasia. Carloman's palaces, mostly in the area between the Marne and Meuse rivers, included Samoussy, Attigny, Ponthion, Thionville, Brumath and Nijmegen. He died at Samoussy in December 771, and was buried at Reims. It was at nearby Corbeny, another of Carloman's palaces, that Charlemagne

---

[75] See below, pp. 82–8.
[76] *RVARF* 769, ed. Kurze, p. 29, Fredegar, Continuations, c. 53, ed. Wallace-Hadrill, p. 121; and *Annales mettenses priores* 768, p. 55; Classen, 'Karl der Große und die Thronfolge', suggested that Neustria was divided.

subsequently met Carloman's inner circle of *fideles*. Charlemagne's principal palaces were north of his brother's group; apart from the assemblies convened at Worms and Valenciennes, they were concentrated between the lower Rhine and Meuse, at Aachen, Orville, Düren and Liège. Charlemagne was also active in Aquitaine in the aftermath of Pippin's military conquest of the region. Not until after Carloman's death did Charlemagne use the palaces of Attigny and Herstal (see Map 1). For neither brother is the area of operation at all large. This may indicate the extent of the regions where they were sure of support, for we have no idea of the extent to which the idea that they should succeed their father in the kingship was fully accepted.

There were no recent precedents for royal succession between more than one heir for the new dynasty to follow, despite the brief partition between Pippin III and his brother Carloman when they were still mayors. They chose, moreover, to elevate only one Merovingian king to the throne rather than two, and Carloman's departure for Mount Soracte soon thereafter left Pippin III in sole charge. The political position on Pippin's early death in any case was not necessarily secure and we cannot assume that the sons' succession was either automatic or straightforward. One source of legitimacy, however, was the anointing of them both by the pope long ago in 754 and the connection sustained by Pippin thereafter, not least in relation to Frankish policies towards the Lombard kingdom. The popes, indeed, had been wont since 754 to address Pippin, Charlemagne and Carloman as kings: 'Dominis excellentibus filiis, Pippino regi et nostro spirituali compatri seu Carolo et Carolomanno, idem regibus et utriusque patritiis romanorum stephanus papa'.[77] Both brothers may have had to work hard to consolidate and extend their power, much as Charles Martel had had to do on his father's death in 714. It would have been in the new kings' interests to work together.

Although the contemporary papal sources report disharmony between the Frankish kings, even this does not give the impression of separate kingdoms. In a letter addressed to both Charlemagne and Carloman, for example, Pope Stephen III reported on the visit of their *missi*, Guazbert and Fulbert, Ansfred and Helmgar, who had brought a letter to the pope in which the brothers had apparently admitted to quarrelling. Nevertheless, they insisted that that was all now in the past and that they were together intent on upholding the rights of St Peter. The pope certainly went on to ask the kings jointly for help in protecting 'the rights of St Peter', that is, to

---

[77] *Codex epistolaris carolinus*, ed. Gundlach, *Ep.* 6 (755), p. 488.

assist the pope against the Lombards, and he spoke of their kingdom, not their kingdoms.[78] Carloman's position in relation to his brother remains ambiguous. It is difficult to know what weight to attach to the fact that it is Carloman who was crowned king in Soissons like his father before him, who initially maintained his father's relationship with St Denis and Fulrad the chaplain, and who called his own son Pippin.

Much has been made by modern scholars of the quarrel between the two brothers.[79] It has been extended from one recorded incident to 'bitter rivalry' and 'fraternal hostility' overall, especially with regard to the Lombard kingdom.[80] It is going too far to assume that this brief quarrel is an indication of lasting and bitter rivalry between the two Frankish kings. Such a reading distorts our understanding of the years in the immediate aftermath of the death of Pippin III. The temporary dissension between the two brothers noted by Pope Stephen III is accounted for in the *Annales regni francorum* and elaborated further by the Revised Version in the context of the conclusion of the subjugation of Aquitaine.

In 769 Charlemagne met Carloman at Duasdives (Moncontour) (either near Vienne or a place just north of Chasseneuil in Aquitaine) and failed to get any help from him.[81] The Revised Version of the *Annales regni francorum* explains that Carloman was led astray by the advice of his magnates on this. The meeting between Bertrada and Carloman at Seltz, just north of Strasbourg, before she went to Italy, which is reported in both versions of the *Annales regni francorum*, has been interpreted as connected with the brothers' quarrel in Aquitaine.[82] The gloss 'in order to make peace' (*pacis causa*) provided by the Reviser seems to relate to Bertrada's mission in Italy. The meeting between Carloman and Bertrada, therefore, should more plausibly be understood as a discussion about Italian policy, possibly in the light of the pope's letter. It is possible, in other words, to read the few

---

[78] Ibid., Ep. 44, pp. 558–60.

[79] M. Lintzel, 'Karl der Große und Karlmann', *Historische Zeitschrift* 140 (1929), pp. 1–22; E. Delaruelle, 'Charlemagne, Carloman, Didier et la politique du mariage franco-lombard (770–771)', *Revue historique* 170 (1932), pp. 213–24. Compare King, *Charlemagne*, pp. 6–8; and Classen, 'Karl der Große und die Thronfolge', Map 4.

[80] J. Jarnut talks in terms of 'Brüderkampf' and 'crisis' and claims it is reported many times ('vielfach bezeugte Feindschaft'): 'Ein Brüderkampf und seine Folgen; Die Krise des Frankenreiches (768–771)', in G. Jenal (ed.), *Herrschaft, Kirche, Kultur: Beiträge zur Geschichte des Mittelalters. Festschrift für Friedrich Prinz zu seinem 65. Geburtstag*, Monographien zur Geschichte des Mittelalters 37 (Stuttgart, 1993), pp. 165–76, repr. in Jarnut, *Herrschaft und Ethnogenese*, pp. 235–46.

[81] *ARF* 769, ed. Kurze, p. 28.

[82] J. L Nelson, 'Making a difference in eighth-century politics: the daughters of Desiderius', in A. C. Murray (ed.), *After Rome's fall: narrators and sources of early medieval history. Essays presented to Walter Goffart* (Toronto, 1998), pp. 171–90. and J. L. Nelson, 'Bertrada', in Becher and Jarnut, *Der Dynastiewechsel von 751*, pp. 93–108.

references we have to Bertrada as dividing her time between the households of the two brothers and actively assisting both kings in Frankish dealings with the Lombard rulers rather than as acting in some way as a mediator between the two kings. If she were keeping the peace between the two brothers, it cannot be assumed that she was on Charlemagne's 'side' rather than Carloman's. Bertrada was also in Charlemagne's household at some stage during these years, for another letter from Pope Stephen was addressed jointly to Bertrada and Charlemagne.[83] If it is correct that Charlemagne was assigned or claimed Aquitaine, but then asked Carloman for assistance, that might be sufficient to account for a sudden flare-up of a quarrel between them. Lintzel, indeed, suggested long ago that Charlemagne had actually seized Carloman's 'portion' of Aquitaine.[84] The confirmation of Pippin III's capitulary for Aquitaine, dated 768 or 769, is unfortunately ambiguous in this respect, for its reference to *genitor Pippinus, nos* and *missi nostri* could apply to either brother (if using a 'royal we') or both.[85] There is no reliable indication of why Carloman refused Charlemagne assistance in Aquitaine. For all we know, Carloman may have felt he had enough on his hands consolidating the Pippinid position north of the Loire, and thus the brothers, both with new and immense responsibilities, may have argued and disagreed about priorities. Alternatively, Carloman may have objected to Charlemagne's policies in Aquitaine itself. A further factor is the degree of agreement on policies towards the Lombards and the papacy. Even Pope Stephen did not remain consistently hostile towards the Lombards.[86]

There is thus a great deal of uncertainty about Carloman's career and the nature of his relations with his brother, largely created by innuendo circulated after his death. In any case, we should always, always, remember that the greater proportion of surviving narrative accounts of 768–71 are written some years after Carloman's death. The pope's report of the brothers' protestation that they had settled their differences should be taken seriously. A serious obstacle to this might be thought to be Cathwulf's definition, in his letter to Charlemagne *c.* 775, of the third proof of Charlemagne's blessedness. Cathwulf claimed that it was Charlemagne's preservation from the treachery of his brother in all things

[83] *Codex epistolaris carolinus*, ed. Gundlach, Epp. 47, 48, pp. 565–7.
[84] Jarnut, 'Ein Brüderkampf', who cites the earlier literature.
[85] *MGH Cap.* I, No. 18, pp. 42–43. The implications of this capitulary for the government of Aquitaine after Pippinid conquest is discussed below, p. 237.
[86] See *Codex epistolaris carolinus*, ed. Gundlach, Ep. 46, and compare ibid., Ep. 85, pp. 564–5 and 621–2.

(*ut de fratris tui insidiis in omnibus*). Cathwulf's fourth blessing, moreover, is that Charlemagne divided the kingdom with his brother, and the fifth, that God took Carloman up 'into the higher kingdom' so that that the whole (Frankish) kingdom came to Charles 'without any loss of blood' as did the Lombard kingdom and the city of Pavia thereafter.[87] Despite the strongly partisan nature of Cathwulf's language, and speculation about the sources of his information aside, this, presented in a chronological sequence as it is, can be read as an overstated reference from hindsight to the disagreement in Aquitaine in 769 in order to celebrate Charlemagne's sole rule. It is presumably, however, what Cathwulf thought Charlemagne might like to hear. The quarrel between the two brothers was known from the papal letters, if nothing else, and it was the *Codex epistolaris carolinus* compiled in 791 which preserved these very letters at Charlemagne's command.[88] Cathwulf's attitude to Carloman is the beginning of a trend, for in the narratives composed later in Charlemagne's reign, such as the *Annales regni francorum*, Carloman's status and integrity were downgraded. All focus on Charlemagne even before he was left as sole ruler in 771.

The notion of an entente maintained between the brothers after 769 is based in part on an appreciation of the pragmatism and political astuteness displayed by Charlemagne throughout his subsequent career. There is no reason to suppose that Carloman was any the less practical. When they first succeeded their father, neither could have had any expectation of the length of their reigns and the difficulties that might lie ahead. The situation as far as precise areas of jurisdiction are concerned may initially have been in the process of definition. Charlemagne's and Carloman's support of each other would have strengthened the Pippinid family's hold on power as a whole, and it has to be acknowledged that factions and the taking of sides among the magnates, paradoxically enough, would have worked to the advantage of one or the other of them and thus also to the Pippinid position in providing a Pippinid focus and an exclusively Pippinid set of choices for political loyalties.[89]

---

[87] *Epistulae variorum Carolo magno regnante*, ed. E. Dümmler, Ep. 7, *MGH Epp.* IV, pp. 501–5, in Paris, BnF lat. 2777, fols 56v–58r. See J. Story, 'Cathwulf, kingship and the royal abbey of Saint-Denis', *Speculum* 74 (1999), pp. 1–20; M. Garrison, 'Letter to a king and biblical exempla: the examples of Cathwulf and Clemens *peregrinus*', *Early Medieval Europe* 7 (1998), pp. 305–28.

[88] See above, pp. 37–8.

[89] A similar point is made in relation to Grifo and the role he played in the consolidation of the position of his half-brothers Pippin III and Carloman by S. Airlie, 'Towards a Carolingian aristocracy', in Becher and Jarnut, *Der Dynastiewechsel von 751*, pp. 109–27.

The similarity in the behaviour of each king on succeeding Pippin III, moreover, is a telling indication of the standard ways in which a political position might be secured. Both had support from ecclesiastical and secular magnates and both confirmed their father's grants to major ecclesiastical institutions within the Frankish kingdom. The brothers' charters for these years in particular reflect a pattern repeated on king's accessions subsequently, namely the confirmation of grants made by their predecessors. The meagre survival rate, however, means that there is only the barest indication of this, such as Carloman's confirmation of grants of immunity and freedom from tolls to St Denis, immunity for Argenteuil, Granfelden, Honau and Münster in Gregoriental, and immunity and freedom of election of the abbot for Novalesa.[90] Carloman's own policies are suggested by the grant, prompted by Abbot Asinarius of Novalesa and addressed to all his bishops, abbots, counts, vicars, *centenarii* and all his agents or *missi*, of freedom from tolls throughout his kingdom to Novalesa for the general benefit of trade.[91] Novalesa, founded by Abbo of Provence, appears to have sustained its support of the Pippin family; Carloman clearly wished to ensure that it continued to do so, though it was eventually Charlemagne who was called on to confirm the founder's original grants of land.[92] Strategic considerations of access to Italy may also have played a role. Further, Carloman restored forested land to his count of the palace, Chrodoald.[93] Charlemagne's charters from the period of joint rule offer a similar combination of confirmations of earlier royal grants to Corbie, St Aubin in Angers, St Bertin and St Maur des Fossés,[94] and new gifts such as the tithe granted to Utrecht.[95] Carloman granted immunity and royal protection to Echternach,[96] and this may indicate competition with his brother for the favour and support of particular monastic houses. Charlemagne's encroachment on his brother's expectations of loyalty might seem to be indicated by the gift of St Dié in the Vosges to St Denis.[97] On the other hand, both Echternach and St Denis had been important for their parents and family as a whole, and thus such gifts might equally well be interpreted as a continuation of filial piety and an aspect of the joint rulership.

If the *Liber pontificalis* is to be trusted on this point, a further indication of joint rule appears to be the decision to send twelve bishops to the Synod

[90] *DKar.* I, Nos. 43–6, 49, 50, 52 and 54. On the charter evidence generally see below, pp. 197–204.
[91] *DKar.* I, No. 47.   [92] See Geary, *Aristocracy in Provence*, pp. 38–9.   [93] *DKar.* I, No. 51.
[94] *DKar.* I, Nos. 57, 58, 59, 60, 61.   [95] *DKar.* I, No. 56.
[96] *DKar.* I, No. 48.   [97] *DKar.* I, No. 79.

of Rome held in 769. Pope Stephen III had sent his envoy Sergius with the request, but Sergius arrived too late to see Pippin III and saw his sons instead. The bishops are listed in one Frankish manuscript of the *Liber pontificalis* only, produced in the Auxerre region between 827 and 844, though the list is apparently confirmed in a later copy of the records of the council itself.[98] The bishops came from the ecclesiastical provinces of Reims (Reims, Amiens, Meaux and Noyons), Sens (Sens and Langres) Bourges, Tours, Narbonne, Lyon and Mainz (Mainz, Worms and Würzburg), and so might be supposed to be representative in some way. It should be noted, however, that the ecclesiastical provinces within the Frankish kingdom without a representative were Cologne, Trier, Bordeaux, Eaux, Arles and Vienne, and there were no bishops present from Bavaria or Alemannia either. It is also noteworthy that seven of the bishops recorded as selected to go to Rome – Wilichar of Sens, Erlolf of Langres, Hermenarius of Bourges, Gavienus/Gaugenus of Tours, Daniel of Narbonne, Ado of Lyon, Gislebert of Noyon – are first recorded as incumbents of their sees in connection with this council. Many of those already installed in their sees did not attend. These new bishops may be newly consecrated supporters of their respective rulers. The other bishops chosen to attend, Tilpin of Reims, George of Ostia/Amiens, Wulfram of Meaux, Lull of Mainz, Ermembert of Worms and Bernulf of Würzburg, may have been those on whose support Charlemagne and Carloman felt able to count. When Charlemagne won over his brother's former faithful men in 771, moreover, Wilichar of Sens at least is specifically mentioned among the bishops. Unfortunately the episcopal *fasti* are generally too lacunose and the dates of episcopal reigns too uncertain to be able to use them with any confidence as an indicator of political support in any specific way, as distinct from allowing the Roman council list of 769 to confirm that in some matters at least Charlemagne and his brother acted in harmony.

The uncertainties surrounding the ability of either king to count on the support of the bishops in the first three years of their reigns may provide a context for Charlemagne's supposed first capitulary. This was largely

---

[98] LP, Life 96, c. 17, ed. Duchesne, I, pp. 473–5. Leiden, Universiteitsbibliotheek, Voss lat. Q 41. See Davis, *Lives*, p. 96 note 43; and compare *MGH Conc.* II.i, pp. 75–6 (repeats the list in the *Liber pontificalis*), and p. 80, the list from the council according to an eleventh-century manuscript. This gives George's see as Ostia (the see he held before coming to Francia). If contemporary and not added later, the *Liber pontificalis* list is the only indication we have that George was already bishop of Amiens as early as 769. On George see J. Story, *Carolingian connections* (Aldershot, 2003), pp. 56–64 and 87–9. For Charlemagne and his bishops see further below, pp. 299–305.

concerned with religious matters, such as the jurisdiction of bishops and the behaviour of the clergy, though it also insists on the importance of attendance at the lawcourts, the *mallus* and *placita*. It may more appropriately be dated to the beginning of Charlemagne's period of sole rule and the attempt to assert his sole authority rather than while he still reigned with his brother.[99]

The development of Frankish relations with both the pope and Lombard kingdom is the most striking aspect of this short period of joint rule, for it built on the cordial relations established by Pippin III with Pope Stephen II and his successor Paul I.[100] After Pope Stephen III's comment on the conclusion of the dispute between the two brothers, a subsequent letter from Pope Stephen returned to the issue of Lombard encroachment on the 'rights of St Peter'. The pope expressed extreme alarm and dismay at rumours of the negotiations Desiderius, king of the Lombards, was apparently setting in train to arrange a marriage between a daughter of Desiderius and one of the brothers – an especially dreadful idea and the devil's contrivance as far as the pope was concerned – for it would bring about the 'pollution of the splendour and great nobility' of the Frankish kings' lineage 'by the perfidious and most foully stinking people of the Lombards', the pope's enemies. Furthermore, both brothers were already married to Frankish women and these marriages had been arranged by Pippin III. Pope Stephen urged them not to accept a foreigner as wife, stressing that none of their forebears had done so.[101] That same summer Pope Stephen addressed a letter to Carloman alone, acknowledging receipt of a letter brought by Carloman's messengers Berald and Audbert. The pope offered to baptize Carloman's son and act as his godfather, and sent loving messages to Carloman's wife, the queen.[102]

An indication that the brothers were already intervening in Italian political affairs is a letter to Bertrada and Charlemagne brought from

[99] *MGH Cap.* 1, No. 19, and see below, pp. 237–9. The capitulary survives within the collection compiled by Benedictus Levita, 3, 123–37, 139–40. See G. Schmitz and W. Hartmann, online edn and discussions at <www.benedictus.mgh.de/haupt.htm>. This section appears to be that on the newly discovered New Haven, Yale University Library, Beinecke fragment MS 1074, announced on that website. On its authenticity see Mordek, *Bibliotheca*, p. 547, who concedes that it is not out of the question that the legal collection, Paris, BnF lat. 4788, of the central decades of the ninth century, may once have contained it.

[100] See McKitterick, *History and memory*, pp. 142–50.

[101] *Codex epistolaris carolinus*, ed. Gundlach, Ep. 45, pp. 560–3, implies that it was the pope who persuaded Pippin not to go ahead with the marriage between Gisela and Constantine. See W. Pohl, '*Alienigena uxor*: Bestrebungen zu einem Verbot auswärtiger Heiraten in der Karolingerzeit', in A. Pečar and K. Trampedach (eds.), *Die Bibel als politisches Argument* (Munich, 2007), pp. 159–88.

[102] *Codex epistolaris carolinus*, ed. Gundlach, Ep. 47, pp. 565–6.

Italy by (H)itherius (the palace notary of Charles) and the pope's response which reported that the Franks had fought on the pope's behalf in Benevento.[103] Sometime after Easter 771, the pope again wrote to report a plot in Rome led by Christopher and Sergius, and supported by Carloman's *missus* Dodo and his troop of Frankish soldiers, to kill the pope himself. The pope made it clear that Dodo was breaking faith with his king as well, but the presence of Frankish soldiers associated with both Charlemagne and Carloman is another indication of a joint Frankish policy towards the Lombards. The pope further reported that peace had been concluded with King Desiderius.[104]

The proposed and actual marriages of the two young kings may throw additional light on the strength of their position and family connections as well as on relations with Italy. The Frankish Queen Bertrada, mother of Charlemagne and Carloman, and Queen Ansa (wife of Desiderius) have been credited with the brokerage of Charlemagne's betrothal with the daughter of Desiderius. In Bertrada's case her role is surmised, as mentioned above, because she is reported in the *Annales regni francorum* as visiting Carloman at Seltz, a palace north of Strasbourg, and going from there to Italy. The *Annales Mosellani*, probably produced after *c.* 797, add a diplomatic role to this Italian visit, saying that she met King Desiderius, many cities were returned to St Peter and she brought Desiderius' daughter back to Francia. Bertrada may, therefore, have been involved in the negotiations concerning a marriage between the daughter of the Lombard King Desiderius and one of her sons.[105] Ansa's role is thought to be indicated by her epitaph by Paul the Deacon, in which he refers to the marriages Ansa arranged for her daughters:

> Discissos nectens rapidus quos Aufidus ambit
> Pacis amore ligans cingunt quos Rhenus et Hister.

> Joining men sundered, whom the swift Ofanto surrounds,
> Binding in love of peace those [men sundered] whom the Rhine and Danube gird.[106]

Although the Ofanto can be taken as an allusion to Benevento and thus the husband of Adalperga, it would seem that 'those whom Rhine and Danube gird' is a reference only to Tassilo, bridegroom of Liutperga, in Bavaria,

---

[103] Ibid., Ep. 46, pp. 564–5. [104] Ibid., Ep. 48, pp. 566–7. [105] Nelson, 'Making a difference'.
[106] *MGH Poet.* 1, p. 46, lines 13–14, and K. Neff (ed.), *Die Gedichte des Paulus Diaconus: kritische und erklärende Ausgabe*, Quellen und Untersuchungen zur lateinische Philologie des Mittelalters 3, fasc. 4 (Munich, 1908), pp. 47–8, trans. J. Ziolkowski, to whom I am grateful for discussion of my interpretation of these lines.

and that no third marriage, to a Frankish king on the Rhine, is indicated.[107] We have Pope Stephen III's word for it that this alliance of *a* daughter with *one* of the Pippinid brothers was discussed, and the discussion at least can be dated in the months of his pontificate between Pippin III's and Carloman's deaths, that is, between 24 September 768 and 30 December 771.[108] As we have seen, Stephen objected violently. He also mentions a suggestion that Gisela, the kings' sister, should be married to Arichis, son of Desiderius.[109] Certainly Carloman is married and producing children, for the *Annales petaviani* as well as the pope mention the son of Carloman and his wife Gerberga. The *Annales petaviani* even give him a name: Pippin, born *c.* 770.[110] It is this boy whom Pope Stephen offered to baptize.[111]

The proposed Lombard–Frankish marriage came to nothing. We do not know exactly when, how, why or even if the Lombard princess ever arrived in Francia (despite the claim of the *Annales Mosellani* referred to above) or whether she was actually married to Charlemagne before the whole thing was called off. Einhard's report fifty years later that Charlemagne was married to a daughter of Desiderius and that Charlemagne subsequently repudiated her may be merely his surmise as a result of reading the papal letters.[112] It is far more likely that the alliance might have been discussed but got no farther, due primarily to the pope's objections. Hammer has even suggested that the discarded fiancée or bride was actually Liutperga, taken to marry Tassilo instead by Bertrada.[113] All there is to indicate that Charlemagne had any liaison with a woman before he married Hildegard in 772 is Pope Stephen's reference to Charlemagne being married already, while Carloman was still alive, and the existence of Charlemagne's eldest son Pippin the Hunchback, who rebelled against his father in 792. This Pippin, born after 768, was the offspring of Charlemagne's first recorded liaison or marriage, to the [possibly noble] Frankish woman Himiltrude,

---

[107] For the argument for the third marriage see Nelson, 'Making a difference'.

[108] His pontificate was 7 August 768 – 24 January 772.

[109] *Codex epistolaris carolinus*, ed. Gundlach, Ep. 45, p. 563.

[110] *Annales petaviani*, ed. G. Pertz, *MGH SS* I, p. 10. This Pippin may have been Carloman's second child.

[111] The *Annales mettenses priores* 771, p. 58 (the only source to name Carloman's wife), claims that Gerberga went with two boys to Italy after Carloman's death in 771, though she could have had the second after this one called Pippin.

[112] Einhard, *Vita Karoli*, c. 18, ed. Halphen, p. 58. For various explanations, but all based on the premise of 'bitter rivalry' between the brothers, see Nelson, 'Making a difference', and Jarnut, 'Ein Brüderkampf'.

[113] C. Hammer, *From* ducatus *to* regnum: *ruling Bavaria under the Merovingians and early Carolingians* (Turnhout, 2007). I am grateful to Carl Hammer for letting me read his text in advance of publication.

before his marriage to Hildegard, a daughter of the Alemannian noble house.[114]

At the end of 771, Charlemagne was quite unexpectedly left as sole ruler of the Frankish kingdom, for his brother Carloman died suddenly, of unknown causes, on 4 December at his palace at Samoussy and was buried in the church of St Remigius of Reims.[115] Carloman's wife Gerberga appears to have fled with her two small sons and a small entourage to Italy.[116] She at least may indeed have lacked confidence in the benevolence of her brother-in-law, but we do not know what prompted her to go to Italy. According to the *Liber pontificalis*, her two boys subsequently figure in the Lombard king's plans for subverting the political order in Francia.[117] The same source says Gerberga was escorted to Italy by Autchar, who had served as an envoy under Pippin III and played a major role in enabling Pope Stephen II to travel to Francia in 753. Autchar is associated with Desiderius by Pope Hadrian's biographer, and is explicitly mentioned as having been taken, together with Gerberga and her sons, by Prince Adalchis to Verona when Charlemagne was besieging Pavia three years later. They might even have been hostages of some kind. Autchar and Gerberga subsequently surrendered to Charlemagne.[118]

One final oddity in all this story is the possible coincidence of the name of Carloman's wife and another daughter of King Desiderius and Ansa.[119] The papal letter objecting to a Lombard liaison on the ground that he was already married to a Frankish woman, his greetings to Carloman's wife and his offer to act as godfather to the couple's new son apparently militate against any suggestion that it was Carloman who took a Lombard bride and that she simply returned home on his death. Supposing the pope to have been confused or misinformed about which brother was already married and which of the brothers had had a son called Pippin could point to Charlemagne, his liaison with Himiltrude and their son Pippin (later called 'the Hunchback').[120] It could then be Carloman who could

[114] On Pippin's rebellion and Einhard, see also J. L. Nelson, 'Charlemagne – *pater optimus*', in P. Godman, J. Jarnut and P. Johanek (eds.), *Am Vorabend der Kaiser Krönung: das Epos 'Karolus magnus et Leo papa' und der Papstbesuch in Paderborn 799* (Berlin, 2002), pp. 269–82.

[115] The *Annales mettenses priores*, 771, p. 57, give the burial place. It is generally accepted as accurate. See Nelson, 'Carolingian royal funerals', pp. 143–5.

[116] Below, p. 109.   [117] *LP*, Life 97, cc. 9 and 23, ed. Duchesne, I, pp. 488 and 493.

[118] *LP*, Life 97, cc. 31 and 34, ed. Duchesne, I, pp. 495–6.

[119] See Nelson, 'Making a difference', p. 183.

[120] K.-F. Werner, 'Die Nachkommen Karls des Großen, 1.–8: Generation', surmised that the liaison with Himiltrude was *c.* 768 (*KdG* IV, Tafel), but omitted any discussion of either Himiltrude or Pippin the Hunchback, ibid., pp. 442–3.

have married Gerberga. But such a notion creates more problems than it solves. What Carloman's wife Gerberga's flight may indicate, however, is a greater warmth towards Desiderius and his Lombard followers on Carloman's part and perhaps less sympathy with the pope's position than it is now otherwise possible to document.

Charlemagne alone, therefore, was left to pursue the various strands of internal and external policy inherited from his father as well as from the three years of joint rule with his brother. What this entailed is discussed in the remainder of this chapter.

SOLE RULE AND ITS CONSEQUENCES: CHARLEMAGNE'S FAMILY, LEGITIMACY AND THE SUCCESSION

After Carloman's death, Charlemagne lost no time in agreeing to a meeting with the leading men of Carloman's household at Corbeny. (It is not clear where the initiative lay, but the Revised Version of the *Annales regni francorum* attribute it to Charlemagne.[121]) The account of this meeting provides a few names. Wilichar, archbishop of Sens, and Fulrad of St Denis have already been mentioned, and Maginarius, Carloman's notary, joined Charlemagne's notarial staff and served subsequently as a *missus* in Italy. Among the secular magnates at Corbeny were Warin and Adalhard, Charlemagne's cousin, who was then about eighteen years old. Warin joined Charlemagne, but that Adalhard was initially less inclined to serve Charlemagne may be indicated by his retreat, voluntarily or otherwise, to the monastery of Corbie. His biographer Paschasius Radbertus claimed decades later that Adalhard left in a state of righteous indignation at Charlemagne's alleged repudiation of the daughter of Desiderius and marriage to Hildegard, but, given the outcome I have outlined above, this is most unlikely. More fundamental disagreements over policy and personal antagonism may have been involved.[122]

Charlemagne's union with Hildegard represents a further extension of his personal relations within an area once his brother's primary responsibility. It had the effect of strengthening links with his wife's family and the

---

[121] *ARF* 771, ed. Kurze, p. 32, and compare *Annales mettenses priores*, 771, pp. 57–8, which even claims that Wilichar of Sens and Fulrad anointed Charlemagne as king over themselves: 'And he auspiciously acquired *monarchia* of the entire kingdom of the Franks' (*et obtinuit feliciter monarchiam totius regni Francorum*).

[122] Paschasius Radbertus, *Vita Adalhardi*, c. 7, *PL* 120, cols. 1507–6 at col. 1511, and extracted in *MGH SS* 2, p. 525. See B. Kasten, *Adalhard von Corbie: die Biographie eines karolingischen Politikers und Klostervorstehers*, Studia humaniora 3 (Düsseldorf, 1986), pp. 24–35.

region from which they came, and seems to have taken place after Carloman's death. Hildegard was the daughter of the Suabian or Alemannian Count Gerold and Imma. Apart from a report from Thegan in the 830s that there was an understanding that Imma was the daughter of the former *dux* of Alemannia, we know little more about her family.[123] Her brother Gerold appears to have flourished in Charlemagne's service, however, and after 788 was appointed by his brother-in-law to administer Bavaria. He was killed while fighting the Avars in 799.[124] According to the epitaph written by Paul the Deacon after Hildegard's death on 30 April 783, Hildegard had been married for eleven years, and died, therefore, in the twelfth year of her marriage.[125] This would put the marriage early in 772. The Frankish narratives say nothing about the event. The *Annales regni francorum* records in passing that she went to Pavia in 773–4 and was with her husband in Rome in 781. It also mentions her death. The *Annales mettenses priores* adds the information that she was buried in the church of St Arnulf in Metz,[126] and a royal charter survives recording Charlemagne's grant of the Villa Cheminot to St Arnulf's for perpetual lights at the tomb of his dearest wife and daily prayers for the repose of her soul.[127] Hildegard

---

[123] Thegan, *Gesta Hludowici imperatoris* c. 2, ed. E. Tremp, *Thegan: Die Taten Kaiser Ludwigs; Astronomus, Das Leben Kaiser Ludwigs*, MGH SRG 64 (Hanover, 1995), p. 176; K. Schreiner, '"Hildegardis regina": Wirklichkeit und Legende einer karolingischen Herrscherin', *Archiv für Kulturgeschichte* 57 (1975), pp. 1–70; and I. Heidrich, 'Von Plectrud zu Hildegard: Beobachtungen zum Besitzrecht adliger Frauen im Frankenreich des 7. und 8. Jahrhunderts und zur politischem Rolle der Frauen', *Rheinische Vierteljahrsblätter* 52 (1988), pp. 1–15.

[124] See below, p. 126. On Gerald, see J. B. Ross, 'Two neglected paladins of Charlemagne, Erich of Friuli and Gerold of Bavaria', *Speculum* 20 (1945), pp. 212–34; K. F. Werner, 'Bedeutende Adelsfamilien im Reich Karls des Großen', *KdG*, I, pp. 85–142 at pp. 111–12; and M. Borgolte, *Die Grafen Alemanniens in merowingischer und karolingischer Zeit: Archäologie und Geschichte*, Freiburger Forschungen zur ersten Jahrtausend in Südwestdeutschland 2 (Sigmaringen, 1982). See also P. Riché, C. Heitz and F. Héber-Suffrin (eds.), Actes du Colloque, *Autour d'Hildegarde*, Centre de recherche sur l'antiquité tardive et le haut moyen âge et Centre d'histoire et civilisation de l'Université de Metz Cahier 5 (Paris, 1987).

[125] Paul the Deacon, *Epitaphium Hildegardis reginae*, MGH Poet. I, p. 58, Pauli et Petri Carmina No. XXII, lines 21–4. I follow Schreiner, '"Hildegardis regina"', p. 7; G. Tellenbach, *Der großfränkische Adel und die Regierung Italiens in der Blütezeit des karolingischen Reiches*, in *Studien und Vorarbeiten zur Geschichte des großfränkischen und frühdeutschen Adels* (Freiburg, 1957), pp. 40–70 at p. 67; and J. F. Böhmer and E. Mühlbacher, *Regesta Imperii*, I: *Die Regesten des Kaiserreichs unter den Karolingern 751–918*, augmented repr. of 2nd 1908 edn (Hildesheim, 1966), p. 66, in this rather than Werner, 'Die Nachkommen', p. 442. Werner cites Paul the Deacon's poem: 13 seems to be a typographical error and should be 12. W. Hartmann, 'Karl der Große', in K. Schnith (ed.), *Mittelalterliche Herrscher in Lebensbildern: von den Karolingern zu den Staufen* (Graz, Vienna and Cologne, 1990), p. 22, simply repeats Werner.

[126] ARF 783, ed. Simson, p. 70. See also P. E. Schramm and F. Mütherich (eds.), *Denkmale der deutschen Könige und Kaiser* (Munich, 1962), p. 122.

[127] DKar. I, No. 149.

Table 2 *The children of Charlemagne and Hildegard*

772/3 – 4 August 812	Charles (the Younger)
773/4 – July/August 774	Adalhaid
775 – 6 June 810	Rotrud
777 – 8 July 810	Pippin (of Italy; *olim* Carloman: name changed 781)
778 (16 April) – 20 June 814	Louis (the Pious)
778 (16 April) – 779/80	Lothar, twin of Louis
779/80 – after 14 January 823	Bertha
781 (before May) – after 800	Gisela
782 (after 8 June) – 8 June 783	Hildegard

appears to have been a pious woman, well able to take advantage of her royal status. The commission of the remarkable Godescalc Gospel lectionary by Hildegard in concert with her husband may be more than the marital association indicated in their gifts to the monasteries of St Denis and St Martin of Tours.[128] She also donated a cloth (*pallium*) for an altar dedicated to St Peter in the church of St Anastasius built by King Liutprand in Olonna in 783,[129] and she appears to have had Leoba, abbess of Tauberbischofsheim (†779), with her at court for a while in order to give her spiritual advice and religious instruction.[130]

Charlemagne's marriage to Hildegard was remarkably fruitful. It is Hildegard who is highlighted in later sources, such as the Frankish history book in Vienna ÖNB cod. 473, as the mother of the Emperor Louis the Pious.[131] In eleven years Hildegard, who is thought to have been thirteen or fourteen years old at the time of her wedding, gave birth nine times and died at the age of twenty-five or twenty-six, probably never having recovered after her ninth delivery[132] (see Table 2).

Charlemagne added further to his family in subsequent marriages. Fastrada bore the king two daughters, Theodrada, who became abbess of

---

[128] See below, pp. 331–3.

[129] Recorded in a verse inscription in Vat. pal. lat. 833 and ed. G. de Rossi, *Inscriptiones Christianae urbis Romae septimo saeculo antiquiores*, 2 vols. (Rome 1857–88), II (1888), pp. 95–118 at pp. 168–9; and *MGH Poet.* I, pp. 105–7 (No. I, x–xiv).

[130] Rudolf of Fulda, *Vita sancti Leobae*, c. 18, ed. G. Waitz, *MGH SS* 15, p. 129.

[131] McKitterick, *History and memory*, p. 123, and Reimitz, 'Ein fränkisches Geschichtsbuch'. On the significance of the choice of Merovingian names for Louis and his twin brother see J. Jarnut, 'Chlodwig und Chlothar: Anmerkungen zu den Namen zweier Söhne Karls des Großen', *Francia* 12 (1984), pp. 645–65, repr. in J. Jarnut, *Herrschaft und Ethnogenese im Frühmittelalter: Gesammelte Aufsätze von Jörg Jarnut. Festgabe zum 60. Geburtstag* (Münster, 2002), pp. 247–53.

[132] Tabulated by K. F. Werner, 'Die Nachkommen', Tafel.

Argenteuil in Paris, and Hiltrude.[133] The king married Fastrada the year Hildegard died and she lived until 794. The *Annales regni francorum* speak with notable warmth of Charlemagne's affection for her, as we have seen.[134] It was thus the domestic and mediating activities of the two queens, Fastrada and her successor, the childless Liutgard who died in 800, and the possible presence of the children born to Himiltrude, Hildegard and Fastrada, with whom the scholars and poets of the royal court were most familiar and on whom their depictions of court life are based.[135] The role of the convent of Chelles, presided over by Charlemagne's sister Gisela, as an alternative sphere of activity and location of female royal presence, and even power, is an intriguing element about which we only have the merest hints.[136]

Much less is known about the female members and children of the royal household after Liutgard's death, or even if they remained at court. Although Charlemagne did not marry again, two girls (Ruothild, later abbess of Faremoutiers, and Adaltrude) and five boys were the fruit of subsequent liaisons. It is this undiminished and extramarital sexual energy of the aging king, rather than unnatural sexual behaviour, which seems to have disturbed Wetti of Reichenau, whose vision of hell included Charlemagne with an (unspecified) animal gnawing his genitals.[137] The boys born after 800 all went on to ecclesiastical careers, and two, Drogo and Hugh, became in due course particularly valuable allies of their half-brother Louis the Pious; they served as his archchaplain and archchancellor respectively (see Table 3).

In addition to these children, Charlemagne added his little granddaughters, the offspring of his son Pippin of Italy, to the royal household after their father's death.[138] Other grandchildren possibly reared at court were the illegitimate sons of Charlemagne's daughters Rotrude and Bertha, who

---

[133] On Fastrada see J. L. Nelson, 'The siting of the council at Frankfurt: some reflections on family and politics', in R. Berndt (ed.), *Das Frankfurter Konzil von 794: Kristallisationspunkt karolingischer Kultur*, I: *Politik und Kirche*; II: *Kultur und Theologie*, Quellen und Abhandlungen zur Mittelrheinische Kirchengeschichte 80 (Mainz, 1997), I, pp. 149–66. See also J. L. Nelson, 'Women at the court of Charlemagne: a case of monstrous regiment?', in J. C. Parsons (ed.), *Medieval queenship* (Stroud, 1993), pp. 43–61, repr. in Nelson, *The Frankish world, 750–900* (London, 1996), pp. 223–42.

[134] Above, p. 47. See also the Epitaph of Fastrada by Theodulf of Orleans, ed. E. Dümmler, *MGH Poet.* I, p. 483; trans. P. E. Dutton, *Carolingian Civilization* (Peterborough, Ont., 1993), p. 45.

[135] See also below, pp. 139–42.   [136] See McKitterick, 'The Rorigo Bible'.

[137] Walafrid Strabo, *Visio Wettini*, ed. E. Dümmler, *MGH Poet.* II, pp. 301–33; English trans. D. Traill, *Walafrid Strabo's* Visio Wettini: *text, translation and commentary*, Lateinische Sprache und Literatur des Mittelalters 2 (Frankfurt, 1974). For full exposition of the significance of this see M. de Jong, *The penitential state* (forthcoming). For the older literature see P. E. Dutton, *The politics of dreaming in the Carolingian empire* (Lincoln, Neb., and London, 1994).

[138] For his grandson Bernard, Pippin of Italy's heir, see below, p. 102. Another granddaughter, Adelheid/Adelaide, died at the age of twelve in 810.

Table 3 *The children of Charlemagne and his other wives and concubines*

c. 769–811	Pippin (the Hunchback) later monk at Prüm (mother: Himiltrude)
c. 784 – after 800	Hruodhaid (mother unknown)
c. 785 – after 844	Theodrada, abbess of Argenteuil before 814 (mother: Fastrada)
c. 787 – after 800	Hiltrude (mother: Fastrada)
after 800 – 852	Ruothild abbess of Faremoutiers (mother: Madelgaud)
after 800	Adaltrude (mother: Gersvind, a Saxon)
801–55	Drogo, bishop of Metz and archchaplain (mother: 'Regina')[a]
802/6–44	Hugh, abbot of St Quentin and archchancellor (mother: 'Regina')
807 – after 818	Theodoric, cleric after 818 (mother: Adalind)
800/5 – 844	Ricbod, abbot of St Riquier (mother: unknown)
after 800 – after 843	Bernard, abbot of Moutier St Jean (mother: unknown)

[a] This may be a description of her function as *de facto* consort rather than her name.

Table 4 *The grandchildren of Charlemagne and possible members of the royal household before 814*

c. 800–67	Louis, abbot of St Denis an archchancellor to Charles the Bald (parents: Rotrude and Count Rorigo)
c. 800/10 – after 810	Atula (parents: Pippin of Italy and his wife)
c. 800/10 – after 810	Gundrada (parents: Pippin of Italy and his wife)
c. 800/10 – after 810	Berthaid (parents: Pippin of Italy and his wife)
c. 800/10 – after 810	Theodrada (parents: Pippin of Italy and his wife)
c. 800–817	Bernard (parents: Pippin of Italy and his wife)
before 800 – 844	Nithard (parents: Bertha and Angilbert)
before 800 – ?	Hartnid (parents: Bertha and Angilbert)

had taken Count Rorigo and the courtier Angilbert (lay abbot of St Riquier) respectively as lovers (see Table 4). Those of Louis the Pious's children born before 814, on the other hand, remained in Aquitaine with their father on his accession to the empire (see Table 5).

As can be surmised from all the uncertainties concerning birth and death dates indicated above, very little is known about many of these children, but it is striking how many in due course were channelled into ecclesiastical careers or, as in the case of Pippin the Hunchback, simply removed from the political scene by incarceration in a monastery.[139] It is important to

[139] B. Kasten, *Königssöhne und Königsherrschaft: Untersuchungen zur Teilhabe am Reich in der Merowinger- und Karolingerzeit*, *MGH* Schriften 44 (Hanover, 1997), pp. 141–50. See also M. de Jong, 'Monastic prisoners or opting out? Political coercion and honour in the Frankish kingdoms', in M. de Jong and F. Theuws with C. van Rhijn (eds.), *Topographies of power in the early middle ages*, The Transformation of the Roman World 6 (Leiden, 2001), pp. 291–328.

Table 5 *The children born before 814 of Louis the Pious and a concubine,
and Louis and Ermengard, married 794*

c. 794	Alpais (mother: concubine)
c. 794 – after 817	Arnulf (later count of Sens) (mother: concubine)
795 – 29 September 855	Lothar, emperor (married 821) (mother: Ermengarde)
797 – 13 December 838	Pippin I of Aquitaine (married 822) (mother: Ermengarde)
c. 800 – ?	Rotrud (mother: Ermengarde)
c. 802/4 – after October 841	Hildegard (mother: Ermengarde)
c. 806 – 28 August 876	Louis the German (married 827) (mother: Ermengarde)

note, however, that the fate of those born after 800, who would all
have been barely of marriageable age or of much political consequence,
was determined by their half-brother Louis the Pious when he came
to the throne in 814. Of the thirty-six children and grandchildren of
Charlemagne, only Louis the Pious and his children before 814, Pippin
of Italy and Pippin's son Bernard were brought up at courts not presided
over by Charlemagne or his queens. Of all these children, moreover, only
Louis the Pious, Pippin of Italy and his son Bernard were actually married
or permitted to marry before 814. They were the only ones among those we
know reached adulthood, apart from the sons of Louis the Pious, who did
not end their days in a monastery, were sentenced to monastic exile or were
directed into an ecclesiastical career.[140]

All this reflects a remarkable degree of patriarchal control exerted by
Charlemagne over his progeny. To some extent this control was emulated
by Louis the Pious, for his three sons and two of his daughters born before
800 were not married until after their father had succeeded Charlemagne.
Einhard commented that Charlemagne loved his daughters too dearly
to be able to contemplate their leaving home to marry.[141] Such paternal
possessiveness might rather be attributed to a careful avoidance of the
complications that marriage alliances with members of the nobility could
bring. More positively, it might reflect Charlemagne's political and social
need for their presence within the royal household, especially in the
absence of queens after 800.[142] The discussions concerning the aborted
marriage proposal to a daughter of the Lombard king Desiderius while

[140] See R. Schieffer, 'Väter und Söhne im Karolingerhause', in R. Schieffer (ed.), *Beiträge zur Geschichte des regnum francorum* (Sigmaringen, 1990), pp. 149–64.
[141] Einhard, *Vita Karoli*, c. 19, ed. Halphen, p. 62.
[142] This is the suggestion made by Nelson, 'Women at the court of Charlemagne', pp. 43–61, repr. in *The Frankish world, 750–900* (London, 1996), pp. 223–42 at pp. 241–2.

Carloman was still alive (discussed above) may have impressed Charlemagne with the unwanted complications of foreign marriages.[143] It was also supposedly Offa of Mercia's bold suggestion that a son of his marry a daughter of Charlemagne that precipitated the breaking off of diplomatic and trade relations between the two kings.[144]

Given disease, infant mortality and the dangers of death in battle, such a restriction on any filial marriages might seem to be a risky policy, and in the event, only Louis the Pious and his children maintained the Carolingian line. Why neither Pippin the Hunchback nor Charles the Younger appears to have been permitted to marry, whereas both Pippin of Italy and Louis the Pious did so at a very young age, is not clear; all four of Charlemagne's elder sons initially might have been expected to be heirs to their father and to have produced more heirs in their turn. Yet Charlemagne only seems to have thought in terms of producing his own offspring rather than promoting the production of grandchildren. Legitimacy is not necessarily such a decisive issue at this stage, however much clerics became bent on making it so.[145] Charles Martel's career, and even that of Pippin the Hunchback before his disastrous rebellion, indicate this. Charlemagne's own marriages, moreover, cannot be described as powerful alliances, and this may have been deliberate on his part. If he married women from respectable but politically unimportant families, the expectation of political advancement would presumably have been quite low. Hildegard's brother is the only relative of one of Charlemagne's wives who can be seen to have benefited from the royal connection.

The active involvement of the queens in politics and the extent of queenly power, as Janet Nelson has shown, was less limited than nineteenth- and even some twentieth-century historians assumed. Little enough information about the contribution of any layman to life at court survives, let alone that of the women, to assume that the fragments of information we have refer to exceptional activity as distinct from a normal set of responsibilities. The queen's role in the royal household is indicated by the *De ordine palatii* and will be discussed in the following chapter. The absence of a designated queen after 800, as already suggested above, and following Janet Nelson, may have necessitated the elder

---

[143] See above, p. 84, and for further discussion of marriage in the context of diplomacy see below, pp. 282–4.

[144] See further below, p. 282.

[145] S. Konecny, *Die Frauen des karolingischen Königshauses: die politische Bedeutung der Ehe und die Stellung der Frau in der fränkischen Herrscherfamilie vom 7. bis zum 10. Jahrhundert* (Vienna, 1976); and W. Affeldt (ed.), *Frauen in Spätantike und Frühmittelalter* (Sigmaringen, 1990).

princesses assuming some of the queen's public functions within the household. But we do not know how many princesses were in residence in the royal household rather than at Chelles, and unfortunately descriptions of the palace say nothing about it.[146] These are much more preoccupied with the assistance rendered to their father by the princes, and with matters to do with the succession. Because of the early deaths of all the queens, moreover, none was able to attempt to advance the interests of her son(s) or play the part of queen dowager.[147]

Even when she was alive, there is no indication that Hildegard did more than acquiesce in the arrangements Charlemagne made in 781 for the government of the newly acquired regions of Aquitaine and the Lombard kingdom. Pippin and Louis, then aged four and three respectively, were created the sub-kings of these regions, each with his own entourage and advisers.[148] Such a scheme increased Charlemagne's own status, as a king with two sub-kings under him, but a further move enhanced the royal and sacral status of the little boys even more: they were actually anointed as kings in Rome by Pope Hadrian I.[149] The Revised Version of the *Annales regni francorum* adds that they were crowned as well. Pippin, moreover, was baptized and given his new name of Pippin on this occasion (hitherto he had been called Carloman), with the pope acting as godfather. This rite made Pope Hadrian the *compater* of Charlemagne, a tie of spiritual kinship that was taken very seriously by the popes and the Carolingian rulers, at least on the level of diplomacy.[150] It is with this event that the Godescalc Gospel lectionary, dated between 781 and 783, with a depiction of the Fountain of Life resembling the Lateran baptistery, is often associated.[151]

On the same visit to Italy, Charlemagne's new daughter Gisela was also provided with spiritual clout, for she was baptized in Milan, with Thomas, archbishop of Milan (759–3), standing as godfather. Political use may also

---

[146] See below, p. 140. The *De ordine palatii*'s silence on any role for the princesses could be a further indication of the text's early date, before the latter years of Charlemagne made them more prominent at the palace. On the daughters see also R. Schieffer, 'Karolingische Töchter', in Jenal, *Herrschaft, Kirche, Kultur*, pp. 125–39.

[147] P. Stafford, *Queens, concubines and dowagers: the king's wife in the early middle ages* (Athens, Ga., 1983).

[148] Kasten, *Königssöhne*, pp. 138–41; and T. Offergeld, *Reges pueri: das Königtum Minderjähriger im frühen Mittelalter*, MGH Schriften 50 (Hanover, 2001).

[149] The event is recorded only in Frankish narratives, for the narrative section of the Life of Hadrian I in the *LP* effectively ceases after 774 and thereafter it is concerned with Hadrian's works in Rome, building, restoring and adorning churches, including the embellishment to St Petronilla's basilica at St Peter's; Life 97, c. 78, ed. Duchesne, I, p. 509.

[150] On the significance see A. Angenendt, 'Das geistliche Bundnis der Päpste mit den Karolingern (754–796)', *Historisches Jahrbuch* 100 (1980), pp. 1–94.

[151] See further below, pp. 331–3.

have been made of another daughter, Rotrud, for according to the *Annales Mosellani* she was betrothed, although only six years old, to Constantine VI of Byzantium.[152] On Christmas Day 800, moreover (as noted above), at the same time as Charlemagne was crowned emperor, his son Charles the Younger was anointed king by Pope Leo III. Whether Charles the Younger was included in the Christmas day rituals by design or a conscious wish on the part of both Charlemagne and the pope to recreate Charlemagne's own anointing by Pope Stephen II in 754 is not clear. It may have been the pope who took the initiative as an insurance policy to strengthen the papal bond with Charlemagne's sons still further, for this part of the events of 800 is mentioned only by the *Liber pontificalis*, not in Frankish sources.[153]

THE SUCCESSION: THE *DIVISIO REGNORUM* (806) AND
CHARLEMAGNE'S WILL (811)

In 806 Charlemagne made his first specific statement concerning the succession, possibly prompted to do so by his sister Gisela.[154] By then he had been emperor for six years and was himself nearing sixty. It was an opportunity to shape the polity territorially and in terms of jurisdiction for his sons. Not only is the assembly at Thionville, at which this arrangement was drawn up, described in the *Annales regni francorum*, but the document recording it was taken by Einhard to the pope in Rome so that he might subscribe it. The pope, accordingly, on receipt of the document, is said to have read it, approved it, and subscribed it with his own hand (*quibus pontifex lectis et adsensum praebuit et propria manu subscripsit*).[155]

Everything about this succession arrangement – conception, content, documentary format, process of agreement and the papal approval – was unprecedented. The realm was divided very precisely (Map 2) between the three eldest sons of Hildegard, namely Charles the Younger, Pippin of Italy and Louis of Aquitaine. Very broadly, Louis was assigned Aquitaine and Gascony, Pippin was allotted Italy and Bavaria, and Charles got the rest,

---

[152] *Annales Mosellani* 781, ed. J. Lappenburg, *MGH SS* 16, p. 497. For a later phase in this connection see below, p. 282, and on Charles the Younger, see above, pp. 52–3.

[153] For further on the events of 800 see below, pp. 114–18 and *LP*, Life 98, c. 24, ed. Duchesne, II, p. 7.

[154] The suggestion made by Nelson, 'Gender and genre in women historians', pp. 183–98, is prompted by the possible connection between Gisela, Chelles and the *Annales mettenses priores* and whether this history can be regarded as effectively a dossier connected to the *Divisio* of 806. See also Y. Hen, 'The Annals of Metz and the Merovingian past', in Hen and Innes, *Uses of the past*, pp. 175–90. A useful assessment of the discussion of the *Divisio regnorum* is Kaschke, *Die karolingischen Reichsteilungen*, pp. 294–323.

[155] ARF 806, ed. Kurze, p. 121; trans. King, *Charlemagne*, p. 97.

Map 2 The *Divisio regnorum* of 806

namely Francia, Austrasia, Neustria, Thuringia, Saxony, Frisia and the Nordgau of Bavaria and Burgundy (except for the part allotted to Louis), and Alemannia (except for the part allotted to Pippin). The arrangement was designed to allow Charles and Louis a route into Italy, Charles via the Aosta valley and Louis by the Susa valley, 'while Pippin may have entry through the Norican Alps and Chur'.[156] This *Divisio* belies the understated record of Charles the Younger's career in the *Annales regni francorum* for 799–814 noted above. Essentially Charles was to inherit everything except the sub-kingdoms already created for his younger brothers a quarter of a century before, and the integrity of his brothers' kingdoms was to be maintained.

---

[156] *Divisio regnorum, MGH Cap.* 1, No. 45, pp. 126–30, c. 3: 'Pippinus vero et exitum et ingressum per Alpes Noricas atque Curiam.'

Charlemagne described his aim as ensuring the future of the realm. His sons henceforth were to be regarded as his partners in ruling and as his heirs in the event of his death. Provision was also made for division should any one of the brothers predecease the others, including succession by the sons of Charles, Pippin or Louis to their own father's portion. Each son was to defend the borders of his allotted kingdom which 'march with those of foreign peoples, and to maintain peace and amity with his brother'.[157] The full implications for Charlemagne's own government will be considered in a later chapter. For the moment what needs to be highlighted is clause 15, in which the brothers have as their joint duty the care and defence of the church of St Peter, 'just as it was once assumed by our grandfather Charles and by our father of blessed memory', and clause 17, in which the daughters are to be permitted to choose a brother with whom to live or to enter a monastery or even to be married. In clause 18, furthermore, Charlemagne made an astonishing provision that none of his sons should cause any of Charlemagne's grandsons/nephews (*nepotes*) accused before any of the sons to be put to death, mutilated, blinded or tonsured against his will without lawful trial and inquiry. 'Rather it is our will that they be honoured by their fathers and uncles and be obedient towards these with all the deference which is fitting in such a blood relationship.' This is a sobering acknowledgment of possible family relations, presumably based on past experience. Lastly, Charlemagne insisted that all this was to come into effect only once he was dead.[158]

The text of the *Divisio regnorum*, as Peter Classen noted, has an obvious relationship with a will.[159] In that it concerns political power, it is an *ad hoc* adaptation of the testamentary diplomatic practice that had developed in the course of the Merovingian period.[160] In this respect it may be helpful to compare it with Charlemagne's will of 811, preserved in Einhard's *Vita Karoli*.

[157] Ibid., preface, p. 127: 'et fines regni sui qui ad alienigenas extenduntur cum Dei adiutorio nitatur defendere, et pacem atque caritatem cum fratre custodire.'
[158] Ibid., cc. 15–20, pp. 129–30, and the final sentence of c. 18, p. 130: 'sed volumus ut honorati sint apud patres vel patruos suos et obedientes sint illis cum omni subiectione quam decet in tali consanguinitate esse.'
[159] Classen, 'Karl der Große und die Thronfolge', p. 217 note 59. See also E. Ewig, 'Überlegungen zu den merowingischen und karolingischen Teilungen', Settimane 27 (1981), pp. 225–53; and R. Schieffer, 'Vater und Söhne im Karolingerhaus', *Beiträge zur Geschichte des regnum francorum: Festschrift Eugen Ewig*, Beihefte der Francia 22 (Sigmaringen, 1990), pp. 149–64.
[160] G. Speckelmeyer, 'Zur rechtlichen Funktion frühmittelalterlicher Testamente', in P. Classen (ed.), *Recht und Schrift im Mittelalter*, Vorträge und Forschungen 23 (Sigmaringen, 1977), pp. 91–114; and U. Nonn, 'Merowingische Testamente: Studien zum Fortleben einer römischer Urkundenform im Frankenreich', *Archiv für Diplomatik* 19 (1982), pp. 1–129. I have not seen the proceedings of a conference on the *Divisio regnorum* of 806, ed. B. Kasten, *Herrscher und Fürstentestmente im westeuropäische Mittelalter*, Proceedings of the 2006 Saarbrücken conference, 15–18 February 2006 (forthcoming).

That also has a claim to be the first post-Roman royal will to have survived and to resemble Anglo-Saxon and Merovingian episcopal wills from the seventh century.[161] Einhard asserts that Charlemagne had intended to make provision for his daughters and the children of his concubines but did not live to complete this will. Instead, Einhard reproduces the text, presumably obtained from the palace archive, of one made three years before his death, whose terms, he insists, were scrupulously carried out by Louis the Pious after his father's death, though in fact the text seems to indicate that the prescriptions concerning alms for the churches were carried out when the will was first drawn up. This will of 811 divided Charlemagne's treasure and the precious objects in his household as well as the vessels and books of the palace chapel, and the king's own books, or proceeds from the sale thereof, for the benefit of the churches of the twenty-one ecclesiastical provinces of his empire, for the poor, and for his heirs in a division into parts strongly reminiscent of canonical regulations for the division of tithes.[162] The exceptions to the scheme are two silver tables: the one depicting Constantinople was to be presented to St Peter's in Rome and that depicting Rome was to be given to Ravenna.[163] Again, one of Charlemagne's motives in setting out such precise divisions and the shares to be allotted to his heirs, listed as his sons and daughters and the sons and daughters of his sons, was to avoid strife between them.[164] The 811 will says nothing at all about the power within the kingdom, but its division of treasure has some similarity to the division of power set out in 806. Innes has also suggested a comparison of the latter with the *Constitutum Constantini*, which survives in the very same St Denis manuscript that contains Cathwulf's letter to Charlemagne and Charlemagne's letter to Queen Fastrada of 791.[165]

The signatories of the 811 will are an indication of Charlemagne's extended network of close advisers, gathered from across his empire and a telling contrast to those he and Carloman sent to Rome in 769. The archbishops present represented the major ecclesiastical provinces of Cologne, Mainz, Reims, Salzburg, Lyons, Besançon and Arles.[166] Additional episcopal

---

[161] M. Innes, 'Charlemagne's will: piety, politics and the imperial succession', *English Historical Review* 112 (1997), pp. 833–55 at p. 851, for example, draws attention to the account of Wilfrid of Hexham's will included in the *Vita Wilfridi* and the will made by Bertram, bishop of Le Mans.

[162] A point made by Innes, 'Charlemagne's will', p. 850.

[163] See below, p. 372.   [164] Einhard, *Vita Karoli*, c. 34, ed. Halphen, p. 96.

[165] Innes, 'Charlemagne's will,' p. 835, and above, on Paris, BnF lat. 2777, pp. 43–6.

[166] On Hildebald/Hildebold of Cologne, see Depreux, *Prosopographie*, pp. 246–7. He was Charlemagne's archchaplain from 794. Ricolf, archbishop of Mainz, had succeeded Lull. On Arn of Salzburg see M. Niederkorn-Bruck and A. Scharer (eds.), *Erzbischof Arn von Salzburg*, Veröffentlichungen des Instituts für Österreichische Geschichtsforschung 40 (Vienna and Munich, 2004). Little is known about Wolfar of Reims, Bernoin of Besançon or John of Arles, but on the last named see Depreux, *Prosopographie*, pp. 274–5. John acted as an intermediary

witnesses were the suffragan bishops Theodulf of Orleans, Jesse of Amiens, Haito of Basle and Waltcaud of Liège, all of whom had played a prominent role in Charlemagne's ecclesiastical reforms. Similarly, the four abbots present were heads of some of the leading royal monasteries of the kingdom – Tours, Lorsch, St Riquier and St Germain des Prés, though it is notable that St Denis is not represented.[167] Among the fifteen lay magnates who acted as witness, only a few can be linked, however tentatively, to particular areas of jurisdiction. Thus Otulf and Hatto may have been based in Bavaria,[168] Gerold in the eastern march of Bavaria,[169] Unruoc in the march of Friuli,[170] Bera/Bero in Barcelona,[171] Stephen in Paris,[172] Burchard and Meginhard in Thuringia, and Ercanger in the Breisgau.[173] Rihwin may have been count of Poitiers.[174] Of the other *comites*, Wala was the king's cousin, but it is not clear where Meginher, Edo, Hildger and Hrocculf served.[175] They too indicate how wide the network of loyalty and

---

between Charlemagne and Louis and subsequently served as a *missus* under Louis. On Leidrad of Lyons, see the letter of Leidrad to Charlemagne and see de Jong, 'Religion', in Story, *Charlemagne*, and below, p. 344.

[167] Fridugis, Adalung, Angilbert and Immo respectively. On Fridugis of Tours who became Louis the Pious's archchancellor, see Depreux, *Prosopographie*, pp. 199–203; on Adalung of Lorsch and St Vaast, see ibid., pp. 84–6. Angilbert of St Riquier was the lover of Charlemagne's daughter Bertha; see S. Rabe, *Faith, art, and politics at Saint-Riquier: the symbolic vision of Angilbert* (Philadelphia, 1995). On Immo (Irmino), famous for his Polyptyque of the abbey of St Germain, see Depreux, *Prosopographie*, pp. 272–3, and his references.

[168] Depreux, *Prosopographie*, pp. 232–3.

[169] Gerold was a nephew of Hildegard's brother; see Depreux, *Prosopographie*, pp. 210–11.

[170] On the Unruochings see Werner, 'Adelsfamilien'; and R. Le Jan, 'Prosopographica neustrica: les agents du roi en Neustrie de 639 à 840', in H. Atsma (ed.), *La Neustrie: les pays au nord de la Loire de Dagobert à Charles le Chauve, 650 à 850*, Beihefte der Francia 16 (Sigmaringen, 1989), pp. 231–70 at No. 188, p. 257.

[171] Depreux, *Prosopographie*, pp. 129–30.

[172] See Le Jan, 'Prosopographica neustrica', No. 265, p. 264. On the capitulary relating to Stephen of Paris, *MGH Cap.* I, No. 39, p. 112, see K.-F. Werner, 'Missus – marchio – comes: entre l'administration centrale et l'administration locale de l'empire Carolingien', in K.-F. Werner and W. Paravicini (eds.), *Histoire comparée de l'administration (IVe–XVIIIe siècles)*, Francia Beihefte 9 (Munich, 1980), pp. 191–239 at p. 199; and Mordek, *Bibliotheca*, pp. 551–2.

[173] Ercanger/Erchangar, possibly count in the Breisgau; see Depreux, *Prosopographie*, pp. 182–3; M. Borgolte, *Geschichte der Grafschaften Alemanniens in fränkischer Zeit*, Vorträge und Forschungen, Sonderband 31 (Sigmaringen, 1984); Borgolte, *Die Grafen Alemanniens in merowingischer und karolingischer Zeit: eine Prosopographie* (Sigmaringen, 1986), pp. 105–9, 248–54; and Borgolte, 'Die Geschichte der Grafengewalt im Elsaß von Dagobert I. bis Otto dem Großen', *Zeitschrift für die Geschichte des Oberrheins* 131 (1983), pp. 3–54 at p. 25.

[174] Rihuin, Ricouin (I) Depreux, *Prosopographie*, p. 365, who prefers to leave it open between Poitiers and Padua but I follow E. Hlawitschka, *Franken, Alemannen, Bayern und Burgunden in Oberitalien (774–962): zum Verständnis der fränkischen Königsherrschaft in Italien*, Forschungen zur oberrheinischen Landesgeschichte 8 (Freiburg im Breisgau, 1960), pp. 296–7, in preferring Poitiers.

[175] On Wala, see Depreux, *Prosopographie*, pp. 390–3; and Le Jan, *Prosopographica neustrica*, No. 282, p. 266.

Map 3 Charlemagne's empire in 814

service was now stretched. There are three notable absences in terms of regions represented: the sub-kingdoms of Aquitaine south of Poitiers and west of Provence, of Italy south of the Alps, and the newly-conquered region of Saxony (see Map 3). In that the archdiocese of Mainz included the new Saxon sees, they may be supposed to be represented in principle; it is possible too that the counts whose areas of jurisdiction are unknown served in these areas. Generally, however, the lack of direct links between the witnesses and the two sub-kingdoms of Aquitaine and Italy echoes the configuration of the inheritance envisaged in the *Divisio regnorum*. This in its turn raises the question of the degree to which either the former Lombard kingdom in Italy or the former *region* of Aquitaine was integrated into the Frankish empire.[176]

The *Divisio regnorum* reflects attention given to a particular, collegiate, model for governing the huge empire created by Charlemagne, the extent of which is clearly summarized in the first three clauses (see Map 3). The death of Pippin of Italy in 810, followed a year later by the death of Charles the Younger, left the king with an attenuated version of that model, but with the understanding that Pippin of Italy's kingdom was to remain autonomous.[177] Charlemagne took public steps to preserve it. At a general assembly at Aachen in 812, Pippin of Italy's son Bernard was recognized king in succession to his father and sent to rule his new kingdom.[178] Bernard's little sisters were given a home with their grandfather. According to the plan of 806, Bernard's kingdom would have included Bavaria except for the Nordgau that had been allocated to Charles the Younger. At another general assembly at Aachen the following September, 813, the sole remaining legitimate son of Charlemagne and Hildegard, Louis the Pious, was summoned to Aachen and crowned emperor by his father. The Chronicle of Moissac adds that Louis was acclaimed by the assembled bishops, abbots, counts and magnates, and that Charlemagne commended Louis's half-brothers Drogo, Theodoric and Hugh to him.[179] The Astronomer elaborates the occasion into a whole summer of preparation and instruction in the art of kingship by the father to the son.

When Charlemagne died shortly thereafter, on 28 January 814, the obsequies were organized that very day and he was buried in the palace chapel at Aachen. Louis himself did not arrive from Aquitaine until a month later. He then allegedly drove his sisters from the palace, and took

---

[176] For fuller discussion see below, pp. 107–14 and 243–4.

[177] Death of Pippin in *ARF* 810, ed. Kurze, p. 132, and of Charles, *ARF* 811, ed. Kurze, p. 135.

[178] *ARF* 812, ed. Kurze, pp. 136–7. Einhard confirms this, *Vita Karoli*, c. 19, ed. Halphen, p. 61. Italian charters issued in the names of Charlemagne and Bernard jointly are also extant: see, for example, E. P. Vicini (ed.), *Regesto della chiesa cattedrale di Modena* (Rome, 1931), Nos. 4 (1 November 811) in Charlemagne's name alone, pp. 5–7, but No. 5, Modena, 10 August 813, is in the name of Charles and Bernard, kings in Italy, ibid., pp. 7–8. No. 6, 25 February 816, ibid., pp. 9–10, cites Bernard in the fourth year of his reign, but Nos. 7 and 8, charters of 10 April and 3 December 816, cite Louis and Bernard, ibid., pp. 10–13.

[179] *ARF* 814, ed. Kurze, p. 140; and Chronicle of Moissac 813, ed. G. Pertz, *MGH SS* 1, pp. 310–11. See also W. Wendling, 'Die Erhebung Ludwigs des Frommen zum Mitkaiser in Jahre 813 und ihre Bedeutung für die Verfassungsgeschichte des Frankenreichs', *Frühmittelalterliche Studien* 109 (1985), pp. 201–38.

over the Frankish realm.[180] The inscription above Charlemagne's tomb, created either during the month of the interregnum or after Louis's arrival, stressed his orthodoxy and how he had 'gloriously extended the kingdom of the Franks' (*qui regnum francorum nobiliter ampliavit*).[181] This was indeed a vastly increased territory in comparison to that which Charlemagne himself had inherited in 771. Within it, as we have seen, Italy and Rome occupied a special place that needs to be explained. It is to the circumstances of this enlargement of Charlemagne's kingdom into an empire extending across much of western Europe, therefore, that I now turn.

THE GROWTH OF THE KINGDOM

Saxony

After his brother's death in December 771, Charlemagne had spent Christmas at Attigny and Easter at Herstal. From there he travelled to an assembly convened at Worms in the spring of 772, from which he launched his first campaign into Saxony. On the face of it, it was a dramatically successful foray. He captured the Eresburg and destroyed a Saxon holy place known as the Irminsul, where he found a great quantity of gold and silver treasure. He advanced as far as the river Weser and, in the *Annales regni francorum*'s version of events, he 'treated with the Saxons and received twelve hostages before returning to Francia'.[182] As if to stress the divine support and favour for this war, the annalist also tells the story of the miraculous provision of water for the army while they were camped near the Irminsul. Yet this campaign was succeeded by many others, almost every year.

It is doubtful whether conquest of the Saxons, or even their conversion to Christianity, was the purpose from the beginning, though these two purposes emerged in due course. The latter in particular became a constant theme of late ninth- and tenth-century Saxon historiography; the Poeta Saxo's celebration of Charlemagne's leading the Saxons to heaven seems to have set the trend.[183] Charlemagne was, after all, continuing a pattern of relations with the Saxons begun in the time of his grandfather Charles

---

[180] On the burial see Einhard, *Vita Karoli*, c. 31, ed. Halphen, pp. 86–8; A. Dierkens, 'Le tombeau de Charlemagne', *Byzantion* 61 (1991), pp. 156–80; and Nelson, 'Carolingian royal funerals', pp. 145–53. On Louis and his sisters see Astronomer, *Vita Hludowici*, cc. 22–3, ed. Tremp, pp. 350–2.

[181] Einhard, *Vita Karoli*, c. 31, ed. Halphen, p. 88.

[182] ARF 772, ed. Kurze, p. 34.   [183] See above, pp. 22–4.

Martel and father Pippin. Carloman, Charlemagne's uncle, had captured
the castle of Hohenseeburg in 743 and Theodoric the Saxon was forced to
submit to him. The following year, Theodoric was captured 'a second time'
when Carloman and Pippin invaded Saxony together, and it was to Saxony
that Grifo fled in 747 in order to gather some armed support. Subsequently
Pippin mounted campaigns in Saxony in 753 and again in 758. As a result of
the 758 expedition, Pippin had secured the payment of an annual tribute of
300 horses from Saxons in the region of Sythen.[184] These campaigns seem
to be responses to occasional raids into Frankish territory from groups of
Saxons or instances of unprovoked Frankish attacks on the Saxons simply
because their proximity was interpreted as threatening. The relationship
involved a forced acknowledgment of superior strength, and was expressed in terms of the payment of tribute.[185] There is no suggestion of
co-ordinated or sustained aggression on either side in the decades before
772, as distinct from a regulation of relations by means of brisk bouts of
fighting and demonstrations of force between the Frankish military contingents and different groups of Saxons within Westphalia and beyond the
Weser who impinged on Frankish territory. Only as Saxon resistance
stiffened and leadership coalesced around Widukind did Charlemagne
settle into a relentless and bloody onslaught and the securing of Frankish
dominance over all the Saxon territories. The war, as Charlemagne pushed
ever farther north towards and even beyond the Elbe, was punctuated by
the Franks' seizing of Saxon strongholds such as Eresburg and erection of
new fortifications and new palaces and churches, notably at Paderborn,
and the Saxons' destruction of these same places. It was further complicated by shifting alliances on the part of both Franks and Saxons, with
other peoples in the north, the Nordliudi or northern (Slavic) people, the
Wilzi and Abodrites, and the Danes.[186]

The first phase culminated in a severe defeat of a Frankish army at Süntel
in 782 and Charlemagne's horrifying reprisal: 4,500 Saxons, who had been
handed over to Charlemagne by other Saxons, were executed at Verden.[187]
It is probably after this event, or else after Widukind's submission in 785,

[184] ARF 758, ed. Kurze, p. 16.
[185] See T. Reuter, 'Plunder and tribute in the Carolingian empire', *Transactions of the Royal Historical Society*, 5th series 5 (1985), pp. 75–94, and below, pp. 135–6.
[186] M. Hardt, 'Hesse, Elbe, Salle and the frontiers of the Carolingian empire', in W. Pohl, I. Wood and H. Reimitz (eds.), *The transformation of frontiers from late antiquity to the Carolingians* (Leiden, 2001), pp. 219–32; and M. Hardt, 'The *limes Saxoniae* as part of the eastern borderlands of the Frankish and Ottonian-Salian empire', in F. Curta (ed.), *Borders, barriers and ethnogenesis: frontiers in late antiquity and the middle ages* (Turnhout, 2005), pp. 35–50.
[187] See above, p. 23.

that the first Saxon capitulary was produced; it is especially striking for its fierce insistence that the Saxons be baptized on pain of death.[188] With Widukind's submission in 785 and his baptism with Charlemagne acting as his godfather, there was a respite; some parts of Saxony and some groups of Saxons were successfully incorporated into the Frankish realm. The annals report contingents of Saxons in Frankish military expeditions thereafter, especially those against the Avars.[189] Rebellion among the Saxons broke out again in 793. Large groups of Saxon men, women and children were deported from northern Saxony to Bavaria. A second, and rather milder, Saxon capitulary was issued in 797.[190] In all, it took Charlemagne thirty-two years to subdue Saxon resistance. Not until the peace of Salz in 803 and the cession of a formerly Saxon region north of the Elbe to the Abodrites was Saxony finally incorporated into the Frankish realm, and the process of Christianization proceeded apace.[191] Again, it is the Poeta Saxo who provides a commentary on the conclusion of peace, for he highlights the relinquishing of the former political structures of the Saxons and their conversion to Christianity. He claims that they were to enjoy their own legates or local administrators, native laws, and freedom under *iudices* appointed by the king. In a formulation adapted from Einhard's *Vita Karoli*, moreover, he adds that the Saxons were federated with the Franks to become a unified nation.[192]

Some impression of the trauma of this long-drawn-out war can be derived from the quantity of military artefacts among the archaeological finds from the Westphalian region and beyond, with huge numbers of beautifully crafted swords (for which the Franks were famous), and many shield bosses, spurs and bridle bits, arrow heads, spears and fragments of

---

[188] *MGH Cap.* I, No. 26, and below, p. 253.
[189] For example, ARF 788, 789, 791, 802, 808, ed. Kurze, pp. 80, 84, 88, 117, 125.
[190] *MGH Cap.* I., No. 27; for the government of Saxony see below, pp. 251–6.
[191] For an excellent summary see A. Lampen, 'Die Sachsenkriege', *799 Kunst und Kultur*, II, pp. 264–72.
[192] Poeta Saxo, ed. P. von Winterfeld, *MGH Poet.* IV (Berlin, 1899), p. 48. 'Tum sub iudicibus, quos rex inponeret ipsis / Legatisque suis permissi legibus uti / Saxones patriis et libertatis honore / Hoc sunt postremo sociati foedere Francis / ut gens et populus fieret concorditer unus / Ac semper regi parens aequaliter uni.' Compare *Vita Karoli*, c. 7, 'et francis adunati sunt unus cum eis populus efficerentur', ed. Halphen, p. 26. And see B. von Simson, 'Der Poeta Saxo und der Friede zu Salz', *Forschungen zur deutschen Geschichte* I (1862), pp. 301–26. See H. Löwe, 'Poeta Saxo', in H. Löwe, W. Wattenbach and W. Levison, *Deutschlands Geschichtsquellen im Mittelalter: Vorzeit und Karolinger*, VI: *Die Karolinger vom Vertrag von Verdun bis zum Herrschaftsantritt der Herrscher aus dem Sächsichen Hause das ostfränkische Reich* (Weimar, 1990), pp. 261–7. The implications of this are considered further in Chapters 4 and 5 below. See also H. Mayr-Harting, 'Charlemagne, the Saxons and the imperial coronation of 800', *English Historical Review* III (1996), pp. 1113–33; and Mayr-Harting, 'Charlemagne's religion', in Godman, Jarnut and Johanek, *Am Vorabend*, pp. 113–24.

chain mail. Even a whetstone for sharpening the blades was found at Büraburg near Fritzlar.[193] Written information about the Saxons in the course of these wars is provided for us by the Franks from their perspective of the Saxons as intransigent rebels against the benefits of Frankish rule and as pagans resistant to the blessings of Christianity. Even this is often considerably after the event. Not until the second half of the ninth century are there any Saxon comments on the process of conquest.

Hostage-taking, as we saw already with Charlemagne's campaign in 772, was a regular feature of peace or truce agreements.[194] A key piece of earlier information about the different groups of Saxons, however, is derived from a hostage list tucked into an early ninth-century legal manuscript from Reichenau. It comprises two leaves of parchment, preserved in St Paul in Lavanttal, Benediktinerstift St Paul Lavant, Cod. 6/1, fols 191r–192v, containing a list, written in 802–5, of the names and fathers' names of thirty-seven Saxon hostages and their Alemannian guards, who included three bishops and many counts. The list is organized into groups of Westphalians, Eastphalians and people from Engern. These hostages were to be brought to Mainz and handed over to Bishop Haito of Basel and Count Hitto.[195] Haito's links with Reichenau may account for the insertion of the leaves into a book of canon law written in Reichenau. The list's division of the Saxons into groups is confirmed by the description provided by the Poeta Saxo, at the end of the ninth century, who described the Saxons at the beginning of his poem. The Saxons had almost as many leaders as they had districts, but were divided into three main groups, Westphalians, Osterliudi or Ostphalians, and Angariani/Engern, whose territory was between that of the Westphalians and Eastphalians.[196] The subjection of these groups in succession, and of possible other groups further to the east, is no doubt one reason why the Saxon wars were so protracted.[197]

---

[193] *799 Kunst und Kultur*, I, pp. 273–311; the whetstone is V. 7, ibid., p. 276. See also M. Becher, 'Die Sachsen im 7. und 8. Jahrhundert: Verfassung und Ethnogenese', in ibid., pp. 188–94. For the practicalities of war and the raising of armies, see below, pp. 270–3.

[194] See A. Kosto, 'Hostages in the Carolingian world (714–840)', *Early Medieval Europe* 11 (2002), pp. 123–47.

[195] See *799 Kunst und Kultur*, II, pp. 327–8 (VI. 4). This is the hostage list ed. Boretius, *MGH Cap.* I, pp. 233–4.

[196] On the Poeta Saxo see also above, pp. 22–4.

[197] I. Wood, 'Beyond satraps and ostriches: political and social structures of the Saxons in the early Carolingian period', in D. H. Green and F. Siegmund (eds.), *The Continental Saxons from the migration period to the tenth century: an ethnographic perspective* (Woodbridge, 2003), pp. 271–86.

Italy

As the sixth, seventh and eighth proofs of Charlemagne's blessedness, Cathwulf's letter to Charlemagne in 775 offered his defeat of the Lombard army without a pitched battle, his capture of the city of Pavia, the king and its treasures, and his entry into 'golden and imperial Rome'. Charlemagne's enemies were equated with God's enemies, and Cathwulf added parallels between Charlemagne and Hebrew rulers and prophets – Moses, Joshua, Ezekiel and Judas Maccabaeus – and clinched these with a quotation from St Paul (Romans 8.31): 'If God is with us who can be against us?'[198] Cathwulf's exultant summary of the conquest of the Lombard kingdom in 773–4, with its association with entry into Rome, is the most immediate Frankish response to Charlemagne's success; the only other contemporary record, written soon after 774, is the first section of the Life of Pope Hadrian I (772–95) in the *Liber pontificalis*. This seems to have been written up with close reference to copies of letters from Pope Hadrian kept in the papal register. The papal letters to the Carolingian rulers preserved in the *Codex carolinus*, on the other hand, have a gap between 771 and the aftermath of the Lombard conquest, though much is implied by Hadrian's comments thereafter. These papal letters reflect an attempt on the part of the pope to secure the Franks' assistance in organizing Italian politics as the pope wished, as well as the limited degree to which Charlemagne complied.

Although written nearly twenty years after the event, the *Annales regni francorum* also preserve earlier memories and knowledge.[199] As we saw in the previous chapter, the early version of the *Annales regni francorum* presents the decision to invade Italy as taken after consulting 'the Franks' and an assembly at Geneva had determined the military strategy to be adopted. The annalist was much more concerned with disturbances in the border region between the Franks and the Saxons, and presented the siege of Pavia, Charlemagne's taking time off from the siege to journey to Rome to celebrate Easter and then his capture thereafter of Desiderius, his wife and daughter and all the treasure of the palace, as an interruption in the smooth course of the new campaign in Saxony.

In the light of the relations between the Lombards and the Franks in the early part of the eighth century on the one hand, and between the popes and the Pippinids on the other, moreover, the conquest of Lombardy has

---

[198] Cathwulf, ed. Dümmler, *MGH Epp.* IV, *karo. aevi*, II (Berlin, 1895), pp. 501–5 at p. 502.
[199] Above, pp. 28–9.

the character of a political *coup d'état* far more than one of aggressive conquest. The notaries recording legal transactions in the former Lombard kingdom made an apparently seamless transition in their dating clauses in early 774 from dating according to the regnal year of Desiderius and his son Arichis to dating according to the first year of Charlemagne's reign as king of the Lombards.[200] Charlemagne's own charters, moreover, described him from 774 as the king of the Franks and the Lombards.

It is difficult to determine precise inclinations of loyalty between Franks and Lombards at any one moment. Instead there is a shifting pattern of alliances and sympathies in the years between 757 and 773. Pippin III, for example, had been sent to the court of the Lombard ruler Liutprand. It was from the king there that he had received his ceremonial haircut on reaching manhood.[201] He can be supposed to have had considerable knowledge of Lombard affairs. He was, besides, a determined enemy of Liutprand's successor Aistulf and a staunch supporter of the papacy. Yet the *Annales mettenses priores* claim that Pippin's assistance had been crucial for Aistulf's successor Desiderius' gaining the throne of the Lombard kingdoms in the first place.[202] As we have seen above, Desiderius had much more nuanced and inconsistent relations with both Pope Stephen III and Pippin III's wife and sons. Although Charlemagne appears to have been consistently inclined to support the pope against the Lombards (though not necessarily to fight them), the same cannot be said of Carloman. With reference to the latter, for example, the *Liber pontificalis* preserves a complaint to Desiderius, king of the Lombards, that Carloman had been a friend of Christopher and Sergius and was ready to avenge their deaths after they had been blinded on Desiderius' orders, allegedly as a favour to Pope Stephen. Somehow, Pippin, Carloman and Charlemagne, and Bertrada too for that matter, as we have seen, were intimately involved in Lombard politics in the 760s and 770s in ways of which we have the merest hint in the fragments of information that survive. Certainly, Lombards and Franks had their own lines of communication with each other, and the latter attempted at one stage to mediate between the

---

[200] On the charter evidence see below, p. 113.
[201] On *barbatoria* see Y. Hen, *Culture and religion in Merovingian Gaul, AD 481–751* (Leiden, 1995), pp. 137–43; see also M. Diesenberger, 'Hair, sacrality and symbolic capital in the Frankish kingdoms', in M. Diesenberger, R. Corradini and H. Reimitz (eds.), *The construction of communities in the early middle ages*, The Transformation of the Roman World 12 (Leiden, 2003), pp. 173–212; and R. Bartlett, 'Symbolic meanings of hair in the middle ages', *Transactions of the Royal Historical Society*, 6th series 4 (1994), pp. 43–60.
[202] *Annales mettenses priores* 773, p. 60.

Lombard king and the pope.[203] The Frankish envoys on that occasion included George of Ostia and a possibly Alemannian count called Albuin, who was described in the *Liber pontificalis* as a favourite of Charlemagne at this very early stage of the king's career.[204]

The peculiar political structure of the Lombard kingdom may have facilitated Charlemagne's takeover, for it was an essentially elective king-ship, with the king chosen from among the leading dukes of the Lombard kingdom.[205] This left room for political factions and the promotion of the interests of rivals into which the Franks could insert themselves. The partial Lombard support for a Frankish seizure of the throne in 774, and the speed with which the initial phase of Charlemagne's takeover was concluded, can be better accounted for in this kind of volatile political context. The attempt of some Spoletans and some dependencies of the Duchy of Spoleto to surrender to the pope before the fall of Pavia in 774, and the intransigence of Friuli and Benevento thereafter, are further indications of a lack of cohesion and strong support for Desiderius and his policies and actions within the Lombard kingdom. Further factors in Italian politics at this time are the aspirations of the archbishop of Ravenna to secure ecclesiastical autonomy,[206] and the Byzantine interest, maintained since the end of the Ostrogothic wars of the sixth century, in the Exarchate of Ravenna in the northeast of Italy, in Rome itself, and in the southern regions of Apulia and Calabria.[207] The *Liber pontificalis* alleges that Desiderius was trying to trick the pope into coming to him so that he would anoint Carloman's sons as kings. This would thereby cause a rift in Francia and alienate Charlemagne from the pope.[208] Given the complexity of the political situation and Desiderius' alleged manoeuverings on behalf of Carloman's sons, it is possible that Charlemagne was doing far more than assisting the pope when he attacked Desiderius, for he had his immediate position within Francia to safeguard.

---

[203] *LP*, Life 97, c. 27, ed. Duchesne, I, p. 494.

[204] As D. Bullough convincingly established, this is not the Englishman Alcuin as has usually been assumed: '*Alboinus deliciosus Karoli regis*: Alcuin of York and the shaping of the Carolingian court', in L. Fenske, W. Rösener and T. Zotz (eds.), *Institutionen, Gesellschaft und Kultur im Mittelalter: Festschrift J. Fleckenstein* (Sigmaringen, 1985), pp. 73–92. See also H. Löwe, 'Zur *Vita Hadriani*', *Deutsches Archiv* 12 (1956), pp. 493–8.

[205] For a summary see P. Delogu, 'Lombard and Carolingian Italy', in *NCMH*, II, pp. 290–319; and C. La Rocca (ed.), *Italy in the early middle ages* (Oxford, 2002).

[206] Letters of Hadrian, *Codex epistolaris carolinus*, Nos. 53–5, ed. Gundlach, pp. 574–80, concerning Leo of Ravenna.

[207] T. S. Brown, *Gentlemen and officers: imperial administration and aristocratic power in Byzantine Italy, AD 554–800* (Rome, 1984).

[208] *LP*, Life 97, c. 9, ed. Duchesne, I, p. 488.

Dominant themes in the papal sources during the three years after Carloman's death were the mounting urgency of appeals from the pope for help against the Lombards, Desiderius' responsibility for his own downfall, due to his obduracy, and the reluctance of Charlemagne on his part to side definitively with the pope and take up arms against the Lombards. According to the *Liber pontificalis*, Pope Hadrian had been approached on his election by Desiderius. The Lombard king had offered peace according to terms that he claimed had been agreed between the Franks the Lombards and the Romans twenty years previously,[209] but simultaneously had captured Faenza and the economically important duchies of Ferrara and Commachio from the Exarchate of Ravenna, thereby cutting the exarchate off from essential supplies and lands.[210] The pope considered these regions to be part of papal territory granted in 757 by Pippin, Charlemagne and Carloman, though the status of this 'grant' and agreement is highly contested.[211] Desiderius refused to discuss the matter unless he could do so with the pope in person. Despite this charge, introduced as if to express the lengths of perfidy to which Desiderius could reach, the subsequent narrative presents Hadrian's prime concern as the retrieval of the cities 'stolen' by Desiderius. He would come to Desiderius, but only if his cities were restored. Desiderius subsequently occupied still more cities with territory regarded as part of the papal territories, and the *Liber pontificalis* reported that this was accompanied by 'much murder, fire and devastation.[212]

At this point in the *Vita Hadriani*'s narrative, Hadrian sent his envoys by sea with letters to Charlemagne asking him to help the pope as his father Pippin had done. Yet Hadrian had failed to inform the Frankish king of his election in 772 and, as far as we know, did not write to him for several months. It was a full year after his consecration that Hadrian called for help. At the same time as the papal envoy, moreover, a Lombard messenger

---

[209] *LP*, Life 97, c. 5, ibid., 1 p. 487.

[210] The economic importance of this region has been confirmed by recent archaeological excavation. See S. Gelichi, 'Le anguille di Venezia: il lungo seculo VIII degli emporia dell'arco nord-orientali adriatico', in S. Gasparri and C. La Rocca (eds.), *774: ipotesi su una transizione: Seminario internazionale, Poggio imperiale, Poggibonsi [SI] (16–18 febbraio, 2006)* (Siena, forthcoming).

[211] See J. Jarnut, 'Quierzy und Rom: Bemerkungen zu den "promissiones donationis" Pippins und Karls', *Historische Zeitschrift* 220 (1975), pp. 265–97; T. F. X. Noble, *The Republic of St Peter: the birth of the papal state, 680–825* (Philadelphia, 1984), pp. 153–81; R. Schieffer, 'Karl der Große und der Ursprung des westlichen Kaisertums', in W. Pohl (ed.), *Die Suche nach den Ursprüngen von der Bedeutung des frühen Mittelalters*, Österreichische Akademie der Wissenschaften, phil.-hist. Klasse Denkschriften 322 (Forschungen zur Geschichte des Mittelalters 8) (Vienna, 2004), pp. 151–8; and F. Hartmann, *Hadrian I (772–795)*, Päpste und Papsttum 34 (Stuttgart, 2006), pp. 113–56.

[212] *LP*, Life 97, c. 18, ed. Duchesne, 1, pp. 491–2.

was at the Frankish court. What made Charlemagne throw in his lot with the papacy rather than with the Lombard kings? The missing element is the quality of Frankish intelligence about Lombard politics. The discussions among the Franks alluded to in the *Annales regni francorum* may well have included assessments of Frankish chances of success for an extremely expensive and chancy venture to assist a pope who had hitherto been less than communicative. Even a pro-papal stance on Charlemagne's part is not sufficient to account for the decision to go to the pope's assistance so wholeheartedly, with two Frankish armies crossing the Alps. Yet it is also noteworthy that Charlemagne initially tried diplomacy rather than force and sent his envoys to try to persuade Desiderius to restore the cities 'to St Peter'. They failed. It is only then that Charlemagne moved with his armies to Italy.

The Frankish annalist appears to have been unwilling to register opposition to Charlemagne from anyone other than Desiderius and his family. He recorded that 'all the Lombards from all the cities of Italy came to Pavia and subjected themselves to the dominion of the glorious king Charles and the Franks'. Charlemagne had the task, nevertheless, of persuading all the Lombard dukes to accept his rule. One important indication of the way in which Charlemagne established order at a time of military upheaval and famine, and presented himself to the Lombards as a strong alternative to the Lombard king, is the *notitia italica*.[213] It is usually dated to 776 in the aftermath of the rebellion of Hrodgaud of Friuli in 776 in which Hrodgaud was killed and Charlemagne took over the cities of Treviso and Cividale.[214]

The notitia italica

The *notitia* is extant in three of the big Italian capitulary collections of the tenth/eleventh century as well as three important early ones.[215] These confirm, if nothing else, the authority of it coming from Charlemagne,

---

[213] *MGH Cap.* I., No. 88; and C. Azzaro and P. Moro (eds.), *I Capitolari italici: storia e diritto della dominazione carolingia in Italia* (Rome, 1998), pp. 50–2. I am very grateful to Mayke de Jong and Jan Ziolkowski for their help with interpreting this *notitia* and its possible context.

[214] C. De Clercq, 'Capitulaires francs en Italie à l'époque de Charlemagne', in *Hommage à Ursmer Berlière*, Bulletin de l'Institut historique belge de Rome, Supplément (Bruxelles, 1931), pp. 251–60, and uncontested since; see F. Manacorda, *Ricercha sugli inizii della dominazione dei Carolingi in Italia*, 2 vols., Studi Storici 71–2 (Rome, 1968), pp. 36–43; and F. Bougard, *La justice dans le royaume d'Italie de la fin du VIIIe siècle au début du XI siècle*, Bibliothèques des Ecoles Françaises d'Athènes et de Rome 291 (Rome, 1995), pp. 37 and 51.

[215] Cava dei Tirreni 4, Milan O.55 sup, BAV, Chigi F.IV.75; Ivrea, Biblioteca capitolare XXXIII s.IX med. N. Italy (includes the 'germanic' *leges*; XXXIV c. 830 Pavia ; St Paul im Lavanttal, 4/1, which is dated between 818 and 825, Pavia or Aquileia. See Mordek, *Bibliotheca*, p. 1089, and below, p. 249.

and there is no non-Italian transmission. The *notitia* is dated 20 February, and the year has been assumed to be 776 simply because 20 February 774 has not been thought to be possible. In February 774, Charlemagne was camped with his army outside Pavia, whither Liutprand had fled. A clause in the *notitia* itself, moreover, is ambiguous: it refers to the charters in the time of Desiderius which because of famine or some other reason will not be effective (*ut cartule ille quae tempore desiderio factae fuerunt per districtionem famis aut per qualecumque ingenio*). The siege of Pavia is thought to have lasted up to ten months before Liutprand finally surrendered, but Charlemagne appears to have been sufficiently confident in its effectiveness to take time off to go to Rome to celebrate Easter. One of Charlemagne's charters drawn up on 19 February 774 was redacted at Pavia by the royal notary Hitherius in the name of Charles as *rex francorum*.[216] It is concerned with a land exchange in the *pagus* of Le Mans, and might offer a hint that Charlemagne had been receiving petitions and/or petitioners while in his camp. The *notitia* also mentions legal disputes and that the decisions he had made had been read out to him. This would make the production of the *notitia* the next day, that is, after the redaction of the Le Mans charter, the less unlikely.

The *notitia*, in short, could be read as a very practical and immediate response to problems created by the presence of Charlemagne's army camped outside Pavia, with an underlying political message to win over the local population. It might help to account for the success and ease with which Charlemagne established himself in Pavia. The *notitia* recognizes a time before Charlemagne ruled and the present situation. It aimed at correcting the abuses caused by war and providing legal security for people worried about their property, with the political outcome still uncertain. It wished to guarantee the legality of sales and donations of property from that day forward (20 February). Unfair legal obligations made under duress were declared null and void but others that were contracted legally and fairly would be upheld. Men who gave themselves into *servitium* with their families would be free 'as before' (*ut primitus*). Men who might not have received the right price for landed property because of damage done by Charlemagne's armies should have the opportunity to prove its former value. Whoever could prove that he sold or gave his land from necessity, during a famine (with or without a charter that mentions this famine), would have his charter declared null and void. He would receive back his goods in the state they were when he sold them. Sales and donations *in loca*

---

[216] *DKar.* I, No. 79.

venerabilia, presumably ecclesiastical institutions, should be suspended until they could be discussed at a *sinodus* with bishops and *comites*.

The reference to charters drawn up in the time of Desiderius may indicate the impossibility of this charter being as early in 774, unless we accept how little we know of the relative status of Desiderius and Charlemagne in the early part of 774 and the *notitia* itself as an invitation to transfer political allegiance. There is no other evidence of the work of the royal notaries in Italy at the time of Hrotgaud's rebellion, that is, before Easter 776. Guigbold, acting for Hitherius, was responsible for a charter drawn up in Vicenza in June, and another charter was redacted at Ivrea in the same month in the king's name.[217] These are, in any case, the only royal charters extant for the entire year. The Revised Version of the *Annales regni francorum* creates a picture of a very swift military campaign and Franks appointed as counts in the retaken cities. Even if a longer period after Charlemagne's takeover, that is, until 776, before the production of the *notitia* is thought to be more plausible, the *notitia* remains an eloquent witness to the practical process of conquest.

By 779 the duke of Spoleto had also accepted Charlemagne as king. By 781 Charlemagne felt sufficiently secure to install a Frankish administration at Pavia with his four-year-old son Pippin as the papally anointed king of Italy.[218] Within Italy, Benevento, and possibly factions in both the other Lombard regions, that is, Spoleto and the north, were restive. The Revised Version of the *Annales regni francorum* hints at a much more prolonged process of establishing control than the original Frankish annalist seems to have been prepared to concede. This is backed up by the papal letters preserved in the *Codex epistolaris carolinus* which make it quite clear that Charlemagne took less and less heed of Pope Hadrian's attempts to control his movements, not least in Spoleto, where Charlemagne made an independent approach to Duke Hildeprand.[219] In 786, twelve years after the conquest, the author of the *Annales regni francorum* noted, as an introduction to a substantial account of Charlemagne's attempt to subdue Benevento, that Charlemagne 'considered it proper that he should take over the rest of the kingdom since he already had control of its ruler, the captive Desiderius and all of Lombardy'. On the face of it, Charlemagne's campaign in Benevento in 786 was successful in that he secured an agreement from Duke Arichis to have Arichis's younger son Grimoald as a

[217] *DKar.* I, Nos. III and II2.   [218] See above, p. 95, for Pippin's baptism by Pope Hadrian.
[219] *Codex epistolaris carolinus*, ed. Gundlach, Epp. 56, 57. and 58, and compare ibid., Epp. 61 and 64, pp. 580–4, 588–9, 591–2.

hostage and Grimoald was subsequently installed as duke in 787 by Charlemagne. Grimoald, however, was no puppet and did not choose to remain loyal to Charlemagne.[220]

Three principal aspects of the Frankish occupation of Italy need to be registered. Firstly, and despite Cathwulf's celebratory effusion, the consolidation of Charlemagne's initial *coup d'état* took many years and there was strong ducal opposition to Frankish rule in some of the Lombard regions, Secondly, the pope found it impossible to make the Frankish ruler fall in with all his plans as far as the control of territory was concerned. Cordial relations were established otherwise, and the pope did his utmost to define the Frankish king's position in Italy in close association with the papacy and Rome. Einhard records the memory of Charlemagne's strong attachment to Rome and St Peter.[221] The Frankish ruler's affection for Hadrian himself was marked by the commissioning of the spectacular epitaph on Hadrian's death in 795, inscribed on black marble and sent by the Franks to Rome. It is still visible in the portico of St Peter's basilica.[222] Thirdly, the Italian venture of 773/4 had long-term consequences that could not have been foreseen at the time, not the least of which were the continued involvement in Italian politics, a new proximity to Byzantine interests, and the papal elevation of Charlemagne as *imperator* and governor of the Romans a quarter of a century after he had seized the throne of the Lombards.

The imperial title

Charlemagne spent only a total of fourteen months in Italy during his forty-six year reign and over half that time was spent in Rome itself. It was on the last of his four visits that he was made emperor by the pope. The immediate context for this famous event was the squalid local politics of Rome. Set upon by his enemies, who attempted to gouge out his eyes and rip out his tongue, Hadrian's successor Pope Leo escaped across the Alps and sought Charlemagne's assistance by travelling north to Paderborn.[223]

---

[220] See below, p. 169.   [221] Einhard, *Vita Karoli*, c. 27, ed. Halphen, pp. 78–80.

[222] J. Story, J. Bunbury, A. C. Felici, G. Fronterotta, M. Piacentini, C. Nicolais, D. Scacciatelli, S. Sciuti and M. Vendittelli, 'Charlemagne's black marble: the origins of the Epitaph of Pope Hadrian I', *Papers of the British School at Rome* 73 (2005), pp. 157–90, illustrated in D. Bullough, *The age of Charlemagne* (London, 1970), p. 66; and see above, p. 4.

[223] M. Becher, 'Die Reise Papst Leos III. zu Karl dem Großen: Überlegungen zu Chronologie, Verlauf und Inhalt der Paderborner Verwandlungen des Jahres 799', in Godman, Jarnut, Johanek, *Am Vorabend der Kaiser Krönung*, pp. 87–112, establishes the context and chronology of the papal visit.

The meeting there between Charlemagne and the pope in September 799 was celebrated almost immediately by the so-called Paderborn epic.[224] The upshot was that first Frankish envoys and then Charlemagne himself went to Rome to deal with Leo's opponents. Leo himself was obliged to stand trial and swear to his innocence of the unsavoury charges made against him. It was in the aftermath of Leo's difficulties that Charlemagne was crowned emperor by the pope on Christmas Day in St Peter's basilica in Rome as part of the Christmas festivities.

The descriptions of this ceremony that are extant indicate that it was a staged occasion, for the congregation was ready to shout the imperial acclamations, and Charles the Younger, Charlemagne's son, was crowned at the same time.[225] There is no agreement, either in the contemporary sources or among modern scholars, as to whether the pope was the prime mover behind the imperial coronation or whether the Franks were, or what its contemporary significance was.[226] The very fact of Charlemagne and the Franks intervening to reinstate a pope has been taken as a crucial indication of Charlemagne's essentially imperial role even before he was actually crowned, as well as an important confirmation of the legal strength of his judgment in the pope's favour after he was crowned.[227] This may be assuming rather greater continuity and punctiliousness in the papal observance of Roman law by the end of the eighth century than we can otherwise document. The coronation certainly represents both a spectacular culmination of the long association of the Pippinids with the popes and a decisive demonstration of the strength of the political support the pope could command.[228] Charlemagne's status as ruler acquired an extra ideological dimension which both the Franks and the pope were swift to exploit in

[224] *Karolus magnus et Leo papa*, ed. H. Beumann, F. Brunhölzl and W. Winkelmann, *Karolus magnus et Leo papa: ein Paderborner Epos vom Jahre 799* (Paderborn, 1966); and W. Hentze, *De Karolo rege et Leone papa: der Bericht über die Zusammenkunft Karls des Großen mit Papst Leo III in Paderborn in einem Epos für Karl den Kaiser* (Paderborn, 1999).

[225] *LP*, Life 98, c. 24, ed. Duchesne, II, p. 7; and see above, p. 96.

[226] An excellent assessment is R. Schieffer, 'Neues von der Kaiserkrönung Karls des Großen', *Sitzungsberichte der Bayerische Akademie der Wissenschaften, phil.-hist. Klasse* (2004), pp. 3–25, with reference to the older literature, among which the most important is P. Classen, 'Karl der Große, das Papsttum und Byzanz: die Begründung des karolingischen Kaisertums', in *KdG*, I, pp. 537–608, and repr. in H. Fuhrmann and C. Märtl (eds.) *P. Classen, Karl der Große, das Papsttum und Byzanz*, Beiträge zur Geschichte und Quellenkunde des Mittelalters (Sigmaringen, 1995).

[227] For somewhat anachronistic suggestions about the legal point see P. Moraw, 'Kaiser gegen Papst – Papst gegen Kaiser: Prozesse und Quasiprozesse als Mittel der theologisch-politisch-rechtlichen Auseinandersetzung von 800 bis 1350', in U. Schultz (ed.), *Große Prozesse: Recht und Gerechtigkeit in der Geschichte*, 2nd edn (Munich, 1996), pp. 55–64 at pp. 56–8.

[228] Angenendt, 'Das geistliche Bundnis'.

terms of theoretical authority and the precedents offered by earlier Roman Christian emperors.[229]

How much practical difference the imperial title made to Charlemagne's power, or even to the Franks' position in Italy, is doubtful, yet attention needs to be paid to the mixed reactions of contemporaries. The *Annales regni francorum* simply records the ceremony in St Peter's and says Charlemagne set aside the name of patrician and was henceforth called emperor and *augustus*. He thereupon set the affairs of the city of Rome and of the whole of Italy in order.[230] Very soon afterwards, Einhard claimed that Charlemagne would not have gone into St Peter's that day had he known what the pope intended. If this is an accurate observation rather than simply a standard topos for humility, it may reflect Charlemagne's ambivalence about the pope's role, as distinct from the consecration itself. Charlemagne's title in his charters and capitularies was, after all, altered immediately from *Carolus gratia dei rex francorum et langobardorum ac patricius Romanorum* to *Karolus serenissimus augustus a deo coronatus magnus pacificus imperator Romanum gubernans imperium, qui et per misercordiam dei rex francorum atque langobardorum.*[231]

On the coinage, on the other hand, the Class 4 or imperial type of coins with the laureate bust of Roman type and the inscription IMP.AUG. were apparently not issued until 812, though *denarii* struck at Rome by Pope Leo III from 800 onwards did bear Charlemagne's name and the monogramme IMPA for imperator.[232] The Class 4 coins issue has been dated 812 and linked with the delayed Byzantine 'recognition' of Charlemagne's imperial title recorded in the *Annales regni francorum*. Envoys from the Byzantine emperor came to Charlemagne in Aachen and acclaimed him according to their custom in Greek and called him emperor and *basileus*.[233] The record of this Byzantine acknowledgment, and the subsequent relations with the eastern empire recorded in the sections of the *Annales regni francorum* written in the reign of Louis the Pious, reflect the later development of Frankish understanding of the historical development of the Roman empire and the potential challenge a Frankish imperial title might present

---

[229] E. Pfeil, *Die fränkische und deutsche Romidee des frühen Mittelalters*, Forschungen zur mittelalterlichen und neueren Geschichte 3 (Munich, 1929); and McKitterick, *Perceptions of the past*, pp. 35–62.

[230] *ARF* 801, ed. Kurze, p. 112, but compare the comments on this section of the annals, above, pp. 49–54.

[231] *DKar.* 1, No. 189, and compare No. 197.

[232] Grierson and Blackburn, *Medieval European coinage*, pp. 209–10 and Catalogue 748, 749; for Leo's coins, pp. 210 and 262.

[233] *ARF* 812, ed. Kurze, p. 136.

to Byzantium. It remains a possibility, however, that the Franks anticipated Byzantine recognition and struck the imperial type of coins some years before 812; it may be incorrect to assume that only Byzantine acknowledgment would have enabled the Franks to strike these coins.

Contemporary observers in the reign of Charlemagne, however, may have taken a more pragmatic attitude. The Lorsch annals, completed in 803, even offered a justification for Charlemagne's elevation in terms of the situation in Byzantium.[234] The author stated that it was due to the absence at that time of the name of emperor (*nomen imperatoris*) among the Greeks because they had female rule (*femineum imperium*) under the Empress Irene.[235]

These references, however, have to be set beside the so-called Kölner Notiz of 798. This records, baldly and perplexingly, that legates came to Charlemagne from the Greeks in order to offer him *imperium*.[236] Even if this is an accurate interpretation of the embassy's purpose on the part of this contemporary observer, the use of the word *imperium* does not necessarily refer to any formal imperial title or position. This Greek embassy is also recorded in the *Annales regni francorum*, but there the annalist concentrated on their peaceful mission, the fact that the legates were sent by Irene, because her son Constantine had been 'blinded by his own men', the names of the legates, and Charlemagne's agreement to their request that Sisinnius, brother of the bishop of Constantinople, be released and allowed to return home.[237] The *Annales mettenses priores* commented merely that the embassy was sent 'solely for the sake of ecclesiastical peace and concord'.[238] Why this embassy might have been offering Charlemagne any kind of *imperium* anywhere, as distinct from acknowledging his authority as far as deciding the fate of Sisinnius was concerned, remains a puzzle. Disputes about influence or ecclesiastical interests in Istria, Dalmatia or Croatia may have been at issue, not least Pippin of Italy's

---

[234] See J. Fried, 'Papst Leo III. Besucht Karl den Großen', *Historische Zeitschrift* 272 (2001), pp. 281–326.

[235] Lorsch annals 801, ed. G. Pertz, *MGH SS* I, p. 38. For a clear summary of the various contemporary reports, each representing different perspectives on the matter, see J. L. Nelson, 'Um 801: warum es so viele Versionen von der Kaiserkrönung Karls des Großen gibt', in B. Jussen (ed.), *Die Macht des Königs: Herrschaft in Europa vom Frühmittelalter bis in die Neuzeit* (Munich, 2005), pp. 38–54.

[236] Cologne, Diözesan und Dombibliothek, Cod. 83(II); Schieffer, 'Neues', pp. 9–14; and Schieffer, 'Karl der Große und der Ursprung des westlichen Kaisertums'.

[237] *ARF* 798, ed. Kurze, p. 104, repeated in *RVARF*, ibid., p. 105.

[238] *Annales mettenses priores* 798, p. 83; and see the studies in *Aquileia e le Venezie nell'alto medioevo*, Antichità altoadriatiche 32 (Udine, 1988); and P. Chiesa (ed.), *Paolino d'Aquileia e il contributo italiano all'Europa carolingia* (Udine, 2003).

activities in that area, the extent of Aquileia's ecclesiastical jurisdiction, and the rivalries with Venice as well as Byzantium.[239]

The indications in the Frankish sources, whatever the ideological capital gained from the comparisons with Roman emperors, are that Charlemagne initially regarded the imperial title as peculiar to him. The *Divisio regnorum* of 806, for example, made no reference to the title being preserved or any unified empire being sustained after his death. Only the deaths of Pippin of Italy and Charles the Younger, in 810 and 811 respectively, altered the situation, so that Louis the Pious was made heir to the imperial title as well as to the Frankish kingdom (apart from Bernard of Italy's kingdom) in 813. It was only under Louis the Pious that imperial ideology was fully elaborated.[240] Even in Louis's reign, however, the place of both Italy and Bavaria within the Frankish empire required special consideration, and it was Louis and his advisers who separated the two. In the *Ordinatio imperii* of 817, Italy became Louis's eldest son Lothar's special responsibility, but Bavaria, Carinthia, Bohemia and the Avars and Slavs in the eastern part of the Bavaria were allocated to Louis (the German).[241] Such an apportionment conceals a major upheaval at an earlier stage within the Carolingian family, for Louis the German's portion was the consequence of Charlemagne's appropriation of the entire inheritance of his cousin Tassilo.

Bavaria and the Agilolfings

Bavaria, like Frankish Gaul, had a Roman past, and parts of the former Roman provinces of Rhaetia and Noricum had been Christian since the late Roman period.[242] Bavaria had its own links with Rome, with the Lombard kingdom, and with the archdiocese of Aquileia. As a consequence of the establishment of the Frankish Christian family of the Agilolfings as *duces* in Bavaria, there were also social and cultural links with the Franks.[243] The Agilolfings' pride in their position is reflected in the confident

---

[239] See the entries in the ARF 806 and 810, ed. Kurze, pp. 120–2 and 132, concerning disputes and legates to the Franks which may indicate earlier Frankish involvement at the end of the eighth century. For a possible context, see F. Curta, *Southeastern Europe in the middle ages 500–1250* (Cambridge, 2006), pp. 100–3.

[240] See, for example, E. Boshof, *Ludwig der Fromme* (Darmstadt, 1996).

[241] *MGH Cap.* 1, No. 136: *Ordinatio imperii*, cc. 1, 2 and 17, pp. 270–3, at pp. 271 and 273.

[242] J. Jahn, *Ducatus Baiuvariorum: das bairische Herzogtum der Agilolfinger*, Monographien zur Geschichte des Mittelalters 35 (Stuttgart, 1991); and H. Wolfram, *Grenzen und Raume: Geschichte Osterreichs von seiner Enstehung* (Vienna, 1995).

[243] H. Friesinger, *Die Bayern und ihre Nachbarn* (Vienna, 1985); and J. Semmler, 'Zu den bayrischen-westfränkischen Beziehungen', *Zeitschrift für bayerische Landesgeschichte* 29 (1966), pp. 372–85.

statement in the *Lex baiuvariorum* that the leader of the Bavarians was and ought to be from the Agilolfing family.[244] Bavaria's distinctiveness and periods of independence, however, are overshadowed by the insistence in Frankish sources that the Bavarians had been subjected, to a greater or lesser degree, to the Merovingian rulers at various times since the late sixth century.[245] The early ninth-century *Annales mettenses priores*, for example, probably represents a standard view of the time in the assertion that Pippin II had attempted to re-establish Frankish power over the various peoples who had once been subjected to the Franks, that is, the Saxons, Frisians, Alemans, Bavarians, Aquitainians, Gascons and Bretons. Both the Continuations of Fredegar and the *Annales mettenses priores*, moreover, record Charles Martel occupying the lands of the Bavarians, conquering the people, and bringing back not only treasure but also Pilitrud (the wife of Duke Grimoald of Bavaria) and her niece Swanahild (Sunnichild). Charles Martel married Swanahild and it is their union that is commemorated in the Salzburg *Liber vitae* in the 780s.[246] Their son, Grifo, later sought support from his relatives in Bavaria against his brothers, Pippin III and Carloman, in the difficult period after Charles Martel's death when the Pippinid mayors fought to consolidate their authority against opposition from the Alemans, Bavarians and Aquitainians, and their allies.[247] The forced annexation of Bavaria by Charlemagne, therefore, needs to be seen against this pattern of intermittent hostility towards the Franks, the occasional success on the Pippinids' part in influencing internal Bavarian politics by supporting the regime, the claims to independence on Bavaria's part, and the crucial blood ties between the Pippinids and the Agilolfing dukes.[248]

Lamentably little is known about Bavarian politics from Bavarian sources at this time. Tassilo's career, for instance, is primarily communicated by the author of the first section of the Royal Frankish annalist. As remarked above, this portion of the text reported the conquest of Bavaria as the

---

[244] *Lex baiuvariorum*, III, 1, ed. E. von Schwind, *MGH Leges nat. germ.* 5, 2 (Hanover, 1926), pp. 312–13.

[245] Paul the Deacon, *Historia langobardorum*, V. 7, ed. G. Waitz, *MGH SRL*, p. 118. See J. Jarnut, *Agilolfingerstudien: Untersuchungen zur Geschichte einer adligen Familie im 6. und 7. Jahrhundert*, Monographien zur Geschichte des Mittelalters 32 (Stuttgart, 1986).

[246] Salzburg, St Peter Archiv A1, ed. in facsimile, K. Forstner, *Das Verbrüderungsbuch von St Peter in Salzburg: Vollständige Faksimile-Ausgabe im Originalformat der Handschrift A1 aus dem Archiv von St Peter in Salzburg* (Graz, 1974); and see McKitterick, *History and memory*, pp. 174–85. See also Astronomer, *Vita Hludowici*, c. 21, ed. Tremp, *Astronomus*, p. 348, for the memory of Tassilo's parents.

[247] *Annales mettenses priores* 741, p. 32. On Grifo see above, pp. 28, 66.

[248] J. Jarnut, 'Genealogie und politische bedeutung der agilofingische Herzöge', *MIÖG* 99 (1991), pp. 1–22.

culmination of the accretion of power by the Pippinids.[249] The *Annales regni francorum*'s determinedly negative portrayal of Tassilo's legal position is designed to make the annexation of Bavaria by his cousin Charlemagne in 788 seem entirely proper and a fitting punishment for Tassilo's behaviour during the thirty years he had been duke. In order to provide some kind of counterbalance to the Carolingian version of events, especially this excessively biased account of Tassilo in the *Annales regni francorum*,[250] much has had to be reconstructed from the eighth-century lives of Rupert, Emmeram and Corbinian, the *Notitiae Arnonis*, the *Breves notitiae*, the simple entries of names of Bavarian dukes and their wives and children set out in the Salzburg *Liber vitae*, and the references to the pre-Carolingian history of Bavaria in the later ninth-century *Conversio bagoariorum et carantanorum*.[251]

The relations between the Franks and the Agilolfings in Bavaria in the Merovingian period before 751 are sometimes difficult to ascertain, but it is clear that direct political interference by the Franks and the Pippinids, as well as more subtle means of exerting a political influence, affected Bavarian political affairs from time to time.[252] Most of the evidence for the history of Bavaria in the late seventh and the eighth centuries is associated with the major sees of Regensburg, Passau, Freising and Salzburg, especially with the last named. The career of St Rupert, missionary to Salzburg, for example, has been associated with anti-Pippinid sentiments in Bavaria as early as the turn of the seventh century.[253] Rupert, bishop of Worms, was invited to Bavaria by Duke Theodo. The Life of Rupert was probably commissioned by Rupert's successor Virgil and perhaps designed to demonstrate the existence of an independent ecclesiastical tradition within Bavaria.[254] Arbeo, bishop of Freising (764–83) established an association of two other early eighth-century Frankish

[249] See above, p. 31.

[250] M. Becher, *Eid und Herrschaft: Untersuchungen zu Herrscherethos Karls des Großen*, Vorträge und Forschungen Sonderband 39 (Sigmaringen, 1993).

[251] *Conversio bagoariorum et carantanorum*, ed. H. Wolfram (Vienna, 1979); *Breves notitiae*, ed. F. Losek, '*Notitia arnonis* und *Breves notitiae*', Mitteilungen der Gesellschaft für Salzburger Landeskunde 130 (1990), pp. 5–192; H. Wolfram, *Salzburg, Bayern, Österreich: Die* Conversio bagoariorum et carantanorum *und die Quellen ihrer Zeit* (Vienna, 1995); and F. Losek, *Die* Conversio bagoariorum et carantanorum *und der Brief des Erzbischofs Theotmar von Salzburg*, MGH Studien und Texte 15 (Hanover, 1997).

[252] J. Jahn, 'Hausmeier und Herzöge: Bemerkungen zur agilolfingisch-karolingischen Rivalität bis zum Tod Karl Martels', in Jarnut, Nonn and Richter (eds.), *Karl Martell*, pp. 317–44.

[253] H. Wolfram, 'Der heilige Rupert und die antikarolingische Adelsopposition', *MIÖG* 80 (1972), pp. 4–34; see also Wolfram, *Salzburg, Bayern, Österreich*, pp. 227–51.

[254] See I. Wood, *The missionary life: saints and the evangelisation of Europe 400–1050* (London, 2001), pp. 147–8.

bishops, Corbinian and Emmeram, with Duke Theodo and with Freising and Regensburg respectively, in the Lives he wrote of each saint between 769 and 772. Yet there is also a hint of Pippinid infiltration; according to Arbeo, Corbinian not only quarrelled with Duke Grimoald and his wife Pilitrud, but was given a very substantial sum of money (900 gold *solidi*) by Pippin II in order to purchase properties in the Freising region.[255] There are indications that Virgil of Salzburg had connections with the Frankish mayor as well.[256]

Under Duke Theodo (696–717/18), Bavaria appears to have enjoyed its greatest period of autonomy. His invitations to Frankish missionary bishops to work in Bavaria appear to have been designed to promote the reorganization of the church in Bavaria for which Boniface of Mainz later claimed the credit.[257] Theodo also travelled to Rome in 715 or 716 to ask the pope for assistance in this enterprise.[258] Theodo, however, divided the rule of Bavaria between his four sons. That such division seems to have left the way open for further political interference in Bavaria on the part of the Pippinid mayors is indicated by the fact that it was Pilitrud, wife of Grimoald (who had in fact been married before that to Grimoald's brother Theodoald), who was taken by Charles Martel to Francia with her niece Swanahild after Charles's attack on Bavaria in 725. Only Hucpert, the son of another of Theodo's sons, survived to rule as duke until 736/7. Odilo, apparently a son of Gotfrid, the Agilolfing duke of Alemannia, became duke in 736/7.[259] Frankish sources naturally, though one suspects disingenuously, claim that he was installed with the direct assistance of Charles Martel, though it is likely that the Lombard ruler Liutprand played a role as well.[260] Odilo, moreover, in a period of disaffection against his rule, took refuge briefly with the Frankish mayors and there appears to have gained the affections of Chiltrud, the sister of the mayors Pippin and Carloman. Their son Tassilo was born in 741.[261] When Odilo returned to Bavaria, Chiltrud was assisted by her stepmother

---

[255] Arbeo, *Vitae sanctorum Haimhrammi et Corbiniani*, ed. B. Krusch, *MGH SRG* 13 (Hanover, 1920).

[256] McKitterick, *History and memory*, pp. 180–4.

[257] Boniface, Ep. 45, ed. Tangl, *Briefe des Bonifatius*, pp. 71–4; and see the earlier letter of Gregory III, ibid., Ep. 44, pp. 70–1.

[258] *LP*, Life 91, c. 4, ed. Duchesne, I, p. 398.

[259] J. Jarnut, 'Studien über Herzog Odilo', *MIÖG* 85 (1977), pp. 273–84; and compare W. Stormer, *Adelsgruppen im früh- und hochmittelalterlichen Bayern*, Studien zur bayerischen Verfassungs- und Sozialgeschichte 4 (Munich, 1972).

[260] Jarnut, *Genealogie und politische Bedeutung*, p. 150.

[261] M. Becher, 'Zum Geburtsjahr Tassilos III', *Zeitschrift für bayerischen Landesgeschichte* 52 (1989), pp. 3–12.

Swanahild to join him and married him, apparently against her brothers' wishes. This is how it came about that when Odilo died in 748, his and Chiltrud's little son Tassilo was established as duke, although still only eight years old, with his uncle Pippin's support.

The opportunity to extend his authority into Bavaria as a magnate in the guise of a helpful uncle to his Agilolfing nephew may well have been regarded by Pippin III as a potential chance to create an alternative theatre of power, before he succeeded in making himself king in Francia.[262] Nevertheless, whatever Pippin had attempted in relation to Bavaria would have needed to have been re-established when he died, with no clear excuse for either Charlemagne or Carloman to interfere further. Tassilo by 768 was of age in his own region and the acknowledged ruler of Bavaria. His reign is notable both for the continuation of much that his predecessor Theodo had begun and for his emulation of many of his uncle Pippin's methods of rule. These are manifested in Tassilo's interest in missionary expeditions in Carinthia and the promotion of ecclesiastical reform within Bavaria, signalled by the convening of major synods such as Ascheim (757), Neuching (771), and Dingolfing (776/7). The last named adopted the idea of prayer associations first set out at Pippin's synod of Attigny, and is one of many instances of interchange between the Bavarian and Frankish churches.[263] Tassilo founded major monasteries such as Mondsee, Kremsmünster, and Innichen, and it was in his reign that religious culture flourished at such centres as Freising and Salzburg with, again, many instances of communication with religious centres in Francia.[264] It is probably with Tassilo that the first redaction of the *Lex Baiuvariorum* is to be associated, though some historians prefer to attribute it to his father Odilo.[265] Tassilo cultivated his own relations with both the Lombard kingdom and with the popes. He married Liutperga, the

---

[262] K. Reindel, 'Bayern im Karolingerreich', *KdG* I, pp. 220–46.

[263] Synod von Dingolfing and *notitia de pacto fraternitatis episcoporum et abbatum bavaricorum*, ed. A. Werminghoff, *MGH Conc.* II.i, No. 15 (Hanover, 1906), pp. 96–7; and K. Schmid and O.-G. Oexle, 'Voraussetzungen und Wirkung des Gebetbundes von Attigny', *Francia* 2 (1974), pp. 71–122.

[264] H. Löwe, 'Salzburg als Zentrum literarischen Schaffens im 8. Jahrhundert', in H. Koller and H. Dopsch (eds.), *Salzburg im 8. Jahrhundert* (Salzburg, 1975), pp. 99–143; and R. McKitterick, 'Unity and diversity in the Carolingian church', in R. N. Swanson (ed.), *Unity and diversity in the church*, Studies in Church History 32 (Oxford, 1996), pp. 59–82.

[265] R. Kottje, 'Die *Lex baiuvariorum* – das Recht der Baiern', in H. Mordek (ed.), *Überlieferung und Geltung normativer Texte des frühen und hohen Mittelalters*, Quellen und Forschungen zum Recht im Mittelalter 4 (Sigmaringen, 1986), pp. 9–24. And compare P. Landau, 'Die *Lex baiwariorum*: Entstehungszeit, Entstehungsort und Character von Bayerns ältester Rechts- und Geschichtsquelle', Sitzungsberichte der bayerischen Akademie der Wissenschaften, phil.-hist. Klasse, Jahrgang 2004, 3 (Munich, 2004), pp. 34–42.

daughter of King Desiderius of the Lombards, some time before 768, and in 772 his son Theodo was baptized by Pope Hadrian I.[266]

In 768 Charlemagne and Carloman, as we have seen, had their own positions to buttress, and it was nearly twenty years before Charlemagne felt strong enough or, conceivably, sufficiently threatened or provoked to overturn his powerful and increasingly ambitious Agilolfing cousin. Apart from a bullying tactic in 781, there is little to indicate that the subjection of Bavaria was on the agenda previously. In that year, however, a reminder was delivered to Tassilo concerning the earlier oath and obligations to Pippin III, his sons and the Franks (*ad partem domni Pippini regis, et domni Caroli magni regis vel Francorum*).[267] It was orchestrated with the help of the pope's *missi* in the aftermath of Charlemagne's creation of the sub-kingdoms of Italy and Aquitaine for his own little sons Pippin and Louis. At the same time Charlemagne, like Tassilo, had become a *compater* with the pope as a consequence of the baptism of Pippin, perhaps deliberately mirroring Theodo's baptism nearly a decade before.

It is important to reiterate that the accounts of Tassilo's downfall are both Frankish and retrospective.[268] There is, for example, the notorious entry in the annals for 788. Here the annalist refers back to his earlier evil deeds and how Tassilo had even deserted the lord king Pippin on campaign.[269] But it is also the annalist who has determined the emphasis on Tassilo's subordination to the Pippinids in the historical record. In 748 Tassilo was established as ruler in Bavaria with Pippin's backing; in 755, when still only fourteen years old, but possibly to mark his achieving his majority, he attended a Frankish assembly, and in the following year he accompanied his uncle on campaign in Italy.[270] In 757, Tassilo is presented as making a solemn oath of fidelity to Pippin and his sons Charles and Carloman, *sicut vassus dominos suos esse deberet* (as a man/vassal should to his lords), sworn on the relics of the saints Denis, Eleutherius and Rusticus, Germanus and Martin.[271] Tassilo deserted the Frankish army on campaign in Aquitaine in 763 *per malam ingenium*.[272] The meeting at Worms in 781, before which Tassilo had insisted on receiving hostages from his cousin, resulted in Tassilo being constrained to renew the oath sworn to Pippin

---

[266] J. Jahn, 'Virgil, Arbeo and Cozroh: Verfassungsgeschichtliche Beobachtungen an bairischen Quellen des 8. und 9. Jahrhunderts', *Mitteilungen der Gesellschaft für Salzburgische Landeskunde* 130 (1990), pp. 201–91 at p. 256; and for Tassilo's careeer see Jahn, *Ducatus baiuvariorum*, pp. 335–550.

[267] *ARF* 781, ed. Kurze, p. 58. [268] Becher, *Eid und Herrschaft*.

[269] For commentary on this account see McKitterick, *History and memory*, pp. 4–5.

[270] Fredegar, Continuations, c. 38, ed. Wallace-Hadrill, p. 107.

[271] *ARF* 757, ed. Kurze, pp. 14–16. [272] Ibid., p. 20.

and his young sons in 757. In his turn, moreover, Tassilo was obliged to deliver twelve hostages of his own. They were brought to Quierzy by Bishop Sindpert of Regensburg (756–91).[273]

Saxon affairs occupied the annalist's account for the next few years, but the persistence of the tension between Tassilo and Charlemagne is suggested by the report of a Bavarian embassy to Rome in 787. Bishop Arn of Salzburg and Abbot Hunric of Mondsee were entrusted by Tassilo, apparently in possession of the information that their visit would coincide with that of Charlemagne, to beg the pope to intercede with Charlemagne on Tassilo's behalf.[274] Unsurprisingly, there is nothing in the *Codex epistolaris carolinus* to indicate that Pope Hadrian so exerted himself on any occasion apart from this. The annalist nevertheless reports that the pope did indeed discuss Tassilo with Charlemagne and, unfortunately for Tassilo, accepted Charlemagne's version of the situation. In consequence, the pope told Tassilo's *missi*, in a remarkable speech preserved in the *Annales regni francorum*, that they were to require Tassilo to be obedient to Charlemagne in all things. If Tassilo chose not to obey the pope, then Charlemagne and his army would be entirely absolved from any charge of sin if they waged war in Bavaria. Any future burning or killing, therefore, would effectively have been brought on the Bavarians by Tassilo's intransigence, 'and the lord king Charles and the Franks would remain innocent of all guilt therefrom' (*et domnus rex carolus ac Franci innoxii ab omni culpa exinde permansissent*).[275] Most of this, interestingly enough, is omitted by the Reviser, who simply reported that the pope interceded forcefully with the king but was infuriated that the legates were unwilling to discuss peace terms. Hadrian thereupon threatened Tassilo with anathema should he not keep his oath of fidelity to Charlemagne.

With such moral authority to back him, on his return to Francia Charlemagne summoned a 'vast army' under his own command, another of Austrasian Franks, Thuringians and Saxons, and a third comprising a force from Italy led by Pippin of Italy, against Bavaria. Tassilo surrendered, was required to renew his oath and deliver the standard twelve hostages, as well as a thirteenth, his son Theodo. At that stage Tassilo remained as duke.[276]

Again, there is a considerable discrepancy between the various accounts of Charlemagne's aggression and Tassilo's response, with only very

[273] Ibid., p. 58.   [274] Ibid., p. 74.   [275] Ibid., p. 76.
[276] See also S. Airlie, 'Narratives of triumph and rituals of submission: Charlemagne's mastering of Bavaria', *Transactions of the Royal Historical Society*, 6th series 9 (1999), pp. 93–120.

occasionally a hint of sympathy at Tassilo's plight. That these occur at all are rare counterweights to the triumphalist narrative of the *Annales regni francorum*.[277] Thus, the original annalist is in no doubt that Charlemagne was in the right and that all the Bavarians were in any case more loyal to Charlemagne than to Tassilo;[278] the Reviser alters this to say that Tassilo's surrender was in consideration of 'the safety of himself and his people', and the *Annales mettenses priores* blame Tassilo's contumaciousness on his heeding the advice of his wicked wife.[279] The briefer accounts, such as the Lorsch Chronicle and the *Annales nazariani*, contrive by their very brevity to be less partisan. The latter, however, a text surviving in a single manuscript from the late eighth century (BAV pal. lat. 966), preserves a significant detail in the report that Tassilo's wife and children were captured together with all the treasure after Tassilo had surrendered to Charlemagne and given up Theodo as a hostage. Only after that was Tassilo himself arrested and charged with plots against the king rather than with a failure to keep an old oath of fidelity.[280]

The official account for 788 in the *Annales regni francorum* relates how Charlemagne returned to his onslaught against Tassilo and summoned him to Ingelheim for what has been described as a show trial.[281] The basis of the quarrel had changed. Tassilo was now accused not only of not observing his former oaths and of the crime of *harisliz* or desertion of Pippin's army back in 763, but also of seeking an alliance with the Avars against Charlemagne. Further, he had persuaded *fideles* of Charlemagne to join him, and plotted their deaths and attempted to subvert the loyalty of his own men towards the Frankish king by advising them to make mental reservation when swearing their oaths. Tassilo's own speech was defiant: 'he confessed to having said that even if he had ten sons he would rather lose every one of them than accept that the agreements should remain as they were or allow what he had sworn to stand: and he had also said that he would be better off dead than living thus'. Tassilo was successfully convicted by the 'Franks, Bavarians, Lombards, and Saxons and those from every province gathered at that assembly', and condemned to death. This

---

[277] See further above, pp. 27–31, and also McKitterick, *Perceptions of the past*, pp. 64–89.

[278] *ARF* 787, ed. Kurze, p. 78.

[279] *RVARF* 787, ed. Kurze, p. 79; *Annales mettenses priores* 788, p. 76. This is a point picked up by the Poeta Saxo, see above, p. 24.

[280] *Lorsch Chronicle*, ed. H. Schnorr von Carolsfeld, *Neues Archiv* 36 (1911), pp. 13–49: see Kaschke, *Die karolingischen Reichsteilungen*, pp. 149–73, and *Annales nazariani*, ed. G. Pertz, *MGH SS* I, p. 43; see McKitterick, *Perceptions of the past*, p. 89.

[281] Jahn, *Ducatus baiuvariorum*, p. 540.

was commuted by Charlemagne, out of love of God, because Tassilo was his blood relation (*ab amorem dei et quia consanguinaeus eius erat*) and, at Tassilo's request, to permission to become a monk and do penance 'for his great sins'.[282] Theodo, Tassilo's son, was similarly dispatched to a monastery, and a similar fate met Tassilo's wife and daughters. The *Annales nazariani* again records what sounds like an eyewitness story: Tassilo is said to have pleaded with the king not to tonsure him in the palace because of the shame and disgrace in which he would be seen by the Franks.[283]

Subsequent references to Bavaria in the *Annales regni francorum* are meagre, and concern Charlemagne's organization of his new territory in 788, 791–3, and 803, and campaigns mounted from Regensburg against the Avars in 791. For reasons which have not entirely been explained, it was not until the Synod of Frankfurt in 794 that Tassilo was finally presented to the assembled lay and ecclesiastical magnates.[284] The synod stressed Tassilo's renouncing and foreswearing all future claims to all his rights and properties and anything legally belonging to his sons and daughters as well. This forced renunciation appears to indicate that the subjugation of Bavaria was not quite so smooth as the Frankish sources would like us to believe. In addition to the political tensions Schieffer has outlined,[285] Tassilo's brief reappearance should probably be related to the extended period Charlemagne had spent in Regensburg and Bavaria between 791 and 793. This period of residence suggests the prolonged effort required to bring the region definitively under Carolingian rule and reorientate all the political and religious networks, as well as legalize claims to land. Charlemagne's confirmation of properties granted to the monastery of Kremsmünster in 791, recorded only in a twelfth-century copy inserted into the late eighth-century *Codex millenarius*, for example, suggests disputes over land rights created by the removal of Tassilo. The abbot was said to be holding specific properties originally granted by Tassilo in free tenure on behalf of the monastery, but because such tenure could scarcely remain firm and stable by the grant of Tassilo alone, he had petitioned to grant and confirm these lands anew and more fully. This Charlemagne had done after inspection of

[282] *ARF* 788, ed. Kurze, p. 80.   [283] *Annales nazariani*, ed. Pertz, *MGH SS* 1, p. 44.
[284] *MGH Cap.* 1, No. 28, c. 3, p. 165. E. Magnou-Nortier went so far as to claim that this clause actually belonged in 788 and was wrongly set in the Frankfurt record: E. Magnou-Nortier, 'L' "Admonitio generalis": étude critique', *Jornades internacionals d'estudi sobre el bisbe Feliu d'Urgell* (Urgel-Litana, 2000), pp. 195–242 at p. 207.
[285] R. Schieffer, 'Ein politischer Prozess des 8. Jahrhunderts im Vexierspiegel der Quellen', in Berndt, *Das Frankfurter Konzil vom 794*, 1, pp. 167–82.

the text of Tassilo's original donation.[286] The Frankfurt decision in 794 marks the last stage of Tassilo's downfall and the legal veneer created by Charlemagne and his advisers. Three copies of the decision were made, one for Tassilo to keep with him in the monastery, one for the palace archive and one to be kept in the palace chapel.[287]

As with Charlemagne's conquest of the Lombard kingdom twenty years years earlier, the Frankish king may have been able to exploit noble factions or disaffection within Bavaria to his advantage. Some Bavarian magnates may even have regarded the prospect of rule by Charlemagne as more attractive, or potentially more profitable, than an independent Bavaria under Tassilo. The rapid escalation of Frankish aggression against Tassilo was no doubt made possible by the conclusion of a major phase in the war against the Saxons, but the extraordinary efforts made by the Franks to claim the annexation of Bavaria as a righteous and just conquest are an eloquent indication of its being precisely the opposite.

If the passages about Tassilo are read in conjunction with those about Saxon rebels, it can be seen that the author of the *Annales regni francorum* refers to the Bavarian leader and his fate in a way similar to that in which he portrays the Saxon rebels and Charlemagne's dealings with them. Similarly, the resistance offered to Charlemagne by the Beneventans and Charlemagne's reprisals, even to the twelve hostages from Duke Arichis and the addition of a thirteenth hostage, Arichis's own son Grimoald, has many resemblances to the account of Tassilo's downfall. Other peoples besides the Beneventans, such as the Avars, the Bretons, Abodrites, the Danes, and the Muslims in Spain, were all brought into contact with the Franks as a result of the expansion of Frankish territory.[288] On the part of these peoples, a number of different patterns of relations with the Carolingians emerge.

EXTERIORES GENTES

Danes

Written reports of the internal affairs of the Danes and their contact with western Europe during the reign of Charlemagne are derived entirely from

---

[286] *DKar.* I, No. 169, pp. 227–8. See also W. Brown, *Unjust seizure: conflict, interest and authority in an early medieval society* (Ithaca, 2001); and C. Hammer, *Charlemagne's months and their Bavarian labours. The politics of the seasons in the Carolingian empire*, BAR International series 676 (Oxford, 1997).

[287] *MGH Cap.* I, No. 28, p. 74: 'Unde tres breves ex hoc capitulo uno tenore conscriptos fieri praecepit: unum in palatio retinendum, alium praefato Tasiloni, ut secum haberet in monasterio, dandum, tertium vero in sacri palacii capella recondendum fieri iussit.' See also below, pp. 250–1.

[288] J. M. H. Smith, '*Fines imperii*: the marches', in *NCMH*, II, pp. 169–89.

observers within Francia. There are few of them before 814 and these are mostly brief news items, apparently quite well informed, of events in a distant kingdom. Some attempts were also made by the Franks to interfere in the internal politics of the Danish peninsula. Only when the Danes chose to attack the Franks themselves, or the Franks' Abodrite allies, did the *Annales regni francorum* concede the amount of trouble they could cause, and the importance of the various shifting alliances among Danes, Abodrites, Wiltzites, Smeldingi, and Linones north of the Elbe.

An embassy from a King Sigifrid of the Danes had been received by Charlemagne as early as 782.[289] In 800 Charlemagne had to strengthen his fleet and coastal defences against pirates in the North Sea, though it should not be assumed that these pirates had anything to do with the Danish rulers. It was Godofrid of the Danes who actually threatened Charlemagne effectively, both militarily and economically. He arrived with his fleet and horsemen at Schleswig in 804. He subsequently invaded Abodrite territory with an army, captured the trading emporium of Reric and relocated the merchants to Haithabu/Hedeby on the Schlei river, drove out the Carolingian ally Duke Thrasco, took Thrasco's son hostage, and killed another Abodrite duke called Gotelaib. Charles the Younger was sent to the Elbe with an army to fight him off. Although Godofrid retreated with severe casualties (or so it was claimed by the Frankish annalist), the Abodrites on this occasion, and the Frisians shortly thereafter, were required to pay tribute to the Danish king.[290] On other occasions, notably that on which Charlemagne himself went with his armies in 810, and his Persian elephant Abul-Abaz died, Godofrid's threats were countered without fighting.[291] The annalist credited Godofrid with the building of the Danevirke. Dendrochronological dating has established that the main part of this impressive rampart across the base of the Jutland peninsula had actually been built in 737, though some extra construction work might date to Godofrid's reign.[292] Godofrid might have been strong enough to

[289] *ARF* 782, ed. Kurze, p. 60.
[290] *ARF* 808, ed. Kurze, p. 125. On the economic implications of Godofrid's seizing of Reric see M. McCormick, 'Um 808: was der frühmittelalterliche König mit der Wirtschaft zu tun hatte', in Jussen, *Die Macht des Königs*, pp. 71–7.
[291] ARF 810, ed. Kurze, pp. 133–5; and see M. Hardt, 'The *Limes saxoniae* as part of the eastern borderlands of the Frankish and Ottonian-Salian empire', in Curta, *Borders, barriers and ethnogenesis*, pp. 35–50.
[292] *ARF* 808, ed. Kurze, p. 126. On the Danevirke see H. H. Andersen, H. J. Madsen and O. Voss, *Danevirke* (Copenhagen, 1976); and H. H. Andersen, *Danevirke og Kovirke: arkøologiscke undersøgelser 1861–1993* (Højbsjerg, 1998). See also H. Jankuhn, 'Karl der Große und der Norden', *KdG* I, pp. 699–707.

establish firm control of the area north of the Elbe, but his murder in 810 by one of his own men left his son Hemming, who was apparently less inclined to make war against the Franks or the Abodrites, to make peace with Charlemagne.[293]

It is a significant indication of the strength of the Danes that the Frankish annalist made no attempt to conceal the fact that legates of the Danes and of the Franks met in ways quite unparalleled by encounters with the other peoples whom Charlemagne subjected to his dominion. The defeated leaders of peoples apart from the Danes were brought to Charlemagne by victorious Frankish generals. Alternatively, legates from the rulers of neighbouring peoples suing for peace were required to come to Charlemagne wherever he was based. The Danish rulers, Godofrid and his successor Hemming, as well as the four sons of Heriold who succeeded Hemming after an internal dispute, however, all successfully demanded special meetings. Peace with Charlemagne in 809, 811 and 813, therefore, was agreed at meetings convened north of the Elbe River with twelve or sixteen *primores* from each side, and confirmed by mutual oaths 'in accordance with their usage and custom' (*secundum ritum ac morem suum sacramentis pax confirmatur*).[294]

Abodrites and other Slavs

Charlemagne's ally, Witzan of the Abodrites, headed a combined army of Franks, Saxons, Frisians, Sorbs and Abodrites against another Slavic people called the Wiltzites north of the Elbe. After Witzan was killed by Saxons in 795, Thrasco had become the client *dux* of the Abodrites and led them against the *Nordliudi* (the second element of whose name may be of Slavic origin) and other enemies of the Franks on a number of occasions. The Danish defeat of the Abodrites in 808, and murder of the Abodrite *dux*, Thrasco, by Godofrid's men in the following year (809), appear to have disrupted the supportive relations Charlemagne had established with the pagan Abodrites since at least the 780s by supporting leaders favourable to

---

[293] *ARF* 808–9, ed. Kurze, pp. 125–6, 128–9. On Abodrites see W. H. Fritze, 'Die Datierung des *Geographicus bavaricus* und die Stammesverfassung der Abodriten', *Zeitschrift für Slawische Philologie* 21 (1952), pp. 326–42; and Fritze, 'Probleme der abodritischen Stammes- und Reichsverfassung und ihrer Entwicklung von Stammesstaat zur Herrschaftsstaat', in H. Ludat (ed.), *Siedlung und Verfassung der Slawen zwischen Elbe, Saale und Oder* (Giessen, 1960), pp. 141–220. See also M. Hellmann, 'Karl und die slawische Welt zwischen Ostsee und Böhmerwald', in *KdG* I, pp. 708–18; and above, pp. 12–13.

[294] *ARF* 809, 811, 813, ed. Kurze, pp. 128, 134–5, 138–9, esp. p. 134.

him. It was not until Louis the Pious's reign that the regime in Abodrite territory was stabilized once more.[295]

Just as proximity had presented Charlemagne with the need to try different methods of maintaining political stability with the northern Slavs and the Danes, so in the east and southeast, contiguity determined the relations between the Franks, Bavarians and Lombards on the one hand, and the Bohemian, Carantanian and Croatian Slavs on the other. In these instances, missionary work also played a part.[296] Again the record during Charlemagne's reign is all too meagre, though in 805 Charles the Younger was sent to fight the Bohemian Slavs. A year later an army from Bavaria, Alemannia and Burgundy was sent against the Bohemian Slavs. Legates (Paul, duke of Zara and Donatus, bishop of Zara) were received from the Dalmatians in 806 and from the Slavs in the Danube region in 811.[297]

Bretons

Others among the peripheral peoples, such as the Bretons, became tributaries. In 786, an army under the seneschal Audalf achieved a victory against the Bretons, and Breton leaders were presented to the king in his assembly at Worms. The Revised Version of the *Annales regni francorum* explained the aggression as being an attempt to reimpose a tribute and adds that the Bretons had also been required to bring hostages. So again, the claim is made that Charlemagne revived older political relations and forced their reimposition. In 799, however, a different author reported that as a result of Count Wido's efforts, the 'whole province of the Bretons was subjugated by the Franks, something which had never happened before'.[298] Brittany was in fact never fully incorporated into the Carolingian empire, though a marcher region was established during Charlemagne's reign which acted as a conduit of Carolingian and Frankish influence further west into Breton territory.[299]

---

[295] Jankuhn, 'Karl der Große und der Norden'.

[296] H. Krahwinkler, *Friaul im Mittelalter: Geschichte einer region vom Ende des fünften bis zum Ende des zehnten Jahrhunderts*, Veröffentlichungen des Instituts für Österreichischen Geschichtsforschung 30 (Vienna, 1992); I. Suicic, *Croatia in the early middle ages: a cultural survey* (London and Zagreb, 1999).

[297] *ARF* 806 and 811, ed. Kurze, pp. 120–1 and 135; and for general context Curta, *Southeastern Europe*.

[298] *ARF* 786 and 799, ed. Kurze, pp. 72 and 108. Compare J. M. H. Smith, 'The sack of Vannes by Pippin III', *Cambridge Medieval Celtic Studies* 11 (1986), pp. 17–27.

[299] See J.-P. Brunterc'h, 'Le duché du Maine et la marche de Bretagne', in H. Atsma (ed.), *La Neustrie: les pays au nord de la Loire de 650 à 850*, Beihefte der Francia 16/1 (Sigmaringen, 1989), pp. 29–128; and J. M. H. Smith, *Province and empire: Brittany and the Carolingians* (Cambridge, 1992).

Avars

Boruth, the ruler of Carinthia, had appealed to his Bavarian neighbours for assistance against the Avars in 741 and 742. A Bavarian mission to Carinthia was inaugurated soon afterwards, accompanied by a limited amount of Bavarian settlement in former Slav territory, some peaceful contact between the Avars and their western neighbours, and the conversion to Christianty of some of the people.[300] The Avar *khagan* and *jugur* had also sent a peaceful embassy to Charlemagne in his camp at Lippeham in 782.[301] One of the charges levelled against Tassilo of Bavaria in 788 was that he had sought to form an alliance with the Avars against his cousin Charlemagne. It is in connection with this allegation and in the immediate aftermath of Tassilo's downfall that the Royal Frankish annalist records three victories against the Avars. The first, in Italy, may have been prompted by an Avar attack. The Franks, however, 'with the Lord's help', were victorious and the Avars returned to their home disgraced (*cum contumelia*) because they had fled the field. The second battle between the Avars and Bavarians, at which Charlemagne's *missi* and some Franks were present, was again won with the Lord's help. Lastly the Avars took 'revenge' and attacked the Bavarians (*qui voluerunt vindictam peragere contra Baioarios*). *Missi* of Charlemagne were present at this battle too, and with the Lord's protection (*et Domino protegente*) another victory fell to the Christians. Many Avars were slain and others drowned in the Danube as they fled. The year entry for 788 concludes with Charlemagne installed at Regensburg and defining a frontier region so that the Bavarians could be safe from the Avars (*et ibi fines vel marcas Baioariorum disposuit, quomodo salvas Domino protogente contra iamdictos Avaros esse potuissent*).[302]

Like the final subjection of Tassilo, the attack on the Avars is presented by the author of the *Annales regni francorum* as a legitimate and Christian act, despite the meagre record of Avar aggression hitherto, and justified by 'the immense and intolerable evil which the Avars had perpetrated against

[300] W. Pohl, *Die Avaren: Ein Steppenvolk in Mitteleuropa 567–822 n. Chr.* (Munich, 2002); W. Pohl, I. Wood and H. Reitmitz (eds.), *The transformation of frontiers from late antiquity to the Carolingians*, The Transformation of the Roman World 10 (Leiden, 2001); H. Goetz, J. Jarnut and W. Pohl (eds.), Regna et gentes: *The relationship between late antique and early medieval peoples and kingdoms in the transformation of the Roman world*, The Transformation of the Roman World 13 (Leiden, 2003); H. Reimitz, 'Grenzen und Grenzüberschreitungen im karolingischen Mitteleuropa', in W. Pohl and H. Reimitz (eds.), *Grenze und Differenz im frühen Mittelalter*, Österreichische Akademie der Wissenschaften phil.-hist. Klasse, Denkschriften 287 (Forschungen zur Geschichte des Mittelalters 1) (Vienna, 2000), pp. 105–66.
[301] *ARF* 782, ed. Kurze, p. 60.   [302] *ARF* 788, Ibid., pp. 82–4.

the holy church and the Christian people' (*propter nimiam malitiam et intolerabilem quam fecit Avari contra sanctam ecclesiam vel populum christianum*). Alternative perspectives are available, even if the pro-Charlemagne stance remains as strong.

The Revised Version of the *Annales regni francorum* reinforced the political case against the Avars but omitted the religious righteousness. Thus it cast doubt on the peaceful purpose of the embassy from the Avars in 782 (*velut pacis causa miserunt*) and claimed that the Avar attacks on Bavaria and Friuli were according to their agreement with Tassilo (*sicut Tassiloni promiserunt*).[303] Again, too, the original annalist presented the decision to attack as the result of the deliberations between Charlemagne and an assembly of Franks, Saxons and Frisians, whereas the Reviser attributes the aggressive and vengeful purpose to the king alone.[304] The Christian zeal is reinforced in Charlemagne's letter to his wife Fastrada[305] and echoed in the *Annales regni francorum* by the army's celebration of litanies and masses for three days, with prayers for God's support for the safety of the army and to Christ for victory and vengeance. In the event battle was not joined, though the Franks destroyed Avar strongholds and the Avars fled further east into Pannonia. Four years later, *missi* from the Avar *tudun* came to Charlemagne's camp on the Elbe to convey the *tudun*'s offer to become a Christian. The Frankish response was represented by Eric of Friuli's raid on the Avar Ring and his sending of the Avars' fabulous treasure, a 'vast treasure amassed by past kings over numerous centuries was sent to the lord king Charles in Aachen' (*thesaurum priscorum regum multa seculorum prolixitate collectum domno regis Carolo ad Aquis palatium misit*). This attack was followed up by Pippin of Italy, who brought still more booty. Only the original annalist, however, notes the internal disputes within the Avar kingdom of which Eric and Pippin quite probably had taken advantage. Another Avar embassy to the Franks followed, but uprisings in which Eric of Friuli and Gerold, the governor of Bavaria, were killed, are recorded under 799.[306]

The Avars were not completely destroyed so much as dispersed by these Frankish raids. In 805 a Christian Avar prince with the baptismal name of Theodore asked for a place to live between Savaria/Szombathely and Carnuntum/Petronell to afford his people some protection from attack by Slavs.[307] As late as 811, Charlemagne sent an army into Pannonia to deal

---

[303] *RVARF* 782 and 788, ed. Kurze, pp. 61 and 83.   [304] *ARF* 791, ed. Kurze, pp. 86–88.
[305] See above, p. 43.   [306] Ross, 'Two neglected paladins'.
[307] *ARF* 805, ed. Kurze, p. 120; and see below, p. 278.

with military aggression between Slavs and Avars.[308] It is possible that Charlemagne and his officials on this occasion were brokering some kind of agreement between the Slavs and Avars in the lower Danube region, for embassies from both groups came to the king at Aachen. Despite the protestations of religious fervour which accompanied the various attacks on the Avars, how much effort the Franks or Bavarians made to convert the Avars is difficult to ascertain.[309]

Muslims, Christian Visigoths and Basques

Although religion was used as an excuse for attacking the Avars, it appears not to have been a consideration in the various dealings Charlemagne had with the peoples of Spain, whether in Muslim Al-Andalus, the Christian Visigothic kingdoms of northern Spain, or the mixed population of the area brought loosely under Carolingian control known as Septimania. The Frankish sources claim great success in Spain, but there was in fact quite a complicated policy of playing off the possibilities of alliance with both Muslim and Christian rulers in a volatile political situation. Just as the Danish rulers and the attacks by northern pirates cannot necessarily be associated, moreover, so with the Muslims it is necessary to distinguish between the Moorish pirate raids on Corsica, Sardinia and the Balearic islands with which the fleets of Pippin of Italy and Count Burchard had to deal,[310] and the struggles for power within Muslim Al-Andalus itself in which the Franks became involved. Embassies bearing gifts from one ruler to another came to Francia from the Christian kings of the Asturias and Galicia and the Muslim rulers of Al-Andalus,[311] but most of Charlemagne's contacts with Spain were with Muslim Spain and Septimania. From the Muslim rulers came not only the embassies and the rich presents but also appeals for help. Charlemagne's response to a similar appeal from Italy, as we have seen, had brought him rich rewards, but he only ever succeeded in making a temporary and slight impact south of the Pyrenees. The policy of attempting to intervene in the internal politics of a particular kingdom or city in order to ensure that an ally was in power was certainly an alternative to outright conquest. Yet it could, of course, be manipulated by both sides. Control of Barcelona, for instance, alternated between those friendly towards the Franks or to the Muslim rulers of Spain. Ermold the Black,

---

[308] *ARF* 811, ed. Kurze, p. 135.
[309] For an analysis of the years 791–811 see Pohl, *Die Awaren*, pp. 315–23.
[310] *ARF* 806, 807, 810, ed. Kurze, pp. 122, 124, 133.   [311] *ARF* 797, Ibid., p. 100.

reporting 'the most recent tales which have reached his uncomprehending ears', described it as a border town with a mixed population, full of Moorish robbers and armed bands, and political refugees from both the north and the south.[312]

The Frankish expedition to Spain in 778 was in response to an appeal for help in an internal power struggle by 'Ibn al-Arabi' brought by an embassy in 777. Unlike the interference in Italy, the launch of an army into Spain is not accompanied in the Frankish sources by any sense of long deliberation or persuasion. An army of men from Burgundy, Austrasia, Bavaria, Provence and Septimania, as well as a contingent of Lombards, converged on Saragossa.

The *Annales regni francorum* presents the expedition as a complete success, with Pamplona destroyed and the Spanish Basques and Navarrans subjugated. The Revised Version of the annals, however, preserves the report of the disastrous ambush by Basques in the Pyrenees as the Frankish army returned home. It is Einhard who tells us that Roland, the count of the Breton march, was one of those killed. Einhard, like Ermold the Black, may have been repeating stories or songs he had heard. Later this expedition to Spain was written up in the epic *Chanson de Roland* as a clash between the forces of Christendom and those of Islam.[313] The severity of the defeat at Roncesvalles may be indicated by the fact that it was another twenty years before the Franks returned to Spain. The Muslim Sadun had seized Barcelona in 797, and had visited Aachen and allied himself with Charlemagne. Louis the Pious was thereupon sent to consolidate the Frankish position in this border area. Again, the Frankish military engagements in the Spanish march between 797 and 803 had mixed success. Sadun himself by 801 was described as a rebel and Barcelona was captured from him. A subsequent campaign led by Louis in 808 to Tortosa was inconclusive. The Muslim commander of Saragossa and Huesca, who replaced the Frankish count Aureolus in 801, was anxious to be regarded as an ally of the Franks but was driven out by Abd al-Rahman, son of Abulaz, ruler of Al-Andalus, with whom Charlemagne concluded peace in 812. It was then left to Louis the Pious, after he had become emperor, to maintain diplomatic relations with the rulers of the various parts of Spain.

---

[312] Ermoldus Nigellus, *In honorem Hludowici pii*, ed. E. Faral, *Poème sur Louis le Pieux et épîtres au roi Pépin*. Les classiques de l'histoire de France au moyen âge 14 (Paris, 1964), pp. 12–14.

[313] *Chanson de Roland*, ed. C. Segre (Geneva, 1989).

CONCLUSION: THE LIMITS OF EXPANSION

The circumstances of Charlemagne's successful conquests and annexation of territory, combined with intermittent political influence exerted on the borders of the realm, have generally been regarded as the process of a transformation of an aggressive military strategy into a concentration on defence in the latter years of Charlemagne's reign, with a concomitant claim that crushing the Avars in 790s was 'the last really large aggressive military operation conducted by the Carolingians'.[314] As we have seen, the seizing of the Avar treasure was the result of two small raiding forays, and the Avars themselves retreated without a fight before a display of force from the Frankish host. A relentlessly systematic process of conquest certainly characterizes the Saxon wars. Most of the campaigns of the 770s were between the Rhine and the Werra, gradually moving further east to the areas between the Werra and the Aller rivers and north beyond the Hase river into eastern Frisia. Only in the 790s were the Franks able to gain a foothold in the Bardengau between the Weser and Elbe.

Certainly the Frankish narrative sources throughout the eighth century rarely let a year pass without recording a military assembly or campaign. In Charlemagne's reign, however, there are significant periods of peace. It is an oversimplification to see these military activities as aggression succeeded by defence, especially if the priorities of the different annal writers, and the various attacks mounted against the northern and eastern Slavs in the first decade of the ninth century, are taken into account. The conquest of Saxony and the quelling of resurgent pockets of Saxon and Frisian resistance account for many of Charlemagne's military campaigns. Once the Saxon wars are taken out of the reckoning, we are left with the completion of Pippin's conquest of Aquitaine in 769, the initial success in Lombard Italy precipitated by the request of the pope for assistance, a plea for help from Spain in 778 which had such a disastrous outcome, the political annexation of Bavaria, the attacks on the Avars, the quelling of at least three revolts (in 785, 786 and 792[315]), a defence against attack from Byzantine forces in 788, the defensive diplomacy in relation to the Danes mentioned above and some retaliatory military expeditions against Slavs. As we have seen, forays beyond the Elbe were primarily in connection with the client rulers among their Slav allies.

---

[314] The most cogent presentation of this view is that of T. Reuter, 'The end of Carolingian military expansion', in P. Godman and R. Colllins (eds.), *Charlemagne's heir: new perspectives on the reign of Louis the Pious* (Oxford, 1990), pp. 391–405.

[315] See McKitterick, *Perceptions of the past*, pp. 63–89.

The political manoeuvering and opportunism displayed in other respects indicate that the motives for Carolingian expansion and the settling of the borders involved more than aggression or defence, and there seems to me to be just as much of an effort to deal with insurgence and to settle borders earlier in Charlemagne's reign as later on. Reuter was right to suggest that the end of expansion was probably a conscious decision, but it needs to be recognized first of all that Bavaria and Saxony were the last expansionist enterprises which actually integrated further territory into the Frankish kingdom.[316]

Secondly, the process of absorbing Saxony under Frankish rule had begun under Charlemagne's grandfather Charles Martel, partly in parallel with missionary enterprises. Bavaria was entirely a family matter. The takeover of the Lombard kingdom had roots in Pippin's actions in support of the papacy. It is also fascinating that the expansion of Charlemagne's empire reached, with the exception of the Danes, the northern and eastern limits of the Germanic peoples of western Europe in his day. The various political relations with those beyond the Romance or Germanic linguistic regions – Bretons, northern and eastern Slavs, Avars, Saracens and Greeks – were such that they remained beyond the frontiers of the Frankish empire. The constant vigilance and skirmishing required in the 780s and 790s to maintain and consolidate the limits of these conquests is striking.

In the later 780s, moreover, a new and religious fervour is manifest in the annalists' account of Charlemagne's military activity, with the zeal to convert pagans or punish pagans for damage inflicted on Christian peoples providing extra motives for dealing with both Tassilo and the Avars. Such a concern coincides with the programmatic reform capitularies of 786 and 789. It coincides with the preparations for the issue of the Capitulary of Herstal in 786 and the *Admonitio generalis*. On one level, this coincidence of reforming legislation and aggressive military Christianity should not be exaggerated, for, as we have noted, the religious preoccupations of Charlemagne did not prevent him forming alliances with pagan Slavs as well as Muslims. On the other hand, the programme of religious reform and expansion of Christian culture was part of an overall strategy of Carolingian rule. It is to the government of the realm, the consolidation of the Frankish empire and the promotion of Carolingian political identity that the rest of this book, therefore, will be devoted.

---

[316] For a further context in which to understand the limits of empire see below, pp. 288–91.

CHAPTER 3

The royal court

INTRODUCTION

Political power and its location had become more decentralized and less institutionalized in the post-Roman world. The Carolingian construction of a network of regional centres of power, a 'topography of power',[1] appears to offer an instance of such decentralization within the much-expanded *regnum francorum*, with a 'great chain of palaces' whose symbolic role was enhanced from time to time by the king's presence or by the conduct of the king's business.[2]

A distinctive feature of Carolingian rule was the plurality of political and administrative centres and the maintenance of communications between these centres and their surrounding regions. How this worked in relation to a 'royal court' or the royal household needs a fresh examination, not least to see how Charlemagne developed a royal court, or a number of royal courts, from the base provided by his father Pippin. Charlemagne's court is too often seen as a static and unchanging institution, and described in terms of conditions during the last few years of his reign and the early period of the reign of Louis the Pious. Both the evidence for the 'court' and the role of the many royal palaces within the empire, therefore, need to be reassessed in relation to the apparent agreement among modern scholars concerning the dominance of the palace at Aachen, and their confidence in the character of the court based there. Neither the role of Aachen nor the court is unproblematic. The complicating factors are the degree to which either the king or the court was itinerant and how integral itinerancy was

---

[1] M. de Jong and F. Theuws, with C. van Rhijn (eds.), *Topographies of power in the early middle ages*, The Transformation of the Roman World 6 (Leiden, 2001).

[2] J. L. Nelson, 'Aachen as a place of power', in Jong, Theuws and Rhijn, *Topographies of power*, pp. 217–42 at p. 222. See also S. Airlie, 'The palace of memory: the Carolingian court as political centre', in S. Rees Jones, R. Marks and A. J. Minnis (eds.), *Court and regions in medieval Europe* (York and Woodbridge, 2000), pp. 1–20 at p. 14.

to the system of Carolingian government as it was developed under Charlemagne. The current perception of the court is of a single itinerant institution which eventually 'settled at Aachen' around 794.[3] Thus the structure of the royal household, the practical manifestations of itinerancy, the stages at which the household and its satellites may or may not have 'settled', and the light these throw on how centralized or dispersed Charlemagne's rule was, are all interconnected issues. I look first, therefore, at the evidence for the royal household and its structure, and the appropriateness of its designation as a court. I then discuss the contemporary evidence about Aachen in relation to the other Carolingian palaces in order to establish Aachen's place alongside many other centres in Charlemagne's topography of power. I turn thereafter to the question of the royal itinerary, for commentary on it hitherto proves to have been based on ill-founded assumptions. Not the least of these is the traditional interpretation of the charter evidence and the work of the notaries of the royal writing office or 'chancery'. I suggest a new approach to the charters and argue that they highlight the crucial role of written documents emanating from the royal household, wherever it was, in maintaining an essential network of communication throughout the empire.

The information which might make it possible to establish whether the court was either an entity or a group of people is scattered, often ambiguous and difficult to date precisely. The most important category of material is that apparently emanating from a group closely associated with the king and recording his decisions in the form of administrative and legislative documents: that is, the extant royal diplomas or charters (documents recording royal grants or judicial decisions produced in the king's writing office), and the capitularies, decrees and decisions of the king and his advisers, sometimes made at a general assembly, organized into *capitula*. The charters' *arengae* (that is, the description of the donor and reasons for the grant being made) or their dating clauses also offer an indication of where they were produced. These are customarily taken as firm evidence of the presence of the king and thus as providing key information for plotting the itinerary.

A further category of material comprises works composed by people who are associated with the king and often described as 'at the court' or even as 'courtiers', 'court scholars' or the like. This extends from the so-called coterie poetry of the 'court scholars' and the handsome manuscripts produced by two groups of scribes and artists associated with the royal

---

[3] See below, pp. 347–50.

court, to letters, didactic treatises, theological works, and historical writing, in particular the Royal Frankish annals. Although this last-named historical text was, as we have seen, designed as a very determined and skilful expression of the Franks' identity and cultural affiliations, its orchestration in terms of the movements of the king, even to the extent of recording where he spent the summer, the winter, Christmas and Easter, provides us with an important contemporary comment on the group of people closest to the king. This will be drawn on below.[4] All this contemporary material in its turn fed information to such later descriptions as the sections allegedly based on an account by Adalhard of Corbie of the early Carolingian palace in Hincmar of Reims's *De ordine palatii*, the capitulary concerning discipline in the palace, the *Vita Karoli* of Einhard, Ermold the Black's poem in honour of Louis the Pious, and Notker Balbulus's *Gesta Karoli*. To this contemporary and later ninth-century written evidence can be added the material remains, whether the buildings and artefacts of the palaces associated with Charlemagne, or the coinage produced by his mints.

THE ROYAL HOUSEHOLD: POETIC IMAGES

Let us look first at some of the contemporary descriptions of the royal household. The creation of a vivid and influential image of the royal family and palace officials during the reign of Charlemagne is primarily due to the impressions and reminiscences recorded by poets patronized by Charlemagne. Alcuin, Modoin, Theodulf and Angilbert in particular celebrated the king as cultured, a lover of poetry and devoted to learning, surrounded by the beautiful members of his family. Angilbert's theme in his poetic epistle, for instance, is the love of poetry. He describes some of the king's children – Charles, Rotrud and Bertha – as well as Charlemagne's sister Gisela and a few of the officials of the household, Meginfred the chamberlain, Hildebold the chaplain, Audulf the seneschal, and lastly the *pueri* in the house where Angilbert once lived, as potential lovers of his verse.[5] He described, with an allusion to Matthew 16.18 ('On this rock I will build my church'), how Charlemagne first had the church at Aachen built. Alcuin's poetic epistle concentrated more on praise of Charlemagne, with a hyperbolic account of a hierarchy of groups serving the king, from the priests and deacons of the chapel, led by 'Jesse', whose

---

[4] Below, pp. 162–71, and see McKitterick, *History and memory*, esp. pp. 84–155.
[5] *MGH Poet.* 1, pp. 360–3.

bull-like voice resounds in the chapel, 'Sulpicius' the reader, and 'Idithun' the cantor, to the boys trained by the cantor to sing in the chapel.[6] Theodulf of Orleans also devoted a large portion of his poem on the court to praise of Charlemagne, stressing his fame, his illustrious antecedents, his wisdom, and his role as guardian of treasure, avenger of crimes, dispenser of *honores* and conqueror of Avars, Arabs and nomads. It is Theodulf who mentioned prayers offered in the chapel, and the king's palace where he gives audience to the common people (*plebs*). Theodulf also offered an idealized family portrait, with the king flanked to left and right by his sons Charles and Louis and daughters Bertha, Rotrud and Gisela (called after her aunt), Hruodhaid, Hiltrud and Theodrada, as well as the king's sister (if she should happen to be there). Oddly enough, there is no reference to the queen, which may indicate that this poem should be dated after 800 and the death of Liutgard.[7] Thereafter there is an account of the royal officials, mostly given nicknames: Meginfrid the chamberlain, Bishop Hildebold the archchaplain, Riculf (later archbishop of Mainz), Ercambald the notary, the unidentified 'Lentulus' who brings apples, Einhard, Fridugis, Oswulf, Audulf the steward, Eppinus/Eberhard the cupbearer, Alcuin and Wigbod. Angilbert is mentioned as absent. All these men are depicted at a feast in the palace and listening to a recitation of Theodulf's poem, before the king retires and each man returns home to his own house (*mansio*). Modoin's eclogue, dated 804–10, describes either the king or the palace as the *caput orbis* (head of the world). Modoin goes on to talk of the rebirth and restoration of Rome in this new Rome of the Franks at the palace and of the many kingdoms forged into an empire with its palaces and lofty walls.[8] Two anonymous poems, the so-called Paderborn Epic or *Karolus magnus et Leo papa* of *c.* 800, and the Lament on the death of Charlemagne (after 814), explore this Roman theme in conjunction with Charlemagne still further.[9] The former describes Charlemagne as the father

---

[6] *MGH Poet.* i, pp. 245–6. I share the views of those who think Alcuin's poem *O mea cella* is about York, not Aachen. See C. Newlands, 'Alcuin's poem of exile *O mea cella*', *Mediaevalia* ii (1985), pp. 19–45; and A. Orchard, 'Wish you were here: Alcuin's courtly poetry and the boys back home', in Rees Jones, Marks and Minnis, *Courts and regions in medieval Europe*, pp. 21–44.

[7] *MGH Poet.* i, pp. 483–9. The lack of reference to the queen and the names of the daughters (two of whom are Fastrada's children) suggests that this poem is to be dated after the death of Liutgard (800) but before the death of the king's sister Gisela in 810.

[8] *MGH Poet.* i, pp. 385–6. Compare Virgil's description of Carthage, R. A. B. Mynors, *P. Vergili Maronis Opera* (Oxford, 1969), pp. 116–17.

[9] A strong case has been made for Modoin as the author of the Paderborn epic: see F. Stella, 'Autore e attribuzioni del "Karolus magnus et Leo papa"', in P. Godman, J. Jarnut and P. Johanek (eds.), *Am Vorabend der Kaiserkrönung: das Epos "Karolus magnus et Leo papa" und der Papstbesuch in Paderborn 799* (Berlin, 2002), pp. 19–34.

of Europe and lord of a city where a second Rome flowers anew, the construction of whose palace and church, as well as such Virgilian elements as a theatre, forum, great wall, towers and baths, are described with exaggerated and fanciful detail.[10] The latter laments the death of Charlemagne, mourned by Rome and Francia alike, and buried in the earth at Aachen.[11]

Interpretation of these poems has usually moved somewhat optimistically beyond the hyperbolic descriptions and extravagant praise to envisage a settled court, located at Aachen, with a king surrounded by family, courtiers and officials. Certainly there is a consistent portrayal of the royal family, the chief servants in charge of the domestic affairs of the household, the clerics of the palace chapel, and a place where the king gave audiences to his people. There are also the references to these officials living in separate houses associated with the main palace complex. The dating of the poems, moreover, has usually been guided by assumptions that they all refer to the court at Aachen. Yet the only place actually specified and named in any of these poems is in the anonymous lament. This states that Charlemagne's burial place was indeed at Aachen. All the rest is supposition.

The persistent assumption that all references to the palace or court concern Aachen might well be legitimate. Yet one of many exceptions is the extravagant description of building work in *Karolus magnus et Leo papa*. It is more likely, given the poem's theme of the famous meeting between pope and Frankish ruler at Paderborn, to be inspired by the construction of the palace and church, not at Aachen, but at Paderborn, whose church was consecrated in 799.[12] The passing allusions to people attending banquets, the common people seeking an audience, and officials returning to their homes, scattered among Theodulf's poem, moreover, serve to warn us that this may be a generalized, if not idealized, description of the orchestration of access to the king at one of his residences rather than secure evidence of a settled court at Aachen. Although of crucial importance in relation to the cultural activity promoted by the ruler, therefore, these poems cannot give us much more than a rosy and stylized picture of a court setting; they cannot be read as descriptions of a specific location, let alone of Aachen.

---

[10] *Carolus magnus et Leo papa*, *MGH Poet.* 1, pp. 366–79, and ed. H. Beumann, F. Brunhölzl and W. Winkelmann, *Karolus magnus et Leo papa: ein Paderborner Epos vom Jahre 799* (Paderborn, 1966); D. Schaller, 'Das Aachener Epos für Karl den Kaiser', *Frühmittelalterliche Studien* 10 (1976), pp. 134–68, makes the case for Einhard as author. See also D. Schaller, *Studien zur lateinischen Dichtung des Frühmittelalters* (Stuttgart, 1995); and C. Ratkowitsch, *Karolus magnus: Alter Aeneas, Alter Martinus, Alter Justinus. Zur Intention und Datierung des Aachener Karlsepos* (Vienna, 1997).

[11] *MGH Poet.* 1, pp. 435–6.   [12] See below on the palace and church at Paderborn, pp. 165–6.

Let us pursue this court setting, comprising the family, officials of the household, the chapel and its staff, before considering specific locations and their implications. Here the evidence provided by the texts which describe the court of Charlemagne from a distance of years and/or geography may be more helpful. Despite the difficulties of charting the precise dissemination of the various categories of sources, their information is derived from a mixture of personal and second-hand memories, the contemporary written material, including the poetry, letters and legislative material emanating from the court, and creative imagination. The most influential of these, at least for modern, if not also for the Franks' own, understanding of the structure and function of the court, is the account of the royal household claimed to be based on a description by Adalhard of Corbie, of the early Carolingian palace in Hincmar of Reims's *De ordine palatii*.

THE ROYAL HOUSEHOLD: THE *DE ORDINE PALATII* OF HINCMAR OF REIMS

The *De ordine palatii* was presented by Hincmar, archbishop of Reims (845–82) to the young King Carloman of the west Franks, in 882.[13] Hincmar claimed that part of his text was derived from an earlier account of the palace by Adalhard of Corbie. Part I of the text (chapters 1–11) has been understood as a text within the genre of the mirrors for princes, for it sets out fundamental precepts for Christian kingship.[14] The second part (chapters 13–35) discussed the administration of the palace and of the kingdom. Hincmar/Adalhard described the residents of the palace, who

---

[13] Hincmar of Reims, *De ordine palatii*, ed. T. Gross and R. Schieffer, *Hinkmar von Reims, De ordine palatii*, *MGH Fontes* 3 (Hanover, 1980). This edition takes account of the sixteenth-century Basle manuscript, containing various works by Hincmar, Basle, Universitätsbibliothek O.II.29, discovered by Karl Christ in 1930, and the work Ernst Perels did on it thereafter in relation to the edition Johannes Busaeus made from a now lost Speier manuscript (burnt in the 1689 fire in Speier's cathedral library): *Hincmari Rhemensis archiepiscopi ... Epistolae, cum coniecturis notisque brevibus Joannis Busaei Noviomagi* (Mainz, 1602), pp. 16–42. Maurice Prou's edition and commentary, Hincmar, *De ordine palatii: texte Latin, traduit et annoté* (Paris, 1884), but published in Bibliothèque de l'école des hautes études 58 (Paris, 1885), although based only on the Busaeus edition, is still of value, for Prou anticipated many of the conclusions and issues others have discussed since. See also J. Fleckenstein, 'Die Struktur des Hofes Karls des Großen im Spiegel von Hincmars De ordine palatii', in Fleckenstein, *Ordnungen und formende Kräfte des Mittelalters: Ausgewählte Beiträge* (Göttingen, 1989), pp. 1–27; and W. Rösener, 'Königshof und Herrschaftsraum: Norm und Praxis der Hof- und Reichsverwaltung im Karolingerreich', in *Uomo e spazio nell'alto medioevo*, Settimane 50 (Spoleto, 2003), pp. 443–79.

[14] H. H. Anton, *Fürstenspiegel und Herrscherethos in der Karolingerzeit*, Bonner Historische Forschungen 32 (Bonn, 1968).

included the king, queen and royal family. The leading person at court was the chaplain, described as usually a bishop licensed to be absent from his see by the pope and who acted as adviser to the king and head of the palace chapel. He had all the clergy of the palace under his supervision. In relation to the royal household, Hincmar/Adalhard included definitions of the role of the officials within the sacred palace (*sacrum palatium*) (c. 16), especially of the chaplain and chancellor, and an account of the process by which one gained access to royal justice, if not to the king himself. Thus Hincmar/ Adalhard stressed that it was the count of the palace who settled disputes which, although rising elsewhere, were brought to the palace for equitable decisions.[15] The author also insisted that the strength of the realm with regard to the matters both great and small that occurred daily rested upon the other officers 'whenever they were gathered at the palace'.[16] In a later chapter he explained that the purpose of all these arrangements was that 'officials of sufficient number and type ... should never be missing from the palace; at all times the palace was to be adorned with worthy council-lors', not least so that legations could be properly received.[17] Attention was also given to the selection of officials. They were to come from different regions in order to facilitate access to the palace, for the people 'recognized that members of their own families or inhabitants of their own region had a place in the palace'.[18] The palace was credited with a clear hierarchy, determined in part by degrees of access to the king, and with the queen and the chamberlain in charge of the internal economy.[19]

The emphasis of the remaining chapters, from chapter 29 onwards, is on the maintenance of order in the kingdom. Here the communication with those in the far-flung regions of the kingdom, orchestrated by the palace officials so prominent in the earlier chapters, is complemented by the discussions at the assemblies, held in the open air in good weather but otherwise with those attending divided up into smaller groups indoors. The process for the consideration of the king's agenda, with messengers going back and forth between the king and the *proceres* who discuss the capitularies, is described in considerable detail, as is the king's wish for news and use of the assemblies both to receive and to broadcast it.[20] Even at the assemblies, access to the ruler was carefully controlled, for the palace officials who accompanied the king would determine if the matter ought to be brought to the king and would arrange to give someone the opportunity

---

[15] Hincmar, *De ordine palatii*, c. 21, ed. Gross and Schieffer, *Hinkmar*, pp. 70–2.
[16] Ibid., c. 17, p. 66.   [17] Ibid., c. 25, p. 78.   [18] Ibid. c. 18, p. 66.
[19] Ibid., cc. 19, and 22, pp. 68, 72–4.   [20] Ibid., cc. 34–6, pp. 90–6.

of speaking. Hincmar/Adalhard also claimed that there were two assemblies each year, one more general and the other restricted to the leading magnates.

Apart from the assemblies, the indications of the king's movements within his kingdom are limited first of all to the description of the duties of the *mansionarius* (master of the lodgings) who informed all local officials of the times, places and seasons of the king's arrival.[21] If local officials learned of this (i.e. the king's coming) too late and performed their duties at an unpropitious time or with excessive haste, the royal party might have been unnecessarily inconvenienced by such negligence. Further, as well as informing local officials, the seneschal had to tell the *susceptores* so that they would know at a suitable time and well in advance when and in what place the king would arrive among them, in order that they might prepare the lodgings.

Because Hincmar claims that he had read and copied a work about the palace (*Cuius libellum de ordine palatii legi et scripsi*) actually written by Adalhard, Charlemagne's cousin and abbot of Corbie from *c.* 815 to 826, this part of Hincmar's text has been optimistically regarded as a description of the early Carolingian court in the reign of Charlemagne.[22] Hincmar uses the word *libellus*, often used as a technical term in Frankish sources in association with admonition and with normative texts, and this may indicate that Adalhard's original should be counted as such.[23] Determining the possible content of Adalhard's original text and what Hincmar may have added has proven so far to be inconclusive. That some of the phrasing in the text as it stands may indeed be Adalhard's, and thus that Hincmar's claim to have used an earlier work can be believed, was persuasively argued by Schmidt, who used Adalhard's Statutes for Corbie for comparison.[24] That is, there are a sufficient number of stylistic reminiscences of Adalhard's phrasing in the Corbie Statutes recurring in the *De ordine palatii* to encourage confidence in Hincmar's claim that the text by Adalhard had indeed once existed, however much Hincmar may have adapted it to his own purpose and used it to enhance his own views. In addition, at particular points in the text which discuss the day-to-day

[21] Ibid., c. 23, p. 76.
[22] Ibid., c. 12, p. 54. On Adalhard, see B. Kasten, *Adalhard von Corbie: die Biographie eines karolingischen Politikers und Klostervorstehers*, Studia humaniora 3 (Düsseldorf. 1986), pp. 42–84, esp. 72–84; see also P. Depreux, *Prosopographie*, pp. 76–9.
[23] I owe this point to Mayke de Jong.
[24] J. Schmidt, *Hinkmars 'De ordine palatii' und seine Quellen* (Frankfurt am Main, 1962), esp. pp. 24–6 and 34–41; and see L. Levillain, 'Les statuts d'Adlahard pour l'abbaye de Corbie', *Le Moyen Age* 13 (1900), pp. 233–386; and Gross and Schieffer, *Hinkmar*, p. 11.

practical details of administrative structure and methods, there is a striking similarity between chapters 13–35 of the *De ordine palatii* and the Statutes of Adalhard, but an equally striking lack of consonance with other writings by Hincmar. Chapters 17 and 35 discuss the rationale for the division of labour among the officials, even those of the higher ranks, and for the varying degrees of access to the king. In chapter 18, as we have seen, the account of the selection of officials stresses the importance of their being drawn from the different regions of the realm and why this is politically advantageous. Yet when Hincmar speaks elsewhere about the selection of officials he simply emphasizes their moral qualities, though these are seen as an essential consideration for the carrying out of public duties.[25]

Nevertheless, the degree to which Hincmar may have offered Adalhard's text with few changes as an inspiring example from a past golden age remains uncertain. Alternatively, he may have energetically updated the text in order to provide real, practical, if idealized, guidance for what a king should strive to make the palace administration achieve at the end of the ninth century. The description of the royal household and government is presented in the imperfect tense. This enhances its character as inspiration from the past. Although the organization of the royal household is presented as an admirable and smooth-running system, the information in chapters 13–35 is also largely practical rather than exhortatory and admonitory and might be thought to be the work of a man still very much engaged in political and public affairs. The details of the particular offices, their principal duties, and how the system as a whole was supposed to work are offered as if they together constituted a model to follow and thus remained pertinent.

In order to assess how closely the *De ordine palatii* might reflect the organization of the palace in the reign of Charlemagne, a complementary approach to the text is to consider the likely degree of stability of the court over a long period in terms of its internal structure and the functions of the palace officials. That is, how much might really have changed in the organization of the Frankish royal household between the late eighth and the late ninth century?

It is not possible to answer this precisely, however one might want to do so. What appears logical in this respect is not to be given the same credence as what is actually attested in the contemporary evidence. That is, even without the claim to have used a portion of an older treatise by Adalhard, it is wishful thinking to suppose that Hincmar's text in itself could be regarded as reflecting the essentially unchanging structure of the Carolingian royal

---

[25] Schmidt, *Hinkmars Quellen*, p. 35; and see above p. 143.

household, its role in the government of the realm, and some of the principles upon which it rested, and thus be applicable to the reign of Charlemagne. An analogy might be the relative stability of the organization of a monastery, especially if it followed a known Rule such as the *Regula sancti Benedicti*, but even here, knowledge of the variable practice among Carolingian monasteries claiming to follow the Rule should make one wary of too uncritical an acceptance of such a proposition except in general terms.

It would perhaps be possible to envisage the *De ordine palatii* nevertheless as an idealized description of an institution that can be labelled the Carolingian royal palace and which drew on Hincmar's own knowledge of the structures and practices of the household and the government of the kingdoms between 840 and 882. It may well be the most reasonable approach. Even so, the acceptance of the *De ordine palatii* as Adalhard's description of the royal court of Charlemagne requires further justification and it is still necessary to consider whether the text could reflect the court of Charlemagne at a certain stage of its development.

Reliance on the practical details provided by Adalhard may not be possible unless the officials and their duties itemized can be corroborated from sources dating from the reign of Charlemagne. This is particularly crucial in relation to the indications in the text about the itinerancy of the king,[26] the role of the palace as a point of convergence for both the providers of justice and those seeking it, and as a centre of communication, and the role of the officials as agents of the king. What needs to be done, therefore, is to take the different elements from this account and compare them with other sources from the period of Charlemagne's rule. Such comparison may provide support for the roles extrapolated by modern historians from Adalhard/Hincmar's description.

Analysis both of the possible Hincmarian additions and of elements of the text that can be corroborated in other early Carolingian sources, however, pulls in opposite directions. One example is the account of the *apocrisiarius* or chaplain and head of the palace chapel (cc. 13–16). *Apocrisiarius* is a word that Löwe argued was not associated with the chaplain until *c*. 860, even though Hincmar himself notes that Pope Gregory had performed this office in Constantinople in the sixth century.[27]

[26] F. L. Ganshof, 'Charlemagne et les institutions de la monarchie franque', *KdG* I, pp. 349–93 at pp. 361–3, with the unequivocal statements that the court was itinerant and Charlemagne was an itinerant ruler.

[27] H. Löwe, 'Hincmar von Reims und der Apocrisiar: Beiträge zur Interpretation von De ordine palatii', in Die Mitarbeiter des Max-Planck-Instituts für Geschichte (eds.), *Festschrift für Hermann Heimpel zum 70. Geburtstag am 19. Sept. 1971* (Göttingen, 1972), pp. 197–225.

On the one hand, the use of the term, the partly fanciful historical development of the office from the late antique Roman court and the papal relationship with Constantine, the claim that the office had existed in the Frankish kingdoms since the time of Clovis, and the examples provided of 'licit and illicit practice' by those who had held the office under Pippin, Charlemagne and Louis the Pious, from Fulrad to Drogo, have been judged to be Hincmar's additions. He notes that the office of chaplain was held successively by Fulrad at the time of Pippin and Charlemagne, by Angilram and Hildebold in the time of Charlemagne, and by Hilduin, Fulco and Drogo in the time of Louis the Pious. Not only is some of this information available only after Adalhard's death, but other aspects, notably the reference to Clovis, have direct parallels in other work by Hincmar, such as his *Vita sancti Remigii*.[28] The history of the post of *apocrisiarius* thus reflects Hincmar's interpretation of the position of chaplain from the vantage point of the later ninth century and after it had changed in emphasis. The presentation of the Frankish rulers as emulators of Constantine in the presence of the *apocrisiarius* at the palace is nevertheless certainly consonant with other tendencies on the part of the Franks to see themselves as heirs to a past that included Constantine, the early church and the popes. Thus Hincmar could here be reflecting a much wider and longer-term understanding of the special relationship of the Franks with the early church.[29]

The office of chaplain at the Frankish royal court, on the other hand, undoubtedly existed. It was indeed much the same as that described under the heading of *apocrisiarius*. The particular permission for the holder of this Frankish office to be absent from his diocese appears to have been required as a consequence of the provision enunciated at the Council of Sardica (347), c. 11: that a bishop should not be absent from his diocese for longer than three weeks. This was renewed by Pope Eugenius II on 15 November 826. It would also appear to have been behind the specific reference at Frankfurt in 794 to papal permission for the replacement of Bishop Angilram of Metz with Bishop Hildebald of Cologne permanently at Charlemagne's palace in order to oversee ecclesiastical affairs.[30] There is a striking insistence on the canonical and legal background and on the consent of the other bishops to this arrangement both in the *De ordine*

---

[28] See the commentary in Prou (ed.), Hincmar, *De ordine palatii*, esp. pp. 40–1; Gross and Schieffer, *Hinkmar*, pp. 58–59 and Schmidt, *Hinkmars Quellen*.

[29] McKitterick, *History and memory*, pp. 218–64.

[30] *Concilium Francofurtense* 794, c. 55, *MGH Conc.* II.i, p. 171. See aslo O.-G. Oexle, 'Die Karolinger und die Stadt des heiligen Arnulf', *Frühmittelalterliche Studien* 1 (1967), pp. 249–364.

palatii and in the 794 Council of Frankfurt. Thus the case for the relevance of the description of the palace administration in the text to conditions in the reign of Charlemagne gains in strength.

Apart from the use of the word *apocrisiarius*, a *capellanus* at the palace is attested as early as 742/3[31] and also in a diploma of Carloman, dated 769, referring to Fulrad as *Folradus capellanus palacii nostri*.[32] Other individuals are also accorded the title *capellanus*.[33] Similarly, of the other officials discussed in some detail in the *De ordine palatii*, even a cursory look at charters and capitularies of the late eighth and the early ninth centuries indicates that the titles *camerarius, comes palatii, senescalcus, buticularius* and *comes stabuli* there used each bear a similar meaning in terms of function or duties to those mentioned in the *De ordine palatii*.[34] The *mansionarius* (master of the lodgings) is slightly less secure. He is first mentioned in texts linked to the early years of Louis's reign, namely the capitulary on the discipline of the palace, but there are closely associated words in other capitularies.[35] For some of the under-officials mentioned in the *De ordine palatii* – the *ostiarius* (porter), *sacellarius* (treasurer) *dispensator* (alms distributor) – there is again sufficient usage in other texts from Charlemagne's reign to indicate that these are not offices of later ninth-century origin. The word *scapoardus* (keeper of the vessels) has been claimed as a distinctively germanic and Lombard word that has been Latinized, attested otherwise in the Lombard laws and a charter of 771. Some of the lesser officials, such as *bersarii* (wardens of the forest), *veltrarii* (keepers of the kennels) and *bevarii* (hunters of beavers) are apparently to be found only in the *De ordine palatii*. The *Lex Salica* has a penalty for the theft of the dogs, and they are highly regarded in the earlier *Lex Burgundionum*, still being copied in the Carolingian period, so to posit a master of the hunting dogs at the palace is entirely feasible.[36] The description of the palace as a *sacrum palatium*, moreover, deploys a term found as early as the middle of the eighth century in Lombard sources,[37] though by Hincmar's day this phrase was probably standard.[38]

---

[31] *Concilium germanicum* 742/3, c. 2, *MGH Conc.* II.i, p. 3.   [32] *DKar.* I, No. 43, p. 62.

[33] Fleckenstein, *Die Hofkapelle*, I, pp. 28–43.

[34] J. F. Niermeyer, *Mediae latinitatis lexicon minus* (Leiden, 1954–76), provides ample instances of contemporary use of these words.

[35] Ibid., and see, for example, *MGH Cap.* I, p. 298, line 12.

[36] *Pactus legis salicae*, 6, 1–4, ed. K. A. Eckhardt, *MGH Leges* nat. germ. IV, I (Hanover, 1962), pp. 35–8.

[37] D. Bullough, 'Baiuli in the Carolingian *regnum langobardorum* and the career of Abbot Waldo', *English Historical Review* 77 (1962), pp. 625–37.

[38] M. de Jong, 'Sacrum palatium et ecclesia: l'autorité religieuse royale sous les carolingiens (790–840)', *Annales* 58 (2003), pp. 1243–69.

THE *CAPITULARE DE VILLIS* AND THE *DE ORDINE PALATII*

The most decisive comparable description of royal administrative structures of direct relevance to the court, famous in relation to the *servitium regis*[39] but not hitherto considered in relation to the *De ordine palatii*, as distinct from in relation to the palace administration,[40] is the famous *Capitulare de villis* of the late eighth century. It is extant in a single manuscript, Wolfenbüttel, Herzog August Bibliothek Helmstedt. 254, dated 825–30, and of disputed origin (variously claimed for Fulda or the Rhineland (? Cologne), containing a group of texts associated with the royal court.[41] This long and detailed account of how the royal estates for the king's own use are to be managed provides an impressive complement to the outline of the royal household given in the *De ordine palatii*. The *Capitulare de villis* makes a series of very specific provisions about the estates established to minister to the king's needs. The wealth of detail about every aspect of the estates' agricultural, craft and industrial activity, and about the men and women working on each estate, has been exhaustively discussed in relation to the Carolingian economy, but there are some aspects that merit highlighting in relation to the royal household and the palace. The sheer wealth implied is immense, but how it is to serve the king in his palaces is also indicated. In clause 15, for example, Charlemagne refers to the need to have the foals sent to the winter palace at the feast of St Martin.[42] The clause concerning the queen's key role in the household completely corroborates the account of the queen's role in the *De ordine palatii*.[43] There are injunctions about the failure of any subordinates (*iuniores*) of the *iudex* in charge of the estates when the *iudex* himself is serving the king elsewhere (in the army, on guard duty, on a mission or away elsewhere: *in exercitu, aut in wacta, seu in ambasciato vel alibi fuerit*.[44] Every *iudex* is to see that the produce is brought to the court in plentiful

---

[39] W. Metz, 'Quellenstudien zum *servicium regis* (900–1250)', *Archiv für Diplomatik* 22, 24, 31, 38 (1976, 1978, 1985, 1992), pp. 187–271, 203–91, 273–326, 17–68, and Metz, *Das karolingische Reichsgut* (Berlin, 1960). See also C. Brühl (ed.), *Capitulare de villis: Cod. Guelf. 254 Helmst. Der Herzog August Bibliothek Wolfenbüttel*, Dokumente zur deutschen Geschichte in Faksimile, Reihe 1: *Mittelalter*, Bd. 1 (Stuttgart, 1971); and K. Gareis (ed.), *Die Landgüterordnung Kaiser Karls des Großen (Capitulare de villis vel curtis imperii): Text-Ausgabe mit Einleitung und Anmerkungen* (Berlin, 1895). See also the phrase-by-phrase commentary in B. Fois Ennas, *Il Capitulare de villis* (Milan, 1981).

[40] See Rösener, 'Königshof und Herrschaftsraum'.

[41] Mordek, *Bibliotheca*, pp. 946–9; and *MGH Cap.* 1, No. 32, pp. 82–91.

[42] Ibid., p. 84: 'Ut poledros nostros missa sancti Martini hiemale ad palatium omnimodis habeant.'

[43] Ibid., c. 16, p. 84, and compare *De ordine palatii*, cc. 13, 19, 22, ed. Gross and Schieffer, *Hinkmar*, pp. 56, 68, 72–4.

[44] *Capitulare de villis*, c. 16 *MGH Cap.* 1, p. 84

supply three or four times a year.[45] The reason for the use of the word *iudex* becomes clear in later sections of the capitulary, for they are responsible for law and order as well as the administration of justice.[46] This too constitutes a supplement to the functions of the count of the palace responsible for the administration of justice described in the *De ordine palatii*,[47] and corroborated by extant charters recording the settlement of disputes, such as those from Düren 775, Thionville, *c.* 782, and Aachen in 812, involving the counts of the palace Anselm, Worad and Amalric respectively.[48]

There are also, of course, ample parallels with other capitularies of Charlemagne concerning the administration of justice, such as the *Capitulare missorum item speciale* c. 48 (802) and the *Capitulare de iustitiis faciendis* (811–13).[49] There is a similar emphasis on the need for communication and dissemination of information in writing and by oral means with the references to the letters containing instructions sent from the queen and king, and concerning the need for the king to be informed in writing about the estates, their revenues and their produce – from vegetables, grain, wine, fish and meat to the shoes, saddles, weapons and tools produced by the leatherworkers, carpenters and smiths for royal use. All this information is to be recorded and sent each year at Christmas to the king so that he might know 'what and how much of each thing [he had] on each of [his] estates'.[50] That these estates are exclusively for royal use is indicated by the clause forbidding the king's *missi* and their retinues on their way to or from the palace, unless on the orders of the king or queen, to lodge in the royal *villae*, for it is the counts who are to continue to supply the *missi* with what they need, as they have done in the past.[51] There are also specific

[45] Ibid., c. 20, p. 84, 'Unusquisque iudex fructa semper habundanter faciat omni anno ad curtem venire, excepto visitationes eorum per vices tres aut quattuor seu amplius dirigant.'
[46] Ibid., cc. 4, 29, 52, 53 and 56, pp. 83, 85 and 88: for example (c. 56), 'Ut unusquisque iudex in eorum ministerio frequentius audientias teneat et iustitiam faciat et praevideat qualiter recte familiae nostrae vivant' (*iudex* is misleadingly translated as 'steward' in the English version by Loyn and Perceval, though this of course may have been one of the functions of the official concerned).
[47] *De ordine palatii*, c. 21, ed. Gross and Schieffer, *Hinkmar*, pp. 70–2.
[48] *DKar.* I, Nos 102, 148, and 216, pp. 146–7, 200–2, 288–9.
[49] *Capitulare missorum item speciale* c. 48 (802) and the *Capitulare de iustitiis faciendis* (811–13), *MGH Cap.* I, Nos. 35 and 80, pp. 104 and 176–7.
[50] Ibid. cc. 47, 55, 62, pp. 87, 88 and 89: c. 47: 'secundum quod nos aut regina per litteras nostras iusserimus; in uno breve conscribi faciant ... nobis per brevem innotescant'; c. 62: 'omnia seposita, distincta et ordinata ad nativitatem Domini nobis notum faciant, ut scire valeamus quid vel quantum de singulis rebus habeamus'. Compare *De ordine palatii*, cc. 34–6, ed. Gross and Schieffer, *Hinkmar*, pp. 90–6.
[51] Ibid., c. 27, p. 85: 'Et quando missi vel legatio ad palatium veniunt vel redeunt, nullo modo in curtes dominicas mansionaticas prendant, nisi specialiter iussio nostra aut reginae fuerit ... Et comes de suo ministerio vel homines illi qui antiquitus consueti fuerunt missos aut legationes soniare ...'

instances of similar terminology in the *Capitulare de villis* and the *De ordine palatii*, such as the offices of the hunters and the falconers (*venatores* and *falconarii*) and the use of *mansionaticus* with reference to lodgings.[52] The way in which each royal *villa* is to be fully equipped with beds, bedding, tableware, kitchen pots and utensils and tools (much as the second or holiday houses of some people nowadays), so that nothing need be borrowed and everything can be ready, accords with the indications in the *De ordine palatii* about the duties of the *mansionarius* and the reception of the king on his travels.[53] Fish was to be sold when the king did not visit his estates.[54] It is clear too, that such journeys are closely associated with the movements of the king on his military campaigns. Reference is made to the produce and tools to be loaded on the carts needed for the army, as well as that sent to the palace, and the records to be made of what was sent.[55]

There are thus a sufficient number of parallels and echoes of the structures described by Hincmar/Adalhard in capitularies from the end of the eighth century and the early ninth century to indicate that the *De ordine palatii* can be accepted as a plausible representation of the Carolingian court as early as the reign of Charlemagne. It may even be appropriate to think of the capitularies providing the information or inspiration for the composition of the various paragraphs of the *De ordine palatii* dealing with officials and their duties. As will be seen below, moreover, contemporary charters from the late eighth and early ninth centuries corroborate the role in hearing disputes ascribed to the count of the palace.[56]

Yet the precise date at which Adalhard might have written this, whether it can be understood as a description of Charlemagne's royal household at the beginning or end of his reign, and the possible political context in

---

[52] *Capitulare de villis*, cc. 11 and 47, *MGH Cap.* 1, pp. 84 and 87, and compare c. 36, ibid., p. 86, on the woods and forests being well stocked for royal hunts.

[53] *Capitulare de villis*, c. 42, *MGH Cap.* 1, p. 87: 'Et unaquaeque villa . . . ita ut non sit necesse aliubi hoc quaerere aut commodare.'

[54] *Capitulare de villis*, c. 65, *MGH Cap.* 1, p. 89: 'quando nos in villas non venimus' and compare *De ordine palatii*, c. 23, ed. Gross and Schieffer, *Hinkmar*, p. 76.

[55] *Capitulare de villis*, c. 64, *MGH Cap.* 1, no. 30, p. 85: 'ex omni conlaboratu eorum servitium segregare faciant, et unde carra in hostem carigare debent . . . et sciant quantum ad hoc mittunt'; c. 64, p. 89, and c. 68, p. 89, on the good barrels bound with iron which can be sent to the army or to the palace: 'quos in hostem et ad palatium mittere possint'; see also c. 42, ibid., p. 87, on the iron tools which they provide for the army, the *iudices* are to see that they are good, and when they are returned they are put back in the storeroom: 'Et ferramenta quod in hostem ducunt . . . et iterum quando revertuntur in camera mittantur.'

[56] See below, pp. 210–11.

which the original work by Adalhard may have been written, also need to be considered.[57]

It has been suggested that the original production of Adalhard's description might have been prepared either in relation to the establishment of the new court for Pippin in Italy in 781, when Adalhard was part of the little team of Frankish officials appointed by Charlemagne to rule during Pippin's minority, or between 810 and 814, when Adalhard played a similar role for Pippin's son Bernard.[58] The brief appointment of Adalhard as regent in Italy for the young Bernard has hitherto been preferred as a possible date and context for Adalhard's original text, though for no very good reason except in accord with Brühl's doubts about how seriously to take the single surviving reference to Adalhard's having been prominent in Pippin of Italy's entourage.[59] It has to be said that the record for Adalhard's acting as regent for Bernard is even more meagre.[60] Because Paschasius does not mention Adalhard's regency for Bernard, Brühl thought he got muddled between the two. Certainly Adalhard appears to have shared the duties of supporting the young Pippin with Abbot Waldo of Reichenau and St Denis, the *dux* Rotchild (*baiulus* to the young king)[61] and Angilbert of St Riquier, who headed the palace chapel, so to assign him a specific post as regent is inappropriate.[62] Time in Italy at the former court of the Lombard king might well account nevertheless for some of the details included in Adalhard's treatise. Nelson has offered an attractive hypothesis supporting the later date (while dismissing the earlier date without discussion), but her suggestion concerning the status of Cunigund's marriage and need for a legitimate heir remains insufficient to take account of the particular needs of the 780s as outlined above.[63]

[57] The alleged title of Adalhard's work reported by Freher, which led Schmidt, *Hinkmars Quellen*, pp. 22–3, to date the text post-814, seems very dubious. For one thing, both Pippin and Charlemagne are described as *imperatores*. For another, Schmidt's focus, and that of subsequent scholars, was more on the implications of the completed text for Hincmar's political ideology than on the possible political context within which Adalhard might himself have been prompted to compose his text.

[58] Kasten, *Adalhard von Corbie*, pp. 72–84.

[59] Paschasius Radbertus, *Vita Adalhardi*, c. 14, *MGH SS* 2, p. 252.

[60] *Translatio sancti Viti martyris*, c. 3, ed. I. Schmale-Ott, Veröffentlichungen der Historischen Kommission für Westfalen, Reihe 41, Fontes minores 1 (Münster, 1979), p. 38: 'Factum est autem, postquam praefatus puer (Bernhard) crevit accepit (Adalhard) ei uxorem et constituit [eum] secundum iussionem principis (Charlemagne) super omne regnum'.

[61] E. Munding, *Abt-Bischof Waldo*, Texte und Arbeiten 1, Heft 10/11 (Beuron and Leipzig, 1924); and Bullough, '*Baiuli*'.

[62] See the full discussion by Kasten, *Adalhard von Corbie*, pp. 42–72.

[63] Nelson, 'Aachen as a place of power', in De Jong, Theuws and van Rhijn (eds.), *Topographies of power*; and see above, pp. 113–14.

Thanks to the Astronomer's account of Louis's early career, we know a little about the arrangements made by Charlemagne for Louis the Pious in Aquitaine. These, as well as the organization of Charlemagne's own administration, may provide an appropriate general context in which to place Adalhard's account of the palace. That is, Adalhard's original text could have been intended to serve as a guide or even a blueprint for the establishment of an essentially new institution or series of institutions within the Frankish realm, and one, moreover, that had to exist within a system of orchestrated communication between the court and the regions.[64] The Astronomer described how Charlemagne consolidated his father Pippin III's conquests by setting up counts and abbots throughout Aquitaine, 'and many others too who are commonly called vassals ... He committed the care of the kingdom to them as far as he judged beneficial, likewise the safety of the frontiers and the revenues of the royal country estates'. When Louis was established as king in Aquitaine several years later, Charlemagne 'assigned Louis Arnold as a *baiulus* (tutor) and he set up in orderly and fitting fashion other officers suited to the safeguarding of the boy'. Elsewhere the Astronomer referred to the magnates 'by whose advice the realm of Aquitaine was administered' and reported that King Louis in that same year held his general assembly in Toulouse. In relation to the common assumption about the economic need for the king to be constantly on the move, the Astronomer has suggestive things to say. He claimed that Louis ordained that he should spend the winter in four different palaces – Doué, Chasseneuil, Angeac and Ebreuil – consecutively so that each would take turns in supporting the young king for the winter and thus relieve the common people of the burden of the military expenses commonly called *fodrum*. For local officials this clearly meant a loss of revenue. The Astronomer added the comment that the measure angered the military men. Nevertheless, he reported:

This man of mercy (Louis) thought about the poverty of those who had to pay and the harshness of those who demanded payment, and the losses suffered by each. Louis judged it enough to support his men from his own resources rather than exposing his men to dangers by permitting them to forage for their supplies ... These actions are said to have been so pleasing to his father the king (that is, Charlemagne) that in imitation he (Charlemagne) forbade the payment as tribute of military fodder in Francia.[65]

---

[64] See below, pp. 215–22.
[65] Astronomer, *Vita Hludovici Pii*, c. 7, ed. E. Tremp, *MGH SRG* 64, pp. 304–6.

The implication is that Charlemagne too expected to live off his own estates during the winter, though the Astronomer here gives Louis the credit for the idea rather than presenting it as a Frankish royal practice introduced into Aquitaine. The Astronomer's account of Louis's early years in Aquitaine, moreover, gives no hint that his movements were anything more than forays to war and on occasion to join his father. The assemblies recorded appear also to be primarily for military purposes.

The establishment of Frankish methods of rule and a Frankish royal court in the former Lombard kingdoms and in Aquitaine provide pertinent contexts for the initial composition of Adalhard's text, especially if the bare bones of the text were some form of the chapters from 12 to 36 of the existing treatise. Unfortunately very little is known, apart from the information yielded by the Astronomer, about the provision for the courts of sub-kings or for king's sons remaining with their father in the reign of Charlemagne, as distinct from the arrangements subsisting under Louis the Pious after 814.[66] There has been a tendency in consequence to project what is known concerning the period back onto the late eighth and early ninth centuries, as well as to read rather more into the sources than they would warrant. A striking instance is the idea of the king's sons and the queen maintaining independent households and the sons having their own entourages. Much rests again on sources from Louis the Pious's reign; but even in the case of Ermold the Black's description of Charles and Pippin, who come to pray in the church of the palace of Charlemagne, the fact that they are accompanied by their boisterous *proceres* and *comitatus* respectively (and they interrupt the proceedings) does not prove the institutionalized presence of a resident *comitatus*. Ermold, moreover, creates a literary contrast between the hurly-burly of the king's two elder sons and their companions clattering into the church and the reverent and solitary arrival of Louis.[67] Alcuin does give one small indication of a *famulus* of Charles the Younger in mentioning Otulf, who belonged to it.[68] This would confirm at least that Charles had an entourage and servants of his own, though we have no way of establishing how large or how separate from the rest of the royal household such a group might have been. Hincmar's comment on the officials answerable to the king alone or in some instances to the queen and the family will also not bear the weight of a special

[66] B. Kasten, *Königssöhne und Königsherrschaft: Untersuchungen zur Teilhabe am Reich in der Merowinger- und Karolingerzeit*, MGH Schriften 44 (Hanover, 1997), pp. 139–64.

[67] Ermold Nigellus, *In honorem Hludowici Pii*, ed. E. Faral (Paris, 1964), pp. 48–50.

[68] Alcuin, *MGH Epp.* IV, No. 188, pp. 315–6. He is also mentioned in Theodulf's poem on the court, lines 175–9, *MGH Poet.* I, p. 487.

household within the palace. Only in the cases of the establishments of Pippin and Louis in Italy and Aquitaine is there evidence of separate households.

Adalhard, as mediated to us by Hincmar, therefore, gives a firm impression of delegated kingship, and of a central and strongly organized palace which acted as a fixed point to a set of royal officials. He places considerable emphasis on the chapel and the chaplains, especially the archchaplain. He does not seem to be describing an itinerant court, though he is describing a travelling king. This too would fit what we know of 781 far better than 810.[69] The establishment of the new sub-kings in the 780s and the promulgation of the *Capitulare de villis*, the capitularies for the *missi*, and the capitularies concerning the administration of justice, are all part of the same concentrated administrative effort within the Frankish realm in which Charlemagne and his chief advisers were involved. It is within this early Carolingian context that the second part of Hincmar's text belongs.

THE ROYAL HOUSEHOLD IN LATER NARRATIVE ACCOUNTS

The *De ordine palatii* was one of a number of later ninth-century texts whose representation of the court of Charlemagne had their own momentum and ideological messages. All were successively fed by earlier accounts. Einhard's *Vita Karoli*, for example, offered a portrait of the king surrounded by his family, eating and travelling with his sons and daughters, and welcoming many foreigners to his court. He enjoyed the hot springs and, for this reason, so Einhard claims, Charlemagne built his palace at Aachen and lived there during the final years of his life. His sons, nobles and friends were invited to join him in the bath, so that there might be up to a hundred bathing together. The king was constantly alert to the duties of ruling. Yet Einhard's text indicates that the core of Charlemagne's household was quite small. This compact nature of the royal household is, incidentally, corroborated by the capitulary on the discipline of the palace [of Aachen] from early in Louis the Pious's reign, which makes a clear distinction between the palace and the houses (*mansiones*) and estates of the officers, servants, estate managers, traders, bishops, abbots and counts of the town surrounding the palace.[70] Einhard also offered an account of the building work of Charlemagne, with the church of Aachen singled out as the most

---

[69] See above, p. 95.   [70] *MGH Cap.* 1, No. 146, pp. 297–8.

outstanding (along with the wooden bridge over the Rhine at Mainz, unfortunately burnt down soon after completion). He mentioned two palaces Charlemagne began to build, at Ingelheim and at Nijmegen, and his care to repair other churches in his kingdom. He stressed Charlemagne's own observance of the Christian religion in the beautiful church he had built at Aachen. The king attended the chapel morning and evening and was very particular about the conduct of the services, not just as far as the vessels and vestments are concerned but also regarding the way in which the lessons were read and the psalms sung.[71] Such concern is reflected too in Charlemagne's will, preserved by Einhard, for there the chapel's endowment, and its property in terms of books, vessels and other objects he had given, were not to be divided up.[72]

Einhard's *Vita* at least, as has been mentioned earlier, was disseminated widely throughout the Frankish kingdom, and such authors as Notker Balbulus had access to it. Notker contrived to add a host of well-turned anecdotes about how he thought the court worked, with a hierarchy of officials to be confronted one after the other before any visitor was finally admitted to the royal presence. When a party of Greek envoys at last met the king, for example, they found him surrounded by his family, abbots, bishops and warriors in an idealized representation of the support offered the king within his kingdom. Notker also portrayed the physical court, and often specifically referred to it as located at Aachen, as a complex of buildings to receive the bishops, abbots, counts and all those who flocked to the court from all over the world. He discussed the number of churches built by Charlemagne, both those belonging to the royal domain and new churches, not least the *basilica* of Aachen itself.[73] He, too, stressed the king's keen interest in his chapel and the liturgy and music performed there. Notker included other anecdotes about the building of his cathedral, 'finer than the ancient buildings of the Romans', which may be a reference either to the chapel at Aachen or to one of the other new cathedrals such as Paderborn. Other anecdotes contain incidental references to Charlemagne's attendance at the services in the chapel or the offices performed there, particularly the early morning lauds attended by the king. Notker commented, indeed, that such was the king's interest that

[71] Einhard, *Vita Karoli*, cc. 17 and 26, ed. Halphen, pp. 50, 52, 76, 78.
[72] Einhard, *Vita Karoli*, c. 33, ed. Halphen, p. 98.
[73] Notker, *Gesta Karoli*, cc. 30–1, ed. H. H. Haefele, *MGH SRG* NS 12 (Berlin, 1959), pp. 40–1, but see also references to the baths, pp. 44, 80; to the church, pp. 38, 41, 59, 60; and to the palace, pp. 19, 38, 41, 44, 59, 70 and 92.

'no new arrival dared to join the emperor's choir unless he could read and chant'.[74]

The tendency of these later ninth-century texts was to amalgamate features of the courts of a number of Carolingian kings, though most of these texts agree on the central importance of the palace chapel and the Christian liturgy in it. Yet what is missing from both these and modern scholars' discussions of the court is a sense of change or development and how many of the characteristics of court life were indeed present at the beginning, in the middle, or by the end of the reign of Charlemagne. Both the recognition of the role of the chapel and this wisdom of hindsight or back projection are particularly important when considering the material evidence for the Carolingian royal court in the light of the archaeology and architectural history of the palaces, not least the considerable prominence that has been accorded to Aachen in modern scholarship.

CHARLEMAGNE'S PALACES AND THE STATUS OF AACHEN

Aachen may well represent an attempt to establish a centre for the Carolingian empire and was certainly a statement of royal wealth and status. Even so, the modern perception of Aachen, inevitably composite and impressed by the magnificence of the surviving chapel buildings within the area of modern Aachen's market, the excavated archaeological layers, and the series of allusions and descriptions from throughout the late eighth and the ninth centuries, has possibly exaggerated its political centrality within Charlemagne's empire, at least for the first three-quarters of his reign. Even then, much of the area seems to have been a building site, with construction continuing into the first two decades of the ninth century. Although Aachen's strategic position, on the spur of the Roman road between Cologne and Maastricht and close (a day's walk) to the Meuse River and water transport, was long ago emphasized by Flach,[75] it still does not seem either geographically or topographically an obvious place to establish a principal residence, let alone a capital. There has also been a considerable amount of circular argument, with architecture and archaeo-logical remains being interpreted in the light of the poetry and the narrative

---

[74] Notker, I, cc. 4, 5, 7 (from which the quotation is taken), 11, 19, 31, 32, 33; II, cc. 7, 8, ed. Haefele, pp. 5–10, 16, 25, 42–6, 58–62. See also below, pp. 340–5.
[75] D. Flach, *Untersuchungen zur Verfassung und Verwaltung des Aachener Reichsgutes von der Karolingerzeit bis zur Mitte des 14. Jahrhunderts*, Veröffentlichungen des Max-Planck-Instituts für Geschichte 46 (Göttingen, 1976).

sources discussed above. These in their turn have sometimes been read as corroboration of the physical structures.

Certainly Charlemagne was buried in the church at Aachen,[76] and he crowned his son Louis the Pious there in 813. Louis was crowned again (together with his wife Ermingard) by Pope Stephen IV in 816, but this time at Reims.[77] Falkenstein regarded it as significant that Aachen was not mentioned in the *Divisio regnorum* of 806 and suggested that our perception of Aachen's preeminence rests on the chance that in 814 the empire was not after all divided.[78] All the indications are that Aachen's central role in Carolingian political ideology is primarily due to Louis the Pious and his heirs, for it is from the sources from his reign that descriptions of the palace at Aachen as a focal point of Louis's kingship and of court life stem.[79] Although the Ingelheim palace was also important for Louis, it was Louis who focussed his government on Aachen. Aachen indeed functioned more like a capital and less like a residence among many for Louis. In this connection, moreover, Christina Pössel has pointed to the very limited nature of Louis's itinerancy. It was confined for the most part to the region between the Meuse and the Rhine, with more, and more prolonged, stays at Aachen than elsewhere.[80] Aachen also became the most usual place for the convening of the assembly, though the precise definition of an assembly, as distinct from a small meeting of leading men, makes it difficult to be precise. Seventeen or eighteen of Louis's assemblies were convened there; if we adopt Seyfarth's criteria of meetings of *optimates* as well as general assemblies we know of five (in 789, 802, 809, 811 and 813) explicitly mentioned as convened at Aachen during the reign of Charlemagne.[81] Aachen became of central importance in the quarrel between the sons of

---

[76] Above, p. 102.

[77] *LP*, Life 99, c. 2, ed. Duchesne, II, p. 49. This is virtually all that Stephen achieved in his six-month pontificate before his death in January 817.

[78] L. Falkenstein, 'Charlemagne and Aix-la-Chapelle', in A. Dierkens and J.-M. Sansterre (eds.), *Souverain à Byzance et en occident du VIIIe au Xe siècle, Hommage à la mémoire de Maurice Leroy, Byzantion* 69 (1991), pp. 231–89.

[79] See P. Classen, 'Bermerkungen zur *Pfalzenforschung am Mittelrhein*, Deutsche Königspfalzen: Beiträge zu ihrer historischen und archäologischen Erforschung I, Veröffentlichungen des Max-Planck-Instituts für Geschichte II/I (Göttingen, 1963), pp. 75–96, repr. in J. Fleckenstein (ed.), *Ausgewählte Aufsätze von Peter Classen*, Vorträge und Forschungen 28 (Sigmaringen, 1983), pp. 475–501 at p. 478.

[80] C. Pössel, 'The itinerant kingship of Louis the Pious', unpublished MPhil in Medieval History dissertation, Faculty of History, University of Cambridge (1999).

[81] E. Seyfarth, *Fränkische Reichsversammlungen unter Karl dem Großen und Ludwig dem Frommen* (Leipzig, 1910), pp. 65–9, and his distinction between general and *optimates'* assemblies. For Louis, I follow Possel. For the ARF words for assemblies see above, pp. 28 and 40. See below on assemblies, pp. 222–33.

Louis the Pious after 840, and Nithard, writing *c.* 844, claimed that Aachen was the *sedes prima* of Francia.[82]

As was noted earlier, the section of the *Annales regni francorum* concerning the last fifteen years or so of Charlemagne's reign, and written early in the reign of Louis the Pious, uses the narrative to enhance the political status of Aachen.[83] In particular, it incorporates a great deal of detail about the embassies received from the Arabic rulers in Spain, the ruler of Persia, the Avars, the Danish kings, Venice, Dalmatia, Jerusalem, Northumbria, and the Greeks, who are said to have brought Charlemagne the Byzantine recognition of his imperial status in 812. Although some of these were received at other palaces, such as Paderborn, Nijmegen, Rome, Thionville and Reims, many are recorded as presenting themselves to the king at Aachen.

An important indication of the particular importance of Charlemagne's Aachen to succeeding generations is, however, evoked with longing and a specific claim to emulate his grandfather by Charles the Bald when he founded the new church dedicated to the Virgin Mary at his palace of Compiègne:

Because our grandfather [Charlemagne], to whom divine providence granted the monarchy of this whole empire, established a chapel in honour of the Virgin in the palace of Aachen, we therefore, wanting to imitate the pattern set by him and by other kings and emperors, namely our predecessors, since that part of the realm has not yet come to us by way of a share in its division, we have built and completed within the territory under our sway, the palace of Compiègne, a new monastery, to which we have given the name 'royal' in honour of the glorious mother of God and ever virgin Mary. . .[84]

Here we need also to recall that Einhard mentions only that Charlemagne constructed a church dedicated to the Virgin Mary at Aachen, and two palaces, one at Nijmegen and the other at Ingelheim.[85] In other words, there are indications that the really important building at Aachen was the chapel and the religious and liturgical significance attached to it.

There is thus no doubt about Aachen's role as a symbol of political success and the link with the past in the later Carolingian and post-Carolingian years, so strongly evoked by the Ottonian and Salian rulers of

[82] Nithard, *Historiarum libri IIII*, at IV, 1, ed. E. Mülle, *MGH SRG* 44 (Hanover, 1907); and P. Lauer, *Nithard: histoire des fils de Louis le Pieux* (Paris, 1964), p. 116.
[83] Above, pp. 49–54.
[84] Charles the Bald, foundation charter for Compiègne, ed. G. Tessier, *Recueil des actes de Charles II le Chauve*, 3 vols. (Paris, 1943–55), II, No. 425; trans. J. L. Nelson, *Charles the Bald* (London, 1992), discussed in Airlie, 'The palace of memory'.
[85] Einhard, *Vita Karoli*, c. 17, ed. Halphen, pp. 50, 52.

Germany.[86] But too much of the role Aachen came to play in Frankish and
German ideology after the death of Charlemagne appears to have been read
into the sources for Charlemagne's reign itself. Even the poems describing
the court in Charlemagne's reign have been assumed, as we have seen, to be
descriptions of Aachen and used to augment its importance and its function.[87] In order to assess Aachen's changing position during the reign of
Charlemagne, therefore, it needs to be seen in relation both to the other
palaces constructed by Charlemagne in the course of his reign and to the
palace system of his predecessors among the Frankish kings. Further, the
religious role of the palace chapel, and especially of Aachen's palace chapel,
needs to be explored further.

   Precise significance is attached to the word *palatium* in Frankish charters
and narrative sources, given its close association with the authority of the
ruler; but significant differences have been observed between the Merovingian
and Pippinid or Carolingian 'palatial system'.[88] The Carolingian mayors
did not use many Merovingian palaces, and accorded preference to Ver,
Verberie and Quierzy instead of Compiègne. The major Merovingian
palace of Clichy was granted in 741 to the monastery of St Denis, where
Charles Martel was subsequently buried.[89] Pippin's usurpation, however,
led to the use of the Merovingian palaces of Compiègne, Berny, Ponthion
and Soissons, while Pippin and Charlemagne also established new palaces
such as Attigny, Corbeny and Samoussy. Excavation of the first and last of
these in the early years of the twentieth century, as well as at Quierzy and
Compiègne, has corroborated the information about the erection of new
structures in the early Carolingian period.[90] The 1917 excavations of

[86] T. Zotz, 'Grundlagen und Zentren der Königsherrschaft im deutschen Südwesten in karolingischer
   und ottonischer Zeit', in *Archäologie und Geschichte des ersten Jahrtausends in Südwestdeutschland*,
   Archäologie in Geschichte 1 (Sigmaringen, 1990), pp. 275–93; and Zotz, 'Carolingian tradition and
   Ottonian-Salian innovation: comparative perspectives on palatine policy in the empire', in
   A. Duggan, ed. *Kings and kingship in medieval Europe* (London, 1993), pp. 69–100.
[87] For example, P. Godman, *Poets and emperors: Frankish politics and Carolingian poetry* (Oxford,
   1987), pp. 38–92.
[88] For discussion of the Merovingian palace and Pippin III on the one hand and Louis the Pious and his
   west Frankish heirs on the other see J. Barbier, 'Le système palatial franc: genèse et fonctionnement
   dans le nord-ouest du regnum', *Bibliothèque de l'Ecole des Chartes* 148 (1990), pp. 245–99.
[89] I. Heidrich, 'Titulatur und Urkunden der arnulfingischen Hausmaier', *Archiv für Diplomatik* 11/12
   (1965/6), pp. 71–279 at A 12 17 Sept. 741, p. 242.
[90] G. Weise, *Zwei fränkische Königspfalzen: Bericht über die an den Pfalzen zu Quierzy und Samoussy
   vorgenommenen Grabungen* (Tübingen, 1923); J. Barbier, 'Quierzy (Aisne): résidence pippinide et
   palais carolingien', in A. Renoux (ed.) *Palais médiévaux (France-Belgique): 25 ans d'archéologie* (Le
   Mans, 1994), pp. 85–6; A. Renoux, 'Karolingische Pfalzen in Nordfrankreich (751–987)', in *799
   Kunst und Kultur*, III, pp. 130–7, though the chapel and monastery at Compiègne were created
   under Charles the Bald: see Nelson, *Charles the Bald*, pp. 247–8.

Quierzy and Samoussy did not yield anything unambiguous, but recent excavations at St Denis have uncovered what seems to be a possible early Carolingian royal palace.[91] Pippin was most often in Attigny, Quierzy, Verberie and Compiègne. Charlemagne has most often been located in Thionville, Mainz, Worms, Ingelheim, Herstal (particularly between 768 and 784) and Aachen, but the number of times he is supposed to have visited Compiègne, Ver, Verberie and Quierzy may well be an indication of the king trying to demonstrate the continuity of Frankish rulership in the Merovingian heartlands.[92]

Just as Pippin and Charlemagne had taken over and extended the system of Merovingian royal residences, so new palaces accompanied an expansion of Carolingian authority and territory. Charlemagne took over Pavia and Regensburg on his conquest of the Lombard kingdom and annexation of Bavaria respectively, and Frankfurt, Nijmegen, Ingelheim and Paderborn were taken over, established or newly built in the regions conquered by the Carolingians.[93]

According to the annal records, Aachen was increasingly favoured by Charlemagne as a winter palace from Christmas until after Easter in the latter years of his reign. His first Christmas is recorded there as early as 768. Not for another twenty years did he spend Christmas there again, however, and thereafter he wintered there in 795 and 796, 798 and 799, 802 and 804, and from 806 to the end of his life. If in the last ten years of the reign we were to hazard a very rough estimate of the number of months Charlemagne spent in Aachen between 804 and his death, it was approximately 64 per cent of his time. In the final four years most of his time was spent in Aachen except for brief trips to Saxony in 810, to Boulogne in 811 to inspect the fleet, and the Ardennes in 813 to go hunting. This can be compared with approximately 30 per cent of his time in the preceding decade, between Christmas 794 and 803. Such estimates can only be very

[91] See above, p. 45.
[92] See A. Gauert, 'Zum Itinerar Karls des Großen', in *KdG*, I, pp. 307–21, who makes this point. Compare Barbier, 'Le système palatiale franque', but see my reservations about the record of visits to all these, and to Quierzy in particular, below, pp. 189–94.
[93] S. Gasparri, 'Pavia longobarda', *Storia di Pavia 2, L'alto medioevo* (Pavia, 1987), pp. 19–65; A. A. Settia, 'Pavia carolingia e post-carolingia', in *Storia di Pavia*, III: *Dal libero comune alla fine del principato indipendente (1024–1535)* (Pavia, 1992), pp. 9–25; F. Bougard, 'Les palais royaux et impériaux de l'Italie carolingienne et ottonienne', in A. Renoux (ed.), *Palais royaux et princiers au moyen âge* (Le Mans, 1996), pp. 181–96; and F. Bougard, 'Public power and authority', in C. La Rocca, *Italy in the early middle ages*, Short Oxford History of Italy (Oxford, 2002), pp. 34–58 at pp. 44–50. See also Classen, 'Bermerkungen zur Pfalzenforschung' pp. 87–91; and D. Leonhardt, *Die alte Kapelle in Regensburg und die karolingische Pfalzanlage*, Monographien des Bauwesens 3 (Munich, 1925).

rough, for there are months at a stretch when we have no idea precisely where the king was, even with the ambiguous charter evidence taken into account. Thus, on the information available to us, only in the last four years of Charlemagne's life, and possibly as much to do with advancing age as any political ideology, was there any degree of stability at Aachen throughout the year rather than only during the winter months. Towards the end of his reign and his life, therefore, the king moved about less and less and was indeed much more constantly at Aachen. An active life when young and growing increasingly sedentary when old is a pattern reflected in the careers of any number of warrior kings and such early modern rulers as Suleiman the Magnificent and Philip II of Spain.[94]

The many palaces where the king spent Christmas or Easter (see below) were nevertheless a select group within quite a limited area among the many other residences visited by the king in the course of his reign. For the most part the principal locations of this Carolingian royal topography of power remain merely names mentioned in passing, but in a few instances it is possible to augment such meagre written references with extant material remains. From these it is clear that the palaces were designed to impress all who saw them with their rich materials and their structures. Unlike the Welsh castles of the English King Edward I,[95] they were not designed to cow the inhabitants of the surrounding region, for they were not fortified, and many rapidly became the nuclei of towns and markets as well as religious centres.[96] Aachen and its chapel and palace buildings, with the classical spolia, bright mosaics and marble columns, some of them antique porphyry imported from Italy, its magnificent bronze doors, the Roman wolf sculpture and Roman pine-cone, and the equestrian statue from Ravenna of Theodoric, the Ostrogothic king, may not be typical. Enough fragments remain of a number of other palace buildings elsewhere, however, to indicate that very accomplished stone carving and masonry, ambitious architecture, coloured wall paintings and fine tableware for the use of the residents were the norm for a royal residence. Above all, in most instances there is evidence of a palace *aula* for the king to preside over

---

[94] M. Kunt, *Süleyman the Magnificent and his age: the Ottoman empire in the early modern world* (London, 1995); and M. Salgado Rodriguez, *The changing face of empire: Charles V, Philip II and Hapsburg authority 1551–1559* (Cambridge, 1988).

[95] M. Prestwich, *Edward I*, 2nd edn (London, 1997), pp. 170–232.

[96] On the nuclei of towns see A. Verhulst, *The rise of cities in north-west Europe* (Cambridge, 1999); and F. Verhaege, 'Urban developments in the age of Charlemagne', in J. Story (ed.), *Charlemagne: empire and society* (Manchester, 2005), pp. 259–87.

meetings on the late Roman imperial model (such as Constantine's great *aula* at Trier), and usually a chapel or church building as well.

Of the two palaces of Charlemagne mentioned by Einhard, little is either known or visible now of the Carolingian palace of Nijmegen in the Valkhof in modern Nijmegen, though it was a substantial place in the tenth century at least. Most of Carolingian Ingelheim is concealed by modern housing, though some masonry of the lower part of the apse of the large hall and part of the church still in use are visible. Ingelheim, however, has been excavated; even within the limited area investigated, an impressive complex of buildings has been identified, with a large *aula* and a very distinctive semicircular building probably erected during the reign of Charlemagne, though the church on the site has been dated *c.* 900.[97] There is also a detailed description both of the church associated with the palace, which seems to have been St Alban's church in Mainz, and of the palace, in the poem *In honour of Louis the Pious* by Ermold the Black. Ermold may have been moved to include such an account by the description in the *Aeneid* of Dido's temple to Juno.[98] Remnants of decorated plasterwork from the *aula* of the Paderborn palace as well as surviving Carolingian wall paintings elsewhere have encouraged confidence in the veracity of Ermold's claim, in his description of the *domus regia*, that the walls at Ingelheim were also painted.[99]

The palace at Ingelheim, according to Ermold, was decorated with a remarkable series of ruler portraits from Ninus of the Assyrians, Phalaris of Sicily and Cyrus of the Persians to the Carolingians. Such historical resonance is fully in keeping with what we know of the use and knowledge of history in the reign of Charlemagne. The rulers chosen to rank beside Charles Martel, Pippin III and Charlemagne in the apse of the *aula* are the Roman emperors Augustus, Constantine and Theodosius. Ermold also

---

[97] For a useful summary see H. Grewe, 'Die Königspfalz Ingelheim am Rhein', in *799 Kunst und Kultur*, III, pp. 142–51. See also J. Autenrieth (ed.), *Ingelheim am Rhein* (Stuttgart, 1964); and generally see *Die deutschen Königspfalzen: Repertorium der Pfalzen, Königshöfe und übrigen Aufenthaltsorte der Könige im deutschen Reich des Mittelalters*, I: *Hessen*, Veröffentlichungen des Max-Planck-Institut für Geschichte (Göttingen, 1983–96).

[98] Ermold, *In honorem Hludowici christianissimi Caesaris Augusti*, ed. E. Faral, *Ermold le Noir: poème sur Louis le Pieux et épîtres au roi Pépin* (Paris, 1964), Bk IV, lines 2068–165; and see *Aeneid* I, 445. See also the virtual architectural reconstruction and an illustration of the reconstruction of the *aula* in E. Wamers and M. Brandt (eds.) *Die Macht des Silbers: karolingische Schätze im Norden* (Regensburg, 2005), p. 161.

[99] See the archaeologists' website, <www.kaiserpfalz-ingelheim.de>. Note that P. Godman, *Poetry of the Carolingian Renaissance* (London, 1985), p. 253, mistakenly translates this section of the poem as if it were also a description of the church. On the paintings at St Germain d'Auxerrre see C. Sapin (ed.), *Archéologie et architecture d'un site monastique: 10 ans de recherche à l'abbaye Saint-Germain d'Auxerre* (Auxerre, 2000), pp. 274–300.

recorded the particular actions of these Roman rulers who served to inspire the Franks, explicitly linking the Franks and Rome: *caesareis actis Romanae sedis opimae / Junguntur Franci gestaque mira simul* (the Franks and their wondrous deeds continue the acts of the Caesars).[100] Thus Constantine had constructed Constantinople; Theodosius was notable for all his deeds. Charles Martel, Pippin and Charlemagne were celebrated as conquerors of the Frisians, the Aquitainians and the Saxons respectively. On the two main walls were the ancient rulers Ninus, Phalaris and Cyrus, Alexander the Great, Hannibal, and Romulus and Remus, whose ambition and wickedness appear to act as warnings, however mighty these kings may have been. Lammers saw these pictures as a visual representation of the historical concept of Orosius's seven books of history against the pagans, though the Chronicle of Eusebius-Jerome also underpins the information for what is essentially an illustrated world history with representatives of the four world monarchies.[101] The theme of the pictures overall concerns conquering kings and founders of new great cities (Rome and Constantinople). These pictures acted as an ideological support for ruler-ship and enhanced the symbolic resonance of the palace itself.

The other principal Rhine/Main land residences were Worms, burnt in the winter of 790–1, and Frankfurt. The royal palace at Worms was probably based on (or identical with) the Merovingian *palatium* in the region of the cathedral. Frankfurt is, like Ingelheim, on a major river. But it was also one obvious stopping point between the eastern and western portions of Charlemagne's realm. It has become famous as the site of the Synod of 794. Some of the walls and foundations of a possibly two-storeyed hall or *aula* of the Carolingian palace and its chapel have been found in front of the present-day cathedral at Frankfurt, and are carefully preserved there still. The palace at Frankfurt was successively augmented by Louis the

---

[100] Ermold, *In honorem Hludowici christianissimi Caesaris Augusti*, ed. Faral, Bk IV, lines 2150–1, p. 164. Faral comments that Ermold expresses this preoccupation with the association of Roman and Frankish history elsewhere in the poem at Bk II, lines 718–719 and Bk II, line 1077, as well as in the second letter to King Pippin: 'caesareum primus Francorum nomen adeptus, / Francis Romuleum nomen habere dedi' (I was the first of the Franks to take the name of Caesar. And I gave this Romulean name to the Franks to keep), and Bk II, line 1077, 'Tum iubet adferri gemmis auroque coronam/quae Constantini Caesaris ante fuit' (Louis is crowned [by Pope Stephen IV] with a crown of gold and jewels that had belonged to Constantine Caesar). 'Jam venit armipotens Carolus, Pippinea proles: Romuleum Francis praestitit imperium' (... Charles ... acquired for the Franks the empire of Romulus). Second letter to Pippin, *ibid.*, p. 228.

[101] W. Lammers, 'Ein karolingisches Bildprogramm in der *Aula regia* von Inghelheim', in Die Mitarbeiter des Max-Planck-Instituts für Geschichte (eds.), *Festschrift Hermann Heimpel zum 70. Geburtstag am 19. September 1971*, III, Veröffentlichungen des Max-Planck-Instituts für Geschichte 36/III (Göttingen, 1972), pp. 226–89.

Pious and Louis the German, but it is not clear how much of the existing remnants are of Charlemagne's palace.[102]

Although Herstelle and Eresburg were Saxon residences in which Charlemagne spent the winter, it is Paderborn which can be identified as the *urbs Karoli* mentioned in the Moselle annals and *Annales petaviani*, and even described as the *urbs Karoli et francorum* in the *Annales maximiani*.[103] This place is given the Saxon name of *Paderbrunn* in the *Annales regni francorum*.[104] Such a late eighth-century perception of the status of Paderborn as the *urbs Karoli*, a new city created by Charlemagne, added to Einhard's singling out of the two other palaces of Ingelheim and Nijmegen, provides an important counterweight to Charlemagne's supposed concentration on Aachen. The founding of Paderborn represents a major addition to a developing palace system that was explicitly part of a process of expansion and consolidation. No doubt there were elements of the sheer display of power and wealth, and the provision of symbols of authority, in their construction. The character of the Carolingian palaces as instruments of ruling was to become very different in the reign of Charlemagne's grandson, Charles the Bald. It is important not to assume that Carolingian palaces functioned in the same way throughout the Carolingian period.[105] The long-term centrality of particular centres could surely not have been foreseen, though their role as a focus for a region was undoubtedly planned. Charlemagne presumably intended Paderborn, in the heart of the newly conquered territory, to be the largest royal and ecclesiastical centre in the region, as well as a frequent site of Carolingian assemblies during the period of conquest and subjugation. It

---

[102] Binding, *Deutsche Königspfalzen*, pp. 117–22, and see also Classen, 'Bemerkungen zur Pfalzenforschung am Mittelrhein', pp. 75–96, and the series *Die deutschen Königspfalzen: Repertorium der Pfalzen, Königshöfe und übrigen Aufenthaltsorte der Könige im deutschen Reich des Mittelalters*, Veröffentlichungen des Max-Planck-Institut für Geschichte (Göttingen, 1983–96). Compare U. Lobbedey, 'Carolingian royal palaces: the state of research from an architectural historian's viewpoint', in C. Cubitt (ed.), *Court culture in the early middle ages: the proceedings of the first Alcuin conference*, Studies in the Early Middle Ages 3 (Turnhout, 2003), pp. 131–54.
[103] *Annales Mosellani* 776 (Charlemagne built a *civitas* Karlsburg on the River Lippe), ed. J. Lappenburg, *MGH SS* 16, p. 496; the *Annales petaviani* 776 says he built *urbs karoli* in Saxony, ed. G. Pertz, *MGH SS* 1, p. 16; and the *Annales maximiani* 776, ed. G. Waitz, *MGH SS* 13, p. 21, refers to the *urbs Karoli et francorum*.
[104] ARF 777, ed. Kurze, p. 48.
[105] T. Zotz, 'Pfalzen der Karolingerzeit: Neue Aspekte aus historischer Sicht', in L. Fenske, J. Jarnut and M. Wemhoff (eds.), *Deutsche Königspfalzen: Beiträge zu ihrer historischen und archäologischen Erforschung* 5, *Splendor palatii: Neue Forschungen zur Paderborn und anderen Pfalzen der Karolingerzeit*, Veröffentlichungen des Max-Plank-Instituts für Geschichte 11/5 (Göttingen, 2001), pp. 13–23; and compare A. Renoux, 'Bemerkungen zur Entwicklung des Pfalzenwesens in Nordfrankreich in der Karolingerzeit, 751–987', in ibid., pp. 25–50.

was at Paderborn that Charlemagne convened important assemblies, such as those in 777 and 785, quite apart from the famous meeting with Pope Leo in 799.

From the remnants of the early Carolingian palace buildings at Paderborn, comprising coloured glass fragments, some with traces of gold, mosaic pieces, and a wide variety of ceramic tableware, tapestry and painted plaster, remnants of inscriptions, decorative stonework, jewellery and even elaborate keys, it is clear that Paderborn was once a resplendent complex of buildings which included a great *aula* and a large three-aisled basilica south of the first single-naved church.[106] At the time of the papal visit, moreover, the large basilica prepared for Charlemagne was to be consecrated by no less a person than the pope. The church itself was dedicated to St Kilian and to the Virgin Mary, and its religious status was further augmented by sacred relics of both saints, as well as the dedication of one of the altars to St Stephen the Martyr. Paderborn was also one of the new Saxon bishoprics created by Charlemagne, with the first bishop of Paderborn being appointed in 805.[107]

The building of Aachen, therefore, was at the end of a long succession of new enterprises and adaptations and extensions of existing palace complexes. The burning of the palace of Worms in the winter of 790–1, reported in the revised version of the *Annales regni francorum* and the Annals of Fulda,[108] may have precipitated a decision to develop the Aachen residence further, though a more likely possibility is that Aachen was designed to supersede Herstal. The palace of Aachen itself had been expanded from the smaller *villa* or *palatium* of Pippin III. It is described as a *villa* where Pippin III spent Christmas in 767; it is given the label *palatium* in charters of Charlemagne dated 13 January and 1 March 769.[109] A small late antique or early medieval church appears also to have existed on the site, quite apart from late Roman baths. The attraction of Aachen as a residence is alleged by Einhard to have been the hot springs and thermal baths. The richness of the surrounding estates and the reasonable proximity to Roman roads and water routes as well as good hunting forest were also undoubtedly factors, for the Ardennes was an immensely rich source of

---

[106] M. Balzer, 'Die Pfalz Paderborn', in *799 Kunst und Kultur*, I, pp. 116–23, with illustrations and catalogue entries for the archaeological finds from the palace complex site, pp. 124–85. See also B. Mecke, 'Die Pfalz Paderborn ', ibid., III, pp. 175–222; and B. Mecke, 'Die karolingische Pfalz Paderborn: Entdeckung und Ausgrabung', in Fenske, Jarnut and Wemhoff, *Deutsche Königspfalzen*, pp. 51–70.

[107] See below, pp. 299–305.

[108] *RVARF* 790, ed. Kurze, p. 87; and also *Annales fuldenses* 791, ed. Kurze, p. 12.

[109] *DKar*. I, Nos. 55 and 56.

game as well as fish. Régine Le Jan, moreover, has stressed how crucial hunting and management of the forest, and the provision of fresh food in large quantities, were for the palace economy. She has also pointed to the large number of royal residences in the Ardennes within up to four days' travelling distance from Aachen.[110]

For much of the late 790s in particular the palace complex itself comprised probably little more than the northern *aula* or great hall, measuring 17.2 × 44 m, and completed between 792 and 804, the chapel complex (including two large two-storeyed buildings) in the south, probably completed *c.* 796, and the covered, possibly two-storeyed, passage connecting the *aula* and chapel, interrupted halfway by a two-storeyed building that was probably the king's residence.[111] The descriptions of labour services due from tenants in the Polyptych of Saint-Rémi indicate that building work at Aachen was still being undertaken in the first and second decades of the ninth century.[112] It was not until 816 and 825 that Reims was exempt from its labour services at Aachen.[113]

In due course, and most likely by the late teens and early 20s of the ninth century, Aachen became a town and even a hub for the region, with 'a market, a role as a central place, a relatively large and dense population, a diversified economic base, houses of urban type, social differentiation, complex religious organization and judicial centre'.[114] Certainly the capitulary on the discipline at the palace of Aachen refers to the *mansiones* of many of the men gathered round the king at Aachen.[115] This is

[110] Flach, *Untersuchungen zur Verfassung und Verwaltung des Aachener Reichsgutes*; and see also R. Hennebicque (R. Le Jan), 'Espaces sauvages et chasses royales dans le Nord de la France', *Revue du Nord* 62 (1980), pp. 35–57; and E. Ewig, 'Les Ardennes au haut moyen âge', *Ancien pays et assemblées d'états* 28 (1963), pp. 3–38.

[111] See Lobbedey, 'Carolingian royal palaces', pp. 131–53.

[112] On the *bos aquensis* see J.-P. Devroey, *Le polyptyque et les listes de cens de l'abbaye de Saint-Rémi de Reims (IXe–XIe siècles)*, Travaux de l'Académie nationale de Reims 163 (Reims, 1984), pp. xliii–xliv, and B. Guérard, *Le polyptyque de l'abbaye de Saint-Rémi de Reims ou dénombrement des manses, des serfs et des revenus de cette abbaye vers le milieu du IXe siècle de notre ère* (Paris, 1853).

[113] Flodoard, *Historia remensis ecclesiae* II, c. 19, ed. M. Stratmann, *MGH SS* 36 (Hanover, 1998), pp. 175–83, and compare the charter from Charles the Bald, ed. G. Tessier, *Recueil* 2, No. 130, p. 340: 'quae tempore avi nostri domni Karoli imperatoris ex eadem casa dei exigebantur ad palatium quod vocatur Aquisgrani'. See J.-P. Devroey, *Puissants et misérables: système social et monde paysan dans l'Europe des Franca (VIe–IXe siècles)* (Brussels, 2006), p. 580.

[114] These criteria are from the formulation of M. Biddle, 'Towns' in D. M. Wilson (ed.), *The archaeology of Anglo-Saxon England* (Cambridge, 1976), pp. 99–150 at p. 100. See also Verhulst, *The rise of cities*, and Verhaeghe, 'Urban developments'.

[115] *MGH Cap.* 1, No. 146, pp. 297–8, from Paris BnF lat. 4788, fol. 114, trans. Nelson, 'Aachen as a place of power', pp. 238–9. See also J. L. Nelson, 'Was Charlemagne's court a courtly society?', in C. Cubitt (ed.), *Court culture in the earlier middle ages* (Leiden, 2001), pp. 39–58.

corroborated by Notker's account of *mansiones* built around the palace.[116]
Einhard, in his *Translatio* of saints Marcellinus and Petrus, moreover,
refers frequently to his own house at Aachen, at some distance from the
palace.[117]

It might have been assumed that there would be a royal mint located at
Aachen during the reign of Charlemagne. Pippin and Charlemagne had re-
established a state monopoly of coin production as it had existed during the
Roman period. In Charlemagne's early years, until the reforms of 793–4, he
continued to use over 100 mints active during Pippin's reign, but thereafter
the number appears to have been reduced to about forty mints determined
for the heavier (1.7 g instead of 1.3 g) Class 3 coinage of 793/4–812 and only
about ten for the Class 4 coinage period, supposedly from 812 to 814. Yet
Aachen does not appear to have been a mint site during the reign of
Charlemagne. Although the capitulary of Thionville in 805, echoed at
Nijmegen in 808, specifically restricted minting to a *palatium*, Grierson
and Blackburn were of the view that minting was not in fact closely
associated with the royal household.[118] No coins have been found that
were minted at Aachen, nor do any survive from such 'favourite royal
residences' of his earlier years as Verberie, Quierzy or Ponthion. There are a
small number of coins with the inscription *palatina moneta*, albeit none
dating to the reign of Charlemagne.[119] In any case, *palatina moneta* cannot
be a general label to cover coins produced by an ambulatory royal household, even though more than one locality was involved.[120]

Despite the striking lack of a precise correlation between principal
palaces and mints identified for the reign of Charlemagne, the clustering
of mint distribution at least mirrors the concentration of the king's movements. That is, as far as can be determined from the surviving coins (from
specific hoards and single finds), mints were mostly situated in *civitates* and
trading centres between the Loire and Rhine rather than in the palaces.
Mints have been identified at Chartres (Class 1); many places in Francia,
such as Dorestad, Limoges, Lyon, Mainz, Sens and Melle, and, in Italy,
Treviso, Milan, Lucca after 774 (+ the Louis 781 coins in Aquitaine); Milan,
Pavia, Treviso, Lucca, Pisa and Ravenna (used Charlemagne's monogram
in Greek) (Class 3); and Arles, Rouen, Trier, Dorestad, Quentovic and

---

[116] Notker, *Gesta Karoli*, I, c. 30, ed. Haefele, p. 41.
[117] Einhard, *Translatio sancti Marcellini et Petri*, II, cc. 1, 3–6, ed. G. Waitz, *MGH SS* 15, I, pp. 238–64 at
       p. 245–7.
[118] Grierson and Blackburn, *Medieval European coinage*, p. 197.
[119] J. Lafaurie, 'Moneta palatina', *Francia* 4 (1976), pp. 59–87.
[120] Grierson and Blackburn, *Medieval European coinage*, p. 198.

Melle (Class 4 Portrait coins). The Italian *tremisses* of 773–81 struck in Charlemagne's name and resembling those of Desiderius were struck at Milan, Bergamo, Pavia, Castel Seprio, Lucca, Pisa and Chur. The gold *solidi* survive from mints at Uzes, *Aurodis* and Dorestad in Francia and from Milan, Pavia, Treviso and Rome in Italy. Exceptionally, for the sub-kings did not have the authority to mint coinage, a few Class 2 (771–93/4) coins were struck in the name of Louis, sub-king of Aquitaine in 781 at Narbonne, Bourges, Saint-Etienne de Bourges, Clermont and Limoges. These appear to have been minted to mark his inauguration as sub-king. Charlemagne's intrusions into Beneventan coinage were limited to 788–90, when Grimoald struck coins with Charlemagne's name on them. From 800 to *c.* 970 all papal coins struck in Rome bore the emperor's name except sometimes during an imperial vacancy.

The remnants of all the buildings at Aachen, apart from the chapel, are so meagre and often ambiguous that reconstructions and interpretations are necessarily inconclusive. The tendency to try to push back the dates of some of the buildings in the light of preconceptions about Aachen's function should probably be resisted. What is nevertheless clear from the excavations, despite the uncertainty about the dating, is the massive proportions of these buildings, and the relationship between the royal residence and the chapel, reminiscent of the arrangement of royal residence in relation to church or mosque and place for public access to the king in Byzantium, Rome and the Abbasid courts.[121] Further, the sumptuousness and eclecticism of the decoration in the chapel at Aachen, as well as the superb design in which the influence of other royal, papal and imperial buildings in Rome (the Lateran palace), Ravenna (San Vitale), Benevento (Arichis II's Santa Sophia), Trier (the Constantinian basilica) and even Constantinople has been detected, are a telling indication of the symbolic resonances of the building itself.[122] The size and magnificence of the chapel, moreover, suggest that the palace and *aula* too would have been as rich and impressive.

If Fleckenstein was correct in supposing, not only that each palace was probably the central focus of a royal estate, such as is indicated by the

---

[121] M. McCormick, 'Emperors', in G. Cavallo (ed.), *The Byzantines* (Chicago and London, 1997), pp. 230–54 at pp. 233–8; and L. Brubaker, 'Topography and the creation of public space in early medieval Constantinople', in De Jong, Theuws and van Rhijn (eds.), *Topographies of power*, pp. 31–43.

[122] M. Untermann, '"Opere mirabili constructa": Die Aachener "Residenz" Karls des Großen, *799 Kunst und Kultur*, III, pp. 152–64. See also H.-K. Siebigs, *Der Zentralbau des Domes zu Aachen: Unerforschtes und Ungewisses* (Worms, 2004).

Capitulare de villis,[123] but would also have had a *capella* and have acted as the estate's *Eigenkirche*, then all the palaces had a crucial religious as well as administrative function; they formed a network of prayer across the empire.[124] In addition, those that received the king for Christmas and/or Easter were arguably part of what Fleckenstein called a *Festitinerar*, that is, a ceremonial celebration of the two principal Christian festivals accompanied by crown-wearing.[125]

Pippin and Charlemagne created a new focus of Frankish power in Austrasia, centred on Cologne, Aachen, Liège, Nijmegen and the northeast, that is the Mosan region. New residences also became prominent in the Rhineland and Saxony. For instance, there were new palaces built at Frankfurt, Ingelheim and Paderborn to supplement the Merovingian, Bavarian and Lombard residences continuing in use such as Soissons, Paris, Chelles, Compiègne and Berny (near Soissons), Regensburg and Pavia.[126] Paris was eclipsed under Charlemagne and his immediate successors, but St Denis appears to have made special provision in a new building for royal visits.[127] Rural palaces such as Attigny, Ponthion, Herstal, Aachen and Thionville were the administrative residences as well as the hunting lodges of the king. An essential accompaniment of the palaces as royal residences was the royal estate or fisc. The fiscal lands of the Frankish kings were concentrated between the Loire and Scheldt rivers but it is likely that all the palaces were the centres of estates. Palaces, moroever, were generally sited with various facilities in mind: strategy, communications, main routes (sea, river, road), lands of the royal fisc for supplies and forests for hunting. The palace complex created at Aachen in the latter years of the eighth century and early years of the ninth was ultimately of lasting importance and symbolic resonance. Yet its status as a capital, to compare with Toledo under the Visigothic rulers of Spain, or Pavia under the Lombard kings of Italy in the seventh and eighth centuries, had not emerged by the end of Charlemagne's reign. It does not appear to have been more than the *de facto* principal residence in the last few years of the emperor's

---

[123] See above, pp. 149–50.
[124] J. Fleckenstein, *Die Hofkapelle der deutschen Könige*, 1: *Grundlegung. Die karolingische Hofkapelle*, *MGH* Schriften 16/1 (Stuttgart, 1959), esp. pp. 86–101; and see below, pp. 295–8.
[125] C. Brühl, 'Fränkische Krönungsbrauch und das Problem der "Festkrönungen"', *Historische Zeitschrift* 194 (1962), pp. 265–326.
[126] G. Binding, *Deutsche Königspfalzen von Karl dem Großen bis Friedrich II. (765–1240)* (Darmstadt, 1996); and de Jong, Theuws and van Rhijn, *Topographies of power*.
[127] M. Wyss, 'Die Klosterpfalz Saint-Denis im Licht der neuen Ausgrabungen', in Fenske, Jarnut and Wemhoff, *Deutsche Königspfalzen*, pp. 175–92.

life.[128] Aachen was distinctive in relation to Charlemagne's other palaces and residences, however, for the functioning of its chapel as the centre of liturgical reform for the empire.[129]

The precise function of these palaces in relation to any notion of the 'court', therefore, still needs to be determined. Were they indeed designed in some way to make the king accessible and visible to his people? To what extent were they part of a system of government or a means of ruling? Did they act as a 'meeting place and centre of elite integration'[130] or as a 'centre of communication'?[131] All these questions have tended to be subsumed into the assumption that the palaces were designed to serve as staging posts on the royal itinerary, whether of the king or of the 'court' as whole, and it is to the question of the itinerary, therefore, that we now turn.

AN ITINERANT COURT OR AN ITINERANT KING?

Much of the discussion of itinerant courts has centred on, and derives its defining characteristics from, the itinerant kingship of the Ottonian and Salian rulers of the tenth and eleventh centuries in Germany, by whom itinerancy, as a method of rule which emphasized the importance of the king's physical presence, was thoroughly institutionalized. Itinerant kingship is generally defined as 'the form of government in which a king carries out all the administrative functions and symbolic representations of governing by periodically or constantly travelling throughout the areas of his dominion'.[132] Thus it is not merely the ceremonial circumambulation of the royal progress to take symbolic possession of the kingdom, but actually a means of ruling. The king's subjects came to him in the places he visited. The *iter* was also a vehicle for the king's sacrality in the Ottonian period.[133] The itinerary is thought to reflect not only the relationship between the importance of personality and personal power, regarded as an essential characteristic of medieval kings, but also the limited extent of the use of

---

[128] E. Ewig, 'Résidence et capitale pendant le haut moyen âge', *Revue historique* 130 (1963), pp. 25–72, repr. in E. Ewig, ed. H. Atsma, *Spätantikes und fränkisches Gallien, Gesammelte Schriften*, I: Beihefte der Francia 3/1(Munich, 1976), pp. 362–408.

[129] See below, pp. 229–30.

[130] M. Kunt and J. Duindam (eds.), *Royal courts and capitals* (Istanbul, forthcoming).

[131] M. Mersiowsky, 'Regierungspraxis und Schriftlichkeit im Karolingerreich: das Fall Beispiel der Mandate und Briefe', in R. Schieffer (ed.), *Schriftkultur und Reichsverwaltung unter den Karolingern*, Abhandlungen der Nordrhein-Westfälischen Akademie der Wissenschaften (Opladen, 1996), pp. 109–66.

[132] J. Bernhardt, *Itinerant Kingship and royal monasteries in early medieval Germany, c. 936–1075* (Cambridge, 1993), p. 45.

[133] Ibid., p. 293.

writing in government. Indeed, both the size of the kingdom and poor written communications have been posited as strong determining factors for the practice of itinerant kingship. Precisely because this notion of itinerant kingship on the Ottonian model has been so dominant in discussions of Carolingian kingship, it needs to be examined at length.

Study of the Ottonian rulers has been influential, first of all, in methodological terms in order to map the kernel or heartlands of the kingdom as well as 'transit zones'.[134] Although much guesswork has been involved in estimating the number of personnel at the tenth- and eleventh-century court of the German kings, the process of planning the itinerary can only be surmised from the end result. A great deal of productive attention has been concentrated, first of all, on the itinerary itself and the routes taken. This has included the identification of places where the king and his court stayed, how long and how frequently they stayed, and the establishment of a hierarchy of royal places visited. For this identification the charters or royal diplomas have provided what have been assumed to be unequivocal indications of where a king was when the charter was issued. Secondly, the means of support of the king *en route*, in terms of goods, food and fodder, and services due to the king have been unearthed. Yet the payment and services that churches and monasteries were obliged to provide in return for royal protection and patronage, known as *fodrum, gistum et servitium regis*, although undoubtedly important for establishing how the king could be fed and housed on his travels, do not prove the existence of itinerant kingship.[135] Thirdly, the research on the itinerary of the Ottonian rulers has highlighted the role of particular places, notably strategically placed monasteries. These fed, accommodated and supplied the royal court as well as securing and maintaining corridors of transit. The royal monasteries presided over by female members of the royal house were particularly prominent in acting as 'five-star hotels' for the king.[136]

---

[134] See E. Müller-Mertens, *Die Reichsstruktur im Spiegel der Herrschaftspraxis Ottos des Großen*, Forschungen zur mittelalterlichen Geschichte 25 (Berlin, 1980), esp. pp. 101–6 and 121–2. Methodologically, Müller-Mertens was pioneering for his use of charter evidence to identify the 'area of influence' of royal government. All this work is summarized by H. Keller, 'Reichsstruktur und Herschaftsauffassung in ottonisch-fränkischer Zeit', *Frühmittelalterliche Studien* 16 (1982), pp. 74–128. See also T. F. X. Noble's review of Müller-Mertens, *Speculum* 56 (1981), pp. 634–7, and his summary of Müller-Mertens's methodology. See also S. D. Keynes, *The diplomas of Aethelred 'the Unready' 978–1016* (Cambridge, 1980).

[135] C. Brühl, *Fodrum, gistum, servitium regis: Studien zu den wirtschaftlichen Grundlagen des Königtums im Frankenreich und in den fränkischen Nachfolgestaaten Deutschland, Frankreich und Italien vom 6. bis zur Mitte des 14. Jahrhunderts*, Kölner Historische Abhandlungen 14/1–2 (Cologne and Graz, 1968).

[136] Bernhardt, *Itinerant kingship*, pp. 136–76.

The current understanding of itinerant kingship, therefore, rests on a number of assumptions. If we look at some of the older historiography, we can see the development of an understanding of itinerancy both as a departure from the ancient practices of the Roman empire and as a primitive phase before the development of post-medieval centralized government. The latter understanding appears to have been fuelled, among other work, by the exposition of the *ambulante Herrschaftsübung* or *Reisekönigtum* offered by Peyer in 1964.[137] Peyer insisted on the notion of a *Kerngebiet* which comprised the main centres of power focussed on royal estates and palaces, connected by land routes and waterways, and an itinerary or *iter* orchestrated in relation to the principal Christian festivals (Christmas, Easter) and festive crown-wearings. The degree to which these notions were part of a romantic perception of the middle ages are evident in Peyer's pleased use of the famous words of Shakespeare's King Lear (Act 1, scene 1) as, effectively, a valid summary comment about medieval kingship, rather than an early seventeenth-century perception of a practice imagined to be medieval:

> Ourself by monthly course,
> with reservation of an hundred knights
> By you to be sustained, shall our abode
> make with you by due turn. Only we shall retain
> the name and all the additions to a king.

Peyer acknowledged gaps in the evidence relating to the earlier middle ages outside Germany, but was confident nevertheless that we could feel secure about the itinerary of Frankish and French kings. Although initially inclined to claim itinerant kingship as a Germanic practice, alluded to by Tacitus and to be regarded as thoroughly characteristic of the method of rule in the kingdoms of western Europe in the middle ages, Peyer went on to discuss forms of itinerant kingship in the medieval British Isles, Scandinavia and the Slav lands, and subsequently in certain regions of nineteenth-century Africa and southeast Asia, and among the modern nomadic peoples of Asia, the Sahara and Arabia. He concluded that itinerant kingship was a worldwide *Grundform*, not specifically Germanic, but linked with special economic and social circumstances and superseded with the rise of towns and a new style of government. Only in the Balkans did Peyer perceive Roman influence in the retention of a capital or main city. He attributed the

---

[137] C. Peyer, 'Das Reisekönigtum des Mittelalters', *Vierteljahrschrift für Sozial- und Wirtschaftsgeschichte* 51 (1964), pp. 1–21.

Crusaders' use of particular cities as their base in the Latin kingdom of Jerusalem, moreover, to their observance of Byzantine or Roman practice. Despite his examples from countries in nineteenth-century Africa and Asia, Peyer's arguments promoted the notion of the itinerant court as something particularly to be associated with medieval Europe. A travelling king or court was due to a lack of sophisticated *and* centralized government institutions. An itinerant court was unfavourably compared with modern government and regarded in consequence as a primitive phase.

Peyer's exposition has a number of weaknesses. Firstly, there is the failure precisely to distinguish between a king and his court. An entourage of unknown size but which is supposed to have included all administrative officials, including notaries, the royal family, the warrior retinue, a royal chapel and its clergy, household servants and noble youths being trained for future careers, is assumed to have travelled with the king. I shall return to this point below.

Secondly, there is the assumption of an institutionalized system for all kings who can be recorded as having failed to stay in one place all the time. At what point does a king who travels about to go to war, visit a sacred site, go hunting, meet foreign legations, or spend Christmas with his family, become an itinerant king in the technical sense in which it is understood for Ottonian Germany? Is the crucial element the administration of justice, or the hearing of petitions? If so, how often can it be established that Charlemagne did this in person, let alone that he travelled to particular places to do it, as distinct from his subjects occasionally seizing the opportunity of his proximity to make their grievances known? In other words, how institutionalized is the procedure for gaining the king's attention?

Thirdly, reading the evidence for all early medieval kings before the Ottonian rulers as if it represents fragments attesting to the same fully fledged system elsewhere fails to allow either for change over time or for the possibility that we may be observing something else instead that simply has some similarities with Ottonian royal government.

Fourthly, the understanding of itinerant rule as it manifests itself in the later tenth and the eleventh centuries has unfortunately been uncritically projected back onto the Carolingian period, without taking the specific contexts or circumstances of the latter and the manifestly contradictory evidence into account.

Lastly, there are the hints in Peyer's paper that the medieval developments he described were a lamentable departure from the Roman system of royal or imperial government based in capital cities.

A major element in the discussion, indeed, has been the one debating whether or not early medieval palaces functioned as capitals or merely as residences. Certainly in the 1960s, discussion of the history of capital cities, in the sense of principal towns and seats of the public powers of the state with government from a fixed residence, was much influenced by the political upheavals and consequent, often deeply distressing, changes of seats of government in the twentieth century, especially in Germany in the aftermath of the Second World War.[138] The survival of what was regarded as the ancient notion of capital cities and what might have replaced them was addressed independently, together with that of the development of itinerancy, by Ewig a year before Peyer's paper.[139] Ewig challenged the notion that courts were itinerant in the early middle ages until capitals began to be established after the twelfth century. Ewig proposed instead that royal cities in the early middle ages were a continuation of the administrative capitals of the provinces of the late Roman empire, and that the Germanic rulers of the Visigoths, Lombards, Merovingian Franks and Carolingian rulers in Italy after 774 chose cities for their main residences. Nevertheless, Ewig posited a change to itinerant rule with the advent of the Carolingians, and insisted that the great builder of the Frankish empire was obliged to keep on the move. Here Ewig implies that this was due to the necessity of the kings' maintaining personal control rather than to economic need. That is, there is an implicit assumption of a lack of effective written communication needing the substitute of the physical presence of the king. As we shall see, however, the communications network within Charlemagne's reign was both extensive and effective.[140]

Although he charted an itinerary for the earlier part of the reign, however, Ewig suggested that Aachen was becoming a 'résidence-capitale' (a principal residence or not quite a capital?) at some stage after 794, and that it represented 'la transformation d'un palais de campagne en capitale'. Brühl was able to accept the idea that the Merovingian kings of the Franks before the eighth century had a stable residence while still moving around their kingdoms, and agreed that Toledo and Pavia could be regarded as capitals along the Roman pattern. But he was convinced that itinerancy was a Carolingian phenomenon. He was disconcerted by the emergence of Charlemagne's palace at Aachen in, so he stated, the 790s, which he could

<hr>

[138] Brühl says as much in C. Bruhl, 'Remarques sur les notions du "capitale" et du "résidence" pendant le haut moyen âge', *Journal des Savants* (1967), pp. 195–215; repr. in C. Bruhl, *Aus Mittelalter und Diplomatik: Gesammelte Aufsätze*, 2 vols. (Hildesheim, 1989), I, pp. 115–37.
[139] E. Ewig, 'Résidence et capitale pendant le haut moyen âge', *Revue historique* 230 (1963) pp. 25–72; repr. in Ewig, *Spätantikes und fränkisches Gallien* I, pp. 362–408.
[140] See below, pp. 215–22.

describe as no more than 'fast von einer Hauptstadt des Reiches, ein festen *sedes regni*'. He preferred the notion of 'principal town' or 'favourite residence'.[141] He further muddied the issue in a later paper. Here, while acknowledging that early modern states did not always have a single capital and that there were a number of princely residences with towns serving them, he tried to make a distinction between a medieval capital and an early modern or modern one. 'Royal residences *naissent et meurent* whereas capitals *demeurent*'; they 'necessarily' differed in function. A royal city was, according to Brühl, also an ecclesiastical capital, a *civitas*. The notion of itinerant monarchy and of a capital are, therefore, mutually exclusive.

Brühl thus went some way towards Ewig's position by saying that in certain respects royal cities of the Germanic successor states of the early middle ages, especially Toledo and Pavia, resembled capitals of the late Roman empire. He still insisted, however, that the passage to the itinerant monarchy of the middle ages took place in the Carolingian period. Brühl's muddled thinking is clear from his assertion that this itinerant monarchy created a new type of capital, characterized by the creation of a permanent *pied à terre* for the higher temporal and spiritual dignitaries, but that Aachen did not develop the 'authentic functions' of a capital. Aachen, being neither a town nor an episcopal *civitas*, failed Brühl's artificial litmus test of being a capital.

The effect of Brühl's and Ewig's work, all the same, has been to establish the erroneous notion of a Frankish itinerant court in the reign of Charlemagne. On this analysis, Aachen represents a temporary departure from this norm. Donald Bullough, for example, is typical of modern histor-ians of the Carolingian period in referring to the Frankish court as 'constantly on the move, except in the winter months and intermittently well housed'. He alludes to the 'previously itinerant court' 'settling in its new palace at Aachen in 794', and later in the same paper to the remarkable assembly of writings of pagan and classical antiquity assembled at the court 'while it was still itinerant from villa to camp and from camp to villa'.[142] Aachen's relation-ship to itinerant kingship and an itinerant court remains uneasy; but so does the relationship of all the other Carolingian palaces.[143] It appears to remain the assumption that the entire court moved from one place to the next.

---

[141] Brühl, 'Remarques sur les notions du "capitale" et du "résidence"'. In the later Carolingian period the evidence for some kind of system of itinerant monarchy appeared to Brühl to be stronger.

[142] D. Bullough, '*Aula renovata*: the Carolingian court before the Aachen palace', *Proceedings of the British Academy* 71 (1985), pp. 267–301, repr. in Bullough, *Carolingian renewal* (Manchester, 1991), pp. 121–60 at p. 127.

[143] Nelson, 'Aachen as a place of power', reiterated in J. L. Nelson, 'Was Charlemagne's court a courtly society?', in Cubitt, *Court culture*, pp. 39–58.

From all these past discussions, two main interlocking elements emerge. The first is the notion of the palace as part of an economic system. It has been assumed, for the Carolingian period as well as for the Ottonian, that the king would not use his own resources from the royal estates and that anyone coming to a royal palace would expect to be fed by the king. Yet there are indications in later ninth-century evidence, such as the letters of Einhard, that this was not the case.[144] We could remember also the Royal Frankish annalist's description of the envoys from Spain at the Frankish court at Aachen in 816, obliged to hang around the palace waiting for the Emperor Louis and desperately wondering after three months if they would ever be able to go home.[145] We do not know whether part of their desperation was due to the dwindling of their own supplies.

Such a focus on the economic logistics of provision has sometimes become confused with necessity, so that a persistent image has been created of the king and his court like nomadic pastoralists eating up the local produce and constantly on the move in search of new pasture. The Carolingians are even claimed to have had to renounce the idea of a fixed centre of government for economic reasons, 'sans aucun doute pour des raisons d'ordres économiques', and to content themselves with different royal residences.[146] While this economic explanation for itinerant kingship may be valid for the Ottonian rulers, in that Saxony was a notoriously poor region in the early middle ages, it does not make sense for the richly endowed early Carolingian rulers and what has been pieced together about the royal estates both in the Frankish heartlands and on newly confiscated land from Westphalian and Bavarian landholders. Most crucially, discussions of the king's economic needs have rarely taken into account the remarkable wealth of the royal estates and the extensive forest support for hunting and fishing, in proximity to agricultural and pastoral land.[147] Le Jan, indeed, has pointed rather to the sociological and political function of the itinerary: it was not the need for food which governed the king's movements.[148]

The second major element is the degree to which the palace is a focus of personal, physically face-to-face political control on the part of the Carolingian kings. The contradictions of the surviving evidence expose a

---

[144] Einhard, *Epistolae*, ed. K. Hampe, *MGH Epp.* v (Berlin, 1899), Ep. 5, pp. 111–12.
[145] *ARF* 816 and 817, ed. Kurze, pp. 144–5.
[146] Brühl, 'Remarques sur les notions du "capitale" et du "résidence"', p. 207.
[147] W. Metz, *Zur Erforschung des karolingischen Reichsgutes*, Erträge der Forschung 4 (Darmstadt, 1971).
[148] Le Jan, 'Espaces sauvage'.

need to discard the notion that Charlemagne and his court had to be either one thing or the other, itinerant or based on a capital. Karl-Ferdinand Werner, furthermore, insisted that the king did not move in order to govern, though the pattern of a movement from one palace to another in a 'residential region' on the one hand and to meet his magnates in the peripheral areas on the other applies more to Louis the Pious and his successors than to Charlemagne.[149] What the evidence suggests for Charlemagne's reign, first of all, is a much more nuanced combination of movement and long periods of residence, as well as use of a number of key residences, one of them being Aachen, onto which it is inappropriate to graft the later Ottonian system. All previous discussions of Charlemagne's government, as we shall see in the succeeding chapter, have underestimated the network of communications Charlemagne established throughout his empire.

It is clear that there were phases in the movements of the king and in his use of palaces in the course of Charlemagne's reign. These need to be charted more precisely. In the early years of Charlemagne's reign, his mode of government was in the process of development. It was modified as the kingdom was expanded and Aquitaine, Italy, Bavaria and Saxony were incorporated. Undoubtedly the royal palaces supported the king when he was on the move, and were designed to do that, but their existence *per se* does not provide a sufficient basis for understanding the purpose of the royal itinerary. We still need to explore some further questions before the role of the itinerary in Charlemagne's kingship can be determined. Did Charlemagne really introduce itinerant kingship in the technical sense defined above? If the king was itinerant, was the court itinerant as well? To what extent do the movements of the king indicate that he did indeed attempt to exert personal control of the kingdom by his physical presence at any stage in his long reign, as distinct from using itinerancy as a means of demonstrating his power and authority?

CHARLEMAGNE'S TRAVELS

Gauert's famous map from the 1965 Charlemagne exhibition at Aachen illustrated how the king at one time or another moved right across western Europe, from the Pyrenees to the Elbe, from the English Channel almost to

---

[149] K.-F. Werner, '*Missus–marchio–comes.* Entre l'administration centrale et l'administration locale de l'empire carolingien', in W. Paravicini and K.-F. Werner (eds.), *Histoire comparée de l'administration (IVe–XVIII siècles)*, Beihefte der Francia 9 (Munich, 1980), pp. 191–239 at p. 193. On the itinerary of Louis the Pious see Pössel, 'The itinerant kingship of Louis the Pious'.

the Danube Bend, and across the Alps as far south as Capua.[150] The places are most concentrated in the area north of the Seine and extending ever east beyond the Moselle, Rhine and Weser rivers to the Elbe, with a scattering of places in Italy, including Rome, a handful south of the Loire, and brief appearances in the Pyrenees and Pannonia. What Gauert's map could not explain without further commentary was either the duration or the reason for the visits and travels of Charlemagne, and how much the pattern of movement may have changed in the course of Charlemagne's reign. Without knowing that all these areas are in fact within the territory inherited, conquered, annexed, or attached as tributary regions by treaty, moreover, the itinerary would simply record an impressive amount of travelling. Places from the Rhine eastwards into Thuringia, Westphalia and Saxony, for instance, are mostly linked with the Saxon campaigns recorded in many different sets of Frankish annals. Those in Italy reflect the conquest of the Lombard kingdom and subsequent interventions by Charlemagne thereafter in the affairs of the Lombard kingdom, Benevento and the papacy. The little flurry in the Pyrenees is the famous defeat at Roncesvalles which inspired the later Chanson de Roland, and the camps placed in the middle Danube region witness to Charlemagne's triumph over the Avars and seizure of their fabulous treasure.

Gauert's map also distinguished between types of place receiving visits from the king: battlefields and camps in the context of war and military campaigns, episcopal sees and monasteries, and a host of what he describes as royal residences and palaces equipped to receive the king and his entourage (though we have no idea of the size of the latter). Because the places on Gauert's map do in fact represent places both within the Frankish heartlands and in the newly conquered territories – Aquitaine in 768, Lombard kingdoms in 774, Bavaria in 788, the Spanish March, Brittany and the Avar lands far to the east in 790, and Saxony between 770 and 804 – the map at first sight certainly reflects the king's movements within his own domains. But there are difficulties with this, not least the information on which Gauert relied, for it included the problematic charter evidence, traditionally thought to indicate the king's presence at the time of a charter's redaction.

A first step is to break down the king's movements by both category and time. This counters the general impression of both a wide expanse of Europe covered and the favouring of particular places. If the extensive series of military campaigns in Aquitaine, Saxony, eastern Bavaria and Spain are removed, then movement is concentrated in the area between the

---

[150] Gauert, 'Zum Itinerar', between pp. 320 and 321.

Seine and the Rhine with subsidiary areas or places in Saxony and Bavaria, such as Paderborn and Regensburg, and a handful of places in the Loire region and northern and central Italy. Italy, however, features in Charlemagne's travels only in 773–4, 776, 781, 786–7 and 800–1. He reached the Loire region or the area beyond it only in 768–9, 778 and 800. Only after the subjection of Tassilo was Charlemagne in Bavaria, in 788, 791–3 and 803, and the expedition to Pannonia was mounted from thence in 791. The king was in Saxony 772 and 775, every year between 777 and 785, 789, every year between 795 and 799, and in 804 and 810. Charlemagne reached the northwestern coast of his kingdom between Rouen and the Low Countries in 769, 800 and 811, the area west of Liège (including Reims, the Paris region, Compiègne, Quierzy and Attigny) in 768, 774, possibly 775, 781[151] (see below), 782–3, 779, 782, 785, 786, 800 and 804 (Map 4).

This pattern of intermittent visits, albeit some of them prolonged, as in Regensburg, does not make a powerful case for a king ruling by means of his physical presence in the areas under Frankish rule beyond the Rhineland and Moselle region, in the sense understood by itinerant kingship, especially when so much of his activity in Saxony was for military reasons. Conversely, only in 787, 800–1 (mostly in Italy) and 792–3, when he spent such an extended period in Bavaria, did Charlemagne apparently not reside in or cross either the Meuse-Moselle region (Aachen-Liège down to Metz) or the Rhineland-Main areas (Mainz, Ingelheim, Worms, Frankfurt). In many years his travelling is between and within these regions, even if only for the winter, Christmas, and/or Easter. This of course includes the years in which he crosses the Rhineland region in order to reach Saxony. If we were to differentiate the Rhineland-Main region from the Meuse-Moselle region, then the king's presence is recorded (including the problematic charter evidence) in the region at some time during the years 768, 769, 772, 775–9, 782, 783, 786, 788, 789, 794–802 and 804–14 in the Meuse-Moselle region and during the years 770–4, 776, 779, 781, 783, 784, 786, 788, 790, 791, 794, 803, 807 and 808 for the Rhineland-Main region. For the most part, therefore, it would appear that the king ruled his empire from the Frankish heartlands and increasingly, in the latter part of his reign, from the Meuse-Moselle region.

One further practical matter that needs to be considered, however, is the distances involved. Let us take some estimates, based on the information for motorists supplied by the Netherlands website Routenet.nl (with

---

[151] See below, pp. 188–97, on the problems of the charter evidence.

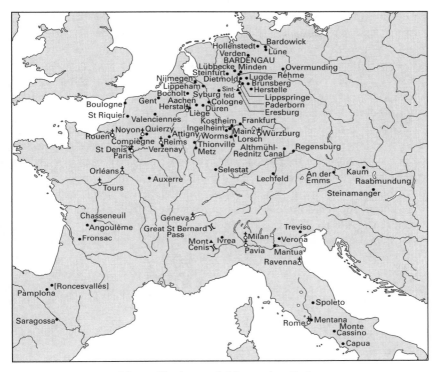

Map 4 Charlemagne's itinerary in 768–814

downloadable maps of all recommended routes). This may give some
indication of distances, even if it can tell us nothing about the time
absorbed by the journey, the speed of travel, the terrain, the conditions
of the roads (ranging from the extensive network of old Roman roads –
many of which were maintained, at least close to towns – to local tracks),
the journeys Charlemagne took by boat on the rivers (as in 793 to
Würzburg[152]) instead of overland, or the weather. Still less do we know
about any of the detours necessary to find fords and bridges to cross rivers,
and the scheduled and, no doubt, unscheduled stops on the way to talk to
people, listen to petitions, eat, rest, pray and the like. It should be noted in
passing that many of the arterial roads of western Europe still follow the
routes of the old Roman roads, so the Routenet.nl suggestions about the

---

[152] *ARF* 793, ed. Kurze, p. 92.

distances involved may not be so very wide of the mark.[153] We can probably assume that Charlemagne himself would have travelled on horseback overland, that there would have been faster riders with the party to carry messages and warn a place of the imminence of the king's arrival, and possibly a slower part of the cavalcade travelling overland with baggage on horses or mules, or in carts, or by water on barges. A conservative estimate might therefore be a speed of 30 km a day.[154]

In 769, for example, Charlemagne, having reached Fronsac near Bordeaux, then travelled to somewhere beyond the Garonne river to the palace at Worms. From Fronsac to Worms is 1081 km or 34 days. In 774 one journey was from Pavia to Ingelheim, a distance of 701 km or about 24 days, but possibly using Worms as a stopping place, which is 46 km from Ingelheim (one very long day or two shorter ones). In 782, one journey was from Thionville to Paderborn, that is, 423 km or a fortnight, and in 788 Charlemagne's travels included the 574 km trip from Regensburg to Aachen (19 days) and in 795 from Aachen to Mainz, that is, 240 km (8 days). If we follow the route of the round trip recorded in the Royal Frankish annals for 800 and 801 the estimate is the following (Map 5):

From Aachen to Boulogne 372 km
From Boulogne to Rouen 183 km
From Rouen to Tours 354 km
From Tours to Orleans 116 km
From Orleans to Paris 130 km
From Paris to Aachen 420 km
From Aachen to Mainz 240 km
From Mainz to Ivrea 696 km (via Strasbourg and Basel)
From Ivrea to Rome (via Florence) 678 km
From Rome to Spoleto 134 km
From Spoleto to Ravenna 237 km
From Ravenna to Pavia 282 km
From Pavia to Ivrea 148 km
From Ivrea to Aachen 894 km

The grand total is 4,884 km, which would involve approximately 162 days on the road. Even during the two decades supposedly 'settled at Aachen',

---

[153] See the *Barrington atlas of the Greek and Roman world* (Princeton, 2000), Maps 7, 10–19, 39–45.

[154] Le Jan, 'Espaces sauvages', also uses the computation of 30 Km per day. M. McCormick, 'Pippin III, the embassy of Caliph al-Mansur, and the Mediterranean world', in Becher and Jarnut, *Die Dynastiewechsel von 751*, pp. 221–42, based his calculations of travel in the eighth century on information relating to the American Civil War and army manoeuvres in the nineteenth century, and calculated similarly, namely, 25 miles per day.

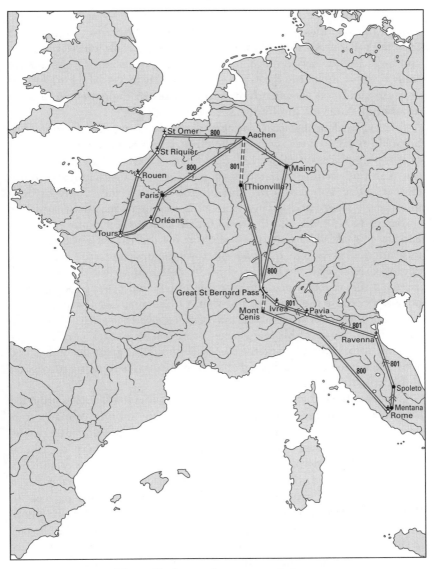

Map 5 Charlemagne's movements in 800–1

the average distance is over 1,000 km per annum between 794 and 804, though this includes the round trip to Rome in 800–1, no travel at all in 802, and the journey to and from Aachen to Mainz, Salz and Regensburg, and back, in 803. Between 805 and 814, the average is 460 km per annum (only 15 days), including the expedition to Saxony in 810 (800 km) and the years 809 and 812–14, when only hunting trips to the Ardennes, a short distance of about 100 km from Aachen, are recorded.[155]

It is self-evident that none of these places can be reached from the one before it in a day. It is necessary, therefore, to envisage an entire network of stopping places on the way.[156] For the most part we can only guess at the planning involved in terms of packing and unpacking weapons, clothes and possibly bedding and utensils as well, the supply of fresh mounts *en route*, and giving notice of intended arrival or ensuring sufficient food, drink and firewood for the entourage (whatever its size) and its animals. The *Capitulare de villis* mentioned earlier gives some indication of a system of *villae* on royal estates kept ready and fully equipped to receive the king, and of the notice of arrival that would be expected. Provision is made for the sale of fish and other goods that are not used because the king did not visit. On the analysis of areas visited, indeed, it looks as if some places may have received the king only once or twice in the course of his reign, whereas he was very often at others. We have no information about the logistics, though a great deal, as noted above, has at least been achieved about the means of supplying provisions and hospitality.

Considerable indications of the reasons for visits to places are provided by the various sources, though there remain many months of many years unaccounted for. There is often uncertainty about the status of a particular place, whether as a customary resting place, a temporary, occasional or unusual stopping place *en route* to somewhere else, or an established royal residence.[157] In Italy, for instance, Charlemagne may have stayed in episcopal residences as well as making use of Lombard palaces. In Rome he probably stayed near St Peter's, though one wonders for whom the nice little Carolingian villa was built in the Forum of Nerva at the end of the eighth century.[158] Occasionally another palace presents itself as very likely, such as Worms for a stay *en route* between Pavia and Ingelheim.

[155] Le Jan, 'Espaces sauvages', p. 47.   [156] Gauert, 'Zum Itinerar'.   [157] Ibid., p. 312.
[158] R. Santangeli Valenziani, 'Profanes Bauwesen in Rom um das Jahr 800', in *799 Kunst und Kultur*, III, pp. 550–7.

Not only do we have the destinations indicated in the narrative sources, but there are also various stopping points, such as the episcopal seats receiving Pippin before 768, including Angoulême, Auxerre, Geneva, Cologne, Liège, Rouen and Würzburg, that Gauert suggested were likely to have continued to offer hospitality to Charlemagne. We also have to remember that Soissons was where Pippin was crowned in 751 and Carloman in 768, and the likelihood that the usurping Carolingians would have made use of the Merovingian palace is strong. The same goes for Noyon, where Charlemagne was crowned. In Metz a palace seems to be testified only from the ninth century near the abbey of St Arnulf. Cologne, a Merovingian royal palace, is only mentioned as a place visited by Charlemagne in connection with excursions against the Saxons, though that does not diminish its importance as a vital staging post, not least when we remember that Cologne was also the see of Hildebold, Charlemagne's chancellor from 791/4 to at least 816 (†818); Hildebold was one of the witnesses of Charlemagne's will.[159] Episcopal seats such as Reims, Metz, Orleans, Noyon, Soissons, Speyer, Worms and Mainz, as well as the abbey of St Denis, seem to have been places where there were palaces or royal houses/estates. Orleans had been the main city of a Merovingian kingdom and there was a palace there, but the abbey of St Mesmin may have had a guest house as well. When the pope visited Francia in 804 and 816 and stayed at Reims, he lodged at the monastery of St Rémi. Louis in 816 chose to stay at the royal palace next to the cathedral at Reims, and so did Charlemagne in 804. In 804 a royal abbey, St Médard at Soissons, was a place for the pope to stay, and probably it was for visiting kings as well.

A royal residence appears to have been a building or estate that the king owned, and was purpose built or designated as royal so that only the king lived or stayed there (as distinct from being a guest there). These may have included secular places that he visited as a guest of the local count, or in town houses in the *civitates* or trading centres, such as Bardowick.[160] It is certainly possible that Charlemagne would have preferred in particular instances to stay with the local bishop. It is also a possibility that he could

---

[159] Depreux, *Prosopographie*, pp. 246–7.
[160] Gauert, 'Zum Itinerar', following up C. Brühl, 'Königspfalz und Bischofstadt in fränkischer Zeit', *Rheinische Vierteljahresblätter* 23 (1958), pp. 161–274, also said the inner organization, the function of these palaces in the itinerary, and their relationship to royal estates, to royal forests and to trade and commerce should be investigated. Some discussion since 1965 has undoubtedly pursued these questions. See, for example, I. L. Hansen and C. Wickham (eds.), *The long eighth century: production, distribution and demand*, The Transformation of the Roman World 11 (Leiden, 2000).

have stayed, if not in his own residence, then in that of the local *missus* or count or even in some kind of public hospice, with rooms commandeered for the occasion if a monastery's guest house were not within reach. The endowment of monasteries and the number of new buildings to serve the king on the move could presumably have been intended for the royal agents as well. Here we need to recall that the *Capitulare de villis* emphasized that the royal estates were intended to administer to the king's needs alone. It expressly forbade the *missi* and their retinues from lodging in the royal manor houses unless he or the queen had given orders that they might; looking after the *missi* was the responsibility of the count.[161] This is echoed in the Capitulary of Herstal for 779. This stated that the count had to provide for the *missus*, or a vassal had to provide for both count and *missus*.[162] As we have seen above, the *Capitulare de villis* also related the organization of the royal estates and houses for receiving the king to the movements of the army. The produce of the estates was among the things that would be loaded onto carts for the campaigns.[163] There is no need for such temporary gatherings to have been confined to the army, for the capitulary and narrative references to assemblies indicate that meetings of secular and clerical magnates were also frequent. In no source is there any reference to billeting on the local populace. The advantage of camps would have been that everyone was there with horses and carts to hand and ready to move very quickly if necessary. Open spaces for camps also offered a major extension of the space within which the king moved.

POLITICAL AND DIPLOMATIC SPACE

Assembly meeting places are an essential feature of the topography of Carolingian royal power. They are the occasions on which we can be certain that large groups of people came together and would need to be housed and fed. There are occasional references in the annals to the huts built for the winter, or to tents (as noted below).[164] It may be that nearby monasteries, particularly the royal abbeys richly endowed by the king, would also offer hospitality to the king and his entourage as well as to visiting abbots and bishops or other clergy and laymen. Choice of a site for

[161] *Capitulare de villis*, cc. 1 and 26, *MGH Cap.* 1, No. 32, pp. 83 and 85.
[162] Capitulary of Herstal, c. 17, *MGH Cap.* 1, No. 20, p. 51.
[163] *Capitulare de villis*, c. 30, *MGH Cap.* 1, No. 32, p. 85, and see also cc. 64 and 68, ibid, p. 89; and above, pp. 149–51.
[164] See below, pp. 187–8.

an assembly or a synod, therefore, would need to bear in mind the provision of sufficient suitable flat and preferably unrocky land for camps, the erection of temporary huts of wood, tents (especially in the summer months), and a good water supply. The sheer organization involved was prodigious. The Revised Version of the *Annales regni francorum*, moreover, occasionally refers to the suitability of weather for army movements, and to the availability or lack of fodder to make it feasible for an army to set out. These phrases are more than mere literary effect.[165]

Paderborn offers an important example of a prominent meeting place which may have had its parallel elsewhere. Paderborn had an excellent water supply, ample supplies of game and pasturage, and a large flat area in which many men could gather. It was thus ideal for a camping army or delegates to an assembly. The large area, including the Domburg, used by Charlemagne, furthermore, has been described as diplomatic space, that is, the space forming the physical and symbolic framework for conveying a particular interpretation of power during diplomatic interaction. This is particularly evoked for Paderborn in the poem *Karolus magnus et Leo papa*.[166] Many of those coming to meetings and assemblies needed to be able to set up their tents and to procure fodder for their horses and livestock, and a good supply of water.[167] Here we should recall the reference in the *De ordine palatii* to sessions of an assembly being conducted outdoors in fair weather.[168] There are a few references to tents and temporary wooden structures in the *Annales regni francorum*, though more permanent town houses may also have been built as the economic role of the settlement developed.

Carolingian palaces were free-standing on river banks and on plains, with a very varied set of designs for the layout of the various buildings. The royal residential buildings, apart from the chapel and *aula* of these palaces, moreover, appear to have been too small to accommodate the crowds of officials and followers with which they have in the past been associated. As we have seen, written texts relating to Aachen indicate that other houses to accommodate those in royal service or wishing to be close to the king

---

[165] *RVARF* 777, 779, 780, 783, 784 (suitable weather), 782, 798 (fodder), ed. Kurze, pp. 49, 53, 55, 65, 67, 59 and 103.

[166] S. Lamb, 'The Frankish expansion and diplomatic space', unpublished essay, MPhil in Medieval History, University of Cambridge (2005) (I am grateful to Sally Lamb for allowing me to cite this work); *Karolus magnus et Leo papa*, ed. E Dümmler, *MGH Poet.* 1, pp. 366–79.

[167] See also the discussion of army matters below, pp. 270–3.

[168] Hincmar, *De ordine palatii*, c. 35, ed. Gross and Schieffer, *Hinkmar*, pp. 92–4.

appear to have been constructed nearby.[169] The political and diplomatic outdoor space surrounding these residences, however, would have been of crucial importance in relation to every Carolingian palace for the gathering of assemblies.

The places apparently visited, moreover, reflect a network of social and political connections that it is sometimes possible to document in greater detail from other sources. This suggests that the distribution of royal residences across the empire needs to be seen as functioning within this network and was far from being higgledy-piggledy.[170] Yet the palaces that have been identified were for the most part too far apart to envisage them as the only stopping place for the ruler or any of his officials. What has to be surmised, rather, is a combination of halts by the side of the road, using tents or rough shelters, the possibly frequent use of the guest houses of abbeys or bishoprics, and use of royal estates and royal residences or palaces *en route* as indicated by the provisions of the *Capitulare de villis*. Although in some instances the route taken – by ship down the Rhine, crossing the Alps by the Great St Bernard pass, by land from Boulogne to Tours via St Riquier, Rouen and Orleans (probably on old Roman roads) – is known, for many of these journeys we know only the destinations (though the exact location cannot always be identified), rather than details about the means of travel or routes followed.

If so much of the itinerary of Charlemagne is to be attributed to war and the consolidation of conquest as a military leader on the one hand, and to religious devotion and the observance of Christian festivals on the other,[171] it would suggest that we need to look more closely at the remainder of the evidence to establish how much, in addition to the information about assemblies, can be assigned to governmental and administrative action.

CHARTERS AND THE ROYAL ITINERARY

Gauert's map was based on the documentary and narrative evidence extant from Charlemagne's reign, particularly the charters emanating from the royal chancery. Royal diplomas reflect royal power and record royal business. Charlemagne's charters grant lands, royal protection, immunity, the revenue from tolls, and free abbatial election to different places. They record the settling of property disputes and the return of confiscated

---

[169] See the salutary remarks of R. Samson, 'Carolingian palaces and the poverty of ideology', in M. Locock (ed.), *Meaningful architecture: social interpretations of buildings* (Avebury, 1994), pp. 99–131.
[170] Here I differ from Airlie, 'The palace of memory'.   [171] See below, pp. 321–30.

land. They are also, of course, crucial witnesses at a number of levels both to the relations between the king and his subjects and to the orchestration of acceptance and recognition of the king's authority, though full study of these aspects cannot be undertaken here. This charter evidence has appeared to scholars in the past to provide an exact and uncontestable source of information about the king's whereabouts with a simple equation: where the charter was drawn up, there was the king and his court. Unfortunately, it is not as simple as that.

Let us look at the year 775 to highlight the problems, though it needs to be registered that 775 was the year from which the greatest number of charters, twenty-two, survives in the whole of Charlemagne's reign. Between 5 January and 26 June there is a series of charters drawn up *ad carisiaco palatii publici* (*sic*), that is, at Quierzy. The dates given are 5 and 22 January; 14 March, 4 April, 24 and 29 May, 9 and 26 June. During these six months one charter was also drawn up at St Denis (*actum in monasterio Sancti Diunysii*) on 25 February and two at Thionville on 3 and 10 May (*apud theodonem*). For the rest of the year charters are recorded at Düren 28 July, 3 August, 25 October, and November. Thionville is recorded again in November, and the last document for the year is at Selestat in December. The Quierzy charters record grants to Hersfeld in Thuringia, Metz, St Denis, Farfa and Honau. The St Denis document is a grant for St Denis. The Thionville documents in the early part of the year make grants to Flavigny and St Martin at Tours and in the latter part to Salonne and Prüm. The Selestat charter records the settling of a dispute between Honau and Corbie. In the case of St Denis in February, Düren in July and Selestat in December, the transactions are actually recorded as being drawn up or enacted at a meeting where the king was to administer justice in the place concerned. The Quierzy documents record business concerning very distant places in Germany and Italy as well as closer to Quierzy at St Denis. The two Thionville charters concern places in Burgundy and the Loire region (Map 6).

Let us look at this sequence again with the distances between the various places in mind. Charlemagne spent Christmas 774 at Quierzy according to the *Annales regni francorum*, and grants were drawn up at Quierzy in favour of Hersfeld and Metz, dated 5 and 22 January 775.[172] Next, at St Denis, 109.8 km or 3 days distant via Noyon and Compiègne, the charter dated 25 February (original, written by Wigbald *ad vicem Hitherii*) recorded land

---

[172] *DKar.* 1, Nos. 89 and 90 (both survive in the original and were written by Hitherius), and 91 (Gorze cartulary copy of s.XII; no scribe recorded).

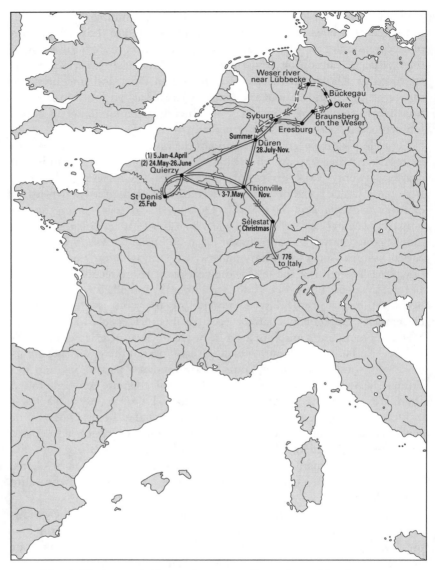

Map 6 Charlemagne's itinerary in 775 according to the traditional accounts

granted to St Denis.[173] Then back again at Quierzy, grants were made to St Denis on 14 March of freedom from tolls, and immunity.[174] In 775, Easter fell on 26 March which, according to the *Annales regni francorum*, Charlemagne spent at Quierzy. A grant of immunity redacted at Quierzy by Wigbald was made to Murbach on 4 April. The king then supposedly moved on to Thionville, a distance of 303 km or ten days' journey, possibly via Reims, Chalons and Metz. At Thionville, freedom from tolls was granted to Flavigny on 3 May, and confirmation of the possession of estates to St Martin of Tours on 10 May. These charters were written by Rado but survive only in later copies.[175] Thereafter, the king apparently returned, another ten-day journey of 303 km, to Quierzy, according to the charters of Quierzy of 24 May, 29 May, 9 June, and 26 June, granting freedom of election to Farfa, and confirming possessions of Honau and of earlier alienated land to St Denis. All four of these charters were written by Wigbald *ad vicem Hitherii*, but only the grant for St Denis survives in the original.[176] The *Annales regni francorum* record an assembly of the army at Düren before setting out for a summer campaign in Saxony. From Quierzy to Düren (between Aachen and Cologne) is 361 km or twelve days' journey. Thereafter the *Annales regni francorum* records the campaigns in the Weser river region, at least ten days' journey away, the capture of Syburg and the rebuilding of the Eresburg. Charters are also recorded at Düren on 28 July, 3 August, 25 October and November.[177] The grants in July, August and October were to Hersfeld, and that in November was to Fulda. Those include one original and one copy each of charters written by Rado and Wigbald, both *ad vicem Hitherii*. The charter of 28 July, how-ever, was written by Theudegarius and records a settlement of a dispute between Fulrad of St Denis and Erchanrad bishop of Paris, presided over by Charlemagne, and in the presence of many *fideles*, including Anselm, count of the palace.[178] From Düren the charter record takes us 267 km or nine days' journey to Thionville and there Rado *ad vicem Hitherii* wrote a grant of land to Salonne which survives in the original in the St Denis archive.[179] The Prüm cartulary records two further grants drawn up at Thionville in November, granting immunity and confirming Pippin III's gifts to Prüm.[180] Lastly, at Sélestat, where Charlemagne spent Christmas

---

[173] *DKar.* I, No. 92.
[174] *DKar.* I, Nos. 93 (this survives in a s.XII/XIII cartulary), and 94 (an original, written by Wigbald *ad vicem Hitherii*).
[175] Wigbald's charter, *DKar.* I, No. 95, and Rado's, *DKar.* I, Nos. 96 and 97.
[176] *DKar.* I, Nos. 98–101.   [177] *DKar.* I, Nos. 102–5.   [178] *DKar.* I, No. 102.
[179] *DKar.* I, No. 107.   [180] *DKar.* I, Nos. 108–9.

785 (according to the *Annales regni francorum*), a dispute was again recorded by Theodegarius in the presence of Anselm, count of the palace, and survives only in early modern copies.[181] With the record of the dispute between Fulrad of St Denis and Bishop Erchanrad of Paris, this is one of the very few to record the king's presence in the charter itself. It explains that the king was in his palace in Sélestat in order to listen to cases and give justice.[182]

What does even this small example tell us about charter redaction in relation to the king's movements? The grants are a combination of royal decisions to exert patronage, and the consequence of petitions, requests for royal favour or the judicial intervention of the ruler in meetings possibly organized by the count of the palace to settle disputes. In the case of Quierzy, the Royal Frankish annals tell us that the king spent Christmas and Easter at Quierzy, so we surmise that he was there for winter and early spring before he is then recorded as setting out for the assembly of the host at Düren, also a royal palace, and the campaign in Saxony. If we were to accept the charter record literally, then we would have to add in the 606 km round trip between Quierzy and Thionville in April and May. If we accept all the charters of Quierzy of 775 as an indication of the king's presence then the campaign in Saxony did not start until July. The charters issued from Düren are dated June, July, August and October which would require Charlemagne to be returning from the Weser river campaign, at least a ten-day journey, at regular intervals before finally reaching the palace of Thionville, in order to grant land to Salonne and Prüm, and Sélestat in December to judge the dispute between Honau and Corbie.

Rather than accepting the charters as an indication of the physical presence of the king, therefore, it is much more likely that we are seeing in many, if not most, instances the activities of the king's officials, with notaries and the scribes working for them sent out or based on site to record transactions in the name of the king, possibly accompanied by the count of the palace. The itinerary for the year is much more likely to have been simply from Quierzy to Düren to Saxony, back to Thionville and then on to Selestat for Christmas (confirmed by the *Annales regni francorum*) before Charlemagne set out for Italy the following year, with none of the zig-zagging back and forth that the charters have hitherto been thought to record. (Map 7)

[181] *DKar.* I, No. 110.
[182] The formula is standard: for example, in D.Kar., I, No. 102, the formula is as follows: 'cum nos in dei nomen Duria villa in palacio nostro ad universorum causas audiendum vel recta iudicia termenandum resederimus.' In *DKar.*, I, No. 110, it is: 'Cum nos in dei nomine sclatistati villa in palacio nostro ad universorum causas audiens dum vel recta iudicia terminandum resideremus.'

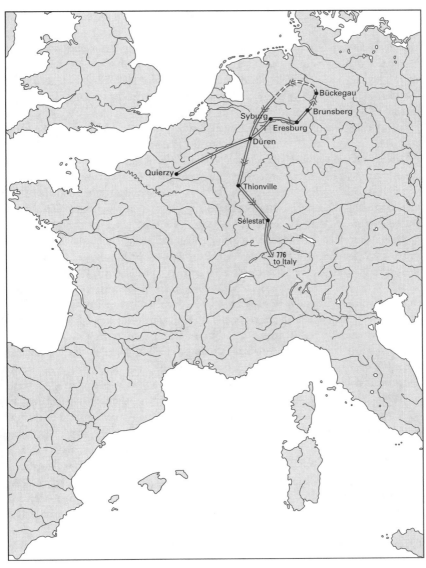

Map 7 Charlemagne's itinerary in 775: revised version

It would also suggest that we should take the *ad vicem* note in the charters more seriously as an indication of a notary acting as a deputy for the *cancellarius* when the latter was elsewhere. The indications are that Wigbald did indeed go to St Denis and remain at Quierzy to oversee transactions in the spring, and that both Rado and Wigbald acted for Hitherius at Düren during the Saxon campaigns of the summer and autumn.

Thus there would appear to have been a system of itinerant scribes and notaries responsible for the correct redaction and the authentication of charters, accompanying officials for the king. The wide range of places where transactions were recorded suggests written petitions being dealt with from one of the palaces where the king has been resident at some stage, and also transactions drawn up as a result of a hearing elsewhere which had indeed been in the presence of the king. One of these is the charter of 6 December 777. It survives in the original written by Rado at Aachen, granting a privilege for the church of Salonne near St Denis, as agreed at the synod of Paderborn in the preceding summer. The meeting in Paderborn, moreover, is confirmed by the *Annales regni francorum*; these recorded the king as holding a *synodum publicum* at Paderborn in spring.[183]

That the sequence of charters for 775 and the charter of 777 are not isolated instances is clear from other charters issued in Charlemagne's name. Use of notaries acting on behalf of the king is also indicated, for example, by the movements for 770–3. According to the various annal accounts, the king was present at an assembly in Worms in 770 with Christmas at Mainz and Herstal in the spring of 771, possibly on the way to the assembly in Valenciennes, with Christmas at Attigny in 771 and then at Herstal again for Easter in 772.[184] The settlement of the dispute at Longlier in 771 is in keeping with the king's movements recorded in the narrative sources, not least the meeting at Corbeny with Carloman's followers after Carloman's death.[185] It is not impossible that Charlemagne was present at Reims for the burial of his brother, for Reims, Samoussy, Attigny and Corbeny are all within one or two days' journey from each other along the Roman road from Reims to Saint-Quentin nearby.[186] The text of the Herstal charter in 772 fits the narrative

[183] *DKar.* I, No. 118, and *ARF* 777, ed. Kurze, p. 48.
[184] *ARF* 770, 771, ed. Kurze, pp. 80 and 82.   [185] *DKar.* I, No. 63.
[186] On Carloman's burial see *Annales mettenses priores 771*, p. 57. Samoussy to Reims is 67 km (2 days) and to Corbeny less than a day (24 km). Corbeny to Attigny is 68 km or two days. From the assembly at Valenciennes down to Reims would take five or six days (172 km).

record of the itinerary, for it describes the settling of a dispute about Lorsch possessions.[187]

Acceptance of other charters from these years as indications of the king's presence, however, would again involve Charlemagne in a great deal of to-ing and fro-ing, with journeys to Worms in 771 and then over to Quierzy and to Longlier *en route* for Geneva in 773; these would have been major detours. In October 778, moreover, at *Goddingas villa* (Godinne) south-west of Liège, a charter to confirm St Denis's immunity was drawn up by Giltbertus *ad vicem Radonis* at a point when Charlemagne would still have been in Saxony, unless he took a circuitous route back from Saxony in the early autumn in order to arrive at Herstal, west of Aachen, for Christmas.[188] In the following year many annals record that Charlemagne retired to Worms for the winter after the Saxon campaigns, yet there is also a charter in favour of Hersfeld drawn up at Herstal in September, by Wigbald *ad vicem Radonis*, many miles from either the Saxon strongholds or the palace at Worms.[189] When returning from Italy in 781 to spend Christmas at Quierzy, the king travelled via Worms. He may also have gone to Herstal again on the way, to be there when an exchange of land between Abbess Eufemia of St Peter's in Metz and Fulrad, abbot of St Denis was written by one scribe and recognized by Widolaicus *ad vicem Radonis*. But the difference in the journeys would have been approximately 112 km, that is, four days on the road.[190] Given the extraordinary distances traversed to Saxony or to Rome, such a detour may be entirely reasonable, but it seems less likely than the charter drawn up by the anonymous notary being sent to Herstal for recognition, or the notary visiting Herstal to get the job done in the king's absence. This is especially the case if the beneficiaries and the lands granted, themselves far removed geographically from the place of redaction, are taken into account.

Some places where charters were drawn up may well have been on the route taken and could have acted as feasible stopping places. Thus in returning to Worms from dealing with the revolt in Friuli in 776, the king may have chosen to go via Vicenza and Ivrea, from which we have two charters dated 9 and 16 June on his way to cross the Alps by either Mont Cenis or, more likely, the Great St Bernard pass. Vicenza and Ivrea are

[187] *DKar.* I, No. 65.   [188] *DKar.* I, No. 120. This survives in the original.
[189] *DKar.* I, No. 126; the editor, Mühlbacher, acknowledged this but thought there might be a mistake in the dating, p. 176.
[190] *DKar.* I, No. 136: see A. Stoclet, *Autour de Fulrad de Saint-Denis (v. 710–784)* (Geneva and Paris, 1993); and *ChLA*, XVI, No. 628, Paris, Archives nationales K7, No. 8. *Folradus abbas* is also written in tironian notes.

approximately ten days (314 km) apart, though it might have been done faster. The Vicenza charter was drawn up by Wigbald *ad vicem Hitherii*, but unfortunately neither the late eighteenth-century copy nor the fifteenth-century cartulary version of the gift of land made at Ivrea to the grammarian Paulinus preserves the name of the scribe.[191] Further on this hypothetical route is *Patris Gaiaggio*, possibly to be identified with present-day Patri Gaggio, where a charter attributed to Rado recorded a land grant to Nonantola. Mühlbacher noted that this place lay 'on one of the routes from Ivrea to the Upper Rhine'. He presumably had in mind that the next destination we can record after Ivrea is Worms. It is a possible route, though a very roundabout one, and a preferable route would have been via Aosta. It may be more practical, therefore, to think of this little Italian group as the consequence of a certain amount of written correspondence or requests delivered orally.

That the process of charter redaction could include a charter being drawn up elsewhere and brought to a palace for confirmation may be suggested by a document from 797. Here the *recognitio* was provided by Ercambald at Aachen but written by Genesius and with Pippin king of Italy acting as *ambasciator*. The charter recorded a transaction confirming the monastery of Nonantola's ownership of land given by a Lombard noble.[192] A further possibility is that the bare outline of the details was sent to the palace and the entire charter was then prepared and returned in due course to Nonantola. A rare instance of such a process is the manu-mission of the woman Sigrada, jotted down on a piece of parchment in tironian notes, that seems to be the draft of a now lost charter.[193] The verso of the parchment was subsequently used to record a grant to Fulda.[194]

Similarly, in 782, the grant recognized by Wigbald at Gondreville, if the king has to be presumed to be present, would have involved doubling back to Thionville and an extra six days' journey at the end of the Saxon campaign that year.[195] The year 786 was one in which Charlemagne, according to all our other evidence, did not get as far north as Aachen, but Ercambald *ad vicem Radonis* drew up a charter there.[196]

---

[191] *DKar.* I, Nos. 111 and 112.   [192] *DKar.* I. No. 183.

[193] *DKar.* I, No. 115: see M. Tangl, 'Der Entwurf einer unbekannten Urkunde Karls des Großen in tironischen Noten', *MIÖG* 21 (1900), pp. 344–50; *ChLA*, XII, No. 540, p. 68, Munich, Bayerisches Hauptstaatsarchiv Kaiserselekt I Rückseite.

[194] Now *DKar.* I, No. 116; and see *ChLA*, XII, No. 539, pp. 65–7.

[195] *DKar.* I, No. 147: immunity granted to Modena.

[196] *DKar.* I, No. 152, a grant of immunity and freedom of election to the abbacy for the monastery of Ansbach. This led Mühlbacher to doubt whether the charter had been drawn up in Aachen.

Occasionally there are direct correlations between the places enjoying the king's presence in the narrative sources and the charter or capitulary record, as in the visit to Rome in 787, the Christmas and Easter of 787–8 spent at Ingelheim and the assembly there on 28 March 788. There is a cluster of charters from Mainz, Worms and Kostheim during the year Charlemagne spent there in 790,[197] and his sojourn in Regensburg in 792 is also reflected in grants for Aniane and Aquileia drawn up there.[198] Conversely, if we look at the last twenty years of Charlemagne's reign in relation both to the places of charter redaction and to the summary above of the winters spent in Aachen or elsewhere, a similar pattern emerges. From the period from 794 to 803, with no charters surviving at all for the years 796 and 798, of twenty-seven charters, one third were redacted at Aachen. In the years after 803, with no charters at all from 804 and 805, and a total of sixteen surviving charters, only four were produced somewhere other than Aachen. Seven of the remainder, dated at Aachen, were written between 811 and 813. On the charter evidence at least, therefore, it is only during the last three years of the reign that charter scribes and the king completely coincide in a prolonged residence at Aachen.

Such details are suggestive, for they undermine the solidity of assumptions about the charter evidence hitherto. Yet three further factors need to be taken into account, namely the uneven pattern of Charlemagne's charter survival, the changing pattern of charter redaction over time, and our lacunose knowledge of the royal writing office itself. These in their turn, moreover, throw further light on the functioning of the royal household.

CHARTER SURVIVAL

Reference has already been made to years for which there are no charters extant. In addition to the lack of Charlemagne's charters in 768 and 814, there are eight otherwise productive years of the reign with no extant charters, namely 784, 785, 789, 793, 796, 798, 804 and 805.[199] Twenty-one charters from 800 or earlier cannot be precisely dated, but even so, in

---

[197] *DKar.*, I, Nos. 163–7, but No. 167 for Salzburg may have been written somewhere else.
[198] *DKar.* I, Nos. 173–5.
[199] In terms of capitularies, for example, there are the *Admonitio generalis, Duplex capitulare missorum ad Breviarium missorum Aquitanicum* of 789 and the *Capitulare missorum* of 789 or 792/3, the *Capitulare de latronibus* of 804 and the *Capitulare missorum in Theodonis villa datum primum et secundum generale* of 805. If the few extant letters from the *Codex epistolaris carolinus* are added, this indicates a continuance of the exchange of letters between the popes and the Carolingian rulers in the years to 793: Nos. 74, 77, 83, 84, 87, 89, 94; and see also *MGH Epp.* III (Berlin, 1899), pp. 59–60, 63–4 and 66–7. See also below, pp. 233–63.

the remaining years of the reign there is, more often than not, a very meagre record, with twenty-five years for which there are three or fewer charters.[200] For only six years are there five or more charters, and the twenty-two remaining from 775 are quite exceptional, especially given that no fewer than ten of these survive in the originals. The year 775 is nevertheless a representative indication of one of the determinants for this meagre survival rate, in that it so happens that grants were made to monasteries in that year which have a better archive record than many of the others, namely St Denis (6) Hersfeld (5), Farfa (3) and Prüm (2). The last two have early cartularies, of the eleventh and tenth century respectively. Other later cartularies which preserve many older documents are the Lorsch, Fulda and Echternach cartularies of the twelfth and thirteenth centuries. Despite the remarkable archive efficiency of St Gallen, however, only two of Charlemagne's charters from the St Gallen archive, a gift to the priest Arnald and the agreement between Abbot John of St Gallen and Bishop Sidonius of Constance, both original, survive, and they happen to be two of the very few royal diplomas from Alemannia as a whole before 814.[201]

Although the dominance of the St Denis archive, so marked for the Merovingian period, is less marked in the Carolingian period, St Denis charters nevertheless make up a substantial proportion of the surviving charters of Charlemagne: fourteen of the forty-seven originals, that is, 25 per cent, are from St Denis. From the 164 genuine diplomas of Charlemagne, fifteen are in favour of St Denis or its dependent cell Salonne, compared with ten for Hersfeld, nine for Fulda and seven for Lorsch.[202]

That this apparent preference for St Denis is more likely to be a consequence of the exceptional survival of documents from St Denis

---

[200] See the clear graph provided in Nelson, 'Aachen as a place of power', p. 241.

[201] *DKar.* I, No. 130 (780). On St Gallen see R. McKitterick, *The Carolingians and the written word* (Cambridge, 1989), pp. 77–134; P. Erhart and B. Zeller (eds.), *Mensch und Schrift im frühen Mittelalter* (St Gallen, 2006), and P. Erhart (ed.), *ChLA*, Part C, Switzerland III, St Gallen, 1 (Dietikon and Zurich, 2006), being the first volume of the St Gallen charters dating from the ninth century in facsimile.

[202] See W. Goffart and D. Ganz, 'Charters earlier than AD 800 from French collections', *Speculum* 65 (1990), pp. 906–32; R. Bautier, 'La chancellerie et les actes royales dans les royaumes carolingiennes', *Bibliothèque de l'Ecole des Chartes* 143 (1984), pp. 5–80; and G. P. A. Brown, 'Politics and patronage at the abbey of St Denis (814–898): the rise of a royal patron saint', unpublished DPhil thesis, University of Oxford (1989). See also H. Fichtenau, 'Archive der Karolingerzeit', in H. Fichtenau, *Beiträge zur Mediävistik*, Ausgewählte Aufsätze 2, Urkundenforschung (Stuttgart, 1977), pp. 115–25; and B.-M. Tock, 'La diplomatique française du haut moyen âge, vue à travers les originaux', in M. Courtois and M. J. Gasse-Grandjean (eds.), *Diplomatique française du haut moyen âge: inventaire des chartes originales antérieure à 1121 conservées en France*, ARTEM 4 (Turnhout, 2001), pp. 54–60.

than a reflection of Charlemagne's policies also affects our understanding of the overall indications of Charlemagne's charters.[203] In terms of the palaces where the *recognovi* was recorded, only one charter can be placed south of the Loire and there is none from Alemannia. Yet the overall pattern of giving in terms of recipients, even once the contested charters have been removed from consideration, is far more widely dispersed.

We have, in short, an imperfect and probably distorted impression in terms both of the geographical and chronological distribution of the charters, and of the relative intensity of charter redaction or final approval. It is dependent on the efficiency of certain archives with the chance of their documents surviving to the present day, and on the orchestration of royal favour for a particular institution. Neither can be assumed to be evenly distributed across the entire reign. Whereas many of Louis the Pious's early charters were confirmations of grants made by his father and grandfather, and there was thus undoubtedly a great burst of activity in the first few years of his reign, the same does not appear to be the case for Charlemagne.[204] On the contrary, he steadily built up his own new and increasing network of royal monasteries and favoured individuals to add to that already fostered by his father.[205]

CHARTER REDACTION

Discussion of Charlemagne's charters hitherto has not taken sufficiently into account either the sphere of operations of the notaries or the implications of the *ad vicem* and *recognovi* notes at the end of the charters. When this is done, the information in the charters and the work of the notaries, however patchy and skewed our evidence, can be interpreted rather differently from the conclusions drawn by scholars hitherto. To demonstrate this, let us first take one example of an original charter from the late eighth

---

[203] D. Songzoni, 'Le chartrier de l'abbaye de Saint-Denis en France au haut moyen âge: essai de reconstitution', *Pecia: resources en médiévistique* 3 (2003), pp. 9–210, esp. pp. 119–49.

[204] On Louis see P. Johanek, 'Probleme einer zukünftigen Edition der Urkunden Ludwigs des Frommen', in Godman and Collins, *Charlemagne's heir*, pp. 409–24; and T. Kölzer, *Kaiser Ludwig der Fromme (814–840) im Spiegel seiner Urkunden*, Nordrhein-Westfälische Akademie der Wissenschaften, Vorträge G 401 (Paderborn, 2005). For some examples of Charlemagne's confirmation of earlier grants see *DKar.* I Nos. 56, 57, 91, 94. For lordship over monasteries more generally see S. Wood, *The proprietary church in the medieval west* (Oxford, 2006), esp. pp. 211–30 and 247–59.

[205] J. Semmler, 'Pippin III und die fränkische Klöster', *Francia* 3 (1975), pp. 88–146; Semmler, 'Karl der Große und das fränkische Mönchtum', in *KdG* II, pp. 255–89, and below, pp. 295–8.

century in order to demonstrate its features and the kind of information it can yield.

In 775, on the occasion of the completion of the building of the new church at St Denis, Charlemagne granted the villas in Luzarches and Messy, in the regions of Paris and Meaux respectively, to the monastery of St Denis.[206] As with all other royal charters written by royal scribes, this is written in a very distinctive chancery cursive script, with elaborate, elongated and even curly ascenders to many of the letters. These are enlarged for the name and titles of the ruler on the first line of the document and again when recording the *signum* of the ruler and the *recognitio* of the chancery official. This St Denis charter is very large, for it measures 505 × 330 mm. Again, this is typical of royal charters, for they are mostly written on very large pieces of parchment, wider than they are tall (often as much as half a metre wide), and the script is parallel to the longer side. The text is usually written on the flesh side of the membrane. The charter starts with the protocol, comprising a chrismon, a distinctive and elaborate symbolic invocation, and the name of the ruler, written in elongated letters and offering the title of the ruler: 'Charles, by the grace of God king of the Franks and Lombards' (*Carolus gratia dei rex francorum et langobardorum*) and his address to the potential audience for the legal transaction, 'to all our faithful subjects both present and future' (*omnibus fidelibus nostris tam praesentis quam et futuris*). The clauses known as the Arenga follow, in which a statement is made about the general motivation or reason for the grant. Such a statement can include reference to specific petitions on the part of the recipient. The charter then mentions the recipient. In this St Denis charter a descriptive account of the church of St Denis, recently rebuilt and dedicated, and of the resting place of St Denis and his companions, is included.

The body of the charter then records what is actually being given and the terms under which it is granted. In this case it is the two *villae*, whose location is precisely described. They are granted 'in perpetuity' and for the salvation of our soul' (*donamus pro anime nostrae remedio . . . donatumque in perpetuo*), that they may be used for the increase of the said monastery and the monks that serve there, for the furnishing of the church itself and for the maintenance of the poor.[207] Like this one, many grants also specify what goes with the villas, such as lands, houses, their tenants, slaves (or serfs or servants), vineyards, woods, meadows, pastures, waters and watercourses, flour mills, and all movable and immovable belongings. This

---

[206] Paris, Archives Nationales K6, No. 4, *ChLA* XVIII, No. 615, for a facsimile.   [207] *DKar.* I, No. 92.

gift of perpetual and complete ownership will be maintained provided it will please these monks 'to pray both day and night for the Lord's mercy upon us and our descendants' (*pro nobis prosequente progenia nostra die noctuque domini misericordia adtencius depraecare*).

Signing-off clauses are then added. This includes the announcement of the signature and of the seal in a standard formula: 'and that this our authority may be more strictly observed and better maintained throughout the years, we have directed that it be confirmed hereunder in our own hand and sealed with our ring' (*manu propria subter eam decrevimus roborare vel de anulo nostro iussimus sigilare*). After a space of two or three lines in width, there is then the portion of the charter text known as the eschatocol, with the *signum* and name of the ruler, his monogram and the name of the notary responsible who provides the *recognovi* note, that is, the official confirmation of the charter. He adds another chrismon and subscription symbol or beehive, beside which, in notarial shorthand or tironian notes, the details of the *recognovi* note are often repeated, sometimes with additional indications of who may have requested that the document be drawn up. So here in this St Denis charter there is the *signum Caroli gloriosissimi regis*. Then the notary's formal recognition of the charter follows: *uuigbaldus ad vicem Hitherii recognovi*, and in tironian notes is added *uuigbaldus advicem Hitherii recognovi et subscripsi* (that is, '[I] Wigbald witnessed/ validated and signed [this charter] on behalf of Hitherius'.

At the very bottom of the charter is the date clause. This is written in the form of a date (day and month) according to the Roman system and the regnal year of the king. This charter, therefore, is dated on the '5th of the Kalends of March [= 25 February] in the seventh year and first year of our rule, enacted in the monastery of St Denis in the name of the Lord. *Feliciter*.'

Most of the elements of the charter are formulaic and provide in their essentials a template for all such grants. This can be seen from other charters as well as from Carolingian formularies compiled for the use of notaries and preserving sample texts of donations as well as of other kinds of document.[208] With the titles given the king in the first line, and in the date clause, a charter provides information about the particular stage of the king's career, in this instance, the seventh year after Charlemagne succeeded his father and the first year after his conquest of the Lombard

---

[208] *Formulae Marculfi* and *Formulae marculfinae aevi karolini*, ed. K. Zeumer, *MGH Formulae*, and see below, pp. 220–2.

kingdom, hence 775. It is quite unusual for the royal charter to be enacted in a monastery as this one was. More usually this part of the clause refers to its enactment in the open or public business in a royal villa or palace in the following formula: *actum . . . palatio publico.*[209] Thus on 13 January 769 a charter was drawn up *actum Aquis palatio publico* (Aachen), and another *actum Audriacum villa* (Orville). The formulaic phrases in other charters are similar: *actum in Theodone villa palacio publico* (Thionville), *actum Haristallio palatio publico* (Herstal), *actum brocgagad palatio publico* (Brunath), *actum Salmunciago palatio publico* (Samoussy), *Carisiaco palacio publico* (Quierzy – also called a *villa* in another charter), *Dura palatio publico* (Düren), *Noiumaga palatio publico* (Nijmegen). The stress is on the public transaction of legal business, and it is echoed in private charters. Such publicness, that is, not secret but open, is a characterization of the accessibility, in principle at least, of the king's justice and munificence, and of that of his officials. Very occasionally, as demonstrated earlier, it is also an indication of the king's presence.

For the purposes of mapping both the itinerary and the activities of the scribes and notaries, it is the eschatocol and date clause which are crucial. It needs to be stressed, however, that any chancery-trained notary, or even a scribe supplied by the recipient, could actually write the charter, but it is one of the royal notaries on his own or on the chief notary's behalf who supplies the *recognovi* note and *subscriptio* and who arranges for the seal to be attached. In the case of this St Denis charter from 775, Wigbald, the royal notary, signed the charter on behalf of the chief notary Hitherius, but the document was actually written by an unnamed royal chancery scribe. The latter's hand can also be found, incidentally, writing the text of a charter granting immunity to St Denis at the palace of Quierzy on 14 March 775, for which Wigbald again supplied the *recognovi* note.[210] Two copies of this March grant of immunity were produced, but the text of the other copy was also not written by Wigbald. Here the work was divided between two scribes, one for lines 1–6 and the other for lines 7–18. I shall return to the significance of this below.

It needs to be conceded, furthermore, that the date of the charter *recognitio* is not necessarily the date recorded at the bottom of the charter. There are some instances, such as a gift Pippin made to Fulda in 766 in memory of his brother Carloman, which has the text written by an

---

[209] *DKar.* I, No. 95, enacted at Quierzy.
[210] *DKar.* I, No. 94, *ChLA* XVI, No. 616 (Paris, Archives Nationales, K6, No. 5(1)).

unknown scribe, and the *recognovi* note and *subscriptio* provided by Baddilo, but the date clause notes that Hitherius wrote it.[211] One further point needs to be made. At one stage in the development of the study of the diplomatic (that is, the technical elements of the charter), it was suggested that one of the two little lines forming the A in the centre of the Karolus monogram on the charters, called the *Vollziehungsstrich* (completion stroke), was supplied by the king himself.[212] There is no way of proving this. Although in some charters this little stroke is indeed in different ink, it is also the case that in many others it looks as if the whole monogramme were written at the same time. Current opinion is rather more sceptical about the notion of the king adding his little mark to each charter in this way. Analogies with the signing of letters by the head of a large office or institution might make this personal completion something that might have happened occasionally, even though it does not appear to have been consistent practice. In other words, the appearance of the monogramme cannot be taken as an uncontestable indication of the king's involvement in the process of charter validation.

All these elements of Carolingian charter production are well known and have been studied intensively.[213] They not only reflect the continuity of many basically Roman forms of documentary practice, but also provided the underlying model for the subsequent forms of royal and local legal records and organization of royal administration and protocol in the middle ages.

The main lines of Carolingian diplomatic practice are also clear, namely, the degree of continuity between Merovingian and Carolingian charter practice,[214] the formulae for the protocol, eschatacol and dating clause, the titles used for the king (*intitulatio*),[215] the chrismons and beehives which varied according to notary and scribe, the seals, the terms of the various

---

[211] *DKar.* I, No. 21, *ChLA* XII, No. 530 (Marburg Hessisches Staatsarchiv Kaiserurkunden Fulda 766.VII).

[212] See H. Bresslau, *Handbuch der Urkundenlehre* (Berlin, 1931), II, pp. 163–4; and see J. Spiegel, 'Vollziehung', *Lexikon des Mittelalters* (1999), cols. 1840–1. Compare the comments by M. Mersiowsky, 'Towards a reappraisal of sovereign charters', in K. Heidecker (ed.), *Charters and the use of the written word in medieval society*, Utrecht Studies in Medieval Literacy (Turnhout, 2000), pp. 15–26.

[213] The classic accounts remain Bresslau, *Handbuch*, I, pp. 374–85; G. Tessier, *La diplomatique royale française* (Paris, 1962); Bautier, 'La chancellerie carolingienne'; and Tock, 'La diplomatique française'.

[214] See esp. P. Classen, *Kaiserreskript und Königsurkunde: Diplomatische Studien zum Problem der Kontinuität zwischen Altertum und Mittelalter* (Thessaloniki, 1977).

[215] H. Wolfram, *Intitulatio*, I, *Lateinische Königs- und Fürstentitel bis zum Ende des 8. Jahrhunderts*, *MIÖG*, Ergänzungsband 21 (Vienna, 1967).

kinds of grants of land, freedom from tolls, privileges of immunity, the freedom of election of the abbot, manumission, land exchange and the settlement of disputes and the classification of documents by content. The petition from the recipient who asked for a grant is quite often specified, and very occasionally there are instances of this recipient providing a scribe to write the body of the charter. One example is a donation of a church and its estates to the monastery of Hersfeld in 782. Although Wigbald signed this on behalf of Rado, the chief royal notary, the text of the charter was actually written by someone who was struggling rather unsuccessfully to imitate royal chancery cursive, possibly a member of the Hersfeld community or else a local notary.[216] An alternative process is suggested by Genesius' charter for Nonantola in 797. It was written by Genesius but has the *recognitio* added by Ercambald at Aachen. It may have been sent, therefore, to Aachen for confirmation.

THE ROYAL WRITING OFFICE AND THE PALACE NOTARIES

The charter evidence thus provides information about the 'chancery' personnel, but the latter's relation to the royal household and to royal government, not least whether the charters actually witness to the king's presence and the royal itinerary, still needs to be explored. It may be most helpful, therefore, to consider the activities of the men who took responsibility for the production of the king's charters, and on occasion even wrote them themselves rather than relying on anonymous underlings. I set these out in chronological order of the chief notary and his named assistants. By convention the chief notary is known as the *cancellarius*, though this term is never used by those supplying the *recognovi* notes and the *subscriptiones* in the royal diplomas of Charlemagne.

Hitherius was the head of the notaries under Pippin III and continued in this role in the early years of Charlemagne's reign. His place was taken in due course by Rado, who had himself served as a notary under Hitherius, and then Ercambald who in his turn had served under Rado. The last surviving charter from Charlemagne's reign was enacted at Aachen on 9 May 813, by *uuitherius diaconus ad vicem Hieremiae* with Gundradus as *ambasciator*, that is, the person transmitting the order to draw up a charter. The document confirmed the Saxon Asig in possession of the lands of his

---

[216] *DKar.* I, No. 144, and *ChLA* XII, No. 538, Marburg, Hessisches Staatsarchiv, Kaiserurkunden Hersfeld 782.VII.28. On local notaries involved in monastic charter production see R. McKitterick, *The Carolingians and the written word* (Cambridge, 1989), pp. 77–134.

father.[217] This been taken to indicate Hieremias taking over from Ercambald, although there is no indication of his having served as a notary previously. Although it is a lovely charter, with most of the royal seal intact, I leave it out of consideration here because it is a little problematic. Hieremias was a chaplain and this is the only instance we have of his being referred to in charter production. Reference to him may be an indication of the general oversight of the writing office rather than involvement in the day-to-day running of it as chief notary. It is comparable to the references to chaplains requesting the production of the charter in others emanating from the royal writing office as early as 772. These are most usually hidden in the tironian notes around the beehive at the bottom of the charter. This particular case may also have involved different personnel to record it.[218]

Hitherius was responsible for charters between 768 and 775 enacted at Aachen, Orville, Herstal, Valenciennes, Blanzy,[219] Brumath,[220] Longlier, Quierzy (773 and 775)[221] and Pavia. Notaries who acted on his behalf were Wigbald and Rado.[222] Wigbald was active between 774 and 782. He was responsible for charters at Düren, Samoussy, St Denis, Quierzy,[223] Vicenza,

---

[217] *DKar.* I, No. 218. It survives in the original in Münster Nordrhein-Westfälisches Staatsarchiv, Kaiserurkunde I, 813 and is illustrated in *799 Kunst und Kultur*, I, VI.5, pp. 328–9, where it is compared with *DKar.*, I, No. 213, recording a grant to Count Benitt.

[218] See the discussion of the possible notarial dimension to the chaplain's role in Fleckenstein, *Die Hofkapelle*, pp. 74–9. The following charters record, in tironian notes, the intervention of a chaplain. *DKar.*, I, No. 139: *ChLA* XII, No. 531, Marburg Hessisches Staatsarchiv Kaiserurkunden Fulda 781.XII at Quierzy 781, with the note *Folradus ordinavit*; *DKar.* I, No. 140: *ChLA* XII, No. 532 Marburg Hessisches Staatsarchiv Kaiserurkunden Fulda 781.XII Rossdorf at Quierzy 781, with the note *Folradus ordinavit*; *DKar* I. 104, Marburg Hessisches Staatsarchiv Kaiserurkunden Hersfeld 775 × 25 with the note 'ordinante domno meo karolo rege Francorum et Fulrado abbate'; *DKar.* I. 116, *ChLA* XII 539, with the note 'domno rege ordinant uuihbaldus recognovi'; *DKar.* I, No. 176, Munich, Bayerische Staatsarchiv, Kaiserselekt 2 (at Frankfurt) *ChLA* XII, No. 541, 'et Angilberto abbate ambasciante'. The scribe Witherius of the 813 charter cannot necessarily be identified with the Witherius who wrote *DKar.*, I, No. 138, in 781 at Quierzy.

[219] *ChLA* XIX, No. 672, Colmar, Archives départmentales du haut-Rhin, fonds de Murbach 10G generalia 3, No. 2, and *DKar.* I, No. 64, in favour of Murbach.

[220] St Gallen, Stiftsarchiv E.E.5.B.44, *DKar.* I, No. 69, in favour of Arnald, priest, and kept at St Gallen. For a facsimile see A. Bruckner (ed.), *Diplomata karolinorum*, I (Basel, 1974), Tafel 3.

[221] *ChLA* XII, Nos. 533 and 534, Marburg Hessisches Staatsarchiv Kaiserurkunden Hersfeld 775 I 5 and 775 I 5 (redacted at Quierzy), *DKar.* I, Nos. 89 and 90 in favour of Hersfeld.

[222] Cited *ad vicem Hitherii* by Rado (772) at Herstal, 774 × 6 at Worms, Düren, Verberie, 775 × 2 at Thionville and Düren, and one at Vicenza by Wigbald (776).

[223] Of the eight charters Wigbald subscribed at Quierzy, three survive in the original: *DKar.* I, Nos. 94, 95 and 101. See *ChLA*, XV, Nos. 616 and 617 (Paris, Archives Nationales K6 5/1 and 5/2), *ChLA*, XIX (Colmar, Archives départmentales du haut-Rhin, fonds de Murbach 10G generalia 3 No. 3) and *ChLA* XCV, No. 618 (Paris, Archives Nationales K6, No. 6) *DKar.* I, No. 101. Of these, two are from the St Denis archive in Paris and one from Murbach, now in Colmar.

Herstal,[224] Pavia, *Cispliaco*(?), Hersfeld[225] and Gondreville. Wigbald served under Hitherius (to 776) and Rado (777–82), but the latter had done a stint as an under-notary between 772 and 783 before heading the writing office. Rado subscribed charters at Thionville,[226] Herstal,[227] Worms,[228] Düren,[229] Verberie,[230] Patris Giagio (possibly Patri Gagio in Lombardy), Aachen,[231] Quierzy, and an unidentified place.[232] At the first five of these Rado provided the *recognovi* notes *ad vicem Hitherii*.

As head of the writing office, **Rado** had a number of notaries working for him between 777 and 799, in addition to Wigbald. Those whose names we know include Gislebertus/Giltbertus,[233] Optatus,[234] Widolaicus,[235] Iacob[236] and Gudulfus.[237] They subscribed charters at the palaces of Herstal, Worms, Hersfeld, Pavia, *Cispliaco*, Capua, Rome and Regensburg. In addition, there was Ercambald, who succeeded Rado as head notary. For Rado, Ercambald

---

[224] Of the four enacted at Herstal two survive in the original: *DKar.* i, Nos. 116 and 123 for Fulda and St Marcel, Chalon, respectively. See *ChLA* xii, No. 539 (Munich, Bayerische Hauptstaatsarchiv Kaiserselekt I) and *ChLA* vii, No. 651 (Paris, BnF Coll. Bourgogne 75, no. 4, CL 8837).

[225] *DKar.* i, No. 144, for Hersfeld. See *ChLA*, xii, No. 538 (Marburg, Hessisches Staatsarchiv Kaiserurkunden Hersfeld 782 vii 28).

[226] Of the four at Thionville, one original, *DKar.* i, No. 107 for Salonne, preserved in the St Denis archive, is extant. See *ChLA* xvi, No. 620 (Paris, Archives Nationales K6 No. 8) and *799 Kunst und Kultur*, i, No. iii.3, pp. 127–8. The scribe's name is recorded in tironian notes as Adarulfus, one of Fulrad of St Denis's notaries.

[227] Three, including one original, *DKar.* i, No. 121, for Hersfeld. See *ChLA*, xii, No. 537 (Marburg, Hessisches Staatsarchivv, Kaiserurkunden Hersfeld 779.iii.13).

[228] One of the two survives in the original, *DKar.* i, No. 130, in St Gallen. St Gallen, Stiftsarchiv A.4. A.1, facsimile in Bruckner (ed.), *Diplomata karolinorum*, Tafel 4.

[229] Two of the four survive in the original. The St Denis archive had two copies, one subscribed by Rado and the other by Wigbald: *DKar.* i, Nos. 84 and 103. The former is for St Denis and the latter for Hersfeld. See *ChLA* xvi, Nos. 613 and 614 (Paris, Archives Nationales K6, No. 5/1, and K6, No. 5/2), and *ChLA* xii, No. 535 (Marburg, Hessisches Staatsarchiv Kaiserurkunden Hersfeld 775.VIII.3).

[230] This survives in the original, *DKar.* i, No. 88, for St Denis. This is a *tractoria* and lacks a royal *subscriptio* or date clause. *ChLA* xvi, No. 621, dated 774–6 by Atsma and Vezin (Paris, Archives nationales K6, No. 9).

[231] *DKar.* i, No. 118, for Salonne. See *ChLA* xix, No. 679 (Nancy, Archives départmentales Meurthe-et-Moselle G. 468).

[232] *DKar.* i, No. 83, for St Denis, preserved in the St Denis archive.

[233] Gi[s]l[e]bertus writes charters from 778 to 781 and in 795 in St Denis: *DKar.* i, No. 120. See *ChLA* xvi, No. 620 (Paris, Archives Nationales K7, No. 3), and in Worms (× 2), Lippspringe, Aachen and Pavia: *DKar.* i, Nos. 128, 129, 131, 133, 151, 179.

[234] Optatus wrote charters in 779 and 788 in Herstal and Regensburg: *DKar.* i, Nos. 122 and 162. See the Herstal original in Regensburg *ChLA*, xvi, No. 625 (Paris, Archives Nationales K7, No. 2); the other survives in a s.XIII Salzburg cartulary.

[235] Widolaicus wrote charters in 781, 794 in Herstal: *DKar.* i, No. 136; see *ChLA* xvi, No. 628 (Paris, Archives nationales K7, No. 8/1), as well as Quierzy × 2 and Frankfurt.

[236] Iacob wrote from 787 to 792 in Capua, Rome, Worms and Regensburg.

[237] Gidulfus wrote one charter in 790 at an unnamed place (No. 168).

provided the *recognovi* note and *subscriptio* in charters between 777 and 797 at Regensburg, Thionville and Aachen, as well as in the cluster of palaces on the Rhine at Worms,[238] Ingelheim, Mainz, Frankfurt and Kostheim. His own charters at Aachen in 797 include one for which Maginardus acted as the *ambasciator*, and one written by Genesius for which Ercambald supplied the *recognitio*.[239]

From 799 to 812, **Ercambald** had notaries under him, including not only Genesius[240] but also Amalbertus,[241] Hadingus,[242] Aldricus,[243] Altfredus,[244] Blado,[245] Ibbo,[246] Suavis[247] and Gilbertus.[248] Apart from the five subscribed by Genesius' hand, and three by Amalbertus, the others were responsible for only one or two charters each, and the places of redaction, apart from Aachen itself, were Thionville, Ingelheim, St Martin's, Tours, Rome, and a place on the Reno river near Bologna.

The apparent increase in the number of notaries in the last two decades of the reign that scholars have remarked on does not take into account the number of additional chancery-trained scribes whose work is evident in the charters from the time of Hitherius and Rado.[249] It is also not

---

[238] Of the two charters written at Worms, one is original: *DKar.* I, No. 150, in favour of Arezzo, *ChLA* xxv, No. 797 (Arezzo, Archivio Capitolare canonica, 783 ottobre).

[239] *DKar.* I Nos 181 and 183. See also *ChLA* xvi, No. 637 (Paris, Archives Nationales K7, No. 15). Maginardus is probably the chaplain Maginarius, abbot of St Denis.

[240] Genesius wrote from 799 to 802 at Aachen, St Martin at Tours, Rome, the Reno river and Schweigen. The last named, in Hersfeld's favour, *DKar.* I, No. 198, survives in the original in the Marburg archive.

[241] Amalbertus wrote charters from 799 and 806 in Thionville, and in Aachen in 799. Amalbertus also wrote *ad vicem Ercambaldi* at an unnamed place, in a charter for Lagrasse near Narbonne: *DKar.* I, No. 189. See *ChLA*, xviii, No. 667 (Carcassonne, Archives départmentales de l'Aude, serie H.ii, No. 1).

[242] Hadingus' charter was dated at Salz and granted Grado immunity: *DKar.* I, No. 200.

[243] Aldricus wrote one charter in 807 in Ingelheim, *DKar.* I, No. 206, which survives in the original. It records an exchange between Bishop Agilward of Würzburg and Count Audulf, and was also confirmed by the chaplain Hildebold.

[244] Altfredus wrote a charter at Aachen in 808, *DKar.* I, No. 207, in favour of Piacenza.

[245] Blado's charter written at Aachen survives in the original, *DKar.* I, No. 208, in Modena. It confirmed Lantreicus (later altered to read Manfred) of Reggio, who had been a hostage in Francia, in possession of lands returned to him.

[246] Ibbo's two charters were copied at Aachen and Verden respectively in 809 and 810, and the latter, *DKar.* I, No. 210, in favour of the monastery of Ebersheim, survies in the original in the municipal archive in Sélestat.

[247] Suavis' two charters are from Aachen, *DKar.* I, No. 213, an original confirming Count Bennit's ownership of land that had once belonged to his father Amalung (a Saxon), see *799 Kunst und Kultur*, I, vi.5, pp. 328–9 (Münster, Nordrhein-Westfälisches Staatsarchiv, Kaiserurkunde I, 813), and an undated charter in an unidentified place in favour of Fulda *DKar.* I, No. 215, copied into the twelfth-century Codex Eberhardi.

[248] Gilbert's sole charter was written at Aachen: *DKar.* I, No. 217.

[249] Nelson's list of notaries, for example, 'Aachen as a place of power', p. 240, did not include these scribes.

accompanied by an increase in charter redaction, at least in terms of the surviving documents. As we shall see below, the usual understanding of an intensification of administrative and judicial activity, on the evidence of the capitularies and references in the narrative sources, cannot be sustained.[250]

If these notaries are plotted on a map (Map 8), it becomes clear that there are different spheres and concentrations of activity as well as areas – Alemannia, Aquitaine, Brittany, Saxony, Septimania and most of Bavaria and Italy – for which we have only one or two palaces, or else none, recorded as places where charters were enacted, even though the gifts and grants of privileges to religious institutions and to lay individuals by Charlemagne extended throughout the empire.[251] The period when Hitherius and Rado presided over the notaries before 782–3 was one in which many charters were drawn up in the palaces of west Francia, especially Quierzy, as well as outlying places such as Regensburg, Lippspringe, and Rome. Ercambald's period of office, on the other hand, from 783 onwards, sees a greater concentration of charters enacted in the Rhine-Main-Moselle region and Aachen, again with outlying charters dated at Verden, Salz, Regensburg, Tours, Rome and near Bologna. It is Genesius who is responsible for the range of places from Tours to Rome. It seems likely that it was he, perhaps with some other scribes as assistants, who went to Rome as Charlemagne's secretary in 800–1, and that it was Hadingus who accompanied the king to Salz, where Charlemagne received envoys from Byzantium on his way to Bavaria.[252] The notary Ibbo appears to have gone with the king on his expedition to Saxony and Verden in 810.[253]

There are instances in the earlier years of local scribes of charters, or scribes writing *ad vicem* a royal notary, that is, on behalf of a royal notary, who do not themselves seem to have been palace notaries. Two charters granting immunity and fishing and other rights respectively to Lorsch in response to requests, and drawn up at Thionville and Herstal in 772 and 777, were given the *recognovi* note *ad vicem Liutbert* (Liudberd) by Rado, which may indicate that a copy had been sent to the palace to be authenticated.[254] We may have another instance of Lorsch supplying a charter in that the *recognovi* note is by Witigowo in a document of 772. This records Charlemagne's taking the monastery under royal protection and granting

---

[250] See below, pp. 234–7.   [251] See the maps of endowed institutions in Prinz, *KdG* I, p. 488.

[252] Compare *ARF* 803, ed. Kurze, p. 118, and *Annales mettenses priores* 803, pp. 89–90.

[253] *DKar.* I, No. 210, and see *Annales sancti Amandi* and Chronicle of Moissac, ed. G. Pertz, *MGH* SS I, pp. 14 and 309.

[254] *DKar.* I, Nos. 67 and 114.

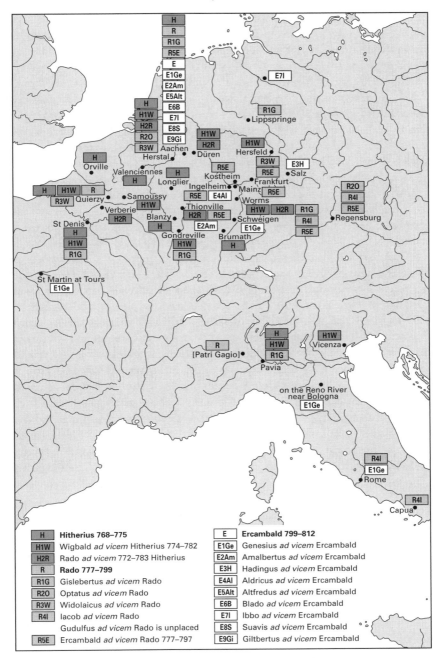

Maps 8 Charlemagne's notaries and their areas of operation

the monks freedom to elect their abbot. All these, unfortunately, are preserved only in the twelfth-century cartulary of Lorsch, so there is no help to
be got from the script.[255] Similar instances are the charter for Bobbio dated at
Pavia in 774 with a *recognovi* note from Enrich. This again may be the work
of a local notary.[256] A gift of lands to Fulda in the Wormsgau and Mainz,
with the *recognovi* note by Egilbertus, *cancellarius* for Fulda, was possibly
redacted at Fulda itself.[257] The charter granting royal protection and immunity to Aniane dated at Regensburg by *Bartolomeus notarius ad vicem
Hludovici* in 792, on the other hand, is a rare witness to the process by
which Louis the Pious's grants in Aquitaine needed to be confirmed in the
palace, though some of its peculiarities may be due to its being a later copy.[258]
Another instance of the drawing up of documents for Louis is the reward of
land made to John for his victory over the Saracens in Barcelona. This was
granted after Charlemagne had received a letter supporting John from
Louis.[259]

The charters also indicate variable documentary practice. The reports of
the settlement of disputes were presented in a different style, and the notary
responsible was not among the usual group of officials. Instead, he was
associated with the count of the palace responsible for the record of
the decisions reached.[260] A few of these distinctive charters survive from
the reign of Charlemagne. They incorporate explicit statements about the
proceedings having been conducted in the king's hearing when he was in
his palace in order to listen to cases and administer justice. The groups
gathered at these hearings are mentioned, such as counts and *fideles* listed
by name,[261] or the 'bishops, abbots, dukes, counts, gastalds and the rest of
our faithful subjects'.[262] Although only one survives in the original and the
scribe was not always recorded in the later copies, we do have Thiotgaudus
acting as notary in 771 at the palace at Longlier in a dispute won by Fulda;
the count of the palace was not mentioned.[263] Similarly Theudegarius

[255] *DKar.* I, No. 72. Compare M. Innes, *State and society in the early middle ages: the middle Rhine valley 400–1000* (Cambridge, 2000), pp. 191–2.

[256] *DKar.* I, No. 80.   [257] *DKar.* I, No. 127.

[258] *DKar.* I, No. 173, and see Mühlbacher's discussion.   [259] *DKar.* I, No. 179.

[260] These scribes are generally known as *Gerichtsschreiber*. See Bautier, 'La chancellerie royale'; and R. Hübner, "Gerichtsurkunden der fränkischen Zeit, I: Die Gerichtsurkunden aus Deutschland und Frankreich bis zum Jahre 1000', *Zeitschrift der Savigny Stiftung für Rechtsgeschichte, Germanistische Abteilung* 12 (1893), pp. 1–118, and II, 'Die Gerichtsurkunden aus Italien bis zum Jahre 1150', ibid., 14 (1893), pp. 1–258.

[261] See *DKar.* I, No. 110.

[262] See, for example, *DKar.* I, No. 196. This is the dispute subscribed by Genesius rather than a count of palace's scribe, though the reference to dukes and gastalds is pertinent to the Italian context.

[263] *DKar.* I, No. 63.

acted as notary to Anselm, the count of the palace at Düren and Sélestat, both in 775.[264] At Quierzy in 781, that is, where the case was heard, Witherius *notarius* wrote, *ad vicem Chrotardi*, the record of the settlement of a dispute in favour of St Denis with the king, and with Warald, count of the palace, present.[265] Similarly, at Aachen in 806, Raphuinus *notarius* recorded the settlement of a dispute between Abbot Fardulf of St Denis and the *camerarius* Eberhard at which the count of the palace was represented by other counts.[266] In a case heard at Aachen in March 812 and recorded by Eldebertus, the count of the palace was Amalric.[267] In May 801, Genesius acted as notary to record a dispute between Bishop Vitalis of Bologna and Abbot Anselm of Nonantola settled in a hearing on the Reno river near Bologna. The charter written by *Witherius diaconus ad vicem Hieremiae*, giving Asig the Saxon his father's lands in 813, with Gundradus acting as *ambasciator*, also belongs with this group.[268] These charters are invaluable documents in affording rare glimpses of the king's judicial hearings in the course of his travels and in the presence of the disputants, witnesses, counts, *scabini*, *fidele*s and the notary, all of whom attended these hearings in the king's presence.

What this long excursus has established is that the charters reflect a network of palace notaries, possibly distributed among the various royal palaces, or who at least journeyed out from a base to serve a particular region. Further, the charter evidence only occasionally corroborates the presence of the king; royal diplomas reflect the conduct of royal business but are of limited value in reconstructing the royal itinerary. A great deal of day-to-day administration in the name of the king was carried out across the kingdom in the king's absence, based in the various palaces, even if some of these notaries actually appear to have accompanied the king himself. A similar case can be made for the clergy of the royal chapel, especially if Fleckenstein was correct in supposing an overlap of personnel between chapel and notariat at a level below that of the principal chaplain. That is, while each palace chapel may have been equipped to conduct the liturgical services the king required on his visits at Christmas, Easter and throughout the year, he was also accompanied by at least a chaplain and

---

[264] *DKar.* I, Nos. 102 and 110.   [265] *DKar.* I, No. 138.   [266] *DKar.* I, No. 204.
[267] *DKar.* I, No. 216. This survives in an original preserved in the St Denis archive.
[268] *DKar.* I, Nos. 197 and 218. See also *DKar.* I, No. 148, but it lacks any indication of date or scribe. No. 211 is in a different form and no scribe or count of palace is mentioned. This is about episcopal jurisdiction in Carinthia.

possibly a number of clerics when on military campaigns, or to other destinations.[269]

CONCLUSION: COURT AND KINGDOM

All the available evidence undermines the traditional notion of an entire court on the move. Occasionally there are hints in the sources of Charlemagne summoning members of the royal household and the court to him at one of his stopping places. Thus, when in Pavia in 774, Charlemagne sent word to Francia and had his wife and his sons brought to him there. In 780, he left his sons Pippin and Charles at Worms and went to Rome with his wife. In 787, the king was joined at Worms by Fastrada and his sons and all the court dignitaries he had left with them, and it was there that he decided to hold an assembly.[270] In 781, Tassilo of Bavaria came to Charles at Worms, where an assembly was held, but it was at Quierzy that Bishop Sundpert of Regensburg received Tassilo's twelve hostages.[271]

That the king travelled with a small entourage is undoubted, but his journeys do not accord with the technical definition of itinerant kingship, for it was not a fundamental aspect of his method of rule. Certainly the assemblies and the meetings to administer justice, as we shall see in more detail in the next chapter of this book, were gatherings of groups of people within a locality or a region who came, or were summoned, to meet the king. These assemblies, as Christina Pössel has argued, were occasions on which the ruler and his secular and ecclesiastical magnates could stage-manage and manipulate consent.[272] The king travelled for specific purposes, to go to war, to honour a saint, to convene assemblies, and to go hunting, but the pattern of his journeys is not that of a systematic or comprehensive system of rule. Courts have been regarded as a reflection of centralized power and the centre for competition for royal favour and

---

[269] On particular palaces and services see the *Capitulare missorum* 808, c. 9, 'de operibus palatii ad Vermeriae'; c. 10, 'de illo broilo ad Attiniacum palatium nostrum', *MGH Cap.* I, No. 53, p. 140, in BnF lat. 9654, fol. 21v and BAV pal. lat. 582, fol. 24v. See also the *Capitula omnibus cognita facienda 801–814* (?801–6), c. 1, 'ut infra regna Christo propitio nostra omnibus iterantibus nullus hospitium deneget, mansionem et focum tantum; similiter pastum nullus contendere faciat, excepto pratum et messem', *MGH Cap.* I, No. 57, pp. 144; and *Capitulare missorum Aquisgranense primum*, c. 1: 'de clamatoribus qui magnum impedimentum faciunt in palatio ad aures domni imperatoris', *MGH Cap.* I, No. 64, p. 153.
[270] ARF 774, 780 and 787, ed. Kurze, pp. 40, 56 and 76.   [271] Ibid., 781, p. 58.
[272] Pössel, 'The itinerant kingship of Louis the Pious'; and Pössel, 'Symbolic communication and the negotiation of power at Carolingian regnal assemblies, 814–840', unpublished PhD thesis, University of Cambridge (2003). And see below, pp. 222–33.

individual prestige.[273] An itinerant court might seem to be a contradiction in terms, for it implies either no centre or a variable centre, and thus a shifting kaleidoscope of power. If, on the other hand, the king was the one who moved, it would make the personal aspect of Carolingian government potentially more prominent.

The energy put into administration and justice by the king himself was also emulated by the officials installed in the localities, and the elaborate system of counties and *missatica* (administrative districts) regularly inspected by the king's agents known as the *missi dominici*.[274] Charlemagne's solution to the problem of royal control and government of his realm was a combination of itinerancy and stability with a complex network of officials empowered to conduct business on his behalf, 'like a great railway junction shunting personnel all over the kingdom'.[275] This undoubtedly was a method of rule that developed gradually. Towards the very end of his reign and his life it is clear that the king moved about less and less and was indeed much more constantly at Aachen. This, as already noted earlier, could have been as much biological as it was ideological, for it is a pattern reflected in the careers of any number of warrior kings.[276] In due course, however, Charlemagne augmented the powers and numbers of the *missi dominici*, especially in 802, so that there would be less need for the king, let alone any of his officials other than the *missi*, to travel. There appears to be a greater dependence on agents and use of communications to secure rule without the king's physical presence. In other words, royal government from the royal household was increasingly dependent less on the king's own movements, for his accessibility was not the key issue, than on the effectiveness of his officials and, above all, on the means of communication. It is to these and to the government of the kingdom as a whole, therefore, that I now turn.

---

[273] See J. Duindam, *Myths of power: Norbert Elias and the early modern court* (Amsterdam, 1994).
[274] Werner, '*Missus–Marchio–Comes*', pp. 191–239. And see below, pp. 256–63.
[275] The evocative phrase is from Airlie, 'The palace of memory'. [276] See above p. 162.

CHAPTER 4

The king and the kingdom: communications and identities

INTRODUCTION

In the course of his reign, as the Frankish realm became ever larger and more disparate in character, so royal government became less dependent on the king's own movements. Charlemagne's accessibility in person, as we established in the preceding chapter, was not the key issue, though from the beginning of his reign he insisted that any man in his kingdom had the right to come to him.[1] Instead, he increasingly relied on the effectiveness of his officials and, above all, on his ability to communicate with them. This can best be observed in the development of the roles of the assemblies, of the capitularies as the principal means of communicating with his people, and of the *missi dominici*, officials drawn from the church and the higher ranks of the laity. All these were part of establishing order in a *regnum* where ecclesiastical and secular concerns were intertwined and interdependent; bringing thieves to justice and combating heresy were equally matters of state.[2] Government of the realm as a whole was complemented by measures designed for particular regions. The assemblies, capitularies and role of the *missi dominici*, therefore, will be the focus of the first sections of this chapter. Yet underlying the processes of communication was a strong purpose, not simply to ensure royal control, peace, stability and order, but also to create a harmonious and Christian whole of a disparate realm. Some of the means by which Charlemagne attempted this, and articulated it with ever greater insistence, will also be explored. The establishment of new churches and monasteries, and the conversion of

---

[1] Capitulary for Aquitaine 768/9, c. 8., *MGH Cap.* 1, No. 18, p. 43.
[2] See the pertinent comments in M. de Jong, '*Ecclesia* and the early medieval polity', in S. Airlie, W. Pohl and H. Reimitz (eds.), *Staat im frühen Mittelalter* (Forschungen zur Geschichte des Mittelalters 11) Denkschriften der Österreichische Akademie der Wissenschaften, phil.-hist. Klasse 334 (Vienna, 2006), pp. 113–32; and also M. de Jong, '*Sacrum palatium et ecclesia*: l'autorité religieuse royale sous les Carolingiens (790–840)', *Annales* 58 (2003), pp. 1243–69.

conquered peoples, most obviously the Saxons, were integral components of Frankish political expansion. The Christian faith offered an essential common culture to bind this huge empire together, however varied the liturgical practice and religious expression might have been. The organization of ecclesiastical institutions, the observance of the faith in ritual, the promotion of Christian morality, the definition of orthodox doctrine, and the dissemination of essential texts were all part of this. The new churches and monasteries established in the landscape, both in the Frankish heartlands and the newly conquered regions, were essential markers of Charlemagne's power. Lastly, war and conquest drew new neighbours into the Frankish orbit. The conduct of war and the consequential peace agreements and diplomacy with the peoples beyond the Frankish frontiers provided still further means of communication with the diverse *gentes/* peoples within and without the Frankish empire. Yet the expansion of the Frankish realm to embrace many peoples created problems, not only of order and control but also of identity and cohesion, with which a system of communications alone could not contend. Such problems, and Charlemagne's methods of confronting them, are underlying themes of both this and the following chapter.

COMMUNICATIONS

The essential element in the dynamic between the court and the rest of the kingdom was Charlemagne's network of communications, both oral and written.[3] In capitulary and letter, Charlemagne insisted on his wish to be kept informed and on the right of his people to be heard. This was extended to all the peoples of the territories he took over.[4] Charlemagne's capitularies provide crucial indications of the increasing expectation that letters and messages would be sent and that the means

[3] R. McKitterick, *The Carolingians and the written word* (Cambridge, 1989), esp. pp. 23–75; J. L. Nelson, 'The use of writing in Charlemagne's government', in R. McKitterick (ed.), *The uses of literacy in early medieval Europe* (Cambridge, 1990), pp. 258–96; R. Schieffer (ed.), *Schriftkultur und Reichsverwaltung unter den Karolingern*, Abhandlungen der Nordrhein-Westfälischen Akademie der Wissenschaften 97 (Opladen, 1996). For general considerations about the notion of communication, see M. Mostert (ed.), *New approaches to medieval communication*, Utrecht Studies in Medieval Literacy (Turnhout, 1999).

[4] *MGH Cap.* I, No. 18 (768/9), c. 8, p. 43; No. 26 (782/5), c. 26, p. 70 (with reference to the Saxons: no-one is to prevent anyone coming to the king to appeal for justice', and compare c. 34 (the role of the counts to hold courts and administer justice), ibid., p. 70; No. 23 (789), c. 27, p. 64; No. 25 (793), c. 5, p. 67; No. 28 (794), c. 6, pp. 74–5 and (to be heard by God in any language) cc. 52, 78; No. 33 (802) cc. 1, 14, 25, 28 and 40, pp. 92, 94, 96 and 98; No. 44 (806), c. 18 (2), 24 (8), pp. 122–4; No. 49 (806/7), c. 4, p. 135; No. 73 (811), pp. 164–5; No. 80 (811), c. 2, p. 176.

were created for the systematic portage of royal commands and summons. In a series of notes on the administration of law by the *missi dominici*, extant only in Paris BnF lat. 4613, an Italian law book of the tenth century, the king explained that he intended to notify the *missi* and counts by letter concerning when and where they were to assemble. He added a general indication that anyone unhappy with the work of the *missi* or counts should report it to the king.[5] The capitulary of 802 explained the system of the *missi* sent throughout the realm and the requirement that they send written reports on their work to the emperor (as he was by then). The final clause of the capitulary reiterated the king's need for information: 'we wish to know by means of our *missi* now sent out throughout our entire realm . . . how laymen are observing the order for the assembly of the army'. The clause lists all the other things on which the king wished to be kept informed, and especially 'the nature of their obedience to our command and will and also how they have observed our *bannus*, and above all how each is striving to keep himself in God's holy service', among ecclesiastics, nuns and laymen, counts and hundredmen.[6] Another circular letter of 806 repeated the requirement that the king be sent, or that the *missi* should bring, written reports of the benefices of the king's men.[7] As a corroboration of the procedure these examples imply, the *De ordine palatii* described a process of discussion and consideration of topics proposed by the king by means of a series of written and oral messages.[8] It also stressed the means by which the king acquired military intelligence. Strategic military planning for the movement of offensive and defensive troops, the maintenance of political stability in the border regions, and alertness to the possibility of insurrection meant that there was a constant need for information. On Charlemagne's return from Italy after Rotgaud of Friuli's rebellion in 776, for example, a messenger (*nuntius*) came reporting that the Saxons had rebelled: 'they had abandoned all their hostages, broken their oaths and induced the Franks at the *castrum* of Eresburg, by means of *mala ingenia* and *iniqua placita*, to evacuate it. With Eresburg deserted by the Franks, the Saxons destroyed the wall and earthworks.' Acting on this information, an assembly was summoned at Worms and the decision was

---

[5] *MGH Cap.* I, No. 25, cc. 5 and 6, p. 67. On the manuscript see Mordek, *Bibliotheca*, pp. 469–76.
[6] *MGH Cap.* I, No. 33, cc. 1 and 40, pp. 92 and 98, trans. P. D. King, *Charlemagne: translated sources* (Kendal, 1987), p. 242.
[7] *MGH Cap.* I, No. 49, c. 4, p. 136.
[8] *De ordine palatii*, c. 34, ed. T. Gross and R. Schieffer, *Hinkmar von Reims, De ordine palatii, MGH Fontes* 3 (Hanover, 1980), pp. 90–2.

made to attack the Saxons.[9] Charlemagne's network of communications, with its great variety of means for acquiring knowledge of all kinds, underlay the remarkable success of Charlemagne's armies.[10]

Royal charters also amply demonstrate that the palace writing office could act on written or oral instructions, or a combination of the two. The extent of the legal investigations and documentation assessed could be very considerable. One example is the confirmation of the grants of freedom from tolls and of immunity made to St Denis as a result of a petition on the part of Abbot Fulrad. Fulrad wanted to have all earlier grants in St Denis's possession confirmed. These grants had been made by Charlemagne's predecessors, that is, both Pippin III and the Merovingian kings. These documents were inspected and accordingly renewed.[11] In this case many of the documents that Fulrad is likely to have produced and that Charlemagne's notaries inspected still survive. It is an impressive run of charters, from Chlothar I, Dagobert II, Chlothar II and other Merovingian kings right up to Chilperic II.[12] The extraordinarily extensive range of places for which charters were drawn up, outlined above, is an eloquent witness to the successful process of petition and grant, and of representations made to the king by individuals which then are responded to by grants of one kind or another.[13] In a summary of complaints received, dated *c.* 811, there is an important indication of the counts' success in relaying to the king the difficulties they encountered in making sure that people did their military service, and their complaints about the habit of the people in their districts of seeking out the *missi* rather than the counts for redress of their grievances.[14] This may also indicate, of course, problems with local counts and a perception on the people's part, by this stage in Charlemagne's reign, of the *missi* being a higher and more reliable authority, and with closer royal connections. Such petitions and claims on the attention of the king's officials were directed to the plethora of centres of

[9] ARF 776, ed. Kurze, p. 44; the phrasing *per mala ingenia* recalls the formal oaths of fidelity in 789 *sine fraude et malo ingenio*, *MGH Cap.* 1, No. 23, c. 18, p. 63; and see below, on oaths, pp. 268–70.

[10] See B. S. Bachrach, 'Charlemagne and the Carolingian general staff', *Journal of Military History* 66 (2002), pp. 313–57, esp. 315–23. On the various means of gathering intelligence, spy networks and the like, see A. D. Lee, *Information and frontiers: Roman foreign relations in late antiquity* (Cambridge, 1993). For the wider background of Carolingian warfare see B. S. Bachrach, *Early Carolingian warfare: prelude to empire* (Philadelphia, 2001); and G. Halsall, *Warfare and society in the barbarian west, 450–900* (London, 2003).

[11] *DKar.* I, Nos. 93 and 94.

[12] *ChLA*, XIII, Nos. 552–571, and XIV, Nos, 574, 586, 589. See D. Songzoni, *Le chartier de Saint-Denis en France au haut moyen âge. Essai de reconstitution*, Pecia 2 (2003).

[13] See above, pp. 188–212, Map 8, and also the map in *KdG*, 1, between pp. 488–9.

[14] *MGH Cap.* 1, No. 73, pp. 164–5.

power which were the means by which the royal household connected the king and his family to the various regions of his kingdom. The *De ordine palatii* described this in its account of how the seneschal, wine steward and constable had to inform local officials of the times, places and seasons of the king's arrival and the duration of his stay so that they could collect and prepare what was needed. This included notifying the *susceptores* in advance 'so that they could prepare the king's lodgings' ... 'From every part of the entire realm, anyone desolate, impoverished, oppressed by debts, overwhelmed by unjust accusations ... widows, orphans, men great and small, each according to his need or situation, was always to have access to the mercy and the pity of the senior officers.'[15]

There are rare instances of surviving letters concerning day-to-day administration and government.[16] One of these, dated to March 806 and addressed to an unnamed count, is clearly a circular letter with many original recipients. It was sent by Charlemagne's *missi* Adalhard, Fulrad, Unruoch and Hrocculf.[17] Given that Bishop Gerbald was apparently himself a *missus dominicus*, albeit in a different district, it is possible that he used this letter as a model when addressing his own counts.[18] In the letter, the *missi* emphasized that they themselves were required to deliver written reports, and so needed information from the counts in their turn.[19] They urged the counts to 'reread their capitularies' to check that they had done all that was required of them as well as recalling what they had been told orally. The combination of written and oral instructions is reiterated. Counts were asked to list the rebellious and disobedient, and either send the names or tell the *missi* personally when they met. Should anything not be clear, they should send a messenger to the *missi* to ask for clarification. Lastly, they should reread the letter and keep it by them as a checklist. The *missi* themselves received advice and instructions from the king, often in

[15] *De ordine palatii*, c. 25, ed. Gross and Schieffer, *Hinkmar*, pp. 78–9.
[16] See M. Garrison, '"Send more socks": on mentality and the preservation context of medieval letters', in Mostert, *Medieval communication*, pp. 69–99; P. Chaplais, 'The letter from Bishop Wealhere of London to Archbishop Brithwold of Canterbury: the earliest original "letter close" extant in the West', in M. B. Parkes and A. G. Watson (eds.), *Medieval scribes, manuscripts and libraries: essays presented to N. R. Ker* (London, 1978), pp. 3–23; and M. Mersiowsky, 'Regierungspraxis und Schriftlichkeit im Karolingerreich: Das Fallbeispiel der Mandate und Briefe', in Schieffer, *Schriftkultur und Reichsverwaltung*, pp. 109–66.
[17] *MGH Cap.* I, No. 85, pp. 183–5. It was preserved in the collection of Gerbald of Liège (Berlin Staatliche Bibliothek, Preussische Kulturbesitz lat. fol. 626, fols 24r–52v at fols 28v–29r). See the edition and commentary by W. A. Eckhardt, *Die Kapitulariensammlung Bischof Ghaerbalds von Lüttich*, Germanenrechte NF, Abt. Beihefte, Deutschrechtliches Archiv 5 (Göttingen, 1955); and further below, pp. 256–63.
[18] See below, pp. 264–5. [19] *MGH Cap.* I, No. 85, p. 184.

response to questions they had sent to him. In one response, extant in two of the major Carolingian capitulary collections of the tenth century, the king is markedly testy about the thick-headedness of the *missus* he is addressing, for he tells him that if answers to questions about legal procedure are not to be found in Roman or Frankish law, the *missus* should raise the question at a general assembly. He also complains he has told this *missus* again and again what to do in the cases of false witness and of failure to appear before the *missus*, as well as of tolls at bridges, but that the *missus* had not understood them.[20] Palace officials could themselves respond to queries from *missi*, especially if what was required was explanatory detail concerning directives already issued by the king.[21] A more programmatic circular letter is the capitulary known as the *Admonitio generalis* of 789, sent via the royal *missi* to lay and ecclesiastical magnates.[22]

There are many general issues raised by these administrative letters, quite apart from the capitularies like the *Admonitio generalis*, but for the moment I wish to note that letters are among the most ephemeral of documents, and far less likely to survive than legal records such as charters. Administrative and business notes, informal letters, letters to or from lay men and women, and love letters, have rarely been preserved. This is in contrast to letters assembled by the sender or the recipients for particular purposes, for their authority, or to serve as models or as literary artefacts, such as the correspondence between the early Carolingian rulers and the popes, preserved by the order of the king in the *Codex epistolaris carolinus*,[23] and the early Carolingian letter collections of Alcuin and of Boniface of Mainz.[24] The papal letters are full of references to the bearers of the letters and of the *missi* sent hither and yon with news, requests, orders, and commissions. Messengers quite clearly supplemented the letters they carried with oral reports. Pope Stephen reported to Carloman in 770 or 771, for example, that the *missi* Berald and Autbert had delivered the letter and also related in detail 'the matters with which Carloman had charged them'. Pope Hadrian

---

[20] *MGH Cap.* 1, No. 58, pp. 145–6, Paris, BnF lat. 9654, fol. 15r–v, and Vat. pal. lat. 582, fol. 18r–v; see also Mordek, *Bibliotheca*, pp. 562–78 at p. 566, and pp. 780–97 at p. 785.

[21] R. Pokorny, 'Eine Brief-Instruktion aus dem Hofkreis Karls des Großen an einen geistlichen Missus', *Deutsches Archiv* 52 (1996), pp. 57–83.

[22] *MGH Cap.* 1, No. 22, pp. 52–62. See below, pp. 239–40.

[23] On the *Codex epistolaris carolinus* see above, pp. 36–7.

[24] Garrison, '"Send more socks"'; and G. Constable, *Letters and letter collections*, Typologie des Sources du Moyen Age Occidental 17 (Turnhout, 1976). On the compilation of Alcuin's letter collections see D. Bullough, *Alcuin: achievement and reputation* (Leiden, 2004), pp. 43–102; and on the Mainz collections of Boniface's letters see M. Tangl, 'Studien zur Neuausgabe der Bonifatius Briefe', in Tangl, *Mittelalter in Geschichte und Diplomatik: ausgewählte Schriften* (Berlin, 1966), pp. 60–175.

sent a letter to Charlemagne, carried by Bishop Andrew and Abbot Pardus, saying that he had also provided full particulars orally with careful instructions as to what the *missi* should say to the king on the pope's behalf.[25] Letters could be deliberately destroyed if the information they contained was too dangerous to keep. Alcuin reported to Arn in 799, for example, that besides Alcuin himself, only Candidus had read Arn's letter reporting the complaints about Pope Leo III's morals, and that they had then burnt the letter to avoid the possibility that 'scandal' (*scandalum*) might arise through carelessness on the part of Alcuin's secretary.[26]

Yet a sufficient number of business letters has survived on both papyrus and parchment, in palimpsest, or copied into a book, to indicate how normal a means of communication they were during the reign of Charlemagne. There is, for example, the report sent of the situation in Benevento in 788 by Maginarius, preserved in its papyrus original. Maginarius informed Charlemagne that he and the other royal *missi*, Atto and Goddramnus, went to the Beneventan frontier by different routes and had agreed to let each other know whatever they learnt about the degree to which people in the region were loyal to Charlemagne. The report is full of references as a matter of course to messengers, messages and letters sent and received.[27] An original letter, written in a cursive documentary script from Charlemagne to the pope about the possibility of Waldo, abbot of St Denis and Reichenau, being elevated to a bishopric, *c.* 791, survives as a palimpsest parchment bifolium. It was reused at Benediktbeuren between 810 and 825 for the text of Jerome-Gennadius, *De viris illustribus.*[28]

The Formulary of Marculf provides a wealth of models for business letters and the situations envisaged in which letters and documents of

---

[25] *Codex epistolaris carolinus,* ed. Gundlach, Epp. 47 and 55, pp. 565–6, 578–80; and for similar references see ibid., Ep. 66, p. 594.

[26] Alcuin, *Epistolae,* 184, ed. E. Dummler, *MGH Epp.* IV, p. 309.

[27] *ChLA* XVI, No. 629 (Paris, Archives Nationales K7, No. 9); *Carolinus,* ed. Gundlach, Appendix 2; and for Hadrian's side of this business see ibid., No. 82.

[28] Munich, Bayerische Staatsbibliothek Clm 6333, fols 90v and 87r; on fol. 32 is a palimpsest letter from an unknown bishop to Charlemagne; see E. Munding, *Königsbrief Karls d. Gr. an Papst Hadrian über Abt-Bischof Waldo von Reichenau-Pavia: Palimpsest-Urkunde aus Cod. Lat. Monac. 6333, Texte und Arbeiten,* 1: *Abteilung,* Beiträge zur Ergründung des älteren lateinischen christlichen Schrifttums und Gottesdienstes 6 (Beuron, 1920); and B. Bischoff, *Die südostdeutschen Schreibschulen und Bibliotheken in der Karolingerzeit,* 1: *Die bayrischen Diözesen,* 3rd edn (Wiesbaden, 1974), pp. 32–4. The arguments for this bifolium being the original letter are convincingly assembled by M. Mersiowsky, 'Preserved by destruction: Carolingian original letters and Clm 6333', in G. Declercq (ed.), *Early medieval palimpsests* (Turnhout, 2007); and M. Mersiowsky, 'Regierungspraxis und Schriftlichkeit im Karolingerreich: das Fallbeispiel der Mandate und Briefe', in Schieffer, *Schriftkultur und Reichsverwaltung,* pp. 109–66.

various kinds would have been required. According to the preface, it was first compiled for a Bishop Landri (thought to be Landri of Meaux rather than of Paris). It has been dated to the end of the seventh century, probably after 688, but all the extant copies are Carolingian and usually preserved with other legal and administrative material.[29] An example is Leiden, Universiteitsbibliotheek BPL 114, compiled at Bourges at the end of the eighth century and still in a Carolingian binding (with an extra part, now in Paris, BnF lat. 4629, added soon after 805).[30] The codex contained selections from Isidore of Seville's *Etymologiae* to do with consanguinity, the *Epitome Aegidii* of Roman law, the letter of Bishop Chrodebert of Tours to Abbess Boba on the verdicts within canon law concerning a professed nun who had committed adultery, and a large portion of the Formulary of Marculf into which other *formulae* were apparently interpolated by the compiler. The Formulary of Marculf was also revised during the reign of Charlemagne and is extant in versions produced in the Paris and Salzburg regions. Collections closely related to it were made at Tours, Bourges, Sens, Flavigny and St Denis.[31] Other regional formulary collections from Charlemagne's reign are associated with Murbach, Reichenau and St Gallen.

The Marculf collection, well known for its models for various kinds of legal documents such as immunities, donations, confirmations of earlier grants, and royal protection, appears to have been devised or adapted for use by a royal official and includes a letter summoning a count to the king's presence.[32] Although much shorter, the Carolingian edition is divided into sections of letters concerning clerics, officials and laymen, letters sent to or received from the king, and letters for the count of the palace concerning the administration of justice. There are also formulae for the records of various kinds of legal transactions. The model letters common to both the original and the Carolingian revision comprise letters about the administration of justice and reports to be made to the king, a recommendation asking the recipient to give every assistance to the bearer, courtesy letters to a mother or a sister who has entered a convent, the response of the king to

[29] K. Zeumer, *Marculfi Formulae*, MGH Formulae merowingici et karolini aevi (Hanover, 1882–6), pp. 32–106; and see also A. Uddholm, *Marculfi Formularium libri duo* (Uppsala, 1962). For a summary of the scholarship see U. Nonn, 'Formelsammlungen, III: Frühmittelalter', *Lexikon des Mittelalters*, III, cols. 648–9.
[30] Mordek, *Bibliotheca*, pp. 502–7.
[31] K. Zeumer (ed.), *Formulae marculfinae aevi karolini*, MGH Formulae, pp. 113–27; and B. Bischoff, *Salzbürger Formelbücher und Briefe aus Tassilonischer und karolingischer Zeit*, Sitzungsberichte der Bayerischen Akademie für Wissenschaften, phil.-hist. Klasse, Heft 4 (Munich, 1973).
[32] Zeumer, *Marculfi Formulae*, I, 28.

the petition concerning the selection of an individual to a bishopric,[33] the royal appointment of a count or *dux*, letters from one king to another (to be augmented by an orally delivered message), advice with a specific legal problem,[34] and the requisition of animals and supplies for a *missus dominicus*. The close relationship between the maintenance of order and confirmation of property rights is confirmed with the model for a letter to the king from landowners who have lost their title deeds as a result of the devastation of armies, the burning of houses and the pillaging of their belongings, asking the king to confirm them in the possession of all their property.[35] These are models, to be sure, so they cannot provide specific instances of the situations they represent. The number of copies of the various redactions of this formulary, and the great variety of independent variants surviving in individual manuscripts, are nevertheless a clear indication of the recognition of the usefulness and continued relevance of formulae such as these. Extant charters, moreover, occasionally witness to the formularies' use.[36]

ASSEMBLIES

The regular assemblies of the lay and ecclesiastical magnates were the obvious occasions for newsgathering and the exchange of information, quite apart from their function as a forum for the ruler's relations with the political community.[37] This, for the most part, has to be surmised from the bald references scattered through the narrative sources to meetings of Franks, of the army, and of lay and ecclesiastical magnates at assemblies. In many instances an assembly was held in conjunction with the mustering of the host for a military campaign, but there are ample indications that an assembly could also be a separate event. Occasionally an annal entry will yield a little detail, as in 787, when Charlemagne convoked an assembly in Worms and reported there to his *sacerdotes* and *optimates* how everything

[33] See below, pp. 299–305.
[34] Zeumer, *Marculfi Formulae*, I, 29; and compare *Formulae marculfinae aevi karolini*, 18.
[35] Zeumer, *Marculfi Formulae*, I, 33 and 34; and *Formulae marculfinae aevi karolini*, 19 and 22. See W. C. Brown, 'When documents are destroyed or lost: lay people and archives in the early middle ages', *Early Medieval Europe* 11 (2002), pp. 337–66.
[36] H. Sproemberg, 'Marculf und die fränkische Reichskanzlei', *Neues Archiv* 47 (1928), pp. 77–142; and H. J. Zatschek, 'Die Benützung der Formulae Marculfi und andere Formularsammlungen in den Privaturkunden der 8. bis 10. Jhts', *MIÖG* 42 (1927), pp. 165–267. See also A. Rio, *Legal practice and the written word: Frankish formulae, c. 500–1000* (Cambridge, forthcoming).
[37] A useful general survey is T. Reuter, 'Assembly politics in western Europe from the eighth to the twelfth century', in P. Linehan and J. L. Nelson (eds.), *The medieval world* (London, 2001), pp. 434–50.

had turned out on his journey to Italy.[38] The Lorsch annals relate how Charlemagne called an assembly of his Franks and his other *fideles* at Regensburg in 792, 'and there the whole Christian people present with the king judged that Pippin (the Hunchback) as well as those who were his accomplices in this abominable plot should lose both their estates and their lives . . . Since the king did not wish [Pippin] to be put to death, the Franks judged that he must be subjected to God's service.'[39]

Military intelligence, both local and about distant events, was frequently brought to the king in his encampments: in 778, for example, the king was at Auxerre, on his way back from the expedition to Saragossa, when he was informed of Widukind's rebellion in Saxony; and in 795 it was while Charlemagne was in his camp near Bardowick that he received the news that Witzan, 'king' of the Abodrites, had been killed by Saxons in an ambush while crossing the Elbe nearby.[40] It was usually at assemblies, as we shall see below, that foreign legates and all their news were received.

The *De ordine palatii*, furthermore, offers a description of how the king would take time during these assemblies to interview men coming from all parts of the realm. Participants in the assembly were required to make themselves well informed about what was happening in their own areas. 'Each was to collect information concerning any relevant matter (in both internal and external affairs) not only from his own people but from strangers and from both friends and enemies.'[41] Both formal discussions and casual conversations would have provided essential opportunities for the formation of policy and the exertion of political influence and patronage. Each assembly was a forum for the negotiation of power relations as well as of personal relationships, not least those between the king and his magnates. The presentation of gifts, the reception of foreign ambassadors, the spectacle of supplicants for peace, the hearing of legal disputes, the discussion of policy and, on occasion, the ceremonial baptism of defeated enemies, were occasions on which group identity could be expressed and confirmed, quite apart from the bonding between colleagues and friends from all parts of the empire. Differentiation between the larger group and the smaller sub-groups, such as the ruler's entourage, could also have been affirmed. Thus the *Annales regni francorum* report the baptism of Saxons and the visit of Saracen envoys from Spain at the assembly at Paderborn in

---

[38] *ARF* 787, ed. Kurze, p. 76.

[39] Lorsch annals 792, ed. Pertz/Katz, *MGH SS* i, p. 35; trans. King, *Charlemagne*, p. 140.

[40] *ARF* 778 and 795, ed. Kurze, pp. 52 and 98–100. For military intelligence and embassies, see also below, pp. 279–87.

[41] *De ordine palatii*, c. 36, ed. Gross and Schieffer, *Hinkmar*, pp. 94–6.

777, and Tassilo's humiliation and conviction were in the sight of all at the general assembly at Ingelheim in 788.[42] A further indication of the way discussions might have been conducted is provided by the description of the Synod of Rome in 769 in the *Liber pontificalis*. That offers a clear sense of the different groups gathered in discussion, how individuals could be questioned, how written texts could be scrutinized and how those deemed to be nefarious could even be burnt in the presence of all. Liturgical rituals were a customary part of the proceedings.[43]

That so many of the assemblies are linked with military campaigns reminds us of two constant elements in the group solidarity of the Franks, namely, their military discipline and their comradeship in arms, whether on the move, in camp or in the heat of battle.[44] Religious and secular rituals undoubtedly enhanced this military solidarity.[45] The three days of litany and prayer performed on the Avar campaign, made so famous by Charlemagne's account of them in his letter to Fastrada,[46] is but one instance of the spiritual preparation of a warrior embodied in a customary sequence of prayers, masses in time of war or the king going out to battle,[47] almsgiving, processions, and fasting to obtain divine assistance for Charlemagne's armies.[48] The army mustered to attack the Avars 'besought God's mercy, that He might deign to grant us peace, health, victory, and a successful campaign'. The army's prayers were reinforced by prayers elsewhere in the kingdom. Priests and bishops accompanied the army and served the pastoral needs of soldiers on campaign, probably including confession.[49] Walter's prayers and confession of his sins on the eve of further battle with Franks, so vividly portrayed in the early ninth-

---

[42] *ARF* 777 and 788, ed. Kurze, pp. 48 and 80.

[43] *LP*, Life 96, c. 16, ed. Duchesne, I, p. 473. See also H. Schneider, *Die Konzilsordines des Früh- und Hochmittelalters*, *MGH* Ordines de celebrando concilio (Hanover 1996).

[44] For useful surveys see Halsall, *Warfare and society*, pp. 134–62 and 177–214; and Bachrach, *Early Carolingian warfare*, pp. 134–201.

[45] J. L. Nelson, 'Violence in the Carolingian world and the ritualization of ninth-century warfare', in G. Halsall (ed.), *Violence and society in the early medieval west* (Woodbridge, 1998), pp. 90–107.

[46] *MGH Epp.* IV, p. 528 lines 28–34; and see above, pp. 43–4.

[47] *Liber sacramentum Engolismensis*, ed. P. Saint-Roch, *CCSL* 159C (Turnhout, 1987), pp. xi–xii; and see M. McCormick, *Eternal victory: triumphal rulership in late antiquity, Byzantium and the early medieval west* (Cambridge, 1986), p. 348.

[48] See M. McCormick, 'The liturgy of war in the early middle ages: crisis, litanies, and the Carolingian monarchy', *Viator* 15 (1984), pp. 1–23; and McCormick, *Eternal victory*, pp. 34–52.

[49] *MGH Epp.* IV, p. 528, and *ARF* 791, ed. Kurze, p. 88; and D. S. Bachrach, *Religion and the conduct of war, c. 300–1215* (Woodbridge, 2005), pp. 31–63. See also F. Prinz, *Klerus und Krieg im früheren Mittelalter: Untersuchungen zur Rolle der Kirche beim Aufbau der Königsherrschaft*, Monographien zur Geschichte des Mittelalters 2 (Stuttgart, 1971); and Prinz, 'King, clergy and war at the time of the Carolingians', in M. H. King and W. M. Stevens (eds.), *Saints, scholars and heroes: studies in medieval culture in honor of Charles W. Jones* (Collegeville, 1979), II, pp. 301–29.

century poem *Waltharius,* are an important indication of the expectations of the poem's audience about the piety as well as the military prowess of a Carolingian warrior.[50]

Only occasionally are there glimpses of the contemporary importance of the military ethos, such as the fragments of Carolingian heroic poetry in the *Waltharius* and the *Hildebrandslied,*[51] victory poems,[52] or the celebration of the martial glory of a mustered army in the poem *Carolus magnus Leo papa* of *c.* 799:

> The whole army, plumed, marvellously shines.
> Javelins sparkle in the light, standards flutter in the wind,
> Armed young men are afire and confident youth
> Rejoices on horseback.[53]

Laments for fallen warriors (though most extant *planctus* postdate Charlemagne's reign) preserve the memory of leading men who had died on campaign as well as of kings.[54] The recurrent performance of such laments, sung to mourn deaths, or their circulation in written form, such as Paulinus of Aquileia's lament for Eric, *dux* of Friuli, may account for the texts being preserved in manuscripts from Aquitaine and from the west Frankish or Breton region in the later ninth, and turn of the ninth, century respectively.[55] Similarly, the *Annales regni francorum* mention Count

---

[50] Bachrach, *Religion and the conduct of war,* pp. 57–8. I summarize the case for an early date for the *Waltharius* in McKitterick, *The Carolingians and the written word,* taking my lead from A. Onnefors, *Die Verfasserschaft des Waltharius-Epos aus sprachlicher Sicht* (Düsseldorf, 1978), pp. 42–6. See also Bachrach, *Early Carolingian warfare,* pp. 74–75 and J. M. Ziolkowski, 'Of arms and the (Ger)man: literary and material culture in the poem of Walter (Waltharius)', in J. R. Davis and M. McCormick (eds.), *The long morning of medieval Europe: new direction in early medieval studies,* Harvard University October 29–31, 2004 (Cambridge, Mass., forthcoming).

[51] *Waltharius: Lateinisch-deutsch; Waldere, Englisch-Deutsch,* ed. and trans. G. Vogt-Spira and U. Schafer (Stuttgart, 1994). See J. M. Ziolkowski, 'Fighting words: wordplay and swordplay on the Waltharius', in K. E. Olsen, A. Harbus and T. Hofstra (eds.), *Germanic texts and Latin models: medieval reconstructions* (Leuven, Paris, and Sterling, VA, 2001), pp. 29–51; and for the *Hildebrandslied* see W. Braune, K. Helm and E. A. Ebbinghaus, *Althochdeutsches Lesebuch* (Tübingen, 1979), pp. 84–5; C. Edwards, 'German vernacular literature: a survey', in R. McKitterick, *Carolingian culture: emulation and innovation* (Cambridge, 1994), pp. 141–70; and below, pp. 315–20.

[52] *De Pippini regis victoria Avarica,* ed. L. A. Berto, *Testi storici e poetici dell'Italia carolingia,* Medioevo europeo 3 (Padua, 2002), pp. xxxiii–xxxiv and 67–72.

[53] *Carolus magnus et Leo papa,* lines 476–9 ed. E. Dümmler, *MGH Poet.* 1 (Berlin, 1881), p. 378; trans. P. Dutton, *Carolingian civilization: a reader* (Peterborough, Ont., 2004). p. 64.

[54] The *planctus* on Charlemagne's death, *A solis ortu,* appears to be the earliest surviving *planctus* and is generally dated *c.* 814, even though the neumes in the manuscript are of the tenth century; see above, p. 140.

[55] J. Yearley, 'A bibliography of *planctus* in Latin, Provençal, French, German, English, Italian, Catalan and Galician-Portuguese from the time of Bede to the early fifteenth century', *Journal of the Plainsong and Renaissance Music Society* 4 (1981), pp. 12–52.

Gerold and Eric of Friuli, both killed in the Avar wars.[56] Einhard subsequently included the names of the Franks – Anselm, count of the palace,
Eggihard the seneschal, and Roland, count of the Breton march – killed in
the rout in the Pyrenees.[57] The Poeta Saxo, decades later, wrote at length
about this ambush.[58]

The social dynamics of assemblies, including the feasting, drinking and
hunting expeditions accompanying them, can for the most part only be
guessed at.[59] The presence of the king himself would have been a crucial
element for the fellowship of both an army and an assembly in its relationship with the king. Assemblies were also symbols of political cohesion, for
they gathered men and their retinues from all parts of the kingdom. They
were examples of the visibility of political power; those travelling to and
from them would have formed distinctive groups along the roads and
wherever they stayed at night,[60] quite apart from the upheaval and demand
on local resources such a great throng would have created at the assembly
place. Something as basic as the supply of sufficient fresh water for larger
numbers of men and beasts than was usual in a particular place at any one
time may be behind the miracle of the provision of water for the army
recounted in the *Annales regni francorum* for 772.[61]

Rather more has been deduced about the 'negotiation of power' between
the local elites and their peers and the role of symbolic communication
which formed an essential element of these meetings. Theatrical meta-
phors, such as *Inszenierung*, choreography, orchestration, and performance
have been invoked to express the complex combination of speech, gesture,

---

[56] *Versus Pauli de Herico duce*, ed. E. Dümmler, *MGH Poet.* I, pp. 131–3; and ed. O. Holder-Egger, *Vita
Karoli*, Appendix, *MGH SRG* 25 (Hanover, 1911), pp. 44–6; *ARF* 799, ed. Kurze, p. 108. See also H,
Krahwinckler, *Friaul im Frühmittelalter: Geschichte einer Region vom Ende des fünften bis zum Ende
des zehnten Jahrhunderts*, Veröffentlichungen des Instituts für Österreichische Geschichtsforschung
(Vienna, Cologne and Weimar, 1992), pp. 154–8.

[57] *RVARF* 778, ed. Kurze, pp. 51–3; and Einhard, *Vita Karoli*, c. 9, ed. Halphen, pp. 28–30. The ambush
was located by eleventh-century texts at Roncesvallles.

[58] Poeta Saxo, 778, ed. P. von Winterfeld, *MGH Poet.* IV (Berlin, 1899), p. 16.

[59] J. Jarnut, 'Die frühmittelalterliche Jagd unter rechts- und sozialgeschichtlichen Aspekten', in *L'uomo
di fronte al mondo animale nell'alto medioevo*, Settimane 31, I (Spoleto, 1985), pp. 765–808, repr. in
Jarnut, *Herrschaft und Ethnogenese im Frühmittelalter: Gesammelte Aufsätze von Jörg Jarnut. Festgabe
zum 60. Geburtstag* (Münster, 2002), pp. 375–418; D. A. Bullough, *Friends, neighbours and fellow
drinkers: aspects of community and conflict in the early medieval west*, H. M. Chadwick Memorial
Lectures, I (Cambridge, 1991); and S. Airlie, 'Talking heads: assemblies in early medieval Germany',
in P. S. Barnwell and M. Mostert (eds.), *Political assemblies in the earlier middle ages* (Turnhout,
2003), pp. 29–59.

[60] See P. S. Barnwell, 'Kings, nobles and assemblies in the barbarian kingdoms', in Barnwell and
Mostert, *Political assemblies*, pp. 11–28 at p. 27.

[61] *ARF* 772, ed. Kurze, p. 34.

ceremony, group bonding, and the physical ordering of both space and personnel as indicators of status and power on these occasions.[62]

On the question of who attended these assemblies, there is no reason to dissent from Seyfarth's broad distinctions, made a century ago, between routinely held annual general assemblies (convened, from the middle of the eighth century onwards, in May[63]) and smaller meetings of *optimates* convened to discuss specific issues, such as the meetings in 773 to decide whether to assist Pope Hadrian against the Lombards, in 775 concerning the continuation of the Saxon campaign, in 806 to discuss the *Divisio regnorum*, in 811 to witness Charlemagne's will, and in 813 to settle the succession to the empire on Louis the Pious.[64] The Lorsch annals, for example, written barely a year after the assembly of 802, stressed the different groups – bishops, priests and deacons, abbots and monks, the dukes, counts and the rest of the Christian people – summoned to Aachen. On this occasion it would appear that there were separate discussions among these three groups about sets of rules and laws regarded as specifically the business of each.[65] Similarly, the record of the assembly at Frankfurt in 794 specifies that the synod included the king with the bishops and priests of the kingdom of the Franks.[66] At Herstal in 779, on the other hand, the assembly 'gathered together in one synod and council the bishops and abbots and illustrious counts' (*congregatis in uno synodali concilio episcopis, abbatibus virisque inlustribus comitibus*).[67] The terminology used for assemblies in the *Annales regni francorum*, such as the older words *synodus* and *placitum* and the more recent *conventus*, indicate that the gatherings could include both secular and clerical men.[68] Further, a

---

[62] See C. Pössel, 'Symbolic communication and the negotiation of power at Carolingian regnal assemblies, 814–840', unpublished PhD thesis, University of Cambridge (2004). See also G. Althoff, *Verwandte, Freunde und Getreue: zum politischen Stellenwert der Gruppenbildung im frühen Mittelalter* (Darmstadt, 1990), trans C. Carroll, *Family, friends and followers: political and social bonds in early medieval Europe* (Cambridge, 2004); G. Althoff, *Spielregeln der Politik im Mittelalter: Kommunikation im Frieden und Fehden* (Darmstadt, 1997); P. Depreux, 'Lieux de rencontre, temps de negotiation: quelques observations sur les plaids généraux sous le règne de Louis le Pieux', in R. Le Jan (ed.), *La royauté et les élites dans l'Europe carolingienne du début du IXe siècle aux environs de 920* (Lille, 1998), pp. 213–31; and Reuter, 'Assembly politics'.

[63] This change of political military gatherings from March to May seems to be agreed: see Reuter, 'Assembly politics', p. 436.

[64] E. Seyfarth, *Fränkische Reichsversammlungen unter Karl dem Großen und Ludwig dem Frommen* (Leipzig, 1910); and compare *ARF* 773, 775, 806, 811 and 813, ed. Kurze, pp. 34, 40, 121, 134 and 138; and Einhard, *Vita Karoli*, c. 33, ed. Halphen, pp. 92–102; and see above pp. 96–103.

[65] Lorsch annals 802, ed. G. Pertz, *MGH SS* I, pp. 38–9; and see the discussion of these laws below.

[66] *MGH Cap.* I, No. 28, c. 1, p. 73.   [67] *MGH Cap.* I, No. 20, prologue, p. 47.

[68] See above, pp. 28 and 40.

mallus, or local convening of a judicial court, was in effect a local assembly, albeit very specific in its aims.

The king summoned these assemblies. Although in some instances the assembled *optimates* in one year might have decided where they would meet in the following year, the notice of the location of an assembly appears to have been sent out from the palace. The capitulary for the *missi* of 802, for example, refers to the need for everyone to be ready [to set out] when the king's order arrived.[69] That letters were indeed sent out to all potential participants informing them of the venue for assemblies (which would often be convened in conjunction with the military campaign planned for that summer) is indicated by a copy, addressed to Abbot Fulrad of St Quentin (near Amiens in Picardy), of a circular letter from the king. It survives in a contemporary marginal addition made in a thirteenth-century codex.[70] This notified the abbot of the venue for the general assembly that year (806), which was to be held in eastern Saxony on the river Bode at the place called Stassfurt (south of present-day Magdeburg). Abbot Fulrad was specifically required to come with his men armed and equipped in readiness to join the army in whichever region the king should decide. That further information would also be available at the assembly is indicated by the requirement concerning the presentation of the gifts, which Fulrad was to present in person at the assembly or wherever the king happened to be in mid-May. Presumably, Fulrad would have been able to find out where to go. The level of organization required for Fulrad himself to bring or send his men fully equipped from St Quentin to eastern Saxony as required, a journey of over 800 km, let alone the logistics for all the other men to whom this letter was sent, is impressive enough. It also implies an elaborate exchange of messages that was taken completely for granted. Charlemagne's letter itself advises Fulrad (and every other recipient) to make sure that he should have provisions in his carts for three months following the assembly, and to plan on the expedition taking half the year altogether. On the route to Stassfurt, moreover, Fulrad and all other recipients of this letter were to take nothing from the land or settlements through which they passed other than grass, firewood and water. That this is a standard requirement is indicated by its also being mentioned almost forty years earlier in relation to military service or travelling to the assembly in the Capitulary of Aquitaine of 768/9.[71]

[69] *MGH Cap.* I, No. 34, c. 13, p. 100.
[70] *MGH Cap.* I, No. 75, p. 168: Munich, Bayerisches Hauptstaatsarchiv, KL Niederaltaich 39, fol. 75r; see Mordek, *Bibliotheca*, p. 281.
[71] *MGH Cap.* I, No. 18, c. 6, p. 43.

Only rarely is there a specific formal record of the outcome of discussions at an assembly.[72] The Capitulary of Herstal of 779, for example, states
explicitly that it records the decisions agreed by the bishops, abbots, counts
and the king.[73] These concerned the jurisdiction of metropolitans and
power of bishops, court procedure and the administration of justice, payment of tithe, appropriate punishments for perjury and robbery and an
affirmation of the provisions of Pippin III's assemblies and synods.
Similarly, the decisions made at the Synod of Frankfurt in 794 on
Christian doctrine and on practical matters such as coinage, weights, and
measures, were the outcome of an assembly. So too, the regulations for the
Saxons were apparently agreed upon at an assembly at Lippspringe in 782.
Another assembly was specifically recorded at Aachen in 797. Prescriptions
for the administration of justice formulated at Aachen in 802–3, and the
Divisio regnorum of 806, are all preserved in capitularies drawn up after
assemblies whose convening is noted in the narrative sources.[74] Christina
Pössel relates the example of a decision taken at a small gathering of *fideles*
in the *pagus* of Le Mans *en route* between Rouen and Tours in the spring of
800. It was a particular local problem on which Charlemagne appears to
have been consulted as he was passing through.[75] The capitularies from
Boulogne in 811, so concerned with military and naval matters as well as
with justice, may represent the outcome of assembly discussions, though
they are simply labelled as *capitula* established by the emperor at Boulogne.
The *Annales regni francorum* for 811 record only the king's visit to the coast
to inspect the fleet, with no mention of an assembly.[76] For the most part,
there are no clues about the contexts in which the capitulary texts might
have been produced.

The capitulary texts of Charlemagne, therefore, to make no greater
claims about other Carolingian rulers, cannot be regarded as invariably

---

[72] See also D. Hägermann, 'Zur Entstehung der Kapitularien', in W. Schlögl and P. Herde (eds.),
Grundwissenschaften und Geschichte: Festschrift für Peter Acht, Münchener Historische Studien, Abt.
Geschichtliche Hilfswissenschaften 15 (Kallmünz, 1976), pp. 12–27.

[73] *MGH Cap.* 1, No. 20, p. 47.

[74] *MGH Cap.* 1, Nos. 26, 27, 33, 45 (and compare Lorsch annals 802, ed. G. Pertz, *MGH SS* 1, pp. 38–9;
and *ARF* 806, ed. Kurze, p. 121) and 77, pp. 68–72, 91–9, 126–30, 170–2. *MGH Cap.* 1, No. 52,
pp. 139–40, dated by Boretius to 808, may also record an assembly's decisions.

[75] *Capitulum in pago cenomannicum datum*, *MGH Cap.* 1, No. 31, pp. 81–2; and C. Pössel, 'Authors and
recipients of Carolingian capitularies, 779–829', in R. Corradini, R. Meens, C. Pössel and P. Shaw
(eds.), *Texts and identities in the early middle ages*, Forschungen zur Geschichte des Mittelalters 12,
Österreichische Akademie der Wissenschaften, Denkschriften 344 (Vienna 2006), pp. 376–412
at p. 384.

[76] *MGH Cap.* 1, Nos. 74 and 80, pp. 166–7 and 176–7: 'Que domnus imperator constituit Bononia qui
est in littore maris', and compare *ARF* 811, ed. Kurze, p. 135.

originating in assemblies, whether general or small. Pössel has demonstrated, contrary to earlier assumptions, that capitularies only occasionally reflect the business conducted at an assembly.[77] The explicitly royally endorsed and edited reports of collective decisions from assemblies actually comprise a tiny proportion – less than 4 per cent – of Charlemagne's surviving capitularies. If the association between capitularies and assemblies is rarely precise, this has important implications for our understanding of the functions of many of the assemblies as well as of the capitularies. It means that the latter cannot all be regarded as legislation in any conventional sense. If it is inappropriate to classify many of the capitularies as legislation, the extent to which capitularies might corroborate the status of the assembly as a legitimating forum, or need the *consensus fidelium*, is also doubtful.[78] Rather, what gives any royal capitulary its authority is that it comes from the king. Even those who made their own versions of the king's wishes, reiterated them in their own letters and capitularies, or merely compiled a list of the topics to which he wished them to attend, mediated the king's voice.[79] Capitularies were sent to the king's officials, notably the *missi*, and to his people (directly or via the *missi*), as an expression in writing of his will.[80] The contents were thereupon to be more broadly communicated. One capitulary manuscript, Paris, BnF lat. 4995, fol. 19v, for example, preserves the requirement for the public pronouncement of the new law in the *Capitulare legibus additum* of 803 at the *mallus publicus* in Paris by Count Stephen.[81]

[77] Pössel, 'Authors and recipients'. For a restatement of the older views see J. L. Nelson, 'The voice of Charlemagne', in R. Gameson and H. Leyser (eds.), *Belief and culture in the middle ages: studies presented to Henry Mayr-Harting* (Oxford, 2001), pp. 76–90 at p. 77 n.13, i.e.: 'these texts need to be set, as to their origins, in assemblies'.

[78] I follow Pössel, 'Authors and recipients', in this; for an alternative view see J. Hannig, *Consensus fidelium: Frühfeudale Interpretationen des Verhältnisses von Königtum und Adel am Beispiel des Frankenreiches*, Monographien zur Geschichte des Mittelalters 27 (Stuttgart, 1982).

[79] See R. McKitterick on episcopal statutes in *The Frankish church and the Carolingian reforms, 789–895* (London, 1977), pp. 45–79; and P. Brommer, 'Capitula episcoporum: Bemerkungen zu den bischöflichen Kapitularien', *Zeitschrift für Kirchengeschichte* 91 (1980), pp. 207–36.

[80] J. L. Nelson, 'Legislation and consensus in the reign of Charles the Bald', in P. Wormald (ed.), *Ideal and reality in Frankish and Anglo-Saxon society: studies presented to J. M. Wallace-Hadrill* (Oxford, 1983), pp. 202–27, repr. in J. L. Nelson, *Politics and ritual in early medieval Europe* (London, 1986), pp. 91–116.

[81] Mordek, *Bibliotheca*, p. 551; and see K-F. Werner, '*Missus–marchio–comes*: Entre l'administration centrale et l'administration locale de l'empire carolingien', in W. Paravicini and K.-F. Werner (eds.), *Histoire comparée de l'administration (IVe–XVIIIe siècles)*, Beihefte der Francia 9 (Munich, 1980), pp. 191–239 at pp. 199–200; and A. Krah, 'Zur Kapitulariengesetzgebung in und für Neustrien', in H. Atsma (ed.), *La Neustrie: les pays au nord de la Loire de 650 à 850*, Beihefte der Francia 16/1 (Sigmaringen, 1989), pp. 565–81 at p. 569.

The long tradition of attempts to distinguish between the legal force of the king's oral pronouncement at an assembly and that of the written capitulary text are relevant only in the cases of those texts specifically related to assemblies. Even then, discussions of the capitularies have become muddled up with the issue of the king's role in relation to *leges* or 'national' lawcodes.[82] They are also based on a now discredited notion that the juridical power of a supposedly illiterate early medieval king had to reside in his oral decisions, without taking into account that any early medieval king would obviously have two principal models for written records of collective oral decisions in Roman and in canon law, let alone the Germanic *leges* themselves.[83] The king's authority would give the oral pronouncement made at an assembly its power. Similarly, the written record of the decisions of an assembly convoked by and presided over by the king was imbued with his authority. Charlemagne's letters repeatedly indicate that the written record of whatever had been decided at an assembly, or what the king required without an assembly, created an essential obligation on the part of whoever it was who was required to do a certain task, especially if that task were part of his job. In the Capitulary of Herstal of 779, furthermore, Charlemagne referred to whatever his father Pippin had established at assemblies and synods. He was not referring to written capitularies but to those decisions which Charlemagne was now recording in writing and insisting were effective in this form. This applied also to legal transactions: the thirteenth clause of the Capitulary of Herstal discusses the importance of renewing *precariae* when already recorded in writing, and writing them down if not. All subsequent capitularies recording the king's requirements or questions endorse the status of the written text.[84]

[82] See, for example, the discussions by P. Wormald, *The making of English law: King Alfred to the twelfth century*, 1: *Legislation and its limits* (Oxford, 1999), pp. 29–69; and Wormald, '*Lex scripta* and *verbum regis*: legislation and germanic kingship from Euric to Cnut', in P. Sawyer and I. N. Wood (eds.), *Early medieval kingship* (Leeds, 1977), pp. 105–138. Compare R. McKitterick, 'Zur Herstellung von Kapitularien: die Arbeit des leges-Skriptoriums', *MIÖG* 101 (1993), pp. 3–16; and H. Nehlsen, 'Zur Aktualität und Effektivität germanischer Rechtsaufzeichnungen', in P. Classen (ed.), *Recht und Schrift im Mittelalter*, Vorträge und Forschungen 23 (Sigmaringen, 1977), pp. 449–502.
[83] See R. McKitterick, 'Bischöfe und die handschriftliche Überlieferung des Rechts im zehnten Jahrhundert' in D. R. Bauer, R. Hiestand, B. Kasten and S. Lorenz (eds.), *Das fränkische Reich 750–1000: Herrschaft – Kirche – Mönchtum, Festschrift für Josef Semmler* (Sigmaringen, 1998), pp. 231–42.
[84] For full exposition see McKitterick, *The Carolingians and the written word*, pp. 22–75. See also J. L. Nelson, 'Literacy in Carolingian government', in R. McKitterick (ed.), *The uses of literacy in early medieval Europe* (Cambridge, 1990), pp. 258–96.

A complicating factor for any assessment of the capitularies is that nearly all these extant texts are preserved in copies postdating their original production by one or more decades, and thus in contexts created by the later compilers. The greater proportion of the later collections incorporating Charlemagne's capitularies are law books containing 'national laws' and/or canon law. It is necessary, therefore, to distinguish between the initial function and production of the capitularies, and their later uses and contexts of preservation.[85] Too often the latter are confused with the former. Too often, moreover, discussion has attempted to generalize across the entire century for Carolingian capitulary production, or what has been deduced for the capitularies of Louis the Pious or Charles the Bald has tended to be assumed to be as valid for those of Charlemagne.[86] These are issues still being debated. They cannot be resolved on a general basis, even for the reign of Charlemagne alone. Determining the function of particular assemblies and individual capitularies is a more attainable enterprise, and one that is being greatly facilitated by the heroic labours of Hubert Mordek.[87]

In summary, whatever their problematic legal status and subsequent use, and whether or not the later law books were put together by lay officials or clerics,[88] the capitularies are among the most fruitful witnesses to Charlemagne's methods and principles of government. Their subsequent incorporation into collections of law and other categories of text indicates an enhanced function as a record of royal pronouncements on the governance of the kingdom, and even an understanding of them as a genre of legislation.

---

[85] On capitulary manuscripts see the indispensable Mordek, *Bibliotheca*; and A. Bühler, 'Capitularia relicta: Studien zur Entstehung und Überlieferung der Kapitularien Karls des Großen und Ludwigs des Frommen', *Archiv für Diplomatik* 32 (1986), pp. 305–501. I am also indebted to the work in progress on capitulary manuscripts of Jennifer Davis and should like to thank her for letting me read her paper 'A king and his law: Carolingian rulers through the lens of the capitulary manuscripts' (with analytical appendices) in advance of publication. See also R. McKitterick, 'Some Carolingian law-books and their function', in P. Linehan (ed.), *Authority and power: studies on medieval law and government presented to Walter Ullmann* (Cambridge, 1980), pp. 13–27, repr. in McKitterick, *Books, scribes and learning in the Frankish kingdoms, 6th–9th centuries* (Aldershot, 1994), Chapter VIII; and below, pp. 263–6.

[86] See also Wormald, *The making of English law*, pp. 30–70.

[87] Mordek, *Bibliotheca*; and H. Mordek, 'Karolingische Kapitularien', in Mordek, *Überlieferung und Geltung normativer Texte des frühen und hohen Mittelalters*, Quellen und Forschungen zum Recht im Mittelalter 4 (Sigmaringen, 1986), pp. 25–50. See also Mordek, 'Karls des Großen zweites Kapitular von Herstal und die Hungersnot der Jahre 778/779', *Deutsches Archiv* 61 (2005), pp. 1–52; and Pokorny, 'Eine Brief-Instruktion', pp. 57–78.

[88] His determination to establish law books as witnessing to 'those most ideologically committed to life by *lex scripta*, the upper ranks of the clergy', distorts the findings of Wormald, *The making of English law*, pp. 30–70 at p. 63.

The legal dimension of the capitularies and the wider context of ecclesiastical reform have been very fully discussed over the past century or so. Yet the capitularies reflect more about Charlemagne's immediate concerns in ruling his kingdom than any other contemporary source. When first circulated, the capitularies of Charlemagne were the principal form in which he communicated his wishes to the officials responsible for carrying them out, whether layman or cleric, even if for the most part we can now read them only in their received and digested, rather than original, form. It is on the primary communicative role of the texts, therefore, that I wish now to concentrate.

THE CAPITULARIES

Capitularies are so named because they comprise *capitula*, that is, short sections or clauses on a variety of topics. This format has a number of precedents. Roman and canon law (incorporating papal decretals and conciliar decisions) have already been mentioned, but one could add first of all the Pauline Epistles, which would have offered a powerful inspiration for combining exhortation and moral and doctrinal fervour with the administrative and practical regulations.[89] Secondly, although also structured like the fifth-century Roman *Theodosian Code* (which, incidentally, also included clauses concerning religion and the church in Book XVI), there are the *leges*, especially the *Leges langobardorum* of Aistulf which actually use the word *capitulare* in the prologue to describe the format of the laws.[90] Since Ganshof's pioneering analysis, it has been accepted that the definition of a capitulary needs to be broad, for some of the documents labelled by Boretius as capitularies, as if all belonged to the same type of text, issued in the aftermath of an assembly and recording its decisions, have since been identified as agendas for assembly discussions.[91] Still others

---

[89] On biblical texts and their inspiration in Carolingian politics see below, p. 233; B. Fischer, 'Bibeltext und Bibelreform unter Karl dem Großen', in *KdG* II, pp. 156–216; R. Kottje, *Studien zum Einfluß des Alten testaments auf recht und Liturgie des frühen Mittelalters (6.-8. Jahrhundert)*, Bonner historische Forschungen 23, 2nd edn (Bonn, 1970); and M. de Jong (ed.), *The power of the word: the influence of the Bible on early medieval politics*, special issue of *Early Medieval Europe* 7 (1998).

[90] Noted by F. Bougard, *La justice dans le royaume d'Italie de la fin du VIIIe siècle au début du XIe siècle*, Bibliothèque des Ecoles françaises d'Athènes et de Rome 291(Rome, 1995), p. 18; and compare F. Bluhme and A. Boretius (eds.), *MGH Leges* 4 (Hanover, 1868), p. 195. On the Theodosian Code see J. Harries and I. Wood (eds.), *The Theodosian Code* (London, 1993).

[91] See F. L. Ganshof, *Recherches sur les capitulaires* (Paris, 1958); German trans. *Was waren die Kapitularien?* (Weimar and Darmstadt, 1961), p. 25. For an original example, sold at Sotheby's in London, 25 June 1985, see H. Mordek, 'Recently discovered capitulary texts belonging to the legislation of Louis the Pious', in P. Godman and R. Collins (eds.), *Charlemagne's heir: new perspectives on the reign of Louis the Pious* (Oxford, 1990), pp. 437–55, and fuller German version, 'Unbekannte Texte zur karolingischen Gesetzgebung: Ludwig der Fromme, Einhard und die

appear to be *aide-mémoires* or checklists of things to be done or matters to be investigated, royal discourses or admonitions, letters, and even texts closely resembling sermons.[92]

Thus capitularies all relate in one way or another to Charlemagne's method of ruling, and most can be regarded as administrative documents. Issues of format, content, responsibility, context of production and function have become blurred, yet they need to be distinguished; the capitulary form – in *capitula* – and the underlying responsibility for them – the king – are the defining characteristics of the capitulary, whereas specific aspects of the context of production, content and function need to be considered in relation to each capitulary on its own merits. The assembly, as indicated above, might have been one place where such texts could have been received and subsequently taken home by the participants. The capitularies identified the duties and goals of the recipients as envisaged by the king.[93]

The many discussions about who may have been responsible for the actual writing of the prose or style of these texts miss the point.[94] The formal capitularies went out in the king's name from the royal writing office initially and represent the substance of his wishes, just as his charters record grants and decisions he had made and his letters say what he wanted said. Even the less formal agendas and the like are associated with royal authority. It may well be the case that the subsequent compilers of the capitularies may have reordered them and added glosses or cross references. It is simply not possible for us to be certain of this or to determine whether the process of mediation through a notary may have altered the language of these documents, though it may well be that some of the capitularies, expressed with greater directness and asperity, allow us to hear Charlemagne's own voice 'without interference'.[95]

Let us look at the surviving capitularies or royal administrative documents in more detail in order to determine the pattern of distribution within the chronology of Charlemagne's reign. One hundred and seven

Capitula adhuc conferenda', *Deutsches Archiv* 42 (1986), pp. 446–70, repr. in H. Mordek, *Studien zur fränkischen Herrschergesetzgebung: Aufsätze über Kapitularien und Kapitulariensammlungen ausgewählt zum 60. Geburtstag* (Frankfurt am Main, 2000), pp. 161–86.

[92] See R. McKitterick, *The Frankish church and the Carolingian reforms, 789–895* (London, 1977), pp. 17–44; McKitterick, *The Frankish kingdoms under the Carolingians, 751–987* (London, 1983), p. 102; and the recent survey by T. M. Buck, *Admonitio und praedicatio: zur religiös-pastoralen Dimension von Kapitularien und kapitulariennahen Texten (507–814)*, Freiburger Beiträge zur mittelalterlichen Geschichte, Studien und Texte 9 (Frankfurt am Main, 1997), esp. pp. 25–31.

[93] This is suggested by Pössel, 'Authors and recipients'.

[94] See for example, F.-C. Scheibe, 'Alcuin und die Admonitio generalis', *Deutsches Archiv* 14 (1958), pp. 221–229.

[95] Nelson, 'The voice of Charlemagne', pp. 76–88, at p. 80.

capitularies (according to Boretius' edition) survive, dated to the reign of Charlemagne as king. They range in date from 768 to 813, to which records of councils convened in his reign but not categorized as capitularies by the *MGH* editors need to be added. These are the Bavarian synods of 796, 798 and 800, and the records of the councils of Aquileia (796/7), Rome (798) and Aachen (809), and the reform councils of 813 convened in Arles, Tours, Reims, Chalon and Mainz. Of these, the greater proportion certainly belongs to the period 801–14. Bühler's categories also need to be taken into account; he distinguished between capitularies partly by format, i.e., *Epistola* or *Constitutio*, and these comprise twelve of the items labelled 'capitulary' in Boretius' edition. Ten of these, however, including the *De litteris colendis* and the *Divisio regnorum*, are very germane to royal rule.[96] For my calculations below, I have included Bühler's ten *Epistolae* and *Constitutiones* as capitularies in the broad sense of royal administrative documents. Less convincingly, Bühler separated out a further group of sixteen documents he designated as *Capitula episcoporum*. Certainly four of these read like episcopal checklists, though they relate to matters required by the king, and a fifth is the episcopal statute of Gerbald of Liège.[97] The remaining eleven, which include the Synod of Frankfurt, however, can be associated more directly with the ruler, so I have included them in my reckoning. The ten undated texts in Boretius' edition have been omitted from the reckoning. In cases where there is a date astride a date band I have counted it in the earlier one, but I freely acknowledge that doubts about particular documents and alternative choices about categories will produce slightly different totals.

With all this taken into account, the distribution of edited capitularies during Charlemagne's reign is as follows. There are eleven capitularies from the first twenty years of Charlemagne's reign, that is, 768–88, up to the acquisition of Bavaria. There are a further eleven capitularies, plus the five synods in Bavaria, Aquileia and Rome, for the period 789–800. In the last thirteen years of the reign, 801–14, there are 79 capitularies, the Aachen council of 809 and the reform councils of 813. It has been customary to accept this greater number of capitularies as evidence of a major increase in administrative and governmental activity, produced by a greater number of chancery personnel. This apparent increase is then attributed to the effect of the imperial title on Charlemagne, even to the extent of

---

[96] For the *De litteris colendis*, see below, pp. 240–1, and for the *Divisio regnorum* see above, pp. 96–8.
[97] Bühler, 'Capitularia relicta, pp. 305–501.

describing the capitulary of 802 as incorporating an 'imperial programme' of government.[98]

Certainly the lack of secure evidence for capitularies from the first year of Charlemagne's reign, together with the small group of ecclesiastical synodal records from Pippin's reign, suggest that Charlemagne was slow to develop this particular form of general communication or record for part of the Frankish political process, and indeed, the production of capitularies in general. The Herstal assembly in 779 is particularly interesting in its affirmation of Pippin III's earlier provisions, eleven years after his death. No capitularies of Charlemagne are preserved from before this date apart from the confirmation of Pippin's provisions for Aquitaine, and the undated 'first capitulary' of Charlemagne. Both, as we shall see, are usually dated to 768 or 769.[99] Even so, neither the notion of a great increase in governmental activity nor that of an 'imperial programme' holds up particularly well on closer examination. On the basic level of relative bulk, it should be acknowledged that many of the post-800 items in Boretius' *Capitularia* volume are very short. The total quantity of text is almost the same for before as for after 800 if we exclude the following: the judgment for Spain in charter form, the undated extracts lumped together as *Capitula francica* and *Capitula italica*, the Saxon hostage list, the episcopal statute of Bishop Gerbald of Liège and the four 'episcopal checklists', the letter from Riculf to Egino,[100] and the undated texts.[101] The Bavarian, Aquileian and Roman council *acta* would weight the pre-800, side of the scale still more.[102]

Once the content is examined, however, it is clear that the principal elements of the so-called post-800 'imperial programme' embodied in the administrative capitularies for the *missi dominici* are first articulated in the earlier, that is, the pre-800, capitularies. The early capitularies of Charlemagne include the problematic 'first capitulary', the Capitulary of

[98] F. L. Ganshof, 'Le programme de gouvernement impérial de Charlemagne', *Renovatio imperii: atti della giornata internazionale di studio per il Millenario, Ravenna 4–5 November 1961* (Faenza, 1963), pp. 63–96, trans. J. Sondheimer, 'Charlemagne's programme of imperial government', in Ganshof, *The Carolingians and the Frankish monarchy* (London, 1971), pp. 55–86; and see also T. M. Buck, '"Capitularia imperatoria": Zur Kaisergesetzgebung Karls des Großen von 802', *Historisches Jahrbuch* 122 (2002), pp. 3–26.
[99] Compare also pp. 237–9.   [100] *MGH Cap.* I, Nos. 76, 104, 105, 115, 123, 81, 117–19, 127.
[101] *MGH Cap.* I, Nos. 107–10; 113, 114, 129–31. There are sixty-eight pages of pre-800 texts as opposed to seventy-two printed pages of text for those certainly post-800 in the Boretius *Capitularia* volume. It should be emphasized that all these figures can only be approximate, given the lack of agreement about the status of particular texts as well as their dates. But the general pattern remains clear.
[102] *MGH Conc.* II.i, Nos. 20–38.

Herstal, the *Admonitio generalis*, the *Capitulare de villis*, the synodal decisions of Frankfurt, and the capitularies for Aquitaine, Italy, Bavaria and Saxony. These set out royal policy and extend the king's aspirations for orderly government, justice and a well-regulated Christian realm to the newly acquired territories. They together merit the label 'programmatic' far more than those of post-800.

The first two capitularies attributed to Charlemagne have been assumed to be at the beginning of his reign. Each has a precarious transmission history. The capitulary for Aquitaine survives in the compilations of capitularies and laws made for an Aquitainian *missus dominicus*, now Leiden Voss. lat. Q.119.[103] The *Capitulare primum* was edited by Etienne Baluze from a now lost manuscript from St Vincent's monastery in Laon, but was also incorporated into the collection of Benedictus Levita.[104] The Aquitainian capitulary, perhaps issued with Carloman in 768 or 769, confirmed their father Pippin's ordering of Aquitaine.[105] Yet it needs to be looked at in conjunction with the other, the *Capitulare primum*. The former's *capitula* attend to some basic preliminary guidelines for the reorganization of the church, the regulation of property ownership, the confirmation of the right of men to appeal to the king for justice, the status of the law (Roman and Frankish) and the role of the *missi dominici* acting for the king. The latter capitulary, supposedly from 769, has long been considered a later ninth-century forgery on the grounds, above all, of its opening clause: *Karolus, gratia dei rex regnique Francorum rector et devotus sanctae ecclesiae defensor atque adiutor in omnibus*. Ferdinand Lot thought this phrasing an unlikely formulation for the third quarter of the eighth century, especially with its articulation of the role of the king as rector and defender of the church. Schmitz has pointed out, however, that similar formulae are to be found at the beginning of both the *Admonitio generalis* and a newly identified

---

[103] *MGH Cap.* I, No. 18. For the Leiden manuscript, see below, p. 265.
[104] Mordek, *Bibliotheca*, pp. 214 and 547, who noted that it was not entirely impossible, even if unlikely, that Baluze's manuscript was the codex now Paris BnF lat. 4788 of the mid to third quarter of the ninth century, and that this capitulary had been on leaves now lost. See also Benedictus Levita, III, cc. 123–37, 139–40. On the case for the contents of Benedictus Levita's collection needing a more positive reassessment see R. McKitterick, 'History, law and communication with the past in the Carolingian period', in *Comunicare e significare nell'alto medioevo*, Settimane 52 (Spoleto, 2005), pp. 941–79 at pp. 969–78. See the online edition by G. Schmitz and W. Hartmann, <www.benedictus.mgh.de/haupt.htm>.
[105] See above, p. 80.

capitulary from 798/9.[106] Further, the papal letters to the Frankish rulers in the *Codex epistolaris carolinus*, from Pope Paul to Pippin III, and especially those of Pope Stephen III to Charlemagne and Carloman and the early letters of Pope Hadrian to Charlemagne, are replete with complimentary affirmations of the Frankish ruler's protective and supportive role in relation to the church.[107]

The opening sentence in the *capitulare primum* could also be understood as a neat summary of the sentiments expressed in Charlemagne's earliest charters, issued between 769 and 775. These affirm the royal duty to care for places of religion for the benefit of God's servants and to care for the clergy, the spiritual rewards which will result from grants made for the love of God to the resting places of the saints, and the duty to make gifts to the church to obtain mercy from God. A telling indication of the need to learn what was fitting in a king's behaviour emerges strongly from these charters. In the first place, many charters confirm things granted and conceded in former times by Charlemagne's predecessors for the stability of his king-dom. In a grant to St Denis in 775, moreover, Charlemagne noted that he had discovered what grants had been made in the past in the precepts and confirmations of earlier kings (*in eorum confirmationis vel preceptionis anteriorum regum invenimus*). Throughout the realms of Francia and Italy which were his by God's favour (*per regna deo propicio nostra*), he now confirmed them anew.[108] This attention to the provisions of his forebears in the Capitulary for Aquitaine, the *Capitulare primum* and the earliest charters is what one might expect from a new king. It is also evident in the echoing in the *Capitulare primum* of clauses from the *Concilium germanicum* of Charlemagne's uncle Carloman, especially clauses 1–8, and from some Merovingian church councils.

Rather than undermining the validity of the *Capitulare primum*, such reiteration of past decrees reinforces it. That some of its clauses are rapidly

---

[106] *MGH Cap.* 1, No. 19, declared a forgery by F. Lot, 'Le premier capitulaire de Charlemagne', *Annuaire de l'Ecole pratique des hautes études, sect. Philologique et historique* 1924/5, pp. 7–13, repr. in F. Lot, *Recueil des travaux historiques de Ferdinand Lot*, 11 (Geneva, 1970), pp. 317–23; but see G. Schmitz, 'Echte Quellen – falsche Quellen: müssen zentrale Quellen aus der Zeit Ludwigs der Frömmen neu bewertet werden', in F.-R. Erkens und H. Wolff (eds.), *Von Sacerdotium und regnum: geistliche und weltliche Gewalt im frühen und hohen Mittelalter. Festschrift für Egon Boshof zum 65. Geburtstag* (Cologne, Weimar and Vienna, 2002), pp. 275–300 at p. 279. Compare the *Admonitio generalis*, *MGH Cap.* 1, No. 21; and Mordek, *Bibliotheca*, Anhang 1: *Texte, Karoli Regis capitula ad Arnonem archiepiscopum Salisburgensem directa* (c. 798/9), pp. 974–5. On the *Admonitio generalis* see further below, pp. 239–40.

[107] *Codex epistolaris carolinus*, ed. Gundlach, Epp. 20, 57, 72, pp. 520–2, 582–3, 602–3; and see further below, pp. 292–8.

[108] DKar. 1, Nos. 55–103, esp. Nos. 87 and 93.

superseded is another indication of its preliminary, even provisional, character. The date, given Charlemagne's description as simply *rex francorum*, can
only be set between 768 and 774, though my inclination would be to follow
Baluze in considering it as one of the earliest attempts at imposing a new order
on Charlemagne's part. I would therefore suggest a date of 768–71. The
Capitulare primum's combination of such general requirements as those for
the maintenance of the *placita* and the work of the *mallus* with a large number
of regulations for church organization and discipline is entirely consistent
with the later capitularies as well as with the Capitulary for Aquitaine.

Certainly the Capitulary of Herstal, one of the few to be endorsed
explicitly by an assembly, is also concerned with internal ecclesiastical
matters for its first six clauses. Like many other capitularies, however, the
topics concerning the church overlap with secular affairs when it comes to
punishments, criminals seeking sanctuary, the regulation of land ownership and property, the conduct of legal transactions, and judicial hearings.
Here too, as in the Capitulary of Aquitaine, the role of the *missi* was
emphasized. Even so many years into his reign, this relatively young king
was anxious to confirm that the provisions of Pippin in his assemblies and
synods were to be maintained.

Some hint of the effort required to maintain order and peace in conditions where, as we saw above, not all were necessarily happy under
Carolingian rule, may be reflected in the clause forbidding sworn associations except for almsgiving, fire or shipwreck.[109] The Capitulary of
Herstal survives in either a 'common' or a 'Lombard' version in an
astonishing number of capitulary collections compiled in Italy, Francia
and Bavaria. It thus witnesses to the effectiveness of the initial dissemination of these clauses agreed at a gathering of bishops, abbots and counts
with the king. The Herstal *capitula* are also echoed in many later capitularies, not least the *Admonitio generalis*, issued a decade later.[110]

Although probably unrelated to a specific assembly, the *Admonitio
generalis* arose out of discussions Charlemagne had had with his lay and
clerical advisers. It is undoubtedly a royal admonition,[111] but also contains a

[109] *MGH Cap.* I, No. 20, c. 16. On the implications of these guilds and *coniurationes* see my discussion in McKitterick, *Perceptions of the past*, pp. 71–3.
[110] E. Magnou Nortier, 'L' "Admonitio generalis". Etude critique', *Jornades internacionals d'estudi sobre le bisbe Feliu d'Urgell* (Urgel-Litana, 2000), pp. 195–242. I am grateful to Dominque Iogna-Prat for this reference. For a robust discussion, not only of the perverse suggestion that this is a forgery but also of the implications of this kind of argument concerning doubts about particular documents, see Schmitz, 'Echte Quellen – falsche Quellen', esp. p. 278 note 13.
[111] See M. de Jong, *Penitential State*, chapter 4 (forthcoming).

wealth of specific provisions drawn from the *Dionysio-Hadriana* canon law collection about the behaviour and conduct of the clergy, and requirements for the setting up of schools, the duties for the clergy, the conformity of monks to the Rule, the singing of Roman chant in the office, the use of equal and correct weights and measures, and the recommended content of sermons. The prologue underlines the conscious formulation of a policy and vision for a Christian Frankish kingdom.[112] Not only was this *Admonitio* rapidly and widely disseminated, but there is every indication, as I have demonstrated elsewhere, of the rapid impact and implementation of this decree. Certainly there was an abundance of moral fervour and idealism expressed in it, but there were also very specific injunctions as to how the Christian society described in the text was to be achieved.[113]

Remarkable though it is, the *Admonitio generalis* needs to be seen in the context of the succession of increasingly elaborate statements about the integration of the Christian faith within the institutional and political framework of the Frankish realm in the first three decades of Charlemagne's reign. Charlemagne's models for these were not just the contents of the earlier synodal texts, but also the crucial role assumed by the Carolingian mayors and kings, and the Bavarian Agilolfing dukes, in presiding over assemblies of ecclesiastical and lay magnates and confirming any decisions. Already signalled at the beginning of the reign and in the Capitulary of Herstal, which in their turn drew on statements developed under Carloman and Pippin III, the provisions of the *Admonitio generalis* were enhanced, reinforced and even modified by subsequent capitularies and letters from the king and statements from assemblies. Most notable among these are the *De litteris colendis*, possibly to be dated as early as 784/5,[114] and the Capitulary of Frankfurt of 794.[115]

The circular letter known as the *De litteris colendis* relates specifically to schools and learning and will be discussed in the following

---

[112] *MGH Cap.* I, No. 22; and McKitterick, *Frankish church*, pp. 1–40. See also M. T. Kloft, 'Das geistliche Amt im Umfeld des Frankfurter Konzils', in R. Berndt (ed.), *Das Frankfurter Konzil von 794: Kristallisationspunkt karolingischer Kultur*, II: *Kultur und Theologie*, Quellen und Abhandlungen zur Mittelrheinische Kirchengeschichte 80 (Mainz, 1997), pp. 885–917 (who highlights *correctio* as well, (p. 904). See also G. Brown, 'The Carolingian renaissance', in McKitterick, *Carolingian culture*, pp. 1–51.

[113] On the dissemination, Mordek, *Bibliotheca*, p. 1082, lists forty-one manuscripts as well as its inclusion in the collection of Ansegisus.

[114] *MGH Cap.* I, No. 29, and re-edited by T. Martin, 'Bemerkungen zur "Epistola de litteris colendis"', *Archiv für Diplomatik* 31 (1985), pp. 227–72 at pp. 231–5. Martin credits Alcuin with a role in its conception and even drafting. See also J. Fleckenstein, *Die Bildungsreform Karls des Großen als Verwirklichung der "norma rectitudinis"* (Bigge-Ruhr, 1953).

[115] *MGH Cap.* I, No. 28, pp. 73–8.

chapter.[116] The capitulary of Frankfurt is a vivid report of a Carolingian assembly. Its *capitula* read more like a summary of decisions, and discussions of various topics, rather than a full set of orders or instructions. Although it starts with the explicit statement that it had been convened at the command of Charlemagne, thereafter the report alternates between indirect third-person reporting of the decisions reached by the king and the synod, and some more direct reportage in the first person. The latter suggests the king's direct intervention in the discussion with his comments or responses. Thus at the beginning of clause 4 there is the statement, 'Our most pious lord decreed, with the approval of the holy synod' .... In clauses 55 and 56, where it is explained that Hildebold can act as chaplain at the palace as a result of papal permission to be absent from his diocese, and Alcuin is presented as a potential member of the religious fellowship of the synod, the phrases used are 'the king also stated' and 'he recommended also'. In clause 16, however, the statement begins, 'We have heard', and continues, 'We and the holy synod have decreed'.[117] In some places, a series of clauses following such statements is set out under this general indication of the source of authority. Their abruptness is striking, 'that priests, deacons, monks and clerics are not to drink in taverns', 'that the Lord's day is to be observed from evening to evening' or 'that a bishop is not to be allowed to remain ignorant of the rule of the canons and the monastic rule'. They certainly draw on similar decisions made at early church councils and incorporated into the *Admonitio generalis* five years earlier. If compared with their counterparts about clerics in pubs, a bishop's knowledge, or the observance of Sunday in the *Admonitio generalis*, the Frankfurt clauses reflect minor adjustments, possibly as reactions to the presentation of anecdotal evidence offered in discussion.[118] Such

---

[116] Below, p. 316.

[117] See H. Mordek, 'Aachen, Frankfurt, Reims: Beobachtungen zu Genese und Tradition des Capitulare Franconofurtense (a. 794)', in Berndt, *Das Frankfurter Konzil von 794*, 1: *Politik und Kirche*, pp. 125–48; and Mordek, 'Das Frankfurter Kapitular Karls des Großen (794)', in J. Fried, R. Koch, L. E. Saurma-Jeltsch and A. Theil (eds.), *794: Karl der Große in Frankfurt am Main: Ein König bei der Arbeit. Austellung zum 1200-Jahre Jubiläum der Stadt Frankfurt am Main* (Sigmaringen, 1994), pp. 46–9; both repr. in H. Mordek, *Studien zur fränkischen Herrschergesetzgebung: Aufsätze über Kapitularien und Kapitulariensammlungen ausgewählt zum 60. Geburtstag* (Frankfurt am Main, 2000), pp. 193–203 and 205–27. See also Kloft, 'Das geistliche Amt', pp. 913–16; and P. Depreux, 'L'expression "statutum est a domno rege et sancta synodo" annonçant certaines dispositions du capitulaire de Francfort (794)', in Berndt, *Das Frankfurter Konzil von 794*, 1, pp. 82–101.

[118] *MGH Cap.* 1, No. 28, cc. 20 and 21, p. 26. See Mordek, 'Aachen, Frankfurt, Reims'; and Mordek, *Bibliotheca*, Anhang 1: *Texte*, pp. 139–47 (in repr., pp. 219–27), where the adaptations are discussed in detail.

reiteration and amendment are striking features of the post-800 capitularies as well.

Yet it should not be forgotten that Frankfurt also contained references to the regulation of prices, weights and measures and to the reform of the coinage as something recently effected. It echoed the Herstal capitulary's clause against secular plots and *coniurationes* or conspiracies,[119] and included several clauses about the administration of justice, especially in the bishops' courts. Even the counts were to come to the bishops' courts, though the implication of the clause as a whole may be that the bishop was to be in charge of cases concerning all clergy and monks. The king in this respect set the metropolitan as the next stage for appeal, and if all else failed, accusers and accused were to come to the king with a letter from the metropolitan. In matters which concerned a cleric and a layman, the bishop and the count were to act together.[120]

The practical elements so briefly signalled in the Frankfurt capitulary are fully developed in the *Capitulare de villis* discussed in the previous chapter, though the principal focus is the network of royal estates on which the king depended for his livelihood, the need to provide the essential supplies, equipment, and horses for his military campaigns, and the arrangements for receiving revenues and renders.[121] So, too, the themes already identified in the other early capitularies are reiterated, namely, the responsibilities of the royal officials, the requirements for information, the use of letters and reports, the care for his people's welfare, the provision for justice, and the possibility in principle of even a *servus* gaining a hearing from the king himself.[122]

The general application of this small but important group of programmatic capitularies from the earlier part of Charlemagne's reign is clear, not only from their content but also from the very wide dissemination of the most comprehensive of them. Thus the capitulary of Herstal survives in thirty-three copies of the common version and seven of the Lombard, and the *Admonitio generalis* is to be found in over forty manuscripts.[123] Of the

[119] But see Mordek, 'Aachen, Frankfurt, Reims', p. 141 (repr. p. 221) for clerical *coniurationes vel insidias*.

[120] *MGH Cap.* 1, No. 28, cc. 6, 30, 44, 45, pp. 74–5, 77.   [121] See above, pp. 149–51.

[122] *MGH Cap.* 1, No. 32, cc. 2, 55, 56, 57, pp. 83 and 88. On the difficulty of translating the word *servus* see H.-W. Goetz, 'Serfdom and the beginnings of a "seigneurial system" in the Carolingian period: a survey of the evidence', *Early Medieval Europe* 2 (1993), pp. 29–51. A precise historical context for the production of the *Capitulare de villis* was suggested by A. Verhulst, 'Karolingische Agrarpolitik: das Capitular de villis und die Hungersnote von 792 und 805/806', *Zeitschrift für Agrargeschichte und Agrarsoziologie* 13 (1965), pp. 175–89; but see above, p. 155.

[123] See Mordek, *Bibliotheca*, pp. 1081–2 and compare Bühler, 'Capitularia relicta', pp. 484.

ninth- and tenth-century manuscripts among these, it is probably reasonable to presume that they were compiled from pre-existing copies, either of
the entire collection, or of individual capitularies available in the same area.
If so, then the distribution of capitularies extended from southern Italy to
Picardy, Burgundy and Aquitaine and from Lotharingia and the Rhineland
to southern Bavaria.

THE REGIONAL CAPITULARIES AND THE BENEFITS OF
CAROLINGIAN RULE

Among these pre-800 programmatic capitularies, however, are also to be
found the special regional capitularies issued soon after Charlemagne's
takeover of the regions concerned. The capitularies concerning Aquitaine,
Italy, Bavaria and Saxony were all produced as part of the consolidation of
Carolingian rule soon after the Carolingian takeover of these territories,
and have a far more local circulation.[124] The Aquitainian capitularies, as
mentioned earlier, are to be found only in the collection formed by a
Carolingian royal official for use in Aquitaine, now in Leiden Voss. lat.
Q 119.[125] A similarly meagre survival is apparent for the Saxon capitularies.
That for 782/5 is extant only in a manuscript produced in Mainz *c.* 825,
which also contains the capitulary for 797. The latter was copied in Corvey
in the tenth century in a compilation that included the *Lex Saxonum* and
the early charters of the monastery.[126] The Bavarian capitulary is exclusively in Bavarian codices. Boretius originally dated it '?810' and Mordek
suggested '?803'.[127] The codicological context may have prompted these
guesses. This short text follows the clauses of another capitulary with a
conjectural date of ?805–13 in the Freising capitulary collection, Munich,
Bayerische Staatsbibliothek Clm 19415, dated to the early ninth century,
and precedes the *Capitulare de legibus* of 803. The earliest copy of the
Bavarian capitulary, Vienna ÖNB 2232, on the other hand, is from the
beginning of the ninth century. While obviously not precluding the assign-
ment of the date 803, the content of its clauses, comprising matters the *missi*
should know, accords with the concerns of the other early capitularies of
Charlemagne.[128] The capitulary making additions to the Bavarian laws is

[124] *MGH Cap.* I, Nos. 18, 24, 26, 27, 68, 69, 88–103, pp. 42–3, 65–6, 68–72, 157–9, 187–12.
[125] See above, p. 237, and also below, pp. 265–6, for fuller discussion of this manuscript.
[126] BAV pal. lat. 289 and Münster, Staatsarchiv msc. VII. 5201. See Mordek, *Bibliotheca*, pp. 769–71 and 378–86.
[127] *MGH Cap.* I, No. 69, pp. 158–9; and Mordek, *Bibliotheca*, p. 1088.
[128] See Mordek, *Bibliotheca*, pp. 911–15. For further discussion of this capitulary, see below, p. 250.

not quite so exclusive, given that the contents of books to do with *leges* are rarely associated with one region only. Beside the Bavarian witnesses to this text it was also included in BAV reg. lat. 991, a product of the *leges* scriptorium associated with the court of Louis the Pious, and a tenth-century manuscript from Burgundy (Paris, BnF lat. 4417).[129] Apart from the inclusion of Pippin's capitulary of 781, the capitulary of 787 and, for the period after 800, the capitulary of 801 and Charlemagne's letter to Pippin, in a small number of non-Italian compilations, the Italian capitularies also have an Italian provenance. They are extant in the great Italian capitulary collections from Pavia, Aquileia and elsewhere in northern and central Italy made from the first quarter of the ninth century onwards.

The regional capitularies reflect the first stages of the imposition of Frankish rule in the newly conquered areas and complement the early programmatic capitularies issued by Charlemagne. These local capitularies articulate the principles on which Carolingian domination and control were based, and the locally produced charters and dispute settlements provide some sense of the degree to which such general administrative arrangements were either effected or effective. The first capitulary for Aquitaine, for example, as already indicated, confirms decisions already made by Pippin III, and thus constitutes an important model for Charlemagne's arrangements thereafter.[130] In addition to the general provisions about the restoration of churches by bishops, abbots or lay *homines* who hold them as benefices, there is stress on the right to justice, respect for the law, and the authority of the *missi*. The notion of personality of the law, perhaps better understood as a mobile territorial law whose content and use were dependent on local consensus, and apparently a Carolingian innovation, is suggested by the clause stating that all men in Aquitaine, Romans as well as Salians (that is, Franks), were to enjoy the use of their laws. A man coming from another region was to live according to the law of that region (*ipsius patriae*).[131] The maintenance of existing legal systems and the negotiation, as well as the confirmation, of legal rights in relation to the laws and customs of the region before the Carolingian takeover, can be documented in each of the new territories incorporated into the Carolingian empire. It is provided for in the short statements in

---

[129] See below, p. 263.   [130] *MGH Cap.* I, No. 18, pp. 42–3.
[131] Ibid., c. 10, p. 43; and compare *Marculfi Formulae*, I.8, and *Formulae marculfinae aevi karolini*, c. 15, ed. K. Zeumer, *MGH Formulae* 15, pp. 47–8 and 120; *Lex Ribuaria* 35.3, ed. F. Beyerle and R. Buchner, *MGH Leges nat. germ.* 3, 2 (Hanover, 1951), p. 87; and *Capitulare missorum item speciale*, c. 48, *MGH Cap.* I, No. 35, p. 104. For discussion see P. Amory, 'The meaning and purpose of the terminology in the Burgundian laws', *Early Medieval Europe* 2 (1993), pp. 1–28 at pp. 19–23.

Charlemagne's capitularies for these regions, it is implied by the attention paid to updating the national *leges*,[132] and it is evident in the extant *notitiae* recording the judging of disputes over property.[133] Herwig Wolfram, for example, has stressed how the reaction to the Frankish takeover in Bavaria is reflected in the charters from Freising, Salzburg, Niederaltaich, Passau and Kremsmünster. Many of these record the negotiations for the confirmation and assertion of legal rights in the face of encroachments from the local aristocracy, some of whom tried to take advantage of the altered political situation at the expense of these monastic and episcopal foundations.[134] The requirement to swear the new oath of loyalty to Charlemagne as emperor in 802, outlined in the capitulary to the *missi* for 802, was referred to by local witnesses in a charter from Freising as having been performed that very year: 'as we promised this year in our oath of fidelity to the lord emperor Charles'.[135] All this gives the lie to the inclination to assume that the capitularies merely reflect an ideal.

Italy

In Italy, as noted above, Charlemagne had to make a rapid decision about the validity of sales and gifts in wartime while still conducting the siege at Pavia in early 774.[136] The importation of Frankish rule into Lombard Italy was a gradual process as the young king Charlemagne devised a means of coping with the sudden acquisition of an entire and well-established polity in addition to the kingdom to which he had succeeded. Pippin was based at

---

[132] On the *leges*, see below, pp. 275–8.
[133] These are listed by R. Hübner, 'Gerichtsurkunden der fränkischen Zeit, I: Die Gerichtsurkunden aus Deutschland und Frankreich bis zum Jahre 1000', *Zeitschrift der Savigny Stiftung für Rechtsgeschichte, Germanistische Abteilung* 12 (1891), pp. 1–118; and II: 'Die Gerichtsurkunden aus Italien bis zum Jahre 1150', *Zeitschrift der Savigny Stiftung für Rechtsgeschichte, Germanistische Abteilung* 14 (1893), pp. 1–258. See also W. Davies and P. Fouracre (eds.), *The settlement of disputes in early medieval Europe* (Cambridge, 1986); and J. Davis, 'Conceptions of kingship under Charlemagne', unpublished MLitt dissertation, University of Cambridge (1999), pp. 152–69. See also above, p. 150.
[134] H. Wolfram, 'Die Notitia Arnonis und ähnliche Formen der Rechtssicherung im nachagilolfingischen Bayern', in P. Classen (ed.), *Recht und Schrift im Mittelalter*, Vorträge und Forschungen 23 (Sigmaringen, 1977), pp. 115–30.
[135] T. Bitterauf (ed.), *Die Traditionen des Hochstifts Freising, 744–926*, Quellen und Erörterungen zur bayerischen Geschichte, NF 4 (Munich, 1905), No. 186. See the discussion by M. Innes, 'Charlemagne's government', in J. Story (ed.), *Charlemagne: empire and society* (Manchester, 2005), pp. 71–89 at p. 81, who adds the example of an Alemannian charter from St Gallen, ed. H. Wartmann, *Urkunden Sankt Gallen* (St Gallen, 1863), No. 187; and for the wider context see W. Brown, *Unjust seizure; conflict, interest and authority in an early medieval society* (Ithaca and London, 2001).
[136] Above, pp. 111–13.

Pavia with his own entourage; any capitularies and charters were issued either in association with his father or by Charlemagne alone. The more regulatory capitularies, moreover, coincide with the establishment of Pippin of Italy as king.[137] They too, notably the Capitulary of Mantua of 781, are preoccupied with the proper administration of justice and officials doing their jobs, the role of the counts in hearing cases, the importance of making records of claims and decisions reached, and the assistance to be rendered to the bishops by the counts or their agents. A recognition that older customs might be observed is the reference to tolls that are to be levied only 'in accordance with ancient custom' (*secundum antiquam consuetudinem*). There is also a strong echo of the regulations articulated already in the Frankish kingdom north of the Alps. The Mantua capitulary, for example, repeated some of the provisions of the Capitulary of Herstal from two years earlier, as well as from the *Capitulare primum*, though its assumption of the integration of ecclesiastical and secular affairs on Frankish lines may well have been a new emphasis within the Lombard kingdom. That the Capitulary of Mantua was produced in association with an assembly suggests that it was as much a public relations exercise of reassurance that the Franks brought peace and order, and to mark the installation of Pippin of Italy as sub-king, as anything else. The subsequent Italian capitularies reinforced and reiterated these earlier decrees. Further, the large number of charters issued by Charlemagne granting land in Italy and confirming privileges looks like a bid to ensure loyalty. They are certainly far more numerous than the surviving land grants he made elsewhere in the Frankish realm, though the different patterns of archive preservation may create a false impression.[138]

One factor in the gradual accommodation of the Franks to Lombard practice, combined with a familiarity with the Frankish attitude to royal power and strong moral imperative, might be termed the colonial

---

[137] See the pioneering study by F. Manacorda, *Ricerche sugli inizii della dominazione dei Carolingi in Italia*, Studi Storici Fasc. 71–72 (Rome, 1968). See also the new collection of texts and translations by C. Azzaro and P. Moro, *I capitolari italici: storia e diritto della dominazione carolingia in Italia* (Rome, 1998). See also the dating sequence suggested by C. De Clercq, 'Capitulaires francs en Italie à l'époque de Charlemagne', in *Hommage à Ursmer Berlière*, Bulletin de l'Institut Historique Belge de Rome (Brussels, 1931), pp. 251–60.

[138] See above, pp. 197–9; and Davis, 'Concepts of kingship under Charlemagne', pp. 108–9. But see above, pp. 199–204, for the limitations of the charter evidence, and below, pp. 295–8, for the endowment of monasteries. I am grateful too to François Bougard for his important observations in his paper 'La production documentaire publique et privée, avant et après 774', in S. Gasparri and C. La Rocca (eds.), *774: ipotesi su una transizione: Seminario internazionale, Poggio imperiale, Poggibonsi [SI] (16–18 febbraio 2006)* (Siena, forthcoming), on which I draw in what follows. This can also be consulted on <www.youtube.com/watch?v=EDP50hQj-58&search=74>.

mentality, that is, the attitude of officials representing the central government who identify with, and adapt to, the particular circumstances of
administering an outlying part of the empire.[139] The extent to which
Frankish officials settled into Lombard society and became advocates of
the law and customs of their adopted regions can only be guessed at in this
early period of Carolingian rule, though it becomes more marked thereafter.[140] Frankish rule entailed inclusion in the wider network of
Carolingian communications and the introduction of Frankish administrative structures such as the counts and the *missi* into Italy. From
Charlemagne's itinerary it is clear that he rarely visited his new territories
himself, relying instead on his officials. Both local men and imported
Frankish personnel served as officials. In Italy at least, such men as came
from north of the Alps – very few can be identified during the reigns of
Charlemagne and Pippin of Italy – were more likely to be in the higher
ranks.[141] Local men, such as the Lombard Aio, moreover, also served as
counts. Aio may have been involved in the revolt of Hrodgaud in 776, for
he is described as formerly *infidelis* (unfaithful) and had taken refuge in the
land of the Avars. But in 799 he received Charlemagne's forgiveness, his
confiscated land in Friuli, Vicenza and Verona was returned to him, and he
served Charlemagne thereafter.[142] Aio was also present at the court hearing
to settle the dispute at Rizana-Risano *c.* 804. The dispute concerned the
villagers' protest against the new levies imposed by the *dux* Johannes,
including the requisitioning of horses. This remarkable discussion was
concluded in the villagers' favour, and the payments and renders from

[139] For a comparative perspective see J. E. Wilson, *The making of a colonial order: information,
uncertainty and law in early colonial Bengal*, Centre for South Asian Studies, Occasional paper
No. 6 (Cambridge, 2004).

[140] See Bougard, *La justice*, esp. pp. 119–38; Bougard, 'Public power and authority', and S. Gasparri,
'The aristocracy', in C. La Rocca (ed.), *Italy in the early middle ages 476–1000*, The Short Oxford
History of Italy (Oxford, 2002), pp. 34–83.

[141] See Bougard, *La justice*, pp. 139–203. See also G. Tellenbach, 'Der grossfränkische Adel und die
Regierung Italiens in der Blütezeit des Karolingerreiches', in G. Tellenbach (ed.), *Studien und
Vorarbeiten zur Geschichte des grossfränkischen und frühdeutschen Adels*, Forschungen zur oberrhein-
ischen Landesgeschichte 4 (Freiburg, 1957), pp. 40–70.

[142] E. Hlawitschka, *Franken, Alemannen, Bayern und Burgunden in Oberitalien (774–962): zum
Verständnis der fränkischen Königsherrschaft in Italien*, Forschungen zur oberrheinischen
Landesgeschichte 8 (Freiburg im Breisgau, 1960). For his prosopography of office-holders see
pp. 98–293, at pp. 113–4 for Aio, and compare T. Reuter, 'Plunder and tribute in the Carolingian
empire', *Transactions of the Royal Historical Society*, 5th series, 35 (London, 1985), pp. 75–94 at p. 88
note 71. On Aio, see H. Krahwinkler, *Friaul im Frühmittelalter: Geschichte einer Region vom Ende des
fünften bis zum Ende des zehnten Jahrhunderts*, Veröffentlichungen des Instituts für Österreichische
Geschichtsforschung 30 (Cologne, Vienna and Weimar, 1992), pp. 137–42.

the pre-Frankish period of rule were restored.[143] Whether Johannes himself was a Lombard, a Greek or a Frank now serving the Carolingian rulers is not known, though his name makes it less likely that he was a Frank. The charter, written by Peter the deacon of Aquileia and on the orders of the patriarch Fortunatus of Aquileia, is an essential indication, not only of the maintenance of pre-Carolingian customs, but also that the fluidity of local power relations should not be underestimated.

Generally the Italian notaries' acceptance of a new ruler was swift, insofar as this is recorded in the change in the dating formulae by the regnal year of Charlemagne in the extant original Lombard charters from June 774 onwards.[144] The famous charter written *tempore barbarici* in May 774, which still uses a dating formula according to the reigns of Desiderius and Arichis,[145] and the will of the *gasindus* Taido of Bergamo in May 774, who refers to the *varietas calamitatum insurgentium*, however, may be indications that the reception of Frankish armies in the Lombard kingdom was not always greeted with enthusiasm.[146] There is a difference in the formula used; some notaries made it look much more final politically than others. Thus the charter from San Salvatore in Monte Amiata records the year as the first year of Charlemagne's reign in Italy as *rex francorum et langobardorum*, whereas others mention the number of years since Charlemagne's arrival in Italy or even in the city of Pavia. Lucca notaries dated their charters according to the year Charlemagne's rule in Lombardy began.[147] The

---

[143] C. Manaresi, *I placiti del regnum Italiae*, 1, Fonti per la storia d'Italia 92 (Rome, 1955), No. 17, pp. 48–56, and discussed fully with a German translation of the text in Krahwinkler, *Friaul im Frühmittelalter*, pp. 199–243 (text, pp. 202–10).

[144] See, for example, ChLA XXIV, Italy 5 (1985), No. 751, and compare ibid., XXXVI, Italy 17 (1990), No. 1046, still dated according to the reign of Desiderius in May 774, and No. 1047, dated 16 July and the beginning of the reign of Charlemagne as king of the Franks and Lombards: ChLA XXVIII, Italy 9 (1988), No. 854, Milan, Archivio di Stato Museo Diplomatico No. 19, August 774: 'In christi nomini regnantes domno nostro Carolo vero excellentissimus rege Langobardorum seo et Francorum anno primo' (*sic*). I am grateful to Walter Pohl for discussion of this point and the dating clauses in general. For further comments on the private charters see also Bougard, 'La production', and the essays in *La giustizia nell'alto medioevo (secoli V–VIII)*; and *La giustizia nell'alto medioevo (secoli IX–XI)*, Settimane 42 and 44 (Spoleto, 1995 and 1997).

[145] ChLA XXVII, No. 827, May 774 (Piacenza, Archivio Capitolare Cantonale 1, Cassetta 4, donazioni No. 5: 'facta carta donationis tempore barbarici anno dominorum nostrorum Desiderius et Adelchis Regis' (!) Written by Andoald *vir clarissimus*.

[146] L. Schiaparelli (ed.), *Codice diplomatico Longobardo*, Fonti per la storia d'Italia 38 (Rome, 1933), No. 291, pp. 426–7 at p. 426, and No. 293, pp. 429–37 at p. 430. See V. Fumagalli, *Il regno italico* (Turin, 1978), pp. 3–4.

[147] ChLA XXV, Italy 6, No. 758 (dated 785); XXV, Italy 6 (1986), no. 795 (dated 782). The slight element of doubt is due to the possibility of these being diplomatic formulae in use since the fifth and sixth centuries, though if so these might even then have been formulated in the period of the political crisis of the Gothic wars. See F. Bougard, 'La production documentaire publique et privée'.

introduction of Frankish legal arrangements, or at least the documents recording them, such as *precaria* (land granted of which the donor retained the use for his lifetime), has also been traced. Most crucial of all, the notaries as a professional group maintained their activities. The original charters extant from the archives of northern Italy yield a number of scribes whose careers spanned the period of the Frankish conquest. A further sign of continuity is the lack of radical changes in the diplomatic structure of the charters from northern Italy until after 810.[148]

At the same time as much of local Lombard traditions was maintained, the Lombards appear to have accommodated the Frankish general and 'Italian' capitularies. There are a number of large Italian capitulary collections comprising both the Italian and more general capitularies.[149] The earliest of these is a law book compiled, probably in Aquileia, which included the Mantua capitulary and copies of the national *leges* (*Lex Ribuaria, Lex Salica, Lex Baiuvariorum, Lex Alamannorum, Lex Burgundionum*, the *Epitome Aegidii* of Roman law) as well as a collection of extracts from the legislation of Charlemagne and Pippin of Italy organized into ninety-two chapters. The emphasis of this collection was on the administration of justice, legal record and ecclesiastical prerogative. It includes a long list of those who had sworn the oath of fidelity to the Carolingian ruler, among whom were such officials as notaries, gastalds (judges) and *scabini* (local experts who oversaw the conduct of justice).[150] It is a book that reflects both the acceptance and the adaptation of specifically Frankish administrative measures in northeast Italy on a local level to suit the requirements of officials in that area. Its contents imply that it was compiled to serve a mixed community.[151] One of the scribes of this

[148] See Bougard, *La justice*, pp. 65–73 and 119–37. For the general development of the notariate in Italy see A. Meyer, *Felix et inclitus notarius: Studien zum italienischen Notariat vom 7. bis zum 13. Jahrhundert* (Tübingen, 2000), pp. 8–10 and 12–14. On Lombard charters see N. Everett, *Literacy in Lombard Italy* (Cambridge, 2003), pp. 197–234.

[149] See above, p. 111, and Bougard, *La justice*, pp. 30–1; and, for details of the contents: Mordek, *Bibliotheca*, pp. 98–111 (Cava dei Tirreni, Biblioteca della Badia, 4); ibid., pp. 131–49 (Gotha, Forschungsbibliothek, Membr. I. 84); ibid., pp. 173–85 (Ivrea, Biblioteca capitolare XXXIII and XXXIV); ibid., pp. 356–68 (Modena, Biblioteca capitolare O.I.2); ibid., pp. 357–64 (Munich, Bayerische Staatsbibliothek Clm 19416); ibid., pp. 469–76 (Paris, BnF lat. 4613); ibid., pp. 756–68 (BAV, Chigi F.IV.75); ibid., pp. 881–3 (BAV Vat. lat. 5359).

[150] See below, pp. 275–6.

[151] St Paul in Lavanttal, Archiv des Benediktinerstiftes 4/1: see R. Eisler, 'Die illuminierten Handschriften Kärnten', in F. Wickhoff (ed.), *Beschreibendes Verzeichnis der illuminierten Handschriften in Oesterreich* (Leipzig, 1907), pp. 100–2; Mordek, *Bibliotheca*, pp. 685–95; and McKitterick, *History and memory*, pp. 253–4. For a discussion of the implications of this manuscript and the two Vatican collections of canon law see McKitterick, 'History, law, and communication with the past', pp. 962–9.

manuscript is also to be found working on a book completed about two decades earlier containing a special collection of ecclesiastical or canon law, now BAV Barberini lat. 679.[152] In its turn, the Barberini manuscript is closely related to another canon law compilation, BAV Vat. lat. 1342. These manuscripts demonstrate how compilers could draw on more general ecclesiastical provisions and resisted the tendency, evident in some other centres in the former Lombard kingdom, to fall in line with Frankish norms. Like the charters, therefore, such books reflect a variable response at the local level to the imposition of Frankish rule in Lombard Italy.

Bavaria

Count Gerold, who had family connections with the Agilolfings as well as being Charlemagne's brother-in-law, was installed in Bavaria after 788.[153] He was effectively the king's principal representative in the area, though Charlemagne based himself at Regensburg in 791–3 and other officials appear to have operated in particular areas. Charlemagne's confirmation of Tassilo's grant to Kremsmünster (3 January 791) describes an inspection of the properties in the original donation, by Arn of Salzburg, Abbot Fater of Kremsmünster, Count Hleodrus and Chunibert the justice. The Capitulary of Thionville of 805 mentions that Audulf at Hallstadt, Forcheim, Pfreimd and Regensburg, and Werinar at Lorch in the far east of Bavaria, had to oversee the trading activities of any merchants in their areas.[154] It was from that period, coupled with the final submission of Tassilo at Frankfurt in 794, that Carolingian rule was secured. After Gerold's death in 799, Bavaria also appears to have been defined as a *missaticum*, with Arn, archbishop of Salzburg, and Count Audulf together acting as *missi dominici* (if this *missaticum* was organized in the same way as the others discussed below).[155] Local procedures and local law and custom, as far as we can tell from the surviving charters, were for the most part maintained and only slowly modified in the course of the late eighth and earlier part of the ninth centuries. The first Capitulary for Bavaria shows a similar concern for the maintenance of justice and the Bavarian law, and for the authority of the judges, and refers to what was done in the time of Tassilo. This may have had much to do with the initial difficulties

---

[152] For a list of contents see Mordek, *Bibliotheca*, pp. 751–7.
[153] H. Wolfram, *Salzburg, Bayern, Österreich: die Conversio Bagoariorum et Carantanorum und die Quellen ihrer Zeit*, MIÖG Ergänzungsband 31 (Vienna and Munich, 1995), pp. 172–3.
[154] *MGH Cap.* I, No. 44, c. 7, p. 123; see also Wolfram, *Salzburg*, p. 182.
[155] See below, pp. 259–60; and Wolfram, *Salzburg*, pp. 185–8.

Charlemagne may have experienced in establishing Carolingian authority within Bavaria as well as the need to avoid disrupting local rights to property.[156] The succession of legal disputes conducted by Atto of Freising (784–810), for example, for the most part investigated and confirmed property rights as they had existed in the Agilolfing period.[157] Some of these had to go to appeal, at which stage they involved Arn, archbishop of Salzburg, acting as Charlemagne's *missus*, even though he had been one of Tassilo's leading men before 788.[158] The Salzburg adaptation of the Carolingian edition of Marculf's formulary, furthermore, preserved in the collection of letters and formulae put together in the time of Archbishop Liuphram of Salzburg (836–59), indicates a willingness to mix Frankish material with Bavarian.[159]

Saxony

Saxony, a largely pagan and non-Roman territory, presents a special case.[160] Establishing and consolidating Frankish rule over the Saxons, and the Saxons becoming what Einhard later called 'one people' with the Franks, took far longer than the actual conquest, though that alone involved three decades of recurrent military campaigning.[161] Here, above all, Charlemagne's ideology of conquest can be observed, with an imposition of the Frankish Christian churches onto the Saxon landscape (*ut ecclesiae Christi que modo construuntur in Saxonia et deo sacratae sunt*) and the forcing of the Saxons into the Frankish Christian mould.[162] The rhetoric of the *Annales regni francorum* and the poem *De conversione saxonum* (dated *c.* 777) implies swift success.[163] Charlemagne certainly founded new bishoprics at Paderborn, Verden, Minden, Münster, Osnabrück and Bremen (the formal creation of Halberstadt and Hildesheim

---

[156] For a reflection on these difficulties in relation to the Bavarian bishops see S. Freund, *Von den Agilolfingern zu den Karolingern: Bayerns Bischöfe zwischen Kirchenorganisation, Reichsintegration und karolingischer Reform (700–847)*, Schriftenreihe zur bayerischen Landesgeschichte 144 (Munich, 2004).

[157] See Brown, *Unjust seizure*, pp. 75–83, for examples; and also G. Bührer-Thierry, 'De la fin du duché au début de l'empire: dix ans de transition à la lumière des chartes (788–799)' in Gasparri and La Rocca, *774: ipotesi di transizione*.

[158] M. Niederkorn-Bruck and A. Scharer (eds.), *Erzbischof Arn von Salzburg*, Veröffentlichungen des Instituts für Österreichische Geschichtsforschung 40 (Vienna and Munich, 2004).

[159] Bischoff, *Salzburgerformelbücher*, pp. 16 and 57–61; and Brown, *Unjust seizure*, pp. 102–23.

[160] P. Johanek, 'Der Ausbau der sächsischen Kirchenorganisation', *799 Kunst und Kultur*, II, pp. 494–506.

[161] Poeta Saxo, *MGH Poet.* IV, p. 71, and Einhard, *Vita Karoli*, c. 7, ed. Halphen, p. 26.

[162] *MGH Cap.* I, no. 26, c. I, p. 68.

[163] See S. A. Rabe, *Faith, art and politics at Saint-Riquier: the symbolic vision of Angilbert* (Philadelphia, 1995), pp. 54–74.

followed early in Louis the Pious's reign), but the installation of bishops in
these new sees, let alone the building of churches and the institutional infra-
structure, did not get properly under way until the first decade of the ninth
century. The church at Paderborn, for example, was consecrated in 799.[164]
Even once the sees were supplied with incumbents, none appears to have been
particularly well endowed.[165] There is ample indication of the Franks' deep
commitment to, and various strategies adopted for, the mission to the Saxons.
Alcuin's *Vita Willibrordi*, for example, although a hagiographical account of
the Anglo-Saxon founder of Echternach in the late seventh century, has been
interpreted as a blueprint, in terms of theory, strategy and attitude, for the
'final stage' of the Christianization of Saxony 100 years later.[166]

Yet the long-drawn-out war of conquest in Saxony is matched by the
slow progress of Christianization and even longer process of conversion.[167]
Paganism itself may have become articulated in opposition to the Frankish
impact.[168] Early work by missionary bishops in the eighth century was
conducted both with and without the secular support of the Carolingian
mayors. That these bishops based themselves either at fledgling monasteries or places subsequently designated as episcopal seats is indicated by
the fragmented account in some of the annals and in the *Vitae* of such
missionary saints as Boniface, Sturm, Lebuin, Liudger and Willehad.[169]
The last named, for example, had to withdraw from Westphalia in the early
780s until it was safe for him to continue work again after the submission
and baptism of Widukind; he was consecrated bishop in Worms in 787 and
subsequently built a church dedicated to St Peter in Bremen, where he had
established his see.[170] Liudger had links with Werden as well as becoming

[164] See above, p. 166.
[165] C. Carroll, 'The bishoprics of Saxony in the first century after Christianisation', *Early Medieval Europe* 8 (1999), pp. 219–45. See also Carroll, 'The archbishops and church provinces of Mainz and Cologne during the Carolingian period, 751–911', unpublished PhD thesis, University of Cambridge (1999).
[166] I. N. Wood, 'An absence of saints? The evidence for the Christianisation of Saxony', in P. Godman, J. Jarnut and P. Johanek (eds.), *Am Vorabend der Kaiserkrönung: das Epos "Karolus magnus et Leo papa" und der Papstbesuch in Paderborn 799*, pp. 335–52 at pp. 346–8; and see I. N. Wood, *The missionary life: saints and the evangelisation of Europe 400–1050* (London, 2001), pp. 79–99.
[167] P. Johanek, 'Die Ausbau der sächsischen Kirchenorganisation', in *799 Kunst und Kultur*, II, pp. 494–506.
[168] For comparison, see the cross-fertilization between pagan Norsemen and Christian English in northern England discussed by L. Abrams, in S. Baxter and J. L. Nelson (eds.), Memorial volume for Patrick Wormald (Aldershot, forthcoming).
[169] See H. Büttner, 'Mission und Kirchenorganisation des Frankenreiches bis zum Tode Karls des Großen', in *KdG*, I, pp. 454–87, esp. 467–73; and see also Wood, *The missionary life*, pp. 89–112.
[170] See R. McKitterick, 'Le scriptorium d'Echternach', in M. Polfer (ed.), *L'évangélisation des régions entre Meuse et Moselle et la fondation de l'abbaye d'Echternach (Ve–IXe siècle)* (Luxemburg, 2000), pp. 499–512.

the first bishop of Münster. The see of Verden was linked with the monastery of Amorbach. Although Münster had links with Utrecht because of Liudger's Frisian origins, Liudger was actually consecrated by Archbishop Hildebold of Cologne in 805.[171] The impression is of *ad hoc* arrangements made when the political situation was favourable. A lot depended on the support of the Rhineland bishops, who were not necessarily working in any co-ordinated fashion. During Charlemagne's reign it appears to have been the bishoprics within the archdiocese of Cologne, especially Münster, Minden and Bremen, which were more active. That this coincided with Hildebold's incumbency of the office of *capellanus* at the palace (from 794) is surely no coincidence.[172]

Saxon legal custom undoubtedly existed and no doubt needed to be respected. The Christian institutional framework had to be created and personnel trained if they were to practise Frankish methods. The two capitularies specifically designed for Saxony, dated 782 and 797, effectively frame the main phases of conquest. The provision of a written form of the *Lex Saxonum*, already in a form greatly affected by such Frankish codes as the *Lex Ribuaria*, followed a few years afterwards, *c*. 802.[173] With hindsight, the first capitulary, even if not as early as 782, appears somewhat premature in its assumption that control had now been established and could be enforced. If it is 782, it can be linked with an assembly at Lippspringe, where counts were appointed, apparently from among the Saxons, to administer the newly conquered territory.[174] Other scholars prefer the date of 785 for the first Saxon capitulary, thus making it coincide with the submission and baptism of Widukind.[175]

The decisions recorded in this capitulary have become notorious in modern scholarship for the uncompromising nature of the insistence,

---

[171] G. Isenberg and B. Rommé (eds.), *805: Liudger wird Bischof: Spuren eines Heiligen zwischen York, Rom und Münster* (Mainz, 2005).

[172] Depreux, *Prosopographie*, pp. 246–47.

[173] G. Theuerkauf, *Lex, speculum, compendium iuris: Rechtsaufzeichnung und Rechtsbewußtsein in Norddeutschland vom 8. bis zum 16. Jahrhundert* (Cologne and Graz, 1968), pp. 38–97, esp. pp. 54–67; and see below, p. 276; and *799 Kunst und Kultur*, I, pp. 326–7. The manuscript containing the *Capitulare saxonum* is Münster Nordrhein-Westfälisches Staatsarchiv Msc. VII.5201, of the mid-tenth century, probably from Corvey. The codex includes the *Lex Saxonum* and the *Lex Thuringorum* as well as the charters of Corvey between 823 and 945.

[174] *ARF* 782, ed. Kurze, p. 58, records a *synodus* (*RVARF* 782, ed. Kurze, p. 59, calls it a general *conventus*) and it is the *Annales maximiniani* 782, *MGH SS* 13, p. 21, which records the counts, implying that they were Saxons.

[175] See M. Becher, *Rex, dux und gens: Untersuchungen zur Entstehung des sächsischen Herzogtums um 9. und 10. Jahrhundert*, Historische Studien 444 (Husum, 1996), p. 111 note 625. See also Theuerkauf, *Lex, speculum, compendium iuris*, pp. 38–54.

often on pain of death, on the observance of Christian practices, abandoning of pagan rites, paying tithe for the support of the churches and the clergy, and respect for the Christian church. Emphasizing or even exaggerating the paganism of the Saxons possibly reflects an underlying Frankish strategy of defining Saxons as pagan enemies in order to justify the Franks' treatment of them. Even contemporaries doubted whether the fierce enforcement of tithe payments was the most productive way to proceed as far as a process of joyful conversion to a new faith might be concerned. Alcuin's reactions fourteen years later, so often repeated in relation to this capitulary, can hardly be understood as more than a general comment in the context of the slow advance of Christianization discussed above.[176] Yet the capitulary of 782/5 also brought administration on Frankish lines to the newly conquered territories; it promised order, with counts and priests together ensuring the proper administration of justice, and the possibility of appealing to the king himself. It even permitted certain aspects of Saxon custom to be maintained.[177]

All the same, in 782, or even in 785, Charlemagne had conquered only a portion of the land. The second Saxon capitulary, on the other hand, issued specifically in relation to an assembly at Aachen on 28 October 797, refers to the Saxons from various districts, Westphalians, Angrarians and Eastphalians, and the Bortrini and the 'northerners' (*septentrionales*), whose custom is invoked at the end of the capitulary.[178] The Saxon hostage list of *c.* 806 as well as the Poeta Saxo confirm the division of Saxons into Westphalians, Eastphalians and Angrarians at least, though this most probably represents only some of those lumped generically together as Saxons in the Frankish sources.[179] This later capitulary of 797 could be regarded as a confirmation and extension of the previous capitulary in order to mark what might have been hoped to be the conclusion of the Saxon campaigns. While the emphasis is, as for the other regional capitularies, on the administration of justice, it is noteworthy that the Saxons

---

[176] Alcuin, Ep. 110, ed. E. Dümmler, *MGH Epp.* 11 (Berlin, 1895), pp. 157–9.

[177] *MGH Cap.* 1, No. 26; for access to the king, cc. 2 and 26; for priests and counts, cc. 29–31 and 34; for the Saxon law penalties to be used for perjurers, c. 33; pp. 67–70.

[178] *MGH Cap.* 1, No. 27, cc. 1 and 11, pp. 71–2.

[179] *MGH Cap.* 1, No. 115; and see *799 Kunst und Kultur*, 1, pp. 327–8. Poeta Saxo, *MGH Poet.* lat., p. 8. See also M. Becher, "'Non enim habent regem idem antiqui Saxones ...'" Verfassung und Ethnogenese in Sachsen währen des 8. Jahrhunderts', in H. J. Hassler (ed.), *Sachsen und Franken in Westfalen: 799 Kunst und Kultur der Karolingerzeit*, Studien zur sachsen Forschung 12 (1999), pp. 1–31; and I. N. Wood, 'Beyond satraps and ostriches: political and social structures of the Saxons in the early Carolingian period', in D. H. Green and F. Siegmund (eds.), *The Continental Saxons from the migration period to the tenth century: an ethnographic perspective* (Woodbridge, 2003), pp. 271–86.

were explicitly included in the discussions; decisions were reached with the consent of the Franks and the Saxons.[180] The third clause, for example, states that it had been decided by all the Saxons that in all cases where Franks were obliged by the law to pay fifteen *solidi*, the nobler Saxons were to pay twelve, freemen six, and *liti* three *solidi* in compensation. Many other clauses seem to indicate an assertion on the part of the Saxons of their own law, and the willingness of the Franks to permit it.[181] Only appeal to the king could override the penalty according to Saxon law. Again, this is entirely in keeping with the preservation of local custom observed in all the other conquered territories.[182]

Even after the issue of this capitulary, the *Annales regni francorum* record expeditions to Saxony in 797, 798 and 799. The assembly at Paderborn in 799 was also, as was noted earlier, the setting of the famous meeting with Pope Leo III, but the Lorsch annals add the information that, in that same year, Charlemagne relocated 'a multitude of Saxon men, women and children and divided their lands among his *fideles*'. He also sent Charles the Younger to the Bardengau to deal with the Nordliudi in 799.[183] Charlemagne returned to Saxony in 804, and the *Annales regni francorum* record another deportation of Saxons, this time from beyond the Elbe into Francia; their land was given to the Abodrites.[184] The Poeta Saxo placed the final peace concluded between Franks and Saxons at Salz in 803.[185]

Conquest of the Saxons brought new neighbours. The Capitulary of Thionville of 805 attempted to regulate the activities of the merchants in territories of the northern Slavs as well, and mentions by name further officials who would oversee the merchants' activities: In addition to the officials in Bavaria mentioned above, there was Hredi at Bardowick, Aito at Magdeburg and Madalgaud at Erfurt. There was also a specific prohibition on selling arms or mail and penalties for any merchants doing so.[186]

[180] *MGH Cap.* I, No. 27, c. 3, p. 71.
[181] Theuerkauf, *Lex, speculum, compendium iuris*, pp. 38–66; and M. Becher, 'Die Sachsen im 7. und 8. Jahrhundert: Verfassung und Ethnogenese', in *799 Kunst und Kultur*, I, pp. 188–94.
[182] Einhard, *Vita Karoli*, c. 7, ed. Halphen, p. 26, who uses the word *populus*; and see *MGH Cap.* I, No. 27, c. 10, p. 72 (referring to the removal of a convicted malefactor outside his *patria*). For discussion of Frankish administration in Saxony see Becher, *Rex, dux und gens*, pp. 110–24.
[183] *ARF* 797, 798, 799, ed. Kurze, pp. 100, 102–4, 106. The *Annales petavaini* 799, ed. G. Pertz, *MGH SS* I, p. 18, adds that Charles the Younger had to deal with the *infideles* among the Nordliudi.
[184] *ARF* 804, ed. Kurze, p. 118.
[185] See also B. von Simson, 'Der Poeta Saxo und der Friede zu Salz', *Forschungen zur Deutschen Geschichte* I (1862), pp. 301–26, and his later reconsideration: 'Der Poeta Saxo und der angebliche Friedensschluss Karls des Großen mit den Sachsen', *Neues Archiv* 32 (1907), pp. 27–50.
[186] *MGH Cap.* I, No. 44, c. 7, p. 123.

Most of the accounts of the Saxon conquest were written some time after the event and gloss over the horrors – the battles, the mass executions in response to rebellions, the forced conversions, the deporting of men, women and children far from their homeland, and the appropriation of land. Some inkling of the social upheaval and opportunities afforded to members of elite groups to assert their social and political status is offered by the Stellinga revolt later in the ninth century,[187] but there are earlier indications of major social adjustments for men who were rehabilitated and whose lands were restored. In 811, for example, Charlemagne confirmed Count Bennit's ownership of lands given to his father Amalung the Saxon for his fidelity, and two years later Asig, Charlemagne's faithful man (*fidelis*), was confirmed in the possession of lands lost by his father Hiddi the Saxon.[188] At some stage Charlemagne appears to have appointed his cousin Wala to oversee administration in Saxony, just as he had elevated his brother-in-law Gerold in Bavaria.[189] Nothing further is known about when this might have happened or how long Wala may have been in this position.[190]

THE ADMINISTRATIVE CAPITULARIES FOR
THE *MISSI DOMINICI*, 802–813

The requirements for hearing the oath and for making known the contents of the capitularies amending the 'national' law, as well as for judging according to the written law, were addressed to the *missi dominici*.[191] In comparison with the programmatic and regional capitularies of the 780s and the 790s, most of those issued by Charlemagne thereafter are administrative communications to or about the *missi dominici* rather than legislation. Again, some statistics may be illuminating. If one were to categorize the post-800 capitulary texts according to their principal focus and intention, four relate to the army, seven directly to justice or amending the *leges*, ten to canon law and matters exclusively to do with the Rule of Benedict, monks and priests, and the rest, more than half the total number, relate to the *missi*'s duties or have directly to do with representing the king's

---

[187] See E. Goldberg, 'Popular revolt, dynastic politics and aristocratic factionalism in the early middle ages: the Saxon *stellinga* reconsidered', *Speculum* 70 (1995), pp. 467–501.

[188] *DKar.* 1, Nos. 213 and 218. Both charters survive in the original. See *799 Kunst und Kultur*, 1, pp. 328–9 for No. 218; and above, pp. 204, 205, 207, 211.

[189] Compare Depreux, *Prosopographie*, pp. 390–3; and L. Weinrich, *Wala: Graf, Mönch und Rebell. Die Biographie eines Karolingers*, Historische Studien 386 (Lübeck and Hamburg, 1963).

[190] See Becher, 'Die Sachsen', *799 Kunst und Kultur*, 1, pp. 120–1, drawing on the *Translatio sancti Viti*.

[191] *MGH Cap.* 1, No. 34, c. 26, p. 96.

authority, including the administration of justice and the attention to be paid by the *missi* to the promotion of Charlemagne's ideals for a Christian realm. This distribution, in short, indicates a formulation of policy and goals in the earlier part of the reign, with continued attention paid to their implementation in the last decade and a half before Charlemagne's death. Just as the earlier capitularies for the *missi*, such as the one sent to the *missi* Mancio and Eugerius in 789, reiterate points from the capitularies of 779 and 789 for the attention of the *missi*, so the later administrative capitularies were taken up and further developed in the years between 802 and 813.

The most famous of these administrative capitularies is that of 802, which provides a comprehensive description of the responsibilities of the *missi*.[192] Ganshof described this as a 'programmatic capitulary of imperial government', but, as I have argued above, it is the earlier capitularies that most deserve this label, whereas this one, extant in its complete form in only one manuscript, should be recognized as a comprehensive exhortation to the *missi dominici*, spelling out their duties and responsibilities.[193] It was supplemented by the checklist that was sent out, preserved for us by a number of *missi dominici* in different regions.[194] The reference to Charlemagne as an emperor puts the general administrative capitulary for the *missi* after 800, but it has also been associated with the Lorsch annals' reference, at the beginning of the entry under 802 considered above, to the sending out of archbishops, abbots, dukes and counts, throughout Charlemagne's whole realm, to do justice 'to the churches, widows and orphans, the poor and the whole of the people'. The annalist attributes the creation of the high-ranking *missi* to do justice to the emperor's anxiety to avoid the risk of bribery; these new officials had no need to receive gifts.[195] The capitulary preamble refers to men from among his *optimates* chosen for their greatest good sense and wisdom, 'archbishops and other bishops as well as venerable abbots and pious laymen', whom he sent out 'throughout

---

[192] *MGH Cap.* I, No. 33, *Capitulare missorum generale.*
[193] Extracts are preserved in the ss.X/XI canon law collection known as the *Collectio canonum V. librorum,* and in a copy of Burchard of Worms's *Decretum* (BAV Vat. lat. 7790) of the early twelfth century, which has cc. 14 and 15: see H. Mordek. '"Quod si non emendent, excommunicetur"', in K. G. Cushing and R. F. Gyug (eds.), *Ritual, text and law: studies in medieval canon law and liturgy presented to Roger E. Reynolds* (Aldershot, 2004), pp. 171–84.
[194] That is, the *Capitulare missorum speciale, MGH Cap.* I, No. 34.
[195] Lorsch annals 802, ed. G. Pertz, *MGH SS* I, pp. 38–39. The contemporary *Annales Guelferbytani* refer to the sending out of *missi* under 801, ed. W. Lendi, *Untersuchung zur frühalemannischen Annalistik: die Murbacher Annalen, mit Edition,* Scrinium Friburgense I (Freiburg in der Schweiz, 1971), pp. 131 and 173. On the gifts and issue of new personnel see J. Hannig, 'Pauperiores vassi de infra palatii? Zur Entstehung der karolingischen Königsbotenorganisation', *MIÖG* 91 (1983), pp. 309–74, who argues convincingly for no great change in personnel.

his entire realm and through them confirmed to all his subjects the right to live according to the appropriate body of law'.[196] As has already been discussed, these new officials were to judge according to the written law. This congruence between the capitulary and the Lorsch annals sheds a new light on the circulation of information. The annals offer the narrative equivalent and the context for the capitulary. It is as if the annals' author, supposedly Ricbod of Lorsch, had attended the assembly, had brought the capitulary back with him and had augmented his summary of it with a description of the discussions at the October assembly in Aachen.[197]

Whether the entire capitulary of 802 should be regarded as a reaction on Charlemagne's part to being made emperor, however, is questionable. Most of the other features of this capitulary, apart from the requirement for a new oath discussed above, were part of a development of structures of government that had been under way since the late 770s. Although the administrative capitulary for 802 (as I shall henceforth refer to it) was issued at the same time as the *missatica* were reorganized, that is, the districts for one of which a pair of *missi dominici* was responsible, this represented a reorganization of an institution that had been a regular and vital part of Carolingian administration since the late 770s at least.[198] The role envisaged for the *missi* in 802, moreover, had its precedents in such documents as the memorandum for the *missi* in Aquitaine and the *edictum legationis* for *missi* issued from Aachen in March 789.[199] The special status of the *missus dominicus* in relation to the provision of justice was indicated by the Capitulary of Herstal in 779: 'If a count fail to administer justice within the area of his jurisdiction, he is to have the needs of our *missus* provided for from his household until justice has been done there and if the vassal fails to administer justice then both the count and the *missus* are to stay in his household and live at his expense until he does administer justice.'[200]

---

[196] *MGH Cap.* I, No. 33, c. I, pp. 91–2: 'in universum regnum suum, et per eos cunctis subsequentibus secundum rectam legem vivere concessit.'

[197] On the Lorsch annals and their composition and authorship see H. Fichtenau, 'Abt Richbod und die Annales Laureshamenses', in *Beiträge zur Geschichte des Klosters Lorsch*, 2nd edn, Geschichtsblätter für den Kreis Bergstraße, Sonderband 4 (Lorsch, 1980), pp. 277–304; McKitterick, *History and memory*, pp. 104–10; and above, p. 25.

[198] On the development of the *missi dominici* see V. Krause, 'Geschichte des Instituts der *missi dominici*', *MIÖG* 11 (1890), pp. 193–300; Werner, '*Missus–marchio–comes*', and R. McKitterick, *The Frankish kingdoms under the Carolingians, 751–987* (London, 1983), pp. 93–7. On the *missatica* see Eckhardt, 'Die *capitularia missorum specialia* 802' and *Die Kapitulariensammlung Ghaerbalds von Lüttich*. See also Hannig, 'Pauperiores vassi de infra palatii?'

[199] *MGH Cap.* I, Nos. 23 and 24, pp. 62–6. [200] *MGH Cap.* I, No. 20, c. 21, p. 51.

Hitherto, the role of the *missus* had been an intermittent one, and the word, as can be seen from the papal letters, retained its additional use as a word to designate ambassadors, those charged with political negotiations or even simply messengers well into the ninth century. The papal letters, for example, are full of references to the political negotiations in Rome, Spoleto and Benevento, conducted by a constant flow of royal *missi* to Italy – Archbishop Wilichar of Sens and Abbot Dodo, Bishop Andreas and Abbot Pardus, Archbishop Possessor of Embrun and Rabegaud in 775, Archbishop Possessor and Duke Hildebrand of Spoleto in 784, the deacon Atto in 778, Wulfuin in 780, Hitherius and Abbot Maginarius of St Denis in 781, 786 and 788, Goddramnus, *ostiarius magnificus*, in 788,[201] Peter, bishop of Pavia in 781, Counts Leuderic and Aruin in 788, Roro the *capellanus*, Betto, Hucbald and many more who are not named.[202] Radbert, a *missus* sent by Charlemagne to Constantinople, died on his journey home in 807.[203]

From 802 at least, however, one clerical *missus* (usually an archbishop) and one lay *missus* acted together within a specific territory known as a *missaticum*. The potential tension this system created in relation to the spiritual role of the ecclesiastical *missi* is indicated in a capitulary to the *missi* sent out nine years later. In this the emperor enquires about the way of life of bishops and abbots and the ways in which those who have left the world can be distinguished from those who still follow it: 'Is the difference only that they do not bear arms and are not publicly married?'[204] The potential tension between the bishop's role as a secular leader and his spiritual responsibilities in the Frankish empire is similar to that experienced by the bishop of late antiquity. As Claudia Rapp has established with her model of spiritual, ascetic and pragmatic authority, the bishop's asceticism both was evidence of his spiritual authority and justified his secular and pastoral role.[205] Charlemagne's admonitions and enquiries to his bishops appear to recognize this.

From four different versions of the special capitulary of the *missi* in 802, and incidental references in relation to judicial disputes elsewhere, a

---

[201] See the account of Maginarius' report in 788, above, p. 88.
[202] *Codex epistolaris carolinus*, ed. Gundlach, Epp. 51, 55–7, 65, 67, 69, 70, 72, 80, 82, 85; pp. 571–3, 578–83, 592–603, 612–16, 621–2.
[203] *ARF* 807, ed. Kurze, p. 123.
[204] *MGH Cap.* I, No. 72, pp. 162–4, re-edited by F. L. Ganshof, 'Note sur les "capitula de causis cum episcopis et abbatibus tractandis" de 811', *Collectanea Stephan Kuttner* 3, Studia Gratiana 13 (1967), pp. 20–5; and discussed with English translation by Nelson, 'The voice of Charlemagne'.
[205] C. Rapp, *Holy bishops in late antiquity: the nature of Christian leadership in an age of transition*, The Transformation of the Classical Heritage 37 (Berkeley, 2005).

number of *missatica* and *missi* have been identified within the ecclesiastical provinces of Sens, Reims, Tours, Salzburg[206] and Rouen. In the last named, the *missi* (Magenaud, archbishop of Rouen, and Count Madelgaud) had the extra responsibility of maintaining coastal defences and the harbours.[207] The version of this capitulary in Paris, BnF lat. 9654, a late eleventh-century legal and capitulary collection from Lotharingia, preserves the copy sent to Magnus of Sens and Count Godefrid. Their *missaticum* extended across a region delimited by an imaginary line which started at Orleans and proceeded to the Seine, to Troyes and Langres, and then to Besançon and Autun before arriving back at Orleans. Each pair of *missi* appointed, therefore, would presumably have had their area of jurisdiction similarly defined.

The *missi dominici* were carriers of royal authority.[208] They could act as judges in court. A hearing from a *missus* was one stage in the legal or judicial appeal process. The activities of a *missus* described by Theodulf of Orleans in his poem *Contra iudices*, combined with a number of *notitiae* of dispute settlements, such as those involving Arn of Salzburg referred to above, provide some notion of the realities of providing justice.[209] They could punish criminals and receive oaths. They were constantly required to inspect and check on the behaviour of both clergy and laity. They were charged with communicating the king's wishes as expressed in his capitularies and letters to everyone else. They enforced the king's *bannus*. These officials were an extra stratum of the political system.

The system of *missi* and *missatica* appears to have extended across the entire kingdom. It therefore constituted a vital means of co-ordinating communication within the empire. The substantial body of capitularies for the *missi*, therefore, merits further examination in order to determine how much they reflect of their use, reception and preservation.[210] The opening words of the most detailed capitulary of them all, that of the 802 administrative capitulary, *De legatione a domno imperatore directa*, if original, indicate a mandate from the king or emperor. In adding all the other

---

[206] See Wolfram, *Salzburg*, pp. 185–8.

[207] Eckhardt, 'Die *capitularia missorum specialia* 802', and *Die Kapitulariensammlung Ghaerbalds von Lüttich*.

[208] See R. Le Jan, 'Justice royale et pratiques sociales dans le royaume franc au IXe siècle', in *La giustizia nell'alto medioevo (secoli IX–XI)*, pp. 47–85; and the discussion between Oliver Guillot and Régine Le Jan, pp. 88–9.

[209] For the context in the normative sources see H. Siems, 'Bestechliche und ungerechte Richter in frühmittelalterlichen Rechtsquellen', *La giustizia nell'alto medioevo (secoli V–VIII)*, pp. 509–63; and Hubert Mordek's comment in the Discussion, pp. 566–7.

[210] Some of these were studied by C. De Clercq, *Neuf capitulaires de Charlemagne concernant son œuvre réformatrice par les "missi"*, Università degli studi di Camerino, Istituto Giuridico, Testi per esercitazioni, Sezione V, n. 3 (Milan, 1968).

matters to do with the administration of justice, an insistence on written law, what the new oath entailed, statements about the procedure to be followed in bringing the perpetrators of certain crimes (such as incest and the murder of kinsmen) to the king for judgment, the need for bishops, abbots and abbesses to have advocates in court, the summons to the army, and the moral behaviour required of all clerics and laymen, the capitulary has again the ring of a general *admonitio* concerned with all matters, secular and ecclesiastical, within the kingdom.[211] Many of the general themes of the earlier capitularies are reiterated, such as the insistence on law, justice and the morality of clerics and laymen, even if new, or more precise, stipulations and recommendations are also added. One of these is the insistence that disputes, including those involving violent killings, should be brought to the royal officials and dealt with through the courts and the law. This was an attempt to inhibit the seeking of vengeance by members of a victim's or even the murderer's kindred.[212]

The administrative capitulary of 802 was perhaps intended as the authorization of the *missi*'s role. It supplied their brief and the credentials that they would need to communicate to any counts or others who might question their authority. Yet the document has also a highly personal ring, for it occasionally slips into first- rather than third-person passages. Thus the king forbade the crime of incest, which included ravishing a nun. The specific instance is offered of a man called Fricco, who had perpetrated incest upon a nun. This has the character of the king's own memory of the case and its relevance. In a later clause he complained about poachers of game in the royal forests. Nevertheless, it is difficult to categorize this capitulary. The first-person elements could represent the king's personal intervention in some way, in the form either of comments on a draft, or comments made in a discussion. Such comments were subsequently incorporated rather raggedly into the text as we have it.[213] The text's survival in only one copy, a tenth-century Italian manuscript, Paris BnF lat. 4613, does not help.[214] The Italian origin, moreover, opens up the possibility that the compilation of Lombard law, Italian and general capitularies in which this capitulary is preserved may have had its origins in a collection made at the

---

[211] Buck, *Admonitio und praedicatio*.

[212] Compare the *Admonitio generalis*, c. 67, *MGH Cap.* 1, No, 22, p. 59, which the 802 capitulary explains more fully, and below, p. 270. For a context see G. Halsall, 'Violence and society: an introductory survey', in Halsall, *Violence and society*, p. 25.

[213] This was a suggestion made by F. L. Ganshof, 'Charlemagne's programme of imperial government', in English in F. L. Ganshof, *The Carolingians and the Frankish monarchy* (London, 1971), pp. 55–85.

[214] Mordek, *Bibliotheca*, pp. 469–76.

Carolingian court of Pavia. The 801/2 capitulary itself could then represent a statement of the new administrative arrangements and their ideological rationale sent to Pippin of Italy for distribution to the relevant officials in their newly defined districts. The capitulary defining the *missatica* created in 802 also mixes the first and third persons; reference to the *bannus* and swearing of the oath, for example, is in the impersonal third person.[215] These two capitularies in their variety of style are typical of the range to be found in the later administrative capitularies, presumably due also to the different personnel of the royal writing office or others at court responsible for their redaction.[216]

Like the records of oath-taking, the system of *missi* and *missatica* relied entirely on Charlemagne's communications system. The *missi* in their turn passed down elements of their own responsibilities to the counts and reiterated the need for a constant flow of information, written reports and consultation. How exactly the distribution of capitularies was managed is not known, given that not one original survives. Various scenarios have been proposed on stylistic or imaginative grounds. One presumes that the notaries responsible for the charters also produced the capitularies. This is suggested by the few references there are in the capitularies to the making of copies and their destination. A capitulary for 808, for example, refers to copies to be made for the *missi*, counts and military commanders; the chancellor was to retain a fourth.[217] That the *missi* received copies cannot be doubted. One group of *missi* wrote to a count in 806 to tell him to 'reread' his capitularies, and to remember what he had been told to do orally.[218] A further consideration in the dissemination of the king's wishes is the possible role of senior members of court. The new *missi* may not always have been completely sure about what they could, or had to, do. Angilbert of St Riquier, for example, has been proposed as the member of the court circle perhaps responsible for the letter answering queries made by an ecclesiastical *missus* about examining canons, monks and laymen concerning their observance of the *canones* and *leges* in connection with the capitularies of 802–3. That Angilbert would have been in a position to offer such advice is supported by the fact that elsewhere Charlemagne refers to Angilbert as the man 'who is close to us and who serves as our intimate

[215] *MGH Cap.* I, No. 34, c. 18 p. 101, and extension to c. 19, pp. 101–2.
[216] P. Bernard, 'Benoît d'Aniane est-il l'auteur de l'avertissement "Hucusque" et du Supplément au sacramentaire "Hadrianum"?', *Studi medievali* 39 (1998), pp. 1–120, esp. pp. 55–61. See also below, p. 342.
[217] *MGH Cap.* I, No. 50, c. 8, p. 138.   [218] *MGH Cap.* I, No. 85, preface, p. 184.

counsellor' and gives him the nickname of Homer.[219] This letter may even have been designed as a formal general letter rather than a personal one. The late tenth- or early eleventh-century copy of it lacks any protocol, so this cannot be established. Thus Angilbert's intention may have been to let his letter act as a gloss to the requirements of the capitulary for 802.[220] Its existence suggests that not all *missi* attended the assembly described by the Lorsch annalist, and they had consequently to conduct such enquiries by letter and messenger.

THE MISSI DOMINICI AND THEIR BOOKS

To understand the capitularies and the possible role of the *missi* we are at the mercy of the choices and selections made by the compilers of the manuscripts in which the capitularies are preserved. Sometimes only one or two capitularies are included in a collection, but there are also major capitulary collections such as that from Reims in BAV pal. lat. 582 and Paris, BnF lat. 10758, the late tenth- or early eleventh-century collection from Lotharingia in Paris, BnF lat. 9654, and the Italian collections already mentioned. This process of reception of the capitularies can also be documented during Charlemagne's reign itself. In the absence of original capitularies, the copies made are assumed to be complete, though in some instances clauses of a particular capitulary might be scattered through a codex according to the compiler's ordering of his material. Although both the principal early capitularies of Charlemagne in due course formed part of the major capitulary collections of the ninth and tenth centuries, the *Admonitio generalis* survives in its earliest manuscripts from the late eighth century, alongside canon law, and liturgical or devotional material (Wolfenbüttel, Herzog-August Bibliothek, Helmst. 496a). The Capitulary of Herstal, on the other hand, was included in an early ninth-century law book containing Roman and Salic law (BAV reg. lat. 846), and in a small capitulary collection (St Gallen, Stiftsbibliothek 733). Even within a capitulary, abridgment or selection may have occurred. The capitulary on matters to be discussed with bishops and abbots, for example, survives in two different tenth-century compilations from Reims and Lotharingia.[221] Its second clause implies that the enquiries were also to be made to counts.

[219] *MGH Epp.* IV, Nos. 92 and 93.
[220] Pokorny, 'Eine Brief-Instruktion aus dem Hofkreis Karls des Großen, pp. 57–83.
[221] *MGH Cap.* I, No. 72, in Paris, BnF lat. 9654, and BAV pal. lat. 582: see Mordek, *Bibliotheca*, pp. 562–78 and 780–97.

It may have been the copyist who decided to omit the counts' clauses rather than their never having existed in the first place.

Concerns about how to categorize the capitularies, how they were organized and the order in which clauses might originally have occurred prevent us from appreciating the historical evidence provided by these collections in their own right. These books are in fact precious indications, not only of the dissemination of the capitularies and their continued application in different contexts, but also of the original *missi*'s reactions to the tasks assigned to them. There is a further set of outward ripples of dissemination created by the capitulary collection of Ansegisus.[222] Arnold Bühler and Jennifer Davis, moreover, have independently analysed the patterns of capitulary preservation in terms of the codicological context: capitularies are gathered together with national laws, with canon law and other religious texts, and with annals and other historical writing.[223] Many of these books were originally designed as handbooks for the *missi* themselves. Two such compilations made by *missi dominici* in the first and second decade of the ninth century are important witnesses to the process of reception of Charlemagne's directions to his *missi*. Let us look at two of them, from Liège and Aquitaine respectively.

One, compiled *c.* 806 by Gerbald of Liège (787–810), survives in a section of a twelfth-century Liège manuscript now in Berlin (Berlin, Deutsche Staatsbibliothek, lat. fol. 626, Part II).[224] The other, originally put together by a *missus* responsible for Aquitaine in the early ninth century, was recopied in the late ninth century in southwest France. It is now in Leiden, Universiteitsbibliotheek Voss. lat. Q 119.[225]

Gerbald's capitulary collection of 806 was formed at about the time of the arrival in Liège, only 60 km, or approximately two days' ride, from Aachen of the four imperial *missi* – Adalhard, Fulrad, Unruoch and Hrocculf – whose letter is also preserved in Gerbald's collection. Gerbald's own episcopal statutes were issued a few years earlier than this. He made his own collection of material; presumably he had himself

[222] See G. Schmitz (ed.), *Die Kapitulariensammlung des Ansegis (Collectio capitularium Ansigisi)*, MGH *Cap.* Nova series I (Hanover, 1996).

[223] Bühler, '*Capitularia relicta*', and Davis, 'A king and his law'.

[224] See Eckhardt, *Die Kapitulariensammlung Bischof Ghaerbalds von Lüttich*; and see also W. A. Eckhardt, 'Review of Ganshof, *Was waren die Kapitularien?*', *Historisches Zeitschrift* 195 (1962), pp. 372–7. Why such a collection should have been preserved in the twelfth century would merit further investigation.

[225] Mordek, *Bibliotheca*, pp. 210–17. For the date and location see B. Bischoff, *Katalog der festländischen Handschriften des neunten Jahrhunderts (mit Ausnahme der wisigotischen)*, Teil II: *Laon–Paderborn* (Wiesbaden, 2004), p. 63, No. 2239.

received it in his capacity as *missus*.[226] Among the capitularies he included were not only the *Admonitio generalis* of 789 and the principal capitularies for the *missi* from 802, 803, 805 and 806, albeit with the clauses rearranged, but also capitularies with additions to the law from 803 and brief notes on the tariffs in the *Lex Salica* and *Lex Ribuaria*. He added his own three diocesan statutes, addressed primarily to the priests in his diocese (though some clauses concern the laity), and an exchange of letters he had enjoyed with Charlemagne.[227] These are all fully in tune with, and augment, in terms of practical provisions, the matters addressed in the capitularies in the rest of his collection. As we saw earlier in this chapter, Bishop Gerbald may himself have acted as a *missus dominicus*, perhaps in a different district.[228]

The collection of an Aquitainian *missus* in Leiden, Universiteits-bibliotheek MS Voss. Lat. Q119, opens with the extract from Isidore of Seville's *Etymologiae* on law and the letter of Bishop Chrodbert of Tours to Abbess Boba. In addition to Merovingian royal edicts amending and adding to the *Lex Salica*, the Carolingian *capitulare legibus additum* of 803, the manuscript contains an Epitome of Roman law (the *Epitome Aegidii* of the *Lex Romana Visigothorum* and the *Lex Salica, Lex Ribuaria, Lex Alamannorum* and *Lex Baiuvariorum*, two Carolingian ordinals, and the following capitularies: the 768 capitulary for Aquitaine and *Breviarium* 789 for Aquitaine, the capitulary for *missi* of 803, the *Duplex capitulare missorum* divided into two separate groups of *capitula*, selections from the *Admonitio generalis* 789 and the Capitulary of Herstal of 779 omitting clause 7, the *capitula per missos cognita facienda*, an extract from a council from the time of Pippin on incest and, lastly (fols 140–141v), the *Capitula legi addita* of 816.[229] It is a collection with clear signs in the manuscript of quire-by-quire copying from its exemplar. This exemplar, despite the changes of hand and the beginning of the capitulary section in the middle of quire 'S' on fol. 132r (on the next leaf after the *Lex Salica* ends), seems originally to have comprised the entire contents, with the possible exception of the 816 additional capitulary and the ordinals. The Aquitainian capitulary straight after the *Lex Salica* in this codex, moreover, is the very one that states that all men, Romans and Salians, are to enjoy the use of

[226] For a detailed contents list see Mordek, *Bibliotheca*, pp. 37–42.
[227] Eckhardt, *Kapitulariensammlung Ghaerbalds von Lüttich*; and P. Brommer, *MGH* Capitula epis-coporum I (Hanover, 1984), pp. 3–42. For the context of these statutes see McKitterick, *Frankish church*, pp. 45–79, esp. pp. 50–2.
[228] See above, p. 218.
[229] *MGH Cap.* I (in the order in which they appear), Nos. 118, 24, 40, 34, 23, 22, 67, 15, 134.

their laws. The sequence of quire signatures throughout the manuscript makes it clear that the compilation was all of a piece.[230] The inclusion of the capitularies for *missi* after the material relating to law and the national *leges* themselves suggest that this was, like Gerbald of Liège's compilation, a collection made to enable the *missus* to fulfil his role. Although it is not possible to determine whether the original compilation was intended for a secular or an ecclesiastical *missus*, the original owner apparently wanted the capitulary texts he needed to fulfil the requirement that he administer justice. This *missus*'s book, therefore, is an eloquent witness to the role of the *missi* in providing essential links between the observance of the customs and laws of all the peoples within the Carolingian empire, the royal administrative structures and Charlemagne himself.

For all the problems of selection and omission, the effectiveness of the distribution of Charlemagne's capitularies is in fact amply attested by the wide geographical range of places with which later capitulary manuscripts can be associated. Some of the later collections appear to be based on earlier exemplars, which could themselves have been earlier collections, or else the single-sheet format in which they most probably were sent. In many cases it was undoubtedly a *missus* who collected and preserved many of the capitularies of Charlemagne.

The *missi dominici* clearly played a crucial role in promoting greater coherence and administrative links across the empire. How much success they may claim for the relative stability of the Frankish realm in the last two decades of Charlemagne's life is difficult to demonstrate, but there were other means of constructing communities and identities within Charlemagne's empire which we should now consider.

MULTIPLE LOYALTIES AND THEIR OBLIGATIONS

Quite apart from the frequent reports of Saxon 'rebellion' against Frankish rule before 803/4, there are occasional traces in the narrative accounts of dissidents and rebellions elsewhere, especially among the Saxons' northern, eastern and southern neighbours. One extraordinary story is a revolt of a group of Thuringian nobles. It is preserved in a contemporary record dating from the end of the eighth century, the so-called *Annales nazariani*,

---

[230] Compare B. Bischoff, *Katalog der festländischen Handschriften*, II, p. 63, who notes incorrectly that the manuscript comprises only 119 leaves rather than 141, and Mordek, *Bibliotheca*, who resolved this by dating the portion from fol. 120 to the tenth century. Although Quire M and a leaf in Quire P are missing, the texts are arranged continuously. Compare the discussion iin Wormald, *Making of English law*, pp. 61–2.

possibly from Murbach. This occupies fols 53v–59v of BAV pal. lat. 966, and is in the same hand as the earlier part of the manuscript which contains the *Liber historiae francorum*. The outcome of this rebellion was grim. Despite the ringleaders' having been tried and apparently forgiven, this is what happened next:

> After some days had passed, therefore, the king sent those Thuringians off in the company of his *missi*, some into Italy and to St Peter and some into Neustria and Aquitaine, sending them to the tombs of the saints so that they might swear fidelity to the king and his children. And this they are attested to have done. Several of them were arrested on their return journey from these places. Their eyes are known to have been torn out. Some however reached the city of Worms and were arrested there and sent into exile and their eyes are known to have been torn out there. And all their possessions and estates are known to have been confiscated by the crown. The king remains unharmed and safe, therefore, ruling the kingdom of the Franks and the Lombards and Romans most excellently inasmuch as the king of heaven is proved to be his protector.[231]

Such evidence of rebellion is rare. Yet, coupled with the repeated prohibitions of sworn associations (*coniurationes*) in the capitularies,[232] the Thuringian revolt is a salutary reminder that the Frankish narratives' presentation of unalloyed Carolingian success must be tempered with the acknowledgment that some groups rejected, or at least resented, the much-vaunted benefits of Carolingian rule. How personally directed at Charlemagne himself this might have been is difficult to establish. Certainly the narrative of the Thuringian revolt included the report that 'one of them said to the king : If my confederates and associates had proved to be of my sentiments, never again would you have been seen crossing to this side of the Rhine alive.' This reported remark is a telling indication of how torn the loyalties of even one small group could be between the claims of the kindred, their former political and social bonds, and the new configurations created by the demands of a new king. The preservation of the story in itself witnesses to the existence of multiple loyalties on the part of the writer and possibly on those of his listeners and readers as well.

---

[231] Lendi, *Die Murbacher Annalen*, p. 159–63, for a modern edition; and compare *Annales nazariani*, ed. G. Pertz, *MGH SS* 1, pp. 40–4 at pp. 41–2; English trans. (from the *MGH* edn) King, *Charlemagne*, pp. 154–5. For full discussion of this story and its implications see McKitterick, *Perceptions of the past*, pp. 84–9.

[232] *Capitulare Haristallense* 779, *MGH Cap.* 1, No. 20, c. 14, pp. 50 and 51; *Concilium Francofurtense* 794, ed. Werminghoff, *MGH Conc.* II.i, No. 19, c. 31. p. 169; *Capitulare missorum in Theodonis villa datum secundum, generale*, *MGH Cap.* 1, No. 44, c. 10, p. 124.

Acceptance of new overlordship could not erase the memory of older or coexisting ties. The revolt of the east Frank Count Hardrad a year earlier is presented as that of a *coniuratio* (a sworn association) against the king (*adversus regem*).[233] The most famous case of all, that of Tassilo, concerned his breaking of faith to his cousin Charlemagne.[234] Pippin the Hunchback's revolt bears all the signs of a resentful son's quarrel with his father, at least as it is presented in the Revised Version of the *Annales regni francorum* and by Einhard.[235]

The oath

After these revolts, a capitulary was sent out to the *missi* explaining why the oath was necessary because it derived from ancient custom (*ex antiqua consuetudine*) and, most crucially, because it was implied that an oath would prevent rebellion. It referred to the 'unfaithful men' (*infideles*) who had conspired against Charlemagne's life and said that when questioned they had not sworn fidelity to him (*quod fidelitatem ei non iurasset*).[236] The condemnation of *coniurationes* and *conspirationes* was reiterated at Frankfurt in 794.[237] Just over a decade later a capitulary for the *missi*, labelled as issued at Thionville in 805/6 in two of the major capitulary collections from the ninth and tenth centuries in which it is preserved, stipulates the punishment for those engaging in a conspiracy (*conspiratio*) of any sort and sealing it with an oath; any such conspiracy, with or without an oath, was forbidden.[238]

Other dissidents, especially those among the recently subjugated, seem more determined to throw off Frankish rule more generally, but even so, the references are couched in terms of fidelity to the king. Thus a recurrent complaint in the annalistic sources is the breaking of oaths and of faith. Hrodgaud the Lombard betrayed his faith.[239] The Saxons broke their oaths and violated their faith, and on another occasion vowed they would be 'Christian and loyal to the king', only to break their promises concerning

---

[233] For the argument that Hardrad's revolt is not to be conflated with that of the Thuringians see McKitterick, *Perceptions of the past*, p. 88.

[234] *ARF* 788, ed. Kurze, p. 80: 'quod Tassilo fidem suam salvam non haberet'.

[235] *RVARF* 792, ed. Kurze, pp. 91–3: 'facta est contra illium coniuratio a filio suo maiore, nomine Pippino'.

[236] *MGH Cap.* 1, No. 25, c. 1, p. 66.   [237] *MGH Cap.* 1, No. 28, c. 31, p. 77.

[238] *MGH Cap.* 1, No. 44, c. 10, p. 124.

[239] *ARF* 775, ed. Kurze, p. 42, 'Hrodgaudus langobardus fraudavit fidem suam.'

the maintenance of Christianity and fidelity to the king the very next year.[240] Avars forsook the faith they had promised.[241]

Oaths were sworn by every man over the age of twelve, whether a cleric or layman. The oath was coupled with the king's *bannus* or right to command and be obeyed. The comprehensive pursuit of confirmation that oaths to the king had been sworn was the task of the *missi* and counts. They were required to draw up lists of those who had sworn the oath and send them to the king. Such a written record is quite unprecedented and, again, relied on the royal communications network. One such surviving list of oath-swearers from northern Italy may date from late in Charlemagne's reign, for it was copied into the capitulary collection in St Paul in Lavanttal 4/1. In five columns, it sets out the names of 174 men, either from one community or several. Whoever compiled the original record had made an effort to distinguish between those with the same name. Thus there is an Urso *infante*, Urso *gastaldo*, Urso Ambrosio, Urso *notario*, Urso de Cornitulo, Urso, *et alio* Urso, and no fewer than three more men called Urso, making ten altogether.[242] In 789, the oath was relatively straightforward in its personal direction to be faithful to Charlemagne and his sons 'all the days of my life without fraud and evil design': *quia fidelis sum et ero diebus vitae meae sine fraude et malo ingenio*.[243]

In 802, everyone was required to swear the oath to Charlemagne as emperor even if he had already done it to Charles as king. This is one of only a few indications of an adjustment in terms of the imperial title. Given that a similar change is observable in the charter protocol and, as we shall see below, a burst of activity in the revision and redaction of the 'national' laws, the new oath at least may well be part of Charlemagne's realization of the potential of his new title. The portmanteau nature of the new oath was spelt out in detail. Fidelity to the emperor now entailed not only loyalty to the ruler, ensuring the loyalty of others, and a refusal to commit treason.[244] Fidelity also meant serving God, not stealing any of the emperor's property, whether moveable or immoveable, not harming any churches,

---

[240] *ARF* 776, 794, 795: 'Saxones ... sacramenta rupta' (776); 'ibi missus nuntiavit Saxones iterum fidem suam fefellisse'. (793); 'et quamvis fraudulenter et christianos se et fideles domno regi fore promiserunt' (794); 'quod Saxones more solito promissionem suam, quam de habenda christianitate et fide regis tenenda fecerant, irritam fecissent'; ed. Kurze, pp. 44, 94, 96.

[241] *ARF* 799, ed. Kurze, p. 108: 'Eodem anno gens Avarum a fide quam promiserat, defecit.'

[242] *MGH Cap.* I, No. 181, pp. 377–8. This copy, entered into the law book, St Paul in Lavanttal, Archiv des Benediktinerstiftes MS 4/1, fol. 184r, as if it were in a register, is presumably a copy of a list sent to the king. It is headed 'Indiculus eorum qui sacramentum fidelitatis iuraverunt.' See also Mordek, *Bibliotheca*, pp. 685–95.

[243] *MGH Cap.* I, No. 23, c. 18, p. 63.   [244] *MGH Cap.* I, No. 33, cc. 2–9, pp. 92–3.

widows, orphans or pilgrims, and not neglecting a benefice of the emperor or trying to pretend it was not the emperor's. Swearing the oath implied an agreement to obey the king's *bannus* or command, and an undertaking not to act in opposition to his will and commands, or to obstruct payment of his dues or rents. It further entailed a commitment to fair judicial procedures, upholding the law, and supporting the *missi* or leading men in their exercise of justice. Fidelity to God and his church, and to the emperor and his government, were thus conflated. A new formula was provided which was far more obviously Christian in its emphasis. It was to be sworn in God's name on holy relics. It also emphasized Charlemagne's right to the throne by describing him as the son of Pippin and Bertrada. It added a phrase that the swearer of the oath would be faithful 'as a man ought rightfully be towards his lord' for the *honor* of his *regnum*. The entire formulation of this oath reflects a major shift in emphasis in Charlemagne's conception of his Christian kingship.[245] But the oath should also be acknowledged as playing a crucial role in providing a common bond of fidelity, focussed on the king, the church, and the law, right across Charlemagne's kingdom, alongside oaths sworn to local lords or professions to the religious life.[246] In insisting on the oath of fidelity from all those of an age to swear, Charlemagne created a means of trumping all other personal and institutional loyalties while yet not negating them. He did this by making the oath uphold the Christian faith, and social and political morality, at the same time as it affirmed his royal power.

Besides the oath, Charlemagne's peoples would have been most conscious of their belonging to the larger polity in four principal ways: military service, general liturgical rites, use of the coinage, and the judicial process.

Military service

Military service in principle was required of men from every region of the Frankish empire. The exact level of requirements at a routine level is difficult to establish, for the handful of extant capitularies on the matter seem to indicate that it depended on particular circumstances or strategic

---

[245] A pioneering study was C. E. Odegaard, 'Carolingian oaths of fidelity', *Speculum* 16 (1941), pp. 284–96; and Odegaard, 'The concept of royal power in Carolingian oaths of fidelity', *Speculum* 20 (1945), pp. 279–89; but see now M. Becher, *Eid und Herrschaft: Untersuchungen zum Herrscherethos Karls des Großen*, Vorträge und Forschungen Sonderband 39 (Sigmaringen, 1993); and J. L. Nelson, 'Kings with justice, kings without justice', in *La giustizia nell'alto medioevo* (secoli IX–XI), pp. 797–823. See also Innes, 'Charlemagne's government', pp. 80–2.

[246] *MGH Cap.* I, No. 44, c. 9, p. 124.

needs. The demands for military service may have become increasingly differentiated in the course of the reign, especially once the more or less constant succession of campaigns to Saxony had ceased. We know too little about the conduct of the Saxon wars to be able to draw hard and fast conclusions about the recruitment to the army in the period 770–800, let alone thereafter. That most of the capitularies touching on military matters are dated from 805 onwards may have created a distorted impression of the processes of conquest and defence generally. The impression is of a concentration on the *heribannus* fines and other penalties for those refusing to go on campaign, but whether this is really a new phenomenon or one with limited application for a short time cannot be ascertained.[247]

What we have are occasional snapshots about the calling-up process which need to be understood as very specific injunctions in relation to particular campaigns, rather than rules applying consistently over many decades. Campaigns were subjected to meticulous strategic planning, and the failure to follow orders for the mobilization and deployment of troops at a particular target, as in the debacle of 782, could have tragic consequences.[248] No Frank, Saxon, Bavarian, Lombard or any of the other peoples incorporated into the Frankish empire would have been unaware of the demands of military service and many went off to fight. Despite the fact that the *Annales regni francorum* is particularly concerned to highlight the many peoples brought under Carolingian rule and their incorporation into the *gens* of the Franks, the authors still make specific reference to the different groups in the armies on a number of occasions. In 778, for example, the army Charlemagne led against Spain gathered *de partibus Burgundiae et Austriae vel Baioariae seu Provinciae et Septimaniae et pars Langobardorum*; in 787, the army assembled to invade Bavaria included *Franci, Austrasi, Toringi* and *Saxones*; in 791, Frisians, Saxons, Ripuarians and Thuringians under Count Theodoric and Maginfred the *camerarius* formed one contingent sent along the north bank of the Danube to fight the Avars, while the Bavarians took the armies' supplies by boat along the Danube, and Charlemagne and the Franks headed the army on the south bank of the river.[249] Here too we can recall the rhetorical effect of the

---

[247] T. Reuter, 'The end of Carolingian military expansion', in Godman and Collins, *Charlemagne's heir*, pp. 391–405.

[248] On 782 see above, pp. 29–31. For discussion of recruitment and the interpretation of the Carolingian capitularies on mobilization of the army see the surveys by Halsall, *Warfare and society*, pp. 71–110; Bachrach, *Early Carolingian warfare*; and the comments by Reuter, 'The end', pp. 396–400, and Bachrach, 'Charlemagne and the Carolingian general staff'.

[249] *ARF* 778, 787, 791, ed. Kurze, pp. 50, 78 and 88; and Lorsch annals 791, ed. G. Pertz, *MGH SS* I, p. 34.

annalist's claim that Franks, Bavarians, Lombards, and Saxons were assembled together at Ingelheim in 788 to condemn Tassilo. All these references helped to create a sense of identity and affiliation under the rule of Charlemagne.[250]

The few surviving directives about mobilization include requirements for the service of men from different regions. We have already noted the letter addressed to Fulrad, abbot of St Quentin, in April 806, concerning the armed men and the equipment for defensive works and making camps, as well as arms, that he was to bring to Stassfurt.[251] Charlemagne wanted Fulrad's men to be equipped with arms, gear, food and clothing. Each horseman should have a shield, lance, sword, dagger, bow and quivers with arrows. In the carts were to be utensils of various kinds, that is, axes, planes, augers, adzes, trenching tools, iron spades or shovels and other tools necessary for an army. Fulrad's *homines* were to march along with the carts and horsemen, with the leader always with them to ensure discipline. In 802–3, the penalties for not coming to the army when summoned were set; each man was to come and the count was to see that each was prepared with a lance, shield, bow with two strings and twelve arrows, breastplate and helmet.[252]

The equipment of the king was to be carried in carts, as was that of bishops, counts, abbots and nobles of the king, and this was to include flour, wine, pork and victuals in abundance, and tools such as adzes, axes, augers and slings, and men who know how to use them; the marshalls of the king were to make sure the whetstones were packed. Each count had to reserve part of the fodder in his country for the army's use, and was responsible for the maintenance of good bridges and good roads. As an exceptional measure in the light of the famine of 806/7, all men beyond the Seine were to do military service; their obligation to do so varied according to ownership of property and the levels of wealth: 'And where two men are found of whom one has two *mansi* and the other one *mansus*, they are to be similarly associated; and one is to equip the other; and he who is the more capable is to come to the army . . .'[253] A fragment of a capitulary on various matters from *c.* 807 refers to the method of mustering soldiers in relation to the assembly for that year:

If it shall be necessary to furnish aid against the Saracens of Spain or the Avars, then five of the Saxons shall equip a sixth, and if it be necessary to bear aid against

[250] I discuss this fully in McKitterick, *History and memory*, esp. pp. 84–132.
[251] *MGH Cap.* I, No. 75, p. 168.   [252] *MGH Cap.* I, No. 77, cc. 9 and 10, p. 171.
[253] *MGH Cap.* I, No. 48, pp. 134–5.

the Bohemians, two shall equip a third; if, indeed, there is a need to defend the native country against the Sorbs, then all shall come together ... Frisians ... and all the horsemen were to come prepared to the assembly; of the remaining poorer men six shall equip a seventh, and thus they shall come well prepared for war to the aforesaid assembly.[254]

Instructions for the *missi* sent out in 808 included a similar scale of property in relation to obligation, as well as requiring the *missi* to find out who had not come when called up the previous year, despite the arrangements made for freemen and poorer men. The king acknowledged that some had bought themselves exemption or stayed at home with the permission of their lords.[255] The fine or *heribannus* for not going to the army was a very lucrative source of revenue; it is mentioned in terms of a fine of three pounds for a man whose wealth was estimated at six pounds, expressed in gold, silver, coats of mail, bronze utensils, clothing, horses, oxen, cows, or other livestock. Some indication of the privation this could cause is indicated by the qualification that the women and children should not have to be deprived of their clothes to pay the fine.[256]

Liturgical prayer for the king

Commemoration of the king in the liturgy and the organization of prayer in times of crisis, especially famine, was widespread in Charlemagne's empire. As a collective expression of supplication, the potential of such prayers to create bonds of association and enhance the sense of loyalty to the king and emperor across the realm was very powerful. A capitulary associated with the assembly at Herstal in 779, for example, requested everyone in the kingdom – bishops, monks and laymen alike – to lend their assistance, in fasting, giving alms, and prayer. The bishops were to offer up three masses and sing three psalters for the king, the army and the present tribulation, priests were to chant three masses; monks, nuns and canons were to chant three psalters.[257] A letter to Bishop Gerbald of Liège in 805 set out an elaborate system of collective fasting.[258] How much this type of general liturgical commemoration, particularly routine masses for the king,

---

[254] *MGH Cap.* I, No. 49, cc. 2 and 3, p. 136.   [255] *MGH Cap.* I, No. 50, pp. 137–8.

[256] *MGH Cap.* I, No. 44, c. 19, p. 125, but compare No. 74 of 811, c. 1, p. 166, where the *heribannus* fine could be commuted into debt servitude if anyone were unable to pay the sixty *solidi* (three pounds) fine.

[257] *MGH Cap.* I, No. 21, p. 52, but see the new edition and commentary by Mordek, 'Karls des Großen zweites Kapitular von Herstal', pp. 1–52, with the edition at pp. 50–1. See further above, p. 43.

[258] *MGH Cap.* I, No. 124, pp. 245–246.

was adopted, is implied by the trial of a politically dissident abbot of San
Vincenzo, who had allegedly refused to chant the customary Psalm 54 for
the safety of the king and his children.[259] Such general liturgical observance
was reinforced by the prayer associations, stemming originally from the
Synod of Attigny (762) in the time of Pippin III, taken up in Bavaria at the
Synod of Dingolfing (*c*. 770), and developed fully in the Frankish kingdom
thereafter.[260]

Coinage

Pippin III and Charlemagne re-established a state monopoly of coinage as
it had existed in the Roman world, and as such represented royal authority
in an uncompromising way. So effective was Charlemagne's reformed
coinage that it was the sole valid currency in his realm and affected the
coinage in all the regions peripheral to his empire, such as Venice, Rome
and Benevento. It was so highly rated as an expression of political influence
that Grimoald of Benevento secured his release from being held hostage at
the Carolingian court after 788 by undertaking to employ the king's name
or monogramme in his charters and on his coins. In Rome after 800, all the
papal coinage carried Charlemagne's name or monogramme. Venice's coinage had to be acceptable with the Franks for trading purposes. Small objects
bearing inscriptions and images which circulated throughout the kingdom,
whose use and value were controlled by the king, were carriers of political
messages. From 793/4 the royal monogramme comprising all the letters of
the name KAROLUS became the main obverse. The essentially cruciform
shape of this monogram has been interpreted as an augmentation of the
Christian symbolism of these coins, especially those with the cross on the
reverse.[261] Coinage was not necessarily used in all commercial transactions,
for each Carolingian silver penny had a high face value in relation to the
cost of living. Limited use would nevertheless have enhanced its symbolic

---

[259] *Codex epistolaris carolinus*, ed. Gundlach, Ep. 67, pp. 594–7. See E. Ewig, 'Der Gebetsdienst der
Kirchen in den Urkunden der späteren Karolinger', in H. Maurer and H. Patze (eds.), *Festschrift für
Berent Schwineköper zu seinem siebzigsten Geburtstag* (Sigmaringen, 1982), pp. 45–86.

[260] McKitterick, *History and memory*, pp. 156–185; and see also M. de Jong, 'Monasticism and
the power of prayer', in *NCMH*, II, pp. 622–53; and H. Reimitz, 'Conversion and control; the
establishment of liturgical frontiers in Carolingian Pannonia', in W. Pohl, I. Wood and H. Reimitz
(eds.), *The transformation of frontiers from late antiquity to the Carolingians*, The Transformation of
the Roman World 10 (Leiden, 2001), pp. 189–208, has highlighted the 'liturgical orchestration of
political negotiations and military events'. See also below, pp. 340–5.

[261] I. H. Garipzanov, 'The image of authority in Carolingian coinage', *Early Medieval Europe* 8 (1999),
pp. 197–215.

effect, for a coin would not have been so familiar to everyone that its images would have gone unremarked, as tends to be the case with much modern coinage. The ceremonial gold coin issues, meagre as the evidence is for them, would also have had a symbolic value.[262] The most dramatic expression of Charlemagne's understanding of his imperial title, however, is the so-called Class 4 Portrait bust coins. These bear a laureate bust depicting Charlemagne as a Roman emperor and an inscription, IMP(erator) AUG(ustus). Just as the oath of 802 celebrated the authority of the Christian king, so the imperial coinage of Charlemagne disseminated an image of the king as a Roman emperor. So, of course, did the seals on Charlemagne's charters, though their circulation and accessibility were necessarily more limited.[263]

The leges: *law and justice*

The inspiration provided by such Roman emperors as Theodosius, moreover, is also arguably behind the close attention Charlemagne paid to the revision and dissemination of the 'national' laws. Many annals preserve a description of Charlemagne's actions in relation to his government. The Lorsch annals version is particularly informative and important. Made more or less immediately after the event by someone with first-hand knowledge, it reports the creation of the *missi dominici* (though it does not use these words), and describes an assembly held in Aachen in 802 which merits quotation in full.

And in October he convoked a universal synod in [Aachen] and there had read out to the bishops, priests and deacons all the canons, which the holy synod admitted, and the decrees of the pontiffs; and he ordered these to be fully expounded before all the bishops, priests, and deacons. In the same synod he likewise gathered together all the monks and abbots who were there present and they formed an assembly of their own; and the rule of the holy father Benedict was read out and learned men expounded it before the abbots and monks. And then he issued a command of general application to all the bishops, abbots, priests, deacons and the

---

[262] P. Grierson and M. Blackburn, *Medieval European Coinage*, 1: *The early middle ages* (Cambridge, 1986), p. 194; and see also P. Grierson, 'Symbolism in early medieval charters and coins' in *Simboli e simbologia nell'alto medioevo*, Settimane 23 (Spoleto, 1976), II, pp. 601–30.

[263] B.-M. Tock, 'Le sceau', in B.-M. Tock, M. Courtois and M.-J. Gasse-Granjean (eds.), *La diplomatique française du haut moyen âge: inventaire des chartes originales antérieures à 1121 conservées en France*, I (Turnhout, 2001), pp. 28–30; and R. H. Bautier, 'Chartes, sceaux et chancelleries', in Bautier, *Études de diplomatique et de sigillographie médiévale*, Mémoires et documents de l'Ecole des Chartes 34, 2 vols. (Paris, 1990), I, pp. 123–66.

entire clergy, that as clerics they were to live in accordance with the canons, each in his own station, whether in a cathedral or in a monastery or in any of the holy churches, as the holy fathers laid down; and that they were to correct in accordance with the precepts of the canons whatever faults or shortcomings might appear in the clergy or the people; and they that were to have corrected in accordance with the rule of St Benedict whatever might be done in monasteries or among monks in contravention of that same rule of St Benedict. And while this synod was being held the emperor also assembled the dukes, counts, and the rest of the Christian people together with men skilled in the laws and had all the laws in his realm read out and each man's law read out to him and emended wherever necessary and the emended law written down. And he declared that the *iudices* should judge in accordance with what was written and not accept gifts and that all men poor or rich should enjoy justice in his realm.[264]

Not only were everyone's laws and regulations considered in both the ecclesiastical and secular spheres, including canon law and the Rule of Benedict for the clergy and monks, but revised 'Caroline' versions of existing 'national' laws, that is, *the Lex Salica, Lex Ribuaria, Lex Alamannorum* and *Lex Burgundionum*, were also produced.[265] Some laws, such as the *Lex Saxonum* and *Lex Thuringorum*, were probably first set down in written form, or even created on the model of existing laws in connection with this assembly.[266] In the manuscripts from the eighth and ninth centuries, these codes resemble Roman law in format, and are often preserved in collections with Epitomes, or the entire text, of Alaric's breviary of Roman law. This passage demonstrates very clearly that the royal recognition of what was appropriate for each group in Charlemagne's realm in terms of the laws and regulations by which each national or institutional group was guided, however old these might be, could act as a unifying rather than divisive measure; all the laws were 'of his realm' (*omnes leges in regno suo*).

---

[264] Annals of Lorsch, *MGH SS* I, p. 39; English trans., P. D. King, *Charlemagne: translated sources* (Kendal, 1987), p. 145.

[265] For full discussion see R. McKitterick, *The Carolingians and the written word* (Cambridge, 1989), pp. 23–75, and the references to the older literature there cited. Pertinent discussions can also be found in H. Siems, 'Textbearbeitung und Umgang mit Rechtstexten im Frühmittelalter: zur Umgestaltung der leges im Liber legum des Lupus', in H. Siems, K. Nehlen-von Stryk and D. Strauch (eds.), *Recht im frühmittelalterlichen Gallien* (Cologne, Weimar and Vienna, 1995), pp. 29–72; and W. Sellert, 'Aufzeichnung des Rechts und Gesetz', in W. Sellert (ed.), *Das Gesetz in Spätantike und frühem Mittelalter*, Abhandlungen der Akademie der Wissenschaften in Göttingen, phil.-hist. Klasse 3, Folge 196 (Göttingen, 1992), pp. 67–102.

[266] Theuerkauf, *Lex, speculum, compendium iuris*, pp. 54–67; and see above, pp. 257–8.

The capitularies to revise the 'national' laws

These laws were not simply historic monuments or symbols of an ancient past now incorporated into the Carolingian empire. Charlemagne's capitularies also proposed modifications to the national laws in general, and to the Ribuarian and Bavarian codes in particular. Or, at least, this is what has survived. These capitularies emending and adding to the laws have all been dated post-802. There was also a spate of amending the laws early in the reign of Louis the Pious, and a fragment of another capitulary relating possibly to the *Lex Ribuaria* from the time of Louis the Pious has also been found.[267] The general capitulary adding to the laws is dated in relation to an assembly at Aachen 'in accordance with the Salic, Roman and Burgundian' laws.[268] The capitulary stipulates that each count should keep a prison and that judges and the *vicarii* were to have gallows. As far as court procedure was concerned, bishops and abbots should have advocates.[269] The capitulary making changes to the Ribuarian laws in some respects appears to have been prompted by some penalty and procedural changes because they had proved impracticable.[270] The number of oath-helpers of people accused of stealing a flock (of sheep?), for example, was reduced to twelve for each person accused rather than seventy-two. A systematic approach to the revision of the lawcode is indicated by the fact that every clause in the capitulary is numbered according to a clause in *Lex Ribuaria*. Fines are altered or the judicial process in court changed. The issues include fines for not answering a summons to court, what to do about sequestrated property, the limits on bequeathing property to freed-men whether by charter or by penny throw (*denarialis*). The need to swear an oath in church or over relics is stated and this overrides the earlier stipulation in the *Lex Ribuaria* that all oaths were to be sworn at the *harahus* or *stafflus regis*.[271] Requirements for the procedure for designating an heir were altered so that instead of being made in the presence of the king, an heir could now be designated in the presence of one of the royal

---

[267] Mordek, 'Recently discovered capitulary texts' and 'Unbekannte Texte zur karolingischen Gesetzgebung'.

[268] *MGH Cap.* 1, No. 77, cc. 1 and 14, pp. 170, 172.

[269] *MGH Cap.* 1, No. 41, c. 8, p. 118 (*Lex Ribuaria* c. LXVIII).

[270] T. G. W. Faulkner, '*Lex Ribuaria*', unpublished MPhil in Medieval History dissertation, University of Cambridge (2005), pp. 42–6. I am grateful to Tom Faulkner for permitting me to cite his thesis.

[271] *MGH Cap.* 1, No. 41, c. 11, p. 118. Compare *Lex Ribuaria*, ed. R. Buchner, *MGH Leges nat. germ.* 3, 2 (Hanover, 1954), pp. 119–20; and R. Buchner, *Textkritische Untersuchungen zur Lex Ribuaria* (Stuttgart, 1940).

officials, namely the count, a *scabinus* or the *missus dominicus*.[272] This is another telling instance of the way officials were increasingly expected to act for the king as the kingdom expanded and the reign progressed.

By far the greater number of manuscripts of the *leges* are from the ninth or tenth century. It is also striking how many of them represent collections of national *leges*, rather than a single *lex* on its own. The practice of combining these *leges* into compilations dates from Charlemagne's reign. These compilations have an interest in common, namely the administration of the law.[273] The officials most responsible for the administration of justice were, as we have seen, the *missi dominici*.[274]

COMMUNICATIONS BEYOND THE EMPIRE

It is unusual behaviour in a ruthless conqueror to know when to stop and make the best of what he has got.[275] That is what Charlemagne seems to have done, yet the strategies of expansion merit a closer look. In the first three decades of his reign Charlemagne's capitularies had offered practical and moral guidance for the consolidation of royal authority and of Frankish rule. Scepticism about the effectiveness of any royal stipulations and an insistence on their largely rhetorical nature can be justified only if there is supporting evidence of general failure, as distinct from occasional and inevitable abuse of power. An acknowledgment that no political regime is perfect, however, should not obstruct the recognition, not only of the power Charlemagne bestowed on his *missi*, but also the moral imperatives he built into their administrative functions. This moral imperative gathered momentum in the last years of Charlemagne's reign, fuelled by the king's own personal piety and conviction of his responsibilities in relation to the promotion of the Christian religion within his realm, most particularly in those regions newly brought under his control.

The peoples in this area had more than Frankish administration or the obligation to serve in the army or to offer tribute imposed upon them. Charlemagne also required the conversion of his defeated enemies to Christianity and the ceremonial baptism of their leaders. It is a pattern first established with mass baptisms of Saxons in 777 and the surrender accompanied by baptism of Widukind and Abbio, the Saxon rebels, in 785.

---

[272] F. N. Estey, 'The *scabini* and the local courts', *Speculum* 26 (1951), pp. 119–29.
[273] See McKitterick, *Carolingians and the written word*, pp. 40–60.   [274] See above, pp. 256–63.
[275] For discussion of the notion of 'limits of expansion' see above, pp. 135–6.

This is repeated with the baptism of the *tudun* of the Avars in 796. In a subsequent visit recorded from an Avar leader it is Theodore, the Christian leader, who is mentioned, presumably by his baptismal name. The St Emmeram annals preserve the memory, moreover, of a Bohemian leader or *khagan* who was baptized and given the name Abraham when he came to Charlemagne (in his camp at) the Fischa river in 805.[276] Despite these demonstrations of aspirations to be accepted as a Christian ally, the Franks, during the reign of Charlemagne at least, did not exploit Christian conversion as a form of exerting cultural influence beyond Frankish borders. They differed greatly from the Byzantine Greeks in this respect.[277] There is no indication that Charlemagne actively initiated missionary endeavours to peoples who were not already subject to him. His policy appears to have been to concentrate on the conversion of peoples once they were conquered and brought under Frankish rule.[278] Certainly, in the case of the Avars, the initial justification for the Frankish war against the Avars was their attacks on the Christian church and people. This lent the Avar campaigns the character of a holy war against the infidel.[279]

The implications of this combination of religious and political control, which played such a major role in Charlemagne's diplomacy, will be explored further in the following chapter. The place of such visits from foreign rulers also needs to be considered within the context of the *Annales regni francorum*'s representation of Charlemagne and his palace as the centre of world affairs, particularly in the section from 799 to 814.[280]

DIPLOMACY AND POLITICAL IDENTITIES

The annalist reported the sending of Frankish embassies to Spain, Byzantium, Persia, Jerusalem and Rome, and the reception of legates from

---

[276] Greater St Emmeram annals 805, ed. G. Pertz, *MGH SS* I, p. 93; and see above, pp. 131–3, and Reimitz, 'Conversion and control'.

[277] F. Dvornik, *Byzantine missions among the Slavs* (New Brunswick, 1970); A. Vlasto, *The entry of the Slavs into Christendom* (Cambridge, 1971); and J. Shepard, 'Slavs and Bulgars', in *NCMH*, II, pp. 228–49.

[278] H. Büttner, 'Mission und Kirchenorganisation des frankenreiches bis zum Tode Karls des Großen', *KdG*, I, pp. 454–87; and Wood, *The missionary life*. For the earlier background see W. Levison, *England and the Continent in the eighth century* (Oxford, 1946); T. Schieffer, *Winfrid-Bonifatius und die christliche Grundlegung Europas* (Freiburg, 1954); L. von Padberg, *Mission und Christianierung: Formen und Folgen bei Angelsachsen und Franaken im 7. und 8. Jahrhundert* (Stuttgart, 1995).

[279] *ARF* 791, ed. Kurze, p. 88; Pohl, *Die Awaren*; and Deer, 'Karl der Große und der Untergang des Awarenreichs', *KdG* I, pp. 726–30.

[280] See above, pp. 50–2.

the Christian and Arabic rulers of Spain, the emperor of Byzantium,[281] the Caliph of Baghdad, the governor of Sicily, the Patriarch of Jerusalem,[282] the kings of the Danes, Mercia and Northumbria,[283] and the *tudun* and *khagan* of the Avars and Slavs.[284] As early as 769, Charlemagne and Carloman had received envoys from the pope, and in 773, Peter, an envoy from Pope Hadrian, who had travelled by sea to Marseilles and thence overland, sought Charlemagne out at Thionville in order to ask for the king's help against the Lombards.[285] The Saracen envoys Ibn al-Arabi and the son and son-in-law of Yusuf had to extend their journey to Paderborn to find the king at his assembly in 777. Similarly, two decades later, Pope Leo III himself had to travel north to the assembly at Paderborn in order to see the king, while in 803 envoys from the Byzantine Emperor Nicephorus came as far as Salz on the Saale river bearing the written draft of a peace agreement.[286] The manner in which such requests were made, with foreign envoys being obliged to find the king wherever he might be, and traversing great tracts of his realm in order to do so, quite apart from the requests in themselves, is an indication of the Frankish king's reputation and an expression of the sheer territorial extent of his power.

As Charlemagne became more often based at Aachen, so his horizons expanded. The king established contact with far distant people and rulers.

---

[281] M. McCormick, 'Diplomacy and the Carolingian encounter with Byzantium down to the accession of Charles the Bald', in B. McGinn and W. Otten (eds.), *Eriugena: east and west. Papers of the Eighth International colloquium of the Society for the Promotion of Eriugenian Studies* (Notre Dame, 1994), pp. 15–48; and McCormick, *Origins of the European economy: communications and commerce* AD *300–900* (Cambridge, 2001), pp. 175–81.

[282] M. Borgolte, *Der Gesandtenaustausch der Karolinger mit den Abbasiden und mit den Patriarchen von Jerusalem*, Münchener Beiträge zur Mediävistik und Renaissance-Forschung 25 (Munich, 1976).

[283] See J. Story, *Carolingian connections: Anglo-Saxon England and Carolingian Francia, c. 750–870* (Aldershot, 2003), esp. pp. 169–211.

[284] There is still no full study of Carolingian diplomacy, though a beginning was made by F. L. Ganshof, *Le moyen âge: histoire des relations internationales*, I (Paris, 1958); Eng. trans. *The middles ages: a history of international relations* (New York, 1971); and see also beginnings made by W. Pixner, 'Foreign relations and internal and external power in the reign of Charlemagne', unpublished MPhil in Medieval History dissertation, University of Cambridge (1996); and M. Tillotson, 'Frankish diplomatic relations in the reign of Louis the Pious', unpublished MPhil in Medieval History dissertation, University of Cambridge (2003). For pertinent comments about diplomacy in the middle ages from the Byzantine perspective see J. Shepard and S. Franklin (eds.), *Byzantine diplomacy* (Aldershot, 1992) esp. A. Kazhdan, 'The notion of Byzantine diplomacy', pp. 3–23, and J. Shepard, 'Byzantine diplomacy, AD 800–1204: means and ends', pp. 41–72. See also T. C. Lounghis, *Les ambassades byzantins en occident depuis la fondation des états barbares jusqu'aux Croisades* (Athens, 1980); D. Nerlich, *Diplomatische Gesandtschaften zwischen Ost.- und West-Kaisern 756–1002* (Bern, 1999); and A. Gillett, *Envoys and political communication in the late antique west, 411–533* (Cambridge, 2003).

[285] *ARF* 773, ed. Kurze, p. 35; and compare *Annales mettenses priores* 773, pp. 59–60.

[286] *ARF* 803, ed. Kurze, p. 118.

Even if the Frankish exertion of political influence outside Charlemagne's realm was limited, the visits of the representatives of foreign rulers also offered recognition and confirmation of Charlemagne's renown outside the Frankish realm, such as the keys of the city of Huesca sent by its governor Hassan in 799, or 'King Sadun' of Barcelona, captured by the Frankish army under Louis the Pious's command and sent in chains to Charlemagne in 803.[287] Nicetas the patrician made peace in relation to Venice with Pippin of Italy in 807. In 808, Eardwulf of Northumbria arrived in Nijmegen and papal and Frankish envoys went back to his kingdom with him.[288] Above all, the Byzantine envoys in 812 hailed Charlemagne as *imperator* and *basileus*.[289] Equally, Charlemagne sent his own legates, both clerics and lay magnates, far and wide, and thus associated members of the political elite with geographically distant and foreign regions. This would undoubtedly have enhanced the legates' own prestige.[290] It was also a means both of representing the geography of conquered territories symbolically and of communicating the possession of a new domain.[291] The accounts of Charlemagne's hunts can also be recognized as part of the portrayal of the ruler's dominance of the landscape. In 803, for example, he came to Regensburg in Bavaria through the Hyrcanina forest bordering Bohemia, hunting aurochs and other wild game.[292]

Diplomacy, and the accompanying protestations of friendship or the offering of peace, were mutually advantageous as statements of the participating rulers' prestige as well as a recognition of their political power. Diplomacy was an elaborate means of recognizing and even orchestrating boundaries between different polities and peoples. Peaceful relations with other political states during the reign of Charlemagne, however, were confirmed by gifts, effusive letters which stress Christian brotherhood

---

[287] *Chronicle of Moissac*, ed. G. Pertz, *MGH SS* I, p. 307.

[288] *ARF* 807 and 808, ed. Kurze, pp. 124 and 126. See also Story, *Carolingian connections*.

[289] E. Chrysos, 'Byzantine diplomacy, AD 300–800: means and ends', in Shepard and Franklin, *Byzantine diplomacy*, pp. 25–39 at p. 35.

[290] For an ethnographic perspective on the involvement of 'political-ideological elites in travels within and without Christendom' in the early modern period, see M. Helms, *Ulysses' sail: an ethnographic odyssey of power, knowledge and geographical distance* (Princeton, 1988), esp. pp. 249–60, and below, pp. 372–7.

[291] This was particularly manifest with the Achaemenid rulers of Assyria as well. I owe this observation to L. Allen, 'The ideology of conquest in the near east in the first millennium BC', unpublished MA dissertation, University of London (2000).

[292] On the significance of hunting in relation to conquest and expansion see Allen, 'Ideology of conquest'; J. M. MacKenzie, *The empire of nature: hunting, conservation and British imperialism* (Manchester, 1988); J. M. Gilbert, *Hunting and hunting reserves in medieval Scotland* (Edinburgh, 1979); and B. Bender (ed.), *Landscape, politics and perspectives, Explorations in anthropology* (Providence, RI, and Oxford, 1993); and see above, p. 170.

and devotion, and agreements about trade or the cessation of hostilities, rather than with marriage alliances. Indeed, Charlemagne's withdrawal from possible alliances by marriage with the Lombard ruler and the Byzantine emperor are notorious incidents from his early years, but it should be noted that it does not appear to be Charlemagne who initiated these proposals.[293] The Reviser of the *Annales regni francorum*, for example, commented that the Emperor Constantine's attack on Italy in 788 was a furious response to being refused by Charlemagne's daughter.[294]

Similarly, Charlemagne's famous anger at the notion of an alliance through marriage with a daughter of Offa of Mercia, reported in the *Gesta abbatum fontanellensium*, may be a figment of the *Gesta* author's imagination.[295] Although the story has been enthusiastically accepted by historians of Anglo-Saxon England, keen to exaggerate Offa's status and political daring, the dating is problematic, and so are the practical details. The *Gesta* presents a marriage alliance with Offa as something sought by Charles the Younger, not his father. If it is to be believed, Charlemagne's reaction may have been as much against this unwonted attempt at independence by his eldest son as umbrage at Offa's presumption.[296]

The *Gesta* was written at St Wandrille between 833 and 843 and Gervold was abbot *c.* 789–807.[297] The incident is usually dated *c.* 790 in relation to a passing reference in a letter from Alcuin to Adalhard. First of all, Alcuin refers to the disturbance in 'his country' and the new king's attitude not being what he would like. Then he asks Adalhard for news and gossip from the palace and adds an opaque request that, should Adalhard know 'any reason for this quarrel between old friends', he tell him of it. No names are mentioned. Rather than being about Mercia, it seems to me more likely that this letter could refer to the volatile politics of Northumbria. The 'new king' would therefore be Osred. As for the 'old friends' and their quarrel, it is unlikely that this refers to Charlemagne and Offa, for describing them as

---

[293] On the Lombard suggestion, see above, pp. 84–7.

[294] *RVARF* 788, ed. Kurze, p. 83, and see above, p. 96.

[295] F. Stenton, *Anglo-Saxon England* (Oxford, 1946), p. 219, set the trend (he did not give much weight to the supposed alllusions in Alcuin's letters), but it has become an established fact in the literature since then.

[296] See the clear discussion of the evidence in Story, *Carolingian connections*, pp. 184–88, though she has followed Wallace-Hadrill and others in assuming Alcuin's unspecific allusions to a quarrel refer to the dispute over the marriage alliance as well as to trading matters. See, for example, J.-M. Wallace-Hadrill, 'Charlemagne and England' *KdG* 1, pp. 683–9, repr. in Wallace-Hadrill, *Early medieval history* (Oxford, 1975), pp. 155–80, and, 'Charlemagne and Offa', in Wallace-Hadrill, *Early Germanic kingship in England and on the Continent* (Oxford, 1971), pp. 98–123.

[297] *Gesta abbatum Fontanellensium*, c. 12, ed. P. Pradié, *Chronique des abbés de Fontenelle* (Saint-Wandrille) (Paris, 1999), p. 136.

'old friends' is hardly appropriate. The 'old friends' could be a reference to Charlemagne and Hadrian, for a further strange element in relations between Mercia and Francia is the alleged plot on Offa's part, implicating Charlemagne, about which Pope Hadrian protested in a letter (dated between 784 and 791) to Charlemagne.[298] It also seems odd that Alcuin does not know what the quarrel was about, if it was indeed between the Mercian and the Frankish king. In the one letter in which Alcuin did refer specifically to difficulties between Charlemagne and Offa, he referred only to trading agreements, not to any political dispute concerning a marriage proposal.[299] The only extant letter from Charlemagne to Offa, however, is dated 796, and makes no reference to any proposed marriage. Instead, it is about politics and trade agreements, the passage of pilgrims through Frankish territory, the movement of merchants, trade in 'black stones' and cloaks, and political exiles, especially Ecgberht, who was the rival for the kingship of Kent in opposition to Offa's ally, Beorhtric of Wessex. Ecgberht had spent the three (? or thirteen) years between 789 and 802 under Charlemagne's protection in Francia.[300] Alcuin said nothing about the political dimension to Charlemagne's relations with Offa. Nor did the *Gesta abbatum fontanellensium*'s account of Gervold, despite being so anxious to claim Gervold's close friendship with Offa. Charlemagne had clearly been badgered by Offa, for he referred to reading over Offa's letters 'which have been brought to us at different times by the hands of your emissaries'.[301]

Even if a lot has got lost, if the *Gesta* account of Abbot Gervold's career, made fifty years after the event, is credible, and if the customary dating of *c.* 790 be accepted, this creates further difficulties. Of the parties allegedly concerned, the only still-unmarried daughter of Offa at that stage was Aelflaed (she married Aethelred king of Northumbria in 792), and it is she whom Stenton suggested was the woman concerned. But this date works only if Alcuin's allusions *c.* 790 are accepted as referring to a quarrel about a marriage alliance. The *Gesta*'s account mentioned Ecgfrith. His date of birth or when (or if) he was married is not known, though he was crowned

---

[298] *Codex epistolaris carolinus*, ed. Gundlach, Ep. 92, pp. 629–30. See Story, *Carolingian connections*, pp. 198–9.
[299] *MGH Epp.* IV (*Aevi karo.*, II), Nos. 7 and 9.
[300] Charlemagne to Offa, ibid., No. 100, *MGH Epp.* IV. See Story, pp. 195–9. On the black stones see D. P. S. Peacock, 'Charlemagne's black stones: the re-use of Roman columns in early medieval Europe', *Antiquity* 71 (1997), pp. 709–15.
[301] Trans D. Whitelock, *English historical documents*, I (London, 1979), No. 197.

king in 787. On the Frankish side, the ages are not impossible: Charles the Younger was about eighteen in 790 and his sister Bertha about ten. There may be mileage in the notion that it is Offa who was pressing more for this alliance. Altogether, however, there is both so much else involved in relations between Charlemagne, Mercia and Northumbria,[302] and Charlemagne's negative attitude to foreign marriages was otherwise so consistent,[303] that this marriage alliance story seems very unlikely. As already noted, those of Charlemagne's male offspring who were permitted to marry (none of his daughters was officially married) did so to women from within the empire.[304]

In 802, legates from Irene, empress of Byzantium, arrived at Aachen. In response, Jesse of Amiens and Count Helmgaud were sent to Constantinople to conclude peace. They returned the following year accompanied by envoys from the Byzantine emperor Nicephorus (who had succeeded Irene) and the 'written draft of a peace agreement'.[305] An elaborate series of meetings with the rulers of the Danes is described by the royal annalist between 811 and 813, and in 812 peace was also made with Abulaz, the *rex* of the Saracens, and Grimoald, duke of the Beneventans. Diplomatic contacts could also obviate or conclude a period of hostility or one in which Charlemagne's assistance might have been claimed. Thus in 795, when Charlemagne was encamped on the Elbe, legates came from Pannonia to announce that their *tudun* would present himself before Charlemagne and that he wished to become Christian. At Herstelle in 797, Charlemagne received the Saracen abd-Allah, described as a son of the *rex* Ibn Muawiya, who had been driven from Spain into exile to Mauretania by his brother. The following year abd-Allah was sent back to Spain in the company of Louis the Pious. Froia and Basiliscus, the legates of Alfonso king of the Asturias and Galicia, brought a pavilion tent, coats of mail, mules and Moorish prisoners. All these, the Reviser reports, were regarded by the Franks as 'tokens of victory' (*insignia victoriae*) rather

---

[302] See N. Brookes, *The early history of the church of Canterbury* (Leicester, 1984), esp. pp. 117–27; and C. Cubitt, *Anglo-Saxon church councils, c. 650–c. 850* (London, 1995), esp. pp. 182–90.

[303] Compare, of course, the papal diatribe on the subject of foreign wives addressed to Carloman and Charlemagne in 773: see above, pp. 84–8.

[304] See above, p. 93, and compare the small number of Byzantine marriage alliances in the early middle ages and their contexts: A. Davids, 'Marriage negotiations between Byzantium and the west and the name of Theophano in Byzantium (eighth to tenth centuries)', in A. Davids (ed.), *The Empress Theophano: Byzantium and the west at the turn of the first millennium* (Cambridge, 1995), pp. 99–120; and J. Shepard, 'A marriage too far? Maria Lekapena and Peter of Bulgaria', in ibid, pp. 121–49.

[305] See Chrysos, 'Byzantine diplomacy', pp. 38–9.

than gifts. This suggests that Alfonso had successfully asked for Frankish support.

These embassies, moreover, were both a channel for information and military and diplomatic intelligence, and a means of bringing exotic goods and new technology within the Frankish realm.[306] Such information would no doubt have included the practicalities of long-distance travel, the hazards encountered and the wonders observed *en route*. Rare survivals like the eighth-century *Hodoeporicon* of Willibald, with its description of his travels from England to the Holy Land via Sicily and Cyprus,[307] or the later ninth-century pilgrimage of Bernard the Frank, Theudmund from the monastery of San Vincenzo al Volturno, and Stephen from Spain, provide a glimpse of what fellow travellers and embassies might have experienced. Bernard and his companions travelled via the church of St Michael on Monte Gargano in Apulia on the Adriatic coast, down through Bari and Taranto and across the sea to Alexandria and Egypt before reaching Jerusalem, where they stayed in the hospice established by 'the most glorious king Charles'. On their journey home, they sailed 'for sixty days in great discomfort because of the lack of a steady wind' before reaching Rome. There they visited the Lateran church and St Peter's; Bernard commented on the 'countless bodies of the saints' buried in the city. Bernard then parted from his two companions and journeyed on to Mont St Michel near Avranches.[308]

In the reports tracking the progress of legates, there are occasional hints of the difficulties such legates might encounter in dealing with customs officials and local governors, or commandeering transport, quite apart from the risk of dying from disease, privation, as a result of being caught in a foreign war, or in ambushes by brigands on the road. In 806, for example, Frankish legates who had been to see the Persian king managed to get through the Greek lines in Dalmatia safely. They turned up in Aachen the following year in the company of the envoys abd-Allah, from the king of the Persians, and monks from Jerusalem called George (by birth

[306] For a comparative perspective see J. Shepard, 'Information, disinformation and delay in Byzantine diplomacy', *Byzantinische Forschungen* 10 (1985), pp. 223–93; A. D. Lee, 'Embassies as evidence for the movement of military intelligence between the Roman and Sassanian empires', in P. Freeman and D. Kennedy (eds.), *The defence of the Roman and Byzantine east* (Oxford, 1986), pp. 457–81, and Lee, *Information and frontiers: Roman foreign relations in late antiquity* (Cambridge, 1993).
[307] Hugeburc of Heidenheim, *Hodoeporicon* (*Vita Willibaldi*), ed. O. Holder-Egger, *MGH SS* 15, 1, pp. 80–117.
[308] Bernard the Monk, *Itinerarium*, ed. T. Tobler and A. Molinier, *Itinera Hierosolymitana et descriptiones terrae sanctae* (Geneva, 1979), pp. 308–20, trans. J. Wilkinson, *Jerusalem Pilgrims before the Crusades* (Warminster, 1977), pp. 141–5.

Egilbald from Germany, who was abbot of the monastery in Mount) and Felix. The monks were acting as legates for the Patriarch Thomas and had presumably been chosen because they could speak the languages necessary to cope while travelling and at their destination. The emperor then sent them off to Italy to wait for a boat home. The late ninth-century 'Paris conversations' phrase books in Latin and Old High German with many Romance spelllings, moreover, offer some suggestions for purportedly useful phrases for the traveller, from the standard and civil opening gambit 'Which country do you come from' ? (*Gueliche lande cumen ger / de qua patria* ?) to the rude rebuff 'A dog's arse up your nose' (*Vnder ars in tine naso / canis culum in tuo naso*). Other glossaries, such as the Kassel glosses, may also have been designed with travellers, among others, in mind.[309]

Diplomatic gifts were eloquent symbols of the cultural connections of the ruler and an essential link with the exotic which raised him far above his ordinary subjects. The knowledge of their existence, and their addition to the palace treasury or menagerie, functioned as a powerful reminder of the ruler's place in the world.[310] The elephant's death on campaign in Saxony eight years after it had arrived in Francia is also noted. Dicuil, writing his *De orbis mensura* some years after Charlemagne's death, for example, commented on the Frankish people's knowledge of Charlemagne's elephant.[311] A scribe at St Denis near Paris very early in the ninth century, moreover, incorporated an unmistakable elephant's head in an initial B of a copy of Cassiodorus' Commentary on the Psalms.[312] The memory appears to have still been strong enough for an artist to insert two elephants in the spandrels of a canon-table page in the Vivian Bible produced at Tours c. 846,[313] and an ivory carver at about the same time and working in the Loire valley included an elephant in his depiction of the Garden of Eden.[314] An organ had been sent by the Byzantine ruler to Pippin III in 757 and the

---

[309] See W. Braune, *Althochdeutsches Lesebuch* (Tübingen, 1969); C. Edwards, 'German vernacular literature', in McKitterick, *Carolingian culture*, pp. 141–70, at p. 143.

[310] See Helms, *Ulysses' sail*; and below, pp. 372–4.

[311] *ARF* 802 and 810, ed. Kurze, pp. 117 and 131; Dicuil, *Liber de mensuris orbis terrae*, ed. and trans. J. J. Tierney, Scriptores Latini Hiberniae 6 (Dublin, 1967), pp. 82–3.

[312] Paris, BnF lat. 2195, fol. 9v, illustrated in P. Périn and L.-C. Feffer (eds.), *La Neustrie: les pays au nord de la Loire de Dagobert à Charles le Chauve (VIIe–IXe siècles)* (Rouen, 1985), No. 114, pp. 283–4.

[313] Paris, BnF lat. 1, fol. 327v ; illustrated in W. Koehler, *Karolingische Miniaturen*, 1: *Die Schule von Tours* (Berlin, 1930), Plate I.84.

[314] Paris, Musée du Louvre, illustrated in *La Neustrie*, ed. Périn and Feffer, No. 120, pp. 292–93, and J. Hubert, J. Porcher and W. Volbach, *Carolingian art* (London, 1970), Fig. 218, p. 237.

pope sent books to Charlemagne.[315] The Persian envoys in 806 brought pavilion and entrance tents of fine-coloured linen dyed many different colours, silk garments, perfumes, unguents, balsam, and a fabulous brass water clock, with a mechanism to make twelve little balls strike bells and twelve figurines of horsemen appear in twelve windows to mark the passing of the hours.[316] At Pavia in 801 Charlemagne was informed of the arrival of envoys from the king of the Persians at Pisa. He received them together with one from the 'Muslim ruler of Africa' (at Fossatum). It was they who reported that Isaac the Jew, whom Charlemagne had sent to Persia four years earlier with the Frankish envoys Lantfrid and Sigismund (who were now dead), was on his way back with presents. One of these gifts proved to be the elephant which was eventually delivered to Aachen in July 802.[317]

The annalists' accounts of Charlemagne's conduct of diplomacy are, therefore, not just highly effective image-making. They are also a crucial indication of the effectiveness of information-gathering, with reports of campaigns mounted, news of famine and rebellion, events in distant parts as well as closer to home, and the degree to which the king himself was at the centre of a network of communications that extended far beyond the limits of his jurisdiction. The information available to the annalists benefited no doubt from the king's own movements, the work of the royal notaries and *missi dominici*, and the constant contacts with envoys bringing letters and oral messages from elsewhere in his kingdom as well as farther afield. In 793, for example, there is a passing reference made by the Reviser to Charlemagne's calling off an expedition to Pannonia because he received news that the army of Frisians that Count Theodoric had been bringing had been intercepted and destroyed at Rüstringen.[318] That same year Charlemagne had also been informed of another Saxon rebellion and of the killing of Frankish counts in Septimania by some invading Saracens.

---

[315] ARF 757, ed. Kurze, p. 14; and, for example, *Codex epistolaris carolinus*, ed. Gundlach, Ep. 89 p. 626: see B. Bischoff, 'Die Hofbibliothek Karls des Großen', in Bischoff, *Mittelalterliche Studien*, III (Stuttgart, 1981), pp. 149–69 at pp. 151–3. On the organ see J. Herrin, 'Constantinople, Rome and the Franks in the seventh and eighth centuries', in Shepard and Franklin, *Byzantine diplomacy*, pp. 91–107. On silk, see A. Muthesius, 'Silken diplomacy', in ibid., pp. 237–48.

[316] *ARF* 807, ed. Kurze, pp. 123–4.

[317] See R. McKitterick, 'The migration of ideas in the early middle ages: ways and means', in R. Bremmer, K. Dekkers and P. Lendinara (eds.), *Storehouses of wholesome learning: accumulation and dissemination of encyclopaedic knowledge in the early middle ages*, Mediaevalia Groningana (Leuven, Paris and Stirling, 2007), pp. 1–17.

[318] *RVARF* 793, ed. Kurze, p. 93.

CONCLUSION: THE MASTERING OF SPACE

We should also pause to consider both the reality of diplomatic contacts underlying these narrative accounts and what such visits suggest, first of all, concerning the role of communications and intelligence-gathering in the maintenance of Charlemagne's relations with the outside world. Secondly, how do they relate to the order within his realm and the mastering of space, which have been the focus of so much of this chapter?[319] The embassies arriving in the Frankish kingdom, together with those sent by Charlemagne elsewhere, suggest demonstrative diplomacy on Charlemagne's part. It was based more on a concept of superiority, if not supremacy, and a careful policy of control of the *limitrophes* principalities in a manner reminiscent of the later Roman emperors.[320] The increasing emphasis on diplomacy may well reflect a change of policy in the course of Charlemagne's reign and thus be part of the consolidation of the process of conquest possible once the Saxons and Avars had been subjugated and defeated. The limits to expansion, in short, were perceived by Charlemagne himself rather than being imposed by the greater strength of some of the peoples on the periphery, even though realism about, and an assessment of, that very strength may well have played a role. Coupled with the archaeological remains of both Frankish and non-Frankish forts and ramparts from this early Carolingian period, some of which no doubt had an important symbolic as well as, or rather than, a strategic function (much like Hadrian's Wall or Offa's Dyke in Britain), the administrative evidence and deployment of officials suggest a carefully structured topography of power.[321] Charlemagne's empire was indeed a 'sophisticated conception of political space', with a clear differentiation between its central and peripheral spheres of influence within a 'network of centres of power and lines of communication'.[322]

---

[319] See L. Agnew and S. Corbridge (eds.), *Mastering space: hegemony, territory and international economy* (London and New York, 1995).

[320] On the latter see A. Kazhdan, 'The notion of Byzantine diplomacy', in Shepard and Franklin, *Byzantine diplomacy*, pp. 3–24.

[321] J. Henning, 'Civilization versus barbarians? Fortification techniques and politics in Carolingian and Ottonian borderlands', in F. Curta (ed.), *Borders, barriers and ethnogenesis: frontiers in late antiquity and the middle ages* (Turnhout, 2005), pp. 23–34; and M. Hardt, 'The *Limes saxoniae* as part of the eastern borderlands of the Frankish and Ottonian-Salian empire', in ibid., pp. 35–55; M. Hardt, 'Hesse, Elbe, Saale and the frontiers of the Carolingian empire', in W. Pohl, I. Wood and H. Reimitz (eds.), *The transformation of frontiers: from late antiquity to the Carolingians*, The Transformation of the Roman World 10 (Leiden, 2001), pp. 219–32.

[322] I have here applied to Charlemagne's Frankish empire a more general definition supplied by W. Pohl, 'Frontiers and ethnic identities: some final considerations', in Curta, *Borders, barriers and ethnogensis*, pp. 255–65, at p. 261.

Recent scholarly discussions have inclined towards the recognition of conscious policy in the consolidation of the Frankish borders by Charlemagne, though the underlying rationale is disputed.[323] His father and uncle had had to regain dominion of the 'provinces' under Merovingian rule that Charles Martel had controlled, according to the Reviser of the *Annales regni francorum*.[324] Charlemagne himself had an understanding of the border areas or marches (*marca*) of his kingdom from very early in his reign.[325] Matthias Hardt has even suggested the possible role of historical recreation in Charlemagne's conquests, to the degree that there is a remarkable, if fleeting, coincidence between what the emperor Augustus had hoped to achieve and what Charlemagne actually did.[326] Certainly, previous limits of conquests by great rulers could be used as the starting point for greater achievements, and there is no reason to doubt the inspiration provided by the knowledge, derived from Roman history, of past conquests.[327] The Roman tradition of defining borders,[328] and the Lombard precision about areas considered foreign,[329] may also have had an influence both on the Franks' definition of their own territory, and on their understanding of themselves in relation to other peoples. Charlemagne established Frankish rule over the western portion of the old Roman empire and expanded beyond the Elbe to embrace Saxon territory. At the same time, he maintained varying degrees of negotiated acknowledgment of Frankish power from the Slavs beyond the Elbe, in Istria, Dalmatia, and eastern Bavaria.[330]

---

[323] Summarized in T. Reuter, 'The end of Carolingian expansion', in Godman and Collins, *Charlemagne's heir*, pp. 391–404.

[324] *RVARF* 741, ed. Kurze, p. 3.

[325] See ARF 788, ed. Kurze, p. 84; the capitularies for Aquitaine (768/9), Herstal (779) and Thionville (805), *MGH Cap.* 1, Nos. 18, 20, 43, 44; and the discussion by H. Wolfram, 'The creation of the Carolingian frontier system, c. 800', in Pohl, Wood and Reimitz, *The transformation of frontiers*, pp. 233–45.

[326] Hardt, 'Hesse, Elbe, Saale and the frontiers of the Carolingian empire'.

[327] See McKitterick, *Perceptions of the past*, pp. 59–61; and below, pp. 370–2.

[328] C. R. Whittaker, *Frontiers of the Roman empire: a social and economic study* (Baltimore and London, 1994).

[329] W. Pohl, 'Frontiers in Lombard Italy: the laws of Ratchis and Aistulf', in Pohl, Wood and Reimitz, *The transformation of frontiers*, pp. 117–42.

[330] M. Hardt, 'Linien und Säume, Zonen und Räume an der Ostgrenze des Reiches im frühen und hohen Mittelalter', and H. Reimitz, 'Grenzen und Grenzüberschreitungen im karolingischen Mitteleuropa', in W. Pohl and H. Reimitz (eds.), *Grenze und Differenz im frühen Mittelalter*, Österreichische Akademie der Wissenschaften, phil.-hist. Klasse, Denkschriften 287 (Forschungen zur Geschichte des Mittelalters 1) (Vienna, 2000), pp. 39–56 and 105–66; J. M. H. Smith, 'Confronting identities: the rhetoric and reality of a Carolingian frontier;', in W. Pohl and M. Diesenberger (eds.), *Integration und Herrschaft: ethnische Identitäten und soziale Organisation im Frühmittelalter*, Österreichische Akademie der Wissenschaften, phil.-hist. Klasse, Denkschriften 301 (Forschungen zur Geschichte des Mittelalters 3) (Vienna, 2002), pp. 169–204 (with reference to Brittany); and the brief comments by I. N. Wood, 'Missionaries and the Christian frontier', in Pohl, Wood and Reimitz, *Transformation of frontiers*, pp. 209–18 at pp. 217–18; and T. Reuter, 'Charlemagne and the world beyond the Rhine', in Story, *Charlemagne*, pp. 184–94.

In meeting and negotiating with foreign envoys and rulers as representatives of Charlemagne, the Franks' own identity and membership of a
distinct political entity would have been reinforced. One major mechanism
in the limits of Carolingian expansion, and one to which insufficient
weight has hitherto been accorded, was the essential negotiation of territorial jurisdiction on both sides and what this implies about the construction of identities and perception of the 'Other' on the Franks' part, quite
apart from the issues of fixing the topography of the borders and the
benefits of peace.[331] In other words, more notice should be taken of the
personal affiliations that expansion and consolidation entailed and how
these might have gained substance within the institutional framework on
which historians have tended to concentrate hitherto.[332] Timothy Reuter
drew attention to the capitularies which mention *defensio patriae*, defence
of the fatherland.[333] We can also note the capitulary relating to military
service which identifies specific groups of people in relation to border
regions.[334]

It was not a matter of the Franks or Charlemagne simply deciding where
and when to stop, being forced to cease expansion as a result of the strength
of resistance, adopting a new defensive posture or an ideology of peace, or
even 'war weariness'.[335] It was, first of all, the case that the Franks' enemies,
as well as those who simply found themselves to be neighbours of the
Franks, had their own position to assert or safeguard. Franks as well as
Danes, Wilzi, Abodrites, Wends, Avars, Greeks, Bulgars, Croats,
Beneventans, Saracens and Bretons had an interest in maintaining internal
and cross-border peace insofar as border regions, sometimes labelled
marches from the Frankish perspective, could be defined or patrolled. In
these shared border regions, the issues of jurisdiction, legal rights to
property, and multiple loyalties among an inevitably mixed population,
would have been at their most volatile, though there is very little documentary material to enable us to work out quite how social and legal affairs
were conducted on a quotidian basis.[336] Their own political systems meant
that the leaders of peoples beyond the Frankish empire could exploit the

---

[331] Wood, 'Missionaries and the Christian frontier', pp. 250–52; and P. Kershaw, *Peaceful like Solomon: peace, power and the early medieval political imagination* (Oxford, forthcoming).
[332] See, however, F. Curta, 'Introduction', in Curta, *Borders, barriers and ethnogenesis*, pp. 1–9, and esp. p. 5.
[333] *MGH Cap.* I, No. 71 (811), c. 2, p. 161.   [334] *MGH Cap.* I, No. 74 (811), c. 8, p. 167.
[335] See Reuter, 'The end of Carolingian expansion'; and Reuter, 'Plunder and tribute in the Carolingian empire', *Transactions of the Royal Historical Society*, 5th series, 35 (1985), pp. 75–94.
[336] Wolfram, 'The creation of the Carolingian frontier system', pp. 233–46, and Kershaw, *Peaceful like Solomon*.

political advantage and prestige of being seen to treat successfully with a foreign ruler and to be on terms of the exchange of knowledge and high-status artefacts. The Frankish ruler benefited in the same way from such an extension of his range of contacts. Differences between peoples, in terms of language or religion, could simply be acknowledged, and did not even have to be resolved in terms of ephemeral or occasional alliances such as that which persisted between the Franks and the Abodrites for so much of Charlemagne's reign. The Lorsch annalist made a telling comment in this respect when he accounted for the success of Thrasco, *dux* of the Abodrites, and his men against the Saxons north of the Elbe. Despite being pagan, the 'faith of the Christians and of the lord king aided them' so that they were able to defeat the Saxons.[337] Political frontiers were key elements in the formation, or affirmation, of ethnic identities, for they assisted the process of definition or self-definition both on the part of the Franks and on that of their political acquaintances.[338]

Secondly, expansion of the empire and deciding on the limits of Frankish royal control did not have to be a process of aggressive confrontation. It could instead be a process of the mutual recognition of identity enacted through the rituals of diplomatic meetings between envoys, audiences offered by the king himself, the presentations of gifts symbolizing the different regions ruled by non-Frankish, and thus (to the Franks) exotic, peoples. During Charlemagne's reign, the Franks' horizons on earth were thus extended to the limits of the known world.

The Franks' Christian faith also directed their gaze to heaven. The larger definition of the political and geographical space of the Frankish realm explored in this chapter entailed the simultaneous expansion of a Christian Latin culture, the wider adoption of a common language and of literate modes of communication and record, and an apprehension of the spiritual dimension of the Franks' place in the world. The practical underpinning of such a cultural strategy is the focus of the following chapter.

---

[337] Lorsch annals 798, ed. G. Pertz, *MGH SS* I, p. 37.
[338] As Curta and Pohl have emphaized; Curta, 'Introduction', in Curta, *Borders, barriers and ethnogenesis*, pp. 1–9 at pp. 8–9; and W. Pohl, 'Frontiers and ethnic identities: some final considerations', in ibid., pp. 255–65.

CHAPTER 5

Correctio, *knowledge and power*

INTRODUCTION

When Charlemagne was six years old, he was placed by his father Pippin
III at the head of the escort provided for Pope Stephen for the final miles
to Ponthion at the end of the pope's long journey across the Alps. Fifty
years later, another pope, Leo III, crossed the Alps and spent Christmas in
the Frankish kingdom. On that occasion it was Charlemagne's principal
heir, Charles the Younger, who escorted the papal entourage from
St Maurice d'Agaune to its winter quarters at the royal palace of
Quierzy. Only after Christmas did Charlemagne proceed to Aachen to
spend the rest of the winter, while the pope was escorted back to Ravenna
via Bavaria.

The arrival of Pope Stephen at Ponthion in 754 coincided with the
Feast of the Epiphany, but thereafter the pope moved to Paris and
St Denis.[1] It was there, in the church of the martyr Denis, and of his
supposed companions Rusticus and Eleutherius, that the pope anointed
Pippin as king of the Franks.[2] Charlemagne and his brother Carloman, in
their turn, were anointed as heirs of the new dynasty, whose ultimate
source of authority was God. The version of this event recorded in the
Clausula de unctione Pippini offers an inkling of how the pope's actions
were understood in subsequent years: the *Clausula* noted that this consecration was by the intercession of the holy apostles Peter and Paul, that
Pippin was made *patricius* as well as *rex*, and that the pope 'bound all, on
pain of interdict and excommunication, never to presume in future to
elect a king begotten by any men other than those whom the bounty of
God has seen fit to raise up and has decided to confirm and consecrate by

---

[1] *LP*, Life 94, cc. 24–9, ed. L. Duchesne, *Le Liber pontificalis* (Paris, 1886–1892), I, pp. 447–8.
[2] There is a possibility that *rusticus* and *eleutherius* were originally epithets describing Denis rather than
references to fellow martyrs.

the intercession of the holy apostles through the hands of their vicar, the most blessed pontiff.[3]

The papal anointing in 754, its role in the legitimation of the Carolingian dynasty and its contribution to the ideology of Carolingian kingship have long been acknowledged.[4] Special links were created with the pope and the Christian church and its saints, not only the Roman apostles Peter and Paul, but also St Denis. Further, there was the explicitly divine source of royal authority. All these entailed certain obligations. Some of these obligations in relation to the papacy during the reigns of Popes Stephen II(III), Paul I, Hadrian I and Leo III, and to the protection of the territorial interests of the Roman church, have already been addressed.[5] Although accustomed to wielding power in the Frankish kingdom, and although Pippin's usurpation undoubtedly needed all the extra bolstering it could find, there remained no guarantee that the Carolingian family would indeed be able to maintain their position. The ideological support lent by the pope's visit and Pippin's actions in relation to the church subsequently were a strong message to Pippin's sons of one means by which the Carolingian family's hold on royal authority could be maintained and developed.

Yet the fulfilment of these religious obligations in terms of personal piety and observance depended on the individual response of each ruler. The alleged reason for Pope Leo's visit in 804, fifty years later, underlines this. The *Annales regni francorum* claims that Charlemagne had asked the pope about a rumour of the discovery of a relic of Christ's blood in Mantua. Although Leo appears to have failed to discover anything and to have converted this enquiry into an invitation to visit Francia, Charlemagne's reported interest in a holy relic acts as a reminder of a practical and material element of his religious devotion, at least in the last years of his reign. An obvious question, however, is whether particular acts of devotion, let alone large attempts to fulfil royal religious obligations, were indeed so consistent or articulated and directed in the same ways throughout his decades as king. Can specific phases or shifting patterns of religious policy and royal piety be observed in the course of his reign? Further, in what instances, if

[3] *Clausula de unctione pippini*, ed. A. Stoclet, 'La "Clausula de unctione Pippini regis": mises au point et nouvelles hypothèses', *Francia* 8 (1980), pp. 1–42; and see Stoclet, 'La Clausula de unctione pippini regis, vingt ans après', *Revue belge de philologie et d'histoire* 78 (2000), pp. 719–71, who argues even more strongly for a tenth-century date and the problematic status of this text. But see above, p. 000.

[4] P. E. Schramm, *Kaiser, Könige und Päpste* (Stuttgart, 1968).   [5] Above, pp. 114–16.

any, was the royal court, however the 'court' is understood, the location or generator of manifestations of royal religious devotion?

Both a preoccupation with legitimation and policy, and an assumption of an uncomplicated applicability of evidence from late in Charlemagne's reign to his early actions, have tended to obscure the dynamic of the practical and devotional arena of the king's cultural and religious activities and interests. Similarly, a concentration on political ideology, related partly to possession of the title of emperor after 800 and partly to retro-spective credit for the conversion of the pagan Saxons, has diverted atten-tion away from the gradual build-up of momentum and definition in Charlemagne's religious and cultural policies. These in their turn, more-over, were part of the workings of communication and government within the kingdom already considered in the previous chapter. Certainly, viewed as a whole, the half century of Charlemagne's rule allows us to appreciate the extraordinary ways in which his promotion of correct thinking and correct language was an essential component of an overall strategy of control. In this, the concept of *correctio*, the acquisition of knowledge and the exercise of power were yoked together. Yet we need to consider how all this was achieved, as well as how far the outcome was to create simply the beginnings of a distinctive cultural identity within the Frankish kingdom.

It is not so much the formation of royal religious ideology with which I shall be principally concerned in this chapter, therefore, for this has been amply considered elsewhere.[6] Nor shall I consider in any detail the phases of the Carolingian reforms, Charlemagne's relations with the church, or Charlemagne's reforms in relation to the Christian religion and learning, for these too are familiar.[7] Instead, and despite the exhaustive consider-ations of the so-called 'Carolingian Renaissance' now available,[8] there remains room to consider the implications of the diverse texts and artefacts, acquired or produced during the decades of Charlemagne's reign and associated with the royal household, within the context of the development of his overall religious and cultural strategies. Many of these texts and objects have already been considered in other contexts in this book, but

[6] N. Staubach, 'Cultus divinus und karolingische Reform', *Frühmittelalterliche Studien* 18 (1984), pp. 546–81; J. L.Nelson, 'Kingship and empire', in R. McKitterick (ed.), *Carolingian culture: emulation and innovation* (Cambridge, 1994), pp. 52–87.
[7] See the excellent discussion by M. de Jong, 'Charlemagne and the church', in J. Story (ed.), *Charlemagne: empire and society* (Manchester, 2005), pp. 103–35.
[8] *KdG* II (1965); McKitterick, *Carolingian culture*; J. J. Contreni, 'The Carolingian Renaissance: education and literary culture', in *NCMH*, II, pp. 709–57.

I wish in this chapter to focus on how they present the many facets of Carolingian cultural identity as it was shaped in the course of Charlemagne's reign.

THE SACRED TOPOGRAPHY OF THE FRANKISH KINGDOM

It is in the light of their early exposure to royal leadership in matters of religion, and the close association with the papacy, that the earliest recorded actions of Charlemagne and his brother Carloman on their accession to the throne need to be seen. Each was anointed king in an episcopal seat (Soissons and Noyon) with strong Merovingian saints (Medard and Eligius) as their patrons. Each insisted on the spiritual dimension of their responsibilities, and spelt out their duties towards the religious institutions which provided a fundamental element of the earthly framework within which their royal power was exercised. The papal letters addressed to Charlemagne by Stephen II and Hadrian I reiterate the pope's expectations of the Frankish king's responsibility to defend St Peter and the Roman church and to heed the pope.[9] Hadrian added the rallying cry in 774 that 'the Lord almighty . . . will prostrate other barbarian races beneath your royal feet'.[10] Although the popes were so urgent about the Frankish king's responsibilities out of the need for military assistance, the insistence on the king's God-given authority and responsibilities in letter after letter in the early 770s and 780s can surely be presumed to have made some impression on a young king shaping his policies.

The mutual duty of the king and church to support each other is, of course, something Pippin and Charlemagne took over from their Merovingian predecessors.[11] Protection of and devotion to the church, and the importance of the connection between the pope and the Carolingian family, were facts of Charlemagne's life from the moment his family became royal. This is most evident in the papal letters already discussed in a previous chapter, and in the prayer clauses and the explanations provided for the king's gifts stated in the surviving donation charters made by Pippin III and Charlemagne.[12] The power of prayer is ranged

---

[9] *Codex epistolaris carolinus*, Epp. 44, 45, ed. Gundlach, pp. 558–63.   [10] Ibid,. No. 53, p. 575.
[11] E. Ewig, 'Zum christlichen Königsgedanken im Frühmittelalter', in T. Mayer (ed.), *Das Königtum*, Vorträge und Forschungen 3 (Constance, 1956), pp. 7–73; J. M. Wallace-Hadrill, *The Frankish church* (Oxford, 1983), esp. pp. 94–110; and above, pp. 69–70, 75.
[12] E. Ewig, 'Der Gebetsdienst der Kirchen in den Urkunden der späteren Karolinger', in H. Maurer and H. Patze (eds.), *Festschrift für Berent Schwineköper zu seinem siebzigsten Geburtstag* (Sigmaringen, 1982), pp. 45–86; and above, p. 82.

alongside worldly demonstrations of authority and physical strength. An early indication of this is the donation charter to Prüm in 762, in which Prüm was taken under Pippin's protection and that of his heirs.[13] Further examples come from the *arengae* in charters from the beginning of Charlemagne's reign and are subsequently reiterated in many of his later charters. Yet there is an additional emphasis: the support of the church is both a royal custom and a royal obligation.

In the confirmation of tithes to the church as early as March 769, for example, the royal charter stated on behalf of the king that 'it is our belief that if in all matters we grant the petitions of the clergy the Lord will reward us for it'.[14] In confirming the grant of immunity to the monks of Corbie later the same month, the charter insisted that the reaffirmation of concessions granted by Charlemagne's royal predecessors, the Merovingian kings (Childeric, Theodoric, Clovis, Childebert, Dagobert and Charlemagne's own father Pippin III), constituted an exercise of royal custom.[15] This charter states, moreover, that such an action redounded to the king's favour and to the stability of his kingdom. Another charter reiterated the inheritance of royal responsibility, when it referred to the king reading 'in the confirmations and instructions of the earlier kings what grants were made from of old and granted them anew'. On 2 September 774, when granting Oppenheim on the Rhine to the monastery of Lorsch on the occasion of the translation of Nazarius and dedication of the church, the charter noted the special royal duty to support the saints: 'Whatever we grant or confirm to the resting places of the saints, we believe without doubt redounds to our eternal bliss though the protection of our Lord.'[16]

In granting Fulda the right to choose its abbot that same year, the king's charter again affirmed the conviction that the king thought he should lend an especially kindly ear to petitions from the clergy, 'seeing that perfect faith fails not to obtain the favour of the Most High'. In return to this positive response to their petition, the monks are continually 'to pray for the eternal safety and felicity of our country and for the wellbeing of our selves, our wife and our children'. Charlemagne's concession of lands in the Breisgau to St Denis in 790 expresses a further dimension to the royal responsibility. It is one that is an essential underlay to every royal grant, whatever else the *arengae* offer concerning the royal office and the king's

[13] *DKar.* 1, No. 16, and see J. Semmler, 'Pippin III. und die fränkische Klöster', *Francia* 3 (1975), pp. 88–146.
[14] *DKar.* 1, No. 56.   [15] Ibid., No. 57.   [16] Ibid., No. 82.

role in respect to the clergy and the saints. Although the gift to St Denis is made for the love of God, the respect due to the saint, the salvation of his soul and the stability of the realm, the grant also constituted a legal decision. Lands once part of the royal fisc had been illicitly acquired and by various means had come into the possession of St Denis, whose abbot then restored them to the king. The king now made over possession back to the monastery.[17]

These charter clauses provide an indication of how the king perceived his role. The officials who drew them up were acting in the name of the king. Even if they may have expressed his wishes formally and formulaically, they nevertheless articulate a special perception of the king's role, and one that is borne out by other royal actions and admonitions. There is a powerful consistency throughout all the statements of pious intent and religious justification in the administrative documents of Charlemagne.

To this manifestation of royal religious observance should be added the substance of the king's gifts, namely grants of immunity and freedom from tolls, freedom to elect the abbot, royal protection, and gifts of land, revenues and moveable goods. The creation of royal monasteries can be regarded as in part prompted by strategy and policy to establish enclaves of support and as a consequence of the acquisition of new territories in Aquitaine, Bavaria and Italy, though it is striking that no new monastery was actually founded by Charlemagne himself.[18] Not one genuine foundation charter survives, and even among all those judged to be spurious by Mühlbacher, only one monastery, Neustadt-am-Main, made a claim to being founded by Charlemagne.[19] Instead, Charlemagne simply took over the patronage of existing foundations by granting lands and various privileges, made some of them into 'royal monasteries' by taking them under his special protection (a move often accompanied by immunity and freedom of abbatial elections), confirmed existing lands or rights to property, or settled disputes over land.[20] The pattern of Charlemagne's monastic

---

[17] Ibid., Nos. 86 and 166.
[18] On the pattern of charter survival see above, pp. 197–9. See also J. Semmler, 'Episcopi potestas und karolingische Klosterpolitik', in A. Borst (ed.), *Mönchtum, Episkopat und Adel zur Gründungszeit des Klosters Reichenau*, Vorträge und Forschungen 20 (Sigmaringen, 1974), pp. 305–95.
[19] *DKar.* I, No. 252. See also A. Remensnyder, *Remembering kings past: monastic foundation legends in medieval southern France* (Ithaca, 1995).
[20] B. Rosenwein, *Negotiating space: power, restraint and privileges of immunity in early medieval Europe* (Manchester, 1999); and compare P. Fouracre, 'Eternal light and earthly needs: practical aspects of the development of Frankish immunities', in W. Davies and P. Fouracre (eds.), *Property and power in the early middle ages* (Cambridge, 1995), pp. 53–81.

endowment and his monastic policy as a whole seems far more directed, from the beginning of his reign onwards, at exerting influence, if not control, over the monasteries. Such control had a moral dimension as well, in that support of each monastery's patron saint became the ultimate responsibility of the king, and it involved the way monks cultivated the saint and lived regular lives, enabling them to offer up effective prayer.[21] In this way, Charlemagne built up a sacred adjunct to his own power as king by promoting monastic prayer, support of the clergy and devotion to the saints, and by placing men loyal to him in abbacies. The abbots played an increasingly integrated role in the politics of the Frankish kingdom in Charlemagne's reign.[22] The abbots' attendance at synods, their role as *missi dominici* and as advisers to the king, such as the little group of abbots from St Germain des Prés, St Martin of Tours, Lorsch and St Riquier who were among the witnesses to his will in 811, are elements of the government of the realm as prominent and essential as those of the bishops and counts.[23]

Nor was it only monasteries that were enriched and abbots who were appointed; Frankish religious energy was also directed towards the re-organization of the metropolitans and ecclesiastical provinces, the creation of new bishoprics in Saxony and Frisia, appointments to bishoprics throughout the empire, and the encouragement of new church-building. In that most of the evidence about these matters is in the royal capitularies and conciliar records of assemblies presided over by the king, his approval of the decisions is clear, even if his own initiative in every such project must remain a strong probability rather than a certainty.[24]

---

[21] See the comments by P. Fouracre, 'The origin of the Carolingian attempt to regulate the cult of saints', in J. Howard Johnston and P. A. Hayward (eds.), *The cult of the saints in late antiquity and the early middle ages* (Oxford, 1999), pp. 143–66. For a case study of the role of patron saints, see T. Head, *Hagiography and the cult of saints: the diocese of Orleans, 800–1200* (Cambridge, 1990). The *locus classicus* remains A. Angenendt, '"Mit reinen Händen": das Motiv der kultischen Reinheit in der abendländischen Askese', in G. Jenal and S. Haarländer (eds.), *Herrschaft, Kirche, Kultur: Beiträge zur Geschichte des Mittelalters. Festschrift für Friedrich Prinz zu seinem 65. Geburtstag*, Monographien zur Geschichte des Mittelalters 37 (Stuttgart, 1993), pp. 297–316. See also F. Felten, *Äbte und Laienäbte im Frankenreich: Studie zum Verhältnis von Staat und Kirche im früheren Mittelalter*, Monographien zur Geschichte des Mittelalters 20 (Stuttgart, 1980), pp. 174–256; S. Wood, *The proprietary church in the medieval west* (Oxford, 2006); and Rosenwein, *Negotiating space*, pp. 99–134.

[22] J. Semmler, 'Karl der Große und das fränkische Mönchtum', *KdG*, II, pp. 255–89; F. Felten, *Äbte und Laienäbte im Frankenreich. Studien zum Verhältnis von Staat und Kirche im früheren Mittelalter*, Monographien zur Geschichte des Mittelalters 20 (Stuttgart, 1980), esp. pp. 174–257; and M. de Jong, 'Carolingian monasticism: the power of prayer', in *NCMH*, II, pp. 622–53.

[23] *Vita Karoli*, c. 33, ed. Halphen, p. 100.   [24] See below, pp. 299–305.

THE BISHOPS

The Frankish bishops' power and influence, their wealth and their closeness to the king are crucial elements of the integration of secular and ecclesiastical matters in the eighth and ninth centuries. An indication of their wealth and emulation of the ruler is their own establishments, of which the traces of the episcopal palace complex at Rouen dating from the end of the eighth and beginning of the ninth century offer a tantalizing glimpse.[25] Such cities as are mentioned in the *Divisio regnorum* of 806, moreover, are predominantly episcopal *civitates* in combination with established political territories such as Austrasia, Neustria, Saxony, Frisia or Bavaria. It is not until the description of the territorial divisions for the grandsons of Charlemagne in 843, however, that Frankish sacred and political topography is most apparent. Then, the kingdoms were defined in terms of regions in relation to major rivers, to *civitates*, that is, to ecclesiastical dioceses, and to counties. Yet the apparent solidity of the ecclesiastical structures of the Frankish realm, and the authority of the bishops that is so prominent a feature of the reign of Louis the Pious, were decades in the making, and the role of the king in this process needs to be determined.

Even by 768, the Frankish church was a complex organization in terms of ecclesiastical provinces, metropolitans and suffragan bishops. Many sees traced their history from the Gallo-Roman period, but few had had an uninterrupted sequence of incumbents. Despite the difficulty of determining who was occupying particular sees, or which sees may have been vacant at the time of Charlemagne's accession (a provisional list is appended below), three points emerge. The first is that Charlemagne inherited a convocation of bishops who had assumed office during Pippin's reign and represented most of the ecclesiastical provinces of Frankish Gaul and the Rhineland insofar as the provinces themselves were clearly defined at that stage. Only the provinces of Embrun, Bordeaux and Eauze/Auch have too many gaps to be certain of the succession of bishops in those sees; there is also little information for many of the sees south of the Loire before the late 780s or early 790s. One important source of information about the bishops at the beginning of Charlemagne's reign, however, is the list of those who

---

[25] J. Le Maho, 'Die erzbischöfliche Pfalz von Rouen', in L. Fenske, J. Jarnut and M. Wemhoff (eds.), *Splendor palatii: Neue Forschungen zu Paderborn und anderen Pfalzen der Karolingerzeit*, Deutsche Königspfalzen: Beiträge zu ihrer historischen und archäologischen Erforschung 5, Veröffentlichungen des Max-Planck-Instituts für Geschichte 11/5 (Göttingen, 2001), pp. 193–210.

attended the Council of Rome in 769, which was included in one Frankish copy of the *Liber pontificalis*.[26]

Wilichar of Sens, in particular, figured prominently in the first session of the Council in Rome in relation to the anti-Pope Constantine.[27] A major item on the agenda was the veneration of images and anathematization of the recent Byzantine iconoclasts (a reference to the council of Hieria of 754). But this council was also closely concerned with Roman and papal politics; it was there that Constantine, the former pretender to the papacy, was examined 'on why he as a layman had presumed to intrude into the apostolic see and perpetrate this error and wicked novelty on God's church'.[28] The council went on to condemn Constantine, annul all his ordinations and consecrations, and declare, along with various other provisions regulating papal elections, that no layman should ever presume to be promoted to the papacy, nor should anyone in orders unless he had already risen through the ecclesiastical grades to be cardinal deacon or priest.[29] Frankish participation in this Roman Council of 769 was an affirmation of the standing the Frankish church had attained over the two decades since the Pippinid mayors, in concert with Boniface of Mainz and Chrodegang of Metz, had first promoted ecclesiastical reform.[30]

Secondly, if we add the names of bishops attending the synod in Rome to those who appear to have been in office when Charlemagne and his brother Carloman became kings, it can be seen from Table 6 that not all sees in each ecclesiastical province were occupied.

Of these, eight bishops – of Reims, Rouen, Verdun, Eichstätt, Mainz, Würzburg, Fritzlar/Buraburg and Nevers – had been in office at the time of the papal visit in 754. The only bishops still in office in 768 who had been the incumbents of their sees for the whole of Pippin's reign as well were the

[26] For the political context, see above, p. 83; and *LP*, Life 96, cc. 16–24, ed. Duchesne, I, pp. 473–7.

[27] *LP*, Life 97, c. 5, ed. Duchesne, I, p. 487; and *Codex epistolaris carolinus*, ed. Gundlach, Ep. 48, pp. 566–7.

[28] *LP*, Life 96, c. 18, ed. Duchesne, I, p. 475; trans. Davis, *Lives*, p. 98. Compare *MGH Conc.* II.i, No. 14, pp. 74–92.

[29] On the context see P. Llewellyn, *Rome in the dark ages* (London, 1993); and T. F. X. Noble, *The republic of St Peter: the birth of the papal state, 680–825* (Philadelphia, 1984). For the Council see W. Hartmann, *Die Synoden der Karolingerzeit im Frankenreich und in Italien* (Paderborn, Munich and Vienna, 1989), pp. 84–6; J. Herrin, *The formation of Christendom* (Oxford, 1987), pp. 393–6; W. Levison, *England and the Continent in the eighth century* (Oxford, 1946), p. 128.

[30] Levison, *England and the Continent*, pp. 70–93; J. Schneider (ed.), *Saint Chrodegang: communications présentées au colloque tenu à Metz à l'occasion du douzième centenaire de sa mort* (Metz, 1967); J. M. Wallace Hadrill, *The Frankish church* (Oxford, 1983), pp. 162–77; and M. Claussen, *The reform of the Frankish church: Chrodegang of Metz and the* regula canonicorum *in the eighth century* (Cambridge, 2004).

Table 6 *Frankish Bishops in 768*
Provinces' names in capitals; the bishops of the sees marked with
an asterisk are listed in the *Liber pontificalis* as attending the Synod
of Rome in 769.

REIMS	Beauvais, Cambrai, Chalon, Soissons, *Reims, Senlis, *Amiens
ROUEN	Bayeux, Evreux, Rouen
TOURS	Angers, Le Mans, Tours
TRIER	Trier, Verdun
MAINZ	Chur, Constance, Eichstätt, *Mainz, Speier, Strasbourg, *Würzburg, Buraburg/Fritzlar
COLOGNE	Utrecht, Cologne, Liège
SENS	Auxerre, *Meaux, Nevers, Paris
BOURGES	Limoges, Bourges, Cahors
NARBONNE	Narbonne
ARLES	Carpentras, Marseille
LYON	Belley, Sitten (Sion), possibly Lyon (Madalbert 754–?)
VIENNE	Vienne, Avignon

missionary bishops Willibald of Eichstätt (741-86) and Witta of Fritzlar/ Buraburg (741–86).

Thirdly, a number of bishops, including many of those who attended the synod of Rome, appear to have assumed office, or to be attested for the first time as holding office, only in late 768 or 769. The new kings, therefore, appear to have sent new bishops to Rome. They are listed in Table 7.

As sees fell vacant and new bishoprics were established, so appointments may have been influenced by the king.[31] In some instances, such as the elevation of Theodulf of Orleans in 788, or of Leidrad of Lyon in 797, scholars from the court circle were preferred. The process of selection of the pioneering incumbents of the new sees in Saxony – Halberstadt, Hildesheim, Paderborn, Verden, Minden, Münster, Osnabrück and Bremen – is also obscure. In the cases of Liudger of Münster and Willehad of Bremen, for example, there is a strong link with the Anglo-Saxon and

---

[31] The classic studies on the eastern sees, A. Hauck, *Kirchengeschichte Deutschlands*, II (Leipzig, 1912), pp. 206–27 and 806–17, and on the western sees in the ninth century, P. Imbart de la Tour, *Les élections episcopales dans l'église de France du IXe au XIIe siècle* (Paris, 1891), are still of value, but see also S. Freund, *Von den Agilolfingern zu den Karolingern: Bayerns Bischöfe zwischen Kirchenorganisation, Reichsintegration und karolingischer Reform (700–847)*, Schriftenreihe zur bayerischen Landesgeschichte 144 (Munich, 2004); and S. Patzold, 'Créer un grade ecclésiastique: métropolitains et archevêques du royaume franc (VIIIe–IXe siècles)' (forthcoming).

Table 7 *Frankish bishops apparently installed in/by 768/9*
Provinces' names in capitals; again, bishops of the sees marked with
an asterisk are listed in the *Liber pontificalis* as attending the Synod
of Rome in 769.

REIMS	*Gislebert of Noyon (768–82)
TOURS	*Gavienus/Gaugenus of Tours (769)
TRIER	Angilram of Metz (768–91, elected after a two-year vacancy)
MAINZ	*Erembert of Worms (768/9)
SENS	*Wilichar of Sens (769–78)
BORDEAUX	Launus of Angoulême (769), Verebulfus of Bordeaux (769)
ARLES	Ratbertus of Arles (769)
BOURGES	*Herminarius of Bourges (769–74); Hermenbert of Toulouse (769)
LYON	Ado of Lyon (769–98), *Herulfus of Langres (769–80), Leduard of Macon (769–802)
NARBONNE	*Daniel of Narbonne (769–91)

Frisian missionary effort.[32] The circumstances of their elections are rarely known. Whether these were Charlemagne's nominees of men loyal to him is clear only if there is evidence of their acting for the king in some capacity, as in the case of Angilram of Metz or Wilichar of Sens. In contrast, in 794, Peter, bishop of Verdun, was required to swear his innocence of a charge of conspiring against the king, and the pseudo-bishop Gaerbod was deposed.[33]

What this brief survey of Charlemagne's bishops indicates, however, is that most of his ecclesiastical magnates had only ever known Carolingian rule. They were essentially men of the new regime. Although a good proportion of them had been active in Pippin's reign and would thus have provided an essential strand of continuity in Frankish reform work, many of the bishops were new men, accustomed only to Charlemagne as king.

Nevertheless, the pattern of filling vacant sees across the whole of Charlemagne's reign provides some indication that there was an attempt

[32] R. Kaiser, *Bischofsherrschaft zwischen Königtum und Fürstenmacht: Studien zur bischöflichen Stadtherrschaft im westfränkisch-französischen Reich im frühen und hohen Mittelalter,* Pariser historische Studien 17 (Bonn, 1981); U. Nonn, 'Zwischen König, Hausmeier und Aristokratie: Die Bischofserhebung im spätmerowingisch-frühkarolingischen Frankenreich', in F. R. Erkens (ed.), *Die früh- und hochmittelalterliche Bischofserhebung im europäischen Vergleich,* Beihefte zum Archiv für Kirchengeschichte 48 (Cologne, 1998), pp. 33–58; and H. H. Anton, '"Bischofsherrschaften" in Spätantike und Frühmittelalter: Reflexionen zu ihrer Genese, Struktur und Typologie', in F. Burgard, C. Cluse and A. Haverkamp (eds.), *Liber amicorum necnon et amicarum für Alfred Heit,* Trierer Historische Forschungen 28 (Trier, 1996), pp. 461–73. See also above, p. 252.

[33] Frankfurt 794, *MGH Cap.* I, No. 28, c. 10, p. 75.

to regularize ecclesiastical organization within the kingdom. It is within this context that the definition of ecclesiastical provinces and the status of the metropolitans needs to be seen. One of the few indications of discussion of provincial boundaries is the conclusion of the dispute about Arles and Vienne recorded in the proceedings of the Synod of Frankfurt in 794. The assembly at Frankfurt settled the quarrel between Ursio of Vienne and Elifant of Arles, who presumably had been summoned to Frankfurt to make their case. It was resolved with the confirmation of the number of suffragan sees in the ecclesiastical provinces of Vienne and Arles.[34]

In Charlemagne's will of 811, preserved in Einhard's *Vita Karoli*, the configurations of the metropolitan provinces listed as recipients of gifts were Rome, Ravenna, Milan, Aquileia, Grado, Cologne, Mainz, Salzburg, Trier, Sens, Besançon, Lyon, Rouen, Reims, Arles, Vienne, Tarantaise, Embrun, Bordeaux, Bourges and Tours, though the suffragans of these sees are not indicated.[35] The point of elevation of particular sees, such as Salzburg in 798, to archbishoprics, and the granting of a *pallium* from the pope, can sometimes be documented.[36] Some provincial reorganization would have been necessary to take account of the new sees created as part of the strategy of the Saxon mission, especially as far as the suffragans of Cologne, Mainz and Salzburg are concerned. Precise indications of the chronological sequence of phases in ecclesiastical organization or of the role the king played in this, however, are rare. For the most part, only general remarks survive, such as the reiteration of the need to respect the sphere of each bishop's jurisdiction, and confirmation of the status of the metropolitans.[37]

The public statements Charlemagne made about the metropolitans all invoke the need to organize the church according to the canons of the early Christian church councils. That is, he acted in accordance with what he understood to be the law of the church and, no doubt, the acceptance of normal arrangements such as are recorded in the seventh-century summary

---

[34] For comments on Provence and the early Carolingians see R. McKitterick, 'The scripts of the Bobbio Missal', in Y. Hen and R. Meens (eds.), *The Bobbio Missal*, Cambridge Studies in Palaeography and Codicology (Cambridge, 2004), pp. 19–52 at pp. 42–4; and P. J. Geary, *Aristocracy in Provence: the Rhône basin at the dawn of the Carolingian age*, Monographien zur Geschichte des Mittelalters 31 (Stuttgart, 1985).

[35] Einhard, *Vita Karoli*, c. 33, ed. Halphen, pp. 92–102; and see M. Innes, 'Charlemagne's will: piety, politics and the imperial succession', *English Historical Review* 112 (1997), pp. 833–55.

[36] M. Niederkorn-Bruck and A. Scharer (eds.), *Erzbishof Arn von Salzburg*, Veröffentlichungen des Instituts für Österreichische Geschichtsforschung Beiträge 40 (Vienna and Munich, 2004).

[37] Capitulary of Herstal 779, especially cc.1, 2 and 4, *MGH Cap.* 1, No.20, p. 47; C. Carroll, 'Archbishops and church provinces of Mainz and Cologne during the Carolingian period, 751–911', unpublished PhD thesis, University of Cambridge (1999).

in Isidore of Seville's *Etymologiae*.[38] At Herstal in 779 for example, the first clause states categorically that suffragan bishops were to be subject to the metropolitans in accordance with the canons, and that they were to 'emend and correct with a willing heart such features of their ministry as the metropolitans identify as in need of correction'.[39] In the *Admonitio generalis* of 789 there is again the assumption of an organization of ecclesiastical provinces with metropolitans and suffragans according to canon law. Among other clauses concerning both metropolitans and suffragans, and episcopal jurisdiction more generally, the Council of Antioch (341) is cited to the effect that suffragan bishops and metropolitans were not to make innovations in their dioceses without each other's knowledge.[40] Certainly conciliar decisions and Boniface of Mainz's letters from the 740s indicate the beginnings of stronger differentiation within the ecclesiastical hierarchy in the course of the eighth century than is apparent in the Merovingian period. First of all came Boniface's own elevation to the position of archbishop and the granting of the *pallium* to Rouen, Reims and Sens.[41] Then there was further regularization of the position of Reims and Trier, both of which had apparently been held by Milo early in the 750s.[42] Steffen Patzold, moreover, has emphasized both the gradualness of the process of ecclesiastical reorganization from the 740s until well into the ninth century, and the extent of Pippin III's contribution evident from the queries he addressed to Pope Zacharias in 747 and the Synod of Ver in 755.[43] Patzold has also suggested that Charlemagne's reign saw the clarification of the metropolitan status of particular bishops as well as the boundaries of each province, as distinct from any explicit decision to create such provinces. The involvement of bishops from the Anglo-Saxon tradition may well have played a role in sensitizing the Franks to the implications of ecclesiastical expansion, the need to define the extent of episcopal jurisdictions and

---

[38] Isidore, *Etymologiae*, ed. W. M. Lindsay, I, 7, c.12.

[39] *MGH Cap.* I, No. 20, c. 1, p. 47.

[40] *MGH Cap.* I, No. 22, c. 8, and compare cc. 10, 13, 44, with reference to metropolitans and their suffragans, and cc. 9, 11, 12, 19, 41, 56, 57, 58 on episcopal jurisdiction, ibid., pp. 54–7.

[41] Boniface of Mainz, *Epistulae*, ed. M. Tangl, *Die Briefe des heiligen Bonifatius und Lullus*, *MGH Epp. Sel.* I (Hanover, 1916), Ep. 57; and Council of Soissons, c. 3, ed. Werminghoff, *MGH Conc.* II.i, No. 34 (Hanover, 1906), pp. 102–5.

[42] Ewig, 'Milo *et eiusmodi similes*', in Ewig, *Spätantikes und fränkisches Gallien*, Gesammelte Schriften 2, Beihefte der Francia 3/II (Zürich and Munich, 1979), pp. 189–219.

[43] Zacharias' response was addressed to Pippin as mayor of the palace, his bishops, abbots and other princes of the Frankish realm, *MGH Epp.* III, pp. 479–87, repr. in R. Rau (ed.), *Briefe des Bonifatius: Willibalds Leben des Bonifatius nebst zeitgenössischen Dokumenten* (Darmstadt, 1968), pp. 414–36; and Synod of Ver, cc. 4 and 9, *MGH Cap.* I, pp. 34–5; and Patzold, 'Créer un grade ecclésiastique'.

diocesan territory and the desirability of securing a papal *pallium* for newly created archbishops.[44] Boniface's own move to have his authority confirmed came very soon after the creation of York as the second ecclesiastical province in Anglo-Saxon England and the consequent alignment of the suffragan bishoprics in the provinces of Canterbury as well as York. The Franks were well informed, as a consequence of their involvement in the papal legation to England in 786, about the attempt on Offa's part to carve out a third ecclesiastical province, based around Lichfield in Mercia. Equally, of course, Offa himself may have been impressed by what he had learnt of Frankish ecclesiastical reorganization and have sought to emulate it.[45]

The clarification of ecclesiastical diocesan territories and the insistence that the underlying principles were established on the historical precedents offered in the canons of the church were combined with the reorganization of the *missatica* discussed in the previous chapter. Within our understanding of the network of counties and dioceses, however, it is also necessary to incorporate the monasteries. They were especially active in promoting networks of communication across the kingdoms. They did this not only by means of the links between masters and pupils and scholars, but also by remarkable prayer associations. Particular institutions formed special prayer bonds and entered the names of the members of other monasteries and convents throughout the empire, as well as local patrons and visitors in the *Libri memoriales*.[46] The overlapping territories of the bishoprics, monasteries, *missatica* and counties, as well as their intertwined networks of communication, combined to create a sacred topography within the Frankish kingdoms. That this elaborate framework of institutions was in the process of development throughout Charlemagne's reign is the necessary context within which to consider his reforms. A brief reiteration of the main phases of Charlemagne's reform policies may therefore be helpful.

---

[44] See Flodoard, *Historia remensis ecclesiae*, 2, cc. 13, 16, 17, ed. M. Stratmann, *MGH SS* 36, pp. 162–3, 167–9.

[45] A. W. Haddan and W. Stubbs, *Councils and ecclesiastical documents* (Oxford, 1871), III, pp. 495–8; N. Brooks, *The early history of the church of Canterbury* (Leicester, 1984), pp. 118–20; C. Cubitt, *Anglo-Saxon church councils, c. 650–c. 850* (London, 1995), pp. 153–90; J. Story, *Carolingian connections: Anglo-Saxon England and Carolingian Francia, c. 750–870* (Aldershot, 2003), pp. 55–92; J. Blair, *The Anglo-Saxon church* (Oxford, 2006), pp. 167–8.

[46] K. Schmid and O. G. Oexle, 'Voraussetzungen und Wirkung des Gebetsbundes von Attigny', *Francia* 2 (1974), pp. 71–122; and McKitterick, *History and memory*, pp. 156–85.

CORRECTIO: ECCLESIASTICAL REFORM

Frankish reform is usually understood as the reformation and reconfigura-
tion of all the peoples under Charlemagne's rule to create a Christian realm
in its institutional structures, moral behaviour and personal convictions.
This is certainly how one might characterize Carolingian reform with
hindsight, but to what degree were these elements present from the beginning of Charlemagne's reign?

Some of the impetus for a programme of religious reform had been
provided earlier in the eighth century by the partnership between the
zealous English missionary, Boniface, bishop of Mainz, and Pippin III's
brother Carloman.[47] Pippin III and his main ecclesiastical adviser,
Chrodegang of Metz, had swiftly followed suit.[48] Their reforming ideals
and specific requirements about discipline, orthodox faith and religious
practice were reformulated in the earliest of Charlemagne's programmatic
capitularies, and subsequently proclaimed at many of the assemblies presided over by the king and his lay and religious advisers in the later eighth
and early ninth centuries. As early as the Aquitainian capitulary in 769,
there is a primary focus on church property and buildings,[49] but in the
Capitulary for Herstal, explicitly designated as the result of agreement
between the king, bishops, abbots and counts, far more is added to the
recurrent concern with church estates. Here there are clauses concerning
archiepiscopal and episcopal jurisdiction, the *ordinatio* (that is, consecration) of bishops not yet consecrated, the imposition of a monastic rule on
male and female monasteries, the delineation of episcopal powers in
relation to the priests and clerics within their dioceses and to any layman
or woman committing incest, and a careful delimiting of sanctuary for
killers or other criminals who took refuge in a church. Tithes were also to
be under the bishops' control.[50]

By the time the Capitulary of Herstal was drawn up in 779, of course, the
Saxon campaign was well under way, and the relationship with the papacy

---

[47] Levison, *England and the Continent*, pp. 70–93; T. Schieffer, *Winfrid-Bonifatius und die kirchliche
Grundlegung Europas* (Freiburg, 1954), pp. 186–254; L. von Padberg, *Mission und Christianierung:
Formen und Folgen bei Angelsachsen und Franken im 7. und 8. Jahrhundert* (Stuttgart, 1995); and
M. Imhoff and G. F. Stasch (eds.), *Bonifatius: vom angelsächsischen Missionar zum Apostel der
Deutschen* (Petersberg, 2004).

[48] Schneider, *Saint Chrodegang*; E. Ewig, 'Beobachtungen zur Entwicklung der Fränkischen
Reichskirche unter Chrodegang von Metz', *Frühmittelalterliche Studien* 2 (1968), pp. 67–77; and
Claussen, *The reform of the Frankish church*.

[49] *MGH Cap.* 1, No. 18, cc. 1, 3, 11, pp. 42–3, though a rule is prescribed for 'bishops, abbots and
abbesses' in c. 2.

[50] *MGH Cap.* 1, No. 20, cc. 1–7, pp. 46–51.

had become more intimate as a consequence of the takeover of the Lombard kingdom. Knowledge of Islam as a result of contact with the Muslim communities of Spain, however difficult this is to document precisely, may have further sharpened awareness of differences between the Franks and their neighbours.[51] Subsequent policies concerning the church and religion within Frankish society need, therefore, to be seen within this context of expansion, conversion and contrast with other religions and people, and the Christian commitment and sense of urgency they generated.

Enormous stress was placed on correct texts, proper conduct, rigorous discipline and tidy organization. Charlemagne's bishops and abbots were to play a key role in implementing these reforms. One of them, Theodulf, bishop of Orleans, retrospectively offered in c. 812 a comprehensive description of Charlemagne's purpose:

For this is always dear to him: to exercise bishops in the search of the Holy Scriptures and prudent and sound doctrine, every cleric in discipline, philosophers in knowledge of things divine and human, monks in religion, all generally in sanctity, primates in counsel, judges in justice, soldiers in practice of aim, prelates in humility, subjects in obedience, all generally in prudence, justice, fortitude, temperance, and concord.[52]

Charlemagne's own statements of his aims not only confirm Theodulf's comment but were clearly in place within a decade of his assuming the throne. They were set out most emphatically, moreover, in the programmatic *Admonitio generalis* of 789.[53] They were reiterated consistently in the capitularies and letters of Charlemagne thereafter, and culminated in the reform councils of 813. These, held in Reims, Tours, Mainz, Arles and Châlons-sur-Saône, added emphasis to the clergy's work for the welfare and salvation of the people and further defined the duties of the bishops and priests. The key texts of the Christian faith and for the conduct of Christian life, often referred to in general terms in earlier royal statements,

---

[51] See the 'first' Saxon capitulary, *MGH Cap.* I, No. 26, discussed above, pp. 251–3; and compare Y. Hen, 'Charlemagne's *jihad*', *Viator* 37 (2006), pp. 33–51; and B. Effros, '*De partibus Saxoniae* and the regulation of mortuary custom: a Carolingian campaign of Christianisation or the suppression of Saxon identity?', *Revue belge de philologie et d'histoire* 75 (1997), pp. 267–86; M. McCormick, 'Pippin III, the embassy of Caliph al-Mansur, and the Mediterranean world', in M. Becher and J. Jarnut (eds.), *Der Dynastiewechsel von 751: Vorgeschichte, Legitimationsstrategien und Erinnerung* (Münster, 2004), pp. 221–42; and T. Kitchen, 'Carolingian diplomatic relations with the Abbasid caliphate 768–840 and their representation in Frankish sources' (forthcoming).

[52] Theodulf of Orleans, *On Baptism*, ed. S. A. Keefe, *Water and the Word*, 2 vols. (Notre Dame, IN, 2002), II, p. 281, trans., I, p. 5.

[53] *Admonitio generalis*, preface and cc. 60–82, *MGH Cap.* I, No. 22, pp. 53–4 and 57–62.

were specified – Gospels, Acts, Epistles, liturgical books, patristic writings, the Rule of Benedict for monks, the *Cura pastoralis* of Gregory the Great for bishops and priests, canon law, and civil laws for lay officials, and the Creed and Lord's Prayer were to be taught to all the faithful.[54] The *Admonitio generalis*, of course, drew on earlier conciliar decisions, not least those of relevant decisions from early church councils included in the *Dionysio-Hadriana* collection of canon law, and topics formulated during the reign of Pippin III. But the *Admonitio generalis* also articulated the king's responsibility for the people of God and the need for everyone in the kingdom, and especially the secular and ecclesiastical elites, to work towards creating order and a polity worthy of salvation. One might here compare King Reccared's statements about royal responsibility for the Christian faith at the Third Council of Toledo and the ambition for one faith and one realm expressed at the Fourth Council of 633. Both were known in north Francia and conceivably in royal circles through a probably later eighth-century compilation of which these conciliar decrees form a part, namely, the so-called Collection of St Amand. This collection is extant in a number of codices, including two early ninth-century manuscripts, and is invariably transmitted with the royally approved *Dionysio-Hadriana* collection which it effectively complements.[55]

That this was no mere posturing is indicated by the many reinforcements and specific requirements issued subsequently for both specific religious acts and more general effort. Two letters can serve to highlight the principal emphases and intent of the ruler's fervour and religious energy. A letter from Charlemagne 'to the lectors', probably to be dated soon after 786, spelt out the necessity for the improvement of learning, the provision of correct books of the Old and New Testaments, and the compilation of volumes of suitable readings for the night office.[56] Another letter, dated between 809 and 812, but from one of Charlemagne's bishops, Leidrad of Lyon, who had been elevated to his see in 797, reported to the

---

[54] *MGH Conc.* II.i, Nos. 34–8. Compare the Lorsch annals entry for 802, ed. G. Pertz, *MGH SS* I, p. 38.
[55] Third Council of Toledo, ed. G. Martínez Díez and F. Rodríguez, *La colección canónica hispana*, V: *Concilios hispanos: segunda parte*, Monumenta Hispaniae Sacra, Serie Canónica 5 (Madrid, 1992), pp. 53–73; Fourth Council of 633, c. 2, ibid., pp. 183–4. The Collection of St Amand would merit further investigation, see ibid., I *Estudios*, ed. G. Martínez Diez and F. Rudríguez, Monumenta Hispaniae Sacra, Serie Canónica 5 (Madrid, 1966), pp. 342–7; and L. Kéry, *Canonical collections of the early middle ages (ca. 400–1140): a bibliographical guide to the manuscripts and literature*, History of Medieval Canon Law (Washington, DC, 1999), pp. 84–5; and Mordek, *Bibliotheca*, pp. 29–34 and 439–42. On the 633 statement see M. de Jong, 'Religion', in R. McKitterick (ed.), *The early middle ages: Europe 400–1000*, The Short Oxford History of Europe (Oxford, 2001), pp. 131–66 at p. 137.
[56] *MGH Cap.* I, No. 30, pp. 80–1.

emperor on all he had done to fulfil the emperor's ideals and expectations. These concerned the ecclesiastical ministry, the construction of new churches and the promotion of the liturgy as it was sung in Charlemagne's own sacred palace (*sacrum palatium*).[57]

Leidrad's letter, the capitularies, and the group of episcopal statutes from early in the ninth century designed to carry the royal statements about ecclesiastical organization, clerical discipline and Christian morality to the local level,[58] together indicate a steady elaboration of the efforts made to implement Charlemagne's reforms. This work was not only directed at religious observance within ecclesiastical institutions or among monks and clergy. Charlemagne's policy from early in his reign was directed towards the transformation of the entire people of the Frankish realm into a Christian people, the salvation of that people, the formation of the whole of the society in the territories under Frankish rule within a Christian framework, and the integration of the concerns of the faith with those of society as a whole.[59] An early indication of the connection perceived between conversion and subsequent teaching, moreover, is the confirmation of tithes to the church of Utrecht in 769. This included the statement that the grant was made for the sustenance of the monks and clergy who 'convert the gentiles (Latin: *gentiles*) to Christianity and ... give teaching to those they have converted'.[60]

The specific means for fulfilling Charlemagne's vision, and particular topics or areas on which to concentrate, however, were identified at various stages from the 780s onwards. There are a number of instances of something conceived in relation to a particular enterprise subsequently being adapted for more general application. Charlemagne's letter of 805, giving instructions to Gerbald of Liège for a three-day fast, for example, echoes in many respects the motives for the special fasts ordered in relation to the Avar campaigns of 791:

Consulting together with our *fideles*, both spiritual and lay, and with their approval no less than counsel, we deem it necessary, because of certain pressing exigencies which we shall indicate below [these are listed later in the letter as 'famine, intemperate weather, pestilence, war of the pagan peoples living around

[57] Leidrad, *Epistola ad Carolum*, ed. E. Dümmler, *MGH Epp.* IV (*karol. aevi*, II), pp. 542–4; and A. Coville, *Recherches sur l'histoire de Lyon au IXme siècle* (Paris, 1928), pp. 283–96. See also M. de Jong, '*Sacrum palatium et ecclesia*: L'autorité religieuse royale sous les Carolingiens (790–840)', *Annales* 58 (2003), pp. 1243–69. On the liturgy, see further below, pp. 340–5.
[58] P. Brommer (ed.) *Capitula episcoporum*, and R. McKitterick, *The Frankish church and the Carolingian reforms, 789–895* (London, 1977), pp. 45–79.
[59] Wallace-Hadrill, *The Frankish church.*   [60] *DKar.* I, No. 56.

our frontiers ... of which we have received information'] that three-day fasts be observed by all of us, without exception, and aid sought from him in whom we live, move and have our being.

This fasting was designed to inspire everyone to repentance, that '[the Lord may] make us his supplicants and subjects in true humility, and that he may convert each of us to the observance of his commandments, driving out all error from us ... it is to the end that we may be able to acquire his grace that we have decreed that these fasts and prayers be undertaken by all of you, without exception'.[61]

The ecclesiastical and the secular spheres, therefore, were envisaged as forming one whole sacred realm, an *ecclesia* in its widest sense, even though clergy and secular officials also had distinctive concerns of their own.[62] Within the Frankish kingdom the *cultus divinus*, that is, the cult of the Christian God, was to be securely established. This particular vision of society is apparent from early in Charlemagne's reign onwards, even if the various elements for its fulfilment were devised piecemeal over the decades of his reign. That so many texts survive in unique copies, not always precisely datable, moreover, opens up the possibility that we are dealing with a tiny proportion of what once existed. Ultimately, all this was observed outwardly in the liturgical offices, the ministry of the clergy and the lay magnates, and creation and care of church buildings. The complementary need for proper instruction in Christian faith, doctrine and morals was constantly reiterated.

How such instruction was carried out is amply illustrated by the example of the proliferation of treatises on baptism. Charlemagne's concern for correct instruction in the faith was specifically focussed as late as 812 when he wrote to his metropolitan bishops to ask how they were teaching the priests and people about baptism and its implications. The responses from one of these archbishops, Magnus of Sens, as well as one of Magnus's suffragans, Theodulf of Orleans, were added to a many different clerical manuals incorporating treatises on baptism within the Frankish realm. These were produced from the latter years of Charlemagne's reign and subsequently. They indicate the diversity of individual interpretations of

---

[61] *MGH Cap.* I, No. 124, pp. 245–6; trans. King, *Charlemagne*, pp. 245–7.
[62] For a full exposition of the equation of *ecclesia* and polity in the Carolingian period see M. de Jong, 'Charlemagne's church', in Story, *Charlemagne: empire and society*, pp. 103–35 at pp. 103–4; and de Jong, 'Ecclesia and the early medieval polity', in W. Pohl, S. Airlie and H. Reimitz, *Staat im frühen Mittelalter*, Österreichische Akademie der Wissenschaften, phil.-hist. Klasse, Denkschriften 301 (Forschungen zur Geschichte des Mittelalters 11) (Vienna, 2006), pp. 113–32.

how Charlemagne's reforms might be implemented.[63] Similarly, the dissemination of creed texts and commentaries on the creed from the late
eighth century onwards reflects the successful communication of royal
concerns about correct doctrine even down to the urban and rural communities of the realm.[64] They reinforced, at parish and diocesan level, the
more general discussions of orthodox doctrine. These eventually focussed
on the orthodox understanding of the Trinity, but the process by which
statements of a general wish to maintain catholic doctrine were articulated,
in relation to particular challenges to orthodoxy, was a gradual one.

ORTHODOXY

That Charlemagne became such a champion of orthodoxy, and that the
Frankish theologians were prompted to write so much about very basic
matters of faith, no doubt has as much to do with Charlemagne's sense of
his obligations as Christian king as with the Franks' self-imposed role as
converters of the heathen Saxons and Slavs. Certainly, the *Admonitio
generalis* had articulated the king's commitment to religion and Christian
conduct according to the rule of law. Without challenges from the fringes,
or even from beyond the Carolingian empire, Frankish discussions of
orthodox belief during the reign of Charlemagne might have remained at
the level of anxious reiteration and merely academic discussions of
Christology and other tenets of the faith on the basis of the Franks'
knowledge of the debates in the early Christian church councils. The
most dramatic statements of Frankish orthodox belief, however, were
collective reactions to developments elsewhere. Five years after the
Admonitio generalis, the meeting at Frankfurt in 794 supported the double
procession of the Holy Spirit expressed in the phrase *filioque* which the
Franks added to the creed, but condemned Adoptionism and the Greek
views on images.[65] The council's decrees also served to express
Charlemagne's power and to emphasize his responsibility, together with
his ecclesiastical and secular magnates, for religious orthodoxy and correct

---

[63] Keefe, *Water and the Word.*
[64] S. A. Keefe, 'Creed commentary collections in Carolingian manuscripts', in K. G. Cushing and
R. F. Gyug (eds.), *Ritual, text and law: studies in medieval canon law and liturgy presented to Roger
E. Reynolds* (Aldershot, 2004), pp. 185–204. Keefe has announced her preparation of a full catalogue
of creed commentaries in Carolingian manuscripts: *Inventarium symbolorum, expositionum et
explanationum fidei in codicibus karolini aevi* (Turnhout, forthcoming). For the work of local parish
priests see C. van Rhijn, *Shepherds of the Lord: priests and episcopal statutes in the Carolingian period*,
PhD dissertation, Universiteit Utrecht, akademische proefschrift (2003) (Turnhout, 2007).
[65] Above, pp. 241–2.

observance of the faith. The emphasis on getting matters straight and teaching what was correct imbues all the early Carolingian theological writing. It is predominantly didactic in tone.

The Synod of Frankfurt condemned Adoptionism somewhat perfunctorily, and it is difficult to be certain that this particular issue was one that engaged Charlemagne himself other than because it was an issue so closely related to the *filioque* doctrine of the creed. Other texts amplify the Frankish response, though its political context needs more investigation and explanation than can be attempted here. Adoptionism, sometimes known as the 'Spanish heresy', concerned the nature of Christ's humanity. The view that Christ was adopted into the Trinity and was the adopted Son of God had actually been condemned at the Council of Toledo in 675. It was revived in the northern part of Spain, the region newly conquered by Charlemagne, by Bishop Felix of Urgel in support of Bishop Elipandus of Toledo, but their arguments had originally been directed against the false teachings of Migetius for Christians within Muslim Spain.[66] Only because of a challenge within the Christian church of the Spanish March (by Beatus of Liebana) and an appeal to the pope did the dispute get taken up within Francia. Even then it is difficult to be certain that it was other than a highly personalized argument. Felix's own recanting of his teaching at Regensburg in 792, and the condemnation of the heresy of Adoptionism at Frankfurt in 794, were apparently insufficient to quell him. Although a cogent and effective refutation of Felix's ideas had already been formulated by Paulinus of Aquileia and affirmed, in the aftermath of Frankfurt, in a synod convened at Aquileia in 796,[67] the English scholar Alcuin in his retirement at Tours seems to have fanned the flames. He addressed a brief treatise on the topic to Elipandus in 797 or 798 and a far longer set of four books, also to Elipandus, in 800. In a perplexing series of events, Felix was condemned again in Rome in 798 and also required to debate the issue with

---

[66] For full discussion see J. Cavadini, *The last Christology of the west: adoptionism in Spain and Gaul, 785–820* (Philadelphia, 1993); and H. Nagel, *Karl der Große und die theologische Herausforderungen seiner Zeit: sur Wechselwirkung zwischen Theologie und Politik im Zeitalter des großen Frankenherrschers*, Frieburger Beiträge zur mittelalterlichen Geschichte, Studien und Texte 12 (Frankfurt am Main, 1998).

[67] Paulinus of Aquileia, ed. D. Norberg, *Paulini Aquileiensis opera omnia*, pars 1: *Contra felicem libri tres*, Corpus Christianorum Continuatio Medievalis 95 (Turnhout, 1990); and see N. Everett, 'Paulinus, the Carolingians and *famosissima* Aquileia', in P. Chiesa (ed.), *Paolino d'Aquileia e il contributo italiano all'Europa carolingia*, Atti del Convegno internazionale de Studi, Cividale del Friuli-Premariacco, 10–13 ottobre 2002 (Udine, 2003). On the general context see Nagel, *Karl der Große*.

Alcuin at Aachen in 799.[68] Only then was Felix deposed from his see and exiled to Lyon for the rest of his life.

The debate on the veneration of images was one in which Charlemagne was personally engaged far more than in that on Adoptionism. In the late 780s and early 790s, the discussions among the scholars in Charlemagne's inner circle were prompted by the Franks' rather belated reception of the Latin translation of the text of the canons of the Second Council of Nicaea in 787. The principal outcome was the extraordinary treatise known as *Opus Karoli regis* or *Libri carolini*, composed by Theodulf of Orleans between 790 and 793.[69] Some of the brief comments approving the argument of the treatise entered in the margins of the manuscript copy sent to the pope have been attributed to Charlemagne.[70] The assembly at Frankfurt in 794 endorsed the *Libri carolini* in bluntly rejecting the decisions of the Greeks concerning the adoration of images.[71] The *Opus Karoli regis* was in part a defence against what was perceived as a Greek attack on Frankish and Roman thinking.[72] It explained the errors of the Greeks' understanding of the place of images of Christ and his saints in the church. It affirmed that images were simply reminders of what they represent. It particularly emphasized the superiority of writing and texts to images as a means of teaching about the faith.[73] Such an emphasis on the power of writing, moreover, is entirely in keeping with other aspects of Charlemagne's policies, as we shall see.

It is ironic that out of the Frankish insistence on correct statements of faith arose the addition to the creed known as the *filioque*. Although theologically impeccable, in terms of such patristic writers as Augustine, who had discussed the relationship between Father, Son and Holy Spirit in

---

[68] See D. Bullough, 'Alcuin, Arn and the creed in the mass', in Niederkorn-Bruck and Scharer, *Erzbischof Arn von Salzburg*, pp. 128–36.

[69] Theodulf of Orleans, *Libri carolini / Opus Caroli regis contra synodum*, ed. A. Freeman with P. Meyvaert, *MGH Conc.* II.i (Hanover, 1998). On the Greek text and the misleading rendering into Latin see H. H. Thümmel, 'Die fränkische Reaktion auf das 2. Nicaenum in den Libri carolini', in R. Berndt (ed.), *Das Frankfurter Konzil von 794: Kristallisationspunkt karolingischer Kultur*, Quellen und Adhandlungen zur mittelrheinischen Kirchengeschichte 80, 2 vols. (Mainz, 1997), II: *Kultur and Theologie*, pp. 965–80. See also F. Hartmann, *Hadrian I (772–795)*, Päpste und Papsttum 34 (Stuttgart, 2006), pp. 278–91.

[70] *Opus Karoli regis*, ed. Freeman, *MGH Conc.* III, pp. 48–50 and BAV, Vat. lat. 7207.

[71] *MGH* Cap. No. 28, c. 2, pp. 73–4. See p. 300 above and the comprehensive discussion of the issues in Berndt, *Das Frankfurter Konzil von 794*, I and II.

[72] See D. Ganz, 'Theology and the organization of thought', in *NCMH*, II, pp. 758–85 at pp. 773–7.

[73] On the relation between texts and images see R. McKitterick, 'Text and image in the Carolingian world', in McKitterick (ed.), *The uses of literacy in the early middle ages* (Cambridge, 1990), pp. 297–318, and the papers assembled in *Testo ed immagine nell'alto medioevo*, Settimane 41 (Spoleto, 1994).

the Trinity, the Frankish insertion of the word into the Niceno-Constantinopolitan creed ultimately caused schism between the western and eastern Christian churches.

By the late eighth century a spectrum of scholarly opinion about the three persons of the Trinity supported the idea of the double procession of the Holy Spirit from the Father *and* the Son, rather than from the Father *through* the Son as the Greeks maintained. This is reflected in the Frankish promotion of particular creeds, notably the *Quicunque vult* or Athanasian creed, as well as in the ultimately successful attempt to get the phrase included in the Niceno-Constantinopolitan creed.[74] These creeds were reproduced in books associated with Charlemagne's royal court, notably the Dagulf Psalter, originally designed as a gift for Pope Hadrian. In a letter to Pope Hadrian written in 794, moreover, Charlemagne made it clear that he understood the double procession of the Holy Spirit from the Father and the Son. The doctrine was also asserted in the *libellus* of the Italian bishops against Elipandus of Toledo associated with the Frankfurt council of 794 and Charlemagne's letter to Elipandus and the Spanish bishops.[75] A letter from Pope Leo III to Charlemagne reported a dispute between the monks of Mount Olivet in Jerusalem and John of Mount Saba concerning the singing of the mass and the use of the *filioque* clause when the creed was sung. According to the discussion record of the meeting between Charlemagne's envoys and the pope in 810, moreover, the Niceno-Constantinopolitan creed was sung in Charlemagne's palace chapel at Aachen with the word *filioque* included, even though this was not the wording of the creed agreed at Chalcedon in 451. The Frankish envoys, Bernhar of Worms and Adalhard of Corbie, argued that singing *filioque* in the creed in the palace chapel communicated the patristic interpretation of the double procession of the Holy Spirit and thus theological orthodoxy, and for this reason it should be officially inserted into the creed. The pope maintained that the conciliar decision about the wording of the creed made in the fifth century could not be altered. Despite the pope's ruling, the Franks' conclusions at the Synod of Aachen eventually prevailed, though Rome was the last to capitulate. The synod's statements were reinforced by

---

[74] On the Gallo-Frankish origins of the Athanasian creed see A. E. Burn, *The Athanasian Creed from eighth and ninth-century texts and early commentaries* (Cambridge, 1896); and J. N. D. Kelly, *The Athanasian Creed* (Oxford, 1964). For the wider context and discussion of the Apostles' Creed see J. N. D. Kelly, *Early Christian creeds*, 3rd edn (London, 1972), pp. 358–425.

[75] *MGH Epp.* v, pp. 5–11 and *MGH Conc.* II.i, pp. 136, 163. For Paulinus and the synod of Cividale 796/7 see *MGH Conc.* II.i, p. 187. See R. McKitterick, 'History, law and communication with the past in the Carolingian period', in *Comunicare e significare nell'alto medioevo*, Settimane 52 (Spoleto, 2005), pp. 941–79; and below, pp. 333–8.

a dossier of patristic opinion, short treatises by Theodulf of Orleans, Smaragdus of St Mihiel, and Arn of Salzburg, and the plethora of creed commentaries referred to above.[76]

The ultimate success of the *filioque* clause also raises the question of the role of the palace chapel, and especially the palace chapel at Aachen, in promoting orthodox expressions of faith, but this will be discussed more fully later in this chapter. Throughout his reign, therefore, but becoming ever more specific and insistent in his later years, Charlemagne promoted orthodoxy in the context of canon law and patristic theology.

It was by means of oral and written communication that orthodox belief was taught and maintained within the Frankish realm. Although the Capitulary of Frankfurt in 794 had stated that 'God can be prayed to and man listened to in any language, if his prayers be just, and that no-one should believe that God cannot be prayed to except in three languages',[77] communication between men depended on the means of being understood.[78] So, too, for the teaching of correct doctrine, much hinged on the correct interpretation of words and phrases in Latin texts, even if they were translated into other vernaculars.[79] It is within this context that Charlemagne's emphasis on correct language should be understood. This recognition of the link between language and faith manifests itself for the first time in the middle decades of his reign.

CORRECTIO: LANGUAGE AND CONTROL

In the letter to the lectors of *c.* 786, Charlemagne articulated not only the relationship between the states of learning and of the Christian faith, but his wish to control and oversee both:

Since it is our concern that the condition of our churches should always advance towards better things, we strive with vigilant zeal to repair the manufactory of learning, almost destroyed by the sloth of our forefathers, and summon whom we can, even by our own example, to master the studies of the liberal arts. In the

---

[76] Council of Aachen 809, ed. H. Willjung, *Das Konzil von Aachen 809, MGH Conc.* II.ii (Hanover, 1998).

[77] *MGH Cap.* 1, No. 28, c. 52, p. 78.

[78] See the pertinent remarks by I. N. Wood, 'Missionaries and the Christian frontier', in W. Pohl, I. N. Wood and H. Reimitz (eds.), *The transformation of frontiers from late antiquity to the Carolingians*, The Transformation of the Roman World (Leiden, 2001), pp. 209–18 at p. 217.

[79] For Latin as the vernacular within a substantial part of the Frankish realm see R. McKitterick, *The Carolingians and the written word* (Cambridge, 1989), pp. 1–22; R. Wright, *Late Latin and early Romance in Spain and Carolingian France* (Liverpool, 1982); and M. Banniard, 'Language and communication in Carolingian Europe', in *NCMH*, 11, pp. 695–708.

course of these we long ago accurately corrected, God helping us in all things, all the books in the Old and New Testaments, corrupted by the ignorance of copyists.[80]

It was Charlemagne who charged Paul the Deacon, 'our client and a man close to us', with the completion of the preparation of readings for the night office. Having himself (or so he claimed) examined the text of Paul's compilation of readings from the treatises and sermons of the various catholic fathers, the king then stated: 'We confirm the said volumes by our authority and deliver them to your religiousness to be read in Christ's churches.'

In the circular letter *De litteris colendis,* sent *c.* 784 by Charlemagne to all his monasteries and bishops (it is the Fulda copy that survives[81]), the king explained that he,

along with our faithful advisers, have deemed it useful that the bishoprics and monasteries . . . should . . . devote their efforts to the study of literature and to the teaching of it, each according to his ability, to those on whom God has bestowed the capacity to learn. Letters have often been sent to us in these last years from certain monasteries . . . in most of these writings their sentiments were sound but their language was uncouth . . . because of their neglect of learning their unskilled tongues could not express it without fault . . . let men be chosen for the task of improving knowledge who have the will and ability to learn and also the desire to instruct others.[82]

Charlemagne emphasized that 'those who seek to please God by right living may not neglect to please him also by right speaking. We are well aware that, although verbal errors are dangerous, errors of understanding are more so.'

This letter was reinforced by the *Admonitio generalis* of 789, in which Charlemagne decreed:

Let the clergy join and associate to themselves not only children of servile condition but also the sons of free men. And let schools be established in which boys may learn to read. Correct carefully the Psalms, *notas,* the chant, the calendar, the grammars in each monastery and bishopric, and the catholic books; because often some desire to pray to God properly, but they pray badly because of the incorrect books.[83]

---

[80] *MGH Cap.* 1, No. 30; and Mordek, *Bibliotheca,* pp. 186–7 and 206–7.

[81] See the discussion by T. Martin, 'Bemerkungen zur "Epistola de litteris colendis", *Archiv für Diplomatik* 31 (1985), pp. 227–72.

[82] *Admonitio generalis,* c. 72; *MGH Cap.* 1 , No. 29, p. 79; trans. King, *Charlemagne,* pp. 232–3.

[83] *MGH Cap.* 1, No. 22, pp. 59–60; trans. King, *Charlemagne,* p. 217. The translation of *notas* is disputed. Some think it means 'musical notation', some 'shorthand' and others 'writing'. The position of *notas* between psalms and chant in the list might seem to favour the meaning as musical notation, though no written musical notation, that is, neumes, survives from quite as early as this.

The Latin language and the Christian faith were part of the Frankish inheritance. After all, once the Saxon wars had concluded, the Carolingian realm extended well beyond the bounds of the areas that had once been part of the Roman empire in the west, and thus which had Latin as the common language. In the early 780s, after the completion of the first major phase of the Saxon conquest in Westphalia, the Christianization of the regions east of the Rhine proceeded apace. The Franks introduced Latin, wherever it was not already established, for purposes of government, law, education and religion. In the Frankish regions west of the Rhine, which emerged as the kingdom of France in due course, Latin continued to function effectively as the vernacular, although it evolved in the course of the ninth and tenth centuries into the Romance form which subsequently became French. Similarly, in Lombard Italy and northern Spain, Latin prevailed at all levels, only gradually developing into Italian, Catalan and Spanish in the late Carolingian period.[84]

Alongside the promotion of correct Latin, there is certainly an indication, in surviving conciliar legislation linked with Charlemagne right at the end of his reign, of an awareness of a need to promote the German language as a means of communication. This is the decree concerning church reform issued from Tours in 813. It advised clerics to translate sermons to the people *in rusticam romanam linguam aut theotiscam*,[85] that is, 'Romance', which in due course became Old French, and 'theotisca', literally, 'language of the people' or German. Those Old High German texts which survive from the early ninth century comprise translations of the Lord's Prayer, creeds, baptismal catechisms and confessions, the Rule of Benedict, St Matthew's Gospel, the Gospel harmonies, the *Exhortatio ad plebem christianum*, the *Muspilli* and a number of prayers and charms, and are linked with the royally promoted missionary endeavours in the pagan Saxon regions, in Bavaria and Alemannia and the older areas of evangelization by missionaries from England. The major centres of Old High German text production were Freising, Fulda, Reichenau, St Gallen, Weissenberg, Werden, Salzburg and Murbach.[86] Yet all of these were major centres of Latin learning as well. The written forms of German vernaculars appear initially to have been a pedagogic device to assist the

---

[84] R. Wright (ed.), *Latin and Romance language in the early middle ages* (London, 1991).
[85] *MGH Conc.* II.ii, c. 17, p. 288. See also H. J. Hummer, *Politics and power in early medieval Europe, 600–1000* (Cambridge, 2005), pp. 133–7.
[86] See W. Haubrichs, *Von den Anfängen zum hohen Mittelalter, 1: Die Anfänge: Versuche volkssprachiger Schriftlichkeit im frühen Mittelalter (ca. 700–1050/60)* (Frankfurt am Main, 1988); and C. Edwards, 'German vernacular literature: a survey', in McKitterick, *Carolingian culture*, pp. 141–70.

process of conversion. They were a key to open the door to Latin Christian culture. The early ninth-century manuscript containing the south Rhenish Franconian 'Weissenburg catechism' is a case in point. As well as the catechism, there is the Latin text of the Lord's Prayer accompanied by a commentary in German, a list of the principal vices in Latin and German, the texts of the creeds known as the Apostles' Creed and *Quicunque vult*, and the Latin *Gloria in excelsis*.[87]

It is hardly surprising that the impetus came from Charlemagne and his group of scholars in the late 780s, for wherever they might be gathered together the need to communicate was most urgent. Charlemagne himself probably spoke a form of Old High German close to Rhenish Franconian. Einhard reported that 'not being content with knowing only his own native tongue, Charlemagne also made an effort to learn foreign languages. Among those, he learned Latin so well, that he spoke it as well as he did his own native language, but he was able to understand Greek better than he could speak it.' Einhard further reinforced the impression of Charlemagne's fluency in Latin by his account of the king's suggestions of German names for the months and the winds, though this seems to have had a symbolic rather than any practical impact.[88]

Even in the regions east of the Rhine, Latin was the principal official language from the beginning of the Carolingian conquest. Latin, moreover, exerted a strong influence on the written forms of the various vernacular dialects of Old High German and Old Saxon.[89] Yet the orthography and structure of Carolingian Latin itself was deliberately altered by the scholars in Charlemagne's reign. As early as the last decade of the eighth century, written Latin began to be made to conform, more strictly than the Latin of the seventh and eighth centuries had done, to old classical and Ciceronian standards. Some of this Latin reform is associated with the little group of grammarians who included Peter the Deacon and Paulinus of

[87] Weissenberg catechism, ed. E. Steinmayer, *Die kleineren althochdeutschen Sprachdenkmaler* (Berlin, 1916), No. 6, pp. 29–38; and H. Butzmann, 'Die Weissenburger Handschriften: Einleitung zum Katalog', repr. in H. Butzmann, *Kleine Schriften: Festgabe zum 70. Geburtstag* (Graz, 1973), pp. 48–103 at pp. 55–6. See also J. Knight Bostock, *A handbook on Old High German* (Oxford, 1976), pp. 112–13; and Haubrichs, *Anfänge*, p. 290. On the significance of the Apostles' Creed, see further below, p. 336.

[88] Einhard, *Vita Karoli*, cc. 25 and 29, ed. Halphen, pp. 74 and 82; and see further below, p. 326.

[89] On aspects of Latin and German see M. Banniard, 'Germanophone, latinophone et accès à la Schriftlichkeit', in D. Hägermann, W. Haubrichs and J. Jarnut (eds.), *Akkulturation: Probleme einer germanisch-romanischen Kultursynthese in Spätantike und frühem Mittelalter*, Ergänzungsbände zum Reallexikon der Germanischen Altertumskunde 41 (Berlin and New York, 2004), pp. 340–58.

Aquileia patronized by Charlemagne, and the Englishman Alcuin, who compiled the treatise on Latin spelling conventions, *De orthographia*.

Effective oral, as well as written, communication was a major imperative. Within the court circles, after all, so many different Latin traditions were represented – from Alcuin's and other Anglo-Saxon, Irish and Greek visitors' knowledge of it as a second learned language, to the variety of Spanish, Italian, Aquitainian, Alemannian and Frankish versions of it as a spoken tongue and written literary language – that there would have been considerable pressure to formalize a written *lingua franca* according to well-established rules and models. This is quite apart from the need to teach Latin to those for whom it was not a first language in any sense at all. It is little wonder, therefore, that there was so much interest in the Latin of antique authors, and in grammar and orthography, within political circles.[90] It was not only older standards that were the aim, but also a degree of conformity within the different Latin traditions and accents represented among the scholars of Francia. It is significant, for example, that some of the changes Alcuin effected in his adaptation and excerpting of Bede's earlier *De orthographia* were to do with pronunciation. Such a desire for uniformity in pronunciation was not simply in relation to the celebration of the liturgy,[91] but is also to be understood as an aid to effective daily communication.[92]

Whatever the degree of Charlemagne's own recognition of the potential or need for his own tongue, therefore, his greater energies, at the same time as his earliest articulation of the need for ecclesiastical reform, appear to have been put towards the promotion of correct Latin, the copying and distribution of correctly spelt and accurate Latin texts, and a stress on the correct understanding of texts and of the Christian faith that might result. One way of enhancing Frankish identity would have been to promote the Frankish Germanic dialects. Instead, the symbolic as well as historic force of Latin was enhanced to the highest level. It became a necessary skill to

---

[90] V. Law, 'The study of grammar', in McKitterick, *Carolingian culture*, pp. 88–110; and see further below, pp. 369–70.

[91] Alcuin's *De orthographia*, ed. S. Bruni (Florence, 1997); Wright, *Latin and early Romance in Spain and Carolingian France*, pp. 104–17; and the essays collected in R. Wright, *A sociophilological study of late Latin*, Utrecht Studies in Medieval Literacy 10 (Turnhout, 2005). See also Banniard, 'Language and communication'.

[92] For an important discussion of Latin as a means of learned (in both sense) communication later in the middle ages see T. Haye, *Lateinische Oralität: gelehrte Sprache in der mündlichen Kommunikation des hohen und späten Mittelalters* (Berlin, 2005); and see also M. Richter, 'Die Sprachenpolitik Karls des Großen', *Sprachwissenschaft* 7 (1982), pp. 412–37.

acquire for communication, let alone political and religious advancement. The Latin itself was changed and reformed according to classical norms. There is no indication that this is something Pippin had started, unless by insisting that his son received a proper education. Latin in Pippin's day had been developing further along the way to Romance. With the aid of Charlemagne's advisers, the process of development towards Old French in the written forms of the language, at least, was diverted.

The written word itself became an essential element of royal administration, law, education and religious expression in the course of Charlemagne's reign. Literacy was both required and rewarded. It was not only a means of social advancement and a way to participate in social and political leadership; the cultivation and possession of literate skills were badges of belonging to Charlemagne's greatly expanded Frankish world.[93]

Such a political promotion of Latin and literacy in an empire in which both Romance and Germanic languages were current had a profound effect on the development of a Frankish cultural identity.[94] Written texts became accessible which had a lasting impact on patterns of thought, styles of argument and outlook.[95] Latin provided the means for the Franks to associate themselves with the Roman past in the most fundamental way possible. It became their own past too. The integration of an aspect of Roman past into the Frankish present is thus explicit, and the models for such a revival, as we shall see, were the Roman texts of classical antiquity and the writings of the early Christian church. Not only did the promotion of Latin literacy give the Franks in Charlemagne's kingdom access to the Latin texts of antiquity and the early Christian church; they made these texts part of their own cultural inheritance and an essential foundation on which to build their own Frankish and Christian culture. How much Charlemagne himself contributed to the identification and provision of such texts will be considered later in this chapter, but we need first to consider further the spatial dimension of the Carolingian reforms in relation to Charlemagne's sacred itinerary.

[93] R. McKitterick, *The Carolingians and the written word* (Cambridge, 1989); and J. Nelson, 'Literacy in Carolingian government', in R. McKitterick (ed.), *The uses of literacy in early mediaeval Europe* (Cambridge, 1990), pp. 258–96.
[94] See W. Haubrichs, '*Veterum regum actus et bella*: zur sog. Heldenliedersammlung Karls des Großen', in W. Tauber (ed.), *Aspekte der Germanistik: Festschrift für Hans-Friedrich Rosenfeld* (Göppingen, 1989), pp. 17–46.
[95] For a stimulating set of parallels and contrasts see the account of the English Atlantic as a 'literate empire, a paper empire', in I. K.Steele, *The English Atlantic, 1675–1740: an exploration of communication and community* (Oxford and New York, 1986), esp. pp. 266–67.

CHARLEMAGNE'S SACRED ITINERARY: CHRISTIAN SPACE
AND TIME

The regular movement of the king to celebrate Christmas and Easter in
cities and palaces across the kingdom is recorded in the *Annales regni
francorum*.[96] The palaces were Aachen, Attigny, Douzy, Düren,
Heristelle on the Weser, Herstal, Ingelheim, Nijmegen, Quierzy, Selestat
and Thionville. The cities (in many of which royal palaces were also sited)
were Florence, Liège, Mainz, Pavia, Regensburg, Rome, Rouen, Worms
and Würzburg. Devotion to particular saints might be offered. When the
king was in Liège for Easter in 770, Lambert was honoured. In 774,
Charlemagne was invited to Lorsch to take part in the celebration of the
translatio of St Nazarius, and in 782 he paid a visit to Fulda and Hersfeld as
a sign of devotion to Boniface and Wigbert.[97] In 788 he attended the
translatio of Kilian, and in 793 Charlemagne again honoured St Kilian at
Würzburg and celebrated Christmas there, but moved on by boat to
Frankfurt for the rest of the winter.[98] Other trips to honour saints are
indicated for St Omer (Audomar and St Bertin), St Riquier (Richarius) and
Rouen (Audoin) in the king's tour of saints' burial places in 800. At
Tours Charlemagne prayed at the tomb of St Martin.[99] It is likely that
visits to Reims, Soissons and Mainz are also to be associated with the
veneration of Remigius, Medard and Alban, while in Italy he visited the
shrines of Benedict at Monte Cassino and Andreas on Mount Soracte. We
should, of course, also add Rome and Charlemagne's prayers at the tombs
of Sts Peter and Paul recorded in the *Liber pontificalis*.[100] Einhard insisted
on Charlemagne's devotion to St Peter, and visits to Rome were primarily
for the purpose for prayer (*orationis causae*) as far as the Royal Frankish
annalists were concerned.[101] In 781, Charlemagne's sons were anointed as
kings in Rome, and Pippin was baptized in Rome. That same year a sacred
connection was formed between the Carolingian family and St Ambrose,
for Charlemagne's daughter Gisela was baptized in Milan, presumably in
the church of San Ambrogio, with the archbishop of Milan standing as
godfather.

---

[96] A. Gauert, 'Zum Itinerar Karls des Großen', *KdG* I, pp. 307–21.
[97] According to different recensions of the *Chronicon laurissense breve*: see R. Corradini, *Die Wiener
Handschrift Cvp 430*: ein Beitrag zur Historiographie in Fulda im frühen 9. Jahrhundert*, Fuldaer
Hochschulschriften 37 (Frankfurt am Main, 2000); and H. Schnorr von Carolsfeld, 'Das *Chronicon
laurissense breve*', *Neues Archiv* 36 (1911), pp. 13–39.
[98] *RVARF* 793, ed. Kurze, p. 94.   [99] *ARF* 800, ed . Kurze, p. 110.
[100] *LP*, Lives 97, cc. 35–6, and 98, cc. 23–5, ed. Duchesne, I, pp. 496–7, and II, pp. 7–8.
[101] For example, *ARF* 786, ed. Kurze, p. 72.

In 775, in relation to wintering in Quierzy, Charlemagne took part in the dedication of the new buildings at St Denis and possibly visited the abbey again *en route* from Tours to Aachen in 800.[102] In Paderborn, as already remarked, he had the new basilica consecrated by the pope, just as Aachen's new chapel dedicated to the Virgin was later visited, if not actually consecrated, by Pope Leo on a subsequent journey to Francia.[103] It should be reiterated that Einhard refers to the wonderful church at Aachen, but the palaces he mentions are the one near the royal estates at Ingelheim and the other at Nijmegen on the Waal river. This implies that the principal building work at Aachen was devoted to the chapel and that it was initially created as a sacred site, enhanced by relics of the Virgin Mary herself. Once completed late in the 790s, the chapel enhanced Aachen's position in Charlemagne's sacred itinerary. There may also be a link between the creation of royal monasteries and the logistics of the royal itinerary. Even taking the patchiness of the charter survival into account, the enrichment of so many monasteries, among them St Denis, St Germain des Prés, St Martin at Tours, St Calais, Fulda, Honau, Hersfeld, Farfa, Nonantula and Kremsmünster, is remarkable.[104]

A sacred itinerary was thus at the core of Charlemagne's journeying from a time even before he became king. This is a strong indication of the part the religious devotion of the ruler, not just his reforming policy, played in his concept of rule and practice as a ruler throughout his reign. These places were presumably singled out among other possible locations as containing buildings both large enough for the royal household and appropriate for the performance of the royal Easter and Christmastide liturgies. Christmas in camp at Lügde in Saxony in 784 was presumably out of necessity rather than choice. Physically as well as spiritually, therefore, these places were set apart and different from those places visited for more mundane reasons, such as an assembly or gathering of the host.

Even the secular occasions could be sacralized, however, by the offering up of prayers and special rituals to indicate the ultimate guidance or the

---

[102] See above, pp. 182–4, 189–90.
[103] Lorsch annals 799, ed. G.Pertz, *MGH SS* I, p. 37 (though the implication of the text is that the pope had departed before the consecration of the new church); *ARF* 804, ed. Kurze, p. 119.
[104] See F. Prinz, 'Schenkungen und Privilegien Karls des Großen', *KdG* I, p. 488; J. Semmler, 'Karl der Große und das fränkische Mönchtum', *KdG* II, pp. 255–89, esp. 273–8. On cult sites see J. M. H. Smith, '*Aedificatio sancti loci*: the making of a ninth-century holy place', in M. de Jong, F. Theuws and C. van Rhijn (eds.), *Topographies of power in the early middle ages*, The Transformation of the Roman World 6 (Leiden, 2001), pp. 361–95; and P. Fouracre, 'The origins of the Carolingian attempt to regulate the cult of saints', in J. Howard Johnston and P. A. Hayward (eds.), *The cult of saints in late antiquity and the early middle ages* (Oxford, 1999), pp. 143–66.

protection of God for the army sought by those assembled. The campaign against the Avars was preceded, as we have seen, by three days of fasting, prayers and litanies.[105] The campaign in Saxony in the 770s is retrospectively sacralized by the annalist of the 'C' version of the *Annales regni francorum*. He inserted the extraordinary stories about the miraculous provision of water for the army in 772, the miracle relating to the saving of the church of Fritzlar from being burnt in 773, and the vision of the red shields and rout of the pagans in 776.[106]

Certainly the *Annales regni francorum* authors' intention was to frame the ruler's movements within explicitly Christian time. It is insufficient to regard this as simply the authors' imposition of a particular rhythm on the ruler, for Charlemagne himself seems to have cultivated a particular interest in the Christian calendar and the necessary calculations to establish the dates of Easter and related moveable feasts. Arno Borst has suggested that there may have been an intention to create an 'imperial' calendar, that is, a standard cycle of Christian festivals based on the material in an 'Encyclopaedia of time' and manuals of time produced within the court circle in the 790s and further augmented in 809.[107] This compendium provided both practical and theoretical information about the reckoning of time.[108]

Charlemagne's own sacred itinerary and interests in the charters and annals, as well as the relics and liturgical books that can be associated with him, are indeed indications, despite recent scepticism, that there was considerable success in establishing harmony in the liturgical calendar of the entire realm, as well as calendrical knowledge more widely.[109]

---

[105] *ARF* 791, ed. Kurze, p. 88, and see above pp. 43, 273, 309–10.

[106] *ARF* 772, 773, 776, ed. Kurze, pp. 34, 38, 44–6.

[107] A. Borst, 'Alkuin und die Enzyklopädie von 809', in P. L. Butzer and D. Lohrmann (eds.), *Science in western and eastern civilization in Carolingian times* (Basle, Boston and Berlin, 1993), pp. 53–78. See also McKitterick, *History and memory*, pp. 86–97.

[108] A. Borst, *Die karolingische Kalenderreform*, MGH Schriften 46. See also B. Englisch, 'Zeitbewusstsein und systematische Zeitordnung in den Kalendern des frühen und hohen Mittelalters', in H.-W. Goetz (ed.), *Hochmittelalterliches Geschichtsbewusstein im Spiegel nichthistoriographischer Quellen* (Berlin, 1998), pp. 117–30.

[109] The arguments of Borst, *Kalender reform*; of A. Graf Finck von Finckenstein, 'Fest- und Feiertage im Frankenreich der Karolinger', in R. Schieffer (ed.), *Beiträge zur Geschichte des regnum francorum: Festschrift Eugen Ewig*, Beihefte der Francia 22 (Sigmaringen, 1990), pp. 121–9; and of M. Sierck, *Festtag und Politik: Studien zur Tagewahl karolingischer Herrscher*, Beihefte zum Archiv für Kulturgeschichte 38 (Cologne, Weimar and Vienna, 1995), have been challenged by D. Starostine, who argues for the importance of the seasons and the secular agricultural cycle: '... *in die festivitatis*: gift-giving, power and the calendar in the Carolingian kingdoms', *Early Medieval Europe* 14 (2006), pp. 465–86 at p. 467. The two positions seem to me not mutually exclusive but rather complementary. See also P. Meyvaert, 'Discovering the calendar (*annalis libellus*) attached to Bede's own copy of *De temporum ratione*', *Analecta Bollandiana* 120 (2002), pp. 1–159.

At the heart of this calendar was the cult of saints. The king himself had encouraged a reverence for the saints of the past – whether apostles, Christian martyrs, Gallo-Roman and Merovingian bishops, Frankish monks or missionary saints – by decreeing that no new saints were to be venerated, but only those already chosen 'on the basis of their passions or lives'.[110] This was not only an endorsement of the historical dimension to Frankish spirituality, but also implies a recognition of the authority of the written accounts of the passions and lives of the saints and martyrs.[111] The Bavarian synods of Reisbach, Freising and Salzburg in 798 may represent an extension of earlier Frankish specifications for the observance of the feasts (in liturgical order) of Christmas, St Stephen, St John the Evangelist, Holy Innocents, the Octave of Christmas, Epiphany and the Octave, the Purification of the Virgin, the Octave of Easter, Ascension, Pentecost, St John the Baptist, Sts Peter and Paul, St Martin, St Andrew, and the Assumption of the Virgin.[112] Allowance is made for local feasts to be added. Right at the end of his reign Charlemagne required a core of uniform religious observance or at least one in harmony with local usage. That there was simultaneously room for local use is apparent in the suggestions made in 813 about the observance of saints' feasts. A group of liturgical feasts and saints' days was to be observed by everyone, but each priest was given the latitude to add local saints as required.[113] In 813, moreover, St Remigius was added to the general list, and other martyrs and confessors were to be added as appropriate in particular dioceses where their bodies rested or churches were dedicated to them.

It is clear from extant mass books and calendars, other synodal statements and the episcopal statutes even in the time of Charlemagne, that both the general observance of the principal feasts and local use and diversity were indeed maintained.[114] In keeping with the latitude for local

[110] *MGH Cap.* I, No. 28, Council of Frankfurt 794, c. 42, p. 77; trans. King, *Charlemagne*, p. 229. P. Fouracre, 'The origins of the Carolingian attempt to regulate the cult of saints', in J. Howard Johnston and P. A. Hayward (eds.), *The cult of saints in late antiquity and the early middle ages* (Oxford, 1999), pp. 143–67, has also interpreted this clause negatively as a limit set on the number of saints as part of a policy of the control of cults. Fouracre builds on the arguments of J. M. H. Smith, 'Oral and written: saints, miracles and relics in Brittany, c. 850–1250', *Speculum* 65 (1990), pp. 309–43.
[111] See the interesting discussion by F. Lifshitz, *The name of the saint: the Martyology of Jerome and access to the sacred in Francia, 627–827* (Notre Dame, Ind., 2006); and see also Smith, 'Oral and written'.
[112] *MGH Cap.* I, No. 81, c. 19, p. 179.
[113] *MGH Conc.* II.i, No. 36, c. 36, p. 269. The list from Mainz 813 was subsequently incorporated by Ansegisus into his capitulary collection, ed. G. Schmitz, *Die Kapitulariensammlung des Ansegis, MGH Cap.* Nova series I (Hanover, 1996), II, 33, pp. 555–6.
[114] Sierck, *Festtag und Politik*, pp. 40–9.

use, the calendars associated with Charlemagne himself give an indication of the saints he favoured. That in the Godescalc Evangelistary, for example (Paris, BnF n.a. lat. 1203, fols 121v–124r) listed a host of Roman martyrs as well as a handful of Italian saints from Milan (Nazarius, Gervasius and Protasius), Ravenna (Vitalis) and Vercelli (Eusebius).[115] It also included the major Gallo-Roman and Merovingian saints (some of them particularly associated with the Frankish kings or with the principal ecclesiastical centres of the realm) such as Martin (Tours), Remigius and Macra (Reims), Geneviève and Denis (Paris), Medard, Crispin and Crispianus (Soissons), Maximin (Trier), Symphorion (Autun), the missionary saints Kilian and Boniface, the church fathers Augustine, Jerome, Benedict, Silvester, Gregory the Great, and the supposed Roman martyr Petronilla, who had a special status for the Carolingian family. It also appears to have been from Charlemagne's palace that the observance of All Saints on 1 November was first introduced.[116] Other calendar material indicates that the king's own devotions are likely to have embraced, in addition to the major Roman saints and the Gallo-Roman and Frankish saints of the Godescalc Evangelistary, others such as Hilary, Maurice, Germanus, Vedastus and Amandus, and his own family saints Gertrude and Arnulf. The latter begins to make his appearance in the saints' calendars at the end of the eighth century.[117]

All this cannot be compartmentalized or marginalized either as a minor aspect of ecclesiastical regulation or as only the private devotions of the ruler. It is quite clear that major political occasions and royal demonstrations of power, from Charlemagne's coronation on the feast of St Denis onwards, were orchestrated within this essentially liturgical framework.[118] The Christian orientation of time was extended across the realm as

---

[115] On the knowledge of the Roman martyrs see McKitterick, *Perceptions of the past*, pp. 42–56.

[116] F. Piper, *Karls des Großen Kalendarium und Ostertafel aus der Pariser Urhandschrift herausgegeben und erläutert* (Berlin, 1858). On All Saints see H. Frank, 'Allerheiligenfest', *Lexikon für Theologie und Kirche* 10 (1965), col. 348; and G. Knopp, 'Sanctorum nomina seriatim: die Anfänge der Allerheiligenlitanei und ihre Verbindung mit den "Laudes regiae"', *Römische Quartalschrift* 65 (1970), pp. 185–231.

[117] See Coens, 'Anciennes litanies des saints', in Coens, *Recueil d'études Bollandiennes*, Subsidia hagiographica 37 (Brussels, 1963), pp. 129–322; and the list of saints in the reconstruction of the litany in Alcuin's prayer book, allegedly offered to Charlemagne, in S. Waldhoff, *Alcuins Gebetbuch für Karl den Großen: seine Rekonstruktion und seine Stellung in der frühmittelalterlichen Geschichte der libelli precum*, Liturgiewissenschaftliche Quellen und Forschungen, Veröffentlichungen des Abt. Herwegen-Instituts der Abtei Maria Laach 89 (Münster, 2003), pp. 347–8. On the cult of Arnulf and the Carolingians see O.-G. Oexle, 'Die Karolinger und die Stadt des heiligen Arnulf', *Frühmittelalterlicher Studien* 1 (1967), pp. 250–364, esp. pp. 361–2. On the development of sanctoral cycles in Merovingian Gaul see Y. Hen, *Culture and religion in Merovingian Gaul, AD 481–751* (Leiden, 1995), pp. 82–120.

[118] Sierck, *Festtag und Politik*, esp. pp. 18–67.

Frankish territory expanded.[119] Even so, the emphasis on Christian time evident in so many of the texts associated with Charlemagne, or those working closely with him, should also be set within the wider context of Charlemagne's own attempts to determine more general perceptions of the monthly, seasonal and agricultural cycle of the year reported by Einhard. These, like the Merovingian king Chilperic's attempts to introduce new letters into the alphabet recorded by Gregory of Tours,[120] or the ideological revision of the calendar by the French Revolutionary government,[121] appear to have had little or only short-term impact, but their character is nevertheless very revealing in terms of the king's general understanding of the year's cycle and how agricultural and Christian time were combined. Thus, most of the new names for the months proposed by Charlemagne are undoubtedly references to the seasons and rural activities, such as winter month (January/Wintermanoth), antler-shedding or mud month (February/ Hornung), hay month (July/Heuuimanoth), wine month (October/ Windumemanoth) or harvest month (November/Herbistmanoth), But three, Lenten month (March/Lentzinmanoth), Easter month (April/ Ostarmanoth) and Holy month (December/Heilagmanoth) are references to the Christian liturgical cycle.[122]

RELICS AND SAINTS

It is within this context of religious devotion associated with particular places and saints, already well developed in the Merovingian period,[123] and Charlemagne's *patroni speciales*,[124] that Charlemagne's own collection of

[119] Ewig, 'Gebetsdienst'. See also J. J. Contreni, 'Counting, calendars, and cosmology: numeracy in the early middle ages', in Contreni and S. Casciani (eds.), *Word, image, number: communication in the middle ages* (Florence, 2002), pp. 43–83.

[120] Gregory of Tours, *Historiae* V, 44, ed. B. Krusch, *MGH SRG* I/1, p. 254, and see P. Riché, *Education and culture in the barbarian west, sixth to eighth centuries*, trans. J. J. Contreni from the 1962 Paris edn with updated bibliography (Columbia, SC, 1976), pp. 223–5.

[121] B. Baczko, 'Le calendrier Républicain', in P. Nora (ed.), *Les lieux de mémoire*, 1: *la République* (Paris, 1984), pp. 37–83.

[122] P. E. Schramm, *Beiträge zur allgemeinen Geschichte*, 1: *Kaiser, Könige und Päpste. Gesammelte Aufsätze zur Geschichte des Mittelalters* 1 (Stuttgart, 1968), pp. 311–13. See also C. Hammer, *Charlemagne's months and their Bavarian labors: the politics of the seasons in the Carolingian empire*, BAR International series 676 (Oxford, 1997), esp. p. 80.

[123] P. Fouracre and R. Geberding, *Late Merovingian France: history and hagiography, 640–720* (Manchester, 1996), pp. 43–52.

[124] H. Nobel, *Königtum und Heiligenverehrung zur Zeit der Karolinger* (Heidelberg, 1956); and O. Guillot, 'Les saints des peuples et des nations dans l'occident des VIe–Xe siècles: un aperçu d'ensemble illustré par le cas des francs en Gaule', in *Santi e demoni nell'alto medioevo occidentale (secoli V–XI)*, Settimane 34 (Spoleto, 1989), I, pp. 205–59.

relics of the saints and his gifts of holy relics to other centres need to be considered.[125] Relics gave the owner special access to the holy, and embodied an element of Christian history.[126] Charlemagne's gift of relics of St Kilian and the Virgin Mary to Paderborn's new church on its consecration has already been noted in an earlier chapter.[127] An inventory of the relics of the cathedral of Sens compiled in 1192 preserves the memory of a large gift of relics made by Charlemagne on the occasion of the dedication of the church at Sens in 809 in the time of Archbishop Magnus, though the actual number was probably very much smaller.[128] A label of the early ninth century from Sens also refers to this gift. It lists a fragment from the Holy Sepulchre and a pebble from the river Jordan, and the *pallium* of the Virgin Mary as well as the relics of a number of early Christian, Roman, Gallo-Roman, Frankish, military and monastic saints, namely Stephen, John the Baptist, Gregory the Great, Isidore, Sulpicius, Anastasius, Martin, Anthony and Pachomius, George, Maurice, Candidus, Exuperius, Victor and Hilary. The Frankish saints included Landebert, Vedastus, Leodegarius, Desiderius, Gangulf and Servatius of Maastricht.[129] Charlemagne's gift may have included a relic of St Peter (described in a tenth-century label as having come from the palace), though this could also be a later royal gift.[130] Among the relics at Sens was at least one of St Andrew donated by Angilbert of St Riquier, famous for his relic collection, and whose new abbey church had been embellished with presents from Charlemagne.[131]

[125] H. Schiffers, *Der Reliquienschatz Karls des Großen und die Anfänge der Aachener Pilgerfahrt* (Aachen 1951); F. Prinz, 'Stadtrömische italienische Märtyrreliquien und fränkische Reichsadel in Maas-Moselraum', *Historisches Jahrbuch* 87 (1967), pp. 1–25; H. Röckelein, 'Über Hagio-Geo-Graphien: Mirakel in Translationenberichten des 8. und 9. Jahrhunderts', in M. Heinzelmann, K. Herbers and D. R. Bauer (eds.), *Mirakel im Mittelalter: Konzeptionen, Erscheinungsformen, Deutungen*, Beiträge zur Hagiographie 3 (Stuttgart, 2002), pp. 166–79.

[126] McKitterick, *Perceptions of the past*, pp. 54–56.

[127] Above, p. 252.

[128] M. Prou, 'Authentiques de reliques conservées au trésor de la cathédrale de Sens', *Mémoires de la Société nationale des Antiquaires de France* , 6th series, 9 (1898/1900), pp. 129–72 at pp. 131–2 and 135–40. See also P. Geary, *Furta sacra: thefts of relics in the central middle ages* (Princeton, 2nd edn, 1990), pp. 28–43.

[129] Prou, 'Authentiques de reliques', p. 162, No. 133 and Plate IX.

[130] Ibid., pp. 141–2, No. 5 and Plate VII; p. 147, No. 28 and Plate X.

[131] See Hariulf, *Chronique de l'abbaye de Saint-Riquier (Ve siècle – 1104)*, II, cc. 8–10, ed. F. Lot (Paris, 1894), pp. 61–7; S. Rabe, *Faith, art and politics at Saint-Riquier: the symbolic vision of Angilbert* (Philadelphia, 1995), pp. 120–1; K. Honselmannn, 'Reliquientranslationen nach Sachsen', in V. Elbern (ed.), *Das erste Jahrtausend* (Düsseldorf, 1962), I, pp. 159–93; H. Röckelein, *Reliquientranslationen nach Sachsen im 9. Jahrhundert: über Kommunikationen, Mobilität und Öffentlichkeit im Frühmittelalter* (Stuttgart, 2002); and M. McCormick, *The origins of the European economy: communications and commerce, AD 300–900* (Cambridge, 2001), pp. 283–4.

Angilbert records his gratitude to Charlemagne for the gift of relics brought from the regions of the whole of Christendom, including those from Rome given to Charlemagne by Popes Hadrian and Leo, and from Constantinople and Jerusalem brought by ambassadors sent there by Charlemagne. Hariulf's preservation of Angilbert's list in the eleventh-century history of St Riquier recorded the Roman saints Clemens, Crispin and Crispianus, Laurence, Sebastian, Petronilla, Anastasia and Paul, and a huge list of relics of virgins and martyrs, many of them also Roman. Petronilla, of course, was a saint with special status for the Carolingian family, devotion to whom had been particularly cultivated by Pippin and Charlemagne.[132] Judging from the script of the relic labels, the Carolingian royal convent of Chelles under Gisela's direction in the late eighth and early ninth centuries added to its remarkable seventh- and eighth-century collection a significant number of new relics : they included some of the water of the rivers Tigris and Euphrates flowing out of Paradise, a piece of the stone on which Moses had stood when he saw God, some water from the river Jordan, relics of such saints as Antony, Bartholomew, Baudilius, Benedict, Benignus, Boniface, Crispin and Crispianus, Desiderius of Vienne, Geneviève, Germanus, Gregory, Emmeram of Regensburg, John the Baptist, Leudegarius, Martial, Martin, Paul, Peter, Petronilla, Stephen the first martyr, and many more.[133]

Relics from the Holy Land, primarily associated with the places of Christ's ministry and passion,[134] reflected the Christian's regard for the holy places and acted as a physical representation of the places. Although many patristic writers, such as Gregory of Nyssa, Jerome and Paulinus of Nola, had sought to dissuade correspondents from undertaking a pilgrimage to the Holy Land itself on the understanding that Christianity is a universal faith irrespective of place, the literal enthusiasm for the biblical remains grew apace in the early medieval west.[135] Such relics constituted observable and historical verification of the events in the New Testament. Similarly, the Roman saints' relics together communicated a particular idea of Rome as a resting place of martyrs and saints who were associated with

[132] See McKitterick, *History and memory*, pp. 146–8.
[133] H. Atsma and J. Vezin (eds.), *Authentiques de reliques provenant de l'ancien monastère Notre-Dame de Chelles (VIIe-VIIIe siècles) découvertes par Jean-Pierre Laporte*; ChLA XVIII (Dietikon and Zurich, 1985).
[134] E. D. Hunt, *Holy Land pilgrimage in the later Roman empire, AD 312–460* (Oxford, 1982).
[135] See Kelly, *Jerome*, p. 71. Compare B. J. Kötting, *Peregrinatio religiosa* (Münster, 1950); A. E. Harvey, 'Melito and Jerusalem', *Journal of Theological Studies* 17 (1966), pp. 401–3; and E. D. Hunt, 'St Silvia of Aquitaine: the role of a Theodosian pilgrim in the society of east and west', *Journal of Theological Studies*, NS 23 (1972), pp. 351–73.

momentous events in the history of the church and of the Roman empire. Through relics not only was a spiritual link formed with the holy saint but also a physical link with the place, and the past of the place, from which the relic had come. The historical framework of the place to which the relic was translated was thereby extended. That the Franks felt a special responsibility for Roman saints is reflected in the famous clause of Pippin III's redaction of the *Lex Salica*, reiterated in the *Lex Salica karolina*, usually dated *c.* 802. There the Franks are represented as rescuing the relics of the blessed martyrs of Rome and revering them and decorating them with gold and precious stones.[136]

The Franks had their own saints too. The association of Frankish saints with Roman and Gallo-Roman saints in relic collections and church dedications further enhanced the status of the Frankish saints. Their past was connected to the Roman past of their own region, quite apart from the Roman past as a whole. Further, Frankish saints introduced into the newly conquered and newly converted areas extended Frankish Christianity, not only in terms of institutional structures and liturgical observance, but also in the specific foci of devotion. Many of the saints' relics in Saxony came via Charlemagne and were part of his strategy of conquest, though many more arrived during the reigns of his successors. Minden and Osnabrück received relics from Soissons and Rome/Gorze, and St Maria in Paderborn received a lock of the hair of the Virgin and relics of Crispin and Crispianus.[137]

We should not underestimate the political and ideological force of the physical presence, in newly conquered regions, of these essentially foreign, that is Gallo-Roman and Frankish, saints.[138] It is striking how many of the shrines visited by Charlemagne or the monasteries he favoured had a Gallo-Roman or Frankish connection. There are also the new

[136] *Lex Salica*, D and E, ed. K. A. Eckhardt, *MGH* leges nationum germanicarum 4.2 (Hanover, 1969), pp. 6 and 8. For a fuller discussion of the place of the Roman martyrs within a Frankish sense of the past see McKitterick, *Perceptions of the past*, pp. 35–61.

[137] See McCormick, *Origins of the European economy*, pp. 283–318; Röckelein, *Reliquientranslationen nach Sachsen*; R. Schieffer, 'Reliquientranslationen nach Sachsen', in *799 Kunst und Kultur*, III, pp. 484–97; J. M. H. Smith, 'Old saints, new cults: Roman relics in Carolingian Francia' and 'Appendix: relic translation from Rome to Francia 750–900', in Smith (ed.), *Early medieval Rome and the Christian west: essays in honour of Donald A. Bullough* (Leiden, 2000), pp. 317–40 at pp. 335–6. Her list makes it clear, however, that the majority of relics from Rome were translated from the 820s onwards. See also K. Honselmann, 'Reliquientranslationen nach Sachsen', in V. Elbern (ed.), *Das erste Jahrtausend: Kultur und Kunst im werdenden Abendland an Rhein und Ruhr*, I (Düsseldorf, 1962), pp. 159–93.

[138] Fouracre, 'The origin of the Carolingian attempt to regulate the cult of saints', p. 150.

missionary saints of the eighth century.[139] The reverence acccorded to relics echoes the devotion to these saints indicated in Charlemagne's calendars.[140] The saints' cults thus observed are a practical manifestation of the acceptance of the power of the saints and thus the role of the divine in Frankish affairs.

By means of royal gifts, particular saints became a focus of local religious loyalties in their new homes. They bound the new places to the old, and linked the newly established religious centres in the present with a Gallo-Roman and Frankish past, with virtual strands of memory and association. These became, both despite and because of their origin, an essential element of their own cultural identity. Relic translations and collections, in other words, played an important political role as part of the cultural 'glue' within the new Frankish empire as a whole. They formed a link between Christian past and future, and between things temporal and things eternal, to which Christians old and new had access.[141]

ROYAL PIETY

So far I have concentrated on the various ways in which Charlemagne promoted the Christianity of his subjects. These are virtually the only glimpses available of his personal convictions, but attempts have been made to get closer to his own expressions of his faith.[142] The tenor of Charlemagne's famous letter to Fastrada, the injunctions in so many of the papal letters to him preserved in the *Codex epistolaris carolinus* and the *arengae* of his charters all point to the articulation of the king's personal piety as well as his sense of religious obligation. The prayer book Alcuin devised for Charlemagne, apparently at his request, also gives us an important indication at least of what a close former associate thought

---

[139] I. N. Wood, *The missionary life: saints and the evangelisation of Europe 400–1050* (London, 2001); and L. von Padberg, *Mission und Christianisierung: Formen und Folgen bei Angelsachsen und Franken im 7. und 8. Jahrhundert* (Stuttgart, 1995).

[140] R. Schieffer, 'Reliquien Translationen nach Sachsen', in *799 Kunst und Kultur*, III, pp. 484–97, and map, p. 485.

[141] D. Bullough. 'Roman books and Carolingian *renovatio*', in D. Baker (ed.), *Renaissance and renewal in Christian history*, Studies in Church History 14 (Oxford, 1977), repr. in D. Bullough, *Carolingian renewal*, pp. 1–33 at p. 11.

[142] See the sensitive reading of the religious urgency of the capitulary of 811 offered by J. L. Nelson, 'The voice of Charlemagne', in R. Gameson and H. Leyser (eds.), *Belief and culture in the middle ages: studies presented to Henry Mayr-Harting* (Oxford, 2001), pp. 76–88. See also J. L. Nelson, 'Charlemagne the man', in Story, *Charlemagne*, pp. 22–37. Compare the remarks by H. Mayr-Harting, 'Charlemagne's religion', in P. Godman, J. Jarnut and P. Johanek (eds.), *Am Vorabend der Kaiserkrönung: Das Epos "Karolus magnus et Leo papa" und der Papstbesuch in Paderborn* (Berlin, 2002), pp. 113–24.

appropriate for the king in terms of daily prayer. Alcuin's work for the king is alluded to in the ninth-century *Vita Alcuini*.[143] A link with King David, who had 'established the canonical hours' for prayer, is mentioned in a letter from Alcuin to Charlemagne. It is this letter which has been proposed as one which originally served as a preface for the prayer book. The prayer book itself has been reconstructed from two later manuscripts containing what has been regarded as appropriate material, namely a confession, prayers (including a prayer in adoration of the cross, the Lord's Prayer, a prayer to the Trinity, Sts Peter and Paul, a prayer beseeching God's pity for a sinner and the *Kyrie eleison*), many psalm texts (including the seven penitential psalms), Jerome's prologue on how to integrate the psalms into daily prayer addressed to Paula and Julia Eustochium, and a litany of saints.[144] Some of these prayers are strongly worded, not least that in which the supplicant accuses himself 'of rushing into evil and bending his knees more often in fornication than in prayer, his belly distorted by greed and drink and his back strong in wickedness, his arms in lascivious embracings, his hands full of blood, his ears deaf to good, his eyes seldom fixed on God and his head rarely inclining to God'. Such personal abasement through these prayers and through the medium of the psalmist[145] may have been Alcuin's way of reminding the king of his human failings. But we have no certainty that the book ever reached the king, let alone that he actually used it.

Charlemagne's personal devotion to prayer is indicated more securely, first of all, in two, or possibly three, books associated with him and, secondly, in the creation of the palace chapel at Aachen for the celebration of the liturgy.

The large-format Godescalc Evangelistary (Paris, BnF n.a. lat. 1203, 310 mm × 210 mm) is most famous for the richness of its decoration, with purple-dyed parchment and gold and silver ink for the uncial script of the text. The codex contains six full-page illustrations: of the four Evangelists writing their books with their inspiring symbols in attendance, the fountain of life, and Christ in Majesty (also with a book), and many

---

[143] *Vita Alcuini*, ed. W. Arndt, *MGH SS* 15, 1, pp. 395–485. For the context of Alcuin's preparation of texts for private devotion see also D. Ganz, 'Le *De laude dei* d'Alcuin', in P. Depreux and B. Judic (eds.), *Alcuin de York à Tours: écriture, pouvoir et réseaux dans l'Europe du haut moyen âge*, Annales de Bretagne et des pays de l'Ouest 111 (Rennes and Tours, 2004), pp. 387–91.

[144] Waldhoff, *Alkuins Gebetbuch*, esp. pp. 341–91.

[145] Compare Charles the Bald's Psalter, Paris BnF lat. 1152; and R. Deshman, 'The exalted servant: the ruler theology of the prayerbook of Charles the Bald', *Viator* 11 (1980), pp. 385–417.

resplendent decorated *incipit* pages and initials.[146] Inserted into the margin of the Easter tables at the end of the codex (fol. 125r) corresponding to the year 781 is a note recording Charlemagne's visit to Rome and the baptism of his son Carloman as Pippin in St Peter's. From the *Annales regni francorum* we know that Queen Hildegard was there as well.[147] It is with this visit to Rome that the Godescalc Evangelistary has been directly associated, for there is also a dedication poem in the codex recording the commissioning of the book from Godescalc (fols. 126v–127r) in the four-teenth year of Charlemagne's reign. In a fascinating parallel, the Evangelistary was used 1,000 years later as a gift from the town of Toulouse to mark the baptism and coronation, as king of Rome, of Napoleon's son. The Godescalc Evangelistary, as we shall see, is regarded as the first of a series of books associated with the Hofschule or palace school of Charlemagne, that is, of a group of books linked with if not actually produced 'at court'.

While the book is acknowledged to be a dramatic celebration of Christ as the Word and of Christianity as a religion of the book, whose teaching was conveyed in texts, attention is usually focussed on the six illustrations which precede the text and other decorated pages in the manuscript. I shall have more to say about this aspect of the book's importance below, but want here to comment on the implications of its contents in relation to Charlemagne's own religious devotion. A book actually commissioned by Charlemagne and his wife, who was herself known for her piety, can be presumed to reflect something at least of the commissioners' choice of text. The book does not contain the full texts of the Gospels, but offers a new type of compilation of pericopes accompanied by the full passage from the Gospels to be read. Thus there are 208 extracts from them used as readings for the major feasts of the liturgical calendar, that is, pericopes, arranged in calendar order, with all the illustrations forming a set of images preceding

---

[146] B. Reudenbach, *Das Godescalc Evangelistar: ein Buch für die Reformpolitik Karls des Großen* (Frankfurt am Main, 1998). See also C. Nordenfalk, 'Der inspirierte Evangelist', *Wiener Jahrbuch für Kunstgeschichte* 36 (1983), pp. 175–90. In McKitterick, 'History, law and communication with the past', I failed to notice at proof stage that a sentence had got deleted which has made the comment there (pp. 952–3) about the Dagulf Psalter (Vienna *ÖNB* 1861) complete nonsense. It is the Godescalc Gospels (Paris BnF n.a. lat. 1203) dated 781 which were commissioned by Charlemagne and Queen Hildegard according to an inscription in them: see F. Mütherich, 'Manuscrits enluminés autour de Hildegarde'', and J. Vezin, 'Les livres dans l'entourage de Charlemagne et d'Hildegarde', in P. Riché, C. Heitz and F. Héber-Suffrin (eds.), *Actes du Colloque Autour d'Hildegarde*, Université Paris X Nanterre, Centre de recherches sur l'antiquité tardive et le haut moyen âge, Cahier V (Paris, 1987), pp. 49–55 and pp. 63–70. For further discussion of the Dagulf Psalter see below, pp. 333–8.

[147] *ARF* 780, ed. Kurze, p. 56.

the text. The pericopes and texts begin with the Christmas reading from Matthew's Gospel 1.18–21 and encompass the principal feasts associated with the life and passion of Christ and the major saints' festivals throughout the year.[148] The book also includes readings for various masses for the dead and votive masses with headings indicating the days for which they are intended. The book thus symbolizes the ecclesiastical chronology within which the king's devotion, and that within the palace, was organized. The calendar at the end, as Reudenbach has commented, reinforces this, though the days of each month are also numbered according to the Roman fashion in Kalends and Ides (similar to the dating practice in Charlemagne's charters). Godescalc's dedicatory poem reiterates how he has written the word of God and Christian teaching in gold and silver. The poem reinforces the themes of baptism and conversion, introduced with the illustration of the 'fountain of life' at the beginning of the codex, and acts as a further reflection of the aims expressed in Charlemagne's *De litteris colendis* and the *Admonitio generalis*. Laurence Nees, moreover, has proposed a further layer of interpretation of the 'fountain of life' picture. He has remarked, firstly, on the possibility that Godescalc might have been associated with Fulrad of St Denis, the palace chaplain, and thus have had a connection himself with St Denis. Consequently, Nees has suggested that Godescalc might have offered an image, in his 'fountain of life' picture, of Cathwulf's metaphor of the eight columns as a symbol of the foundations of a just and righteous realm and of a just king. This text, as we have seen, was preserved in a unique copy of a St Denis manuscript.[149] The codex as a whole, therefore, is a statement of the king's religious faith and obligations.

To the celebratory and baptismal theme of the Godescalc Evangelistary can be added the didactic and doctrinal emphases of the Dagulf Psalter (Vienna, ÖNB Cod. 1861), a sumptuous little book created by a member of the so-called Hofschule group of scribes and artists.[150] It is written entirely in gold apart from the crimson headings. The Dagulf Psalter is so called for

---

[148] A. G. Martimort, *Les lectures liturgiques et leurs livres*, Typologie des sources du moyen âge occidental 64 (Turnhout, 1992). See also C. Vogel, *Medieval liturgy: an introduction to the sources*, revised English edn by W. Storey and N. Rasmussen (Washington, DC, 1986), pp. 291–303; and T. Klauser, *Das römische Capitulare evangeliorum, 1: Typen*, Liturgiegeschichtliche Quellen und Forschungen 28 (Münster, 1935).

[149] On Cathwulf, see above, p. 44, and L. Nees, 'Godescalc's career and the problems of influence', in J. Lowden and A. Bovey (eds.), *Under the influence: the concept of influence and the study of illuminated manuscripts* (London and Turnhout, 2007), pp. 21–43. I am very grateful to Larry Nees for letting me read this important article in advance of publication.

[150] See further below, pp. 351–63.

the name of the scribe recorded in the book after a dedication poem addressed to Pope Hadrian I.[151] The book was completed before Hadrian's death in 795. Without any evidence for its location between its production and its presentation by the Emperor Henry IV to Archbishop Adalbert of Bremen in 1065, the Dagulf Psalter is usually assumed to have been a gift prevented by Hadrian's death, dated close to 795, and thus not to have reached Rome at all. The palaeographical and decorative features of the book, however, are consistent with a date in the early 780s. Long ago, James Mearns suggested that the Psalter had indeed reached the Lateran on Charlemagne's visit there in 787 (the earlier visit of 781 is not impossible) and became a gift in its turn from the then Pope Gregory VI to the Emperor Henry III on his visit to Rome in 1046–7.[152] This codex is one of a number of Carolingian royal manuscripts which ended up in the treasure of the Saxon kings of Germany as a consequence of royal gifts.[153] The exquisite late eighth-century ivory plaques forming the book's binding, depicting David the Psalmist and Jerome the translator, are judged to be an example, among a considerable number extant, of the work of ivory carvers producing book covers for the king. They were detached from the rest of the codex, probably during the seventeenth century, and are now in the Louvre.[154]

The Dagulf Psalter's commissioning by the king, however, means that its contents can be taken to represent texts used and approved by him, and it has rightly been interpreted as a statement of orthodoxy.[155] Although a psalter for Queen Hildegard produced at the same time has been lost since

[151] Facsimile in K. Holter (ed.), *Der goldene Psalter 'Dagulf-Psalter': Vollständige Faksimile-Ausgabe im Originalformat von Codex 1861 der Österreichischen Nationalbibliothek* (Graz, 1980); F. Mütherich, 'Die Erneuerung der Buchmalerei am Hof Karls des Großen', in *799 Kunst und Kultur*, III, pp. 560–609 at pp. 565–6; and H. Fillitz, 'Die Elfenbeinarbeiten des Hofes Karls des Großen', in ibid., pp. 610–22 at 610–13. See also R. Beer, *Monumenta palaeographica Vindobonensia: Denkmäler der Schreibkunst aus der Handschriftensammlung des Hapsburg-Lothringischen Erzhauses*, I (Leipzig, 1910), pp. 29–68 and Plates 17–26.

[152] J. Mearns, *The canticles of the Christian church eastern and western in early and medieval times* (Cambridge, 1914), p. 62.

[153] F. Mütherich, 'The library of Otto III', in P. Ganz (ed.), *The role of the book in medieval culture*, Bibliologia: Elementa ad librorum studia pertinentia 4 (Turnhout, 1986), pp. 11–26; and R. McKitterick, 'Ottonian intellectual culture and the role of Theophanu', *Early medieval Europe*, II (1993), pp. 53–74, repr. in McKitterick, *The Frankish kings and culture in the early middle ages* (Aldershot, 1995), Chapter XIII.

[154] D. Gaborit-Chopin and H. Fillitz, 'Die Elfenbeinarbeiten des Hofes Karls des Großen', in *799 Kunst und Kultur*, III, pp. 610–22 at pp. 610–11.

[155] D. Hägermann, 'Der Dagulf-Psalter: ein Zeugnis fränkischer Orthodoxie', in F.-R. Erkens and H. Wolff (eds.), *Von sacerdotium und regnum: geistliche und weltliche Gewalt im frühen und hohen Mittelalter. Festschrift für Egon Boshof zum 65. Geburtstag* (Cologne, Weimar and Vienna, 2002), pp. 83–201.

the fifteenth century, it has been surmised that its contents were similar.[156] The Gallican version of the Psalter, current in Frankish Gaul since the fifth century, and translated by Jerome from the Septuagint text included in the various versions presented in the *Hexapla* of Origen, was chosen in preference to the Roman Psalter (Jerome's corrected edition of the *Vetus Latina* text) used in Rome and Italy.[157] Such a choice would appear to spring from scholarly assessment of Jerome's enterprise. Indeed, the *incipit* of the book emphasizes the source of the Latin text. The teaching of doctrine is evident in the preliminary material supplied in the beginning on fols 5–22. These comprise three separate quires (of eight, eight and two leaves respectively). This material comprises a collection of creeds and creed commentaries, namely, the Nicene creed, the 'Ambrosian' creed and the creeds credited to Pope Gregory the Great and Gregory of Neocaesarea, the commentary on the creed by Jerome, the *Gloria*, an explanation of the Psalms taken from Jerome's letter 47 (to Pope Damasus) and his preface to the Psalms, chapters 1–4 of Cassiodorus' preface to his commentary on Psalms, a letter of Damasus (no. 5), further extracts from Jerome's letter 47, Isidore of Seville's section on the Psalter from his *Proemia* to the books of the Old and New Testaments, and some brief comments by Augustine on the Psalms.[158] This preliminary material is also to be found in a Lyon manuscript donated by Leidrad to St Stephen's monastery, *c.* 800. Delisle surmised that it had been compiled by Leidrad to provide him with ammunition against Adoptionism.[159]

The respect for the liturgical traditions of the early Christian church is evident in the selection of the canticles, or songs of praise taken from the Old and New Testaments, which accompany the Psalm text. Yet these diverse traditions were pulled together and regularized; the set of canticles first presented in the Dagulf Psalter became the standard in Carolingian Psalters thereafter.[160] They comprise the canticles of Isaiah (*Confitebor tibi*, Isaiah 12.1–6), Hezekiah (Isaiah 38.10–20, *Ego dixi in dimidio*), Anna,

[156] Mütherich, 'Manuscrits enluminés autour de Hildegarde', and Vezin, 'Les livres dans l'entourage de Charlemagne et d'Hildegarde'.

[157] B. Fischer, *Lateinische Bibelhandschriften des frühen Mittelalters, vetus Latina*, Aus der Geschichte der lateinischen Bibel 2 (Freiburg, 1985), p. 91; and J. N. D. Kelly, *Jerome* (London, 1975), pp. 159–63.

[158] Identified in Beer, *Monumenta*, p. 32.

[159] L. Delisle, 'Notice sur un manuscrit de l'église de Lyon au temps de Charlemagne', *Notices et extraits de la Bibliothèque Nationale et autres bibliothèques* 35 (1896), pp. 831–42 (on a manuscrit then in the Bibliothèque des Pères Maristes de Sainte-Foi lès Lyon).

[160] Mearns, *Canticles*, and see also H. Schneider, *Die altlateinischen biblischen Cantica*, Texte und Arbeiten 29–30 (Beuron, 1938).

mother of Samuel (*Exultavit cor meum*, Samuel 2.1–10), Moses in Exodus
(*Cantemus domino*, Exodus 15.1–19), Habakkuk (*Domine audivi*, Habakkuk
3.2–19) and another canticle of Moses (*Audite coeli*, Deuteronomy 32.1–43),
the hymn of the three boys from the book of Daniel (*Benedicite omnia opera*:
added to the Hebrew Book of Daniel in the Septuagint at Daniel 3.57–88),
the famous hymn *Te deum laudamus* (attributed here to Ambrose and
Augustine), the Canticle of Zacharias (father of John the Baptist)
Benedictus dominus deus Israhel, Luke 1.68–79, the canticle of the Virgin
(*Magnificat*, Luke 1.46–55) and the *Nunc dimittis* of Simeon (Luke 2.29–32).
These are followed in the Dagulf Psalter by the *Gloria*, the Lord's Prayer, the
Apostles' Creed and the so-called *Fides Athanasii* (Athanasian creed) or
Quicunque vult. The Apostles' Creed, of course, is the baptismal creed in
the version promoted by Charlemagne. Forms very close to the final received
text of this creed are found in late seventh- and eighth-century Frankish
books and it was virtually paraphrased in the *Admonitio generalis*. The
Quicunque vult includes the crucial support for the *filioque* addition to
the creed in specifying that the Holy Spirit proceeded from the Father and
the Son (*spiritus sanctus a patre et filio non factus nec creatus nec genitus sed
procedens*).[161]

Interestingly, the closest earlier parallels to the Dagulf Psalter's set of
canticles are the Vespasian Psalter, probably produced in Canterbury in the
eighth century, which has most of the canticles and five of the same
introductory pieces as in the Dagulf Psalter,[162] and the Psalter now BAV
reg. lat.11 (though the latter includes a group of canticles also found in the
Mozarabic Psalter). This Frankish *Psalterium Duplum* has been linked to
the early Carolingian royal court and may later have belonged to Eberhard
of Friuli whose wife Gisela was a granddaughter of Charlemagne).[163] It was
written in a distinctive Frankish uncial in the same scriptorium as the
Missale francorum, BAV reg. lat. 257.[164] I have suggested elsewhere that
these two books not only were to be linked to the liturgical reforms of

---

[161] *Admonitio generalis*, cc. 32 and 82, *MGH Cap.* 1, No. 22, pp. 56 and 61. See Kelly, *Early Christian creeds*, pp. 368–425, though his location of some of these Frankish books, such as the Bobbio Missal and Sacramentary of Gellone, is too far south.

[162] On the contents of the Vespasian Psalter see D. H. Wright (ed.), *The Vespasian Psalter, British Museum, Cotton Vespasian A.1*, Early English Manuscripts in Facsimile 14 (Copenhagen, 1967).

[163] A. Wilmart, 'Le psautier de la reine n. XI: sa provenance et sa date', *Revue bénédictine* 27 (1911), pp. 341–76; McKitterick, *Carolingians and the written word*, pp. 245–8; and R. McKitterick, 'Royal patronage of culture in the Frankish kingdoms under the Carolingians: motives and consequences', in *Committenti e produzione artistico-letteraria nell'alto medioevo occidentale*, Settimane 39 (Spoleto, 1992), pp. 93–129 at pp. 100–1, repr. in McKitterick, *Frankish kings and culture*, Chapter VII.

[164] *CLA* 1, 101 and 103.

Pippin III and his wife Bertrada,[165] but have affinities in terms of decoration and script with the books produced at Jouarre and the Carolingian royal monastery of Chelles in the eighth century. This Psalter, therefore, can be attributed to the Seine basin constellation of nunneries in this period, which may have been active in supplying liturgical books for the churches in their own or in adjoining dioceses.[166] This possible supply of liturgical books from religious houses enjoying other connections with the royal court has important implications for any assessment of the production of Charlemagne's books. I shall return to these below.

It is the canticles in the Dagulf Psalter which make the likelihood of its offering evidence of Carolingian royal devotion, whether in private prayer or in the palace chapel, more than mere wishful thinking. This regularized set of canticles, together with the entire Gallican Psalter text and, sometimes, a selection of the preliminary material as well, was subsequently repeated in Psalters written for other members of the Carolingian royal house by groups of scribes associated with each king, namely the Psalter of Lothar (London, British Library Add. MS 37768),[167] the Psalter of Charles the Bald (BnF lat. 1152),[168] and the Psalter of Louis the German (Berlin, Preussische Kulturbesitz / Deutsche Staatsbibliothek theol. lat. fol. 58).[169] Other early Carolingian psalters reproducing this set of canticles, and thus attesting to the effectiveness of the liturgical and textual examples set by books produced in association with Charlemagne, are Amiens, Bibliothèque Municipale 18 (the 'Corbie Psalter') and the so-called Psalter of Charlemagne from St Germain des Prés (Paris, BnF lat. 13159), dated *c.* 795–800. The latter, another Gallican psalter with additional prayers and written in a distinctive north Frankish uncial, has strong insular features in its codicology, orthography and decoration. Pope Leo and Charlemagne (as *rex*) are mentioned in one of the prayers, and the saints in the litany – Gereon of Cologne, Aldegonde of Mauberge,

---

[165] D. Bullough and A. L. H. Correa, 'Texts, chants and the chapel of Louis the Pious', in P. Godman and R. Collins (eds.), *Charlemagne's heir: new perspectives on the reign of Louis the Pious* (Oxford, 1990), pp. 489–508 at p. 496, repr. in Bullough, *Carolingian renewal*, pp. 161–240.

[166] R. McKitterick, 'Nuns' scriptoria in Francia and England in the eighth century', *Francia* 19/1 (1992) pp. 1–35 at pp. 20–2, repr. in R. McKitterick, *Books, scribes and learning in the Frankish kingdoms, 6th – 9th centuries* (Aldershot, 1994), Chapter VII.

[167] R. McKitterick, 'Carolingian uncial: a context for the Lothar Psalter', *The British Library Journal* 16 (1990), pp. 1–15, repr. in McKitterick, *Books, scribes and learning*, Chapter VI; and see also E. Screen, 'The importance of the emperor: Lothar I and the Frankish civil war, 840–843', *Early Medieval Europe* 12 (2003), pp. 25–52 at pp. 50–1.

[168] See Deshman, 'The exalted servant'.

[169] See E. Goldberg, *Struggle for empire: kingship and conflict under Louis the German, 817–876* (Ithaca, 2006), pp. 35–6, 46–7 and 285–6.

Gertrude of Nivelles, Lambert of Liège and Bavo of Ghent – endorse its Austrasian origins.[170] Later psalters closely connected with the court such as the Utrecht Psalter, produced at Reims *c.* 820, continue this tradition.[171] A later Reims psalter, for instance, that known as the Psalter of Count Achadeus of *c.* 880, also contains this set of canticles.[172]

A third book which seems to have ended up in Charlemagne's family circle is the Montpellier or Mondsee psalter. It was probably originally prepared at Mondsee for Tassilo and his family and was subsequently brought to Francia by a member of the family.[173] A magnificently decorated if rather small book (213 × 125 mm), with many letters in silver and gold and richly ornamented coloured initials, as well as two full-page miniatures of David and Christ, it contains the *Psalterium Romanum*. It includes a commentary on the Psalms inserted in the form of glosses throughout the text. These make reference to the *Psalterium Gallicanum*. There is also a Hebrew alphabet accompanied by the names of the letters at the beginning of the manuscript. Between 788 and 792, the same set of canticles as in the Dagulf Psalter, a litany of saints linking the book with Soissons, and *laudes* were added in two separate quires at the end of the original text.[174] A little later than this a St Amand-trained hand added a further prayer on fol. 345r–v. The script of the Canticles and *laudes* also resembles that of the Dagulf Psalter. The *laudes* celebrate many members of the Carolingian royal family, including Pippin the Hunchback, Pippin of Italy, Louis of Aquitaine, Charlemagne (described as *magnus et pacificus rex* and *a deo coronatus*) and Queen Fastrada as well as Pope Hadrian, all judges and the Frankish army. The *laudes* end with a prayer to 'Rotrude', who is thought to be the daughter of either Charlemagne or Tassilo of that name. The *laudes* also insert invocations in the Romance language to particular

---

[170] *CLA* v, No. 652, and *799 Kunst und Kultur*, II, XI, 19, pp. 808–10.

[171] K. van der Horst, W. Noel and H. Wustemann (eds.), *The Utrecht Psalter* (Utrecht, 1997).

[172] Cambridge, Corpus Christi College 272: see R.McKitterick, 'Psalter of Count Achadeus', in S. Panayotova and P. Binski (eds.), *The Cambridge illuminations: ten centuries of book production in the medieval west* (London, 2005), pp. 68–9.

[173] *CLA* vi, No. 795; and see F. Unterkircher, *Die Glossen des Psalters von Mondsee (vor 788) (Montpellier, Faculté de Médecine MS 409)*, Spicilegium Friburgense 20 (Freiburg in der Schweiz, 1974), esp. pp. 30–43 and 512; McKitterick, *Carolingians and the written word*, pp. 252–4; J. Semmler, 'Zu den bayerisch-westfränkischen Beziehungen in karolingischer Zeit', *Zeitschrift für Bayerische Landesgeschichte* 29 (1966), pp. 344–424; Waldhoff, *Alcuins Gebetbuch*, pp. 80–90; *799 Kunst und Kultur*, II, XI, 18, pp. 805–8; and C. Hammer, *From* ducatus *to* regnum*: ruling Bavaria under the Merovingians and early Carolingians* (Turnhout, 2007).

[174] Only the *Te deum* is in a different position: see Unterkircher, *Die Glossen des Psalters von Mondsee*, pp. 32–37. On the litany see M. Coens, 'Les Litaniae Carolinae de Soissons', *Analecta Bollandiana* 62 (1944), pp. 129–43. On the *laudes* see Unterkircher, *Die Glossen des Psalters von Mondsee*, pp. 38–43; and E. Kantorowicz, 'Ivories and litanies', *Journal of the Warburg and Courtauld Institutes* 53 (1935), pp. 56–81, esp. pp. 68–69.

saints after each royal name: St John after Pippin the Hunchback, St Maurice after Pippin of the Lombards, St Martin after Louis, and virgins of Christ after Fastrada. The interpretations of the Psalms, largely historical and christological in character, appear to have been designed to assist the reader in his or her study of the Psalms. That is, the layout of this book made it unsuitable for liturgical use. These books reinforce the evidence already provided by Alcuin's prayer book and the Dagulf Psalter for the important role of the Psalms as an aid to private devotion, and more particularly of the type of prayers, religious texts and didactic commentaries used by members of the ruling family.

These books also provide some clues to the king's own piety. How much this was privately expressed and how much more publicly before an audience is a matter of conjecture, but the creation of the palatine chapel at Aachen may provide some clues. For one thing, there is the extraordinary placing of his throne, which was constructed, it must be remembered, of reused stone brought from the Holy Land. Charlemagne's position on his throne in his chapel was not exactly one of abasement (as the wording of the penitential prayers in Alcuin's prayer book might otherwise have suggested). Instead, the one earthly king on his throne in the gallery looked the heavenly king, Christ in Majesty, who was depicted in mosaic close to Charlemagne's own level, straight in the eye across the space of the octagon. There is also the striking resemblance between Aachen's chapel dedicated to the Virgin and possibly consecrated as late as the papal visit of 804, Ravenna's imperial church of San Vitale, built in the reign of Justinian and famous for its mosaics depicting Justinian and his wife Theodora, and a number of other buildings in Ravenna. Between 788 and 791, furthermore, Pope Hadrian had given his consent to Charlemagne for the removal of mosaics and marble from Ravenna.[175] Even before his coronation as emperor, Charlemagne surely intended his chapel to be a resplendent statement of his religious devotion in the Roman imperial tradition, coupled with his effectively imperial might, raised above all other men, and commanding many *gentes*. The chapel, as already stressed above, displays Roman sculptures from antiquity as well as the wealth and splendour of many nations in the form of marble columns, fine building stone, ornamental metal work, and gold and silver ecclesiastical vessels.[176]

---

[175] *MGH Epp.* III, No. 81.
[176] On the ideological importance of Ravenna for the creation of the palace chapel at Aachen see above, p. 169. On the metalwork see K. Pawalec, *Aachener Bronzgitter: Studien zur karolingischen Ornamentik um 800* (Cologne, 1990).

Even more crucially, the palace chapel, and especially the chapel at Aachen once it was completed in the late 790s, served as the centre of the liturgical celebrations and reforms promoted by the ruler. The music, chant and readings in the chapel were supported by the attention given to procuring and reproducing the liturgical texts for use in the chapel, all of which were claimed to be Roman. Associated with these books was the production of corrected editions of the Bible and a court edition of the Gospels. All made the palace chapel, and arguably specifically the palace chapel at Aachen by the last two decades of Charlemagne's reign, the principal engine room of the Carolingian liturgical reforms. It should again be reiterated that Einhard refers to the wonderful church dedicated to the Virgin Mary at Aachen, but the palaces he mentions are the one near the royal estates at Ingelheim and the other at Nijmegen.[177]

Thus, as argued above, Aachen was initially created as a sacred site, enhanced by relics of the Virgin Mary herself, to form the principal focus of the king's sacred itinerary, symbolized in the growing use of the church at Aachen for the royal celebration of Christmas and Easter already noted.

THE PALACE CHAPEL AND THE LITURGY

Pippin III's religious policies, once he had assumed the kingship, had concentrated on establishing Carolingian political control of many monasteries and bishoprics, and on the general reform of religious practice and discipline. Ninth-century Frankish sources stress Pippin's patronage of the liturgy and his effort to replace the Gallican chant with what were claimed to be Roman chant traditions, though in many respects Pippin himself continued a tradition of liturgical patronage inaugurated by the Merovingian rulers of Gaul.[178] Yet the references to Pippin's reforms are all in general terms, and the only place specifically mentioned as promoting

---

[177] Einhard, *Vita Karoli*, c. 17, ed. Halphen, p. 50.
[178] Compare Walafrid Strabo, *Liber de exordiis et incrementis quarundam in observationibus ecclesiasticis rerum*, ed. A. L. Harting-Correâ, Mittellateinische Studien und Texte 19 (Leiden, 1996), pp. 168–9; Theodulf of Orleans, *Opus Caroli regis contra synodum (Libri I Carolini)*, c. 6, ed. A. Freeman, *MGH Conc.* II, Supp. 1, pp. 135–6; and the suggestions of P. Bernard, *Du chant romain au chant grégorien (VIe–XIIIe siècles)* (Paris, 1996), pp. 656–60 and 698–704. For discussion see J. Semmler, 'Pippin III und die fränkischen Klöster', *Francia* 3 (1975), pp. 88–146; and Semmler, 'Episcopi potestas und karolingische Klosterpolitik', in A. Borst (ed.), *Mönchtum, Episkopat und Adel zur Gründungszeit des Klosters Reichenau*, Vorträge und Forschungen 20 (Sigmaringen, 1974), pp. 305–96. On the liturgy see Y. Hen, *The royal patronage of the liturgy in Frankish Gaul to the death of Charles the Bald (877)*, Henry Bradshaw Society Subsidia 3 (London, 2001), pp. 42–64, with analysis of the older literature; and Claussen, *The reform of the Frankish church*, pp. 263–89.

'Roman' chant in Pippin's day was Metz under the direction of Bishop Chrodegang.[179] Charlemagne was a worthy heir to his father insofar as he too is associated with the promotion of a liturgy claimed to be Roman. He claimed, moreover, to be following in his father's footsteps. Again, it is the *Admonitio generalis* of 789 which stated this. The clergy were directed 'to learn the Roman chant thoroughly . . . it is to be employed throughout the office, night and day, in the correct form, in conformity with what our father of blessed memory, King Pippin, strove to bring to pass when he abolished the Gallican chant for the sake of unanimity with the apostolic see and the peaceful harmony of God's holy church.'[180] Apart from the extant liturgical books associated with the royal court, to be discussed below, the firmest evidence for the role of the palace chapel in promoting liturgical texts, liturgical music and orthodox faith comes from the reports of monks visiting Charlemagne's palace at Aachen. It was there in the chapel, so they claimed, that they had heard the Frankish clergy singing the version of the creed which included the word *filioque*. We learnt more about the singing of this *filioque* phrase in the discussion (above) of the meeting between Pope Leo III and Charlemagne's envoys in Rome in 810.[181] This dispute highlights both the practice of singing the liturgy of the palace chapel at Aachen by that time, and the role of the liturgy in communicating and expressing orthodox belief as well as promoting the harmony in texts and the singing of chant.[182] In Ermold the Black's elaborate account of the reception of Harald the Dane at the court of Louis the Pious in 826, he included a description of the procession into the church for the mass and Harald's baptism, and some indication of the music provided. The king was flanked by his chaplains Hilduin and Helisachar and the princes accompanying them. Theoto and his *tuba*, who kept the choirs in order, then led the clergy and choir. The *tuba Theutonis* has been suggested as referring, not literally to a trumpet or, more ingeniously, to a pitching instrument, but in fact to Theoto's own

[179] By Paul the Deacon, *Gesta episcoporum mettensium*, ed. G. Pertz, *MGH SS* 2, p. 268. Walafrid Strabo, *De exordiis,* ed. Harting-Correâ, p. 168 simply records Roman clergy who arrived with Pope Stephen (in 754).

[180] *Admonitio generalis*, c. 80, *MGH Cap.* 1, No. 22, p. 61. On these more general liturgical reforms see McKitterick, *The Frankish church*, pp. 115–54; and Hen, *The royal patronage of liturgy*, pp. 65–94.

[181] *ARF* 807 (and compare 799 and 809), ed. Kurze, pp. 108, 123, 129; and Willjung, *Konzil von Aachen 809, MGH Conc.* 11, Supp. 2, pp. 287–300. See also above, pp. 313–15.

[182] See R. McKitterick, 'Unity and diversity in the Carolingian church', in R. N. Swanson (ed.), *Unity and diversity in the Christian church*, Studies in Church History (Oxford, 1996), pp. 59–82; and K. Morrison, "Know thyself": music in the Carolingian renaissance', in *Committenti e produzione artistico-letteraria nell'alto medioevo occidentale*, Settimane 39 (Spoleto, 1992), pp. 369–479.

great voice intoning the beginning of the chant, that is, singing the first few words before everyone else joined in.[183]

Although the Godescalc Evangelistary is an early instance of the production of a new type of liturgical book for the king's private devotion, it is not until the end of the 790s that there is an indication that the palace chapel was beginning to act as a liturgical focus for the general promotion of 'Roman' liturgy announced in the *Admonitio generalis*. The close association of Charlemagne and his scholars, especially Benedict of Aniane, with the production of the famous *Hucusque* prologue and Supplement to the *Hadrianum* mass book is well known.[184] The prologue alludes to the sacramentary attributed to Gregory the Great but explains that material (comprising masses for Sundays, and occasions such as marriages, consecration of churches, funerals and the like) omitted by Gregory and drawn from other sacramentaries available in Francia has been appended to the main part of the sacramentary. The preface reassures its readers that 'we have inserted nothing in this book except the careful compositions of authors of the highest reputation for virtue and learning'. The outcome of this amalgamation was a combination of current late eighth-century Roman prayers, older practice understood to be Roman, and Frankish and Gallican texts.

The formation in the early ninth century of a new hymnary, made up of poetic texts to be sung during the Office, has been tentatively credited to the court and chapel of Louis the Pious, under the headship of the palace chaplains. The chaplains included, however, Hildebold of Cologne, who was Charlemagne's archchaplain from 791 and continued to hold the office until early in Louis's reign.[185] There is every likelihood, therefore, that the first stage of this 'New Hymnary' is also to be associated with the palace chapel in the reign of Charlemagne and, by the first and second decades of the ninth century, with the palace chapel at Aachen itself. The hymnary, therefore, should be added to the array of so many of the other 'authorized' or authentic texts of liturgical books produced in connection with or disseminated from the palace. In any case this new hymnary replaced a

---

[183] Ermold Nigellus, *In honorem Hludowici Pii*, lines 2482–2503, ed. Faral, *Ermold le noir*, pp. 188–90.

[184] P. Bernard, 'Benoît d'Aniane est-il auteur de l'avertissement "Hucusque" et du Supplément au sacramentaire "Hadrianus"?', *Studi medievali*, 3rd series, 39 (1998), pp. 1–120; and see above, p. 348, note 178. For the text see J. Deshusses, *Le 'sacrementaire grégorien': ses principales formes d'après les plus anciens manuscrits*, 3 vols., Spicilegium Friburgense 16, 24, 28 (Freiburg in der Schweiz, 1971, 1979, 1982); and see Vogel, *Medieval liturgy*, pp. 85–90. See also McKitterick, 'Unity and diversity'.

[185] See J. Mearns, *Early Latin hymnaries* (Cambridge, 1913); J. Szövérffy, *Die Annalen der lateinischen Hymnendichtung*, 1 (Berlin, 1964); H. Gneuss, *Hymnar und Hymnen im englischen Mittelalter* (Tübingen, 1968); and Bullough, 'Texts, chant and the chapel of Louis the Pious'.

north Frankish hymnary that itself appears to have been the first stage in a revision of the old Roman hymnary also associated with a royal chapel. Extant in six manuscripts of the second half of the eighth century and early ninth century, its earliest witness is BAV reg. lat. 11, the *Psalterium Duplum*, connected, as we have seen, with the royal court. It had reached Corbie, St Denis, Reichenau and St Gallen by the beginning of the ninth century.[186] Towards the end of Charlemagne's reign, the liturgy of the sacred palace is claimed to have had an exemplary function, for Leidrad of Lyon said the royal liturgy was the inspiration for his own liturgical innovations in Lyon.[187]

A major problem remains, namely, the location of any palace chapel with a principal role in the liturgy before the early ninth century. The surviving evidence has been presumed to indicate a settled place in one major palace chapel, somewhat on the lines of a Cambridge or Oxford college chapel, the royal chapel at Windsor, or the foundations of choristers associated with major cathedrals in England and Germany. This, rather than a small group established in each of the principal palaces of the Carolingian realm, among which that at Aachen gradually assumed pre-eminence, may well be correct. Yet what seems more likely, in the light of the sacred itinerary outlined above, is that there was a network of chaplains and priests, as well as of cantors and those able to sing the liturgy.[188] This network had presumably become established during the decades since 768, or even from the time that Pippin, with Chrodegang's support, had begun to take an interest in the liturgy. Once the palace chapel at Aachen was completed, it gradually began to provide a model, in both the texts used and the chants sung, to the various members of this network. It may then have begun to attract the most promising singers from within the network.

[186] H. Gneuss, 'Zur Geschichte des Hymnars', *Mittellateinisches Jahrbuch* 35 (2000), pp. 227–48 at pp. 233–5. The other manuscripts are Paris, BnF lat. 14088 (s.VIII/IX Corbie); Paris, BnF lat. 528 (s.IXin St Denis); Paris, BnF lat. 13159 (795–800, Austrasia); Oxford, Bodleian Library, Junius 25 (s.IXin Reichenau); Zurich, Zentralbibliothek, Rheinau 34 (s.IXin Reichenau or St Gallen).

[187] Leidrad, *Epistola ad Carolum*, ed. E. Dümmler, *MGH Epp.* IV (aevi karo., 11) (Berlin, 1895), pp. 542–4; and compare K. Levy, *Gregorian chant and the Carolingians* (Princeton, 1998), pp. 82–108 and 178–86; and the review by R. McKitterick, *Early Music History* 19 (2000), pp. 279–90. On other aspects of the possible function of particular palaces as a model, see M. Innes, 'A place of discipline: aristocratic youth and Carolingian courts', in C. Cubitt (ed.), *Court culture in the early middle ages* (Turnhout, 2003), pp. 59–76; and S. Airlie, 'The palace of memory: the Carolingian court as political centre', in S. Rees Jones, R. Marks and A. Minnis (eds.), *Courts and regions in medieval Europe* (York, 2000), pp. 1–20.

[188] Such a development is also suggested by the later anecdotes recorded by Notker Balbulus, *Gesta Karoli*, 1, cc. 5, 7 and 8, ed. Rau, *Quellen*, III, pp. 328–9; and H. H. Haefele, *MGH SS* rerum germanicarum, Nova series 12 (Hanover, 1959), pp. 8–10.

Chant, however, could not at this stage be disseminated in written form. It had to be promoted by means of living cantors who would teach chant, much as is described by Notker in the story already mentioned in an earlier chapter.[189] The main places for teaching the musical reforms of Pippin and Charlemagne were Metz[190] and the palace chapel, wherever that might have been in the early decades of Charlemagne's reign. The *Admonitio generalis* of 789 specified that the clergy were to learn Roman chant and the night Office and mass, and alluded to Pippin's efforts to do away with Gallican chant. The schools for training boys mentioned in the same capitulary included the need for them to learn singing. The incidental references to the *pueri* at the palace and singing in the chapel, together with the recurrent importance of the chapel, thus acquire greater significance. The letter from Leidrad of Lyon to Charlemagne already mentioned, moreover, records that Charlemagne had sent a cleric from Metz to teach singers so that in the *scola cantorum* at Lyon 'the rite of the holy palace (*sacrum palatium*) may be seen to be practised'.[191] Although Walafrid Strabo in the 820s recorded the coming of Roman chant to Francia in the time of Pippin III, John the Deacon claimed that it was Charlemagne who had noticed the lack of harmony between Roman and Frankish singing.[192] Notker related that the king was so unhappy about the fact that the churches throughout the kingdom differed so much in the way they worshipped God and in the rhythms of their chanting that he asked the pope to send him monks skilled in church singing. But the Roman monks decided to plot to prevent the Franks from achieving uniformity. Charlemagne heard the Advent or Christmas liturgies at 'Metz or Trier' and the following year 'at Paris or at Tours', and discovered that these monks had actually subverted Frankish chant and taught different ways of singing. Once discovered, two of Charlemagne's Frankish monks were then dispatched to Rome in order to learn it properly.[193]

---

[189] Above, pp. 156–7.

[190] Claussen, *The reform of the Frankish church*, pp. 274–5; and Paul the Deacon, *Gesta episcoporum mettensium*, ed. G. Pertz, MGH SS 2 (1829), p. 268.

[191] Leidrad, Ep., *MGH Epp.* V, ed. E. Dümmler; *MGH Epp.* IV (*karo. aevi*, II) (Berlin, 1895), pp. 542–4: 'ut iuxta vires nostras secundum ritum sacri palatii nunc ex parte agi videatur quicquid ad divinum persolvendum officium ordo deposcit.' Compare A. Coville, *Recherches sur l'histoire de Lyon du Vme siècle au IXme siècle (450–800)* (Paris, 1928), pp. 283–4.

[192] Walafrid Strabo, *Liber de exordiis*, ed. Harting-Correâ, p. 168; John the Deacon, *Vita sancti Gregorii magni*, PL 75, cols. 63–242 at cols. 90–1.

[193] Notker, *Gesta Karoli*, I, C. 10, in Rau, *Quellen*, III, pp. 334–6; ed. Haefele, p. 12. See the discussion by S. Rankin, 'Carolingian music', in McKitterick, *Carolingian culture*, pp. 274–316.

The available evidence suggests that there was a period of liturgical experimentation in the palace chapels and cathedrals during the reign of Charlemagne, especially in the chapel dedicated to Mary the Virgin at Aachen. The Franks in the late eighth and the early ninth centuries built on the liturgical innovations and practice of the late Merovingian period. New books and arrangements of liturgical prayers and readings were compiled. A major means of dissemination of liturgical texts, correct doctrine and liturgical melodies was in the chant; the cantors' expert memory was vital for the spreading of these innovations.[194] In the light of the claims the Franks made for their chants being Roman, the Frankish notion of Aachen as a new Rome thus acquires extra, liturgical and musical, dimensions. As with the latitude given for the observance of local saints' cults, however, so local and indigenous liturgical traditions were preserved alongside new liturgical texts and new types of liturgical books within the general context of *correctio* and orthodoxy.

ROYAL BOOKS

Royal piety and the palace chapel's pivotal role in the development of the liturgy manifested themselves above all in special editions of the key texts required. As we have seen, the letter to the lectors of *c.* 786, for example, also referred to the work of Paul the Deacon in preparing 'from the treatises and sermons of the various catholic fathers ... two volumes of readings suitable for each separate reading throughout the Christian year', which Charlemagne himself claimed to have examined and authorized to be read in the churches of his realm.[195] The *Hadrianum* sacramentary text purported to be a copy of an 'authentic' exemplar.[196] The promotion of the *Dionysio-Hadriana* collection of canon law has already been noted.[197] The text of the Bible itself was corrected and edited in the early Carolingian period.[198] From the Godescalc Gospel lectionary, it would appear that as

---

[194] J. Billett, 'Cantors, cantatoria, and the dissemination of Carolingian ecclesiastical reform in the ninth century', unpublished essay for the MPhil in Medieval History, Faculty of History, University of Cambridge (2003). I am grateful to Jesse Billett for permitting me to cite his work. See also R. Crocker, 'Carolingian chant: Roman, Frankish-Roman, Frankish', in R. Sullivan (ed.), *"The gentle voices of teachers": aspects of learning in the Carolingian age* (Columbus, Oh., 1995), pp. 142–70.

[195] *MGH Cap.* I, No. 30, pp. 80–1.

[196] Vogel, *Medieval liturgy*, p. 86; Deshusses, *Le sacramentaire grégorien*.

[197] See also L. Kéry, *Canonical collections of the early middle ages (ca. 400–1140): a bibliographical guide to the manuscripts and literature*, History of Medieval Canon Law (Washington, DC, 1999), pp. 13–20.

[198] B. Fischer, 'Bibeltext und Bibelreform unter Karl dem Großen', *KdG*, II, pp. 156–216; A. von Euw, 'Die Textgeschichte des Lorscher Evangeliar', in H. Shefers (ed.), *Das Lorscher Evangeliar*, Kommentar Band (Luzern, 2000), pp. 33–53; and see also R. McKitterick, 'Carolingian Bible

early as 781 Charlemagne had commissioned a text of the Gospels. The particular edition of the Gospels in the Godescalc lectionary, and the selection of Gospel texts, are also to be found in other Gospel books associated with a group of scribes and artists who appear to have been producing books for the king.[199] These were either for his own use or his family's, or were intended to act as royal gifts in order to promote the use of authoritative and correct texts. With such gifts as the Abbeville Gospels, given to St Riquier, and the Lorsch Gospels, donated to Lorsch, Charlemagne extended and developed what may have begun as the provision of a clear text for use in the palace chapel into the provision of a Carolingian Gospel text for the entire Frankish kingdom.[200] Thus the Christian ruler ensured that the word of God in a proper form was disseminated to all his leading monasteries and cathedrals. The written word in these books became an additional symbol of royal power and authority.[201] Yet these texts were also the practical means of communicating the king's wishes and preferences, and thus of exercising power and authority in the Carolingian world. Books and writing are crucial components of early Carolingian culture.

In the course of this book I have considered the origin, the audience(s) and groups of people among whom they might have circulated of many distinctive texts and categories of evidence. There remains a further group of sources exhaustively discussed by modern literary scholars, palaeographers and art historians, namely the manuscripts associated with Charlemagne and his court. In many ways these codices represent the best-known material dating from Charlemagne's lifetime. They comprise both those books assumed to have been produced in court circles and those the king is supposed to have owned. As with most of the other evidence

production: the Tours anomaly', in R. Gameson (ed.), *The early medieval Bible: production, decoration and use* (Cambridge, 1994), pp. 63–77, and F. Ronig, 'Bemerkungen zur Bibelreform in der Zeit Karls des Großen: Funktion und Ikonologie', in *799 Kunst und Kultur*, III, pp. 711–17.

[199] W. H. Frere, *Studies in the Roman liturgy*, I: *The Roman Gospel lectionary* (London, 1930). See also D. Bullough, 'Charlemagne's court library revisited', *Early Medieval Europe* 12 (2003), pp. 339–63, at p. 341 note 9. Koehler, *Karolingische Miniaturen*, II, pp. 14–16, discerned further textual affinities of the Gospel texts between the Coronation Gospels and the Abbeville Gospels in the Ada group in particular, whereas the text of the Soissons Gospels and the three minuscule codices in the Coronation Gospels group is different. The Godescalc Evangelistary, with its choice of Gospel readings for the liturgical year, needs to be compared with the *Breviarium* of Gospels included at the back of the other Gospel books in the Hofschule group. Two somewhat different selections can be identified. See above, p. 332

[200] For facsimiles see W. Braunfels (ed.), *The Lorsch Gospels* (New York, n.d); and Schefers, *Das Lorscher Evangeliar*.

[201] R. McKitterick, 'Essai sur les représentations de l'écrit dans les manuscrits carolingiens', in F. Dupuigrenet Desroussilles (ed.), *La symbolique du livre dans l'art occidental du haut moyen âge à Rembrandt*, *Revue française d'histoire du livre* 86–7 (Bordeaux, 1995), pp. 37–64.

relating to Charlemagne, however, discussions have proved far from conclusive. In the last few pages of this book, therefore, I return to this material and assess it anew.

The books associated with Charlemagne raise a number of questions. Some, as we have seen, may be books he himself commissioned for his own use in the palace chapel. Others may have been intended to be royal gifts of particular significance, for there are many Gospel books among them. Still other books may have been given to him. The circumstances of these books' production may shed further light on the notion of the royal court and its relation to the royal palaces. More importantly, they may have something to tell us concerning the personal interests of Charlemagne himself.

The thinking about the books associated with Charlemagne, however, has become increasingly muddled. Firstly, the efforts of modern scholars devoted to identifying books that might be associated with members of the court circle, however that circle might be defined, have failed to distinguish between these and those that might have been acquired by the king himself. Of course, it may not be possible to establish such a distinction, but that it may have existed should be acknowledged. Secondly, the assumptions concerning Aachen and the role of the court exposed in a previous chapter have greatly influenced not only current understanding of the evidence of Charlemagne's interest in education and learning and his patronage of various scholars, but also judgments concerning the link between various manuscripts and the court. Thirdly, the palace complex at Aachen has continued to be an attractive, if distracting, choice for modern historians as the venue for Carolingian scholarly and artistic activity, to the extent that 'pre-Aachen' and 'Aachen' phases have become established in modern understanding. The most productive period in Charlemagne's reign, in terms of chronology, was the 780s and early 790s. But in terms of geography it is not helpful to impose Aachen as a location of cultural activity, as distinct from recognizing the energizing effect Charlemagne appears to have had upon many individuals in a number of different places.[202]

There is, therefore, a clear disjunction in the chronology framing these assumptions, quite apart from other practical difficulties, such as where the scholars described as 'at court' found their board and lodging. As I concluded earlier, Aachen was one of a number of new palace complexes initiated under Charlemagne, particularly in the region of Austrasia, and

---

[202] D. Bullough, '*Aula renovata*: the Carolingian court before the Aachen palace', in Bullough, *Carolingian renewal*, pp. 132–60.

it is the liturgical role of the chapel that gave Aachen its pre-eminence.[203] The earliest evidence for Charlemagne's interest in learning and encouragement of scholars is from the late 770s and early 780s. The supposed completion of the Aachen chapel *c.* 795, its dedication as much as a decade later, and the king's eventual favouring of Aachen above all other centres as a residence for long periods in the last few years of his reign thus postdate the enticement of many foreign scholars to the Frankish kingdom. Many of these valued scholars, moreover, had moved to their prizes of abbacies and bishoprics by the time the palace complex at Aachen was completed, even if it is assumed that this was finished at about the same time as the chapel. Paul the Deacon, for example, returned to Italy in 786; Paulinus, bishop of Aquileia, was active in his see from 787; Angilbert was lay abbot St Riquier from 789/90; Theodulf was bishop of Orleans by 798; and Leidrad was established in Lyon from 797. Alcuin arrived only in 786 at the earliest, but was back in Northumbria between 790 and 793. He returned to Francia in the latter part of 793, and not until 794 was he formally received by the assembled bishops into their consortium and *confraternitas* of prayer at Frankfurt, at Charlemagne's request. It is supposed, on little more evidence than Einhard's later claim that Alcuin was personal tutor to Charlemagne, that Alcuin was residing in one of Charlemagne's palaces before he became abbot of Tours in 796.[204] Yet the poem by Theodulf in which Alcuin is mentioned in attendance at a special royal audience proves nothing about Alcuin's residence, or, for that matter, the residence of any other scholar or 'courtier'.[205] Confidence in Alcuin or any other scholar being based at Aachen at any stage between 786 and 796 seems ill founded. It was observed in an earlier chapter, for instance, that the poem *O mea cella* refers to Alcuin's life at York rather than at Aachen. In any case, most of Alcuin's writings date from his time at Tours and very few of his letters can be dated before 793.[206] In the later years of Charlemagne's reign, visiting scholars and others seeking patronage or political favours may well have established town houses clustered near the palace complex, like the one mentioned by Einhard as his own in Aachen in the 820s in his *Translatio*

---

[203] On Aachen's possible function as a church for the local community see J. L. Nelson, 'Aachen as a place of power', in de Jong, Theuws and van Rhijn (eds.), *Topographies of power*, pp. 217–42.

[204] Einhard, *Vita Karoli*, c. 25, ed. Halphen, p. 74.

[205] Theodulf, ed. E. Dümmler, *MGH Poet.* I, pp. 483–9, esp. lines 189–200.

[206] See above, p. 219; W. Edelstein, *Eruditio und sapientia: Weltbild und Erziehung in der Karolingerzeit. Untersuchungen zu Alcuins Briefen* (Frieburg im Breisgau, 1965); D. Bullough, *Alcuin: reputation and achievement* (Leiden, 2004); and P. Depreux and B. Judic (eds.), *Alcuin de York à Tours: écriture, pouvoir et réseaux dans l'Europe du haut moyen âge*, Annales de Bretagne et des pays de l'Ouest III (Rennes and Tours, 2004).

sancti Petri et Marcellini. In the early years, however, we may have to envisage favoured scholars simply joining the king in, or more likely staying near, one or other of his residences for short periods or for special meetings and ceremonial occasions from time to time, especially during the winter months when Charlemagne was not in the field.

Einhard's famous account of Charlemagne's pursuit and patronage of learning and cultivation of the liberal arts (*artes liberales*: a reference to grammar, rhetoric, dialectic, music, astronomy, arithmetic and geometry) has dominated historians' imagination. Charlemagne was taught grammar by Peter of Pisa and the other disciplines, especially rhetoric, dialectic, astronomy and *computus*, by Alcuin.[207]

It is important to remember that Einhard did not arrive at court until late in the reign, and he was writing with hindsight after Charlemagne's death. Even if Einhard's published account of Charlemagne's scholarly activities is not as early as I have postulated above, his description is that of an obituarist, a summary of achievements rather than a narrative, and was inevitably influenced by Einhard's most immediate recollections. He does not provide an historical account of the development of Charlemagne's interest in learning. He comments on Charlemagne's personal interests and the instruction the king himself received from a few scholars, some of which appears to have been in the form of letters rather than face to face.

Certainly Einhard's portrayal of a king who enticed teachers to his presence in order that he might be taught the liberal arts appears to be vindicated when the remarkable manifestations of the king's encouragement of learning and pursuit of knowledge across the kingdom are taken into account. These range from the many didactic and pedagogic tracts on grammar and spelling, the abundance of poetry and letters, to the commentaries on the Bible, sophisticated theological and philosophical discussion, encyclopaedias, and historical writing.[208] Yet the court's role in the transformation of personal interest into a kingdom-wide strategy, and

---

[207] Einhard, *Vita Karoli*, c. 25, ed. Halphen, p. 74. On *computus* and arithmetic, see W. Stevens, 'A present sense of things past: Quid est enim tempus?', in G. Jaritz and G. Moreno-Riaõ (eds), *Time and eternity: the medieval discourse*, International Medieval Research 9 (Turnhout, 2003), pp. 9–28; on astronomy, see B. S. Eastwood, 'The astronomy of Macrobius in Carolingian Europe: Dungal's letter of 811 to Charles the Great', *Early Medieval Europe* 3 (1994), pp. 117–34.

[208] For introductions to the enormous range of material and extensive secondary literature thereon see J. J. Contreni, 'The Carolingian Reniassance: education and literary culture', in *NCMH*, II, pp. 758–85; the essays assembled in McKitterick (ed.), *Carolingian culture*, esp. M. Garrison, 'The emergence of Carolingian Latin literature and the court of Charlemagne (780–814)', at pp. 111–40; and V. Law, *Grammar and grammarians in the early middle ages* (London, 1997), pp. 129–63.

specifically the role of the court's symbolic representative, Aachen, as the engine room for the promotion of learning, remain problematic. They are particularly so when attempting to identify, let alone locate, the books associated with Charlemagne.

The supposition in much of the current literature on Charlemagne's court that Aachen, 'where Charlemagne and his court almost never were', could not be a location of book production before 794 exposes the false expectation that the presence of the king and his 'court' was a necessary condition for the activity of scribes and artists writing for the king.[209] That is, it has been assumed that scribes and artists were based at court, so that the fantasy must necessarily envisage a workshop for scribes, artists, ivory-carvers and metalworkers, and space for those who worked there to live as well. Bullough, for example, referred to the king's *bibliotheca* in both the 'pre-Aachen and in the Aachen years'. Such assumptions about the role of the 'court', as well as that of Aachen itself, are nowhere more apparent than in the discussions of the production of books associated with the king and assigned to a 'court scriptorium' on the one hand, and in the notion of a 'royal library' on the other. The court scriptorium has even been defined as a non-monastic scriptorium with a high turnover of personnel of both scribes and artists.

All these scenarios may well be correct, but the evidence to support them is meagre, to say the least. Groups of scribes and artists undoubtedly produced books of very high quality, some of which can be specifically linked with the king. The scripts and decoration of these have enabled other books with similar script and/or decoration to be added to the group. The first matter that needs to be addressed, therefore, is whether Koehler and Bischoff and their adherents were correct in surmising that the books associated with this 'court scriptorium' were the work of a single atelier, or conceivably two ateliers, producing books for the king. Secondly, can the suggestion that these ateliers were located at 'court', that is, in one of Charlemagne's royal residences, let alone at Aachen, be sustained?

The court atelier

The study of the books associated with the court of Charlemagne rests on analyses of their script and decoration. The outstanding craftsmanship of the scribes and artists included in the so-called Hofschule group, formerly known as the Ada Gospels group, and associated with Charlemagne, is

---

[209] D. Bullough, 'Charlemagne's court library revisited', *Early Medieval Europe* 12 (2003), pp. 338–63.

Table 8 *The 'court atelier': the 'Coronation Gospels' group*

Coronation Gospels, Vienna Weltliche Schatzkammer der Hofburg (*CLA*, x, 1469) written
  in Rustic capitals and uncial in gold on purple parchment
Aachen Domschatzkammer Gospels caroline minuscule
Brescia, Biblioteca capitolare E.II.9 Gospels caroline minuscule
Brussels, Bibliothèque royale 18723 Gospels caroline minuscule

justifiably famous. The decoration of these books is astounding and very
beautiful. It is characterized by a stylized form of figure-painting, elaborate
architectural settings with painted representations of marble columns,
capitals, and arches and frames for the text set with cameos and engraved
gems, simulated jewelled bands and decorated borders framing the text, an
ambitious programme of introductory pages to the Gospels, canon tables,
and initials ornamented in insular interlace, and a wide-ranging palette of
colours. Many of the books are written in gold or silver on purple-dyed or
purple-painted parchment. The predominant script is a graceful Frankish
uncial, though there are pages in the new caroline minuscule and occasional use of rustic and square capitals in headings and the like.

The style of the 'Coronation Gospels' group, all members of which are
Gospel books, on the other hand, is far more realistic and 'painterly' (see
Table 8). The evangelists, for example, are set in landscapes or austere
classical architectural frames. Again, however, there is a lavish use of
purple-dyed parchment and gold and silver script.[210] The decorated
pages lack the elaborate simulated jewelled borders and ornate initials of
the Hofschule group, but the use of purple, gold and silver in both groups
suggests that these are indeed books to be associated with royalty.[211]

The style and script of this Coronation Gospels group, formerly associated with Charlemagne, appear to differ in too many respects from those
of the Hofschule group for us to be able to think of them as books
produced by the same group of scribes and artists. All four codices were

[210] B. Bischoff, 'Panorama der Handschriftenüberlieferung aus der Zeit Karls des Großen', *KdG* II,
  pp. 233–45, repr. in Bischoff, *Mittelalterliche Studien* 3 (Stuttgart, 1981), pp. 5–38; English trans.
  M. Gorman, 'Manuscripts in the age of Charlemagne', in Bischoff, *Manuscripts and libraries in the
  age of Charlemagne* (Cambridge, 1994), pp. 20–55; W. Koehler, *Die karolingische Miniaturen*, II: *Die
  Hofschule Karls des Großen* (Berlin, 1958); and III, *Die Gruppe des Wiener Kronungs-Evangeliars:
  Metzer Handschriften* (Berlin, 1960).
[211] McKitterick, *Carolingians and the written word*, p. 150, drawing on C. de Hamel, 'Books for
  emperors', in de Hamel, *An introduction to medieval illuminated manuscripts* (London, 1986), p. 46.

dated before 810 on art-historical grounds by Koehler,[212] but Bischoff subsequently considered these books, on the basis of the rustic capitals and minuscule scripts they contain, to be the work of several scribes early in the reign of Louis the Pious. He also suggested that the four scribes of the Brussels Gospels, dated to the first quarter of the ninth century, were trained in two places other than the 'court scriptorium', even though their artistic style was similar, and that the minuscule of the Aachen and Brescia Gospels is quite distinct from that of the Brussels Gospels.[213] Because this group is to be associated with Charlemagne's son, the Emperor Louis the Pious, it will not be prominent in the following discussion.

The relationship of the scribes and artists of the 'Hofschule group' to each other, their presumed membership of a 'court scriptorium', and where either scribes or artists might have been trained or based, however, are simply not clear. The very notion of a 'court scriptorium' in itself also needs to be examined afresh. A further consideration is the role of Charlemagne as patron; Bischoff at least became more inclined to see the use of special scripts and the choice of specific forms employed in the *de luxe* ('court school') manuscripts as having been decided 'at the highest level'.[214]

In order to assemble all the small details that need to be considered, I set out below a list of the books attributed to the 'court atelier', that is, the Hofschule (court school). This is compiled on the basis of Koehler's art-historical analysis, offered in 1958 and 1960, which was modified on palaeographical grounds by Bischoff in 1965 and again a decade later when he addressed the question of the books that might be associated with Charlemagne's son Louis the Pious. I then consider the implications of the books themselves in the light of their principal characteristics (of which I provide a brief summary).[215] As we shall see, both the codicology

---

[212] Koehler, *Kronungs-Evangeliargruppe*.

[213] B. Bischoff, 'Die Hofbibliothek unter Ludwig dem Frommen', in J. J. G. Alexander and M. T. Gibson (eds.), *Medieval learning and literature: Essays presented to Richard William Hunt* (Oxford, 1976), pp. 3–22, repr. in Bischoff, *Mittelalterliche Studien*, III (Stuttgart, 1981), pp. 170–186; English trans. M. Gorman, 'The court library under Louis the Pious, in Bischoff, *Manuscripts and libraries*, pp. 76–92, at p. 85.

[214] Ibid., p. 65.

[215] For a full account of the characteristics of these books see the relevant entries in *CLA*. J. A. Harmon, *Codicology of the court school of Charlemagne: Gospel book production, illumination, and emphasized script*, European Univerity Studies, series 28, History of Art 21 (Frankfurt, 1984), esp. pp. 260–83, offers supplementary observations on the display scripts and layout.

and the contents of the books themselves need to be taken into account, for both raise questions about the possible training and contacts of the men (and conceivably women) involved.

The books comprising the Hofschule have been divided into seven 'groups' of single books, pairs or trios of codices, with apparently only ten hands responsible altogether from a span of two or three decades (see Table 9).[216]

A further set of criteria for grouping these codices is their texts, namely the Gospels texts themselves, the prefatory letters and prefaces by Jerome, and the *Capitulare evangeliorum*. Analysis of these three elements led Koehler to group them as follows, in a manner that actually accords with the palaeographical grouping: I: Ada I, Arsenal and Harley; II: Soissons, Ada II and Lorsch. The Abbeville Gospels differ from both of these, and the Godescalc lectionary is a different type of book.

Other codices in which a hand from one of these groups occurs also need to be considered briefly, though they would merit a far fuller study than is possible here. A minuscule similar to that of the Harley Gospels is to be found in the additions at the end of the Moore Bede, Cambridge University Library Kk.5.16.[217] A copy of Tertullian's *Apologeticum* (St Petersburg, Saltykov-Schedrin National Library Q.v.I.40) was written in a minuscule similar to that of the Lorsch Gospels. The hand of the calligraphic minuscule below the miniature in the Cotton evangelistary fragment, moreover, appears to be the same as that which entered the list of six ecumenical councils in Einsiedeln, Stiftsbibliothek, MS 191, a copy of the *Collectio Quesnelliana* which Bischoff described as an excellent product of an 'unidentified North Frankish school' and a work 'fit for a king'. This canon law collection is chronologically arranged and is notable for the dossier of the first Synod of Nicaea and the letters of Pope Leo I that it contains. It appears to have been the favoured collection of canon law in Austrasia before it was superseded by the *Dionysio-Hadriana*.[218] It has obvious relevance as a handbook supporting Christian orthodox doctrine, especially in relation to Charlemagne's fervent commitment to orthodoxy stressed above. Like so many of the books connected with Hofschule group, it has some insular characteristics. In this manuscript, for instance,

---

[216] Listed and subdivided by Bischoff, 'The court library of Charlemagne', at p. 65 n. 45.

[217] *CLA*, II, 139.

[218] See R. McKitterick, 'Knowledge of canon law in the Frankish kingdoms before 789: the manuscript evidence', *Journal of Theological Studies* NS 36/1 (1985), pp. 97–117, repr. in McKitterick, *Books, scribes and learning*, Chapter 2; and J. van der Speeten, 'Le dossier de Nicée dans la Quesnelliana', *Sacris Erudiri* 28 (1985), pp. 383–450.

Table 9 *The 'court atelier': The Hofschule group*

GROUP I

Godescalc Evangelistary (Paris, BnF n.a. lat. 1203; *CLA* v, 681)
Script: gold Frankish uncial for text in ornamental frames; gold caroline minuscule for dedication poems (and some insular features)
Scribes: one, 'Godescalc'
Layout: 2 columns of 29 lines.
Quire marks: last page of quire has a Q under the left-hand column and a Roman numeral under the right-hand column
Decoration: 6 full-page illustrations (Christ in Majesty, Fountain of Life, four evangelists) in a set at the beginning of the codex.
Codicology: regular quires, ruled after folding, pricking in both margins

Ada Gospels Part I (Trier, Dombibliothek Cod. 22, fols. 17–38v; *CLA* ix, 1366)
Script: minuscule; headings in gold, square or rustic capitals
Scribes: 2 or more, one of whom, fols 17–38v, is Godescalc
Layout: 2 columns of 32 lines
Decoration: lovely ornamented initials, canon tables and decorated borders for the text pages. Note that the fact that the borders were done before the text is clearly visible.
Codicology: regular quires, ruling mostly after folding, prickings in both margins
Origin: book written at the order of Ada *ancilla dei*

Arsenal Gospels (Paris Bibliothèque de l'Arsenal 599; *CLA* v, 517)
Script: gold caroline minuscule with square capitals and uncial for headings
Scribe: one, hand very similar to that of Godescalc; begs the reader 'ORA PRO ME' on fol. 58r
Layout: 2 columns of 28 lines
Quire marks: Q below left-hand column on the last page of the quire and Roman numeral under the right-hand column
Decoration: fancy capitals and *incipit* pages, canon tables, but no evangelist portraits
Codicology: ruled after folding, prickings in both margins
Additions: Contemporary scholarly corrections to the *nomina sacra* with *dns* and *sps* expanded to *dominus* and *spiritus* when they referred to a secular lord and to an evil spirit respectively

GROUP II

Harley Gospels (London, British Library, Harley 2788; *CLA* ii, 198)
Script: uncial in gold for the text; *comes* in caroline minuscule; square capitals and red uncial for headings; Rustic capitals at line ends
Scribe: one, with some similarities to the Ada and Godescalc books, but with a different approach to the layout of the text
Layout: 2 columns of 32 lines

Table 9 (*cont.*)

Decoration: Evangelist portraits precede each Gospel; elaborate initials, *incipit* pages and canon tables. A prefatory frontispiece is provided for the Gospels as a whole, and the columns of text have decorated borders.
Codicology: ruled one leaf at a time; prickings in outer margins

GROUP III

Soissons Gospels (Paris, BnF lat. 8850)
Script: gold and silver square capitals, uncial and caroline minuscule
Scribes: probably one
Layout: 2 columns of 32 lines
Decoration: monumental *incipit* pages; evangelist portraits, heavenly Jerusalem and Fountain of Life miniatures, canon tables; decorated borders for the text columns

GROUP IV

Dagulf Psalter (Vienna, ÖNB lat. 1861; *CLA* X, 1504)
Script: gold minuscule text with headings in red uncial and some insular abbreviations
Scribes: 2; Dagulf wrote the psalm text and the other scribe wrote the canticles from fol. 146r
Layout: long lines (small format), 23 lines per page
Decoration: initial pages in gold and paint on purple background and many beautiful initials
Codicology: insular preparation of membrane, ruling after folding and prickings in both margins

A lost Psalter written in gold letters for Queen Hildegard; it has been lost since the fifteenth century but its contents may well have resembled those of the Dagulf Psalter.[a]

GROUP V

Cotton evangelistary fragment, London, British Library, Cotton Claudius B.V, fol. 132v.
Script: minuscule
(Burnt in Cotton fire so condition too poor for much useful comparison)

GROUP VI

Ada Gospels II (Trier 22, fols 38–172; *CLA* IX, 1366) ADD
Script: caroline minuscule for the main text; capitals; and uncials in headings and *incipits*.
Scribes: one? A younger hand than in Ada Gospels.
Layout: 2 columns of 32 lines
Decoration: evangelist portraits on single leaves inserted into the book

Table 9 *(cont.)*

Abbeville Gospels (Abbeville 4, *CLA* VI, 704)
Script: running titles in gold uncial colophon of Rustic capitals; gold uncial on purple-dyed parchment minuscule finishes a line on fol. 75r. Caroline minuscule on non-dyed parchment for the Breviarium with headings in red and green.
Scribes: one scribe
Layout: 2 columns of 32 lines
Decoration: evangelist portraits, magnificent *incipit* pages, initials and canon tables
Codicology: regular quires of 8 leaves, but no quire marks; ruled after folding with prickings in both margins
Origin: probably the codex given to Angilbert of St Riquier by Charlemagne and recorded in the inventory of St Riquier of 831.[b]

GROUP VII
Lorsch Gospels (Alba Julia, Roumania, Biblioteca Documentara Batthyáneum, R.II.1 + Rome, BAV pal. lat. 50)
Script: gold uncial for text; some Rustic capitals in red; caroline minuscule in gold for the *comes*
Scribes: one or two
Layout: 2 columns of 31 lines with decorated borders, a different design for every page
Decoration: canon tables, evangelist portraits, Christ in Majesty, illustrations of the *argumentum* for each Gospel; elaborate *incipit* pages
Codicology: prickings in both margins

---

[a] Mütherich, 'Manuscrits enluminés autour de Hildegarde'.
[b] Hariulf, *Gesta Centulensis*, ed. F. Lot Hariulf *Chronique de l'abbaye der Saint Riquier, Ve siècle–1104* (Paris, 1894), p. 88.

there are corrections from an insular scribe (Anglo-Saxon) on folios 10v and 33 and elsewhere, and the scribe demonstrated his knowledge of insular minuscule on lines 1 and 18 of folio 8v.[219]

The *Libri carolini*, of course, is closely associated with the discussions of the veneration of images within the court circle. The first hand of the *Libri*

---

[219] Ibid, and *CLA* VII, 874. According to Kéry, *Canonical collections of the early middle ages*, p. 27, another copy of this collection, Arras, Bibliothèque Municipale MS 644 (572) (*CLA* VI, 713), is from the same scriptorium (possibly in the Arras region). It is of significance that two further early copies of this collection, *c.* 780, are from the Lorsch region: Vienna ÖNB lat. 2141 and 2147 (*CLA*, X, 1505 and 1506). No modern edition or study of this text in its Carolingian context exists; H. Wurm, *Studien und Texte zur Dekretalsammlung des Dionysius Exiguus*, Kanonistische Studien und Texte 16 (Bonn, 1939), pp. 240–57, published only an inventory of the papal decretals it contains.

carolini manuscript begun 'at the court' is also related to that of the Cotton Evangelistary fragment,[220] while its second hand appears on the Ludwig Evangelistary, a codex written in gold caroline minuscule with some purple parchment pages, 'which was copied not far from the court'.[221] The text of the Ludwig codex is also related to that of the Godescalc Evangelistary. Similar hands are found in the Paterius manuscript, Munich, Bayerische Staatsbibliothek Clm 5255, fols 1.65v, with an insular 'g' in the hand of folios 66–117v and some insular ornamentation in the initials. One of these, on folio 152v, reminded Bischoff of the Dagulf Psalter, folio 146. Some corrections in this codex, moreover, are by a hand similar to that of Martinus the scribe in Paris, BnF lat. 1603, a codex containing the *Vetus gallica* canon law collection and some liturgical texts.[222] Brussels, Bibliothèque royale, II 2572, contains extracts from the grammar by Diomedes made by Peter of Pisa, written before 800.[223] If its contents, works by scholars associated with the court, could establish that this was the royal copy, then several more hands could be included in this group of scribes working in books associated with the court. A further book, namely Paris, BnF lat. 1718, a copy of Ambrose's *Hexameron*, whose 'graceful script' beginning on fol. 17v seemed to Bischoff to be slightly similar to that of the Godescalc evangelistary.[224] There is a note mentioning Hildebold in this manuscript (*Ego Hildebaldus haec*) written in the tironian notes employed by royal notaries in the royal writing office. This cannot of itself prove that the codex was written at court, as distinct from having been in Hildebold's hands at some stage, though Hildebold did serve as the royal chaplain from 791 to 818. It is significant that the text of this book has close kinship with two other north Frankish scriptoria of a similar date.[225] The hand which wrote folios 1–16v and folios 52–152 of the Paris copy of Ambrose also wrote some of the additions in Berlin theol. lat. fol. 354.[226] In addition, Lawrence

[220] *CLA* I, 52; and see A. Freeman, 'Theodulf of Orleans and the *Libri carolini*', *Speculum* 32 (1957), pp. 663–705, and 'Further studies in the Libri carolini', *Speculum* 40 (1965), pp. 203–69; and A. Freeman (ed.), *Opus Caroli Regis contra synodum (Libri carolini)*, MGH Conc. II.i, pp. 67–70 and Plates 2c–12.
[221] Ludwig IV.1 in Getty Museum, Los Angeles California: A. von Euw and J. M. Plotzek, *Die Handschriften der Sammlung Ludwig* (Cologne, 1979), I, pp. 203–5 with plate; and *799 Kunst und Kultur*, II, XI, 17, p. 805.
[222] *CLA* V, 531.
[223] *CLA* X, 1553; and see M. Gorman, 'Peter of Pisa and the *Quaestiunculae* copied for Charlemagne in Brussels II 2572, with a note on the Codex Diezianus from Verona', *Revue Bénédictine* 110 (2000), pp. 238–60.
[224] *CLA* V, 533. Compare Bischoff, 'The court library of Charlemagne', p. 65 note 45.
[225] Compare Bullough, 'Charlemagne's library revisited', p. 353, referring to Cambridge, Corpus Christi College Library, MS 193, and Paris, BnF lat. 12135.
[226] *CLA* VIII, 1067b.

Table 10 *Books linked to the Hofschule by*
coincidence of scribe

Tertullian, *Apologeticum*
Paterius, extracts from Gregory the Great
Ambrose, *Hexameron*
Eusebius-Jerome, *Chronicon*
Collectio Quesnelliania (canon law)
Penitiential material appended to Bede's *Historia ecclesiastica*
Evangelistary (Ludwig)
Libri carolini (*Opus Karoli regis*)
Peter of Pisa's extracts from the grammar of Diomedes
Gospels (of St Denis)

Nees has argued on the basis of the ornament that the 'St Denis Gospels', Paris, BnF lat. 9387, written in caroline minuscule, might be a late work of Godescalc from the 790s. A late addition to the group is the magnificent copy of Eusebius-Jerome, *Chronicon* (Leiden, Universiteitsbibliotheek, Scaliger 14).[227] This not only extends the network of scribal connection still further, but significantly augments the type of book associated with the court. These can be listed as in Table 10.

In general, books linked palaeographically by the common incidence of a scribe need not indicate their connection with the court. They could also represent other work done by these scribes for other centres or patrons elsewhere. The connections between these books on stylistic grounds are not doubted, but what such connections may signify is less certain. They may indicate occasional scribes in association with the court or on commission from the court producing books, as well as books written elsewhere being acquired by the king. They could also, of course, be a sign that the scribes producing books for the king's use were also producing books for other people and other centres.

To summarize, there are six Gospel books, two (possibly three) evangelistaries and one (possibly two) psalter(s) with sufficient stylistic and textual affinities to posit them as the product of a discrete group of scribes and artists, some of whom had been trained in the same place. These are of such magnificence and quality as to make it very probable that only someone of great wealth and resources, such as the king, could command

[227] B. Bischoff, *Katalog der festländischen Handschriften des neunten Jahrhunderts (mit Ausnahme der wisigotischen)*, Teil II: *Laon–Paderborn* (Wiesbaden, 2004), No. 2179, p. 48.

such work. There is a further group, mostly of patristic and canon law texts linked palaeographically or textually to the core of liturgical books. The coincidences of script, and of decorative style, link them together.

Any discussion of these books as the work of one atelier, a 'court atelier', also needs to bear in mind what the notion of a scriptorium implies. It rests on evidence, in the script and layout of each scribal portion of a book, of a degree of cohesion among members of a group and thus of scribal discipline. A scriptorium, in short, is an atelier which creates or perfects a calligraphic script of sufficient common discipline and uniformity to be termed a 'house style', and thus is the work of a group of scribes with a special set of attitudes and intentions in book production. The confidence with which the scripts of the books associated together as the Hofschule group were written indicates accomplished scribes writing in an already well established tradition. That is, this is the work of scribes at the peak of their form, with reputations already well established when they wrote these books. The character of their scripts indicates that they were somewhere in the middle to lower Rhine and Moselle regions. Our understanding of all the early Carolingian 'script provinces' rests on scripts which had become sufficiently distinctive to enable us to group them in such a way.[228] A lead-time for the training of such scribes has to be allowed for, furthermore, in order to account for the emergence of individuals whose scribal discipline was so well established and within whose handwriting the evolution of the new caroline minuscule had already been accommodated. Scribes such as those whose work is visible in the books produced for Charlemagne, or for institutions he patronized, therefore, would have had to be well trained before their earliest work of such a high standard can be recorded. How long such training might take is unfortunately impossible to determine. Nevertheless, the level of training and expertise points to an establishment or establishments equipped with appropriate personnel and with access to exemplars for the copying of books, open to the introduction of the new minuscule, prosperous enough to afford the initial outlay on writing and painting materials, and with connections with the royal household or royal family.

There is thus probably sufficient coincidence in script, decoration, text and codicology among the Hofschule books listed in Tables 9 and 10 for them to be attributed to a scriptorium. But their location, as distinct from the destination of the books produced, cannot be proven. Discussion has

---

[228] B. Bischoff, 'Panorama der handschriftlichen Überlieferung aus der Zeit Karls des Großen', *KdG* II, pp.233–45, repr. in B. Bischoff, *Mittelalterliche Studien*, III (Stuttgart, 1981), pp. 5–38.

become confused by a persistent but misguided tendency among some historians, on the one hand, to equate the evident scribal characteristics of a particular manuscript indicating where the scribe was trained with the actual origin of the books. On the other hand, it is not necessarily the case that the regular recipient of the books produced by a centre had them produced for him or her 'in house'. It is also essential to remember that scribes could move and are arguably most likely to have done so if their skill were such as to have brought them to the notice of the king or to the attention of those responsible for supplying the king's and the royal chapel's textual needs.

A body of accomplished scribes of diverse origins, who might have been diverted to write books as well as charters, were the notaries and chaplains of the royal household. Examples from St Gallen make it clear that scribes could write both chancery cursive and book hands. Both Godescalc and Dagulf refer to themselves as members of the *famulus* of Charlemagne. If they and their peers among the Hofschule scribes were indeed members of the royal household, then the notion of a 'court atelier' producing books for the king's use finds some firmer ground.

Bischoff long ago noted, however, a number of stylistic peculiarities in the production, writing and decoration of these books which throw light on the training of the scribes responsible. In the first place, the minuscule in the Godescalc Evangelistary and Dagulf Psalter resembles that of the early or 'Alter Stil' of Lorsch and also bears some resemblance to that of Metz and other unidentified centres in an 'Austrasian writing province'.[229] Further, the decoration of the Hofschule manuscripts includes insular motifs, such as interlace. The codicology of the Hofschule group includes preparation of the membrane in the insular manner. These striking insular features might be accounted for by the proximity to known centres of insular presence, such as Trier and Echternach. Many of these books are written in uncial script, though some also contain passages in a variant of the new caroline minuscule that was written in the region between the Rhine and the Moselle. An additional consideration is that the scribes may have received already decorated pages on which to copy the text, if the order in which decoration and writing were done in the Ada Gospels, for example, is anything to go by.

---

[229] For discussion of the notion of writing provinces see D. Bullough, 'Review article: a scholar's work is never done', *Early Medieval Europe* 12 (2003), pp. 399–407; and R. McKitterick, 'Carolingian book production: some problems', *The Library*, 6th series, 12 (1990), pp. 1–33, repr. in McKitterick, *Books, scribes and learning*, Chapter XII.

The Frankish uncial of these book, indeed, is too often ignored in discussions of the Hofschule codices, yet it provides one of the clearest indications possible of the books' affiliations. Bischoff's hypothesis concerning an Austrasian writing province at the end of the eighth century indicated possible parallels among the early caroline minuscule scripts associated with Metz, Lorsch and Weissenburg and those of Charlemagne's books. Godescalc's hand itself closely resembles the 'old style' of Lorsch and is linked to a centre where insular influence in the style of decoration and preparation of the membrane is also apparent.[230] The same can be said of other books produced within the diocese of Trier in the last two decades of the eighth century.[231] If one wanted to retain the notion of a group of scribes assembled at a palace in the region in the final decades of the eighth century, then that of Thionville, a short distance from both Trier and Echternach and accessible by boat, would be an obvious candidate.[232] All that the palaeographical and art-historical evidence permits, however, is the identification of groups of scribes and artists, not necessarily all based in the same place, who had been trained in the principal convents and abbeys of Austrasia where insular influence (associated with Echternach and Trier in particular) was present and whose connections with each other have long been recognized. Principal centres in this region where these groups might have been based included Pfalzel at Trier,[233] the community at St Maximin in Trier, where insular and Frankish scribes are known to have worked side by side,[234] Echternach,[235]

[230] B. Bischoff, *Die Abtei Lorsch im Spiegel ihrer Handschriften*, 2nd edn (Lorsch, 1989), pp. 21 and 27.
[231] H. H. Anton, *Trier im frühen Mittelalter*, Quellen und Forschungen aus dem Gebiet der Geschichte, NF 9 (Paderborn, Munich, Vienna and Zurich, 1987), p. 167.
[232] ARF, 773, 782, 805, 806, ed. Kurze, pp. 34, 64, 120, 121; and *Capitulare missorum in theodonis villa datum secundum, generale*, MGH Cap. 1, No. 44, pp. 122–6.
[233] M. Werner, *Adelsfamilien im Umkreis der frühen Karolinger: die Verwandtschaft Irminas von Oeren und Adelas von Pfalzel*, Vorträge und Forschungen Sonderband 28 (Sigmaringen, 1982).
[234] N. Netzer, *Cultural interplay in the eighth century: the Trier Gospels and the making of a scriptorium at Echternach* (Cambridge, 1995); and compare R. McKitterick, 'Frankish uncial: a new context for the work of the Echternach scriptorium', in A. Weiler and P. Bange (eds.), *Willibrord: zijn wereld en zijn werk* (Nijmegen, 1990), pp. 374–88, repr. in R. McKitterick, *Books, scribes and learning*, Chapter V.
[235] M. C. Ferrari, *Sancti Willibrordi venerantes memoriam: echternacher Schreiber und Schriftsteller von den Angelsachsen bis Johann Bertels. Ein Überblick*, Publications du CLUDEM 6 (Luxemburg, 1984); R. McKitterick, 'The diffusion of insular culture in Neustria between 650 and 850: the implications of the manuscript evidence', in Atsma, *La Neustrie*, pp. 395–432, repr. in McKitterick, *Books, scribes and learning*, Chapter III; McKitterick, 'Le scriptorium d'Echternach aux huitième et neuvième siècles', in M. Polfer (ed.), *L'évangelisation des régions entre Meuse et Moselle et la fondation de l'abbaye d'Echternach (Ve–IXe siècle)*, Publications du CLUDEM 16 (Luxembourg, 2000), pp. 499–522; and McKitterick, 'Buch, Schrift, Urkunden und Schriftlichkeit in der Karolingerzeit', in W. Pohl and P. Herold (eds.), *Vom Nutzen des*

Metz[236] and, given the connection between Trier and Lorsch through Ricbod, who was abbot of Lorsch between 784 and 804 and also archbishop of Trier from 791, Lorsch as well.[237]

Analogies with the supply of books from particular scriptoria such as Chelles in the eighth century to bishoprics such as Meaux or Cologne, and the functioning of the scriptorium and atelier of Reichenau in the later tenth and eleventh centuries in relation to the Ottonian rulers, provide an alternative. Similarly, the groups of scribes and artists associated with the royal court need not have been based at the court itself. Each group was, rather, working somewhere in Austrasia producing books for the king, and could also have produced books for other centres or individuals. A further group writing for the court may have been the accomplished scribes among the women at Chelles, presided over by their abbess, Gisela, Charlemagne's sister.[238]

There are textual links connecting writing centres too. The prolegomena of the Dagulf Psalter, for example, include four *capita* from the commentary on the Psalms by Cassiodorus. But this is one of the books copied by the nuns of Chelles and then completed at Corbie.[239] The characteristics of Chelles book production include a number of parallels (such as the use of Frankish uncial script) with those of the Austrasian region. There is some indication that the encyclopaedic compilation and codification of knowledge known as the *Liber glossarum* can also be linked to the court via Chelles. The earliest manuscripts of it are associated with the a-b scriptorium, a centre or group of scribes that has so far eluded location. As a development from the b-minuscule of the late Merovingian period, a-b has sometimes been linked with Corbie and Adalhard of Corbie, and the scribes responsible may have been female. Some years ago I suggested

---

Schreibens: soziales Gedächtnis, Herrschaft und Besitz, Österreichischen Akademie der Wissenschaften, phil.-hist. Klasse, Denkschriften 306 (Forschungen Zur Geschichte des Mittelalters 5) (Vienna, 2002), pp. 97–116.

[236] On Metz see Bischoff, 'Panorama', pp. 6–7.

[237] On Ricbod, see H. Fichtenau, 'Abt Richbod und de Annales lauteshamenses', in *Beiträge zur Geschichte des Klosters Lorsch*, 2nd edn, Geschichtsblätter für den Kreis Bergstraße, Sonderband 4 (Lorsch, 1980) pp. 277–304.

[238] B. Bischoff, 'Die Kölner Nonnenhandschriften und das Skriptorium von Chelles', in Bischoff, *Mittelalterliche Studien*, I (Stuttgart, 1966), pp. 16–34; and McKitterick, 'Nuns' scriptoria', pp. 1–35.

[239] Ganz, editorial addition to Bullough, 'Charlemagne's court library revisited', p. 349 note 42, notes that the Corbie copy is Paris BnF lat. 12239, and the Chelles copies are Paris BnF lat. 12240 and 12241. Compare J. W. Halporn, 'The modern edition of Cassiodorus' Psalm commentary', *Texte und Untersuchungen* 133 (1987), pp. 239–47. Bullough actually made a different point about the Cassiodorus *capita*, citing Theodulf of Orleans's use of Cassiodorus' commentary on the Psalms in order to suggest that a copy was available at court.

that the constellation of nunneries in the Paris basin, notably Chelles and Jouarre, with impeccable royal and Carolingian connections, produced books in the eighth century, a number of whose texts can be associated with the royal court. Not the least of these is the text of Cassiodorus' *Historia ecclesiastica tripartita*.[240] Chelles, therefore, may be another centre to be taken seriously as a location for scribes copying books for royal use.

Overall, it is not possible to locate the scribes producing books for the king. The strongest likelihood is of groups of very accomplished scribes working in one or more ateliers. There is nothing to prove or disprove that these were located at one of Charlemagne's Austrasian palaces, as distinct from some of the major monastic or cathedral centres in the Rhineland or Moselle regions. Two at least of the scribes, Dagulf and Godescalc, had personal connections with the royal court. Some of the non-liturgical texts produced, notably the *Libri carolini*, are undoubtedly closely related to royal interests. The scribes may also have produced books for other individuals and institutions, just as the artists may have worked for a number of different centres.

The royal library

The books linked palaeographically with the 'court atelier' manuscripts demonstrate how easily the question of the 'court atelier' merges into that of books associated with the court more generally. Conflating the royal library with texts used in their own writings by scholars known to have had some connection with the king certainly produces very interesting insights into intellectual activity in the late eighth and early ninth centuries more generally.[241] Unfortunately, however, it tells us nothing of Charlemagne's own books, for it rests on unprovable assumptions about where any scholar was when he wrote. A further factor is the extraordinary concentration of the earliest surviving manuscripts of classical Latin texts in manuscripts produced in early Carolingian Francia. An element of deliberate collection and preservation on the Franks' part has been inferred, not only from the sheer number of classical texts extant from this period, but also from Wigbod's dedicatory poem to his extracts on the Octateuch, customarily dated between 775 and 800. There, Wigbod referred to the collection of books which Charlemagne's *sententia* brought together from many lands

---

[240] McKitterick, *History and memory*, p. 240. For the significance of this as well as the Eusebius-Jerome *Chronicon* codex see further below.

[241] For a summary see Bullough, 'Charlemagne's court library revisited'.

and how he had revived the written heritage of the fathers.[242] Wigbod appears to be referring to Christian patristic works. Bischoff suggested that this statement might indicate that Charlemagne had issued some kind of appeal for rare or interesting ancient texts c. 780. A further hypothesis is that ancient codices were sent to the palace and copied, or else copies were made *in situ* in the ancient Gallo-Roman repositories that may have held them since the late Roman period, such as Reims, Tours or Lyon.[243] Certainly the number of Carolingian copies of classical and patristic texts implies a heightened consciousness of this type of text on the Franks' part. This would also accord with Charlemagne's own insistence on correct language and Latin and Christian learning.

That Charlemagne possessed books of his own is not in doubt. His collection is referred to by contemporaries in passing as the source of such texts as the *Historia naturalis* by Pliny or Augustine's letter to Jerome on the origin of the soul,[244] but was first broadcast by Einhard in preserving Charlemagne's will. In Charlemagne's instructions for the disposal of his possessions, the books in the chapel and the great number of books in his own library (*de libris, quorum magnam in bibliotheca sua copiam congregavit*) are distinguished.[245] The contents of this royal *bibliotheca* have proved difficult to determine. Bischoff first attempted a reconstruction in 1957, and six years later he presented a series of incremental hypotheses 'which enjoyed a high degree of probability'.[246] By 1976 the library was described as one 'founded on Charlemagne's orders' that 'contained rare and recently-discovered works as well as well-known items' and contributed

---

[242] Wigbod, *MGH Poet.* I, p. 96, trans. Bullough, 'Charlemagne's court library revisted', p. 340. On Wigbod see M. Gorman, 'The encyclopedic commentary on Genesis prepared for Charlemagne by Wigbod', *Recherches Augustiniennes* 17 (1982), pp. 173–201, and 'Wigbod and biblical studies under Charlemagne', *Revue Bénédictine* 107 (1997), pp. 40–76, both repr. in Gorman, *Biblical commentaries from the early middle ages* (Florence, 2002), pp. 1–29 and 200–36. On the preface see L. Munzi, 'Compilazione e riuso in età carolingia: il prologo poetica di Wigbodo', *Romanobarbarica* 12 (1992/93), pp. 189–210. Alcuin mentioned the possibility of Augustine's works on the soul being in a royal collection (*si forte in armario imperiali*), *PL* 101 col. 645 ; see Bullough, 'Charlemagne's court library', p. 354.

[243] See R. McKitterick, 'The scriptoria of Merovingian Gaul: a survey of the evidence', in H. B. Clarke and M. Brennan (eds.), *Columbanus and Merovingian monasticism*, BAR International series 113 (Oxford, 1981), pp. 173–207, repr. in McKitterick, *Books, scribes and learning*, Chapter 1.

[244] For example, Alcuin, *Epp.* 155, 162, 170, 309; *MGH Epp.* 4, pp. 250, 260, 280, 474; and Paul the Deacon, preface to the Epitome of Festus, ed. K. Neff, *Die Gedichte des Paulus Diaconus* (Munich, 1908), p. 124, and *MGH Epp.* IV, p. 508.

[245] Einhard, *Vita Karoli*, c. 33, ed. Halphen, p. 98.

[246] B. Bischoff, 'Die Hofbibliothek Karls des Großen', *KdG* II, pp. 42–62, repr. with revisions in B. Bischoff, *Mittelalterliche Studien*, III (Stuttgart, 1981), pp. 149–69; English trans. M. Gorman, in Bischoff, *Manuscripts and libraries in the age of Charlemagne* (Cambridge, 1994), pp. 56–75, esp. at pp. 62, 89 and 75 respectively.

to 'the preservation and diffusion of classical and patristic works and to the new educational ideas which depended on them'.[247] Speculation about the contents of this library has centred first of all on the relatively secure ground of books and texts mentioned as having been read by, given to or dedicated to Charlemagne, such as the *Dionysio-Hadriana* collection of canon law sent by Pope Hadrian in 774, the Epitome of Festus sent by Paul the Deacon in the mid-780s, and Wigbod's work on Genesis.

More problematic is the key piece of evidence in Bischoff's argument, namely, a list of classical and fourth-century works entered into a late eighth-century collection of grammatical texts and poems by scholars associated with the royal court. This is the famous codex Berlin, Deutsche Staatsbibliothek Preussische Kulturbesitz Diez B. Sant. 66, a collection of grammars by Donatus, Servius and Pompeius, a text entitled *De litteris*, and excerpts from Books I and III of the *Etymologiae* of Isidore of Seville concerning grammar and music.[248] The codex was written by two main scribes, one trained in north Francia and the other a contemporary north Italian. Some insular symptoms are to be noted as well. It was the Italian hand that added, on spare leaves and empty spaces on various pages (pp. 2, 66, 67, 116–28, 217, 363), not only the list of books but also some early court poetry and other short texts. The latter include an anonymous commentary on the *Centrimetrum* of Servius, which mentions *Pippinus rex francorum et omnium galliarum* in the introduction, and a short extract from Porphyrius' *Carmen figuratum*. The added poems, all composed before 791, include that celebrating Pippin of Italy's victory over the Avars (pp. 127–8), poems addressed to Peter of Pisa by Angilbert, Charlemagne and Paul the Deacon, and two poems from *Fiducia* to Angilram, written before 791 by someone who knew Charlemagne and Angilram. It is these verses which seemed to Bischoff to militate against an Italian origin for this section of the manuscript (he did not see how they could have come into the hands of Peter of Pisa), and this excluded for him the possibility that the list was of books in an Italian centre. He may have been too quick so to rule out this possibility (Angilbert himself could have shown them to Peter) but it is very difficult to be certain one way or the other.

[247] B. Bischoff, 'Die Hofbibliothek unter Ludwig dem Frommen', in Alexander and Gibson, *Medieval learning and literature*, pp. 3–22 at p. 3, repr. in Bischoff, *Mittelalterliche Studien*, III, pp. 170–86 at p. 170; English trans. M. Gorman in Bischoff, *Manuscripts and libraries*, pp. 76–92 at p. 76.
[248] *CLA* VIII, 1044. See the facsimile edition, B. Bischoff (ed.), *Sammelhandschrift Diez. B Sant. 66: grammatici latini et catalogus librorum*, Codices selecti (Graz, 1973).

Table 11 *The list of classical and late antique works in Berlin, Preussische Kulturbesitz Diez. B. Sant. 66, pp. 218–19, as identified by Ullmann.*[a]

Extracts from Bk IX of Virgil's *Aeneid* and Book III of the *Georgics* (from a *Cento*?)

Lucan, *De bello civilis* (On Caesar, Pompey and the destruction of Rome's freedom)

Terence, *Andria* (and the other comedies)

Iuvenal, *Satires*, Bk II, Satire 6 (invective on the affectations and immorality of Roman women)

Tibullus, elegiac rural and love poems (in two books; or, Book II)

Horace, *Ars poetica* (500 lines about epic poetry and drama)[b]

Claudian, *De raptu Proserpinae* (epic myth about Persephone's descent into the underworld; the capture of Proserpina was also the scene depicted on Charlemagne's sarcophagus)

Claudian, *Ad Rufinum* (invective)

Claudian, *In Eutropium* (invective)

Claudian, *De bello Gothico* (contemporary history written against Alaric the Goth, 401–2)

Claudian, *De bello Gildonico* (an historical epic on the African warlord Gildo)[c]

Martial, *Epigrams*, Bks I–IX (the *incipit* given is from Book I, epigram 36)

Julius Victor, *Ars rhetorica* (a short manual on rhetoric) (a part thereof)

Servius, *De finalibus* (a grammatical text)

Cicero, Catiline orations (political invective) (seven books, so this may includer the 3 Caesarian speeches)

Cicero, oration for King Deiotarius (defence speech)

Cicero, *In Verrem* (prosecution speeches, numbers I, II and III?)

Sallust, on the Catiline conspiracy

Cato, *Sententia in senatu* (presumably the *Dicta Catonis*, a collection of moral maxims in prose and verse)[d]

Sallust, *Iugurtha* (history of the Roman war against Jugurtha, king of Numidia)

Sallust, *Histories* (on the period 78–67 BC)

Alcimus, *Dictiones* or *Controversiae* (texts now lost)

Messius Arusianus, *Exempla elocutionum* (a grammarian writing *c.* 400 who quotes Cicero, Virgil, Sallust and Terence)

---

[a] B. L. Ullmann, 'A list of classical manuscripts (in an eighth-century codex) perhaps from Corbie', *Scriptorium* 8 (1954), pp. 24–37.

[b] This manual by Horace became very influential subsequently.

[c] By the eighth century Claudian was assumed to have been a Christian. His work was full of narrative descriptions, speeches and allusions to classical poets.

[d] Ullmann, 'A list', overlooked this item.

The texts listed are identified by author, *incipits* or *explicits* of particular volumes of the works mentioned, and occasionally by title. It may be helpful to set out the list as in Table 11 with some explanatory comments about the texts.

Discussion of this list has become sidetracked onto the possible relation of particular items to extant manuscripts (especially those connected with Corbie), whether the list is Frankish or Italian, and whether it can be regarded as linked with the court.[249] These discussions have established that the texts were current in the early Carolingian period, and that many scholars knew them, allude to them or actually quote from them, quite apart from the number of extant ninth-century manuscript witnesses to them.

Script and contents alike of this codex appear to suggest a Carolingian court connection in the reign of Charlemagne. Of the two Frankish courts at this time, either the Frankish court of Pippin of Italy or the Frankish court of his father is possible. In that the Frankish script in this book is joined by an Italian minuscule script, the book has seemed to modern scholars to offer two principal alternatives. Firstly, it was written and compiled by a Frank and a Lombard at the Frankish court of Charlemagne and the list is of books in Charlemagne's court library. Alternativly, it was compiled in Italy and the list represents a list of books in Northern Italy.[250] The possibility of a book started in Francia and taken to Italy and completed there is a variant of this.

As I have commented elsewhere, the list's possible origin at the court of Pippin of Italy would offer a glimpse of a court circle there. Such an origin would have the merit of leaving room for the other elements of Bischoff's thesis concerning later north Frankish copies of the texts listed, in contrast to the very meagre evidence for extant ninth-century copies of classical texts from northern Italy.[251] The procurement of exemplars could have benefited from links between Pippin's and his father's households. One might, nevertheless, need to ask about the possible object of the poem celebrating Pippin's victory and the circumstances in which both it and the grammars comprising the bulk of the book's contents might have been copied. One could envisage such a poem arriving at the court of Charlemagne as a form of report and homage for his son.

The character of the list as a whole, however, is crucial, and is the one matter consistently not addressed in discussions of this list hitherto. The codex is predominantly devoted to Latin grammar and style. The list of

[249] See also B. Bischoff, 'Hadoardus and the manuscripts of classical authors from Corbie', in S. Prete (ed.), *Didascaliae: studies in Honor of Anselm M. Albareda* (New York, 1961), pp. 41–57; revised version in Bischoff, *Mittelalterliche Studien*, I, pp. 49–63.
[250] For the royal library see Bischoff, 'Die Hofbibliothek Karls des Großen'. A case specifically for Verona was made by C. Villa, 'Die Horazüberlieferung und die "Bibliothek Karls des Großen": zum Werkverzeichnis der Handschrift Berlin, Diez B. 66', *Deutsches Archiv* 51 (1995), pp. 29–52, but the precise link is disputed; see T. Licht, 'Additional note on the "Library catalogue of Charlemagne's court"', *Journal of Medieval Latin* 11 (2001), pp. 210–13. See also Gorman, 'Peter of Pisa and the *Quaestiunculae*', pp. 248–50.
[251] McKitterick, *History and memory*, pp. 80–1.

texts complements the rest of the contents of the book, for it effectively presents a syllabus for learning to read Latin.[252] It is significant that portions of particular texts are specified, and that others are rather short.[253] Thus this is neither a random list nor a shopping list. It is also not necessarily a list of the contents of any particular collection of books. The works listed form a teaching collection. The list offers texts which require varying degrees of competence, from the relatively basic to the more advanced. They would have assisted the process of acquiring literary skills. Five of the authors, Arusianus Messius and the quadriga of Virgil, Terence, Sallust and Cicero, were part of the Latin syllabus by late antiquity.[254] Three of the authors, Statius, Claudian and Cato, are among the *sex auctores* associated with the medieval school curriculum before the thirteenth century. In addition to the late antique authors Avianus (*Fabulae*) and the Elegies of Maximinian of the sixth century, a Carolingian member of these *sex auctores* was the *Eclogue* of the writer known as Theodulus (a name Paul Winterfeld suggested was a Latinization of Gottschalk), though he probably wrote his *Eclogue* during the reign of Louis the Pious or Charles the Bald.[255] The texts specified in the Diez B Sant. 66 list offer comments on moral worth, a sample of different types of Latin prose and poetry, variants in style such as the smooth, plain and elegant language of Tibullus or the terse style of Sallust, and convey something of classical mythology, Roman history and culture. The list is not, in short, a record of books that were necessarily together in any library, royal or otherwise, but of texts useful for teaching purposes. It offers a glimpse of the process of the formation of a teaching canon of texts in the early middle ages.

---

[252] I owe this suggestion to David McKitterick.

[253] On Carolingian teaching and curricula, see the many studies by J. J. Contreni gathered in his *Carolingian learning, masters and manuscripts* (Aldershot, 1992); Contreni, 'The Carolingian renaissance: education and literary culture', in *NCMH*, II, pp. 709–57; and Contreni, 'The pursuit of knowledge in Carolingian Europe', in R. Sullivan (ed.), *'The gentle voices of teachers': Aspects of learning in the Carolingian age* (Columbus, Oh., 1995), pp. 106–41. Note too the cautionary remarks of D. Ganz, 'Conclusion: visions of Carolingian education, past, present and future', in Sullivan, *'The gentle voices of teachers'*, pp. 261–84.

[254] H. Marrou, *A history of education in antiquity* (Madison, Wis., 1982), trans. from the original French edition of 1948 in London, 1956, pp. 277–8.

[255] See N. Orme, *English schools in the middle ages* (London and New York, 1976), p. 103; G. L. Hamilton, 'Theodulus: a medieval text book', *Modern Philology* 7 (1909), pp. 1–17 (pp. 169–85) and the text in J. Osternacher (ed.), *Theoduli ecloga* (Linz, 1902). Despite some of these authors being mentioned in Carolingian discussions of school books he surveyed, Günter Glauche was disinclined to define the books in the Diez B. Sant. 66 list as 'Schullektüre': G. Glauche, *Schullektüre im Mittelalter: Entstehung und Wandlungen des Lektürekanons bis 1200 nach den Quellen dargestellt*, Münchener Beiträge zur Mediävistik und Renaissance-Forschung 5 (Munich, 1970), pp. 21–2.

Frustratingly little, therefore, can be established with any confidence about the royal library of Charlemagne, as distinct from a large number of major classical and patristic works possessing possible or even probable links with the king and his family, or with scholars patronized by the king. As we have seen, the production of a corrected and revised text of the books of the Bible, particularly the text of the Gospels and the Psalter, can be attributed to royal initiative. Alcuin of Tours, Theodulf and others combined Old Latin versions of different books of the Bible with the Vulgate translations made by Jerome in the early fifth century.[256] Similarly, versions of other books for the mass, the homiliary, hymnary, secular laws, and canon law, appear to have been produced or procured on the prompting of the king. Further, 'authentic' versions of texts, such as the Rule of Benedict or the *Dionysio-Hadriana* collection of canon law, were recommended. I have argued elsewhere, moreover, that the extraordinary concentration of Roman and ecclesiastical history books from the late eighth and the early ninth centuries suggests a systematic provision of history books more generally in Charlemagne's kingdom. There are a number of history books that have been linked, on palaeographical grounds, to members of the royal family, to the scribes writing the liturgical books intended for royal use, or to royal monasteries particularly favoured by the king. These include such codices as the magnificent copy of the Chronicle of Eusebius-Jerome, now in Leiden,[257] the *Liber Albini Magistri*, which Walafrid Strabo saw at the court of Louis and from which he extracted a world history down to the year 809,[258] the Tripartite History of Cassiodorus, connected to Chelles, and the copy of Bede's *Historia ecclesiastica*. Then there is the composition of the annals of Frankish history, let alone the extensive and related recourse to historical precedent and historical example referred to so often in Charlemagne's charters, letters and capitularies. All these together offer a substantial indication of the cultivation, within the royal circle, of an interest in Roman history, secular historiography and early Christian history in the late eighth and early ninth century.[259]

---

[256] Above, pp. 308–9.

[257] On the wider context see McKitterick, *Perceptions of the past*, pp. 7–33.

[258] See Bischoff, 'Eine Sammelhandschrift Walafrid Strabos', *Mittelalterliche Studien*, II (Stuttgart, 1967), pp. 34–51 at p. 43.

[259] McKitterick, *History and memory*, esp. pp. 208–10.

A tradition of writing: the Roman past and the Roman present

Two common elements emerge from all these disparate pieces of evidence and the various texts associated in one way or another with the king and his principal associates. The first is the network of scholars and centres devoted to education and learning within the Frankish realm, rather than one solitary place where culture is focussed. The inability to pin down cultural activity to 'the court' is in fact the strongest possible indication of the achievement of the king in promoting its dispersal throughout the kingdom. The attendance at the assembly at Frankfurt in 794 of bishops from all the regions of the Frankish realm, for example, is just one sign of the sheer reach of Charlemagne's cultural network and the influx of cultural and intellectual traditions from all corners of the realm. The discussions at Frankfurt display Charlemagne as a ruler in the late Roman imperial style as well as a *rex sapiens*. Just as effective communications underpinned Charlemagne's authority and government, so communication by letter, poem, treatise and book secured Christian Latin learning in a myriad of different centres of production from the Paris Basin to eastern Bavaria, and from the north of Saxony to the Pyrenees.

Secondly the formation of a tradition of writing and learning to be observed in all the compositions of Charlemagne's scholars as well as in his own capitularies, letters and charters was securely anchored in the Roman, Christian and Frankish past. The Latin language was the principal medium for this. Its conservation and promotion entailed the continuance of many of the cultural emphases written in that language. The Christian religion and the association with Rome on many different levels also transmitted a complex understanding of the Roman past.[260] Yet at every point, the seventh- and eighth-century Merovingian antecedents of the Franks continued to have a place in Carolingian cultural patterns, just as they had done in the political and religious spheres.[261]

Charlemagne's consciousness of a very diverse cultural and political inheritance, and the keenness to cherish, correct, enhance, augment and regularize (insofar as this was consistent with local traditions) the books and artefacts that formed that inheritance, are apparent from all the various enterprises discussed so far in this book. All the scholars who claimed to

[260] McKitterick, 'The Franks and Rome', in McKitterick, *Perceptions of the past*, pp. 35–61.
[261] See P. Fouracre, 'The long shadow of the Merovingians', in Story, *Charlemagne*, pp. 5–21; R. McKitterick, 'Eighth-century foundations', in *NCMH*, II, pp. 681–94; and McKitterick, 'Das Konzil im Kontext der karolingischen Renaissance', in Berndt, *Das Frankfurter Konzil von 794* II, pp. 635–76.

have been personally encouraged by Charlemagne aligned themselves with a particular intellectual tradition that explicitly based itself on an expectation of continuity with the Roman and Merovingian past. As a consequence of Charlemagne's political expansion, this tradition embraced the cultural and intellectual traditions of regions outside or incorporated within the Frankish realm, including the British Isles, northern Spain, Bavaria and Italy. It formed the practical underpinning of a distinctive sacred topography and cosmic ideology.

While Charlemagne was at St Peter's basilica in Rome in 800, Zacharias and two monks – one from the monastery of Mount Olivet and the other from Saba in the Holy Land – came to see him, bearing special gifts: the keys of the Lord's sepulchre and of Calvary, and the keys of Jerusalem and Mount Sion. On one level these were familiar political and diplomatic gestures acknowledging the extent of Charlemagne's earthly power. Yet because of all that Charlemagne had done by then to promote orthodoxy in relation to Adoptionism and the veneration of images, these gifts also recognized the spiritual and religious dimension of Charlemagne's kingship. With his authority coming from God and his *ministerium* serving the entire *ecclesia*,[262] Charlemagne's rule combined earthly and heavenly concerns. Four years before the meeting in Rome, moreover, Pope Leo III had sent legates to Charlemagne to inform him of Leo's election in succession to Pope Hadrian. These legates presented the Frankish ruler with the keys to the tomb of St Peter and the banners of the city of Rome. Again, the symbolic force of the connection with the sacred by the granting of keys was reinforced.

Just as Charlemagne manipulated the political and geographical space of his empire, so the sacred territory of the Franks expanded to embrace heaven and the realm of Christ and his saints; the horizons of the Carolingian empire reached towards the heavenly Jerusalem. Indeed, one of the court school Gospel books included a representation of the heavenly Jerusalem in the prefatory images before the main text.[263] A further dimension of the Frankish empire is that of time. The slow rise of the Carolingian family to conquest and dominance throughout the Frankish realms was recorded, as we have seen, in the principal Frankish annals in the later eighth and early ninth centuries. Yet contemporary Frankish history was also placed by its authors in the context of the history of Rome and of the Franks in the

---

[262] M. de Jong, 'Ecclesia and the early medieval polity', in Airlie, Pohl and Reimitz, *Staat im frühen Mittelalter*, pp. 113–32.

[263] B. Kühnel, *From the earthly to the heavenly Jerusalem: representations of the holy city in Christian art of the first millennium*, Römische Quartalschrift für christliche Altertumskunde und Kirchengeschichte, Supplementband 42 (Rome, Freiburg im Breisgau and Vienna, 1987).

372 *Charlemagne*

Merovingian period, even back to their origins in Troy. Frankish universal chronicles, moreover, coupled with Carolingian knowledge of biblical history and the rise and fall of empires charted in the *Chronicon* of Eusebius-Jerome, reflect the Franks' perception of both a new age and the continuity of human history. The Franks, Merovingian and Carolingian, were clearly represented as successors to the Romans but with their own special place in a past that stretched back to the creation of the world.[264]

CONCLUSION: SPACE, TIME AND THE GEOGRAPHY OF LEARNING

Towards the end of his life, Charlemagne left instructions in his will, as reported by Einhard, for the disposal of three inscribed silver tables (*mensae*) and one made entirely of gold. A round table depicting Rome was to be given to the bishopric of Ravenna. A square table depicting Constantinople was to be presented to the pope in Rome. Agnellus of Ravenna reported the safe arrival of its table, so it is likely that the gift for Rome was also duly delivered.[265] The gold table and the third silver table, on which was engraved a depiction (*descriptio*) of the world (*totius mundi*) within three concentric circles (*quae ex tribus orbibus*), were to be counted as part of the emperor's wealth to be divided among his heirs and for charity.[266]

The symbolism of these table-top images is apparently straightforward. It has been taken to reflect Frankish imperial domination of the known world and relations with both old and new Rome on the part of their owner. Parallels have been drawn with Augustus and Theodosius.[267] In the association of geography and imperial power, in particular, there are many parallels with the Roman empire of Augustus.[268] So too, Charlemagne's

---

[264] I argue this in detail in McKitterick, *Perceptions of the past*. See also W. Rösener, 'Königshof und Herrschaftsraum: Norm und Praxis der Hof und Reichsverwaltung im Karolingerreich', in *Uomo e spazio nell'alto medioevo*, Settimane 50 (Spoleto, 2003), pp. 443–78.

[265] Agnellus of Ravenna, *Liber pontificalis*, c. 170, ed. D. M. Deliyannis, Corpus Christianorum, Continuatio medievalis 199 (Turnhout, 2006), pp. 350–1.

[266] Einhard, *Vita Karoli*, c. 33, ed. Halphen, p. 98. P. E. Dutton, *Charlemagne's courtier* (Peterborough, Ont., 1998), p. 39, offers the translation: 'the whole universe set within three linked circles'.

[267] See E. Albu, 'Imperial geography and the medieval Peutinger map', *Imago mundi* 37 (2005), pp. 136–48.

[268] D. Dueck, 'The Augustan concept of an "Empire without limits"', in M. Dickhardt and V. Dorofeeva-Lichtman (eds.), *Göttingen Beiträge zur Asienforschung* 2–3 (Göttingen, 2003) pp. 211–27; P. Gauthier-Dalché, 'Principes et modes de la représentation de l'espace géographique durant le haut moyen âge', in *Uomo e spazio nell'alto medioevo*, Settimane 50 (Spoleto, 2003), pp. 117–50; P. Gauthier-Dalché, *Géographie et culture: La représentation de l'espace du VIe au XIIe siècle* (Aldershot, 1997), esp. Chapters II, IV and VIII; and N. Lozovsky, 'Roman geography and ethnography in the Carolingian empire', *Speculum* 81 (2006), pp. 325–364.

ambitions are expressed as much in the promotion of learning, and the royal links with the encyclopaedia of human knowledge in the form of the massive *Liber glossarum* (Paris, BnF lat. 11529 and 11530, and Cambrai 693) formerly regarded as produced at Corbie but actually written in the unlocated 'a-b' scriptorium, and the encyclopaedia of time, as in his territorial expansion.[269] The *Liber glossarum* was a particularly ambitious project, both in terms of the compilation of its contents and the complexity of the layout and copying process. Copies of it were rapidly disseminated throughout the empire, suggesting that it was designed as a teaching tool. Such books as this, coupled with Charlemagne's insistence that so many aspects of government and the religious life be grounded in particular texts, created a textual embodiment of the empire and helped both to institutionalize knowledge within a particular conceptual framework and to present the king as its ultimate centre.[270] Einhard's perception of Charlemagne's function as a ruler, so influential in subsequent generations, included the patronage of learning that is corroborated by the remarkable number of letters and treatises sent to the king on scholarly matters.

Einhard may well have intended his audience to appreciate the obvious symbolism of the account of the tables, especially in association with his portrayal of Charlemagne's assertion of the control of knowledge and of the elements and time by renaming the winds and the months.[271] Charlemagne's possession of three such tables is sufficient to indicate his access to knowledge, quite apart from the imperial symbolism the tables themselves invoke. The *Mensuratio orbis*, associated with the Emperor Theodosius II, was used by Godescalc in composing his dedicatory verses to his Evangelistary.[272] In 825, Dicuil also reminded his readers at the Carolingian court of Louis the Pious that the Emperor Theodosius had commissioned a measurement of the provinces of the earth.[273] Dicuil

[269] T. A. M. Bishop, 'The prototype of *Liber glossarum*', in M. B. Parkes and A. G. Watson (eds.), *Medieval scribes, manuscripts and libraries: essays presented to N. R. Ker* (London, 1978), pp. 69–86; and D. Ganz, *Corbie in the Carolingian Renaissance*, Beihefte der Francia 29 (Sigmaringen, 1990), pp. 48–56. On the 'a-b' script and its possible location see also McKitterick, 'Nuns' scriptoria in England and Francia'.

[270] For Augustan parallels see T. Murphy, *Pliny the Elder's Natural history* (Oxford, 2004) and C. Nicolet, *Space, geography and politics in the early Roman empire* (Ann Arbor, 1991, trans. from the French edn of 1988).

[271] See P. E. Schramm, 'Karl der Große: Denkart und Grundauffassungen', in Schramm, *Beiträge zur allgemeinen Geschichte*, 1: *Von der Spätantike bis zum Tode Karls des Großen (814)* (Stuttgart, 1984), pp. 302–41.

[272] L. Traube, 'Zur Chorographie des Augustus', *Vorlesungen und Abhandlungen*, 3 vols. (Munich, 1920), III, pp. 17–20.

[273] Dicuil, *Liber de mensura orbis terrae*, Prologus I.1 and V. 4, in J. J. Tierney (ed.), *Dicuili Liber de mensura orbis terrae*, Scriptores latini Hiberniae 6 (Dublin, 1967), pp. 45 and 56–8.

reproduced from his sources the names and dimension of the old Roman provinces. This has usually been regarded as an instance of early medieval geographers describing their physical world in terms, not of a physical reality as we would perceive it, but of the bygone world of a bookish tradition. In consequence, there is a correspondence with biblical and classical conceptions of the world rather than with contemporary reality. This preservation of a classical image can nevertheless be interpreted more positively as an indication of a perception and evocation of a past world which needed to be held within the understanding of contemporaries in the ninth century. In other words, Dicuil offered a geography to readers already versed in the history of the regions he was describing, and therefore maintained a consistent frame of reference.

The world map on Charlemagne's third table has further resonance. If we consider, first of all, what it might have depicted, this may indicate the possible understanding of the world and the extent of knowledge about it in the late eighth century. Secondly, the world map serves as a symbol in its turn of how knowledge, learning and religious devotion were intrinsic to Charlemagne's political interests and ideologies. The effort he made to conquer and control the geographical extent of his empire was complemented by the diverse means adopted to promote the Christian faith and learning. It is within this framework that Carolingian culture developed. The political utilization of knowledge of distant peoples and places, things and events, and the control and conquest of distance, as Mary Helms has demonstrated in her study of 'traditional' or 'pre-industrial' societies, may together be considered a significant part of an overall body of once esoteric knowledge that becomes an essential element of a new composite political, intellectual and cultural tradition.[274] A world was created in texts and in reality.

No trace of any of Charlemagne's tables survives. Earlier speculation about the appearance of the third table in particular has proceeded from the assumption that this was the table retained by Charlemagne's son and heir, Louis, 'out of love for his father',[275] and which Lothar, Louis's eldest son and co-emperor, according to the *Annales bertiniani*, found in the treasury at Aachen and had cut up into pieces to be distributed among his men to win support during the civil wars of 840–2.[276] Thegan said the table

[274] M. W. Helms, *Ulysses' sail: an ethnographic odyssey of power, knowledge and geographical distance* (Princeton, 1988).
[275] Thegan, c. 8; *Gesta Hludowici*, ed. Tremp, p. 188.
[276] *Annales bertiniani* 842, ed. Rau, *Quellen*, II, p. 56.

was three-layered in form, like three shields joined into one, and made no reference to any other decoration. Prudentius of Troyes, however, described the large *discus* broken up by Lothar as depicting a map of the whole world (*in quo et orbis totius descriptio*) and said that 'it also showed the stars, and the various movements of the planets at proportionate distances from each other, with the more important signs of the Zodiac'.[277] Given the difference in description, there is some doubt that Charlemagne's table (*mensa*) and Lothar's large plate (*discus*) should be identified with each other. A tabletop, of course, might have been regarded as a 'large plate', though equally there might, by 842, have been other silver plates or tables in the Aachen treasury. Nevertheless, it is on the questionable basis of the description of the table Lothar destroyed to bribe his troops that a reconstruction of the 'celestial' table has been proposed.[278]

Einhard's description of the third table has a lack of precision that suggests he had not seen it. Whether it was kept in the treasury, used to hold eucharistic vessels in the palace chapel, displayed in the *aula* or audience hall or kept in Charlemagne's private bedchamber cannot be established. Nor does the description accord with contemporary representations of the earth, the stars or the planets. Obvious parallels for the latter might be the Leiden *Aratus*, or the Fulda or Salzburg planispheria of 825 and 816–18 respectively.[279] For the former, if it is understood to be a depiction of the 'whole world', there are indications in surviving contemporary representations of the world in diagrams and maps which give some notion of what might have been in the design engraved on Charlemagne's table's surface. Rather than the purely celestial sphere with personifications of stars, the most likely comparisons are to be found in the variety of world maps in texts relating to *computus* (calendar calculations), Isidore of Seville's *Etymologiae*, or the commentary on the Apocalypse by Beatus of

---

[277] English trans. J. L. Nelson, *Annals of St Bertin* (Manchester, 1991), p. 33. The German translation by Rau, *Quellen*, ii, p. 57, reads: 'eine Karte des ganzen Erdkreises, ein Bild des gestirnten Himmels und die verschiedenen Planetenbahnen in erhabener Arbeit strahlten'. For discussion, see K. Kupfer, 'Medieval world maps: embedded images, interpretive frames', *Word and image* 10 (1994), pp. 262–88; D. Mauskopf Deliyannis, 'Charlemagne's silver tables: the ideology of an imperial capital', *Early Medieval Europe* 12 (2003), pp. 161–77.

[278] For the suggestion of a celestial sphere see F. N. Estey, 'Charlemagne's silver celestial table', *Speculum* 18 (1943), pp. 112–17.

[279] W. Stevens, 'Astronomy in Carolingian schools', in P. L. Butzer, M. Kerner and W. Oberschelp (eds.), *Karl der Große und sein Nachwirken: 1200 Jahre Kultur und Wissenschaft in Europa*; *Charlemagne and his heritage: 1200 years of civilisation and science in Europe* (Turnhout, 1997), pp. 417–88 at pp. 457 and 458 (Figs. 10 and 11); Leiden, Universiteitsbibliotheek Voss lat. Q 79, fol. 93v; Basle, Universitätsbibliothek AN.IV.18, fol. 1v; Munich, Bayerische Staatsbibliothek Clm 210, fol. 113v.

Liebana (though the earliest surviving illustrated copy, New York, Pierpont Morgan Library MS 644, fols 33v–34r, is mid-tenth century).[280] The late eighth-century representations of the world offered in codices now in Albi and the Vatican, and probably from Septimania and northern Italy respectively, for example, have the merit of being contemporary with Charlemagne.[281] The Albi manuscript (Albi, Bibliothèque Municipale, MS 29, fol. 57v)[282] contains geographical information about the seas and the winds, the geographical chapter from Orosius' seven books of history against the pagans,[283] and a version of Julius Honorius' *Cosmographia*. The map in the codex depicts a world bounded by seas but extending from Britannia to Babylon. The map in the Vatican codex (BAV Vat. lat. 6018, fols. 63v–64r) superimposes Christian topography onto a classical representation of the world; it includes the location of Paradise in the land of Eden and features Jerusalem, Rome and Constantinople, together with the Mediterranean Sea, at the heart of the map. Britain, Taprobane (Sri Lanka) and the 'unknown southern land' represent the farthest lands of the known world.[284] This map, therefore, charts both space and time. It includes Paradise as if it were a real place on earth with a place in human history rather than a place to be understood allegorically.[285] The oceans on the perimeter and the unknown 'fourth part of the world' (the southern land) do not disguise the underlying structure of this drawing as the 'T-O' world map found in so many copies of Isidore of Seville's *Etymologiae*. This divided the world according to the classical geographers, into three portions – Europe, Asia and Africa, separated by the Mediterranean Sea and the Tanais (Don) and the Nile rivers. A schematic map such as this might have given rise to a description of the whole world within three concentric circles, in which somehow heavenly bodies were included as well. Such a map, if it were depicted on Charlemagne's table, would signal the

---

[280] J. Williams and B. A. Shailor, *A Spanish Apocalypse: the Morgan Beatus manuscript* (New York, 1991).

[281] D. Woodward, 'Medieval *mappae mundi*', in D. Woodward and J. B. Harley (eds.), *The history of cartography*, I: *Cartography in prehistoric, ancient and medieval Europe and the Mediterranean* (Chicago, 1987), pp. 286–368.

[282] Illustrated in diagrammatic form in A. Scafi, *Mapping Paradise: a history of heaven on earth* (London, 2006), p. 138.

[283] See A. Merrills, *History and geography in late antiquity* (Cambridge, 2004).

[284] P. Gauthier-Dalché, 'De la glose à la contemplation: place et fonction de la carte dans les manuscrits du haut moyen âge', in *Testo e immagine nell'alto medioevo*, Settimane 41 (Spoleto, 1994), pp. 693–771 at pp. 759–61, repr. in Gauthier-Dalché, *Géographie et culture*, Chapter VIII.

[285] For discussion, see N. Lozovsky, *'The earth is our book': geographical knowledge in the Latin west ca. 400–1000* (Ann Arbor, 2000), pp. 50–67. This was apparently overlooked by Scafi, *Mapping Paradise*, pp. 95–104. See also Lozovsky, 'Roman geography'.

congruence of physical geography, sacred topography and cosmic ideology within Charlemagne's kingdom. The enticing symbolic resonance offered by the possible imagery of Charlemagne's tables is thus in accord with the king's recognition of the power of knowledge that underlies the topics rehearsed in this chapter.[286] Christian Latin culture and the Christian religion were the means of moulding Charlemagne's empire into a coherent polity.

As I have stressed both in this chapter and throughout this book, Charlemagne and his aims cannot be taken for granted. Nor should these aims be exaggerated or assumed to be the equivalent of his achievements. Much of the evidence relating to Charlemagne's reign has had precarious edifices built upon it, compounded of speculation, creative hypotheses, wishful thinking and political ideologies. In examining the primary and contemporary evidence from Charlemagne's reign afresh, I have sought to distinguish what we know from what we have merely assumed. This has entailed a new assessment of the dynamic pace of change during the half-century of Charlemagne's rule, and his contribution to the forging of a coherent Christian polity within the context of rapid expansion.

One of my principal concerns in this book has been to explore the degrees to which the Franks communicated with the past in order to form or to inform their own contemporary concerns, to heighten their sense of identity and cultural affiliations and to shape their political purpose.[287] As has become clear, diverse elements of the Franks' past, whether biblical, early Christian, Roman or Merovingian Frankish, were drawn on and combined to create a solid underpinning of the Frankish polity. There is no single source of inspiration in the forming of Carolingian political identity.[288]

The character of my analysis has been entirely determined by the nature of the surviving evidence, from the problematic information provided by the Frankish annals to the huge variety of other kinds of documentary and material evidence emanating from the reign. It became clear in the second chapter that the political manoeuvering and opportunism displayed in

---

[286] For comparable recognitions in entirely different historical contexts see T. Blanning, *The culture of power and the power of culture: old-regime Europe 1660–1789* (Oxford, 2002); and D. Ali, *Courtly culture and political life in early medieval India*, Cambridge Studies in Indian History and Society (Cambridge, 2004).

[287] For another instance of how specific varieties of social and political activity are founded upon different perceptions of the past see N. Peabody, *Hindu kingship and polity in precolonial India*, Cambridge Studies in Indian History and Society (Cambridge, 2003).

[288] See J. L. Nelson, *Charlemagne and the paradoxes of power*, The Reuter Lecture 2005 (Southampton, 2006).

other respects indicate that the motives for Carolingian expansion and the settling of the borders involved more than aggression or defence. Although all of these successes in territorial aggrandizement involved at least a show of force, there is relatively little substance to any assumption of Charlemagne as a great warrior or military leader. Given how much Roman history was known and cultivated within his orbit, it is striking that one of the most obvious, Caesar's *Gallic wars*, has not so far been linked to Charlemagne's court.[289] I have also stressed that the process of absorbing Saxony under Frankish rule had begun under Charlemagne's grandfather Charles Martel, partly in parallel with missionary enterprises, and that the annexation of Bavaria was entirely a family matter. The takeover of the Lombard kingdom had roots in Pippin's actions in support of the papacy. I have argued that a new and religious fervour becomes manifest in the 780s, not only in the annalists' account of Charlemagne's military activity, but also in the programmatic reform capitularies of 786 and 789.

This programme of religious reform and expansion of Christian culture was part of an overall strategy of Carolingian rule which maintained both the plurality of political and administrative centres and communications between these centres and their surrounding regions. How this worked in relation to a 'royal court' or the royal household I have investigated in detail, with particular attention to the structure of the royal household, the practical manifestations of itinerancy, the stages at which the household and its satellites may or may not have 'settled', and the light these threw on how centralized or dispersed Charlemagne's rule was. Aachen has emerged as but one of many centres in Charlemagne's topography of power. The charter evidence, moreover, highlighted the crucial role of written documents emanating from the royal household, wherever it was, in maintaining an essential network of communication throughout the empire. Although it is clear that the king travelled for specific purposes – diplomacy, military campaigns, devotion to a saint, assemblies, hunting and to visit Rome – the pattern of his journeys was not that of a systematic or comprehensive system of rule. I have suggested that Charlemagne's solution to the problem of royal control and government of his realm was a combination of itinerancy and stability, with a complex network of officials empowered to conduct business on his behalf. Royal government

[289] The earliest surviving manuscripts are indeed Frankish, but date from the first and second quarters of the ninth century; they may of course depend on an earlier exemplar that might have had a link with the court: see Reynolds, *Texts and transmission*, pp. 35–6.

from the royal household became increasingly dependent on the effectiveness of the king's officials and, above all, on the means of communication. This was particularly apparent in the government of a realm that became ever larger and more disparate in character in the course of Charlemagne's reign. This was observed in the development of the roles of the assemblies, of the capitularies as the principal means of communicating with his people, and of the royal officials, especially the *missi dominici*. All these were part of establishing order in a *regnum* where ecclesiastical and secular concerns were intertwined and interdependent.

Yet underlying the processes of communication was a strong purpose, not simply to ensure royal control, peace, stability and order, but also to create a harmonious and Christian whole of a disparate realm. The Christian faith offered an essential common culture to bind this huge empire together, however varied the liturgical practice and religious expression might have been. The building of churches, the imposition of ecclesiastical institutions, the introduction of Christian ritual, the insertion of Christian morality into social relations, the uncompromising insistence on orthodoxy, the teaching of correct Latin and Christian education, and the definition and dissemination of a canon of selected texts were all part of this.

It is evident that the expansion of the Frankish realm so far to the north, east and south, and the inclusion of so many new peoples, created problems not only of order and control but also of identity and cohesion with which a system of communications alone could not contend. I have demonstrated Charlemagne's methods of confronting these problems in the final two chapters of this book. A preoccupation with legitimation and policy, and an assumption of an uncomplicated applicability of evidence from late in Charlemagne's reign to his early actions, have tended in the past to obscure the dynamic of the practical and devotional arena of the king's cultural and religious activities and interests. Similarly, a concentration on political ideology, related partly to possession of the title of emperor after 800 and partly to retrospective credit for the conversion of the pagan Saxons, has diverted attention away from the gradual build-up of momentum and definition in Charlemagne's religious and cultural policies. These in their turn, moreover, were part of the workings of communication and government within the kingdom considered in Chapter 4. Certainly, viewed as a whole, the half-century of Charlemagne's rule allows us to appreciate the extraordinary ways in which his promotion of correct thinking and correct language was an essential component of an overall strategy of control. In this, the concept of *correctio*, the acquisition of knowledge and the exercise of power were yoked together. Thus in my final chapter I have considered the implications of the diverse texts and artefacts, acquired or produced during the decades of Charlemagne's reign and associated with the royal household, within the context of the development of his overall religious and cultural strategies. Together they present the many facets of Carolingian cultural identity as it was shaped in the course of Charlemagne's reign.

Such reality as underpins the extraordinary range of evidence analysed in this book has proved to be more complex, less secure and, in consequence, far more interesting than any modern textbook synthesis has indicated. Charlemagne was not just a conqueror and emperor who patronized learning, though none of those labels can actually be discarded. His own personality has remained elusive. Even with Einhard's help, it would not have been possible to present this account of his reign as a biography. Yet the effect of Charlemagne's emphasis on Christian Latin learning and Christian orthodoxy, taken up by Franks and by peoples newly incorporated into the Frankish realm alike throughout his realm, was to align the whole of Carolingian Europe to Rome. His insistence on the Roman, Christian and Merovingian past, in all its complexity, as the foundation for the style of rulership, law, communications and culture of his kingdom, was the essential element of the formation of the political and cultural identity of the peoples over whom he ruled within the present. Culture, religion, law and the written text were intrinsic to the exercise and maintenance of political power. As it turned out, these were his most lasting legacies.

Bibliography

SELECTED PRIMARY SOURCES

Sources mentioned briefly are not listed here but are cited fully in the text and can be found by using the Indexes. The list is organized according to author wherever possible, otherwise either according to the title and modern editor or, where appropriate, by category of source (*annales, capitularia, chartae, concilia, diplomata, formulae*, grammars, relic labels, *traditiones*, treasure lists, etc.).

Agnellus of Ravenna, *Liber pontificalis*, ed. D. Mauskopf Deliyannis, Corpus Christianorum, Continuatio medievalis 199 (Turnhout, 2006)

Alcuin, *Carmina*, ed. E. Dümmler, *MGH Poet.* I (Berlin, 1888)

De orthographia, ed. S. Bruni (Florence, 1997)

Epistolae, ed. E. Dümmler, *MGH Epp. kar. aevi*, II (Berlin, 1895); facsimile edn, ed. F. Unterkircher, *Alkuin-Briefe und andere Traktate*, Codices Selecti 20 (Graz, 1969)

Annales fuldenses, ed. G. Pertz and F. Kurze, *MGH SS* 7 (Hanover, 1891); trans. T. Reuter, *The Annals of Fulda* (Manchester, 1992)

Annales laureshamenses, ed. E. Katz, *Annalium laureshamensium editio emendata secundum codicem St Paulensem, Separatabdruck vom Jahresbericht des Öffentlichen Stiftsuntergymnasium der Benediktiner zu St Paul* (St Paul, 1889); and facsimile edn, ed. F. Unterkircher, *Das Wiener Fragment der Lorscher Annalen, Christus und die Samariterin, Katechese des Nicetz von Remesiana. Codex Vindobonensis 515 des Österreichischen Nationalbibliothek, Faksimile Ausgabe*, Codices Selecti 15 (Graz, 1967); ed. G. H. Pertz, *MGH SS*, I (Hanover, 1826), 22–39

Annales maximiani, ed. G. Waitz, *MGH SS* 13 (Hanover, 1881), pp. 19–25

Annales mettenses priores, ed. B. von Simson, *MGH SRG* 10 (Hanover, 1905)

Annales mosellani, 703–97, ed. J. M. Lappenberg, *MGH SS* 16 (Hanover, 1859), pp. 494–9

Annales nazariani, ed. G. Pertz, *MGH SS*, I (Hanover, 1826), pp. 40–4; and W. Lendi, *Untersuchungen zur frühalamannischen Annalistik: Die Murbacher Annalen*, Scrinium Friburgense I (Freiburg in der Schweiz, 1971), pp. 159–63

Annales petauiani, ed. F. Kurze, *MGH SS*, I (Hanover, 1826), pp. 6–18

Annales q.d. Einhardi (= 'Revised' version of *Annales regni francorum*), ed. F. Kurze, *MGH SRG* 6 (Hanover, 1895)

Annales regni francorum unde ab. a. 741 usque ad a. 829, qui dicuntur Annales laurissenses maiores et Einhardi, ed. F. Kurze, *MGH SRG* 6 (Hanover, 1895)

Annales sancti Amandi, ed. G. Pertz, MGH SS 1 (Hanover, 1826), pp. 6–14

Ansegisus, *Capitularia*, ed. G. Schmitz, *Die Kapitulariensammlung des Ansegis*, MGH Cap. Nova series 1 (Hanover, 1996)

Arbeo, *Vitae sanctorum Haimhrammi et Corbiniani*, ed. B. Krusch, *MGH SRG* 13 (Hanover, 1920)

Astronomer, *Vita Hludowici*, ed. E. Tremp, *Thegan: die Taten Kaiser Ludwigs. Astronomus, Das Leben Kaiser Ludwigs*, MGH SRG 64 (Hanover, 1995)

Bede, *Historia ecclesiastica gentis anglorum*, ed. B. Colgrave and R. A. B. Mynors, Oxford Medieval Texts (Oxford, 1969)

Benedictus Levita, ed. G. Schmitz and W. Hartmann, online edn, <www.bene dictus.mgh.de/haupt.htm>

Bluhme, F., and A. Boretius (eds.), *MGH Leges* 4 (Hanover, 1868)

Boniface, *Epistolae*, ed. M. Tangl, *Die Briefe des heiligen Bonifatius und Lullus*, MGH *Epp. Sel.* 1 (Berlin, 1916); ed. R. Rau, *Briefe des Bonifatius: Willibalds Leben des Bonifatius nebst einigen zeitgenössischen Dokumenten* (Darmstadt, 1968)

Breves notitiae, ed. F. Losek, '*Notitia arnonis* und *Breves notitiae*', *Mitteilungen der Gesellschaft für Salzburger Landeskunde* 130 (1990), pp. 5–192

Capitula episcoporum, 1, ed. P. Brommer, MGH *Capitula episcoporum* (Hanover, 1974)

Capitulare de villis, ed. C. Brühl, *Capitulare de villis: Cod. Guelf. 254 Helmst. Der Herzog August Bibliothek Wolfenbüttel*, Dokumente zur deutschen Geschichte in Faksimiles, Reihe 1: *Mittelalter*, Bd. 1 (Stuttgart 1971); ed. K. Gareis, *Die Landgüterordnung Kaiser Karls des Großen (Capitulare de villis vel curtis imperii): Text-Ausgabe mit Einleitung und Anmerkungen* (Berlin, 1895); ed. B. Fois Ennas, *Il Capitulare de villis* (Milan, 1981)

Capitularia, ed. A. Boretius, *MGH Capitularia, Legum Sectio II, Capitularia regum francorum*, 1 (Hanover, 1883); A. Werminghoff, *MGH Concilia aevi karolini*, II.i (Hanover and Leipzig, 1906); and C. Azzaro and P. Moro, *I capitolari italici: storia e diritto della dominazione carolingia in Italia* (Rome, 1998)

Carolus magnus et Leo papa, ed. E. Dümmler, MGH *Poetae*, 1; ed. H. Beumann, F. Brunholzl and W. Winkelmann, *Karolus magnus et Leo papa: Ein Paderborner Epos vom Jahre 799* (Paderborn, 1966)

Chanson de Roland, ed. C. Segre (Geneva, 1989)

Chartae latinae antiquiores, Facsimile edition of Latin charters prior to the ninth century, 1–, ed. A. Bruckner *et al.* (Olten and Lausanne 1954–98)

Chartae latinae antiquiores, Facsimile edition of the Latin charters, 2nd series, ninth century, 1–, ed. G. Cavallo, G. Nicolaj *et al.* (Olten and Lausanne, 1997–)

Chartae (St Gallen), ed. H. Wartmann, *Urkunden Sankt Gallen* (St Gallen, 1863)

Chartae (St Gallen), ed. P. Erhart, *Facsimile edition of the Latin charters, 2nd series, ninth century, Part C, Switzerland III, St Gallen*, 1 (Dietikon and Zurich, 2006)

Chelles (relic labels), ed. H. Atsma and J. Vezin, *Authentiques de reliques provenant de l'ancien monastère Notre-Dame de Chelles (VIIe–VIIIe siècles) découvertes par Jean-Pierre Laporte*, ChLA XVIII (Dietikon and Zurich, 1985), No. 669, pp. 84–108

Chronica minora, saec. IV–VII, ed. Theodor Mommsen, *Chronica minora saec. IV–VII*, 2 vols, MGH *Auctores Antiquissimi* 9 (Berlin, 1892) and 11 (Berlin, 1894)

Cicero, *De oratore*, ed. and trans. G. L. Henderson and H. M. Hubbell, *Cicero, Brutus, Orator* (Cambridge, Mass., 1962); ed. E. W. Sutton and H. Rackham (Cambridge, Mass., and London, 1976)

Clausula de unctione pippini, ed. A. Stoclet, 'La "Clausula de unctione Pippini regis": mises au point et nouvelles hypothèses', *Francia* 8 (1980), pp. 1–42

Codex epistolaris carolinus, ed. W. Gundlach, MGH *Epp.* III, *Epistolae merowingici et karolini aevi*, 1 (Hanover, 1892), pp. 469–657; and facsimile edn, ed. F. Unterkircher, *Codex epistolaris carolinus*, Codices Selecti 3 (Graz, 1962)

Concilia (Aachen, 809), see under *Decretum* . . .

Concilia, ed. A. Werminghoff, MGH *Concilia, Legum Sectio*. III, *Concilia*, II (Hanover, 1906–8)

Constitutum Constantini, ed. H. Fuhrmann, MGH *Fontes* 10 (Hanover, 1968)

Conversio bagoariorum et carantanorum, ed. H. Wolfram (Vienna, 1979)

De Pippini regis victoria Avarica, ed. L. A. Berto, *Testi storici e poetici dell'Italia carolingia*, Medioevo europeo 3 (Padua, 2002), pp. 67–72

Decretum Aquisgranense de processione spiritus sancti a patre et filio (809), ed. H. Willjung, *Das Konzil von Aachen 809*, MGH *Concilia* 2. *Supplementum* 2 (Hanover, 1998)

Dionysius Exiguus, *Libellus de cyclo magno paschae / cyclus paschalis (Liber de paschate)*, PL 67, cols. 483–508

Diplomata (Charlemagne), ed. E. Mühlbacher, MGH *DKar*. I (Berlin, 1906)

Diplomata (Charles the Bald), ed. G. Tessier, *Recueil des Actes de Charles II le Chauve*, 3 vols (Paris, 1943–1955)

Diplomata (facsimiles), ed. A. Bruckner, *Diplomata karolinorum*, 1 (Basel, 1974)

Diplomata (Lombard), ed. L. Schiaparelli, *Codice diplomatico Longobardo*, Fonti per la storia d'Italia 38 (Rome, 1933)

Diplomata (Merovingian), ed. T. Kölzer, *Die Urkunden der Merowinger*, 2 vols (Hanover, 2001)

Dicuil, *Liber de mensura orbis terrae*, ed. J. J. Tierney, *Dicuili Liber de mensura orbis terrae*, Scriptores latini Hiberniae 6 (Dublin, 1967)

Dutton, P. E. (trans.) *Carolingian civilization* (Peterborough, Ont., 1993)

Einhard, *Translatio sanctorum Marcellini et Petri*, ed. G. Waitz, MGH SS 15, 1 (Hanover, 1887), pp. 238–64

Vita Karoli, ed. O. Holder-Egger, MGH SRG 25 (Hanover, 1911); G. Waitz, repr. in R. Rau, *Quellen zur karolingischen Reichsgeschichte*, 1 (Darmstadt, 1974), pp. 163–212; and L. Halphen, *Eginhard: vie de Charlemagne*, 2nd edn (Paris, 1947); trans. P. Dutton, *Charlemagne's courtier: the complete Einhard* (Peterborough, Ont., 1998)

Erconrad, *Translatio S. Liborii episcopi*, ed. and French trans. A. Cohausz and R. Latouche, *La translation du S. Liboire du diacre Erconrad* (Le Mans, 1967)

Ermold, *In honorem Hludowici christianissimi Caesaris Augusti*, ed. E. Faral, *Ermold le Noir: poème sur Louis le Pieux et épîtres au roi Pépin* (Paris, 1964)

Eusebius-Jerome, *Chronicon*, ed. R. Helm, *Eusebius Werke 7: Die Griechischen christlichen Schriftsteller der ersten Jahrhundert 70*, 2nd edn (Berlin, 1956); ed. J. K. Fotheringham, *Chronici canones, Latini verti adauxit ad sua tempora produxit S. Eusebius Hieronymus* (London and Oxford, 1923)

Flodoard, *Historia remensis ecclesiae*, ed. M. Stratmann, MGH SS 36 (Hanover, 1998)

Formulae, ed. B. Bischoff, *Salzbürger Formelbücher und Briefe aus Tassilonischer und karolingischer Zeit*, Sitzungsberichte der Bayerischen Akademie für Wissenschaften, phil.-hist. Klasse, Heft 4 (Munich, 1973)

Formulae, see also under Marculf

Frec<ulf>, *Chronicon*, ed. M. Allen, *Frecvlfi Lexoviensis episcopi opera omnia*, Corpus Christianorum Continuatio Mediaevalis 169 (Turnhout, 2003)

Fredegar, Chronicle Book IV with Continuations, ed. J. M. Wallace-Hadrill, *The fourth book of the Chronicle of Fredegar and its continuations* (London, 1960); ed. H. Haupt and H. Wolfram, *Chronicarum quae dicuntur Fredegarii Continuationes, Quellen zur Geschichte des 7. und 8. Jahrhunderts* (Darmstadt, 1982)

Gabáltais searluis móir (The conquests of Charlemagne), ed. D. Hyde, Irish Texts Society (London, 1917)

Gerbald of Liège, *Capitularia*, ed. W. A. Eckhardt, *Die Kapitulariensammlung Bischof Ghaerbalds von Lüttich*, Germanenrechte NF, Abt. Beihefte, Deutschrechtliches Archiv 5 (Göttingen, 1955)

Gesta abbatum Fontanellensium, ed. G. Pertz, MGH SS 2 (Hanover, 1929), and P. Pradié, *Chronique des abbés de Fontenelle* (Saint-Wandrille) (Paris, 1999)

Glosses (Psalter), ed. F. Unterkircher, *Die Glossen des Psalters von Mondsee (vor 788) (Montpellier, Faculté de Médicine MS 409)*, Spicilegium Friburgense 20 (Freiburg in der Schweiz, 1974)

Grammars, ed. B. Bischoff, *Sammelhandschrift Diez B. Sant 66: Grammatici latini et catalogus librorum* (Graz, 1973)

Gregorian Sacramentary, ed. J. Deshusses, *Le sacramentaire grégorien ses principales formes d'après les plus anciens manuscrits*, 3 vols, Spicilegium Friburgense 16, 24, 28 (Freiburg in der Schweiz, 1971, 1979, 1982)

Haddan, A. W., and W. Stubbs (eds.), *Councils and ecclesiastical documents* (Oxford, 1871)

Hariulf, *Chronicon Centulense*, ed. F. Lot, Hariulf, *Chronique de l'abbaye de Saint-Riquier, Ve siècle–1004* (Paris, 1894)

Heidrich, I., *Die Urkunden der Arnulfinger* (Bad Münstereifel, 2001) and online edn, <www.igh.histsem.uni-bonn.de>

Hildebrandslied, ed. W. Braune, K. Helm and E. A. Ebbinghaus, *Althochdeutsches Lesebuch* (Tübingen, 1979)

Hincmar of Reims, *De ordine palatii*, ed. T. Gross and R. Schieffer, *Hinkmar von Reims, De ordine palatii*, MGH Fontes 3 (Hanover, 1980); ed. M. Prou, *Hincmar, De ordine palatii: texte Latin, traduit et annoté* (Paris, 1884), published in Bibliothèque de l'école des hautes études 58 (Paris, 1885)

Hincmari Rhemensis archiepiscopi . . . Epistolae, cum coniecturis notisque brevibus Joannis Busaei Noviomagi (Mainz, 1602)

John the Deacon, *Vita sancti Gregorii magni*, PL 75, cols. 63–242

Karolus magnus et Leo papa, ed. E. Dümmler, MGH Poet. I (Berlin, 1881), pp. 366–79; ed. Helmut Beumann, Franz Brunhölzl and Wilhelm Winkelmann, *Karolus magnus et Leo papa: ein Paderborner Epos vom Jahr 799* (Paderborn, 1966); ed. W. Heintz, *De Karolo rege et Leone papa*, Studien und Quellen zur westfälischen Geschichte 36 (Paderborn, 1999)

Leidrad, *Epistola*, ed. E. Dümmler, MGH Epp. IV, kar. aevi, II (Berlin, 1895), pp. 542–44

Lex Alamannorum, ed. K. Lehmann and K. A. Eckhardt, MGH *Leges nat. germ.* 5, 2 (Hanover, 1966)

Lex Baiuvariorum, ed. F. E. von Schwind, MGH Leges *nat. germ.* 5, 2 (Hanover, 1926)

Lex Ribuaria, ed. F. Beyerle and R. Buchner, MGH *Leges nat. germ.* 3, 2 (Hanover, 1954)

Lex Salica, ed. K. A. Eckhardt, *MGH Leges nat. germ.* 4, 2 (Hanover, 1969)

Lex Saxonum et Lex Thuringorum, ed. C. von Schwerin, MGH *Fontes* 4 (Hanover and Leipzig, 1918)

Liber pontificalis, ed. L. Duchesne, *Le Liber pontificalis: texte, introduction et commentaire*, 2 vols (Paris, 1886–92); I: English trans. R. Davis, *The book of the pontiffs*, rev. edn (Liverpool, 2000), *The lives of the eighth-century popes (Liber pontificalis)* (Liverpool, 1992), *The lives of the ninth-century popes* (Liverpool, 1995)

Liber sacramentum Engolismensis, ed. P. Saint-Roch, CCSL 159C (Turnhout, 1987)

Liber vitae (Salzburg), ed. K. Forstner, *Das Verbrüderungsbuch von St Peter in Salzburg: Vollständige Faksimile-Ausgabe im Originalformat der Handschrift AI aus dem Archiv von St Peter in Salzburg* (Graz, 1974)

Libri Memoriales, and Libri Memoriales et Necrologia, Nova series (Hanover, 1979–)

Marculf, *Formulae*, ed. K. Zeumer, MGH *Formulae merowingici et karolini aevi* (1882–6), pp. 32–106; ed. A. Uddholm, *Marculfi Formularium libri duo* (Uppsala, 1962); ed. K. Zeumer, *Formulae Marculfi karolini: Formulae marculfinae aevi karolini*, MGH *Formulae merowingici et karolini aevi* (1882–6), pp. 113–27

Mühlbacher, E. (ed.), *Die Urkunden der Karolinger*, I: *Urkundens Pippins, Karlmanns und Karl der Großen*, MGH *Diplomata karolinorum* (Hanover, 1906)

Nelson, J. L. (trans.), *Annals of St Bertin* (Manchester, 1991)

Nithard, *Historiarum libri* IV, at IV, I, ed. E. Mülle, *MGH SRG* 44 (Hanover, 1907), and P. Lauer, Nithard: *Histoire des fils de Louis the Pieux* (Paris, 1964)

Notker Balbulus, *Gesta Karoli*, ed. H. H. Haefele, MGH SRG NS 12 (Berlin, 1959)
Ordines, ed. H. Schneider, *Die Konzilsordines des Früh- und Hochmittelalters*, MGH Ordines de celebrando concilio (Hanover, 1996)
Paderborn epic, see *Karolus Magnus et Leo Papa*
Paul the Deacon, *Carmina*, ed. K. Neff, *Die Gedichte des Paulus Diaconus: kritische und erklärende Ausgabe*, Quellen und Untersuchungen zur lateinische Philologie des Mittelalters 3, fasc. 4 (Munich, 1908)
    Gesta episcoporum mettensium, ed. G. Pertz, MGH SS 2 (Hanover, 1829)
    Historia langobardorum, ed. G. Waitz, MGH *SRL* (Hanover, 1878)
Paulinus of Aquileia, ed. D. Norberg, *Paulini Aquileiensis opera omnia,* pars I: *Contra felicem libri tres*, Corpus Christianorum Continuatio Medievalis 95 (Turnhout, 1990)
Placiti, ed. C. Manaresi, *I placiti del regnum Italiae*, I, Fonti per la storia d'Italia 92 (Rome, 1955)
Poeta Saxo, ed. P. von Winterfeld, MGH *Poet.* IV (Berlin, 1899)
Polyptych (Reims), ed. B. Guérard, *Le Polyptyque de l'abbaye de Saint-Rémi de Reims ou dénombrement des manses, des serfs et des revenus de cette abbaye vers le milieu du IXe siècle de notre ère* (Paris, 1853); ed. J.-P. Devroey, *Le Polyptyque et les listes de cens de l'abbaye de Saint-Rémi de Reims (IXe–XIe siècles)*, Travaux de l'Academie Nationale de Reims 163 (Reims, 1984)
Prou, M., and E. Chartraire (eds.), 'Authentiques de reliques conservées au trésor de la cathédrale de Sens', *Mémoires de la Société Nationale des Antiquaires de France*, 6th series, 9 (1900), pp. 129–72
Regum francorum genealogiae, ed. G. Pertz, *MGH SS* 2 (Hanover, 1929), pp. 304–14
Relic labels, see Chelles and Sens
Rossi, G. de (ed.), *Inscriptiones Christianae urbis Romae septimo saeculo antiquiores*, 2 vols (Rome, 1857–88)
Rudolf of Fulda, *Vita sancti Leobae*, c. 18, ed. G. Waitz, MGH SS 15, 1 (Hanover, 1887), pp. 127–331
Sens (relic labels), ed. Maurice Prou and Eugène Chartraire, 'Authentiques de reliques conservées au trésor de la cathédrale de Sens', *Mémoires de la Société Nationale des Antiquaires de France*, 6th series, 9 (1900), pp. 129–72
Suetonius, *De vita caesarum*, ed. O. Wittstock (Berlin, 1993)
Synod von Dingolfing and *notitia de pacto fraternitatis episcoporum et abbatum bavaricorum*, ed. A. Werminghoff, *MGH Conc.* II. i, No. 15 (Hanover, 1906), pp. 96–7
Tacitus, *Agricola*, in Tacitus, *Agricola, Germania and Dialogus*, ed. and trans. R. M. Ogilvie, E. H. Warmington and M. Winterbottom (revised from M. Hutton and W. Peterson's translations) (London and Cambridge, Mass., 1970)
Thegan, *Gesta Hludowici*, ed. E. Tremp, *Thegan: die Taten Kaiser Ludwigs; Astronomus: Das Leben Kaiser Ludwigs*, MGH SRG 64 (Hanover, 1995)
Theodulus, *Ecloga*, ed. J. Osternacher, *Theoduli Ecloga* (Linz, 1902)
Theodulf of Orleans, *Opus Caroli regis contra synodum (libri I Carolini)*, ed. A. Freeman, MGH Conc. II. i (Hanover, 1998)

Tobler, T., and A. Molinier (eds.), *Itinera Hierosolymitana et descriptiones terrae sanctae* (Geneva, 1879)

Traditiones (Freising), ed. T. Bitterauf, *Die Traditionen des Hochstifts Freising, 744–926*, Quellen und Erörterungen zur bayerischen Geschichte, NF 4 (Munich, 1905)

Translatio sancti viti martyris, ed. I. Schmale-Ott, Veröffentlichungen der Historischen Kommission für Westfalen, Reihe 41, Fontes minores 1 (Münster, 1979)

Treasure lists, ed. B. Bischoff, *Mittelalterliche Schatzverzeichniße* (Munich, 1967)

Versus Pauli de Herico duce, ed. E. Dümmler, MGH *Poet.* 1, pp. 131–3; ed. O. Holder-Egger, *Vita Karoli*, Appendix, MGH SRG 25 (Hanover, 1911), pp. 44–6

Virgil, *Aeneid*, ed. R. A. B. Mynors, *P. Vergili Maronis Opera* (Oxford, 1969)

Walafrid Strabo, *Liber de exordiis et incrementis quarundam in observationibus ecclesiasticis rerum*, ed. A. L. Harting-Correâ, Mittellateinische Studien und Texte 19 (Leiden, 1996)

Waltharius: Lateinisch-deutsch; Waldere: Englisch-Deutsch, ed. and trans. G. Vogt-Spira and U. Schafer (Stuttgart, 1994)

Whitelock, D. (ed.), *English Historical Documents*, 1 (London, 1979)

Wilkinson, J. (trans.), *Jerusalem Pilgrims before the Crusades* (Warminster, 1977)

Wright, D. H. (ed.), *The Vespasian Psalter, British Museum, Cotton Vespasian A. 1*, Early English Manuscripts 1, Facsimile 14 (Copenhagen, 1967)

SECONDARY LITERATURE

Adams, J. N., 'The vocabulary of the *Annales regni francorum*', *Glotta* 55 (1977), pp. 257–82

Affeldt, W. (ed.), 'Untersuchungen zur Königserhebung Pippins: das Papsttum und die Begründung des karolingischen Königtums im Jahre 751', *Frühmittelalterliche Studien* 14 (1980), pp. 95–187

(ed.), *Frauen in Spätantike und Frühmittelalter* (Sigmaringen, 1990)

Agnew, J., and S. Corbridge, *Mastering space: hegemony, territory and international political economy* (London and New York, 1995)

Airlie, S., 'Charlemagne and the aristocracy: captains and kings,' in Story, *Charlemagne: empire and society*, pp. 90–102

'Narratives of triumph and rituals of submission: Charlemagne's mastering of Bavaria', *Transactions of the Royal Historical Society*, 6th series, 9 (1999), pp. 93–120

'The palace of memory: the Carolingian court as political centre', in Rees Jones, Marks and Minnis, *Court and regions in medieval Europe*, pp. 1–20

'Talking heads: assemblies in early medieval Germany', in Barnwell and Mostert, *Political assemblies in the earlier middle ages*, pp. 29–59

'Towards a Carolingian aristocracy', in Becher and Jarnut, *Der Dynastiewechsel von 751: Vorgeschichte, Legitimationsstrategien und Erinnerung*, pp. 109–28

Albu, E., 'Imperial geography and the medieval Peutinger map', *Imago mundi* 37 (2005), pp. 136–48

Ali, D., *Courtly culture and political life in early medieval India*, Cambridge Studies in Indian History and Society (Cambridge, 2004)

Allen, L., 'The ideology of conquest in the near East in the first millennium BC', unpublished MA dissertation, University of London (2000)

Althoff, G., *Amicitiae and Pacta: Bündnis, Einung, Politik und Gebetsgedenken im beginnenden 10. Jahrhundert*, MGH Schriften 37 (Hanover, 1992)

  Spielregeln der Politik im Mittelalter: Kommunikation im Frieden und Fehden (Darmstadt, 1997)

  Verwandte, Freunde und Getreue: zum politischen Stellenwert der Gruppenbildung im frühen Mittelalter (Darmstadt, 1990), trans. C. Carroll, *Family, friends and followers: political and social bonds in early medieval Europe* (Cambridge, 2004)

Amory, P., 'The meaning and purpose of the terminology in the Burgundian laws', *Early Medieval Europe* 2 (1993), pp. 1–28

Andersen, H. H., *Danevirke og Kovirke: arkølogiscke undersøgelser 1861–1993* (Højbsjerg, 1998)

Andersen, H. H., H. J. Madsen and O. Voss, *Danevirke* (Copenhagen, 1976)

Angenendt, A., 'Das geistliche Bundnis der Päpste mit den karolingern (754–796)', *Historisches Jahrbuch* 100 (1980), pp. 1–94

  '"Mit reinen Händen": das Motiv der kultischen Reinheit in der abendländischen Askese', in G. Jenal and S. Haarländer (eds.), *Herrschaft, Kirche, Kultur: Beiträge zur Geschichte des Mittelalters: Festschrift für Friedrich Prinz zu seinem 65. Geburtstag*, Monographien zur Geschichte des Mittelalters 37 (Stuttgart, 1993), pp. 297–316

Anon., *Charlemagne* (Brussels, 1848)

Anton, H. H., '"Bischofsherrschaften" in Spätantike und Frühmittelalter. Reflexionen zu ihrer Genese, Struktur und Typologie', in F. Burgard, C. Cluse and A. Haverkamp (eds.), *Liber amicorum necnon et amicarum für Alfred Heit*, Trierer Historische Forschungen 28 (Trier, 1996), pp. 461–73

  Fürstenspiegel und Herrscherethos in der Karolingerzeit, Bonner Historische Forschungen 32 (Bonn, 1968)

  Trier im frühen Mittelalter, Quellen und Forschungen aus dem Gebiet der Geschichte, NF 9 (Paderborn, Munich, Vienna and Zürich, 1987)

Aquileia e le Venezie nell'alto medioevo, Antichità altoadriatiche 32 (Udine, 1988)

Atsma, H. (ed.), *La Neustrie: les pays au Nord de la Loire de 650 à 850*, Beihefte der Francia 16 (Sigmaringen, 1989)

Autenrieth, J. (ed.), *Ingelheim am Rhein* (Stuttgart, 1964)

Auwera, J. van de, *Adverbial contructions in the languages of Europe* (Berlin, 1998)

Auzépy, M.-F., 'Francfort et Nicée II', in Berndt (ed.), *Das Frankfurter Konzil von 794*, I, pp. 279–300

Bachrach, B. S., 'Charlemagne and the Carolingian general staff', *Journal of Military History* 66 (2002), pp. 313–57

  Early Carolingian warfare: Prelude to empire (Philadelphia, 2001)

Bachrach, D., *Religion and the conduct of war, c. 300–1215* (Woodbridge, 2003)

Baczko, B., 'Le calendrier Républicain', in P. Nora (ed.), *Les lieux de mémoire, I: la République* (Paris, 1984), pp. 37–83

Balzer, M., 'Die Pfalz Paderborn', in *799 Kunst und Kultur*, I, pp. 116–23

Banniard, M., 'Germanophone, latinophone et accès à la Schriftlichkeit', in D. Hägermann, W. Haubrichs and J. Jarnut (eds.), *Akkulturation: Probleme einer germanisch-romanischen Kultursynthese in Spätantike und frühem Mittelalter*, Ergänzungsbände zum Reallexikon der Germanischen Altertumskunde 41 (Berlin and New York, 2004), pp. 340–58

'Language and communication in Carolingian Europe', in McKitterick, *NCMH*, II, pp. 695–708

Barbero, A., *Charlemagne: father of a continent* (New Haven, 2004), trans. from the Italian edn of 2000 by A. Cameron

Barbier, J., 'Quierzy (Aisne): résidence pippinide et palais carolingien', in Renoux, *Palais médiévaux (France-Belgique)*, pp. 82–6

'Le système palatial franc: genèse et fonctionnement dans le nord-ouest du regnum', *Bibliothèque de l'Ecole des Chartes* 148 (1990), pp. 245–99

Barnwell, P. S., 'Kings, nobles and assemblies in the barbarian kingdoms', in Barnwell and Mostert (eds.), *Political assemblies*, pp. 11–28

Barnwell, P. S., and M. Mostert (eds.), *Political assemblies in the earlier middle ages*, Studies in the Early Middle Ages 7 (Turnhout, 2003)

Barrington Atlas of the Greek and Roman world (Princeton, 2000)

Bartlett, R., 'Symbolic meanings of hair in the middle ages', *Transactions of the Royal Historical Society*, 6th series, 4 (1994), pp. 43–60

Bastert, B. (ed.), *Karl der Große in der europäischen Literaturen des Mittelalters: Konstruktion eines Mythos* (Tübingen, 2004)

Bauer, F. A., 'Das Bild der Stadt Rom in der Karolingerzeit: der Anonymus Einsiedlensis', *Römische Quartalschrift* 92 (1997), pp. 190–228

Bauman, H., *Ideengeschichtliche Studien zu Einhard und anderen Geschichtsschreibern des frühen Mittelalters* (Darmstadt, 1962)

Bautier, R., 'La chancellerie et les actes royales dans les royaumes carolingiennes', *Bibliothèque de l'Ecole des Chartes* 143 (1984), pp. 5–80

Bautier, R. H., 'Chartes, sceaux et chancelleries', in Bautier, *Etudes de diplomatique et de sigillographie médiévale*, Mémoires et documents de l'Ecole des Chartes 34, 2 vols (Paris, 1990), I, pp. 123–66

Becher, M., 'Drogo und die Königserhebung Pippins', *Frühmittelalterliche Studien* 23 (1989) pp. 131–51

Eid und Herrschaft: Untersuchungen zum Herrscherethos Karls des Großen, Vorträge und Forschungen Sonderband 39 (Sigmaringen, 1993)

Karl der Große (Munich, 1999); English trans. D. Bachrach, *Charlemagne* (New Haven, 2003)

'Neue Überlegungen zum Geburtsdatum Karls des Großen', *Francia* 19 (1992), pp. 37–60

'"Non enim habent regem idem antiqui Saxones . . .": Verfassung und Ethnogenese in Sachsen währen des 8. Jahrhunderts', in Hassler, *Sachsen und Franken in Westfalen*, pp. 1–31

'Die Reise Papst Leos III zu Karl dem Großen: Überlegungen zu Chronologie, Verlauf und Inhalt der Paderborner Verwandlungen des

Jahres 799', in Godman, Jarnut and Johanek, *Am Vorabend der Kaiser Krönung*, pp. 87–112

Rex, dux und gens: Untersuchungen zur Entstehung des sächsischen Herzogtums um 9. und 10. Jahrhundert, Historische Studien 444 (Husum, 1996)

'Die Sachsen im 7. und 8. Jahrhundert: Verfassung und Ethnogenese', in *799 Kunst und Kultur*, I, pp. 188–94

'Eine verschleierte Krise: die Nachfolge Karl Martells 741 und die Anfänge der karolingischen Hofgeschichtsschreibung', in Laudage, *Von Fakten und Fiktionen*, pp. 95–134

'Zum Geburtsjahr Tassilos III', *Zeitschrift für bayerischen Landesgeschichte* 52 (1989), pp. 3–12

Becher, M., and J. Jarnut (eds.), *Der Dynastiewechsel von 751: Vorgeschichte, Legitimationsstrategien und Erinnerung* (Münster, 2004)

Beer, R., *Monumenta palaeographica Vindobonensia: Denkmäler der Schreibkunst aus der Handschriften der Hapsburg-Lothringischen Erzhauses*, I (Leipzig, 1910)

Beiträge zur Geschichte des Klosters Lorsch, 2nd edn, Geschichtsblätter für den Kreis Bergstraße, Sonderband 4 (Lorsch, 1980)

Bender, B. (ed.) , *Landscape, politics and perspectives*, Explorations in anthropology (Providence, R.I., and Oxford, 1993)

Bernard, P., 'Benoît d'Aniane est-il auteur de l'avertissement "Hucusque" et du Supplément au sacramentaire "Hadrianus"?', *Studi medievali*, 3rd series, 39 (1998), pp. 1–120

Du chant romain au chant grégorien (IVe–XIIIe siècle) (Paris, 1996)

Berndt, R. (ed.), *Das Frankfurter Konzil von 794: Kristallisationspunkt karolingischer Kultur*: I: *Politik und Kirche*; II: *Kultur und Theologie*, Quellen und Abhandlungen zur Mittelrheinische Kirchengeschichte 80 (Mainz, 1997)

Bernhardt, J. W., *Itinerant kingship and royal monasteries in early medieval Germany, c. 936–1075* (Cambridge, 1993)

Berschin, W., *Biographie und Epochenstil im lateinischen Mittelalter*, Quellen und Untersuchungen zur lateinischen Philologie des Mittelalters 8–10, 12, 4 vols (Stuttgart, 1986–99)

Greek letters and the Latin middle ages (Washington, D.C., 1988)

Bertelli, C., and G. P. Brogiolo (eds.), *Il futuro dei Longobardi: L'Italia e la costruzione dell'Europa di Carlo Magno* (Milan, 2000)

Bertolini, O., 'Il *Liber pontificalis*', in *La Storiografia altomedievale*, Settimane 17 (Spoleto, 1970), pp. 387–455

Biddle, M., 'Towns', in D. Wilson (ed.), *The archaeology of Anglo-Saxon England* (Cambridge, 1976), pp. 99–150

Bierbrauer, K., 'Konzilsdarstellungen der Karolingerzeit', in Berndt (ed.), *Das Frankfurter Konzil von 794*, II, pp. 751–65

Billett, J., 'Cantors, cantatoria, and the dissemination of Carolingian ecclesiastical reform in the ninth century', unpublished essay for the MPhil in Medieval History, Faculty of History, University of Cambridge (2003)

Binding, G., *Deutsche Königspfalzen von Karl dem Grossen bis Friedrich II (765–1240)* (Darmstadt, 1996)

Bischoff, B., *Die Abtei Lorsch im Spiegel ihrer Handschriften*, 2nd edn (Lorsch, 1989)
'Frühkarolingische Handschriften und ihre Heimat', *Scriptorium* 22 (1968), pp. 306–14
'Hadoardus and the manuscripts of classical authors from Corbie, in Prete, *Didascaliae*, pp. 41–57; revised German version in Bischoff, *Mittelalterliche Studien*, I, pp. 49–63
'Die Hofbibliothek Karls des Großen', in *KdG* II, pp. 42–62; repr. with revisions in Bischoff, *Mittelalterliche Studien*, III, pp. 149–69; English trans. M. Gorman, 'The court library of Charlemagne', in Bischoff, *Manuscripts and libraries in the age of Charlemagne*, pp. 56–75
'Die Hofbibliothek unter Ludwig dem Frommen', in J. J. G. Alexander and M. T. Gibson (eds.), *Medieval learning and literature: Essays presented to Richard William Hunt* (Oxford, 1976), pp. 3–22, repr. in Bischoff, *Mittelalterliche Studien*, III (Stuttgart, 1981), pp. 170–86; English trans. M. Gorman, 'The court library under Louis the Pious', in Bischoff, *Manuscripts and libraries in the age of Charlemagne*, pp. 76–92
'Die Kölner Nonnenhandschriften und das Skriptorium von Chelles', in Bischoff, *Mittelalterliche Studien*, I, pp. 16–34
Katalog der festländischen Handschriften des neunten Jahrhunderts (mit Ausnahme der wisigotischen), Teil I: *Aachen–Lambach* (Wiesbaden, 1998); Teil II: *Laon–Paderborn* (Wiesbaden, 2004)
Latin palaeography: antiquity and the middle ages, trans. D. Ó Cróinín and D. Ganz (Cambridge, 1990, from the 2nd revised German edn, 1986)
Manuscripts and libraries in the age of Charlemagne (Cambridge, 1994)
Mittelalterliche Studien, 3 vols (Stuttgart, 1966–81)
'Panorama der Handschriften Überlieferung aus der Zeit Karls des Grossen', *KdG*, II, pp. 233–45, repr. in Bischoff, *Mittelalterliche Studien*, III, pp. 5–38; English trans. M. Gorman, 'Manuscripts in the age of Charlemagne', in Bischoff, *Manuscripts and libraries in the age of Charlemagne*, pp. 20–55
'Eine Sammelhandschrift Walafrid Strabos', in *Mittelalterliche Studien* II, pp. 34–50
Die sudostdeutschen Schreibschulen und Bibliotheken in der Karolingerzeit, I: *Die bayrischen Diözesen*, 3rd edn (Wiesbaden, 1974); II: *Die Vorwiegend Österreichischen Diözesen* (Wiesbaden, 1980)
'Das Thema des Poeta Saxo', in *Mittelalterliche Studien*, III, pp. 253–59
(ed.), *Sammelhandschrift Diez. B Sant. 66: grammatici latini et catalogus librorum*, Codices selecti (Graz, 1973).
Bischoff, B., and J. Hofmann, *Libri sancti Kyliani: Die Würzburger Schreibschule und die Dombibliothek im VIII. und IX. Jahrhundert* (Würzburg, 1952)
Bishop, T. A. M., 'The prototype of *Liber glossarum*', in M. B. Parkes and A. G. Watson (eds.), *Medieval scribes, manuscripts and libraries: Essays presented to N. R. Ker* (London, 1978), pp. 69–86
Blair, J., *The Anglo-Saxon Church* (Oxford, 2006)
Blanning, T., *The culture of power and the power of culture: old-regime Europe 1660–1789* (Oxford, 2002)

Bloch, H., review of Monod, 'Etudes critiques', *Göttingische gelehrte Anzeigen* 163 (1901), pp. 872–97

Böhmer, J.-F., and E. Mühlbacher, *Regesta Imperii*, I: *die Regesten des Kaiserreichs unter den Karolingern 751–918*, augmented reprint of 2nd edn of 1908 (Hildesheim, 1966)

Bohne, J., *Der Poeta Saxo in der historiographischen Tradition der 8.–10. Jahrhundert* (Frankfurt am Main, 1965).

Borgolte, M., *Der Gesandtenaustausch der Karolinger mit den Abbasiden und mit den Patriarchen von Jerusalem*, Münchener Beiträge zur Mediävistik und Renaissance-Forschung 25 (Munich, 1976)

"Die Geschichte der Grafengewalt im Elsaß von Dagobert I. bis Otto dem Großen', *Zeitschrift für die Geschichte des Oberrheins* 131 (1983), pp. 3–54.

Geschichte der Grafschaften Alemanniens in fränkischer Zeit, Vorträge und Forschungen, Sonderband 31 (Sigmaringen, 1984)

Die Grafen Alemanniens in merowingischer und karolingischer Zeit, Archäologie und Geschichte: Freiburger Forschungen zur ersten Jahrtausend in Südwestdeutschland 2 (Sigmaringen, 1982)

Borst, A., 'Alkuin und die Enzyklopädie von 809', in P. L. Butzer and D. Lohrmann (eds.), *Science in western and eastern civilization in Carolingian times* (Basle, Boston and Berlin, 1993), pp. 53–78

Die Karolingische Kalenderreform, MGH Schriften 46 (Hanover, 1998)

Boshof, B., *Ludwig der Fromme*, Gestalten des Mittelalters und der Renaissance (Darmstadt, 1996)

Bougard, F., 'La justice dans le royaume d'Italie aux IX–Xe siècles', in *La giustizia nell'alto medioevo (secoli IX–XI)*, Settimane 44 (Spoleto, 1997), pp. 133–76

La justice dans le royaume d'Italie de la fin du VIIIe siècle au début du XI siècle, Bibliothèques des Ecoles Françaises d'Athènes et de Rome 291 (Rome, 1995)

'Les palais royaux et impériaux de l'Italie carolingienne et ottonienne', in A. Renoux (ed.), *Palais royaux et princiers au moyen âge* (Le Mans, 1996), pp. 181–96

'La production documentaire publique et privée, avant et après 774', in Gasparri and La Rocca, *774: ipotesi su una transizione*, available at <www.youtube. com/watch?v=EDP50hQj-58&search=74>

'Public power and authority', in C. La Rocca (ed.), *Italy in the early middle ages*, pp. 34–58

Bowman, A., and G. Woolf (eds.), *Literacy and power in the ancient world* (Cambridge, 1994)

Boyd, C. P., *Historia Patria: Politics, history, and national identity in Spain, 1875–1975* (Princeton, 1997)

Braunfels, W. (ed.), *Karl der Große / Charlemagne* (Aachen, 1965)

(ed.), *Karl der Große: Lebenswerk und Nachleben*, 4 vols I: H. Beumann (ed.), *Persönlichkeit und Geschichte*; II: B. Bischoff (ed.), *Das geistige Leben*; III: W. Braunfels and H. Schnitzler (eds.), *Karolingisches Kunst*; IV: W. Braunfels and P. E. Schramm (eds.), *Das Nachleben* (Düsseldorf, 1965)

(ed.), *The Lorsch Gospels* (New York, n.d.)

Bresslau, H., *Handbuch der Urkundenlehre*, 2 vols (Berlin, 1931)

Brommer, P., 'Capitula episcoporum: Bemerkungen zu den bischöflichen Kapitularien', *Zeitschrift für Kirchengeschichte* 91 (1980), pp. 207–36

Brooks, N., *The early history of the church of Canterbury* (Leicester, 1984)

Broun, D., *The Irish identity of the kingdom of the Scots in the twelfth and thirteenth centuries*, Studies in Celtic History (Woodbridge, 1999)

Brown, G., 'Introduction: the Carolingian Renaissance', in McKitterick, *Carolingian culture*, pp. 1–51

'Politics and patronage at the abbey of St Denis (814–898): the rise of a royal patron saint', unpublished DPhil dissertation, University of Oxford (1989)

Brown, T. S., *Gentlemen and officers: imperial administration and aristocratic power in Byzantine Italy, AD 554–800* (Rome, 1984)

Brown, W. C., *Unjust seizure: conflict, interest and authority in an early medieval society* (Ithaca, 2001)

'When documents are destroyed or lost: lay people and archives in the early middle ages', *Early Medieval Europe* 11 (2002), pp. 337–66

Brubaker, L., 'Topography and the creation of public space in early medieval Constantinople', in de Jong, Theuws and van Rhijn (eds.), *Topographies of power*, pp. 31–43

Brühl, C., *Fodrum, gistum, servitium regis: Studien zu den wirtschaftlichen Grundlagen des Königtums im Frankenreich und in den fränkischen Nachfolgestaaten Deutschland, Frankreich und Italien vom 6. bis zur Mitte des 14. Jahrhunderts*, Kölner Historische Abhandlungen 14/1–2 (Cologne and Graz, 1968)

'Fränkische Krönungsbrauch und das Problem der "Festkrönungen"', *Historische Zeitschrift* 194 (1962), pp. 265–326

'Königspfalz und Bischofstadt in fränkischer Zeit', *Rheinische Vierteljahrsblätter* 23 (1958), pp. 161–274

Palatium und Civitas, I: *Gallien* (Cologne, 1975)

'Remarques sur les notions du "capitale" et du "résidence" pendant le haut moyen âge', *Journal des Savants* (1967), pp. 195–215; repr. in C. Bruhl, *Aus Mittelalter und Diplomatik: Gesammelte Aufsätze*, 2 vols (Hildesheim, 1989), I, pp. 115–37

Brunhölzl, F., *Histoire de la littérature latine au moyen âge*, I/1: *L'époque mérovingienne* (Turnhout, 1990)

Histoire de la littérature latine du moyen âge, II: *De l'époque carolingienne au milieu du onzième siècle* (Turnhout, 1996; revised edn trans. H. Rochais from German edn of 1992)

Brunner, K., *Oppositionelle Gruppen im Karolingerreich*, Veröffentlichungen des Instituts für Österreichische Geschichtsforschung 25 (Vienna, 1979)

Brunterc'h, J.-P., 'La duché du Maine et la marche du Bretagne', in Atsma, *La Neustrie*, I, pp. 29–128

Buc, P., 'Nach 754: warum weniger die Handelnen selbst als eher die Chronisten das politische Ritual erzeugten – und warum es niemanden auf die wahre Geschichte ankam', in Jussen, *Die Macht des Königs*, pp. 27–37

Buchner, M., *Die Clausula de unctione Pippini: eine Fälschung aus dem Jahre 880*, Quellenfälschungen aus dem Gebiete der Geschichte, 1 (Paderborn, 1926)

'Zur Überlieferungsgeschichte des *Liber pontificalis* und zu seiner Verbreitung im Frankenreich im IX. Jahrhundert: zugleich ein Beitrag zur Geschichte der karolingischen Hofbibliothek und Hofkapelle', *Römische Quartalschrift* 34 (1926), pp. 141–65

Buchner, R., *Textkritische Untersuchungen zur Lex Ribuaria* (Stuttgart, 1940)

Buck, T. M., *Admonitio und praedicatio: zur religiös-pastoralen Dimension von Kapitularien und kapitulariennahen Texten (507–814)*, Freiburger Beiträge zur mittelalterliche Geschichte: Studien und Texte 9 (Frankfurt am Main, 1997), especially pp. 25–31

'"Capitularia imperatoria": zur Kaisergesetzgebung Karls des Großen von 802', *Historisches Jahrbuch* 122 (2002), pp. 3–26

Bühler, A., 'Capitularia relicta: Studien zur Entstehung und Überlieferung der Kapitularien Karls des Großen und Ludwigs des Frommen', *Archiv für Diplomatik* 32 (1986), pp. 305–501

Bührer-Thierry, G., 'De la fin du duché au début de l'empire: dix ans de transition à la lumière des chartes (788–799)', in Gasparri and La Rocca, *774: ipotesi su una transizione*

Bullough, D., *The age of Charlemagne* (London, 1965)

'Alboinus deliciosus Karoli regis: Alcuin of York and the shaping of the Carolingian court', in L. Fenske, W. Rösener and T. Zotz (eds.), *Institutionen, Gesellschaft und Kultur im Mittelalter: Festschrift J. Fleckenstein* (Sigmaringen, 1985), pp. 73–92

Alcuin: Achievement and reputation. Being part of the Ford Lectures delivered in Oxford in the Hilary Term 1980 (Leiden and Boston, 2004)

'Aula renovata: the Carolingian court before the Aachen palace', *Proceedings of the British Academy* 71 (1985), pp. 267–301, repr. in Bullough, *Carolingian renewal*, pp. 123–60

'Baiuli in the Carolingian *regnum langobardorum* and the career of Abbot Waldo', *English Historical Review* 77 (1962), pp. 625–37

Carolingian renewal: sources and heritage (Manchester, 1991)

'Charlemagne's court library revisited', *Early Medieval Europe* 12 (2003), pp. 338–63

'Europae pater: Charlemagne's achievement in the light of recent scholarship', *English Historical Review* 85 (1970), pp. 59–105

Friends, neighbours and fellow drinkers: aspects of community and conflict in the early medieval west, H.M. Chadwick Memorial Lectures, 1 (Cambridge, 1991)

'Roman books and Carolingian *renovatio*', in D. Baker (ed.), *Renaissance and renewal in Christian history*, Studies in Church History 14 (Oxford, 1977), repr. in Bullough, *Carolingian renewal*, pp. 1–33

'Review article: a scholar's work is never done', *Early Medieval Europe* 12 (2003), pp. 399–407

Bullough, D., and A. L. H. Correa, 'Texts, chants and the chapel of Louis the Pious', in Godman and Collins (eds.), *Charlemagne's heir*, pp. 489–508

Burn, A. E., *The Athanasian Creed from eighth- and ninth-century texts and early commentaries* (Cambridge, 1896)

Büttner, H., 'Mission und Kirchenorganisation des Frankenreiches bis zum Tode Karls des Grossen', in *KdG*, I, pp. 454–87

Butzer, P. L., and D. Lohrmann (eds.), *Science in Western and Eastern Civilization in Carolingian Times* (Basle, Boston and Berlin, 1993)

Butzmann, H., 'Die Weissenburger Handschriften: Einleitung zum Katalog', repr. Butzmann, *Kleine Schriften: Festgabe zum 70. Geburtstag* (Graz, 1973), pp. 48–103

Canisius, H., *Antiquae Lectiones*, III (Ingolstadt, 1603)

Capo, L., 'Paolo Diacono e il mondo franco: l'incontro di due esperienze storiografiche' in Chiesa, *Paolo Diacono*, pp. 39–74

  'Paolo Diacono e il problema della cultura dell'Italia Longobarda', in Gasparri and Commarosano, *Langobardia*, pp. 169–235

Caroli, M., 'Bringing saints to cities and monasteries: *translationes* in the making of a sacred geography (9th–10th centuries)', in G. Brogiolo, N. Gauthier and N. Christie (eds.), *Towns and their territories between late antiquity and the early middle ages*, The Transformation of the Roman World 4 (Leiden, 2000), pp. 259–74

Carroll, C., 'The archbishops and church provinces of Mainz and Cologne during the Carolingian period, 751–911', unpublished PhD thesis, University of Cambridge (1999)

  'The bishoprics of Saxony in the first century after Christianisation', *Early Medieval Europe* 8 (1999), pp. 219–45

Cavadini, J., *The last Christology of the West: adoptionism in Spain and Gaul, 785–820* (Philadelphia, 1993)

Chaplais, P., 'The letter from Bishop Wealhere of London to Archbishop Brithwold of Canterbury: the earliest original 'letter close' extant in the West', in M. B. Parkes and A. G. Watson (eds.), *Medieval scribes, manuscripts and libraries: Essays presented to N. R. Ker* (London, 1978), pp. 3–23

Chatelain, E., *Les classiques latins*, 2 vols. (Paris, 1894–1900)

Chazelle, C., *The crucified God in the Carolingian era: theology and art of Christ's passion* (Cambridge, 2001)

  (ed.), *Literacy, politics and artistic innovation in the early medieval West* (London and New York, 1992)

Chazelle, C., and B. van Name Edwards (eds.), *The study of the Bible in the Carolingian era*, Medieval Church Studies 3 (Turnhout, 2003)

Chiesa, P. (ed.), *Paolino d'Aquileia e il contributo italiano all'Europa carolingia* (Udine, 2003)

  (ed.), *Paolo Diacono e l'origine dell'Europa medievale: uno scrittore fra tradizione longobarda e rinnovamento carolingio* (Udine, 2000)

Chrysos, E., 'Byzantine diplomacy, AD 300–800: means and ends', in Shepard and Franklin, *Byzantine diplomacy*, pp. 25–40

Chrysos, E., and I. Wood (eds.), *East and west: modes of communication*, The Transformation of the Roman World 5 (Leiden, 1999)

Classen, P., 'Bermerkungen zur *Pfalzenforschung am Mittelrhein*, Deutsche Königspfalzen: Beiträge zu ihrer historischen und archäologischen Erforschung 1, Veröffentlichungen des Max-Planck-Instituts für Geschichte 11/1 (Göttingen, 1963), pp. 75–96, repr. in J. Fleckenstein (ed.), *Peter Classen: Ausgewählte Aufsätze*, Vorträge und Forschungen 28 (Sigmaringen, 1983), pp. 475–501

Kaiserreskript und Königsurkunde: Diplomatische Studien zum Problem der Kontinuität zwischen Altertum und Mittelalter (Thessaloniki, 1977)

'Karl der Große, das Papsttum und Byzanz: Die Begründung des karolingischen Kaisertums', in *KdG*, 1, pp. 537–608, repr. in H. Fuhrmann and C. Märtl (eds.), *P. Classen, Karl der Grosse, das Papsttum und Byzanz*, Beiträge zur Geschichte und Quellenkunde des Mittelalters 9 (Sigmaringen, 1968/85)

'Karl der Große und die Thronfolge im Frankenreich', in *Festschrift für Hermann Heimpel*, Veröffentlichungen des Max-Planck-Instituts für Geschichte 36/3 (Göttingen, 1972), pp. 109–34, repr. in J. Fleckenstein (ed.), *Peter Classen: Ausgewählte Aufsätze*, Vorträge und Forschungen 28 (Sigmaringen, 1983), pp. 205–29

(ed.), *Recht und Schrift im Mittelalter*, Vorträge und Forschungen 23 (Sigmaringen, 1977)

Claussen, M., *The reform of the Frankish church: Chrodegang of Metz and the regula canonicorum in the eighth century* (Cambridge, 2004).

Clausula de unctione pippini, ed. A. Stoclet, 'La "Clausula de unctione Pippini regis": mises au point et nouvelles hypothèses', *Francia* 8 (1980), pp. 1–42

Coens, M., 'Les Litaniae Carolinae de Soissons', *Analecta Bollandiana* 62 (1944), pp. 129–43

Coens, M., 'Anciennes litanies des saints', in M. Coens, *Recueil d'études Bollandiennes*, Subsidia hagiographica 37 (Brussels, 1963), pp. 129–322

'Les litanies bavaroises du "Libellus precum" dit de Fleury (Orléans MS 194)', *Analecta Bollandiana* 77 (1959), pp. 373–91

'Litanies carolines de Soissons et du Psautier de Charlemagne', *Recueil d'études Bollandiennes*, Subsidia hagiographica 37 (Brussels, 1963), p. 297

Coffin, B., 'The production of the *Codex carolinus* in its historical context', unpublished short essay, MPhil in Medieval History, University of Cambridge (2003)

Collins, R., *Charlemagne* (London, 1998)

'Charlemagne's imperial coronation and the annals of Lorsch', in Story, *Charlemagne*, pp. 52–70

'Deception and misrepresentation in early eighth-century Frankish historiography: two case studies', in Jarnut, Nonn and Richter, *Karl Martell in seiner Zeit*, pp. 227–48

Fredegar, Authors of the Middle Ages: Historical and Religious Writers of the Latin West, IV, no. 13 (Aldershot, 1996)

'The "Reviser" revisited: another look at the alternative version of the *Annales regni francorum*', in Murray, *After Rome's fall*, pp. 191–213

Constable, G., *Letters and letter collections*, Typologie des Sources du Moyen Age Occidental 17 (Turnhout, 1976)

Contreni, J. J., 'Carolingian biblical culture', in G. van Riel, C. Steel and J. McEvoy (eds.), *Johannes Scottus Eriugena: The Bible and hermeneutics*, Ancient and Medieval Philosophy series 1 (Leuven, 1996), pp. 1–23

'Carolingian biblical studies', in U.-R. Blumenthal (ed.), *Carolingian essays* (Washington, D.C., 1983), pp. 71–98, repr. in Contreni, *Carolingian learning*, Chapter V

Carolingian learning, masters and manuscripts (Aldershot, 1992)

'The Carolingian Renaissance: education and literary culture', in *NCMH*, II, pp. 709–57

'Counting, calendars, and cosmology: numeracy in the early middle ages', in J. J. Contreni and S. Casciani (eds.), *Word, image, number: communication in the middle ages* (Florence, 2002), pp. 43–83

'The pursuit of knowledge in Carolingian Europe', in Sullivan, '*The gentle voices of teachers*', pp. 106–41

Corradini, R., *Die Wiener Handschrift Cvp 430*: ein Beitrag zur Historiographie in Fulda im frühen 9. Jahrhundert*, Fuldaer Hochschulschriften 37 (Frankfurt am Main, 2000)

Corradini, R., 'Überlegungen zur sächsischen Ethnogenese anhand der Annales Fuldenses und deren sächsisch-ottonischer Rezeption', in W. Pohl (ed.), *Die Suche nach den Ursprüngen: von der Bedeutung des frühen Mittelalters*, Forschungen zur Geschichte des Mittelalters 8, Österreichische Akademie der Wissenschaften, phil.-hist. Klasse Denkschriften 322 (Vienna, 2004), pp. 211–32

'Zeiträume – Schrifträume: Überlegungen zur Komputistik und marginalchronographie am Beispiel der Annales Fuldenses antiquissimi', in W. Pohl and P. Herold (eds.), *Von Nutzen des Schreibens: Soziales Gedächtnis, Herrschaft und Besitz*, Forschungen zur Geschichte des Mittellalters 5, Österreichische Akademie der Wissenschaften, phil.-hist. Klasse Denkschriften 306 (Vienna, 2003), pp. 113–66

Corradini, R., M. Diesenberger and H. Reimitz (eds.), *The construction of communities in the early middle ages: texts, resources and artefacts*, The Transformation of the Roman World 12 (Leiden, 2003)

Coville, A., *Recherches sur l'histoire de Lyon du Vme siècle au IXme siècle (450–80)* (Paris, 1928)

Crick, J., 'An Anglo-Saxon fragment of Justinus' Epitome', *Anglo-Saxon England* 16 (1987) pp. 181–96

Crocker, R., 'Carolingian chant: Roman, Frankish-Roman, Frankish', in R. Sullivan (ed.), '*The gentle voices of teachers*', pp. 142–70.

Crook, J., *The architectural setting of the cult of saints in the early Christian West c. 300–c. 1200* (Oxford, 2000)

Crosby, S. M., *The royal abbey of Saint-Denis from its beginning to the death of Suger, 475–1151*, ed. P. Blum (New Haven, 1987)

Crossley, P. K., *A translucent mirror: history and identity in Qing imperial ideology* (Berkeley, 1999)

Cubitt, C., *Anglo-Saxon church councils, c. 650–c. 850* (London, 1995)

Curta, F. (ed.), *Borders, barriers and ethnogenesis: frontiers in late antiquity and the middle ages* (Turnhout, 2005)

 Southeastern Europe in the middle ages 500–1250 (Cambridge, 2006)

Dahlhaus-Berg, E., *Nova antiquitas et antiqua novitas: typologische Exegese und isidorianisches Geschichtsbild bei Theodulf von Orléans* (Cologne, 1975)

Davids, A., 'Marriage negotiations between Byzantium and the West and the name of Theophano in Byzantium (eighth to tenth centuries)', in Davids (ed.), *The Empress Theophano: Byzantium and the west at the turn of the first millennium* (Cambridge, 1995), pp. 99–120

Davies, W., and P. Fouracre (eds.), *The settlement of disputes in early medieval Europe* (Cambridge, 1986)

 (eds.), *Property and Power in the early middle ages* (Cambridge, 1995)

Davis, J., 'The conception of kingship in Charlemagne's capitularies', unpublished undergraduate thesis, Harvard University (1997)

 'Conceptions of kingship under Charlemagne', unpublished MLitt dissertation, University of Cambridge (1999)

 'A king and his law: Carolingian rulers through the lens of the capitulary manuscripts' (forthcoming)

De Clercq, C., 'Capitulaires francs en Italie à l'époque de Charlemagne', in *Hommage à Ursmer Berlière*, Bulletin de l'Institut historique belge de Rome, Supplément (Brussels, 1931), pp. 251–60

 Neuf capitulaires de Charlemagne concernant son œuvre réformatrice par les "missi", Università degli studi di Camerino, Istituto Giuridico, Testi per esercitazioni, Sezione v, n. 3 (Milan, 1968)

Declercq, G., *Anno domini: les origines de l'ère chrétienne* (Turnhout, 2000)

Delaruelle, E., 'Charlemagne, Carloman, Didier et la politique du mariage franco-lombard (770–771)', *Revue Historique* 170 (1932), pp. 213–24

Delisle, L., 'Notice sur un manuscript de l'église de Lyon au temps de Charlemagne', *Notices et extraits de la Bibliothèque Nationale et autres bibliothèques* 35 (1896), pp. 831–42

Deliyannis, D. M., 'Charlemagne's silver tables: the ideology of an imperial capital', *Early Medieval Europe* 12 (2003), pp. 159–78

 (ed.), *Historiography in the middle ages* (Leiden, 2003)

Delogu, P., 'Carolingian Italy', in *NCMH*, II, pp. 290–319

 An introduction to medieval history, trans. M. Moran, (London, 2002)

 'Longobardi e Romani: altre congetture', in Commarosano and Gasparri, *Langobardia*, pp. 112–67

Depreux, P., 'L'expression "statutum est a domno rege et sancta synodo" annonçant certaines dispositions du capitulaire de Francfort (794)', in Berndt, *Das Frankfurter Konzil von 794*, I, pp. 82–101

 'Lieux de rencontre, temps de negotiation: quelques observations sur les plaids généraux sous la règne de Louis le Pieux', in R. Le Jan (ed.), *La royauté et les élites dans l'Europe carolingienne du début du IXe siècle aux environs de 920* (Lille, 1998), pp. 213–31

Prosopographie de l'entourage de Louis le Pieux (781–840), Instrumenta 1 (Sigmaringen, 1997)

'Tassilon III et le roi des Francs: examen d'une vassalité controversée', *Revue Historique* 593 (1995), pp. 23–73

Depreux, P., and B. Judic (eds.), *Alcuin de York à Tours: écriture, pouvoir et réseaux dans l'Europe du haut moyen âge*, Annales de Bretagne et des pays de l'Ouest 111 (Rennes and Tours, 2004)

Deshman, R., 'The exalted servant: the ruler theology of the prayerbook of Charles the Bald', *Viator* 11 (1980), pp. 385–417

Die deutschen Königspfalzen: Repertorium der Pfalzen, Königshöfe und übrigen Aufenthaltsorte der Könige im deutschen Reich des Mittelalters, Hessen, Veröffentlichungen des Max-Planck-Institut für Geschichte (Göttingen, 1983–96)

Devroey, J.-P., *Puissants et misérables: système social et monde paysan dans l'Europe des Francs (VIe–IXe siècles)* (Brussels, 2006)

Dierkens, A., 'La mort, les funérailles et la tombe du roi Pépin le Bref (768)', *Médiévales* 31 (1996), pp. 37–52

'Le tombeau de Charlemagne', *Byzantion* 61 (1991), pp. 156–80

Diesenberger, M., 'Hair, sacrality and symbolic capital in the Frankish kingdoms', in Corradini, Diesenberger and Reimitz, *The Construction of communities*, pp. 173–212

Doherty, H., 'The maintenance of royal power and prestige in the Carolingian *regnum* of Aquitaine under Louis the Pious', unpublished MPhil dissertation, University of Cambridge (1998)

Dopsch, H., and R. Juffinger (eds.), *Virgil von Salzburg: Missionar und Gelehrter* (Salzburg, 1984)

Dueck, D., 'The Augustan concept of an 'empire without limits', in M. Dickhardt and V. Dorofeeva-Lichtman (eds.), *Göttingen Beiträge zur Asienforschung* 2–3 (Göttingen, 2003) pp. 211–27

Duindam, J., *Myths of Power: Norbert Elias and the early modern court* (Amsterdam, 1994)

Dutton, P. E., *The politics of dreaming in the Carolingian empire* (Lincoln, Neb., and London, 1994)

Dvornik, F., *Byzantine missions among the Slavs* (New Brunswick, 1970)

Eastwood, B. S., 'The astronomy of Macrobius in Carolingian Europe: Dungal's letter of 811 to Charles the Great', *Early Medieval Europe* 3 (1994), pp. 117–34

Eckhardt, W. A., 'Die *capitularia missorum specialia* 802', *Deutsches Archiv* 14 (1956), pp. 495–516

Die Kapitulariensammlung Bischof Ghaerbalds von Lüttich, Germanenrechte NF. Deutschrechtliches Archiv, Heft 3 (Göttingen, 1956)

'Review of Ganshof, *Was waren die Kapitularien?*', *Historisches Zeitschrift* 195 (1962), pp. 372–7

Edelstein, W., *Eruditio und sapientia: Weltbild und Erziehung in der Karolingerzeit. Untersuchungen zu Alcuins Briefen* (Freiburg im Breisgau, 1965)

Edwards, C., 'German vernacular literature', in McKitterick, *Carolingian culture*, pp. 141–70

Effros, B., '*De partibus Saxoniae* and the regulation of mortuary custom: a Carolingian campaign of Christianisation or the suppression of Saxon identity?', *Revue belge de philologie et d'histoire* 75 (1997), pp. 267–86

Ehlers, J. (ed.), *Deutschland und der westen Europas im Mittelalter*, Vorträge und Forschungen 56 (Stuttgart, 2002)

Eisler, R., 'Die illuminierten Handschriften Kärnten', in F. Wickhoff (ed.), *Beschreibendes Verzeichnis der illuminierten Handschriften in Oesterreich* (Leipzig, 1907)

Englisch, B., 'Zeitbewußtsein und systematische Zeitordnung in den Kalendern des frühen und hohen Mittelalters', in H.-W. Goetz (ed.), *Hochmittelalterliches Geschichtsbewußtein im Spiegel nichthistoriographischer Quellen* (Berlin, 1998), pp. 117–30.

Erhart, P., and B. Zeller (eds.), *Mensch und Schrift im frühen Mittelalter* (St Gallen, 2006)

Erinem, H. von, 'Die Tragödie der Karlsfresken Alfred Rethels', in *KdG* IV, pp. 306–25

Erkens, F.-R. (ed.), *Karl der Große und das Erbe der Kulturen* (Berlin, 2001)

Ernst, R., 'Karolingische Nordostpolitik zur Zeit Ludwigs des Frommen', in C. Goehrke, E. Oberländer and D. Wojtecki (eds.), *Östliches Europa: Spiegel der Geschichte. Festschrift für Manfred Hellmann zum 65. Geburtstag*, Quellen und Studien zur Geschichte des östlichen Europa 9 (Wiesbaden, 1977), pp. 81–107

Estey, F. N., 'Charlemagne's silver celestial table', *Speculum* 18 (1943), pp. 112–17
'The scabini and the local courts', *Speculum* 26 (1951), pp. 119–29

Euw, A. von, 'Die Textgeschichte des Lorscher Evangeliar', H. Shefers (ed.), *Das Lorscher Evangeliar*, Kommentarband (Luzern, 2000), pp. 33–53

Euw, A. von, and J. M. Plotzek, *Die Handschriften der Sammlung Ludwig* (Cologne, 1979)

Everett, N., *Literacy in Lombard Italy, c. 568–774* (Cambridge, 2003)

Ewig, E., 'Les Ardennes au haut moyen âge', *Ancien pays et assemblées d'états* 28 (1963), pp. 3–38
'Beobachtungen zur Entwicklung der Fränkischen Reichskirche unter Chrodegang von Metz', *Frühmittelalterliche Studien* 2 (1968), pp. 67–77
'*Descriptio Franciae*', in *KdG*, I, pp. 143–77
'Die fränkischen Königskataloge und der Aufstieg der Karolinger', *Deutsches Archiv* 51 (1995), pp. 1–28
'Der Gebetsdienst der Kirchen in den Urkunden der späteren Karolinger', in H. Maurer and H. Patze (eds.), *Festschrift für Berent Schwineköper zu seinem siebzigsten Geburtstag* (Sigmaringen, 1982), pp. 45–86
'Milo *et eiusmodi similes*', in Ewig, *Spätantikes und fränkisches Gallien*, Gesammelte Schriften 2, Beihefte der Francia 3/II (Zürich and Munich, 1979), pp. 189–219
'Résidence et capitale pendant le haut moyen âge', *Revue historique* 130 (1963), pp. 25–72, repr. in Ewig, ed. H. Atsma, *Spätantikes und fränkisches Gallien, Gesammelte Schriften*, I: Beihefte der Francia 3/I (Munich, 1976), pp. 362–408

'Saint Chrodegang et la réforme de l'église franque', in Schneider, *Saint Chrodegang*, pp. 25–53

'Überlegungen zu den merovingischen und karolingischen Teilungen', *Settimane* 27 (1981), pp. 225–53

'Zum christlichen Königsgedanken im Frühmittelalter', in T. Mayer (ed.), *Das Königtum*, Vorträge und Forschungen 3 (Constance, 1956), pp. 7–73

Falkenstein, L., 'Charlemagne and Aix-la-Chapelle', in A. Dierkens and J.-M. Sansterre (eds.), *Souverain à Byzance et en occident du VIIIe au Xe siècle, Hommage à la mémoire de Maurice Leroy, Byzantion* 69 (1991), pp. 231–289

Faulkner, T. W. G., '*Lex Ribuaria*', unpublished MPhil in Medieval History dissertation, University of Cambridge (2005)

'The representation of the past in the *Annales mettenses priores*', unpublished short essay, MPhil in Medieval History, University of Cambridge (2004)

Favier, J., *Charlemagne* (Paris, 2000)

Felten, F., *Äbte und Laienäbte im Frankenreich: Studie zum Verhältnis von Staat und Kirche im früheren Mittelalter*, Monographien zur Geschichte des Mittelalters 20 (Stuttgart, 1980)

Fenske, L., J. Jarnut and M. Wemhoff (eds.), *Deutsche Königspfalzen: Beiträge zu ihrer historischen und archäologischen Enforschung* 5, *Splendor palatii. Neue Forschungen zur Paderborn und anderen Pfalzen der Karolingerzeit*, Veröffentlichungen des Max-Planck-Instituts für Geschichte 11/5 (Göttingen, 2001)

Ferrari, M. C., *Sancti Willibrordi venerantes memoriam: echternacher Schreiber und Schriftsteller von den Angelsachsen bis Johann Bertels. Ein Überblick*, Publications du CLUDEM 6 (Luxembourg, 1984)

Fichtenau, H., *Das karolingische Imperium; soziale und geistige Problematik eines Grossreiches* (Zurich, 1949), trans. P. Munz, *The Carolingian empire* (Oxford, 1957)

Fichtenau, H., 'Abt Richbod und die *Annales Laureshamenses*', in *Beiträge zur Geschichte des Klosters Lorsch*, Geschichtsblätter für den Kreis Bergstraße, Sonderband 4 (Lorsch, 1980), pp. 277–304, a reprint with afterword of H. Fichtenau, 'Karl der Große und das Kaisertum', *MIÖG* 61 (1953), pp. 287–309

'Archive der Karolingerzeit', in Fichtenau, *Beiträge zur Mediävistik*, Ausgewählte Aufsätze 2, Urkundenforschung (Stuttgart, 1977), pp. 115–25

Fillitz, H., 'Die Elfenbeinarbeiten des Hofes Karls des Großen', in *799 Kunst und Kultur*, III, pp. 610–22

Finck von Finckenstein, A. Graf, 'Fest- und Feiertage im Frankenreich der Karolinger', in R. Schieffer (ed.), *Beiträge zur Geschichte des regnum francorum*, Beihefte der Francia 22 (Sigmaringen, 1990), pp. 121–9

Fischer, B., 'Bibeltext und Bibelreform unter Karl dem Großen', in *KdG*, II, pp. 154–216

Fischer, B., *Lateinische Bibelhandschriften des frühen Mittelalters, Vetus Latina. Aus der Geschichte der lateinischen Bibel* 2 (Freiburg, 1985)

Flach, D., *Untersuchungen zur Verfassung und Verwaltung des Aachener Reichsguter von der Karolingerzeit bis zur Mitte des 14. Jahrhunderts*, Veröffentlichungen des Max-Planck-Instituts für Geschichte 46 (Göttingen, 1976)

Fleckenstein, F., *Die Bildungsreform Karls des Großen als Verwirklichung der 'norma rectitudinis'* (Bigge-Ruhr, 1953)

'Die Struktur des Hofes Karls des Großen im Spiegel von Hincmars *De ordine palatii*', in J. Fleckenstein, *Ordnungen und formende Kräfte des Mittelalters: Ausgewählte Beiträge* (Göttingen, 1989), pp. 1–27

Fleckenstein, J., *Die Hofkapelle der deutschen Könige, 1: Grundlegung: die karolingische Hofkapelle, MGH* Schriften 16/1 (Stuttgart, 1959)

Folz, R., *The concept of empire in western Europe from the fifth to the fourteenth century* (London, 1969) (from the 1953 French edition)

Etudes sur le culte liturgique de Charlemagne dans les églises de l'empire (Paris, 1951)

Le souvenir et la légende de Charlemagne dans l'empire germanique médiéval (Paris, 1950)

Foot, S., 'Finding the meaning of form: narrative in annals and chronicles', in N. Partner (ed.), *Writing medieval history* (London and New York, 2005), pp. 88–108

Forstner, K., 'Das Salzburger Skriptorium unter Vergil und das Verbrüderungsbuch von St Peter', in H. Dopsch and R. Juffinger, *Virgil von Salzburg*, pp. 135–40

Fouracre, P., *The Age of Charles Martel* (Harlow, 2000)

'Carolingian justice: the rhetoric of reform and the contexts of abuse', in *La giustizia nell'alto medioevo (secoli V–VIII)*, Settimane 42 (Spoleto, 1995), pp. 771–803

'Conflict, power and legitimation in Francia in the late seventh and eighth centuries', in I. Alfonso, H. Kennedy and J. Escalona (eds.), *Building legitimacy: Political discourses and forms of legitimacy in medieval societies*, The Medieval Mediterranean: Peoples, Economies and Cultures 400–1500, 53 (Leiden, 2004), pp. 3–26

'Cultural conformity and social conservatism in early medieval Europe', *History Workshop Journal* 33 (1992), pp. 152–60

'Eternal light and earthly needs: practical aspects of the development of Frankish immunities', in Davies and Fouracre, *Property and power in the early middle ages*, pp. 53–81.

'Frankish Gaul to 814', in *NCMH*, II, pp. 85–109

'The long shadow of the Merovingians', in J. Story (ed.), *Charlemagne: empire and society* (Manchester, 2005), pp. 5–21

'Merovingian history and Merovingian hagiography', *Past and Present* 127 (1990), pp. 3–38

'Observations on the outgrowth of Pippinid influence in the "Regnum Francorum" after the Battle of Tertry (687–715)', *Medieval Prosopography* 5 (1984), pp. 1–31

'The origins of the Carolingian attempt to regulate the cult of saints', in J. Howard Johnston and P. A. Hayward (eds.), *The cult of saints in late antiquity and the early middle ages* (Oxford, 1999), pp. 143–67

Fouracre, P., and R. Geberding, *Late merovingian France: history and hagiography, 640–720* (Manchester, 1996)

Fox, M., 'Alcuin the exegete: the evidence of the *Quaestiones in Genesim*', in Chazelle and van Name Edwards, *The study of the Bible in the Carolingian era*, pp. 39–60

Freeman, A., 'Further studies in the Libri carolini', *Speculum* 40 (1965), pp. 203–69

'Theodulf of Orleans and the Libri carolini', *Speculum* 32 (1957), pp. 663–705

Frere, W. H., *Studies in the Roman liturgy*, I: *The Roman Gospel lectionary* (London, 1930).

Freund, S., *Von den Agilolfingern zu den Karolingern: Bayerns Bischöfe zwischen Kirchenorganisation, Reichsintegration und karolingischer Reform (700–847)*, Schriftenreihe zur bayerischen Landesgeschichte 144 (Munich, 2004)

Fried, J., 'Papst Leo III. besucht Karl den Großen', *Historische Zeitschrift* 272 (2001), pp. 281–326

Donation of Constantine and Constitutum Constantini: the misinterpretation of a fiction and its original meaning, Millennium Studien 3 (Berlin and New York, 2007)

Fried, J., R. Koch, L. E. Saurma-Jeltsch and A. Theil (eds.), *794 – Karl der Grosse in Frankfurt am Main: ein König bei der Arbeit. Austellung zum 1200-Jahre Jubiläum der Stadt Frankfurt am Main* (Sigmaringen, 1994)

Friesinger, H., *Die Bayern und ihre Nachbarn* (Vienna, 1985)

Fritze, W. H., 'Die Datierung des *Geographicus bavaricus* und die Stammesverfassung der Abodriten', *Zeitschrift für Slawische Philologie* 21 (1952), pp. 326–42

'Probleme der abodritischen Stammes- und Reichsverfassung und ihrer Entwicklung von Stammesstaat zur Herrschaftsstaat', in H. Ludat (ed.), *Siedlung und Verfassung der Slawen zwischen Elbe, Saale und Oder* (Giessen, 1960), pp. 141–220

Fulbrook, M., and M. Swales (eds.), *Representing the German Nation: history and identity in twentieth-century Germany* (Manchester, 2000)

Gaborit-Chopin, D., and H. Fillitz, 'Die Elfenbeinarbeiten des Hofes Karls des Großen', in *799 Kunst und Kultur*, III, pp. 610–22

Gameson, R. (ed.), *The early medieval Bible: its production, decoration and use* (Cambridge, 1994)

Gameson, R., and H. Leyser (eds.), *Belief and culture in the middle ages: studies presented to Henry Mayr-Harting* (Oxford, 2001)

Ganshof, F.-L., 'Charlemagne et les institutions de la monarchie franque', in *KdG*, I, pp. 349–93

'Eginhard, biographe de Charlemagne', *Bibliothèque d'Humanisme et Renaissance* 13 (1951), pp. 217–230 ; trans. J. Sondheimer, 'Einhard, biographer of Charlemagne', in Ganshof, *The Carolingians and the Frankish monarchy* (London, 1971), pp. 1–16

'L'Historiographie dans la monarchie franque sous les Mérovingiens et les Carolingians: monarchie franque unitaire et Francie occidentale', *La storiografia altomedievale*, Settimane 17 (Spoleto, 1970), pp. 631–85

Le Moyen age: histoire des relations internationales, I (Paris, 1958); trans R. Hall, *The Middle Ages: a history of international relations* (New York, 1971)

'Note sur les "capitula de causis cum episcopis et abbatibus tractandis" de 811', *Collectanea Stephan Kuttner* 3, Studia Gratiana 13 (1967), pp. 20–5

'Le programme de gouvernement impérial de Charlemagne', in *Renovatio Imperii: atti della giornata internazionale di studio per il Millenario, Ravenna 4–5 November 1961* (Faenza, 1963), pp. 63–96, trans. J. Sondheimer, 'Charlemagne's programme of imperial government', in Ganshof, *The Carolingians and the Frankish monarchy* (London, 1971), pp. 55–86

Recherches sur les capitulaires (Paris, 1958); German trans. *Was waren die Kapitularien?* (Weimar and Darmstadt, 1961)

Ganz, D., 'Conclusion: visions of Carolingian education, past, present and future', in Sullivan, '*The gentle voices of teachers*', pp. 261–84

Corbie in the Carolingian Renaissance, Beihefte der Francia 29 (Sigmaringen, 1990)

'Le *De laude dei* d'Alcuin', in P. Depreux and B. Judic (eds.), *Alcuin de York à Tours: écriture, pouvoir et réseaux dans l'Europe du haut moyen âge*, Annales de Bretagne et des pays de l'Ouest III (Rennes and Tours, 2004), pp. 387–91

'Einhard's Charlemagne: the characterization of greatness', in Story, *Charlemagne*, pp. 38–51

'Humor as history in Notker's *Gesta Karoli magni*', in E. B. King (ed.), *Monks, friars and nuns in medieval society* (Sewanee, 1989), pp. 171–83

'The preface to Einhard's "Vita Karoli"', in H. Schefers (ed.), *Einhard: Studien zu Leben und Werk* (Darmstadt, 1997), pp. 299–310

'Theology and the organization of thought', in McKitterick, *NCMH*, II, pp. 758–85

Garipzanov, I. H., 'The image of authority in Carolingian coinage', *Early Medieval Europe* 8 (1999), pp. 197–215

Garrison, M., 'The emergence of Carolingian Latin literature and the court of Charlemagne (780–814)', in McKitterick, *Carolingian culture*, pp. 111–140

'English and Irish and the court of Charlemagne', in P. L. Butzer, M. Kerner and B. Oberschelp (eds.), *Karl der Große und sein Nachwirken: 1200 Jahre Kultur und Wissenschaft in Europa*, I: *Wissen und Weltbild* (Turnhout, 1997), pp. 97–124

'The Franks as the New Israel? Education for an identity from Pippin to Charlemagne', in Hen and Innes, *The uses of the past*, pp. 114–61

'Letters to a king and biblical exempla: the examples of Cathwulf and Clemens peregrinus', in de Jong, *The power of the word*, pp. 305–28

'"Send more socks": on mentality and the preservation context of medieval letters', in Mostert, *New approaches to medieval communication*, pp. 69–99

'The social world of Alcuin: nicknames at York and at the Carolingian Court', in Houwen and MacDonald, *Alcuin of York*, pp. 59–79

Gasparri, S., 'The aristocracy', in La Rocca, *Italy in the early middle ages*, pp. 34–83

'Pavia longobarda', *Storia dei Pavia*, II: *L'alto medioevo* (Pavia, 1987), pp. 19–65

Gasparri, S., and P. Commarosano (eds.), *Langobardia* (Udine, 1990)

Gasparri, S., and C. La Rocca (eds.) *774: ipotesi su una transizione: Seminario internazionale, Poggio imperiale, Poggibonsi [SI] (16–18 febbraio 2006)* (Siena, forthcoming)

Gaudemet, J., 'Survivances romaines dans le droit de la monarchie franque, du Ve au Xe siècle', *Tijdschrift voor Rechtsgeschiedenis* 23 (1955), pp. 149–206

Gauert, A., 'Zum Itinerar Karls des Großen', *KdG*, I, pp. 307–21

Gauthier-Dalché, P., 'De la glose à la contemplation: place et fonction de la carte dans les manuscrits du haut moyen âge', in *Testo e immagine nell'alto medioevo*, Settimane 41 (Spoleto, 1994), pp. 693–771, at pp. 759–61, repr. Gauthier-Dalché, *Géographie et culture*, Chapter VIII

  Géographie et culture: la représentation de l'espace du VIe au XIIe siècle (Aldershot, 1997)

  'Principes et modes de la représentation de l'espace géographique durant le haut moyen âge', in *Uomo e spazio nell'alto medioevo*, Settimane 50 (Spoleto, 2003), pp. 117–50

Geary, P. J., *Aristocracy in Provence: the Rhone basin at the dawn of the Carolingian age*, Monographien zur Geschichte des Mittelalters 31 (Stuttgart, 1985)

  Furta sacra: thefts of relics in the central middle ages (Princeton, 2nd edn, 1990)

  The myth of nations: the medieval origins of Europe (Princeton, 2002)

  Phantoms of remembrance: memory and oblivion at the end of the first millennium (Princeton, 1994)

Geberding, R., *The rise of the Carolingians and the* Liber historiae francorum (Oxford, 1987)

Geertman, H., *More veterum: il Liber pontificalis e gli edifici ecclesiastici di Roma nella tarda antichità e nell'alto medioevo*, Archaeologia Traiectini 10 (Groningen, 1975)

Geith, K. E., *Carolus Magnus: Studien zur Darstellung Karls des Großen in der deutschen Literatur des 12. und 13. Jarhrhunderts*, Bibliotheca Germanica 19 (Bern and Munich, 1977)

Gelichi, S. 'Le anguille di Venezia: il lungo seculo VIII degli emporia dell'arco nord-orientali adriatico', in Gasparri and La Rocca (eds.), *774: ipotesi su una transizione*

Gerchow, J., *Die Gedenküberlieferung den Angelsachsen* (Berlin, 1988)

Gilbert, J. M., *Hunting and hunting reserves in medieval Scotland* (Edinburgh, 1979)

Gillett, A., *Envoys and political communication in the late antique West, 411–533* (Cambridge, 2003)

  (ed.), *On barbarian identity: critical approaches to ethnicity in the early middle ages*, Studies in the Early Middle Ages 4 (Turnhout, 2002)

La giustizia nell'alto medioevo (secoli V–VIII), and *La giustizia nell'alto medioevo (secoli IX–XI)*, Settimane 42 and 44 (Spoleto, 1995 and 1997)

Glauche, G., *Schullektüre im Mittelalter: Entstehung und Wandlungen des Lektürekanons bis 1200 nach den Quellen dargestellt*, Münchener Beiträge zur Mediävistik und Renaissance-Forschung 5 (Munich, 1970), pp. 21–2

Gneuss, H., *Hymnar und Hymnen im englischen Mittelalter* (Tübingen, 1968),

  'Zur Geschichte des Hymnars', *Mittellateinisches Jahrbuch* 35 (2000), pp. 227–48

Godman, P., *Poetry of the Carolingian Renaissance* (London, 1985)

  Poets and emperors: Frankish politics and Carolingian poetry (Oxford, 1987)

Godman, P., and R. Collins (eds.), *Charlemagne's heir: new perspectives on the reign of Louis the Pious (814–840)* (Oxford, 1990)

Godman, P., J. Jarnut and P. Johanek (eds.), *Am Vorabend der Kaiser Krönung: das Epos "Karolus Magnus et Leo Papa" und der Papstbesuch in Paderborn* (Berlin, 2002)

Goetz, H.-W., 'Serfdom and the beginnings of a "seigneurial system" in the Carolingian period: a survey of the evidence', *Early Medieval Europe* 2 (1993), pp. 29–51

Strukturen der spätkarolingischen Epoche im Spiegel der Vostellungen eines zeitgenössischen mönchs: eine Interpretation des Gesta Karoli Notkers von Sankt Gallen (Bonn, 1981)

Goetz, H., J. Jarnut, and W. Pohl (eds.), *Regna et gentes: the relationship between late antique and early medieval peoples and kingdoms in the transformation of the Roman world*, The Transformation of the Roman World 13 (Leiden, 2003)

Goffart, W., 'Paul the Deacon's *Gesta episcoporum mettensium* and the early design of Charlemagne's succession', *Traditio* 42 (1986), pp. 59–94

Goffart, W., and D. Ganz, 'Charters earlier than AD 800 from French collections', *Speculum* 65 (1990), pp. 906–32

Goldberg, E., 'Popular revolt, dynastic politics and aristocratic factionalism in the early middle ages: the Saxon *stellinga* reconsidered', *Speculum* 70 (1995), pp. 467–501

Struggle for empire: kingship and conflict under Louis the German, 817–876 (Ithaca, 2006)

Gorman, M., *Biblical commentaries from the early middle ages*, Millennio Medievale 32, Reprints 4 (Florence, 2002)

'The encyclopedic commentary on Genesis prepared for Charlemagne by Wigbod', *Recherches Augustiniennes* 17 (1982), pp. 173–201, repr. in Gorman, *Biblical commentaries from the early middle ages*, pp. 1–29

'Peter of Pisa and the *Quaestiunculae* copied for Charlemagne in Brussels II 2572, with a note on the Codex Diezianus from Verona', *Revue Bénédictine* 110 (2000), pp. 238–60

'Wigbod and biblical studies under Charlemagne', *Revue Bénédictine* 107 (1997), pp. 40–76, repr. in Gorman, *Biblical commentaries from the early middle ages*, pp. 200–36

Green, D. H., and F. Siegmund (eds.), *The Continental Saxons from the migration period to the tenth century: an ethnographic perspective* (Woodbridge, 2003)

Grégoire, R., *Homéliaires liturgiques médiévaux: analyse des manuscrits* (Spoleto, 1980)

Grewe, H., 'Die Königspfalz Ingelheim am Rhein', in *799 Kunst und Kultur*, III, pp. 142–51

Grierson, P., 'Symbolism in early medieval charters and coins', in *Simboli e simbologia nell'alto medioevo*, Settimane 23 (Spoleto, 1976), II, pp. 601–30

Grierson, P., and M. A. S. Blackburn, *Medieval European coinage, 1: The early middle ages (5th–10th centuries)* (Cambridge, 1986)

Grimme, E. G., 'Karl der Grosse in seiner Stadt', in Braunfels (ed.), *Karl der Große*, IV, pp. 228–73

Grosjean, P., 'Virgile de Salzbourg en Irlande', *Analecta Bollandiana* 78 (1960), pp. 92–123

Guillot, O., 'Les saints des peuples et des nations dans l'occident des VIe–Xe s.: un aperçu d'ensemble illustré par le cas des francs en Gaule', in *Santi e demoni nell'alto medioevo occidentale (secoli V–XI)*, Settimane 34 (Spoleto, 1989), 1, pp. 205–59

Hack, A. T., *Codex carolinus: Studien zur päpstlichen Epistolographie im 8. Jahrhundert*, Päpste und Papsttum (Stuttgart, 2007)

Hageneier, L., *Jenseits der Topik: die karolingische Herrscherbiographie*, Historische Studien 483 (Husum, 2004)

Hägermann, D., 'Der Dagulf-Psalter: ein Zeugnis fränkischer Orthodoxie', in F.-R. Erkens and H. Wolff (eds.), *Von sacerdotium und regnum: geistliche und weltliche Gewalt im frühen und hohen Mittelalter. Festschrift für Egon Boshof zum 65. Geburtstag* (Cologne, Weimar and Vienna, 2002), pp. 83–201

Karl der Grosse: Herrscher des Abendlandes: Biographie (Berlin, 2000)

'Zur Entstehung der Kapitularien', in W. Schlögl and P. Herde (eds.), *Grundwissenschaften und Geschichte: Festschrift für Peter Acht*, Münchener Historische Studien, Abt. Geshichtliche Hilfswissenschaften 15 (Kallmünz, 1976), pp. 12–27

Halphen, L., *Etudes critiques sur l'histoire de Charlemagne* (Paris, 1921)

Halporn, J. W., 'The modern edition of Cassiodorus' Psalm commentary', *Texte und Untersuchungen* 133 (1987), pp. 239–47

Halsall, G., 'Violence and society: an introductory survey', in Halsall, *Violence and society in the early medieval West*, pp. 1–45

Warfare and society in the barbarian West, 450–900 (London, 2003)

(ed.), *Violence and society in the early medieval West* (Woodbridge, 1998)

Hamel, C. de, *An introduction to medieval illuminated manuscripts* (London, 1986)

Hamilton, G. L., 'Theodulus: a medieval text book', *Modern Philology* 7 (1909), pp. 1–17 (169–85)

Hammer, C., *Charlemagne's months and their Bavarian labours: the politics of the seasons in the Carolingian empire*, BAR International series 676 (Oxford, 1997)

'The social landscape of the Prague Sacramentary: the prosopography of an eighth-century mass book', *Traditio* 54 (1999), pp. 41–80

From ducatus to regnum: ruling Bavaria under the Merovingians and early Carolingians (Turnhout, 2007)

Hannig, J., *Consensus fidelium: frühfeudale Interpretationen des Verhältnisses von Königtum und Adel am Beispiel des Frankenreiches*, Monographien zur Geschichte des Mittelalters 27 (Stuttgart, 1982)

'Pauperiores vassi de infra palatii? Zur Entstehung der karolingischen Königsbotenorganisation', *MIÖG* 91 (1983), pp. 309–74

Hansen, I. L., and C. Wickham (eds.), *The long eighth century: production, distribution and demand*, The Transformation of the Roman World 11 (Leiden, 2000)

Hardt, M., 'Hesse, Elbe, Salle and the frontiers of the Carolingian empire', in W. Pohl, I. Wood and H. Reimitz (eds.), *The transformation of frontiers from late antiquity to the Carolingians* (Leiden, 2001), pp. 219–32

'The *limes Saxoniae* as part of the eastern borderlands of the Frankish and Ottonian-Salian empire', in Curta, *Borders, barriers and ethnogenesis*, pp. 35–50

'Linien und Säume, Zonen und Räume an der Ostgrenze des Reiches im frühen und hohen Mittelalter', in Pohl and Reimitz, *Grenze und Differenz im frühen Mittelalter*, pp. 39–56

Harmon, J. J., *Codicology of the court school of Charlemagne: Gospel book production, illumination, and emphasized script*, European University Studies, series 28, History of Art 21 (Frankfurt, 1984)

Hartmann, F., *Hadrian I (772–795)*, Päpste und Papsttum 34 (Stuttgart, 2006), pp. 29–36

Hartmann, W., *Die Synoden der Karolingerzeit im Frankenreich und in Italien* (Paderborn, Munich and Vienna, 1989)

Harvey, A. E., 'Melito and Jerusalem', *Journal of Theological Studies* 17 (1966), pp. 401–3

Haselbach, I., *Aufstieg und Herrschaft der Karlinger in der Darstellung der sogenannten Annales Mettenses priores: ein Beitrag zur Geschichte des politischen Ideen im Reiche Karls des Großen*, Historische Studien, 412 (Lübeck and Hamburg, 1970)

Hassler, H. J. (ed.), *Sachsen und Franken in Westfalen. 799 Kunst und Kultur der Karolingerzeit*: Studien zur Sachsen Forschung 12 (Paderborn, 1999)

Haubrichs, W., *Die Kultur der Abtei Prüm zur Karolingerzeit: Studien zum Heimat des althochdeutschen Georgsliedes*, Rheinisches Archiv 105 (Bonn, 1979)

'*Veterum regum actus et bella*: zur sog. Heldenliedersammlung Karls des Großen', in W. Tauber (ed.), *Aspekte der Germanistik: Festschrift für Hans-Friedrich Rosenfeld* (Göppingen, 1989), pp. 17–46

Von den Anfängen zum hohen Mittelalter, 1: Die Anfänge: Versuche volkssprachiger Schriftlichkeit im frühen Mittelalter (ca. 700–1050/60) (Frankfurt am Main, 1988)

Hauck, A., *Kirchengeschichte Deutschlands*, II (Leipzig, 1912)

'Von einer spätantiken Randkultur zum karolingischen Europa', *Frühmittelalterliche Studien* 1 (1967), pp. 3–93

Haye, T., *Lateinische Oralität: gelehrte Sprache in der mundlichen Kommunikation des hohen und späten Mittelalters* (Berlin, 2005)

Head, T., *Hagiography and the cult of saints: the diocese of Orleans, 800–1200* (Cambridge, 1990)

Heidrich, I., 'Titulatur und Urkunden der arnulfingischen Hausmeir', *Archiv für Diplomatik* 11/12 (1965/66), pp. 71–279

'Die Urkunden Pippins d.M und Karl Martells: Beobachtungen zu ihrer zeitlichen und räumlichen Steuerung', in Jarnut, Nonn and Richter, *Karl Martell in seiner Zeit*, pp. 23–34

'Von Plectrud zu Hildegard. Beobachtungen zum Besitzrecht adliger Frauen im Frankenreich des 7. und 8. Jahrhunderts und zur politischem Rolle der Frauen', *Rheinische Vierteljahrsblätter* 52 (1988), pp. 1–15

Heine B., and T. Kuteva (eds.), *The changing languages of Europe* (Oxford, 2006)

Heinzelmann, M., *Gregor von Tours (538–594): Zehn Bücher Geschichte Historiographie und Gesellschaftskonzept im 6. Jahrhundert* (Darmstadt, 1994), trans. C. Carroll, *Gregory of Tours: history and society in the sixth century* (Cambridge, 2001)

Translationsberichte und andere Quellen der Reliquienkulte, Typologie des sources du moyen âge occidental 33 (Turnhout, 1979)

Hellgardt, E., 'Zur Mehrsprachigkeit im Karolingerreich: Bermerkungen aus Anlaß von Rosamond McKittericks Buch "The Carolingians and the Written Word"', *Beiträge zur Geschichte der deutschen Sprache und Literatur* 118 (1996), pp. 1–48

Hellmann, M., 'Karl und die slawische Welt zwischen Ostsee und Böhmerwald', in *KdG*, I, pp. 708–18

Helms, M. W., *Ulysses' sail: an ethnographic odyssey of power, knowledge and geographical distance* (Princeton, 1988)

Hen, Y., 'The Annals of Metz and the Merovingian past', in Hen and Innes, *The uses of the past*, pp. 175–90

'Charlemagne's *jihad*', *Viator* 37 (2006), pp. 33–51

Culture and religion in Merovingian Gaul, AD 481–751, Culture, Beliefs and Tradition: Medieval and Early Modern Peoples 1 (Leiden, 1995)

'Paul the Deacon and the Frankish liturgy', in Chiesa (ed.), *Paolo Diacono*, pp. 205–23

The royal patronage of the liturgy in Frankish Gaul to the death of Charles the Bald (877), Henry Bradshaw Society Subsidia 3 (London, 2001)

Hen, Y., and M. Innes (eds.), *The uses of the past in the early middle ages* (Cambridge, 2000)

Hennebicque, R., see under Le Jan

Henning, J., 'Civilization versus barbarians? Fortification techniques and politics in Carolingian and Ottonian borderlands', in Curta (ed.), *Borders, barriers and ethnogenesis*, pp. 23–34

Herbers, K., 'Das Bild Papst Leo III in der Perspective des *Liber pontificalis*,' in Niederkorn-Bruck and Scharer, *Erzbischof Arn von Salzburg*, pp. 137–54

'Mobilität und Kommunikation in der Karolingerzeit: die Reliquienreisen der heilige Chrysanthus und Daria', in N. Miedema and R. Suntrup (eds.), *Literatur – Geschichte – Literaturgeschichte: Beiträge zur mediävistischen Literaturwissenschaft. Festschrift für Volker Honemann zum 60. Geburtstag* (Frankfurt am Main, 2003), pp. 647–60

Herrin, J., 'Constantinople, Rome and the Franks in the seventh and eighth centuries', in Shepard and Franklin, *Byzantine diplomacy*, pp. 91–107

The formation of Christendom (Oxford, 1987)

Hill, J. D. (ed.), *History, power and identity: ethnogenesis in the Americas, 1492–1992* (Iowa City, 1996)

Hlawitschka, E., *Franken, Alemannen, Bayern und Burgunden in Oberitalien (774–962): zum Verständnis der fränkischen Königsherrschaft in Italien*, Forschungen zur oberrheinischen Landesgeschichte 8 (Freiburg im Breisgau, 1960)

'Die Vorfahren Karls des Grossen', in *KdG*, I, pp. 51–82

Hobsbawm, E., and T. Ranger, *The invention of tradition* (Cambridge, 1983)

Hodges, R., *Light in the dark ages: the rise and fall of San Vincenzo al Volturno* (London, 1997)

Hoffmann, H., *Untersuchungen zur karolingischen Annalistik*, Bonner Historische Forschungen 10 (Bonn, 1958)

Hofmann, H., *'Roma caput mundi*: Rom und *"imperium romanum"* in der literarischen Diskussion zwischen Spätantike und dem 9. Jht', *Roma fra oriente e occidente*, Settimane 49 (Spoleto 2002), I, pp. 492–556

Holter, K. (ed.), *Der goldene Psalter 'Dagulf-Psalter': Vollständige Faksimile-Ausgabe im Originalformat von Codex 1861 der Österreichischen Nationalbibliothek* (Graz, 1980)

Honselmann, K., 'Reliquientranslationen nach Sachsen', in V. Elbern (ed.), *Das erste Jahrtausend: Kultur und Kunst im werdenden Abendland an Rhein und Ruhr*, I (Düsseldorf, 1962), pp. 159–93

Horst, K. van der, W. Noel and H. Wustemann (eds.), *The Utrecht Psalter* (Utrecht, 1997)

Houts, E. van, *Memory and gender in medieval Europe 900–1200* (Basingstoke, 1999)
'Women and the writing of history: the case of Abbess Matilda of Essen and Aethelweard', *Early Medieval Europe* 1 (1992), pp. 53–68

Houwen, L. A. J. R., and A. A. MacDonald (eds.), *Alcuin of York: Scholar at the Carolingian court*, Germania Latina 3, Mediaevalia Groningana 22 (Groningen, 1999)

Howard-Johnson, J., and P. A. Hayward (eds.), *The cult of saints in late antiquity and the early middle ages: essays on the contribution of Peter Brown* (Oxford, 1999)

Hubert, J., J. Porcher and W. Volbach, *Carolingian art* (London, 1970)

Hübner, R., 'Gerichtsurkunden der fränkischen Zeit I: Die Gerichtsurkunden aus Deutschland und Frankreich bis zum Jahre 1000', *Zeitschrift der Savigny-Stiftung für Rechtsgeschichte, Germanistische Abteilung* 12 (1891), pp. 1–118; and II, 'Die Gerichtsurkunden aus Italien bis zum Jahre 1150', ibid., 14 (1893), pp. 1–258

Hummer, H., *Politics and power in early medieval Europe: Alsace and the Frankish realm, 600–1000* (Cambridge, 2005)

Hunt, E. D., *Holy Land pilgrimage in the later Roman empire, AD 312–460* (Oxford, 1982)
'St Silvia of Aquitaine: the role of a Theodosian pilgrim in the society of East and West', *Journal of Theological Studies*, NS 23 (1972), pp. 351–73

Ihm, M., 'Beitrage zur Textgeschichte des Sueton', *Hermes* 36 (1901), pp. 343–63

Imbart de la Tour, P., *Les élections épiscopales dans l'église de France du IXe au XIIe siècle* (Paris, 1891)

Imhoff, M., and G. F.Stasch (eds.), *Bonifatius: vom angelsächsischen Missionar zum Apostel der Deutschen* (Petersberg, 2004)

Innes, M., 'Charlemagne's government', in Story, *Charlemagne: empire and society*, pp. 71–89

'Charlemagne's will: piety, politics and the imperial succession', *English Historical Review* 112 (1997), pp. 833–55

'The classical tradition in the Carolingian Renaissance: ninth-century encounters with Suetonius', *International Journal of the Classical Tradition* 3 (1997), pp. 265–82

'Memory, orality and literacy in an early medieval society', *Past and Present* 158 (1998), pp. 3–36

State and society in the early middle ages: the middle Rhine valley 400–1000 (Cambridge, 2000)

'Teutons or Trojans? The Carolingians and the Germanic past', in Hen and Innes, *The uses of the past in the middle ages*, pp. 227–49

Innes, M., and R. McKitterick, 'The writing of history', in McKitterick, *Carolingian culture*, pp. 193–220

Iogna-Prat, D., 'Lieu de culte et exégèse liturgique à l'époque carolingienne', in Chazelle and van Name Edwards (eds.), *The study of the Bible in the Carolingian era*, pp. 215–44

Isenberg, G., and B. Rommé (eds.), *805: Liudger wird Bischof: Spuren eines Heiligen zwischen York, Rom und Münster* (Mainz, 2005)

Jacobsen, W., 'Die Pflazkonzeption Karls der Großen', in Saurma-Jeltsch, *Karl der Große als vielberufener Vorfahr*, pp. 23–48

Jahn, J., *Ducatus Baiuvariorum: das bairische Herzogtum der Agilolfinger*, Monographien zur Geschichte des Mittelalters 32 (Stuttgart, 1991)

Jahn, J., 'Hausmeier und Herzöge: Bemerkungen zur agilolfingisch-karolingischen Rivalität bis zum Tod Karl Martels', in Jarnut, Nonn and Richter, *Karl Martell in seiner Zeit*, pp. 317–44

'Virgil, Arbeo und Cozroh, verfassungsgeschichtliche Beobachtungen an bairischen Quellen des 8. und 9. Jahrhunderts', *Mitteilungen der Gesellschaft für Salzburgische Landeskunde* 130 (1990), pp. 201–91

Jankuhn, H., 'Karl der Große und der Norden', in *KdG*, 1, pp. 699–707

Jarausch, K., 'Normalization or renationalization? On reinterpreting the German past', in R. Alter and P. Monteath (eds.), *Rewriting the German past: history and identity in the new Germany* (Atlantic Highlands, NJ, 1997)

Jarnut, J., *Agilolfingerstudien: Untersuchungen zur Geschichte einer adligen Familie im 6. und 7. Jahrhundert*, Monographien zur Geschichte des Mittelalters 32 (Stuttgart, 1986)

'Chlodwig und Chlothar: Anmerkungen zu den Namen zweier Söhne Karls des Grossen', *Francia* 12 (1984), pp. 645–65, repr. in Jarnut, *Herrschaft und Ethnogenese*, pp. 247–53

'Ein Bruderkampf und seine Folgen: die Krise des Frankenreiches (768–771)', in G. Jenal and S. Haarländer (eds.), *Herrschaft, Kirche, Kultur: Beiträge zur Geschichte des Mittelalters. Festschrift für Friedrich Prinz zu seinem 65. Geburtstag*, Monographien zur Geschichte des Mittelalters 37 (Stuttgart, 1993), pp. 165–76, repr. in Jarnut, *Herrschaft und Ethnogenese*, pp. 235–46

'Die frühmittelalterliche Jagd unter rechts- und sozialgeschichtlichen Aspekten', *L'uomo di fronte al mondo animale nell'alto medioevo*, Settimane 31 (Spoleto,

1985), pp. 765–808 reprinted in Jarnut, *Herrschaft und Ethnogenese*, pp. 375–418

'Genealogie und politische Bedeutung der agilofingische Herzöge', *MIÖG* 99 (1991), pp. 1–22

Herrschaft und Ethnogenese im Frühmittelalter: Gesammelte Aufsätze von Jörg Jarnut. Festgabe zum 60. Geburtstag (Münster, 2002)

'Quierzy und Rom: Bemerkungen zu den "promissiones donationis" Pippins und Karls', *Historische Zeitschrift* 220 (1975), pp. 265–97

'Studien über Herzog Odilo (736–748)', *MIÖG* 85 (1977), pp. 273–84

Jarnut, J., U. Nonn and M.Richter (eds.), *Karl Martell in seiner Zeit*, Beihefte der Francia 37 (Sigmaringen, 1994)

Joch, W., *Legitimität und Integration: Untersuchungen zu den Anfängen Karl Martells*, Historische Studien 456 (Husum, 1998)

Johanek, P., 'Der Ausbau der sächsischen Kirchenorganisation', in *799 Kunst und Kultur*, II, pp. 494–506

'Probleme einer zukünftigen Edition der Urkunden Ludwigs des Frommen', in Godman and Collins (ed.), *Charlemagne's heir*, pp. 409–24

Jones, L., *The script of Cologne from Hildebald to Hermann* (Cambridge, Mass., 1932)

Jong, M. de, 'Carolingian monasticism: the power of prayer', in *NCMH*, II, pp. 622–53

'Charlemagne and the church', in Story, *Charlemagne*, pp. 103–35

'*Ecclesia* and the early medieval polity', in S. Airlie, W. Pohl and H. Reimitz (eds.), *Staat im frühen Mittelalter*, Österreichische Akademie der Wissenschaften, phil.-hist. Klasse, Denkschriften 334 (Forschungen zur Geschichte des Mittelalters 11) (Vienna, 2006), pp. 113–32

'The empire as ecclesia: Hrabanus Maurus and biblical *historia* for rulers', in Hen and Innes, *The uses of the past in the early middle ages*, pp. 191–226

'Het woord en het zwaard: aan de grenzen van het vroegmiddeleeuwse christendom', *Tijdschrift voor Geschiedenis* 118 (2005), pp. 464–82

In Samuel's image: child oblation in the early medieval West, Studies in Intellectual History 12 (Leiden, 1996)

'Monastic prisoners or opting out? Political coercion and honour in the Frankish kingdoms', in de Jong, Theuws and van Rhijn (eds.), *Topographies of power in the early middle ages*, pp. 291–328

'Old law and new found power: Hrabanus Maurus and the Old Testament', in J. W. Drijvers and A. A. MacDonald (eds.), *Centres of learning: learning and location in pre-modern Europe and the near East* (Leiden, New York and Cologne, 1995), pp. 161–76

The penitential state (Cambridge, forthcoming)

'*Sacrum palatium et ecclesia*: L'autorité religieuse royale sous les carolingiens (790–840)', *Annales* 58 (2003), pp. 1243–69

(ed.), *The power of the word: the influence of Bible on early medieval politics*, special issue of *Early Medieval Europe* 7 (1998)

'Religion', in R. McKitterick (ed.), *The early middle ages: Europe 400–1000*, The Short Oxford History of Europe (Oxford, 2001), pp. 131–66

Jong, M. de, and F. Theuws with C. van Rhijn (eds.), *Topographies of power in the early middle ages*, The Transformation of the Roman World 6 (Leiden, 2001)

Jussen, B. (ed.), *Die Macht des Königs: Herrschaft in Europa vom Frühmittelalter bis in die Neuzeit* (Munich, 2005)

Kaczynski, B. E., 'Edition, translation, and exegesis: the Carolingians and the Bible', in Sullivan, *'The gentle voices of teachers'*, pp. 171–85

Kaiser, R., *Bischofsherrschaft zwischen Königtum und Fürstenmacht: Studien zur bischöflichen Stadtherrschaft im westfränkisch-französischen Reich im frühen und hohen Mittelalter*, Pariser historische Studien 17 (Bonn, 1981)

Kantorowicz, E. H., 'Ivories and litanies', *Journal of the Warburg and Cortauld Institutes* 53 (1935), pp. 56–81

Laudes regiae: a study in liturgical acclamations and medieval ruler worship (Berkeley, CA, 1946)

Karl der Große oder Charlemagne? Acht Antworten deutscher Geschichtsforscher (Berlin, 1935)

Kaschke, S., *Die karolingische Reichsteilungen bis 831: Herrschaftspraxis und Normvorstellungen in zeitgenössischer Sicht* (Hamburg, 2006)

Kasten, B., *Adalhard von Corbie: die Biographie eines karolingischen Politikers und Klostervorstehers*, Studia humaniora 3 (Düsseldorf, 1986)

Königssöhne und Königsherrschaft: Untersuchungen zur Teilhabe am Reich in der Merowinger- und Karolingerzeit, MGH Schriften 44 (Hanover, 1997)

(ed.), *Herrscher und Fürstentestamente im westeuropaische Mittelalter*, Proceedings of the 2006 Saarbrücken conference, 15–18 February 2006 (forthcoming)

Kazhdan, A., 'The notion of Byzantine diplomacy', in J. Shepard and S. Franklin (eds.), *Byzantine diplomacy* (Aldershot, 1992), pp. 3–23

Keefe, S. A., 'Creed commentary collections in Carolingian manuscripts', in K. G. Cushing and R. F. Gyug (eds.), *Ritual, text and law: studies in medieval canon law and liturgy presented to Roger E. Reynolds* (Aldershot, 2004), pp. 185–204

Inventarium symbolorum, expositionum et explanationum fidei in codicibus karolini aevi (Turnhout, forthcoming)

Water and the Word, 2 vols (Notre Dame, In., 2002)

Keller, H., 'Reichsstruktur und Herschaftsauffassung in ottonisch-fränkischer Zeit', *Frühmittelalterliche Studien* 16 (1982), pp. 74–128

Kelly, J. N. D., *The Athanasian Creed* (Oxford, 1964)

Early Christian creeds, 3rd edn (London, 1972)

Jerome: his life, writings and controversies (London, 1975)

Kempf, D., 'Paul the Deacon's *Liber de episcopis Mettensibus* and the role of Metz in the Carolingian realm', *Journal of Medieval History* 30 (2004), pp. 279–99

Kempshall, M. S., 'Some Ciceronian aspects of Einhard's Life of Charlemagne', *Viator* 26 (1995), pp. 11–38

Kershaw, P., *Peaceful like Solomon: peace, power and the early medieval political imagination* (Oxford, forthcoming)

Kéry, L., _Canonical collections of the early middle ages (ca. 400–1140): a biblio-graphical guide to the manuscripts and literature_, History of Medieval Canon Law (Washington, D.C., 1999)

Kessler, H. L., _The illustrated Bibles from Tours_, Studies in Manuscript Illumination 7 (Princeton, 1977)

Keynes, S. D., _The diplomas of Aethelred 'the Unready' 978–1016_ (Cambridge, 1980)

King, P. D., _Charlemagne: translated sources_ (Kendal, 1987)

Kitchen, T., 'Carolingian diplomatic relations with the Abbasid caliphate 768–840 and their representation in Frankish sources' (forthcoming)

Kleinklausz, A. J., _Eginhard_ (Paris, 1942)

Kloft, M. T., 'Das geistliche Amt im Umfeld des Frankfurter Konzils', in Berndt, _Das Frankfurter Konzil von 794_, II, pp. 885–917

Klopsch, P., 'Anonymität and Selbstnennung mittellateinischer Autoren', _Mittellateinisches Jahrbuch_ 4 (1967), pp. 9–25

Knight Bostock, K., _A handbook on Old High German literature_, 2nd edn (Oxford, 1976)

Knopp, G., 'Sanctorum nomina seriatim: die Anfänge der Allerheiligenlitanei und ihre Verbindung mit dem "Laudes regiae"', _Römische Quartalschrift_ 65 (1970), pp. 185–231

Koehler, W., _Karolingische Miniaturen_, I: _Die Schule von Tours_ (Berlin, 1930); II: _Die Hofschule Karls des Großen_ (Berlin, 1958); III: _Die Gruppe des Wiener Krönungsevangeliar: Metzer Handschriften_ (Berlin, 1960)

Kolarova, L., 'The transmission and dissemination of Carolingian annals', unpub-lished MPhil dissertation, University of Cambridge (1995)

Kölzer, T., 'Die letzen Merowinger: rois fainéants', in Becher and Jarnut, _Der Dynastiewechsel von 751_, pp. 33–60

Kaiser Ludwig der Fromme (814–840) im Spiegel seiner Urkunden, Nordrhein-Westfälische Akademie der Wissenschaften, Vorträge G 401 (Paderborn, 2005)

Konecny, S., _Die Frauen des karolingischen Königshauses: die politische Bedeutung der Ehe und die Stellung der Frau in der fränkischen Herrscherfamilie vom 7. bis zum 10. Jahrhundert_ (Vienna, 1976)

Kosto, A., 'Hostages in the Carolingian world (714–840)', _Early Medieval Europe_ 11 (2002), pp. 123–47

Kötting, B. J., _Peregrinatio religiosa_ (Münster, 1950)

Kottje, R., 'Die _Lex baiuvariorum_ – das Recht der Baiern', in Mordek, _Überlieferung und Geltung normativer Texte_, pp. 9–24

Studien zum Einfluß des Alten Testaments auf Recht und Liturgie des frühen Mittelalters (6.-8. Jahrhundert), Bonner historische Forschungen 23, 2nd edn (Bonn, 1970)

'Zum Geltungsbereich der Lex Alamannorum', in H. Beumann and W. Schröder (eds.), _Die transalpinen Verbindungen der Bayern, Alemannen und Franken bis zum 10. Jahrhundert_, Nationes: Historische und philologi-sche Untersuchungen zur Entstehung der europäischen Nationen im Mittelalter 6 (Sigmaringen, 1987), pp. 359–78

Kötzsche, D., 'Darstellungen Karls des Großen in der lokalen Verehrung des Mittelalters', in *KdG*, IV, pp. 155–214

Krah, A., 'Zur Kapitulariengesetzgebung in und für Neustrien', in Atsma, *La Neustrie*, pp. 565–81

Krahwinckler, H., *Friaul im Frühmittelalter: Geschichte einer Region vom Ende des fünften bis zum Ende des zehnten Jahrhunderts*, Veröffentlichungen des Instituts für Österreichische Geschichtsforschung 30 (Vienna, Cologne and Weimar, 1992)

Krause, V., 'Geschichte des Instituts der *missi dominici*', *MIÖG* 11 (1890), pp. 193–300

Krüger, K. H., *Königsgrabkirchen: der Franken, Angelsachsen und Langobarden bis zur Mitte des 8. Jahrhunderts. Ein historischer Katalog*, Münstersche Mittelalter-Schriften 4 (Munich, 1971)

'Neue Beobachtungen zur Datierung von Einhards Karlsvita', *Frühmittelalterliche Studien* 32 (1998), pp. 124–45

Krusch, B., 'Das älteste fränkische Lehrbuch der dionysianischen Zeitrechnung', *Mélanges offerts à Emile Chatelain* (Paris, 1910), pp. 232–42

Kühnel, B., *From the earthly to the heavenly Jerusalem: representations of the holy city in Christian art of the first millennium*, Römische Quartalschrift für christliche Altertumskunde und Kirchengeschichte, Supplementband 42 (Rome, Freiburg im Breisgau and Vienna, 1987)

Kunt, M., *Süleyman the Magnificent and his age: the Ottoman empire in the early modern world* (London, 1995)

Krönungen Könige in Aachen: Geschichte und Mythos: Austellungs Katalog (Mainz, 2000)

Kunt, M., and J. Duindam (eds.), *Royal courts and capitals* (Istanbul, forthcoming)

Kupfer, A., 'Medieval world maps – embedded images, interpretive frame', *Word and image* 10 (1994), pp. 262–88

Kurze, F., 'Über die karolingischen Reichsannalen von 741–829 und ihre Überarbeitung', *Neues Archiv* 19 (1894), pp. 295–339; 20 (1895), pp. 9–49; and 21 (1986), pp. 9–82

'Zur Überlieferung der karolingischen Reichsannalen und ihrer Überarbeitung', *Neues Archiv* 28 (1903), pp. 619–69

La Rocca, C., *Pacifico di Verona: il passato carolingio nella costruzione della memoria urbana*, Istituto storico italiano per il medio evo, Nuovi studi storici 31 (Rome, 1995)

(ed.), *Italy in the early middle ages, 476–1000*, The Short Oxford History of Italy (Oxford, 2002)

Lafaurie, J., 'Moneta palatina', *Francia* 4 (1976), pp. 59–87

Lamb, S. E., 'The Frankish expansion and the creation of diplomatic space', unpublished short essay, MPhil in Medieval History, University of Cambridge (2004)

Lammers, W., 'Ein karolingisches Bildprogramm in der *Aula regia* von Ingelheim', in Die Mitarbeiter des Max-Planck-Instituts für Geschichte (eds.), *Festschrift Heinrich Heimpel zum 70. Geburtstag am 19. September*

1971, Veröffentlichungen des Max-Planck-Instituts für Geschichte 36/III (Göttingen, 1972), pp. 226–89

Lampen, A., 'Die Sachsenkriege', in *799 Kunst und Kultur*, II, pp. 264–72

Landau, P., 'Die *Lex baiwariorum*: Entstehungszeit, Entstehungsort und Character von Bayerns ältester Rechts- und Geschichtsquelle', Sitzungsberichte der bayerischen Akademie der Wissenschaften, phil.-hist. Klasse, Jahrgang 2004, 3 (Munich, 2004), pp. 34–42

Laporte, J.-P., *Le trésor des saints de Chelles*, Société archéologique et historique de Chelles (Chelles, 1988), pp. 115–60

Laudage, J. (ed.), *Von Fakten und Fiktionen: Mittelalterliche Geschichtsdarstellungen und ihre kritische Aufarbeitung* (Cologne, Weimar and Vienna, 2002)

Law, V., *Grammar and grammarians in the early middle ages* (London, 1997)

'The study of grammar', in McKitterick, *Carolingian culture*, pp. 88–110

Le Jan, R., 'Espaces sauvages et chasses royale dans le Nord de la France', *Revue du nord* 62 (1980), pp. 35–57

'Justice royale et pratiques sociales dans le royaume franc au IXe siècle', in *La giustizia nell'alto medioevo (secoli IX–XI)*, Settimane 44 (Spoleto, 1997), pp. 47–85

'Prosopographica neustrica: les agents du roi en Neustrie de 639 à 840', in Atsma (ed.), *La Neustrie*, pp. 231–70

Le Maho, J., 'Die erzbischöfliche Pfalz von Rouen', in L. Fenske, J. Jarnut and M. Wemhoff (eds.), *Splendor palatii: Neue Forschungen zu Paderborn und anderen Pfalzen der Karolingerzeit*, Deutsche Königspfalzen: Beiträge zu ihrer historischen und archäologischen Erforschung 5, Veröffentlichungen des Max-Planck-Instituts für Geschichte 11/5 (Göttingen, 2001), pp. 193–210

Lee, A. D., 'Embassies as evidence for the movement of military intelligence between the Roman and Sassanian empires', in P. Freeman and D. Kennedy (eds.), *The defence of the Roman and Byzantine east* (Oxford, 1986), pp. 457–81

Information and frontiers: Roman foreign relations in late antiquity (Cambridge, 1993)

Lehmann, P., 'Erzbischof Hildebold und die Dombibliothek von Köln', *Zentralblatt für Bibliothekswesen* 25 (1908), pp. 153–8

Lendi, W., *Untersuchungen zur frühalemannischen Annalistic: die Murbacher Annalen, mit Edition*, Scrinium Friburgense I (Freiburg in der Schweiz, 1971)

Leonhardt, D., *Die alte Kapelle in Regensburg und die karolingische Pfalzanlage*, Monographien des Bauwesens 3 (1925)

Levillain, L., 'De l'authenticité de la *Clausula ad unctione Pippini*', *Bibliothèque de l'Ecole des chartes* 88 (1927), pp. 20–42

'Les Nibelungen historiques et leurs alliance de famille', *Annales du Midi* 49 (1937), pp. 337–408

'Les statuts d'Adalhard pour l'abbaye de Corbie', *Le Moyen Age* 13 (1900), pp. 233–386

Levison, W., *England and the Continent in the eighth century* (Oxford, 1946)

'Das Formularbuch von Saint-Denis', *Neues Archiv* 41 (1919), pp. 283–304

Levy, K., *Gregorian chant and the Carolingians* (Princeton, 1998)

Lewis, B., *History remembered, recovered, invented* (Princeton, 1975)

Lexikon des Mittelalters (1999)

Lhotsky, A., *Quellenkunde zur mittelalterlichem Geschichte Österreichs*, MIÖG Ergänzungsband 19 (Vienna, 1963)

Licht, T., 'Additional note on the "Library catalogue of Charlemagne's court"', *Journal of Medieval Latin* 11 (2001), pp. 210–13

Lifshitz, F., *The name of the saint: the Martyrology of Jerome and access to the sacred in Francia, 627–827* (Notre Dame, In., 2006

Lintzel, M., 'Karl der Große und Karlmann', *Historische Zeitschrift* 140 (1929), pp. 1–22

Llewellyn, P., *Rome in the dark ages*, 2nd edn (London, 1993)

Lobbedey, U., 'Carolingian royal palaces: the state of research from an architectural historian's viewpoint', in C. Cubitt (ed.), *Court culture in the early middle ages: the proceedings of the first Alcuin conference*, Studies in the Early Middle Ages 3 (Turnhout, 2003), pp. 129–54

Losek, F., *Die* Conversio bagoariorum et carantanorum *und der Brief des Erzbishofs Theotmar von Salzburg*, MGH Studien und Texte 15 (Hanover, 1997)

'*Notitia Arnonis* und *Breves notitiae*', *Mitteilungen der Gesellschaft für Salzburger Landeskunde* 130 (1990), pp. 5–192

Lot, F., 'Le premier capitulaire de Charlemagne', *Annuaire de l'Ecole pratique des hautes études*, sect. *Philologique et historique* (1924/5), pp. 7–13, repr. in Lot, *Recueil des travaux historiques de Ferdinand Lot*, 11 (Geneva, 1970), pp. 317–23

Lounghis, T. C., *Les ambassades byzantins en occident depuis la fondation des états barbares jusqu'aux Croisades* (Athens, 1980)

Lowe, E. A., *Codices latini antiquiores: a palaeographical guide to Latin manuscripts prior to the ninth century*, 11 vols + Supplement (Oxford, 1935–71)

Löwe, H., 'Die Entstehungszeit der *Vita Karoli* Einhards', *Deutsches Archiv* 39 (1963), pp. 85–103

'Hincmar von Reims und der Apocrisiar: Beiträge zur Interpretation von De ordine palatii', in Die Mitarbeiter des Max-Planck-Instituts für Geschichte (eds.), *Festschrift für Hermann Heimpel* (Göttingen, 1972), pp. 197–225

'Das Karlsbuch Notkers von St. Gallen und sein zeitgeschichtliche Hintergrund', *Schweizerische Zeitschrift für Geschichte* 20 (1970), pp. 269–302

'Lateinisch-christliche Kultur im karolingischen Sachsen', *Angli e Sassoni al di qua e al di là del mare*, Settimane 32 (Spoleto, 1986), pp. 491–531

'Ein literarischer Widersacher des Bonifatius: Virgil von Salzburg und die Kosmographie des Aethicus Ister', *Abhandlungen der Akademie der Wissenschaften und der Literatur in Mainz. Geistes- und sozialwissenschaftliche Klasse 1951* (Wiesbaden, 1952), pp. 899–988

'Salzburg als Zentrum literarischen Schaffens im 8. Jahrhundert', in H. Koller and H. Dopsch (eds.), *Salzburg im 8. Jahrhundert* (Salzburg, 1975), pp. 99–143

(ed.), *Wattenbach-Levison: Deutschlands Geschichtsquellen im Mittelalter. Vorzeit und Karolinger*, VI: *Die Karolinger vom Vertrag von Verdun bis zum*

Herrschaftsantritt der Herrscher aus dem Sächsischen Hause. Das ostfränkische Reich (Weimar, 1990)

'Zur Vita Hadriani', *Deutsches Archiv* 12 (1956), pp. 493–98

Lozovsky, N., 'Carolingian geographical tradition: was it geography?', *Early Medieval Europe* 5 (1996), pp. 25–44

"The earth is our book": geographical knowledge in the Latin West ca. 400–1000 (Ann Arbor, 2000)

'Roman geography and ethnography in the Carolingian empire', *Speculum* 81 (2006), pp. 325–64

Lynch, J. H., *Godparents and kinship in early medieval Europe* (Princeton, 1986)

Mackenzie, J. M., *The empire of nature: hunting, conservation and British imperialism* (Manchester, 1988)

McCormick, M., *Les annales du haut moyen âge*, Typologie des sources du moyen âge occidental, 14 (Turnhout, 1975)

'Byzantium and the West, 700–900', in McKitterick, *NCMH*, II, pp. 349–80

'Diplomacy and the Carolingian encounter with Byzantium down to the accession of Charles the Bald', in B. McGinn and W. Otten (eds.), *Eriugena: East and West: papers of the Eighth International Colloquium of the Society for the Promotion of Eriugenian Studies* (Notre Dame, 1994), pp. 15–48

'Emperors', in G. Cavallo (ed.), *The Byzantines* (Chicago and London, 1997), pp. 230–54

Eternal victory: triumphal rulership in late antiquity, Byzantium and the early medieval west (Cambridge, 1986)

'The liturgy of war in the early middle ages: crisis, litanies, and the Carolingian monarchy', *Viator* 15 (1984), pp. 1–23

'A new ninth-century witness to the Carolingian mass against the pagans', *Revue Bénédictine* 97 (1987), pp. 68–86

Origins of the European economy: communications and commerce AD 300–900 (Cambridge, 2001)

'Pippin III, the embassy of Caliph al-Mansur, and the Mediterranean world', in Becher and Jarnut, *Die Dynastiewechsel von 751*, pp. 221–42

'Um 808: was der frühmittelalterliche König mit der Wirtschaft zu tun hatte', in Jussen, *Die Macht des Königs*, pp. 71–7

McKitterick, R., 'Bischöfe und die handschriftliche Überlieferung des Rechts im zehnten Jahrhundert', in D. R. Bauer, R. Hiestand, B. Kasten and S. Lorenz (eds.), *Das fränkische Reich 750–1000: Herrschaft – Kirche – Mönchtum. Festschrift für Josef Semmler* (Sigmaringen, 1998), pp. 231–42

Books, scribes and learning in the Frankish kingdoms, 6th–9th centuries (Aldershot, 1994)

'Buch, Schrift, Urkunden und Schriftlichkeit in der Karolingerzeit' in Pohl and Herold, *Vom Nutzen des Schreibens*, pp. 97–112

'Carolingian Bible production: the Tours anomaly', in Gameson, *The early medieval Bible*, pp. 63–77

'Carolingian book production: some problems', *The Library*, 6th series, 12 (1990), pp. 1–33; repr. in McKitterick, *Books, scribes and learning*, Chapter XII

'Carolingian uncial: a context for the Lothar Psalter', *The British Library Journal* 16 (1990), pp. 1–15, repr. in McKitterick, *Books, scribes and learning*, Chapter VI

The Carolingians and the written word (Cambridge, 1989)

'Charles the Bald and his library: the patronage of learning, *English Historical Review* 95 (1980), pp. 28–47, repr. in McKitterick, *Frankish kings and culture*, Chapter V

'The diffusion of insular culture in Neustria between 650 and 850: the implications of the manuscript evidence', in Atsma, *La Neustrie*, pp. 395–432, repr. in McKitterick, *Books, scribes and learning*, Chapter III

'Essai sur les représentations de l'écrit dans les manuscrits carolingiens', in F. Dupuigrenet Desroussilles (ed.), *La symbolique du livre dans l'art occidental du haut moyen âge à Rembrandt*, *Revue française d'histoire du livre* 86–7 (Bordeaux, 1995), pp. 37–64

The Frankish church and the Carolingian reforms, 789–895, Royal Historical Society, Studies in History 2 (London, 1977)

The Frankish kingdoms under the Carolingians, 751–987 (London, 1983)

The Frankish kings and culture in the early middle ages (Aldershot, 1995)

'Frankish uncial: a new context for the work of the Echternach scriptorium', in A. Weiler and P. Bange (eds.), *Willibrord: zijn wereld en zijn werk* (Nijmegen, 1990), pp. 374–88, repr. in McKitterick, *Books, scribes and learning*, Chapter V

History and memory in the Carolingian world (Cambridge, 2004)

'History, law and communication with the past in the Carolingian period', in *Comunicare e significare nell'alto medioevo*, Settimane 52 (Spoleto, 2005), pp. 941–79

'The illusion of royal power in the Carolingian annals', *English Historical Review* 115 (2000), pp. 1–20

'Knowledge of canon law in the Frankish kingdoms before 789: the manuscript evidence', *Journal of Theological Studies* NS 36/1 (1985), pp. 97–117, repr. in McKitterick, *Books, scribes and learning*, Chapter II

'Das Konzil im Kontext der karolingischen Renaissance', in Berndt, *Das Frankfurter Konzil von 794*, II, pp. 635–76

'The migration of ideas in the early middle ages: ways and means', in R. Bremmer, K. Dekkers and P. Lendinara (eds.), *Storehouses of wholesome learning: accumulation and dissemination of encyclopaedic knowledge in the early middle ages*, Mediaevalia Groningana (Leuven, Paris and Stirling, 2007), pp. 1–17

'Nuns' scriptoria in Francia and England in the eighth century', *Francia* 19/1 (1992), pp. 1–35, repr. in McKitterick, *Books, scribes and learning*, Chapter VII

'Ottonian intellectual culture and the role of Theophanu', *Early Medieval Europe* 2 (1993), pp. 53–74, repr. in McKitterick, *Frankish kings and culture*, Chapter XIII

'Perceptions of justice in western Europe in the ninth and tenth centuries', in *La giustizia nell'alto medioevo (secoli IX-XI)*, Settimane 44 (Spoleto, 1997), pp. 1075–1102

Perceptions of the past in the early middle ages (Notre Dame, 2006)

'Psalter of Count Achadeus', in S. Panayotova and P. Binski (eds.), *The Cambridge illuminations: ten centuries of book production in the medieval West* (London, 2005), pp. 68–9

'The renaissance of culture and learning' in Story, *Charlemagne*, pp. 151–67

'Review article', K. Levy, *Gregorian chant and the Carolingians* (Princeton, 1998), *Early Music History* 19 (2000), pp. 279–90

'The Rorigo Bible in its ninth-century context', in L. Gatto and P. Supino Martini (eds.), *Studi sulle società e le culture del medioevo per Girolamo Arnaldi* (Rome, 2002), pp. 409–22

'Royal patronage of culture in the Frankish kingdoms under the Carolingians: motives and consequences', in *Committenti e produzione artistico-letteraria nell'alto medioevo occidentale*, Settimane 39 (Spoleto, 1992), pp. 93–129, repr. in McKitterick, *The Frankish kings and culture*, Chapter VII

'The scriptoria of Merovingian Gaul: a survey of the evidence', in H. B. Clarke and M. Brennan (eds.), *Columbanus and Merovingian monasticism*, BAR International series 113 (Oxford, 1981), pp. 173–207, repr. in McKitterick, *Books, scribes and learning*, Chapter I

'Le scriptorium d'Echternach aux huitième et neuvième siècles', in Polfer, *L'évangélisation des régions entre Meuse et Moselle*, pp. 499–522

'The scripts of the Bobbio Missal', in Y. Hen and R. Meens (eds.), *The Bobbio Missal*, Cambridge Studies in Palaeography and Codicology (Cambridge, 2004), pp. 19–52

'Some Carolingian law-books and their function', in P. Linehan (ed.), *Authority and power: studies on medieval law and government presented to Walter Ullmann* (Cambridge, 1980), pp. 13–27, repr. in McKitterick, *Books, scribes and learning in the Frankish kingdoms, 6th–9th centuries* (Aldershot, 1994), Chapter VIII

'The study of Frankish history in France and Germany in the sixteenth and seventeenth centuries', *Francia* 8 (1980), pp. 556–72

'Text and image in the Carolingian world', in McKitterick (ed.), *The uses of literacy in early mediaeval Europe* (Cambridge, 1990), pp. 297–318

'Unity and diversity in the Carolingian church', in R. N. Swanson (ed.), *Studies in Church History* (Oxford, 1996), pp. 59–82

'Women and literacy in the early Middle Ages', in McKitterick, *Books, scribes and learning*, Chapter XIII

'Zur Herstellung von Kapitularien: die Arbeit des leges-Skriptoriums', *MIÖG* 101 (1993), pp. 3–16

(ed.), *Carolingian culture: emulation and innovation* (Cambridge, 1994) (ed.), *The new Cambridge medieval history,* II: *700–900* (Cambridge, 1995)

McLaughlin, M., *Consorting with saints: prayer for the dead in early medieval France* (Ithaca and London, 1994)

MacLean, S., *Kingship and politics in the late ninth century: Charles the Fat and the end of the Carolingian empire,* Cambridge Studies in Medieval Life and Thought (Cambridge, 2003)

Magnou-Nortier, E. 'L'"Admonitio generalis": étude critique', *Jornades internacionals d'estudi sobre le bisbe Feliu d'Urgell* (Urgel-Litana, 2000), pp. 195–242

Manacorda, F., *Ricerchi sugli inizii della dominazione dei Carolingi in Italia,* 2 vols, Studi Storici 71–72 (Rome, 1968)

Manitius, M., *Geschichte der lateinischen Literatur des Mittelalters,* I: *Von Justinian bis zur Mitte des 10. Jahrhunderts* (Munich, 1911), pp. 646–7

'Zu den Annales laurissenses maiores', *MIÖG* 10 (1889), pp. 410–27

'Zu den Annales laurissenses und Einharti (zur Sprache und Entstehung)', *MIÖG* 13 (1892), pp. 232–8

Marenbon, J., 'Carolingian thought', in McKitterick, *Carolingian culture,* pp. 171–92

Marrou, H., *A history of education in antiquity* (Madison, Wis., 1982, trans. from the original French edition of 1948 in London, 1956)

Martimort, M., *Lectures liturgiques et leur livres,* Typologie des sources du moyen âge occidental 64 (Turnhout, 1992)

Martin, T., 'Bemerkungen zur "Epistola de litteris colendis"', *Archiv für Diplomatik* 31 (1985), pp. 227–72

Masai, F., 'Observations sur le Psautier dit de Charlemagne', *Scriptorium* 6 (1952), 299–303

Mayr-Harting, H., 'Charlemagne, the Saxons and the imperial coronation of 800', *English Historical Review* III(1996), pp. 1113–33

'Charlemagne's religion', in Godman, Jarnut and Johanek, *Am Vorabend der Kaiser Krönung,* pp. 113–24

Mearns, J., *The canticles of the Christian church eastern and western in early and medieval times* (Cambridge, 1914)

Early Latin hymnaries (Cambridge, 1913)

Mecke, B., 'Die karolingische Pfalz Paderborn: Entdeckung und Ausgrabung', in Fenske, Jarnut and Wemhoff, *Deutsche Königspfalzen,* pp. 51–70

'Die Pfalz Paderborn' in Fenske, Jarnut and Wemhoff, *Deutsche Königspfalzen,* pp. 175–222

Meens, R., 'Politics, mirrors of princes and the Bible: sins, kings and the well-being of the realm', *Early Medieval Europe* 7 (1998), pp. 345–57

Mendels, D., *Identity, religion and historiography: studies in Hellenistic history,* Journal for the study of the Pseudepigrapha Supplement series 24 (Sheffield, 1998), pp. 13–34

Merrills, A., *History and geography in late antiquity* (Cambridge, 2004)

Mersiowsky, M., 'Preserved by destruction: Carolingian original letters and Clm 6333', in G. Declercq (ed.), *Early medieval palimpsests* (Turnhout, 2007), pp. 73–98

'Regierungspraxis und Schriftlichkeit im Karolingerreich: das Fall Beispiel der Mandate und Briefe', in Schieffer, *Schriftkultur und Reichsverwaltung unter den Karolingern*, pp. 109–66

'Towards a reappraisal of sovereign charters', in K. Heidecker (ed.), *Charters and the use of the written word in medieval society*, Utrecht Studies in Medieval Literacy (Turnhout, 2000), pp. 15–26

Metz, W., *Das karolingische Reichsgut* (Berlin, 1960)

'Quellenstudien zum *servicium regis* (900–1250)', *Archiv für Diplomatik* 22 (1976), pp. 273–326; 24 (1978), pp. 203–91; 31 (1978), pp. 187–271; 38 (1992), pp. 17–68

Zur Erforschung des karolingischen Reichsgutes, Erträge der Forschung 4 (Darmstadt, 1971)

Meulen, J. van der, and A. Speer, *Die fränkische Königsabtei Saint-Denis: Ostanlage und Kultgeschichte* (Darmstadt, 1988)

Meyer, A., *Felix et inclitus notarius: studien zum italienischen Notariat vom 7. bis zum 13. Jahrhundert* (Tübingen, 2000)

Meyvaert, P., 'Discovering the calendar (*annalis libellus*) attached to Bede's own copy of *De temporum ratione*', *Analecta Bollandiana* 120 (2002), pp. 1–159

Milde, W. (ed.), *Der Bibliothekskatalog des Klosters Murbach aus dem 9. Jahrhundert: Ausgabe und Untersuchungen von Beziehungen zu Cassiodors 'Institutiones', Euphorion, Zeitschrift für Literaturgeschichte*, Beiheft 4 (Heidelberg, 1968)

Miles, R. (ed.), *Constructing identities in late antiquity* (London, 1999)

Mitchell, J., 'Artistic patronage and cultural strategies in Lombard Italy', in G. P. Brogiolo, N. Gauthier and N. Christie (eds.), *Towns and their territories between late antiquity and the early middle ages*, The Transformation of the Roman World 9 (Leiden, 2000), pp. 347–70

Monod, G., *Etudes critiques sur les sources de l'histoire carolingienne*, Bibliothèque de l'Ecole des Hautes Etudes 119 (Paris, 1898)

Moraw, P., 'Kaiser gegen Papst – Papst gegen Kaiser: Prozesse und Quasiprozesse als Mittel der theologisch-politisch-rechtlichen Auseinandersetzung von 800 bis 1350', in U. Schultz (ed.), *Große Prozesser: Recht und Gerechtigkeit in der Geschichte*, 2nd edn (Munich, 1996), pp. 55–64

Mordek, H., 'Aachen, Frankfurt, Reims: Beobachtungen zu Genese und Tradition des Capitulare Franconofurtense (a. 794)', in Berndt, *Das Frankfurter Konzil von 794*, I, pp. 125–48 repr. in Mordek, Studien, pp. 205–28

Bibliotheca capitularium regum francorum manuscripta: Überlieferung und Traditionszusammenhang der fränkischen Herrschererlasse, MGH Hilfsmittel 15 (Munich, 1995)

'Das Frankfurter Kapitular Karls des Großen (794)', in Fried, Koch, Saurma-Jeltsch and Theil, *794: Karl der Große in Frankfurt am Main*, pp. 46–9, repr. in Mordek, Studien, pp. 193–204

'Karolingische Kapitularien', in Mordek, *Überlieferung und Geltung normativer Texte*, pp. 25–50

'Karls des Großen zweites Kapitular von Herstal und die Hungersnot der Jahre 778/779', *Deutsches Archiv* 61 (2005), pp. 1–52

Kirchenrecht und Reform in Frankenreich: Die Collectio Vetus Gallica, die älteste systematische Kanonensammlung des fränkischen Gallien. Studien und Edition, Beiträge zur Geschichte und Quellenkunde des Mittelalters 1 (Berlin and New York, 1975)

'"Quod si non emendent, excommunicetur": Rund um ein neues Exzerpt des Capitulare generale Kaiser Karls des Großen (802)', in K. G. Cushing and R. F. Gyug (eds.), *Ritual, text and law: studies in medieval canon law and liturgy presented to Roger E. Reynolds* (Aldershot, 2004), pp. 171–84

'Recently discovered capitulary texts belonging to the legislation of Louis the Pious', in Godman and Collins, *Charlemagne's heir*, pp. 437–55, and fuller German version, 'Unbekannte Texte zur karolingischen Gesetzgebung: Ludwig der Fromme, Einhard und die Capitula adhuc conferenda', *Deutsches Archiv* 42 (1986), pp. 446–70, repr. in Mordek, *Studien zur fränkischen Herrschergesetzgebung*, pp. 161–86

Studien zur fränksichen Herrschergesetzgebung: Aufsätze über Kapitularien und Kapitulariensammlungen ausgewählt zum 60. Geburtstag (Frankfurt am Main, 2000)

Überlieferung und Geltung normativer Texte des frühen und hohen Mittelalters, Quellen und Forschungen zum Recht im Mittelalter 4 (Sigmaringen, 1986)

Moreton B., *The eighth-century Gelasian sacramentary: a study in tradition* (Oxford, 1976)

Morrison, K., 'Know thyself': music in the Carolingian Renaissance', in *Committenti e produzione artistico-letteraria nell'alto medioevo occidentale*, Settimane 39 (Spoleto, 1992), pp. 329–479

Morrissey, R., 'Charlemagne', in P. Nora (ed.), *Les lieux de mémoire*, III: *Les Frances* (Paris, 1992/1997), pp. 4389–425

Charlemagne and France: A thousand years of mythology, trans. C. Tihanyi (Chicago, 2003) (from the French edn of 1997)

Mortensen, L. B., 'Impero romano, historia romana and historia langobardorum', in Chiesa, *Paolo Diacono*, pp. 355–64

Mostert, M. (ed.), *New approaches to medieval communication*, Utrecht Studies in Medieval Literacy 1 (Turnhout, 1999)

Müllejans, H., *Karl der Große und seine Schrein in Aachen: eine Festschrift* (Aachen, 1988)

Mullen, E. T., *Narrative history and ethnic boundaries: the Deuteronomistic historian and the creation of Israelite national identity* (Atlanta, Ga., 1993)

Müller-Mertens, E., *Die Reichsstruktur im Spiegel der Herrschaftspraxis Ottos des Großen*, Forschungen zur mittelalterlichen Geschichte 25 (Berlin, 1980)

Munding, E., *Abt-Bischof Waldo*, Texte und Arbeiten 1, Heft 10/11 (Beuron and Leipzig, 1924)

Königsbrief Karls d. Gr. an Papst Hadrian über Abt-Bischof Waldo von Reichenau-Pavia: Palimpsest-Urkunde aus Cod. Lat. Monac. 6333, Texte und Arbeiten, 1: Abteilung, Beiträge zur Ergründung des älteren lateinischen christlichen Schrifttums und Gottesdienstes 6 (Beuron, 1920)

Munzi, L. 'Compilazione e riuso in età carolingia: il prologo poetica di Wigbodo', *Romanobarbarica* 12 (1992/3), pp. 189–210

Murdoch, B. (ed.), *German literature of the early middle ages*, 11 (Rochester, N.Y., 2004)

Murphy, T., *Pliny the Elder's Natural history* (Oxford, 2004)

Murray, A. C. (ed.), *After Rome's fall: narrators and sources of early medieval history. Essays presented to Walter Goffart* (Toronto, 1998)

Mütherich, F. 'Die Erneuerung der Buchmalerei am Hof Karls des Großen', in *799 Kunst und Kultur*, III, pp. 560–609

'The library of Otto III', in P. Ganz (ed.), *The role of the book in medieval culture*, Bibliologia: elementa ad librorum studia pertinentia 4 (Turnhout, 1986), pp. 11–26

'Manuscrits enluminés autour de Hildegarde', in P. Riché, C. Heitz and H. Heber-Suffrin (eds.), *Actes du Colloque 'Autour de Hildegarde'* Université Paris X Nanterre, Centre de recherches sur l'antiquité tardive et le haut moyen âge, cahier V (Paris, 1987), pp. 49–55

Muthesius, A., 'Silken diplomacy', in Shepard and Franklin, *Byzantine diplomacy* (Aldershot, 1992), pp. 237–48

Nagel, H., *Karl der Grosse und die theologischen Herausforderungen seiner Zeit: zur Wechselwirkung zwischen Theologie und Politik im Zeitalter des großen Frankenherrschers*, Freiburger Beiträge zur mittelalterliche Geschichte, Studien und Texte 12 (Bern, 1998)

Nebbiai Dalla Guarda, D., *La bibliothèque de l'abbaye de Saint-Denis en France du IXe au XVIIIe siècle* (Paris, 1985)

Nees, L., 'Godescalc's career and the problems of influence', in J. Lowden and A. Bovey (eds.), *Under the influence: the concept of influence and the study of illuminated manuscripts* (London and Turnhout, 2007), pp. 21–43

A tainted mantle: Hercules and the classical tradition at the Carolingian court (Philadelphia, Pa., 1991)

Neff, K., *Die Gedichte Paulus Diaconus: Kritische und erklärende Ausgabe*, Quellen und Untersuchungen zur lateinischen Philologie des Mittelalters 3.4 (Munich, 1908)

Nehlsen, H., 'Zur Aktualität und Effektivität germanischer Rechtsaufzeichnungen', in Classen, *Recht und Schrift*, pp. 449–502

Nelson, J. L., 'Aachen as a place of power', in de Jong, Theuws and van Rhijn, *Topographies of power in the early middle ages*, pp. 217–42

'Bertrada', in Becher and Jarnut, *Der Dynastiewechsel von 751*, pp. 93–108

'Carolingian contacts', in M. Brown and C. Farr (eds.), *Mercia: An Anglo-Saxon kingdom in Europe* (London, 2001), pp. 126–43

'Carolingian royal funerals' in F. Theuws and J. L. Nelson, *Rituals of power from late antiquity to the early middle ages*, The Transformation of the Roman World 8 (Leiden, 2000), pp. 131–84

Charlemagne and the paradoxes of power, The Reuter Lecture 2005 (Southampton, 2006)

'Charlemagne: pater optimus', in Godman, Jarnut and Johanek, *Am Vorabend der Kaiser Krönung*, pp. 269–82

Charles the Bald (London, 1992)

The Frankish world, 750–900 (London, 1996)

'Gender and genre in women historians of the early middle ages', in Nelson, *The Frankish world*, pp. 183–97

'History writing at the courts of Louis the Pious and Charles the Bald', in Scharer and Scheibelreiter, *Historiographie im frühen Mittelalter*, pp. 435–42

'Kings with justice, kings without justice: an early medieval paradox', in *La giustizia nell'alto medioevo (secoli IX–XI)*, Settimane 44 (Spoleto, 1997), pp. 797–825

'Kingship and empire in the Carolingian world', in McKitterick, *Carolingian culture*, pp. 52–87

'Kingship and royal government', in *NCMH*, II pp. 383–430

'Legislation and consensus in the reign of Charles the Bald', in P. Wormald (ed.), *Ideal and reality in Frankish and Anglo-Saxon society: studies presented to J. M. Wallace-Hadrill* (Oxford, 1983), pp. 202–27, repr. in J. L. Nelson, *Politics and ritual in early medieval Europe* (London, 1986), pp. 91–116

'Literacy in Carolingian government', in McKitterick, *The uses of literacy in early mediaeval Europe*, pp. 258–96

'Making a difference in eighth-century politics: the daughters of Desiderius', in Murray, *After Rome's fall*, pp. 171–90

'Perceptions du pouvoir chez les historiennes du haut moyen âge', in M. Rouche (ed.), *Les femmes au moyen âge* (Paris, 1990), pp. 77–85

Politics and ritual in early medieval Europe (London, 1986)

'Public histories and private history in the work of Nithard', *Speculum* 60 (1985), pp. 251–93, repr. in Nelson, *Politics and ritual*, pp. 195–238

'The siting of the Council at Frankfurt: some reflections on family and politics', in Berndt, *Das Frankfurter Konzil von 794*, pp. 149–66

'Um 801: warum es so viele Versionen von der Kaiserkrönung Karls des Großen gibt', in Jussen, *Die Macht des Königs*, pp. 38–54

'Violence in the Carolingian world and the ritualization of ninth-century warfare', in Halsall, *Violence and society in the early medieval West*, pp. 90–107

'The voice of Charlemagne', in Gameson and Leyser, *Belief and culture in the middle ages*, pp. 76–88

'Was Charlemagne's court a courtly society?', in C. Cubitt (ed.), *Court culture in the earlier middle ages* (Leiden, 2001)

'Women at the court of Charlemagne: a case of monstrous regiment?', in J. C. Parson (ed.), *Medieval queenship* (Stroud, 1993), pp. 43–61, repr. in Nelson, *The Frankish world*, pp. 223–42

Nelson, J. L., and M. Gibson (eds.), *Charles the Bald: court and kingdom*, 2nd edn (London, 1990)

Nerlich, D., *Diplomatische Gesandtschaften zwischen Ost.- und West-Kaisern 756–1002* (Bern, 1999)

Netzer, N., *Cultural interplay in the eighth century: the Trier Gospels and the making of a scriptorium at Echternach* (Cambridge, 1995)

Newlands, C., 'Alcuin's poem of exile *O mea cella*', *Mediaevalia* 11 (1985), pp. 19–45

Nicolet, C., *Space, geography and politics in the early Roman empire* (Ann Arbor, 1991), trans. from the French edn of 1988

Niederkorn, M., 'Das *sanctorale* Salzburgs um 800. Liturgie zwischen Norm und Praxis', Habilitationschrift Universität Wien (1999)

Niederkorn-Bruck, M., 'Das Salzburger historische Martyrolog aus der Arn-Zeit und seine Bedeutung für die Textgeschichte des "Martyrologium Bedae"', in Niederkorn-Bruck and Scharer, *Erzbischof Arn von Salzburg*, pp. 155–71

Niederkorn-Bruck, M., and A. Scharer (eds.), *Erzbischof Arn von Salzburg*, Veröffentlichungen des Instituts für Österreichische Geschichtsforschung 40 (Vienna and Munich, 2004)

Niermeyer, J. F., *Mediae latinitatis lexicon minus* (Leiden, 1954–76)

Nineham, D., 'Gottschalk of Orbais: reactionary or precursor of the Reformation?', *Journal of Ecclesiastical History* 40 (1989), pp. 1–18

Nixon, C. E. V., and B. Saylor Rodgers (eds.), *In praise of later Roman emperors: the Panegyrici Latini. Introduction, translation and historical commentary with the Latin text of R. A. B. Mynors* (Berkeley, 1994)

Nobel, H., *Königtum und Heiligenverehrung zur Zeit der Karolinger* (Heidelberg, 1956)

Noble, T. F. X., 'From brigandage to justice: Charlemagne: 785–794', in Chazelle, *Literacy, politics and artistic innovation*, pp. 49–75

'A new look at the *Liber Pontificalis*', *Archivum Historiae Pontificiae* 23 (1985), pp. 347–58

'The papacy in the eighth and ninth centuries', in McKitterick, *NCMH*, II pp. 563–86

Review of Müller-Mertens, *Die Reichsstruktur im Spiegel der Herrschaftspraxis Ottos des Großen*, in *Speculum* 56 (1981), pp. 634–7

The republic of St Peter: the birth of the papal state, 680–825 (Philadelphia, 1984)

'Tradition and learning in search of ideology: the Libri carolini', in Sullivan, *The gentle voices of teachers*, pp. 227–60

Nonn, U., 'Formelsammlungen, III: Frühmittelalter', *Lexikon des Mittelalters*, III, cols. 648–9

'Merowingische Testamente: Studien zum Fortleben einer römischer Urkundenform im Frankenreich', *Archiv für Diplomatik* 19 (1982), pp. 1–129

'Zwischen König, Hausmeier und Aristokratie: Die Bischofserhebung im spätmerowingisch-frühkarolingischen Frankenreich', in F. R. Erkens (ed.), *Die
früh- und hochmittelalterliche Bischofserhebung im europäischen Vergleich*,
Beihefte zum Archiv für Kirchengeschichte 48 (Cologne, 1998), pp. 33–58

'Zur Königserhebung Karls und Karlmanns', *Rheinische Vierteljahrsblätter* 39
(1975), pp. 386–7

Nordenfalk, C., 'Der inspirierte Evangelist', *Wiener Jahrbuch für Kunstgeschichte*
36 (1983), pp. 175–90

Odegaard, C. E., 'Carolingian oaths of fidelity', *Speculum* 16 (1941), pp. 284–96

'The concept of royal power in Carolingian oaths of fidelity', *Speculum* 20
(1945), pp. 279–89

Oexle, O.-G., 'Die Karolinger und die Stadt des heiligen Arnulf',
Frühmittelalterliche Studien 1 (1967), pp. 249–364

Oexle, O.-G., and K. Schmid, 'Voraussetzungen und Wirkung des Gebetbundes
von Attigny', *Francia* 2 (1975), pp. 71–122

Offergeld, T., *Reges pueri: das Königtum Minderjähriger im frühen Mittelalter*,
MGH Schriften 50 (Hanover, 2001)

Onnefors, A., *Die Verfasserschaft des Waltharius-Epos aus sprachlicher Sicht*
(Düsseldorf, 1978)

Orchard, A., 'Wish you were here: Alcuin's courtly poetry and the boys back
home', in Rees Jones, Marks and Minnis, *Courts and regions in medieval
Europe*, pp. 21–44

Orme, N., *English schools in the middle ages* (London and New York, 1976)

Padberg, L. von, *Mission und Christianisierung: Formen und Folgen bei Angelsachsen
und Franken im 7. und 8. Jahrhundert* (Stuttgart, 1985)

Paolo Diacono e il Friuli altomedievale (secc. VI–X), Atti del XIV congresso
internazionale di studi sull'alto medioevo, 2 vols (Spoleto, 2001)

Patzold, S., 'Créer un grade ecclésiastique: métropolitains et archévêques du
royaume franc (VIIIe–IXe siècles)' (forthcoming)

Pawalec, K., *Aachener Bronzgitter: Studien zur karolingischen Ornamentik um 800*
(Cologne, 1990)

Paxton, F. S., *Christianizing death: the creation of a ritual process in early medieval
Europe* (Ithaca, 1990)

Peabody, N., *Hindu kingship and polity in precolonial India*, Cambridge Studies in
Indian History and Society (Cambridge, 2003)

Peacock, D. P. S., 'Charlemagne's black stones: the re-use of Roman columns in
early medieval Europe', *Antiquity* 71 (1997), pp. 709–15

Pearse, R., 'Tacitus and his manuscripts', <www.tertullian.org/rpearse/tacitus>

Pearson, K., *Conflicting loyalties in early medieval Bavaria: a view of socio-political
interaction, 680–900* (Aldershot, 1999)

Pecere, O., and M. D. Reeve (eds.), *Formative stages of classical traditions: Latin
texts from antiquity to the Renaissance* (Spoleto, 1996)

Peitz, W. B. *Dionysius Exiguus Studien* (Bonn, 1960)

Peril, R., *La genealogie et descente de la tres illustre maison Dautriche* (Antwerp,
1535)

Pérrin, P., and L.-C. Feffer (eds.), *La Neustrie: les pays au nord de la Loire de Dagobert à Charles le Chauve (VIIe–IXe siècles)* (Rouen, 1985)

Peters, E., *The shadow king: rex inutilis in medieval law and literature 751–1327* (New Haven and London, 1970)

Peyer, C., 'Das Reisekönigtum des Mittelalters', *Vierteljahrschrift für Sozial- und Wirtschaftsgeschichte* 51 (1964), pp. 1–21

Piper, F., *Karls des Großen Kalendarium und Ostertafel aus der Pariser Urhandschrift herausgegeben und erläutert* (Berlin, 1858)

Pfeil, E., *Die fränkishe und deutsche Romidee des frühen Mittelalters*, Forschungen zur mittelalterlichen und neueren Geschichte 3 (Munich, 1929)

Pixner, W., 'Foreign relations and internal and external power in the reign of Charlemagne', unpublished MPhil in Medieval History dissertation, University of Cambridge, (1996)

Pocock, J. G. A., *Barbarism and religion*, 3 vols (Cambridge, 1999–2003)

Pohl, W. 'Alienigena uxor: Bestrebungen zu einem Verbot auswärtiger Heiraten in der Karolingerzeit', in A. Pečar and K. Trampedach (eds.), *Die Bibel als politisches Argument,* Voraussetzungen und Folgen biblizistischer Herrschafts-legitimation in der Vormoderne (Munich, 2007), pp. 159–88

Die Awaren: Ein Steppenvolk in Mitteleuropa 567–822, n.Chr. (Munich, 2002)

'Frontiers and ethnic identites: some final considerations', in Pohl, Wood and Reimitz, *Transformation of frontiers*, pp. 255–65

'Frontiers in Lombard Italy: the laws of Ratchis and Aistulf', in Pohl, Wood and Reimitz, *Transformation of frontiers*, pp. 117–42

(ed.) *Die Suche nach den Ursprungen: von der Bedeutung des frühen Mittelalters*, Österreichischen Akademie der Wissenschaften, phil.-hist. Klasse, Denkschriften 322 (Forschungen zur Geschichte des Mittelalters 8) (Vienna, 2004)

Pohl, W., and M. Diesenberger (eds.), *Integration und Herrschaft: ethnische Identitäten und soziale Organisation im Frühmittelalter*, Österreichische Akademie der Wissenschaften phil.-hist. Klasse, Denkschriften 301 (Forschungen zur Geschichte des Mittelalters 3) (Vienna, 2002)

Pohl, W., and P. Herold (eds.), *Vom Nutzen der Schreibens: soziales Gedächtnis, Herrschaft und Besitz*, Österreichische Akademie der Wissenschaften, phil.-hist. Klasse, Denkschriften 306 (Forschungen zur Geschichte des Mittelalters 5 (Vienna, 2002)

Pohl, W., and H. Reimitz (eds.), *Grenze und Differenz im frühen Mittelalter*, Österreichische Akademie der Wissenschaften phil.-hist. Klasse, Denkschriften 287 (Forschungen zur Geschichte des Mittelalters 1) (Vienna, 2000)

(eds.), *Strategies of distinction: the construction of ethnic communities, 300–800*, The Transformation of the Roman World 2 (Leiden, 1998)

Pohl, W., I. Wood and H. Reimitz (eds.), *The transformation of frontiers from late antiquity to the Carolingians*, The Transformation of the Roman World 10 (Leiden, 2001)

Pokorny, R., 'Eine Brief-Instruktion aus dem Hofkreis Karls des Grossen an einen geistlichen Missus', *Deutsches Archiv* 52 (1996), pp. 57–83

Polfer, M. (ed.), *L'évangelisation des régions entre Meuse et Moselle et la fondation de l'abbaye d'Echternach (Ve–IXe siècle)*, Publications du CLUDEM 16 (Luxembourg, 2000)

Pössel, C., 'Authors and recipients of Carolingian capitularies, 779–829', in R. Corradini, R. Meens, C. Pössel, and P. Shaw (eds.), *Texts and identities in the early middle ages*, Österreichische Akademie der Wissenschaften, phil.-hist Klasse, Denkschriften 344 (Forschungen zur Geschichte des Mittelalters 12) (Vienna, 2006), pp. 376–412

'The itinerant kingship of Louis the Pious', unpublished MPhil in Medieval History dissertation, University of Cambridge (1999)

'Symbolic communication and the negotiation of power at Carolingian regnal assemblies, 814–840', unpublished PhD thesis, University of Cambridge (2004)

Pratt, D., 'Problems of authorship and audience in the writings of King Alfred the Great', in P. Wormald and J. L. Nelson (eds.), *Lay intellectuals in the Carolingian world* (Cambridge, 2007), pp. 162–91

Prestwich, M. *Edward I*, 2nd edn (London, 1997)

Prete, S. (ed.), *Didascaliae: studies in Honor of Anselm M. Albareda* (New York, 1961)

Prinz, F., 'King, clergy and war at the time of the Carolingians', in M. H. King and W. M. Stevens (eds.), *Saints, scholars and heroes: studies in medieval culture in honor of Charles W. Jones* (Collegeville, 1979), II, pp. 301–29

Klerus und Krieg im früheren Mittelalter: Untersuchungen zur Rolle der Kirche beim Aufbau der Königsherrschaft, Monographien zur Geschichte des Mittelalters 2 (Stuttgart, 1971)

'Schenkungen und Privilegien Karls des Großen', *KdG* I, p. 488

'Stadtrömische italienische Märtyrreliquien und fränkische Reichsadel in Maas-Moselraum', *Historisches Jahrbuch* 87 (1967) pp. 1–25

Prou, M., 'Authentiques de reliques conservées au trésor de la cathédrale de Sens', *Mémoires de la Société nationale des Antiquaires de France*, 6th series, 9 (1898/1900), pp. 129–172

Rabe, S. A., *Faith, art and politics at Saint-Riquier: the symbolic vision of Angilbert* (Philadelphia, 1995)

Rand, E. K., *A survey of the manuscripts of Tours* (Cambridge, Mass., 1929)

'On the history of the *De vita caesarum* of Suetonius in the early middle ages', *Harvard Studies in Classical Philology* 37 (1926), pp. 1–48

Ranke, L. von, 'Zur Kritik fränkisch-deutscher Reichsannalen', *Abhandlungen der königlichen Akademie der Wissenschaften* (Berlin, 1854), pp. 415–56

Rankin, S., 'Carolingian music', in McKitterick, *Carolingian culture*, pp. 274–316

Rapp, C., *Holy bishops in late antiquity: the nature of Christian leadership in an age of transition*, The Transformation of the Classical Heritage 37 (Berkeley, 2005)

Ratkowitsch, C., *Karolus magnus: alter Aeneas, alter Martinus, alter Justinus. Zur Intention und Datierung des Aachener Karlsepos* (Vienna, 1997)

Rauch, C. D., and H. J. Jacobi, *Die Ausgrabungen in der Königspfalz Ingelheim 1909–1914* (Mainz, 1976)

Ray, R. D., 'Bede, the exegete, as historian', in G. Bonner (ed.), *Famulus Christi: essays in commemoration of the thirteenth centenary of the birth of the Venerable Bede* (London, 1976), pp. 125–40

Rees Jones, S., R. Marks and A. J. Minnis (eds.), *Courts and regions in medieval Europe* (York and Woodbridge, 2000)

Reimitz, H., 'Anleitung zur Interpretation: Schrift und Genealogie in der Karolingerzeit', in Pohl and Herold, *Vom Nutzen des Schreibens*, pp. 167–81

'Conversion and control; the establishment of liturgical frontiers in Carolingian Pannonia', in Pohl, Wood and Reimitz, *Transformation of frontiers*, pp. 189–208

'Ein fränkisches Geschichtsbuch aus Saint-Amand und der Codex Vindobonensis palat. 473', in C. Egger and H. Weigl (eds.), *Text–Schrift–Codex: Quellenkundliche Arbeiten aus dem Institut für Österreichische Geschichtsforschung*, Mitteilungen des Instituts für Österreichische Geschichtsforschung Ergänzungsband 35 (Vienna and Munich, 2000), pp. 34–90

'Grenzen und Grenzüberschreitungen im karolingischen Mitteleuropa', in Pohl and Reimitz, *Grenze und Differenz im frühen Mittelalter*, pp. 105–66

'Die Konkurrenz der Ursprünge in der fränkischen Historiographie', in Pohl, *Die Suche nach den Ursprüngen*, pp. 191–210

'Social networks and identities in Frankish historiography: new aspects of the textual history of Gregory of Tours' *Historiae*', in Corradini, Diesenberger and Reimitz, *The construction of communities in the early middle ages*, pp. 229–68

'Der Weg zum Königtum in historiographischen Kompendien der Karolingerzeit', in Becher and Jarnut, *Der Dynastiewechsel von 751*, pp. 283–326

Reindel, K., 'Bayern im Karolingerreich', in *KdG*, I, pp. 220–46

Remensnyder, A., *Remembering kings past: monastic foundation legends in medieval southern France* (Ithaca and London, 1995)

Renoux, A., 'Bemerkungen zur Entwicklung des Pfalzenwesens in Nordfrankreich in der Karolingerzeit, 751–987', in Fenske, Jarnut and Wemhoff, *Deutsche Königspfalzen*, pp. 25–50

'Karolingische Pfalzen in Nordfrankreich (751–987)', in *799 Kunst und Kultur*, III, pp. 130–7

(ed.), *Palais médiévaux (France-Belgique): 25 ans d'archéologie* (Le Mans, 1994)

Reudenbach, B., *Das Godescalc Evangelistar: ein Buch für die Reformpolitik Karls des Großen* (Frankfurt am Main, 1998)

Reuter, T., 'Assembly politics in western Europe from the eighth to the twelfth century', in P. Linehan and J. L. Nelson (eds.), *The medieval world* (London, 2001), pp. 434–50

'Charlemagne and the world beyond the Rhine', in J. Story (ed.), *Charlemagne: empire and society* (Manchester, 2005), pp. 184–94

'The end of Carolingian military expansion', in Godman and Collins, *Charlemagne's heir*, pp. 391–404

'Plunder and tribute in the Carolingian empire', *Transactions of the Royal History Society*, 5th series, 35 (1985), pp. 75–94

'Saint Boniface and Europe', in T. Reuter (ed.) *The greatest Englishman* (Exeter, 1980), pp. 69–94

Reynolds, L. D. (ed.), *Texts and transmission: a survey of the Latin classics* (Oxford, 1983)

Rhijn, C. van, *Shepherds of the Lord: priests and episcopal statutes in the Carolingian period* (Turnhout, 2007)

Riché, P., *Education and culture in the barbarian West, sixth to eighth centuries*, trans J. J. Contreni from the 1962 Paris edn with updated bibliography (Columbia, SC, 1976)

Riché, P., C. Heitz and F. Héber-Suffrin (eds.), *Actes du Colloque 'Autour d'Hildegarde'*, Université Paris X Nanterre, Centre de recherches sur l'anti-quité tardive et le haut moyen âge, Cahier V (Paris, 1987)

Richter, M., *The formation of the medieval West: studies in the oral culture of the barbarians* (Dublin, 1994)

'Die Sprachenpolitik Karls des Großen', *Sprachwissenschaft* 7 (1982)

Rio, A., *Legal practice and the written word: Frankish formulae, c. 500–1000* (Cambridge, forthcoming)

Robinson, R. P., *The Germania of Tacitus* (Middletown, Conn., 1935)

Röckelein, H., *Reliquientranslationen nach Sachsen im 9. Jahrhundert: über Kommunikationen, Mobilität und Öffentlichkeit im Frühmittelalter* (Stuttgart, 2002)

'Über Hagio-Geo-Graphien: Mirakel in Translationsberichten des 8. und 9. Jahrhunderts', in M. Heinzelmann, K. Herbers and D. R. Bauer (eds.), *Mirakel im Mittelalter: Konzeptionen, Erscheinungsformen, Deutungen*, Beiträge zur Hagiographie 3 (Stuttgart, 2002), pp. 166–79

Roma fra oriente e occidente, Settimane di studio del Centro Italiano di studi sull'alto medioevo 49 (Spoleto, 2002)

Ronig, F., 'Bemerkungen zur Bibelreform in der Zeit Karls des Großen: Funktion und Ikonologie', in *799 Kunst und Kultur*, III, pp. 711–17

Rösener, W., 'Königshof und Herrschaftsraum: Norm und Praxis der Hof- und Reichsverwaltung im Karolingerreich', in *Uomo e spazio nell'alto medioevo*, Settimane 50 (Spoleto, 2003), pp. 443–79

Rosenwein, B., *Negotiating space: power, restraint and privileges of immunity in early medieval Europe* (Manchester, 1999)

Ross, J. B., 'Two neglected paladins of Charlemagne, Erich of Friuli and Gerold of Bavaria', *Speculum* 20 (1945), pp. 212–34

Salgado Rodriguez, M., *The changing face of empire: Charles V, Philip II and Hapsburg authority 1551–1559* (Cambridge, 1988)

Samson, R., 'Carolingian palaces and the poverty of ideology', in M. Locock (ed.) *Meaningful architecture: social interpretations of buildings* (Avebury, 1994), pp. 99–131

Sansterre, J.-M. (ed.), *L'autorité du passé dans les sociétés médiévales*, Collection de l'Ecole Française de Rome 333 (Rome, 2004), pp. 139–62

Santangeli Valenziani, R., 'Profanes Bauwesen in Rom um das Jahr 800', in *799 Kunst und Kultur*, III, 550–7

Sapin, C. (ed.), *Archéologie et architecture d'un site monastique: 10 ans de recherche à l'abbaye Saint-Germain d'Auxerre* (Auxerre, 2000)

Sassel, J., 'L'organizzazione del confine orientale d'Italia nell'alto medioevo', in *Aquileia e le Venezie nell'alto medioevo*, Antichità altoadriatiche 32 (Udine, 1988), pp. 107–14

Saurma-Jeltsch, L. E. (ed.), *Karl der Große als vielberufener Vorfahr: sein Bild in der Kunst der Fürsten, Kirchen und Städte*, Schriften des historischen Museums: im Auftrag des Dezernats für Kultur und Freizeit 19 (Sigmaringen, 1994)

Sawyer, P., and I. Wood (eds.), *Early medieval kingship* (Leeds, 1977)

Scafi, A., *Mapping Paradise: A history of heaven on earth* (London, 2006)

Schaller, D., 'Das Aachener Epos für Karl den Kaiser', *Frühmittelalterliche Studien* 10 (1976), pp. 134–68

Studien zur lateinischen Dichtung des Frühmittelalters (Stuttgart, 1995)

Scharer, A., and G. Scheibelreiter (eds.), *Historiographie im frühen Mittelalter*, Veröffentlichungen des Instituts für Österreichischen Geschichtsforschung 32 (Vienna and Munich, 1994)

Scharer, A., *Herrschaft und Repräsentation: Studien zur Hofkultur Königs Alfreds des Großen*, MIÖG Ergänzungsband 36 (Vienna and Munich, 2000)

Scharff, T., *Die Kämpfe der Herrscher und der Heiliger: Krieg und historische Erinnerung in der Karolingerzeit* (Darmstadt, 2002)

Schefers, H. (ed.), *Einhard: Studien zu Leben und Werk* (Darmstadt, 1997)

Scheibe, F.-C., 'Alcuin und die Admonitio generalis', *Deutsches Archiv* 14 (1958), pp. 221–9

Schiaparelli, L., *Il codice 490 della biblioteca capitolare di Lucca e la scuola scrittoria Lucchese (sec. VIII–IX): contributi allo studio della minuscola precarolina in Italia*, Studi e Testi 36 (Vatican City, 1924)

Schieffer, R., *Die Entstehung von Domkapiteln in Deutschland* (Bonn, 1976)

Schieffer, R., 'Charlemagne and Rome', in J. M. H. Smith, *Early medieval Rome*, pp. 279–95

'Karl der Große und der Ursprung des westlichen Kaisertums', in Pohl, *Die Suche nach den Ursprüngen*, pp. 151–8

'Karolingische Herrscher in Rom', *Roma fra oriente e occidente*, Settimane 49/1, pp. 101–28

'Karolingische Töchter', in G. Jenal and S. Haarländer (eds.), *Herrschaft, Kirche, Kultur: Beiträge zur Geschichte des Mittelalters. Festschrift Friedrich Prinz zum 65. Geburtstag*, Monographien zur Geschichte des Mittelalters 37 (Stuttgart, 1993), pp. 125–39

'Neues von der Kaiserkrönung Karls des Großen', *Sitzungsberichte der Bayerische Akademie der Wissenschaften, phil.-hist. Klasse* (2004), pp. 3–25

'Ein politischer Prozess des 8. Jahrhunderts im Vexierspiegel der Quellen', in Berndt, *Das Frankfurter Konzil vom 794*, pp. 167–82

'Reliquientranslationen nach Sachsen', in *799 Kunst und Kultur*, III, pp. 484–93

(ed.), *Schriftkultur und Reichsverwaltung unter den Karolingern*, Abhandlungen der Nordrhein-Westfälischen Akademie der Wissenschaften 97 (Opladen, 1996)

'Vater und Söhne im Karolingerhaus', in Schieffer (ed.), *Beiträge zur Geschichte des regnum francorum: Festschrift Eugen Ewig*, Beihefte der Francia 22 (Sigmaringen, 1990), pp. 149–64

Schieffer, T., *Winfrid-Bonifatius und die christliche Grundlegung Europas* (Freiburg, 1954)

Schiffers, H., *Der Reliquienschatz Karls des Grossen und die Anfänge der Aachener Pilgerfahrt* (Aachen, 1951)

Schmid, K., 'Über das Verhältnis von Person und Gemeinschaft im früheren Mittelalter', *Frühmittelalterliche Studien* 1 (1967) pp. 225–49

Schmid, K., and O.-G. Oexle, 'Voraussetzungen und Wirkung des Gebetbundes von Attigny', *Francia* 2 (1974), pp. 71–122

Schmidinger, H., 'Das Papsttum und die Salzburger Kirche im 8. Jahrhundert', in E. Zwink (ed.), *Frühes Mönchtum in Salzburg*, Salzburg Diskussionen (Salzburg, 1983), pp. 145–55

Schmidt, J., *Hinkmars 'De ordine palatii' und seine Quellen* (Frankfurt am Main, 1962)

Schmidt, P. G., 'Perché tanti anonymi nel medioevo? Il problema della personalità dell'autore nella filologia mediolatina', *Filologia mediolatina* 6–7 (1999–2000), pp. 1–8

Schmitz, G., 'Echte Quellen – falsche Quellen: Müssen zentrale Quellen aus der Zeit Ludwigs der Frömmen neu bewertet werden', in F.-R. Erkens and H. Wolff (eds.), *Von Sacerdotium und regnum: geistliche und weltliche Gewalt im frühen und hohen Mittelalter. Festschrift für Egon Boshof zum 65. Geburtstag* (Cologne, Weimar and Vienna, 2002), pp. 275–300

Schneider, H., *Die altlateinischen biblischen Cantica*, Texte und Arbeiten 29–30 (Beuron, 1938)

Schneider, J. (ed.), *Saint Chrodegang: communications presentées au colloque tenu à Metz à l'occasion du douzième centenaire de sa mort* (Metz, 1967)

Schneider, O., 'Die Königserhebung Pippins 751 in der Erinnerung der karolingischen Quellen: Die Glaubwürdigkeit der Reichsannalen und die Verformung der Vergangenheit', in Becher and Jarnut, *Der Dynastiewechsel von 751*, pp. 243–75

Schnith, K. (ed.), *Mittelalterliche Herrscher in Lebensbildern: von den Karolingern zu den Staufen* (Graz, Vienna and Cologne, 1990)

Schnorr von Carolsfeld, H., 'Das *Chronicon laurissense breve*', *Neues Archiv* 36 (1911), pp. 13–39

Schoenen, P., 'Das Karlsbild der Neuzeit', in *KdG* IV, pp. 274–305

Schramm, P. E., *Beiträge zur allgemeinen Geschichte*, I: *Kaiser, Könige und Päpste. Gesammelte Aufsätze zur Geschichte des Mittelalters*, I (Stuttgart, 1968)

'Karl der Große: Denkart und Grundauffassungen', in Schramm, *Beiträge zur allgemeinen Geschichte, I: von der Spätantike bis zum Tode Karls des Großen (814)* (Stuttgart, 1984), pp. 302–41

'Karl der Große oder Charlemagne? Stellungnahme Deutscher Historiker in der Zeit des Nationalsozialismus', in Schramm, *Kaiser, Könige und Päpste*, I, pp. 342–4

Schramm, P. E., and F. Mütherich (eds.), *Denkmale der deutschen Könige und Kaiser* (Munich, 1962)

Schreiner, K., '"Hildegardis regina": Wirklichkeit und Legende einer karolingischen Herrscherin', *Archiv für Kulturgeschichte* 57 (1975), pp. 1–70

Schröer, N., *Die Annales S. Amandi und ihre Verwandten: Untersuchungen zu einer Gruppe karolingischer Annalen des 8. und frühen 9. Jahrhunderts*, Göppinger Akademische Beiträge 85 (Göppingen, 1975)

Screen, E., 'The importance of the emperor: Lothar I and the Frankish civil war, 840–843', *Early Medieval Europe* 12 (2003), pp. 25–52

Sellert, W., 'Aufzeichnung des Rechts und Gesetz', in Sellert, *Das Gesetz in Spätantike und frühem Mittelalter*, pp. 67–102

(ed.), *Das Gesetz in Spätantike und frühem Mittelalter*, Abhandlungen der Akademie der Wissenschaften in Göttingen, phil.-hist. Klasse 3, Folge 196 (Göttingen, 1992)

Semmler, J., 'Episcopi potestas und karolingische Klosterpolitik', in A. Borst (ed.), *Mönchtum, Episkopat und Adel zur Gründungszeit des Klosters Reichenau*, Vorträge und Forschungen 20 (Sigmaringen, 1974), pp. 305–95

Der Dynastiewechsel von 751 und die fränkische Königssalbung, Studia humaniora: Düsseldorfer Studien zu Mittelalter und Renaissance, series minor 6 (Düsseldorf, 2003)

'Karl der Grosse und das fränkische Mönchtum', *KdG*, II, pp. 255–89

'Der Neubau Karls des Großen: die fränkische Reichskirche', in *Isti moderni: Erneuerungskonzepte und Erneuerungskonflikte in Mittelalter und Renaissance* (forthcoming)

'Pippin III. und die fränkische Klöster', *Francia* 3 (1975), pp. 88–146

'Verdient um das karolingische Königtum und den werdenden Kirchenstaat: Fulrad von St Denis', in O. Münsch and T. Zotz (eds.), *Scientia veritatis: Festschrift für Hubert Mordek zum 65. Geburtstag* (Stuttgart, 2004), pp. 91–115

'Zeitgeschichtsschreibung und Hofhistoriographie unter den frühen Karolingern', in Laudage (ed.), *Von Fakten und Fiktionen*, pp. 135–64

'Zu den bayerisch-westfränkischen Beziehungen in karolingischer Zeit', *Zeitschrift für Bayerische Landesgeschichte* 29 (1966), pp. 344–424

Settia, A. A., 'Pavia carolingia e post-carolingia', in *Storia di Pavia*, III: *Dal libero comune alla fine del principato indipendente (1024–1535)* (Pavia, 1992), pp. 9–25

Seyfarth, E., *Fränkischer Reichsversammlungen unter Karl dem Großen und Ludwig dem Frommen* (Leipzig, 1910)

Shepard, J., 'Byzantine diplomacy AD 800–1204: means and ends, in Shepard and Franklin, *Byzantine diplomacy*, pp. 41–72

'Information, disinformation and delay in Byzantine diplomacy', *Byzantinische Forschungen* 10 (1985), pp. 233–93

'A marriage too far? Maria Lekapena and Peter of Bulgaria', in A. Davids (ed.), *The Empress Theophano: Byzantium and the West at the turn of the first millennium* (Cambridge, 1995), pp. 121–49

'Slavs and Bulgars', in McKitterick, *NCMH*, II, pp. 228–49

'The uses of "history" in Byzantine diplomacy: observations and comparisons', in C. Dendrino, J. Harris, E. Harvalia-Crook and J. Herrin (eds.),

Porphyrogenita: essays on the history and literature of Byzantium and the Latin East in honour of Julian Chrysostomides (London, 2003), pp. 91–115

Shepard, J., and S. Franklin (eds.), *Byzantine diplomacy* (Aldershot, 1992)

Sichard, D., *Le liturgie de la mort dans l'église latine des origines à la réforme Carolingienne* (Münster, 1978)

Siebigs, H.-K., *Der Zentralbau des Domes zu Aachen: Unerforschtes und Ungewisses* (Worms, 2004)

Siems, H., 'Bestechliche und ungerechte Richter in frühmittelalterlichen Rechstquellen', *La giustizia nell'alto medioevo (secoli V–VIII)*, Settimane 42 (Spoleto, 1995), pp. 509–63

'Textbearbeitung und Umgang mit Rechtstexten im Frühmittelalter: zur Umgestaltung der *leges* im *Liber legum* des Lupus', in Siems, Nehlen-von Stryk and Strauch, *Recht im frühmittelalterlichen Gallien*, pp. 29–72

Siems, H., K. Nehlen-von Stryk and D. Strauch (eds.), *Recht im frühmittelalterlichen Gallien* (Cologne, Weimar and Vienna, 1995)

Sierck, M., *Festtag und Politik: Studien zur Tagewahl karolingischer Herrscher*, Beihefte zum Archiv für Kulturgeschichte 38 (Cologne, 1995)

Simson, B. von, 'Der Poeta Saxo und der angebliche Friedensschluss Karls des Großen mit den Sachsen', *Neues Archiv* 32 (1907), pp. 27–50

'Der Poeta Saxo und der Friede zu Salz', *Forschungen zur Deutschen Geschichte* I (1862), pp. 301–26

Smith, A. D., *The ethnic origins of nations* (Oxford, 1986)

Smith, J. M. H., '*Aedificatio sancti loci*: the making of a ninth-century holy place', in de Jong, Theuws and van Rhijn, *Topographies of power*, pp. 361–95

'Confronting identities: the rhetoric and reality of a Carolingian frontier', in Pohl and Diesenberger, *Integration und Herrschaft*, pp. 169–204

'Einhard: the sinner and the saints', *Transactions of the Royal Historical Society*, 6th series, 13 (2003), pp. 55–77

'"Emending evil ways and praising God's omnipotence": Einhard and the uses of Roman martyrs', in K. Mills and A. Grafton (eds.), *Conversion in late antiquity and the early middle ages: seeing and believing* (Rochester, 2003), pp. 189–223

'*Fines imperii*: the marches', in *NCMH*, II, pp. 169–89

'Old saints, new cults: Roman relics in Carolingian Francia', and 'Appendix: relic translations from Rome to Francia 750–900', in Smith, *Early medieval Rome and the Christian West*, pp. 317–40

'Oral and written: saints, miracles and relics in Brittany, c. 850–1250', *Speculum* 65 (1990), pp. 309–43

Province and empire: Brittany and the Carolingians (Cambridge, 1992)

'The sack of Vannes by Pippin III', *Cambridge Medieval Celtic Studies* 11 (1986), pp. 17–27

(ed.), *Early medieval Rome and the Christian West: essays in honour of Donald A. Bullough* (Leiden, 2000)

Songzoni, D., *Le chartrier de l'abbaye de Saint-Denis en France au haut moyen âge: essai de reconstitution*, Pecia: Resources en médiévistique 3 (2003), pp. 9–210

Sot, M., 'Local and institutional history (300–1000)', in Deliyannis, *Historiography in the middle ages*, pp. 89–114

Speckelmeyer, G., 'Zur rechtlichen Funcktion frühmittelalterlicher Testamente', in Classen, *Recht und Schrift im Mittelalter*, pp. 91–114

Speeten, J. van der, 'Le dossier de Nicée dans la Quesnelliana', *Sacris Erudiri* 28 (1985), pp. 383–450

Sproemberg, H., 'Marculf und die fränkische Reichskanzlei', *Neues Archiv* 47 (1928), pp. 77–142

Staab, F., 'Die Königin Fastrada', in Berndt, *Das Frankfurter Konzil von 794*, pp. 183–218

Stafford, P., *Queens, concubines and dowagers; the king's wife in the early middle ages* (Athens, Ga., 1983)

Starostine, D., '. . . in die festivitatis*: gift-giving, power and the calendar in the Carolingian kingdoms', *Early Medieval Europe* 14 (2006), pp. 465–86

Staubach, N., 'Cultus divinus und karolingische Reform', *Frühmittelalterliche Studien* 18 (1984), pp. 546–81

Steele, I. K., *The English Atlantic, 1675–1740: an exploration of communication and community* (Oxford and New York, 1986)

Steinmayer, E., *Die kleineren althochdeutschen Sprachdenkmaler* (Berlin, 1916)

Stella, F., 'Autore e attribuzione del "Karolus Magnus et Leo Papa"', in Godman, Jarnut and Johanek, *Am Vorabend der Kaiser Krönung*, pp. 19–34

Stenton, F., *Anglo-Saxon England* (Oxford, 1946)

Stevens W., 'Astronomy in Carolingian schools', in P. L. Butzer, M. Kerner and W. Oberschelp (eds.), *Karl der Große und sein Nachwirken: 1200 Jahre Kultur und Wissenschaft in Europa; Charlemagne and his heritage: 1200 years of civilisation and science in Europe* (Turnhout, 1997), pp. 417–88

Cycles of time and scientific learning in medieval Europe (Aldershot, 1995)

'A present sense of things past: Quid est enim tempus?', in G. Jaritz and G. Moreno-Riaô (eds.), *Time and eternity: the medieval discourse*, International Medieval Research 9 (Turnhout, 2003), pp. 9–28

Stiegemann, C., and M. Wemhoff (eds.), *799 Kunst und Kultur der Karolingerzeit: Karl der Grosse und Papst Leo III in Paderborn*, 3 vols (Mainz, 1999)

Stoclet, A., *Autour de Fulrad de Saint-Denis (v. 710–784)* (Geneva and Paris, 1993)

'La "Clausula de unctione Pippini Regis": mises au point et nouvelles hypothèses', *Francia* 8 (1980), pp. 1–42

'La Clausula de unctione Pippini Regis, vingt ans après', *Revue belge de philologie et d'histoire* 78 (2000), pp. 719–71

Stormer, W., *Adelsgruppen im früh- und hochmittelalterlichen Bayern*, Studien zur bayerischen Verfassungs- und Sozialgeschichte 4 (Munich, 1972)

Story, J., *Carolingian connections: Anglo-Saxon England and Carolingian Francia, c. 750–870* (Aldershot, 2003)

'Cathwulf, kingship and the royal abbey of Saint Denis', *Speculum* 74 (1999), pp. 1–21

Charlemagne and Rome: the epitaph of Pope Hadrian I (Oxford, forthcoming)

'The Frankish annals of Lindisfarne and Kent', *Anglo-Saxon England* 34 (2005), pp. 59–110

Story, J., J Bunbury, A. C. Felici, G. Fronterotta, M. Piacentini, C. Nicolais, D. Scacciatelli, S. Sciuti and M. Vendittelli, 'Charlemagne's black marble: the origins of the Epitaph of Pope Hadrian I', *Papers of the British School at Rome* (2005), pp. 157–90

(ed.), *Charlemagne: empire and society* (Manchester, 2005)

Strecker, K., 'Studien zu karolingischen Dichtern', *Neues Archiv* 43 (1922), pp. 477–511

Suicic, I., *Croatia in the early middle ages: a cultural survey* (London and Zagreb, 1999)

Sullivan, R. (ed.), *'The gentle voices of teachers': aspects of learning in the Carolingian age* (Columbus, OH, 1995)

Szövérffy, J., *Die Annalen der lateinischen Hymnendichtung*, I (Berlin, 1964)

Tangl, M., 'Der Entwurf einer unbekannten Urkunde Karls des Großen in Tironischen Noten', *MIÖG* 21 (1900), pp. 344–50

Das Mittelalter in Quellenkunde und Diplomatik: Ausgewählte Schriften, I, Forschungen zur mittelalterlichen Geschichte 12 (Berlin, 1966)

'Studien um den heiligen Bonifatius', repr. in Tangl, *Quellenkunde und Diplomatik*, pp. 25–274

'Studien zur Neuausgabe der Bonifatius-Briefe, Teil 1', *Neues Archiv* 40 (1916), pp. 639–790, repr. in Tangl, *Quellenkunde und Diplomatik*, pp. 60–175

'Das Testaments Fulrads von Saint-Denis', *Neues Archiv* 32 (1907), pp. 167–217, repr. in Tangl, *Quellenkunde und Diplomatik*, pp. 540–81

Tanz, S., 'Aspekte der Karlsrezeption im Frankreich des 19. Jahrhunderts', *Das Mittelalter* 4/2 (1999), pp. 55–64

Tellenbach, G., 'Der grossfränkische Adel und die Regierung Italiens in der Blütezeit des Karolingerreiches', in Tellenbach (ed.), *Studien und Vorarbeiten zur Geschichte des grossfränkischen und frühdeutschen Adels*, Forschungen zur oberrheinischen Landesgeschichte 4 (Freiburg, 1957), pp. 40–70

Testo e immagine nell'alto medioevo, Settimane 41 (Spoleto, 1994)

Thacker, A., and R. Sharpe (eds.), *Local saints and local churches in the early medieval West* (Oxford, 2002)

Theuerkauf, G., *Lex, speculum, compendium iuris: Rechtsaufzeichnung und Rechtsbewußtsein in Norddeutschland vom 8. bis zum 16. Jahrhundert* (Cologne and Graz, 1968)

Theuws, F., 'Centre and periphery in northern Austrasia (6th–8th centuries): an archaeological perspective', in J. Besteman, J. Bos and H. Heidinga (eds.), *Medieval archaeology in the Netherlands: studies presented to H. H. van Regteren Altena* (Assen and Maastricht, 1990), pp. 41–69

Thieroff, R., 'The German tense-aspect-mood system from a typological perspective', in S. Watts, J. West and H.-J. Solms (eds.), *Zur Verbmorphologie germanischer Sprachen*, Linguistische Arbeiten 146 (Tübingen, 2001), pp. 211–30

Thomas, H., 'Die Namenliste des Diptychon Barbarini und der Sturz des Hausmeiers Grimoald', *Deutsches Archiv* 25 (1969), pp. 17–63

Till, R., *Handschriftliche Untersuchungen zu Tacitus Agricola und Germania* (Berlin and Dahlem, 1943)

Tillotson, M., 'Carolingian sub-kings and kingship, 781–864', unpublished short essay, MPhil in Medieval History, University of Cambridge (2003)

'Frankish diplomatic relations in the reign of Louis the Pious', unpublished MPhil in Medieval History dissertation, University of Cambridge (2003)

Tischler, M., *Einharts Vita Karoli: Studien zur Entstehung, Überlieferung und Rezeption*, MGH Schriften 48 (Hanover, 2002)

Tock, B.-M., 'La diplomatique francaise du haut moyen âge, vue à travers les originaux', in B. M. Tock, M. Courtois and M. J. Gasse-Grandjean (eds.), *La diplomatique française du haut moyen âge: inventaire des chartes originales antérieures à 1121 conservées en France* I, Atelier de Recherche sur les Textes Médiévaux 4 (Turnhout, 2001), pp. 54–60

'Le sceau', in Tock, Courtois and Gasse-Granjean, *La diplomatique française*, pp. 28–30

Traube, L., 'Zur Chorographie des Augustus', *Vorlesungen und Abhandlungen*, 3 vols (Munich, 1920), III, pp. 17–20

Tremp, E., *Studien zu den Gesta Hludowici imperatoris des Trierer Chorbischofs Thegan*, MGH Schriften 32 (Hanover, 1988)

'Thegan und Astronomus, die beiden Geschichtsschreiber Ludwigs des Frommen', in Godman and Collins, *Charlemagne's heir*, pp. 691–700

Tremp, E., *Die Überlieferung der Vita Hludowici imperatoris des Astronomus*, MGH Studien und Texte 1 (Hanover, 1991)

Ullmann, B., 'A list of classical manuscripts (in an eighth-century codex) perhaps from Corbie', *Scriptorium* 8 (1954), pp. 224–37

Untermann, M., '"Opere mirabili constructa": Die Aachener "Residenz" Karls des Großen', *799 Kunst und Kultur*, III, pp. 152–64

Verhaege, F., 'Urban developments in the age of Charlemagne', in Story, *Charlemagne*, pp. 259–87

Verhulst, A., 'Karolingische Agrarpolitik: Das *Capitulare de villis* und die Hungersnote von 792 und 805/806', *Zeitschrift für Agrargeschichte und Agrarsoziologie* 13 (1965), pp. 175–89

The rise of cities in northwest Europe (Cambridge, 1999)

Verschaffel, T., *Beeld en geschiedenis: het Belgische en Vlaamse verleden in de romantische boekillustraties* (Turnhout, 1987)

Vezin, J., 'Les livres dans l'entourage de Charlemagne et d'Hildegarde', in Riché, Heitz and Heber-Suffrin, *Actes du Colloque 'Autour de Hildegarde'*, pp. 63–70

Vicini, E. P. (ed.), *Regesto della chiesa cattedrale di Modena* (Rome, 1931)

Villa, C., 'Cultura classica e tradizione Longobarde; tra latino e volgari', in Chiesa (ed.), *Paolo Diacono*, pp. 575–600

'Die Horazüberlieferung und die "Bibliothek Karls des Grossen": zum Werkverzeichnis der Handschrift Berlin, Diez B. 66', *Deutsches Archiv* 51 (1995), pp. 29–52; in Italian: 'La traditione di Orazio e la "bibliotheca di Carlo Magno": per l'elenco di opere nel codice Berlin Diez B. Sant. 66', in O. Pecere and M. D. Reeve (eds.), *Formative stages of classical traditions: Latin texts from antiquity to the Renaissance* (Spoleto, 1996), pp. 299–322

'Lay and ecclesiastical culture', in La Rocca, *Italy in the early middle ages*, pp. 189–203

Viret, J., 'La réforme liturgique carolingienne et les deux traditions du chant romain', in Riché, Heitz and Héber-Suffrin, *Actes du Colloque 'Autour de Hildegarde'*, pp. 117–27

Vlasto, A., *The entry of the Slavs into Christendom* (Cambridge, 1971)

Vogel, C., *Medieval liturgy: an introduction to the sources*, revised edn and trans. of the 1981 edn, by N. K. Rasmussen and W. G. Storey (Washington, D.C., 1986)

'Saint Chrodegang et les débuts de la romanisation du culte en pays franc', in *Saint Chrodegang*, pp. 91–109

Voss, J., *Das Mittelalter im historischen Denken Frankreichs: Untersuchung zur Geschichte des Mittelalterbegriffes und der Mittelalterbewertung von der zweiten Hälfte des 16. bis zur Mitte des 19. Jahrhunderts* (Munich, 1972)

Vry, V. de, *Liborius: Brückenbauer Europas: die mittelalterlichen Viten und Translationsberichte* (Paderborn, 1997)

Waitz, G., 'Ueber die handschriftliche Ueberlieferung und die Sprache der Historia Langobardorum des Paulus', *Neues Archiv* 1 (1876), pp. 533–66

'Zur Geschichtsschreibung der Karolingischer Zeit', *Neues Archiv* 5 (1880), pp. 475–91

Waldhoff, S., *Alcuins Gebetbuch für Karl den Großen: seine Rekonstruktion und seine Stellung in der frühmittelalterlichen Geschichte der libelli precum*, Liturgiewissenschaftliche Quellen und Forschungen, Veröffentlichungen des Abt. Herwegen-Instituts der Abtei Maria Laach 89 (Münster, 2003)

Wallace-Hadrill, J. M., *Early Germanic kingship in England and on the Continent* (Oxford, 1971)

'Charlemagne and England', in *KdG*, I, pp. 683–89, repr. in Wallace-Hadrill, *Early medieval history* (Oxford, 1975), pp. 155–80

The Frankish church (Oxford, 1983)

The long-haired kings and other studies in Frankish history (London, 1962)

Wamers, E., and M. Brandt (eds.), *Die Macht des Silbers: karolingische Schätze im Norden* (Regensburg, 2005)

Wattenbach, W., W. Levison and H. Löwe, *Deutsche Geschichtsquellen im Mittelalter: Vorzeit und Karolinger*, II. Heft, *Die Karolinger vom Anfang des 8. Jahrhunderts bis zum Tode Karls des Großen* (Weimar, 1953); III. Heft, *Die Karolinger vom Tode Karls des Großen bis zum Vertrag von Verdun* (Weimar, 1957)

Webster, B., *Medieval Scotland: the making of an identity* (London, 1997)

Wehlen, W., *Geschichtsschreibung und Staatsauffassung im Zeitalter Ludwigs des Frommen* (Lübeck and Hamburg, 1970)

Weinrich, L., *Wala: Graf, Mönch und Rebell. Die Biographie eines Karolingers*, (Lübeck and Hamburg, 1963)

Weise, G., *Zwei fränkische Königspfalzen: Bericht über die an den Pfalzen zu Quierzy und Samoussy vorgenommenen Grabungen* (Tübingen, 1923)

Wendling, W., 'Die Erhebung Ludwigs des Frommen zum Mitkaiser im Jahre 813 und ihre Bedeutung für die Verfassungsgeschichte des Frankenreiches', *Frühmittelalterliche Studien* 19 (1985), pp. 201–38

Werner, K. F., 'Bedeutende Adelsfamilien im Reich Karls des Großen', in *KdG*, I, pp. 83–142

Werner; K.-F., 'Das Geburtsdatum Karls des Großen', *Francia* I (1973), pp. 115–57

'*Hludowicus Augustus*: gouverner l'empire chrétien: idées et réalités', in Godman and Collins, *Charlemagne's heir*, pp. 3–123

'*Missus – marchio – comes*: entre l'administration centrale et l'administration locale de l'Empire', in W. Paravicini and K.-F. Werner (eds.), *Histoire de l'Administration comparée (IVe–XVIIIe siècles)*, Beihefte der Francia 9 (Munich, 1980), pp. 190–239

'Die Nachkommen Karls des Großen bis um das Jahr 1000 (1.–8. Generation)', in *KdG*, IV, pp. 403–83

Werner, M., *Adelsfamilien im Umkreis der frühen Karolinger: die Verwandschaft Irminas von Oeren und Adelas von Pfalzel*, Vorträge und Forschungen Sonderband 28 (Sigmaringen, 1982)

West, G. V. B., 'Charlemagne's involvement in central and southern Italy: power and the limits of authority', *Early Medieval Europe* 8 (1999), pp. 241–67

Whittaker, C. R., *Frontiers of the Roman empire: a social and economic study* (Baltimore and London, 1994)

Wibel, H., *Beiträge zur Kritik der Annales regni francorum und der Annales q.d. Einhardi* (Strasbourg, 1902)

Wickham, C., 'Gossip and resistance among the medieval peasantry', *Past and Present* 160 (1998), pp. 3–24

Williams, J., and B. A. Shailor, *A Spanish Apocalypse: the Morgan Beatus manuscript* (New York, 1991)

Willsdorf, C., 'Le monasterium scottorum: Ettonau et la famille des ducs d'Alsace au VIIIe siècle. Vestiges d'un cartulaire perdu', *Francia* 3 (1975), pp. 1–87

Wilmart, A., 'Le psautier de la reine n. XI: sa provenance et sa date', *Revue bénédictine* 27 (1911), pp. 341–76

'Reliques réunies à Jouarre, *Analecta reginensia*, Studi e testi 59 (Vatican City, 1933), pp. 9–17

Wilson, J. E., *The making of a colonial order: information, uncertainty and law in early colonial Bengal*, Centre for South Asian Studies, Occasional paper No. 6 (Cambridge, 2004)

Wilson, K. (ed.), *A new imperial history: culture, identity and modernity in Britain and the empire, 1660–1840* (Cambridge, 2004)

Wolf, G., 'Grifos Erbe, die Einsetzung König Childerichs III. und der Kampf um die Macht: zugleich Bemerkungen zur karolingischen, Hofhistoriographie"', *Archiv für Diplomatik* 38 (1992), pp. 1–16

'Die Königssöhne Karl und Karlmann und ihr Thronfolgerecht nach Pippins Königserhebung 750/51', *Zeitschrift der Savigny Stiftung für Rechtsgeschichte, Germanistische Abteilung* 108 (1991), pp. 282–96

Wolfram, H., 'The creation of the Carolingian frontier system c. 800', in Pohl, Wood and Reimitz, *Transformation of frontiers*, pp. 233–45

Grenzen und Räume: Geschichte Österreichs vor seiner Entstehung (Wien, 1995)

'Der heilige Rupert und die antikarolingische Adelsopposition', *Mitteilungen des Instituts für Österreichische Geschichtsforschung* 80 (1972), pp. 7–34

Intitulatio, I Lateinische Königs- und Fürstentitel bis zum Ende des 8. Jahrhunderts, MIÖG Ergänzungsband 21 (Graz, Vienna and Cologne, 1967)

'Die Notitia Arnonis und ähnliche Formen der Rechtssicherung im nachagilolfingischen Bayern', in Classen, *Recht und Schrift im Mittelalter*, pp. 115–30

'Political theory and narrative in charters', *Viator* 26 (1995), pp. 39–52

Salzburg, Bayern, Österreich: die Conversio Bagoariorum et Carantanorum und die Quellen ihrer Zeit, Mitteilungen des Instituts für Österreichische Geschichtsforschung Ergänzungsband 31 (Vienna and Munich, 1995)

Wolfram, H., and M. Diesenberger, 'Arn und Alkuin bis 804: zwei Freunde und ihre Schriften', in Niederkorn-Bruck and Scharer, *Erzbischof Arn von Salzburg*, pp. 81–106

Wood, I., 'An absence of saints? The evidence for the Christianisation of Saxony', in Godman, Jarnut and Johanek, *Am Vorabend der Kaiserkrönung*, pp. 335–52

'Beyond satraps and ostriches: political and social structures of the Saxons in the early Carolingian period', in D. H. Green and F. Siegmund (eds.), *The Continental Saxons from the migration period to the tenth century: an ethnographic perspective* (Woodbridge, 2003), pp. 271–86

'Genealogy defined by women: the case of the Pippinids', in L. Brubaker and J. M. H. Smith (eds.), *Gender in the early medieval world, East and West, 300–900* (Cambridge, 2004), pp. 234–56

'In praise of uncertainty', in Pohl and Diesenberger, *Integration und Herrschaft*, pp. 303–14

The Merovingian kingdoms, 482–751 (London, 1994)

'Missionaries and the Christian frontier, in Pohl, Wood and Reimitz, *Transformation of frontiers*, pp. 209–18

The missionary life: saints and the evangelisation of Europe 400–1050 (London, 2001)

Wood, S. *The proprietary church in the medieval West* (Oxford, 2006)

Woodward, D., 'Medieval *mappae mundi*', in Woodward and Harley, *The history of cartography*, I, pp. 286–368

Woodward, D., and J. B. Harley (eds.), *The history of cartography, I: Cartography in prehistoric, ancient and medieval Europe and the Mediterranean* (Chicago, 1987)

Wormald, P., '*Lex scripta and verbum regis*: legislation and germanic kingship from Euric to Cnut', in Sawyer and Wood, *Early medieval kingship*, pp. 105–38

The making of English law: King Alfred to the twelfth century, I: legislation and its limits (Oxford, 1999)

Wright, R., *Late Latin and early Romance in Spain and Carolingian France* (Liverpool, 1982)

(ed.), *Latin and the Romance languages in the early middle ages* (London, 1991, and Philadelphia, 1996)

A sociophilological study of late Latin, Utrecht Studies in Medieval Literacy 10 (Turnhout, 2005)

Wurm, H., *Studien und Texte zur Dekretalsammlung des Dionysius Exiguus*, Kanonistische Studien und Texte 16 (Bonn, 1939)

Wyss, M., 'Un établissement carolingien mis au jour à proximité de l'abbaye de Saint-Denis: la question du palais de Charlemagne', in A. Renoux (ed.), *'Aux marches du palais': qu'est-ce-qu'un palais médiéval?* (Le Mans, 2001), pp. 191–200

'Die Klosterpfalz Saint-Denis im Licht der neuen Ausgrabungen', in Fenske, Jarnut and Wemhoff, *Deutsche Königspfalzen*, III, pp. 175–92

'Saint-Denis', in *799 Kunst und Kultur*, III, pp. 138–41

Yearley, J., 'A bibliography of *planctus* in Latin, Provençal, French, German, English, Italian, Catalan and Galician-Portugese from the time of Bede to the early fifteenth century', *Journal of the Plainsong and Renaissance Music Society* 4 (1981), pp. 12–52

Zatschek, H. J., 'Die Benützung der Formulae Mareculfi und andere Formularsammlungen in den Privaturkunden der 8. bis 10. Jhts', *MIÖG* 42 (1927), pp. 165–267

Zettler, A., 'Eine Beschreibung von Saint-Denis aus dem Jahre 799', in Zettler, *Die Franken* (Mannheim/Mainz 1996), I, pp. 435–7

Ziolkowski, J. M., 'Blood, sweat and tears in the "Waltharius"', in G. R. Wieland, C. Ruff and R. G. Arthur (eds.), *Insignis sophiae arcator: medieval Latin studies in honour of Michael Herren on his 65th birthday*, Publications of the Journal of Medieval Latin 6 (Turnhout, 2006), pp. 149–64

'Fighting words: wordplay and swordplay in the Waltharius', in K. E. Olsen, A. Harbus and T. Hofstra (eds.), *Germanic texts and Latin models: medieval reconstructions* (Leuven, Paris and Sterling, VA, 2001), pp. 29–51

'Of arms and the (Ger)man: literary and material culture in the poem of Walter (Waltharius)', in J. R. Davis and M. McCormick (eds.), *The long morning of medieval Europe: new directions in early medieval studies, Harvard University, October 29–31, 2004* (Cambridge, Mass., forthcoming)

Zotz, T., 'Carolingian tradition and Ottonian-Salian innovation: comparative perspectives on palatine policy in the empire', in A. Duggan (ed.), *Kings and kingship in medieval Europe* (London, 1993), pp. 69–100

'Grundlagen und Zentren der Königsherrschaft im deutschen Südwesten in karolingischer und ottonischer Zeit', in *Archäologie und Geschichte des ersten Jahrtausends in Südwestdeutschland*, Archäologie in Geschichte 1 (Sigmaringen, 1990), pp. 275–93

'Pfalzen der Karolingerzeit: Neue Aspekte aus historischer Sicht', in Fenske, Jarnut and Wemhoff, *Deutsche Königspfalzen*, pp. 13–23

Index of manuscripts

General index

Aachen 54, 170, 178, 187, 197, 280, 292, 350, 378; in
Annales regni francorum 159; assemblies at 158,
(797 and 802–3) 22, 227 229, (809) 235;
building work 167; as 'capital'? 175–6; chapel 8,
169, 171; chapel dedicated to Virgin Mary 322;
chapel, hymnary of 342; chapel, liturgical
function of 340, 348; chapel mosaic 339;
Charlemagne's burial at 158; charters redacted
at 194, 204; chronology of 347–8; coronation of
Louis at 158; hot springs at 9, 12; market 3; new
Rome 345; palace 137–8; portico collapse at
11–12; Rathaus 4; as sacred site 340; site of
166–7; stability at 162; status of 157–71; town
167; travel to 182; treasury of 374–5; without a
mint 168
a-b minuscule 362, 373
Abbeville Gospels 346, 353
Abbio, baptism of 278
Abbo of Provence 71 n. 51
abbots, political role of 298
Abd al-Rahman 134
abd-Allah 284
Abodrites 11, 12–13, 104–5, 128–30, 254, 290–1; allies
of Franks 128
Abraham, Christian Bohemian 279
Abul-Abaz, elephant 128
Abulaz, ruler of Al-Andalus 134, 284
access, to justice 218; to king 141, 143, 145, 174,
177–8, 213–14, 254 n. 177
acclamations 115
Achadeus, count, Psalter of 338
Achmaenid rulers of Assyria 281
Ada, *ancilla dei* 354
Ada Gospels 353, 360
Ada group, *see under* Hofschule group
Adalbert of Bremen 334
Adalchis, prince of the Lombards
Adalgis, *camerarius* 29
Adalhard, abbot of Corbie and cousin of
Charlemagne 23, 88, 151, 282, 363; authorship

of *De ordine palatii* 142, 144–5; *missus* 218, 264,
314; regent in Italy 152
Adalperga, duchess of Benevento 85
Adaltrude, daughter of Charlemagne 91, 92
(Table 3)
Adalung, abbot of Lorsch 100
Adams, J. 378
Adarulfus, St Denis notary 206 n. 226
Ademar 25
administration, increase in 207–8, 235–6; of
justice 215 n. 4; new ideas for 153
admonitio 233, 239, 261
Admonitio generalis (789) 197 n. 99, 219, 237,
239–41, 265, 304, 307–8, 311, 333, 336, 341; on
chant 344; on correct language 316; on
liturgical reform 342; survival of 242
Adoptionism 50, 311–13, 335, 371
Aelflaed, princess of Mercia 283
Aethelred, king of Northumbria 283
Agilolfings 118–19, 240
Agilward, bishop of Würzburg 207 n. 243
Agius of Corvey 23
Agricola, Roman general 17–20
Aio, Lombard count 247
Aistulf, king of the Lombards 108, 233
Aito, royal official 255
Alaric, breviary of 276
Alban, saint 321
Albuin, envoy of Charlemagne 109
Alcuin 139–40, 220, 240 n. 114, 312–13; arrival at
court 348; on Charles the Younger 154; on
conversion of the Saxons 254; *De orthographia*
of 319; on England 282–3; on Latin spelling 319;
letter collection of 219; prayer book by 330, 339;
received at Frankfurt 241; revised text of Bible
by 369; teacher of Charlemagne 349; *Vita
Willibrordi* by 252; York poem by 23
Aldricus, notary 207, 209 (Map 8)
Alexander III, Pope 2
Alexander the Great 164